WAYNESBURG COLLEGE LIBRARY
WAYNESBURG, PA.

966 012w
Obichere, Boniface Ihewunwa
West African States and European
94652

966 012w
Obichere, Boniface Ihewunwa
West African States and European Expansion
94652

MAR 6 1992

West African States and European Expansion

West African States and European Expansion

The Dahomey-Niger Hinterland, 1885–1898

by Boniface I. Obichere

New Haven and London, Yale University Press, 1971

Copyright © 1971 by Yale University.
All rights reserved. This book may not be
reproduced, in whole or in part, in any form
(except by reviewers for the public press),
without written permission from the publishers.
Library of Congress catalog card number: 71–140535
International standard book number: 0–300–01299–3

Designed by John O. C. McCrillis
and set in Granjon type.
Printed in the United States of America by
The Colonial Press Inc., Clinton, Massachusetts.

Distributed in Great Britain, Europe, and Africa by
Yale University Press, Ltd., London; in Canada by
McGill-Queen's University Press, Montreal; in Mexico
by Centro Interamericano de Libros Académicos,
Mexico City; in Central and South America by Kaiman
& Polon, Inc., New York City; in Australasia by
Australia and New Zealand Book Co., Pty., Ltd.,
Artarmon, New South Wales; in India by UBS Publishers'
Distributors Pvt., Ltd., Delhi; in Japan by John
Weatherhill, Inc., Tokyo.

Contents

	Page
Preface	ix
Introduction	1
Chapter 1—The Dahomey-Niger Hinterland and Its Traditional Rulers	7
Physical Features	7
Climate, Vegetation, and Resources	8
Political Situation in the Dahomey-Niger Hinterland in the 1890s	9
The Mamprussi Group	10
The Borgu Group	13
Dahomey	14
Chapter 2—From Berlin to Brussels, 1885–1890	18
The Conference and Questions Concerning the Hinterland	19
The Third Basis	23
The Partition of the West Coast of Africa after Berlin, 1885–90	26
Territorial Settlements after 1885	28
The Slave Coast after 1885	28
France and Porto Novo	29
The Partition of the Slave Coast after 1885	31
France and Portugal: Conflict and Agreement, 1885–87	31
France and Germany on the Slave Coast, 1885–90	33
Britain and Germany: Togo–Gold Coast Boundary, 1885–90	37
Difficulties between France and Britain on the Slave Coast, 1885–90	41
The General Act of the Brussels Conference: Mandate for the Occupation of the Hinterland	49
Chapter 3—The Conquest and Occupation of Dahomey, 1890–1894: Part 1—The First Dahomey War, 1890	51
The Kingdom of Dahomey: Foundation and Extent	51
Development of Diplomatic Relations between Dahomey and France	53
Unwillingness of Britain and France to Intervene in Dahomey	54
The International Setting: Britain and Germany Removed from the Dahomey Area by 1889	55
Remote and Proximate Causes of the First Dahomey War, 1890	57
Bayol's Mission to Abomey, 1889	60
The First Dahomey War, February–October 1890: A New King Faces an Old Problem	66
French Government's Insistence on Negotiations with Dahomey	76
Père Dogère's Diplomatic Mission to Abomey	80

	Page
The Peace Treaty of 3 October 1890	82
Chapter 4—The Conquest and Occupation of Dahomey, 1890–1894: Part 2 —The Second Dahomey War, 1892–1894	86
I. Interlude of Uneasy Peace, 1890–92	86
Admiral Cuverville's Appeasement Measures	87
Béhanzin's Military and Economic Measures Evoke Criticism	90
French Alarm at Dahomey's Rearmament	91
Changed Attitude in France toward War in Dahomey	95
Béhanzin's Intransigence	100
II. The Campaigns of 1892–94	103
The Second Dahomey War Begins	103
The Expedition to Abomey	105
Béhanzin's Peace Overtures and the Occupation of Abomey, November 1892	108
Béhanzin Renews Peace Overtures	111
The Third Campaign: 1893–94: Surrender of Béhanzin, January 1894	113
Resumption of Operations for the Capture of Béhanzin	115
Reorganization of Dahomey by General Dodds	116
Results of the Conquest and Occupation of Dahomey	118
Chapter 5—European Expeditions into the Hinterland, 1890–1894	123
Theoretical Bases of French Expeditions	124
The Anglo-French Declaration of 5 August 1890	128
French Expeditions into the Hinterland	132
British Reaction to the French Expeditions into the Hinterland	141
Anglo-French Niger–Lake Chad Commission, 1892–94	149
Chapter 6—The Scramble for and the Occupation of the Hinterland, 1895–1897	159
The Changed Situations in West Africa, France, and Britain	159
French Expeditions and Occupation of the Hinterland, 1895–97	164
The German Togo Hinterland Expedition	174
Britain Tries to Contain French and German Expansionism	177
Negotiations with France	181
The Resumption of Effective Occupation and Expeditions	191
Chapter 7—The Anglo-French Crisis of 1897–1898	194
Effective Occupation by French Expeditions: The Volta Region	194
Expeditions from Dahomey: Baud, Vermeesch, Bretonnet, Ganier, Ricour	200
Franco-German Negotiations and the Settlement of 23 July 1897	207
British Reaction to French Expeditions and Effective Occupation	209
A West African Force	213

	Page
Chapter 8—The Work of the Niger Commission, October 1897–June 1898	221
The Niger Commission Resumes Negotiations	222
Controversy over African Treaties	226
The Emergence of Draft Conventions	228
The Settlement and Reactions to It	241
Chapter 9—Conclusion	245
Appendix 1—General Act of the Brussels Conference, 2 July 1890: Chapter 1	255
Appendix 2—Franco-Dahomey Peace Treaty, 3 October 1890	256
Appendix 3—Delcassé Circular to the Governors of French Colonies, 20 June 1894	258
Appendix 4—Anglo-Mossi Treaty of 2 July 1894, Concluded by George E. Ferguson	260
Appendix 5—Convention between the United Kingdom and France (14 June 1898)	263
Abbreviations	273
Notes	275
Selected Bibliography	363
Index	385

Maps

1. Spheres of Influence Controversies, 1890–1894 (adapted from Boniface I. Obichere, 1966)	122
2. Dahomey-Niger Hinterland (adapted from Jules Huré, 1 Dec. 1895)	158
3. Penetration Routes into the Niger Bend (1895)	183
4. Frontiers Proposed by Germans (adapted from Kreuz Zeitung, 2 Oct. 1895)	208

Preface

Though this book focuses on the states in the area that I have designated as the Dahomey-Niger hinterland, it does not ignore the expansionist activities of the major European powers in other parts of west Africa. The expansionist enterprise of Europeans in these other areas could be seen as either a prelude or an adjunct to the struggle for territory in the region under study. Since the states in the Dahomey-Niger hinterland were among the last to be conquered, occupied, and partitioned, it is evident that Afro-European competition for power and territory in other parts of Africa (such as the Upper Nile basin, East Africa, the Zambezi basin, the Congo basin, and especially west Africa) had varying degrees of impact on the developments in these states in the 1890s.

This book belongs to the familiar class of monographs that result from refurbished doctoral dissertations; it has developed from the doctoral thesis which I completed at Oxford University in 1967. It deals with the progress of European enterprise from the Atlantic Coast to the innermost recesses of the Dahomey-Niger hinterland from the 1880s to the turn of the twentieth century. The reaction and resistance of the states in this region to the violent intrusion of European imperialism into their very existence is studied through the actions and measures taken by their leaders, rulers, chiefs, and kings, as well as by the subjects and supporters of these leaders. The Franco-Dahomey wars (1890–94) are studied in detail from hitherto unused primary sources. The implications of the conquest of Dahomey for the states of the hinterland are also examined.

The motivations of the European powers for the acquisition of territories in the Dahomey-Niger hinterland after 1885 are opened to investigation. These motives were as complex as the actual operations for the acquisition of territories. Negotiations in Europe and military operations and expeditions in Africa were delicately balanced. The failure of the African states to form a united front against the invading European forces is examined and evaluated in light of the African state systems in the area and also in light of the nature of the relations that existed between these states prior to the onslaught of the European imperial forces. The perception of European enterprise in their domains affected the reaction of some African rulers. In Mossi, for example, it was believed that Europeans were merely a phenomenon which would pass away very quickly. A one-factor theory of historical explanation would prove very unsatisfactory in dealing with the complex of events and men involved in the historical development of European expansion and conquest of the west African states in the Dahomey-Niger hinterland from 1885 to 1898. The period between 1885 and 1898 is seen as that in which the foundations of the present nation-states of west Africa were laid by European action and African reaction.

I want to express my sincere gratitude to all those who helped me in the protracted process of writing this book. Professor John A. Gallagher of Balliol College, Oxford University, who was my supervisor during the preparation of my thesis, deserves my thanks; his vast knowledge of the location of primary sources was of tremendous value to me. I am also indebted to Dr. Colin W. Newbury, Dr. A. F. Madden, the late George Bennett, and Thomas Hodgkin, all of the Institute of Commonwealth Studies, Oxford University; and to Miss Agatha Ramm of Sommerville College, Oxford, who helped me with the diplomacy of the Gladstone administration. In addition, I should like to thank the principal, Mr. J. B. Bamborough, and the fellows of Linacre College, Oxford, for the encouragement and support they gave me during my work at Oxford.

My debt of gratitude is also great to those who aided me in locating primary sources in France and in Africa, especially to M. Luc Zaba, Professor Henri Brunschwig of the Sorbonne, Mlle. Germaine Ganier of Versailles, and Mlle. Antoinette Menier and M. La Roche of the Archives Nationales, Section d'Outre-Mer. I am indebted to many Africans who lightened the burdens of the frustrations and pressures of research with their good humor, especially Rigobert Ladipo of Dahomey; Dr. Abdul A. Jalloh of Sierra Leone; and Dr. Godfrey N. Uzoigwe, Uga Onwuka, Esq., and Dr. B. O. Oloruntimehin of Nigeria. The librarians and archivists at Rhodes House, Oxford; the British Museum; the Public Record Office, London; the Archives Nationales; and the Archives Centrales de la Marine, Paris; and the keepers of the many private papers used in the preparation of this book deserve my thanks. And, of course, I am grateful to those who provided me with the financial support that made this book possible. To Oxford University I am beholden for the Beit Senior Research Scholarship in Commonwealth History and for grants from the Committee For Advanced Studies, the Cyril Foster Fund, and the Beit Fund. My thanks also go to the Commonwealth Scholarship Board of Nigeria, Lagos. Finally, I should like to express my deep gratitude to my wife, without whose support and encouragement the completion of this book would have been impossible.

BONIFACE IHEWUNWA OBICHERE

Legon, Accra, Ghana
15 April 1971

Introduction

This book is an inquiry into the process of the occupation and the partition of the Dahomey-Niger hinterland by Britain and France. The area covered embraces the ancient kingdom of Dahomey and the territory north of it, especially from 9° North Latitude to the banks of the Niger and including Borgu, Gurma, Mangu (Chakosi), Mamprussi, Gurunsi, and Mossi in the Niger bend. The motives and factors which influenced and determined this process are examined and analyzed.

The study is not confined to a single political entity but embraces a wider area, thus cutting across present national frontiers. In general, a chronological approach has been adopted to impose order, but I have felt free to depart occasionally from this approach for the purposes of analysis, criticism, and assessment.

Hitherto there have been accounts of isolated events, articles on single military episodes or expeditions, and a few studies of selected districts or tribes of the interior, but none have taken the whole area as a unit. There is only one article on the military history of the Dahomey hinterland, written by Commandant Lorho in the *Revue des Troupes Coloniales* in 1903. This is not a serious historical study, and it is somewhat inaccurate, since it was based not on official documents but on journalistic reports and military bulletins. There are, however, cursory references to the events of the period in histories of the political units into which the hinterland has been divided, such as Robert Cornevin's *Histoire du Togo* (Paris, 1962) and *Histoire du Dahomey* (Paris, 1963). Elliot P. Skinner's *The Mossi of Upper Volta* (Stanford, 1964) is more an anthropological than a historical work. Recently Dr. Kenneth Vignes has published articles on the rivalry between European powers for territorial acquisitions in equatorial and west Africa in *Revue Française d'Histoire d'Outre-Mer* (1961, 1965). There is therefore no substantial, detailed, and systematic historical work on the history of the area considered as a whole.

This study has tried to trace coherently the process and manner in which the vast Dahomey-Niger hinterland was occupied and finally brought under British, French, and German authority. It has shown the relation between British and French competition for territory in the Niger bend and other international colonial disputes in Africa, Asia, and the Pacific, especially in China and Siam. It has attempted to demonstrate the link between considerations of the balance of power in Europe and the rivalry for territorial acquisition in the Niger territories.

What has emerged from the analysis of the official policies of Britain and France in this area from 1885 to 1898 is that economic considerations and national honor were the paramount factors that influenced and determined the occupation of the Dahomey-Niger hinterland and the manner in which this area was partitioned between Britain, France and Germany. Local factors were important in affecting the process of occupation. First, the strength of a local African kingdom was crucial in determining the speed with which it might be occupied. Obviously, Dahomey was a hard nut to crack. Second, Europeans were able to break into these kingdoms by supporting local dissension; thus the British and French alike sometimes backed pretenders who were merely imposters. Local dissension prevented African resistance from forming military alliances across kingdom lines. Furthermore, the resistance lacked strong centralized administrations and, apart from Dahomey, well-equipped and well-trained standing armies. Consequently, resistance to European occupation tended to be shortlived, although resentment of foreign domination survived. The civil war in Gurma and the weakness of the kingdom of Mossi as a result of the growth of the political powers of the provincial *Nabas* during this period are cases in point.

Other factors such as the humanitarian convictions of missionaries, the spirit of adventure, and French militarism have been reckoned with. The "one factor theory" of historical explanation could not be applied to this study, in view of the ever-widening options and constantly shifting priorities of Britain and France during this period.

The question of the hinterland of west Africa was raised at the Berlin Conference (1884–85) during the discussions of the second and third bases of the conference. Freedom of navigation on the Niger was not sought for its own sake but for the commercial intercourse with the inhabitants of the Niger basin to which it would lead. The Niger question was introduced into the agenda of the conference by Jules Ferry. British delegates succeeded in staving off the internationalization of the control of the Lower Niger and securing for Britain the right to determine navigation regulations, though freedom of navigation was assured for all shipping under such regulations. This was the first international expression of Britain's official policy of excluding France and Germany from acquiring any political control of the Lower Niger, a policy which had been adopted by the British government by 1883.

The competition for territory in the hinterland was primarily a result of the desire to ensure the economic viability of those coastal possessions whose commerce and prosperity depended on the uninterrupted flow of trade with the hinterland. Raw materials were tapped from the hinterland, and manufactured goods were sent from the coast to markets in the hinterland. It was necessary to have access to these markets, and gaining exclusive control of them and the populations they served was desirable if not imperative. Exaggerations about the wealth of the hinterland in natural resources influenced policy makers in London and Paris.

The Brussels Conference (1889–90) concerned itself with the hinterland of the African continent as a source of the Slave Trade. It decided that the Slave Trade should be tackled at its source if the other efforts to suppress it were to be successful. The General Act of the Brussels Conference (2 July 1890), chapter 1, articles 1–7, in effect gave the powers an international mandate for the occupation of the hinterland of Africa in order to suppress the Slave Trade.

The powers undertook this solemn obligation with humanitarian motives, but soon the process of fulfilling the obligation turned into a means of serving the political and economic ambitions of most of the signatory powers. France went to war against the formidable kingdom of Dahomey ostensibly to stop slave dealing and human sacrifice and to avenge the Dahomean insult to French national honor. She ended up by acquiring the whole Dahomean domain. The two wars which resulted in the conquest of Dahomey have been studied in some detail for the first time from the records of the Ministère de la Marine in conjunction with the documents in the Section d'Outre-Mer des Archives Nationales and the Archives Nationales of Dahomey. Among the conclusions of this study is that the reason for Dahomey's position as the most powerful kingdom in west Africa during this period was her advanced military organization, her free access through her own ports to European trade in arms and ammunition, her prosperity, and her strong centralized political organization.

Soon after the Berlin Conference the entire coast of west Africa except for Dahomey was partitioned by the European powers. The subsequent conquest of Dahomey gave the only stretch still in African hands to the French. Logically the next field open for expansion was the hinterland, the most attractive portion of which lay between the coastal colonies of the Gold Coast, Togo, Dahomey, Lagos, and the Niger. The territory east of the Niger had been pegged out by Britain; that of the Upper Niger was being fought for by Ahmadu, Samory, and the French. Thus, according to the *res nullius* doctrine of Berlin and Brussels, the Dahomey-Niger hinterland was open for acquisition.

First the hinterland, which was scarcely known, was explored by several British and French expeditions. Both powers concluded treaties of friendship and protection as well as friendship and commerce with African rulers. Then France initiated the effective occupation of specific regions as a way of giving meaning to the treaties and as an instrument of acquiring rights over any given area. French representatives at the Berlin Conference had contended that England hoped to use treaties of friendship and commerce or protection to exclude France and Germany from territories with the best commercial potential. This led to the insertion of articles 33 and 34 in the General Act of the Berlin Conference, enjoining both effective occupation and the notification of any new acquisitions on the African coast to the signatory powers.

Considerable friction soon developed between Britain, France, and Germany in the hinterland as a result of effective occupation and the scramble for treaties with African rulers. By 1889 these European powers had, by a series of arrangements, partitioned the entire coastline and littoral up to 9° North Latitude. Both Germany and France desired to extend their possessions of Togo and Dahomey respectively to the navigable Niger to ensure to their possessions some of the riches and markets of the hinterland. To Britain this was a *non sequitur*. Britain had chartered the Royal Niger Company on 10 July 1886 to safeguard her interests in the Niger territories. Her predominance in the Lower Niger was reinforced by the Anglo-French declaration of 5 August 1890, which defined the Say-Barruwa Line. The Niger Company was reluctant to expend money to meet the challenge of France and Germany, so the British government entered into the contest and instructed the governors of the Gold Coast and Lagos to bestir themselves and thwart the efforts of France and Germany to appropriate the hinterlands of their colonies.

France and Britain entered into negotiations in 1892–94, but the efforts of Phipps and Hanotaux came to nothing. These diplomatic negotiations were renewed in 1896 but again failed to settle the territorial disputes which by then were assuming alarming proportions and intensity. The 1896 talks were broken off because of French insistence on territorial access to the Lower Niger and the inclusion of the Upper Nile question in the agenda of the negotiations.

The adjournment of the negotiations in May 1896 ushered in a period of intensive scramble for the occupation of the Niger territories. France quickly conquered and occupied Mossi and Bussa in the desire to acquire a foothold on the navigable Niger and to link it with Nikki. By an ingenious invocation of the traditional social and political structure of Borgu, she claimed Nikki by condemning Lugard's treaty there in November 1894 and upholding her own as the only valid treaty with the rightful king of Nikki, Siré Tourou. Several other military expeditions were launched by Governor Ballot into Gurma, Borgu, Mossi, and Gurunsi for France at this time.

Chamberlain quickly organized the West African Frontier Force under Lugard and demanded the counter-effective occupation of Borgu by British forces in what has been described as the checkerboard system. The governor of the Gold Coast was instructed to send expeditions into the Mamprussi, Gurunsi, and Mossi regions, including Bona and Lobi, to counteract the French efforts to penetrate southward and eastward from Wagadugu. The result of this crisis was the assumption of responsibility for the Niger territories by the British government and the abandonment of the fear of additional expenditure arising from further colonial responsibility.

Soon British military power in the disputed areas outstripped that of France. Chamberlain's brinkmanship softened Hanotaux, who called for the resumption of the negotiations. The French government wanted a peaceful settlement of the problems between Britain and France. The Niger Commission was reconstituted in October 1897 to deal with the disputes involving territories in the Niger territories. The problems with which the Niger Commission grappled fell under the broad headings of disputes about African treaties, the Say-Barruwa Line, the freedom of navigation of the Niger, the establishment of uniform tariffs in French and British possessions, and the validity of effective occupation as a means of acquiring territory irrespective of prior treaties. There were also disputes about specific points occupied by French or British forces such as Bussa, Bona, Lobi, Ilo, and Wagadugu.

Britain constrained France to withdraw her forces from Bussa, thus carrying to the logical end the policy of excluding France from the navigable Niger. After several months of diplomatic haggling at Paris and of military expeditions in the disputed areas a settlement was reached by the two powers. Britain conceded Mossi, Nikki, Gurunsi, Gurma, and Bona. France evacuated Bussa and agreed to a regime of identic tariffs in British and French possessions for a period of thirty years. France was granted the right to establish two comptoirs on the Lower Niger, and she recognized the Say-Barruwa Line of 1890. The convention was signed on 14 June 1898.

The effects of this settlement on Anglo-French relations were important in paving the way to the rapprochement which resulted in the Entente

Cordiale of April 1904. After the agreement of 1898, the British government assumed direct responsibility for her possessions in the Niger territories, and France established her authority in the areas acquired by her. A new period in the political, social, and economic development of the peoples of the Dahomey-Niger hinterland had begun. This period continued till the political units created by the imperial powers were granted independence in the middle of the twentieth century.

1

The Dahomey-Niger Hinterland and Its Traditional Rulers

The Niger, the third longest river on the African continent, rises within 150 miles of the sea in the Fouta Jallon highlands on the present borders of Sierra Leone and Guinea. It flows northeast, east, then southeast, "décrivant une immense boucle" whose summit is Timbuktu, and finally empties itself into the Gulf of Guinea through a great delta. The length of the Niger is approximately 2,600 miles. Its basin covers an area of about 580,000 square miles, including the lacustrine region between Sansanding and Kabara.[1]

It was part of this vast Niger basin, especially the territory that lay north of the kingdom of Dahomey to the Niger bend, that formed the cockpit of bitter rivalry and struggle for territory between Britain, France, and Germany in the late nineteenth century. This meant roughly the territory north of 9° North Latitude to 15° North Latitude and between 5° West Longitude and 2° East Longitude. The Dahomey-Niger hinterland covered the territory lying between Carnotville, Gambaga, Wagadugu, Say, and Badjibo. Included in this area of approximately 300,000 square miles was all the land belonging to the kingdoms that had some of these towns as their capitals.

Physical Features

Most of this territory is a vast undulating plateau of between 200 and 500 meters. It has a few spots of high altitude, mainly in Mossi and in the middle and northwestern regions of Dahomey in the Atakora range. The other few high points are the Hombor mountains (800–1,000 meters), the Mossi and Kipirsi heights (700 meters), and the Naouri peak (1,800 meters). Very near Carnotville are located the Mahi highlands, the main peak of which is now known as Mount Delcassé.[2]

The territory is drained by many rivers and small streams (*marigots*), some of which swell considerably in the rainy season but are reduced to dry beds in the dry season. After the Niger, the Volta is the most important waterway of this region. There are a few marshes, such as the Lama Marsh, between Abomey and Alada; the Soui Marsh, between Paraku and Okuta; and the marshes in Gurma, in the low-lying basin of the Pandjari between

Yorgu, Pama, and Kodjar. There are only a few lakes in this territory, the largest of which are located in the central part of the Niger bend—Lac de Bama and Lac Dori.[3]

Climate, Vegetation, and Resources

The climate of the Dahomey-Niger hinterland is tropical with two clearly defined seasons—rainy and dry. Tornadoes and violent storms characterize the change of seasons. The dry season lasts from October to March; the rains dominate the period from April to October. The period between November and February is marked by a special cold, dry weather. This is called the Harmattan and is caused by the northeast winds from the Sahara, which also fill the atmosphere with dust particles that cause haze. The farther north one goes from the Atlantic coast, the less rainfall there is, until one reaches the fringes of the Sahara desert across the Niger.

Most of the region is covered by open savanna. However, occasional patches of forest are sandwiched between the savanna zones. The extreme north of Gurma and Mossi is in the transitional zone between grassland and semidesert.[4] This well-wooded territory is rich in timber of all sorts, and there are many tropical hardwoods in the southern section of the region. The grasslands favor animal husbandry. Cattle, sheep, goats, donkeys, and horses abound in this area. Mossi horses are very good and are probably crossbred with Arab stock. Toutée noted the "pasteurization of milk among the Baribas. Women washed their hands in hot water before milking the cows. They also washed the cow's mammary glands and nipples with warm water. The milk container was also passed through boiling water before storage."[5]

In addition to its vegetable and animal resources, the Dahomey-Niger hinterland has substantial mineral wealth. Iron is available all over the granite plateaus of the region. Gold, silver, and antimony were exploited in the Djenne and Bandiagra districts. Gold was known to be abundant in the hinterland of the Gold Coast. Other minerals of the area are manganese and cobalt. During the period of European occupation, the existence of these minerals was known, but reports of their abundance were exaggerated. A French contemporary observed: "Without believing that there are lodes there like those of California, or Australia we should be serious in saying that there *are* minerals in the area."[6] In conjunction with these natural resources were the human resources. There were many centers of large population in areas such as Mossi, Dahomey, Borgu, and Mamprussi, and in cities like Sansanne Mango, Fada N'Gurma, Bussa, Say, and Matiacuali.[7]

The natural resources of this territory constituted desirable raw materials. The population offered prospects of unlimited consumer markets. A consideration of these factors would influence and even accentuate the scramble by European imperialists for the acquisition of the best part of the Dahomey-Niger hinterland. Furthermore, the physical characteristics of the vast area in which European expeditions were to operate in the period after 1885 constituted veritable, often fatal obstacles to all the expeditions. The luxuriant tropical vegetation and the lack of good all-season roads made trekking in this area very difficult. These, with other problems which arose from social and political factors, would affect the course and the speed of European penetration of the hinterland.

Political Situation in the Dahomey-Niger Hinterland in the 1890s

The center of the Niger bend and the region around the watershed of the Volta is inhabited by "a block of Negro peoples who, for the most part, belong to the Voltaic subfamily of the Nigritic linguistic stock." [8] Among these the most important are the Mossi, the Gurunsi, the Gurmantche, and the Bariba. To the south and southeast of this block of peoples are the Mahi, the Fon, and the Yoruba (Nago) of Dahomey.

In the second half of the nineteenth century, these peoples of the Dahomey-Niger hinterland lived under several political divisions entirely independent of one another.[9] These political units differed in their size, structure, organization, and power. However, certain unifying factors were common to most of them, as was their racial similarity. The political divisions fall into three main groups—the Mamprussi, the Borgu, and the Dahomey groups—based on the origins of their peoples. In addition, there were numerous small-scale societies, both kingdoms and chieftaincies, sandwiched between these large political units.

The Mamprussi group comprised the parent dynasty of Mamprussi and the kingdoms of Mossi, Dagomba, Gurunsi, Chakosi, and Gurma.[10] In the Borgu group were the four Bariba kingdoms based at Bussa, Nikki, Kouandé, and Ilo. Bussa was the parent dynasty of the Borgu complex of kingdoms and chieftaincies.[11] The Dahomey group comprised the kingdoms of Dahomey, Ketu,[12] Mahi, and Schabe. The Mahi territory was not organized politically on the same scale as its neighbors but was more or less a conglomeration of independent villages upon which the Bariba to the north and the Dahomeans to the south preyed at will.[13]

The Mamprussi Group

The peoples of the Voltaic Region could be regarded as belonging to the Mamprussi group of kingdoms and chieftaincies. The basic similarity in the social and political organization of these peoples lends credibility to the legends which attribute a common origin to them.[14] It is possible to regard the region as a homogeneous cultural unit belonging to the same linguistic stock. The strong evidence of convergent evolution in this region renders untenable the earlier view of the area "as a mosaic comprising a welter of tongues and divergent customs." [15]

The tri-dominion of Dagomba, Mossi, and Mamprussi was the most advanced form of political organization in this area at the time of European occupation. Gurma also had a well-established monarchy, but by the 1890s the decentralization of the power of the monarch had begun. The other territories which lay outside the jurisdiction of these kingdoms were organized into petty and paramount chieftaincies, the most important of which were Chakosi, Kilinga, Tem, Dagari, and Gurunsi. In Gurunsi there were struggles for paramountcy at the time of the European scramble for territory in the 1890s. The protagonists of the struggle were Hamaria and Babato, the latter of whom moved into the area with hordes of warriors from the north.[16] Babato was fighting not only wars of pillage but also wars of conquest, with a view to establishing his authority in the Gurunsi area.[17]

Another disturbed zone in the Voltaic group was the Dagomba area, where there was a civil war between Yendi and Salaga.[18] As a result of the wars with Yendi, the commerce of Salaga dropped and its population fled. The persistent efforts of Chief Tsafa to repatriate his subjects after the battles met with little success.[19] The disturbances in the Neutral Zone affected the German expedition into the hinterland at that time, whereas Ferguson's earlier treaty-making expeditions into this area encountered no such difficulties.[20]

The Chakosi were of considerable importance during this period, not because of their reputation as professional warriors[21] but because their capital, Sansanne-Mango, had become an important commercial center. It served the caravan routes from Kintampo and Salaga to the north, and traders from the north made their way southward through Sansanne-Mango. The occupant of the Chakosi throne at this period was Chief Nambema, who could look back on a line of valiant predecessors.[22] They arrived from the south as mercenaries serving the rulers of Gonja and Mamprussi during the wars of succession which plagued these kingdoms early in the nineteenth century, fought their way through Konkomba and Bimbla, and settled in the territory which they conquered. They were called the Mango because they came from Mango Ture in Akan territory. Their capital town was called Sansanne-Mango by the Hausa traders from the north, who used it as an entrepot caravan junction.[23] It was this strategic location of Sansanne-Mango which attracted the agents of European expansion to it and caused Britain, France, and Germany to conclude treaties with Chief Nambema in quick succession.

By the 1890s Mossi was the most renowned of all the kingdoms of the Volta region. The kingdom of Mossi, with its capital at Wagadugu, had successfully withstood the Moslem invasions of many centuries and thus built up a reputation of invincibility. The Tokolors of Macina had no designs for the conquest of Mossi because they believed it was invincible. During his flight from the French, Ahmadu of Segu avoided Mossi on his devastating eastward march toward Sokoto.[24]

The kingdom of Mossi was subdivided into eleven provinces for administrative purposes. All the provinces were under the jurisdiction and authority of the Morgho Naba of Wagadugu, who was at the same time the king and chief high priest of his subjects.[25] The Nabas of all the provinces except three were directly elected and invested by the Morgho Naba; those of Yatenga, Busumo, and Rissama "achieve their thrones by themselves but do notify Wagadugu to approve their investiture." All the *Nabas* of the provinces had permanent representatives at the court of Wagadugu.[26]

This constitutional weakness led to frequent internal struggles in Yatenga, Busumo, and Rissama for succession to the nabaship of these provinces. Yatenga, the most important province, was also most affected by the constant civil wars of succession. The apparent inability of the Morgho Naba of Wagadugu to settle these problems or to make his edicts run in Yatenga affected his hold on that province. The French occupation of Bandiagara in 1893 brought them closer to the weakest link in the chain of Mossi provinces. During the 1894–95 civil war in Yatenga, Naba Bagare invited the French at Bandiagara to aid him against his adversaries, mainly princes of the royal house of Yatenga who were pretenders to the throne. Commandant Destenave profited from this situation, moving in and occupying Yatenga. He propped up Bagare with French military force after concluding a treaty of protection with him.[27] Destenave's efforts to enter Wagadugu and treat with the Morgho Naba were unsuccessful because the king refused to deal with any white man and turned away the messenger sent to him. Destenave retreated because of the weakness of his forces.[28] The occupation of Yatenga by the French drove the thin end of the wedge into the Mossi empire.[29] The decentralized nature of Mossi power would be a handicap in its resistance against French forces when they returned a few years later in full strength to occupy Wagadugu effectively.

Gurma, to the east of Mossi, had traditional ties with the states of the Mamprussi group. Like Mossi, Gurma had a well-established monarchy which was based at Fada N'Gurma.[30] In the 1890s Gurma was in the grips of civil war, with the central throne at Fada N'Gurma claimed by rival princes. The main contestants were Bantchande and Yacom-Bato; the latter refused to recognize the former's authority and challenged him militarily. The chiefs of certain districts allied themselves with one or the other claimant. This state of affairs reduced the effectiveness of the central authority and tended to foster independent action by the chiefs. With three out of the eleven provinces of Gurma[31] in revolt against the central authority, the power of Bantchande over the rest of the kingdom was shaky, if not in jeopardy.

Gurma was of considerable importance in the commercial activities of the Dahomey-Niger hinterland. It was traversed by seven principal trade routes, connecting the Niger and the kingdoms to the south of Gurma, as well as the Niger, Sokoto, and Kano with Wagadugu. These trade routes were as follows, according to Molex:

1. Say—Matiacuali—Fada N'Gurma
2. Dori—Bilanga—Yamba—Fada N'Gurma
3. Wagadugu—Kupela—Fada N'Gurma—Say—Kano
4. Fada N'Gurma—Yanga—Djebiga—Samka
5. Fada N'Gurma—Gambaga—Yendi—Salaga—Krachi
6. Say—Botou—Matiacuali—Madjori—Pama—Sansanne—Mango
7. Ilo—Kandi—Baniguara—Kodjar—Kouandé

Gurma therefore shared considerably in the commerce of the hinterland. The local products of Gurma entered the interstate trade of the area. Important among these products were sheep, cattle, horses, ostrich feathers, eggs, and grains. Kola nuts, from the southern forest belt, were needed in Gurma and were used as a means of exchange in the barter for salt, cloth, and horses from Mossi, Macina, and Torodi. Salt bars came from Mossi; grey salt in sacks were brought from Sokoto and Bilma.[32]

The political situation in Gurma in the 1890s disrupted its economic life by diverting caravans to safer routes. Bantchande, who claimed to be the twenty-third successor of Biaba Lompo, the founder of the Gurma dynasty, played the French against the Germans during the scramble for Gurma by these European powers. With French aid he overcame his adversaries Adama and Yacom-Bato before Gurma was finally annexed by France.[33] On the eastern periphery of Gurma, bordering on the Niger, were the intrusive peoples known as the Dendi or Songhay and the Djerma. These peoples migrated southward down the Niger by the beginning of the eighteenth century. They overcame the Tienga, among whom they settled. By degrees they acquired both banks of the Niger around Gaya and established themselves firmly in the lands they conquered.[34] The Dendi chiefs affirmed their descent from the Askia dynasty of Gao.

The Dendi were strategically located and controlled several crossing points on the Niger. Kola nuts and other forest products from Dahomey and Borgu passed through Dendi into Sokoto, and cloth from Kano and Sokoto were taken through Dendi to the markets west of the Niger. Salt production in Dendi was a commercial asset.[35] In addition, the Dendi were reported to be good agriculturists. The Tienga of Fongha produced salt as an adjunct to farming. Fishing was also an important occupation among the Dendi, the Djerma, and the Songhay.[36]

Toutée reported that constant civil war plagued the Dendi region in the 1890s, and Hourst confirmed this, pointing out that Ahmadu of Segu ravaged the area in 1896. "In reality, it was the Chief of Karimama who invited Ahmadu to help him against the Chief of Gaya," observed Perron.[37] It is among the Dendi that we meet the first people of the hinterland whose predominant religion is Islam, though the Tienga are fetishists.[38]

The Borgu Group

The Baribas inhabited the territory known as Borgu. This territory was divided into several kingdoms and chiefdoms. The principal kingdoms were Bussa, Nikki, Kouandé, Bouay, and Ilo. Bussa was the cradle of the Borgu dynasties. Nikki was founded in the fourteenth century by Sunon Sero, who ventured off from Bussa, and the kingdom gained ascendancy over all the other Bariba kingdoms and guarded the sacred drums as a sign of its superiority.[39] In the eighteenth century a prince exiled from Nikki fled to the northwest and established himself at Kouandé, where he started his own dynasty, unmolested by Nikki.[40]

The basic political organization of the Bariba was not understood by the first Europeans who penetrated into Borgu. Their common origin apart, these kingdoms and their subordinate chiefdoms were independent political units, sovereign in all respects and hardly ever in conflict with one another. The Bariba reputation as warriors was earned by them in conflicts with their neighbors—the Mahi and the Nupe—and any intruders into Bariba territory.[41]

Bariba social structure and traditions were strongly hierarchical. The king was at the top of the social pyramid. He delegated authority to chieftains whose authorities were graded. Bariba respect for their traditions accounted for their indifference, if not resistance, to Islam. The king combined his political and social position with religious functions in which the veneration of ancestors played an important part.[42] The cultural unity of the Bariba marked them out from intrusive groups who lived among them, such as the Dendi and other Moslem minorities. The hierarchical structure of Bariba society affected adversely the possibility of political integration. With a total population of under 100,000 in the 1890s, the Bariba kingdoms did not possess the human resources[43] necessary for the creation of large standing armies on the Dahomey scale. According to Jacques Lombard, the ever-broadening horizontal ties between the Bariba aristocracy, as well as the vertical hierarchical ties between them and the rest of society, rendered political integration impossible. Furthermore, no alliances existed between the Bariba kingdoms, neither defensive nor offensive.

Most parts of northern Borgu were barren and unfit for agriculture. However, Borgu was on the whole an agricultural territory. Horses, cattle, goats, sheep, and other livestock were raised by the Bariba. On the whole, agricultural production was low, and much of it was for subsistence and did not enter into commerce.[44]

Dahomey

Dahomey was the only kingdom of the section of the hinterland under consideration which was below 9° North Latitude.[45] Its importance lay in the fact that it was the most important gateway to the interior (in the 1890s) from the Slave Coast, where three European colonies were perched closely together. The presence of Dahomey made this gateway inaccessible to Europeans who wished to go into the hinterland, unless they skirted Dahomey. Not until this local obstacle to European expansion into the interior was removed, either by peaceful settlement or by force, could agents of expansion traverse Dahomey freely to and from the hinterland.

Because of its nearness to the sea, Dahomey came into early contact with

Europeans[46] and established commercial relations with them. Her ports of Whydah and Cotonou were important centers of the slave trade. By the middle of the nineteenth century, King Gezo elevated the Dahomey monarchy to new heights of prestige. His successor, Gléglé, continued this aggrandizement of the power and wealth of Dahomey.[47] By the end of his reign, in December 1889, the relations between France and Dahomey were so strained that war seemed inevitable (see chap. 3 below).

Dahomey was a centralized state, highly organized for effective political and military action. Her standing army of about 20,000 men and women was the largest on the west coast of Africa at that time. The economic base of the kingdom was the most solid of the African kingdoms in the area. Unlike Ashanti and Mossi or the Bariba kingdoms, the fiscal policy of Dahomey was highly developed; taxes, duties, and customs were collected by efficient agents of the central authority, not by vassal chieftains who paid annual tribute to the king only as long as they maintained good relations with him. There were royal farms and plantations on a much larger scale than in Mossi.[48] Colonies of captives lived at Savi and Whydah, where they were employed in the production of palm oil and palm kernels under the supervision of royal agents known as *Ahisinon*. These products were exchanged at the coast for European goods and weapons.

Fon traditional cooperative institutions such as the *gbe*, the *so*, and the *dopkwe* were employed to fulfill royal demands in the new situations that arose in the nineteenth century, especially during the wars with the Egba (Yoruba) and with France. The *gbe, so,* and *dopkwe* were nonsecret, self-help associations of young men. They regularized and solemnized their relationships by the "drinking of the *vodun*," which imposed "absolute fidelity, unlimited confidence and continual assistance to one another and to each other's families," according to Paul Hazoumé. Under the supervision of the *dopkwegan,* the chief of the *dopkwe,* the young men of the villages joined together to build houses, cultivate the farms, construct and repair roads, and erect ramparts and walls. The *so* organized for cooperative work in the cultivation of fields belonging to its members. In times of national emergency, the king of Dahomey relied on them for feeding the troops. The nineteenth century saw the reinterpretation and expansion of the functions of Fon cooperative institutions.

In addition to her other assets, Dahomey was densely populated in comparison with the rest of the hinterland. According to the estimates published by the Dahomey government in 1899, the population of Lower Dahomey was 258,574.[49] Recent estimates put the Fon population of Dahomey at about

1 million.[50] The people of Dahomey held their king in high esteem and even regarded him as an idol. "After God, the King" was the pithy way in which Dahomeans expressed veneration of their king.[51]

Finally, the wealth of the kings of Dahomey was exaggerated. The pomp and ceremony which attend the several traditional festivals at which the king officiated must have contributed to this exaggeration. At the time of Béhanzin in the early 1890s, the total revenue of the court of Abomey was estimated at 2.5 million francs, including all the taxes and duties in money and kind.[52]

From the foregoing survey of the situation in the Dahomey-Niger hinterland just before the period of European exploration and occupation of this territory, we see a mosaic of political entities. When not disturbed by internal strife or by wars against one another, these kingdoms and chieftaincies were in regular commercial contact with one another. A network of caravan routes linked the whole area. According to Barth, Mossi was traversed by sixteen caravan routes because of its location in the center of the Niger bend. Products of local industries and agriculture entered into the trade of the hinterland. The Mossi were not only good farmers but also "excellent smiths." [53]

The lack of political and military alliances is evident. The Mamprussi-Mossi nonaggression pact was a negative one[54] containing no mutual assistance clause. Even among the Bariba kingdoms there was no defensive alliance. The lack of centralized authority, except in Dahomey, affected the speed and efficiency with which mobilization against foreign invasion could be effected. The absence or the weakness of regular armies was another handicap. Of course, communications between the various political units of the hinterland were poor, since messages took several days or weeks to go from one capital to another in times of peace or war respectively. Traders provided the link between the political divisions of the hinterland. Stories of events in one section were likely to be embellished and exaggerated as they were transmitted to other areas. By this same process, the wealth and natural resources of the hinterland were grossly exaggerated by most European explorers and their informants. For instance, two French administrators in Upper Dahomey resigned their posts and established their own business at Djougou,[55] probably lured by the caravans that passed through Kouandé and Gurma. In 1901 Lugard reinforced the glorious economic prospects of the hinterland and expressed amazement at the volume of merchandise that flowed through the caravan routes.[56]

All these local factors affected the development of events in the Dahomey-Niger hinterland in the period from 1885 to 1898. The European imperial powers could not neglect these local factors during their scramble for and occupation of the Dahomey-Niger hinterland.

2

From Berlin to Brussels, 1885–1890

The beginning of the 1880s ushered in a period of increased activity on the part of colonizing European powers in western Africa. The determined action of France in Senegambia and her armed penetration of the Upper Niger territories was common knowledge in Europe.[1] The course of this penetration was as fitful as that of a mountain stream, and periods of sustained activity alternated with those of comparative inaction and sluggish preparation for further advance. Both France and Britain were consolidating their possessions on the west coast of Africa at this time. Farther down the western coast, Portugal, Britain, Germany, and France were busy acquiring new territories or consolidating previous acquisitions. In this area, the Congo basin was the main bone of contention; Angra Pequena,[2] over which Britain and Germany had a sharp dispute, was the second. The Congo question involved Belgian, Portuguese, British, French, and German interests and was thus a potentially explosive one. The need for a peaceful international settlement of this question seemed to be a necessity and was discussed as early as 1882 by Emile Banning.[3] In addition, Chambers of Commerce in Germany and America—the Manchester Chamber of Commerce and that of Rotterdam—called for an international solution of the Congo question. The Institut de Droit International, at its annual conferences held at Paris in 1878 and at Munich in 1883, discussed the Congo question. Sir Travers Twiss, a British member of the Institute, supported the idea of a regime on the Congo similar to that of the Lower Danube.

In September 1883, M. G. Moynier presented a treatise to the Institut de Droit International on the Congo question, to which he appended a ten-article project for an international treaty on the Congo. These were circulated to the powers by the Institute.[4]

What added fuel to the burning question of the Congo was the Anglo-Portuguese Treaty, signed, after two years of negotiations, on 26 February 1884.[5] Objections were raised in Europe, during the protracted negotiations for this treaty,[6] about Portugal's claims to territories in the Congo basin. Germany and France refused to recognize the Anglo-Portuguese Treaty of

26 February 1884. The question became vexatious for European diplomacy, and it was realized that an understanding between all the powers was indispensable for its solution.[7]

The Angra Pequena affair and the Anglo-Portuguese Treaty[8] decided Bismarck to call an international conference on the Congo and western Africa. Bismarck's aims were stated clearly to the French Ambassador in Berlin, Baron de Courcel:

> L'étendue des possessions coloniales n'est pas l'objet de notre politique; nous ne visons qu'à assurer au commerce allemand l'accès de l'Afrique sur des points jusqu'ici indépendants de la domination d'autres Puissances européennes. . . . Les deux Gouvernements sont également désireux d'appliquer à la navigation du Congo et du Niger les principes que le Congrès de Vienne avait adoptés pour assurer la liberté de la navigation de quelques fleuves internationaux, et qui plus tard ont été appliqués au Danube.
>
> Pour assurer le développement régulier du commerce européen en Afrique, il serait en même temps utile d'arriver à un accord sur les formalités à observer pour que des occupations nouvelles sur les côtes d'Afrique soient considerées comme effectives." [9]

Germany and France collaborated fairly closely in paving the way for the conference. Jules Ferry declined the offer made by Bismarck that the invitations to the conference be issued in the names of Germany and France. However, he conceded that the invitations could be issued in the name of Germany "avec l'accord de la France." [10]

The Conference and the Questions Concerning the Hinterland

When the conference opened on 15 November 1884, Sir Edward Malet, the chief British delegate and ambassador to Berlin, stated in his first speech that Great Britain wished to control the navigation of the Niger alone, but that the question was still open to discussion.[11] Britain's position as far as the Niger was concerned was clearly stated: the Niger should be treated separately, and there should be no international commission for it. Sir Edward Malet insisted that "the establishment of an international commission on the Niger appeared impracticable." [12] The peculiarities of the Niger were outlined by the head of the British delegation. First, most of its middle course between Timbuktu and Bussa was riddled with impracticable rapids—1,000 miles approximately—and was unnavigable,[13] thus cutting off the Upper from the Lower Niger. "The river itself, for most part of its course, is very imperfectly explored," observed Sir Edward Malet. Second, the commerce of the Niger basin owed its "development almost exclusively to British enterprise," and the trade of the area was then "altogether in British hands." [14] It was possible for Britain to make the assertion that all the commerce in the Lower Niger was altogether in British hands, because Sir George Goldie had bought out the French firms in the area a few weeks before the conference opened in Berlin. Commandant Mattei, whose position on the Lower Niger had become untenable[15] following a period of intense cutthroat competition with Sir George Goldie,[16] sold his Comptoirs to the National Africa Company in October 1884.[17] Though the French owners of C.F.A.E. ratified the deal, most of the leaders of French opinion on colonial matters were displeased by it. Edouard Viard thought the sale of the trading posts of a few merchants did not imply the abandonment of French rights in the Lower Niger.[18] Furthermore, General Faidherbe, a well-known figure in French colonial circles and a member of the Conseil Supérieur des Colonies, stated that the sale of their business by two French companies in the Lower Niger was a simple commercial transaction which bound only the parties concerned and not the French nation. It did not confer on the British any exclusive or prohibitive rights in the area from the international point of view.[19]

Finally, the British held that the principles of the Congress of Vienna could not be entirely applied to the Niger. The coastline and the lower course of the river were under sufficient British control. Therefore, navigation could be regulated and "the principles of free navigation" guaranteed by a formal declaration by Britain.[20]

How did the Niger and the Niger basin come to form an integral part of the agenda of a conference called solely to discuss and settle the Congo question? The prelude to the Berlin Conference on west Africa was marked by Franco-German cooperation and the opposition of both powers to Britain.[21]

The strained relations between France and Britain at this time were not only discussed by the press but were also bluntly reviewed in official circles in Paris, where much concern was expressed about the "démêlés avec les Britanniques" [22] in western Africa. Even during the conference, the Colonial Department in Paris issued instructions to its agents in western Africa calculated "pour prévenir les actions inconsidérées" of the agents of British expansion.[23] It is small wonder then that Jules Ferry initially proposed the inclusion of the Niger in the discussion of the Congo.[24] This French demand seems to have arisen as a result of the acute commercial rivalry in the Lower Niger between Britain and France, and because of the considerable friction between these two imperial powers all along the Guinea Coast.

Furthermore, the French government felt that if they secured free navigation of the Niger through the Berlin Conference, they would have won adequate compensation for and repaired sufficiently their failure to aid the C.F.A.E. and save it from going out of business.[25]

Bismarck was well disposed to this suggestion. It would emasculate Ferry's demand for a quid pro quo by an amendment of article 11 of the Treaty of Frankfurt, which dealt with the cession of Alsace-Lorraine to Germany. On this point Courcel received a cold and evasive response from the Iron Chancellor.

Her Majesty's government did not receive favorably the proposals that the Niger would be discussed pari passu with the Congo. In the Foreign Office, the common view was that the call for freedom of navigation on the Niger was definitely anti-British, and that the idea of establishing an international commission on the Niger was unacceptable.[26] Historically, the Niger was tied to Britain.[27] It was British initiative and energy and the expenditure of British money that explored it and opened it up. British enterprise had started to flower in the lower reaches of this great river and its delta. In addition, the Oil Rivers district and "the Lower Niger up to its confluence with the Benue" were British protectorates.[28] Great Britain intended to retain control of the Lower Niger, though she was willing to permit freedom of navigation to all on it.[29] Her proposal that the terms of the Congress of Vienna be applied to other African rivers such as the Zambezi was not accepted.

Bismarck, who at first questioned British claims on the Niger, finally came around and threw in all his heavy weight in support of Britain's claims. It seems he adopted the position in order to improve his chances of securing early British recognition of the International Association while he gave France a sop by recognizing her authority in the Upper Niger.[30]

While the commission was discussing the Niger question, an envoy from the Djerma of Timbuktu was in Paris on a diplomatic mission. Abdel Kader, the envoy, met the leaders of the French government. Ferry thought this event strengthened the position of France at the conference.[31] On the other hand, the recognition of the International Association by Great Britain on 16 December 1884 won for Sir Edward Malet the sympathetic cooperation of the German, Belgian, and American delegates over the Niger question.[32] But Britain's proposal that the principle of free navigation should apply to other African rivers, especially the Zambezi, was opposed by Portugal and France.[33]

Underlying the deliberations of the conference and its commissions on the questions of the navigation of the Congo and the Niger were considerations of the African hinterland.[34] In the case of the Congo, the conference explicitly defined the "conventional basin" of this river.[35] As for the Niger, it was envisaged that "powers who already exercise, or who eventually shall exercise, sovereign powers or those of a Protectorate in the Niger" shall apply the provision of the Acts of Navigation on this river.

Thus the future acquisition of territory in the basin of the Niger was recognized as probable. In any case, both rivers were veritable highways of communication with the hinterland.

> "Gentlemen, a vast market is open in the heart of Africa. All nations will there be treated under conditions of perfect equality, and commerce is subject neither to import duties nor vexatious formalities. . . . Nature has created vast waterways by which commerce, and with it, it is to be hoped, progress in every form, will penetrate to the centre of the African continent. But, to enable them to realize such hopes, it is requisite to place them under a beneficent system of immunities and guarantees. Such is the object of the Acts of Navigation which are to apply to the Congo and the Niger, in such different degree as circumstances render necessary, the principles which render the free navigation of these rivers one of the highest achievements of modern law.[36]

To the merchants of Europe, the second basis was the most important task of the Berlin Conference. They would have been indifferent if the conference had ended in December 1884, after it had completed its work on the Acts of Navigation.[37] For them, the conference was summoned in order to regulate "les conditions les plus favourables au developpement du commerce . . . dans certaines régions de l'Afrique." [38] A study of the discussions of the Niger in the conference reveals three main points. First of all is the exaggerated importance of the Niger in Europe at this time. The French even christened it with assurance "le Nil occidentale." [39] Second, the statesmen and their advisers possessed very little factual knowledge of the river. Their ignorance of the Middle Niger was almost complete, as Captain Toutée and Lieutenant Hourst proved a few years later.[40] Third, Great Britain successfully carried through her jealous policy of keeping the Germans and the French away from the Lower Niger.[41] However, when the press in England claimed that the powers who were at the Berlin Conference had endorsed British sovereignty in the Lower Niger and its basin, it evoked immediate refutation from Germany, probably under the instigation of Prince von Bismarck.[42]

The Third Basis

The official invitation to the powers stated that the third basis on the agenda of the conference would deal with the essential conditions to be observed so that new occupations on the coasts of the African continent would be held to be effective.[43] To the British Foreign Office this was the most sinister of the three bases; it seemed calculated to eject Great Britain from certain of her important commercial posts where her only claims dangled on a thin quasi protectorate.[44] The Foreign Office was right. Bismarck wished to formulate a code or method of occupation to be applied to African territories. This he sincerely hoped would muzzle Great Britain, who was, according to the Germans, expanding in all directions, especially in the Middle Niger and in Adamawa.[45] The intensity of Bismarck's anti-British plans was only reduced because Jules Ferry received them warily and with the utmost circumspection. His coldness was not even thawed by Bismarck's tempting suggestion that he should bring up again the Egyptian question with vigor.[46] The same perceptiveness with which the British Foreign Office defined the problem was applied to the search for its possible solution.

Lord Granville delayed sending instructions to Sir Edward Malet on the third basis until the British Government's position on it was clarified.[47] There was serious divergence of views on this subject in official circles and even in the cabinet.[48] By the time the conference adjourned for Christmas in 1884, the British position on the third basis was still far from clear. The insecure situation was exacerbated by the anxiety of Sir Edward Malet to return to England for his wedding, which had been scheduled for that December. Granville pleaded with him to hold on till the end of the conference and condoled with him and his betrothed, "to whom the delay must be very annoying."[49] Furthermore, efforts to ascertain from Germany the meaning and import of certain words and phrases contained in the third basis met with peremptory and evasive replies. For instance, Sir Edward Malet, in accordance with orders from London, inquired at the German Foreign Office as to the import of the word *coasts*. He was informed that it meant "territories bordering on the sea"![50]

In the meantime, intense activity had begun in the Foreign Office. Sir Julian Pauncefote obtained the opinion of the Law Officers of the Crown on "effective occupation."[51] To this, Lord Selborne contributed the fine distinction between *annexations* and *protectorates*. He benefited from an earlier memorandum prepared in 1883 by Sir E. Hertslet.[52] Pauncefote had doubts about the merits of these subtle distinctions and wondered if they would not "upset the coach on the third basis," thus doing Britain more harm than good.[53] Be that as it may, Sir Edward Malet was instructed to press for the exclusion of protectorates from the clause on jurisdiction because they did not entail the same obligations as annexations and were thus outside the terms of the third basis.[54]

On the other hand, Great Britain wished to make some additions to the Franco-German project on effective occupation. The first of these was the extension of the area to be covered by the new regulations from the coasts to the whole of the African continent. "The African coasts are very near being occupied for the whole of their extent, and that, if reduced to this zone, the formalities we have in view will have but little practical value," argued Sir Edward Malet.[55] The British Foreign Office had strong suspicions that the term *coasts* would be subjected later to "an elastic interpretation" which would possibly give the proposed formalities a "wide territorial application." To anticipate this, Granville originated the idea of applying the two propositions of the third basis to "the whole African continent."[56] Baron de Courcel opposed the amendment proposed by Britain. He contended that although there was little unclaimed territory on the coast, it possessed an importance which justified making new arrangements. Furthermore, lines were clearly defined along the seashore, whereas, in regard to territorial delimitations, there was much that was uncertain and unknown in the interior of Africa.[57] Germany was not "hostile in principle" to the British proposal but felt that it necessarily implied the precise and early settlement of the state of possessions of each power in Africa. John A. Kasson, the minister from the United States,[58] observed that such a delimitation would present important advantages in addition to the prevention of future territorial disputes. He was countered by the remark that "a precise definition of present possessions would lead in fact to a partition of Africa" and that the conference could not deal with acquired positions.[59]

Britain's second demand was that any act of notification by any power be accompanied by a statement of the area occupied, in order to avoid exaggerated claims later. This proposal was not accepted by the commissioners because of its impracticable nature at that time.[60] Jules Ferry instructed Courcel to subscribe to the British proposals on notification only if there was unanimous agreement on this point.[61] Difficulties of a practical order prevented unanimity of views on the two preceding British proposals. But the amendment proposed by Britain that the provisions of the third basis apply equally to powers already possessing territories in western Africa as well as to any newcomers was adopted.[62]

Third, Malet submitted to the commission the British proposal which sought to remove the term *protectorates* from the jurisdiction clause of the provisions by arguing that these were very different from annexations or outright occupations.[63] The German delegates opposed it vehemently when the commission met on 16 January. The apple cart was almost upset; Pauncefote was vindicated.[64] Britain was accused of selfishness. Her aim was to acquire territories by treaties of protectorate, thus excluding other powers from these areas without undertaking any obligations herself. Sir Edward Malet was not supported by the powers. Bismarck was ill-disposed to the omission of the word *protectorates* from the draft project when Busch consulted him on this matter.[65] Back in the Foreign Office in London the question of annexations and protectorates evoked a clash of views after Malet had written home signaling the problems he had encountered and the advice he had received from Sir Travers Twiss, A. Hemming, and R. Mead.[66] Pauncefote and Sir William Harcourt were prepared to concede the point, but Lord Selborne resolutely opposed any concession. He stated that principles should take precedence over the smooth functioning of the conference, because the principles would matter long after the ephemeral diplomatic success at the conference had been forgotten.[67] It seems that Lord Selborne had the backing of Gladstone but not of the other members of the cabinet who desired German cooperation in the Egyptian problem.[68] Renewed pressure on Bismarck by Malet irritated the chancellor, who threatened to disrupt the negotiations if an end to the delay was not in sight. This threat softened the British government. At a special cabinet meeting it was decided to bury the hatchet and accept the amended version of the project. Malet was advised accordingly. On the other hand, Bismarck, on second thought, had instructed Busch to drop the word *protectorates* from the third basis. The commission's work was done, and the proposals were ratified by the conference on 31 January.[69] A parallel thaw on both sides had produced the desired result.

All through the discussion of the third basis, the hinterland was ever present, directly or indirectly. Germany accused Britain of the desire to block the interior to other powers by ill-defined treaties of protectorate. Bismarck had his eyes on the hinterland. He inveighed against the "territorial appetite" of France and Britain, which, by appropriating land before the Germans, would have the advantageous result of "girdling in the German settlements and cutting them off from the interior." [70] The French were not oblivious of the hinterland either. After all, they were engaged in expansion in the Upper Niger at this time, and Ferry had at one point thought it desirable to initiate the occupation of Timbuktu toward the end of 1884.[71]

With reference to the third basis, the hedging and the introduction of checks and balances into the provisions was proof that the interested powers wished "garder les coudées franches" for future maneuvers in the hinterland.[72] Though the proposal for a delimitation of possessions in Africa was not carried by the conference, it was shelved. General knowledge of the interior of west Africa, especially the Dahomey-Niger hinterland, was very sketchy in this period. Even the coastal lands were not as well known as one might imagine. The next decade was to witness the relentless and resolute effort by the interested European powers to remove a barrier to the partition of Africa—the Europeans' ignorance of the hinterland.

Though the conference succeeded impressively in its political, economic, and juridical work, it failed, if not woefully, in its humanitarian aims. Slavery and the slave trade, the liquor problem, and the welfare of the Africans received but cursory and superficial attention.[73]

According to Emile Banning, the Berlin Conference, through its General Act, ordained "la code diplomatique de l'Afrique moderne." Moreover, by implication, it declared African territories not occupied by any European power *res nullius* and thereby ushered in a new epoch in the relationship between Africa and Europe. As Maurice Baumont observed, the Berlin Conference "élaborait une sorte de code international en vue du partage de l'Afrique noire." [74] The General Act of the Berlin Conference set down the rules of the game of territorial acquisition in Africa. It was referred to in cases of dispute between the powers over territories, in questions of notification of treaties and protectorates, and in claims of the right to freedom of navigation of the Niger. In fact, the arbitration of the Mizon affair by M. Lambermont was based on the provisions of this General Act. In international law, it had important and far-reaching juridical effects throughout the partition of Africa.[75]

The Partition of the West Coast of Africa after Berlin, 1885–90

As Baron de Courcel was quick to point out during the Berlin Conference, what was left unappropriated by European powers of the coasts of west Africa was of considerable commercial importance, even if there was not much of it. Since the General Act of the Berlin Conference had implicitly ordained that any territory in these parts belonged to the first comer, the powers and their agents actively began not only to "peg out claims" but to make good their claims. The areas involved were defined, and, by a series of bilateral arrangements and treaties, the entire coast of western Africa was partitioned by the European imperial powers by 1890. Only those arrangements concluded with reference to the Slave Coast and the Gold Coast affected directly the later developments in the Dahomey-Niger hinterland.

When Great Britain proposed the extension of the provisions of the third basis of the Berlin Conference to the whole of the African continent, she buttressed her proposal with the argument that there was not much left on the west coast of Africa in the way of unoccupied territories. How right was Lord Granville, who invented this argument which was aired in Berlin by Sir Edward Malet? Two days after the conference commenced the discussion of the formalities to be observed in order that new acquisitions of territory on the west coast of Africa could be considered effective, Spain proclaimed a protectorate over Rio de Oro and Spanish Guinea.[76] These two new additions increased to about sixteen the total number of ill-defined colonies and comptoirs under European control in western Africa. The comptoirs occupied considerably less space than the colonies. These colonies themselves, such as Lagos, Gambia, and Sierra Leone, did not stretch far along the coast from their respective headquarters. In view of this, the length of coastline between Cape Verde and Cape Lopez occupied by European powers at the beginning of 1885 could be placed at approximately 500 miles.[77] The length of the Upper Guinea coast is approximately 2,500 miles.[78] It follows that roughly 2,000 miles of coastline was then unappropriated and available for imperial enterprise. The two longest stretches were those between the colony of Lagos and the nascent German Cameroons, and between Grand Bassam and Sierra Leone. The most important, from a commercial point of view, was the section between Lagos and the Cameroons, which included the Niger delta region.[79]

Four-fifths of the coastline was by no means an insignificant remnant of the whole. Therefore, the British argument was not founded on fact. This illustrates once again the paucity of general knowledge about Africa at the time, when regulations that would influence her future were being fashioned with good intentions, even if on false premises.

Territorial Settlements after 1885

The life of the Berlin Conference was intentionally prolonged to provide time for the solution of those territorial questions whose amicable settlement was essential to the successful completion of the work of the conference.[80] Those territorial arrangements that were made were not definitive, but they paved the way for the peaceful resolution of future territorial questions. Since the General Act of the Berlin Conference had set up new norms for effective occupation and notification, the powers had to tie together their comptoirs and notify each other about their rights. In the wake of the Berlin Conference there followed a series of proclamations of protectorates on the west coast. As we have seen, Spain initiated this new phase of the partition of Guinea by proclaiming a protectorate over Rio de Oro and Spanish Guinea on 9 January 1885. German Cameroons was recognized by Great Britain on 7 May 1885, and soon after a British protectorate was announced over the Niger Delta and Oil Rivers on 5 June 1885. France was not to be left behind. Her agents began an energetic and systematic collection of treaties in selected areas, usually around their long-established coastal trading stations. This staccato effort covered places scattered along the coast from Dubreka (Rivières du Sud) to Benito.[81] As each power tried to establish itself effectively on the coast, it discovered the necessity of defining the limits of its authority and jurisdiction. Britain and Liberia settled the Liberia–Sierra Leone frontier by 11 November 1885. The Bight of Benin and the Slave Coast provoked more serious problems than the rest of the Upper Guinea coast, and to these we now turn our attention.

The Slave Coast after 1885

As has been pointed out above, most of the Slave Coast and the coasts of the Bights of Benin and Biafra was unoccupied by European powers by 1885. Between the British colonies of the Gold Coast and Lagos, the only occupations were the then rudimentary German protectorate of Togo[82] and the dubious French protectorate of Porto Novo.[83] All the span of coast between Lagos and the Cameroons was free except for the diminutive Mahin Beach enclave,[84] which G. L. Gaiser had acquired by purchase on 29 January 1885. The strip of coast between Grand Popo and Porto Novo belonged to the kingdom of Dahomey. Its main port was Whydah, where the Yevogan[85] appointed by the king of Dahomey lived and exercised sovereign rights.

France and Porto Novo

The French position in Porto Novo had been very vague indeed, and the British colony of Lagos had had cause to intervene in the Porto Novo area several times. The climax had been the blockade of 1876 and the occupation of Ketenu by Governor Ussher of Lagos in 1879. The intermittent friction on the Slave Coast forced France to initiate measures for strengthening her position in Porto Novo and at Cotonou (also spelled Kotonou). It was strongly suspected at the Quai d'Orsay and at the Rue Royale that Britain had the intention of occupying the Slave Coast, and memories of the insistence of Governor John H. Glover that Britain should annex all the Slave Coast were still fresh in the official circles in Paris.[86] Though Cotonou was ceded to France by the treaty of 23 April 1878,[87] French rights there remained vague. The Yevogan, under pressure from Abomey, began a campaign of disengagement from the treaty and even disclaimed his signature on it. The French vice-consul on the Slave Coast, Antin d'Elteil, recommended armed occupation, but the officials in Paris had their doubts about the virtues of an action which might embroil them in more serious disputes with Britain.[88] The passage of time aggravated matters on the Slave Coast. The prospects of a comprehensive settlement of west African questions between Britain and France became more remote.[89] Though the Sierra Leone frontier problem was successfully adjusted, the events that unfolded in Egypt were not conducive to harmonious Anglo-French relations generally.[90] However, repeated offers of his kingdom to France for protection, insistent pleas from French consuls on the spot, and a desire on the part of the French government to conserve with great caution their prior anterior treaty rights on the Slave Coast combined to produce a new mood which made practicable the establishment of a new French protectorate over Porto Novo in 1883.[91] A treaty of friendship and protection was concluded between King Toffa and France on 25 July 1883, and this marked the beginning of the "second French Protectorate" at Porto Novo.[92] The first resident, Bonaventura Colonna de Lacca, died soon after taking office and was succeeded by Guilmin. Then followed a rapid succession of honorary residents,[93] until Colonel L. Dorat took office in May 1884 as the first paid resident. The new resident soon found himself uttering the same warnings as his predecessors Antin d'Elteil, Serval, and Bareste about the British threat to French authority on the Slave Coast. He reiterated with great concern that the French presence at Porto Novo was an obstacle to the expansionist plans of Britain and that the British would spare no efforts to render this presence untenable or at least useless, saying:

> L'Angleterre dont l'objectif est de relier ses possessions de Lagos et celles de la Côte-de-l'Or afin d'être maîtresse du Golfe de Guinée et des embouchures du Niger, entretient avec soin les dissentiments entre les indigènes et les pousse à ces idées d'indépendance; le gouvernement colonial intervient alors et établit son protectorat, réclamé ou non, sur ces petits Etats qu'elle feint de considérer comme ne faisant pas partie du royaume de Porto Novo.[94]

Colonel Dorat and his predecessors were not mistaken in their suspicions concerning British objectives on the Slave Coast. There is abundant evidence that British administrators such as J. H. Glover, Hewett, Ussher, Moloney, and Governor S. Rowe wished to annex Porto Novo.[95] After the Union Jack was hoisted over Ketenu and its environs, Ussher boasted proudly that Britain held the "key to the road between Cotonou and Porto Novo." He hoped that if Toffa were skillfully pressed Porto Novo would be ceded to Great Britain. If annexed, this "magnificent town under the misrule of a tyrant" would bring in to Lagos a minimum annual revnue of £200,-000.[96] In May 1881 A. Moloney told Bareste, the French consul, without reserve that Lagos expected an annual revenue of £25,000 from Ketenu.[97] The French agents, therefore, were not guilty of misjudgment, even though some of their reports were embellished with exaggerations. But for several reasons, both the Foreign and the Colonial Office in London were not enthusiastic for a forward policy in west Africa at this time. First of all, "the persisting economical spirit of the country still resisted increased imperial liabilities."[98] Second, the policy of the Colonial Office, according to the Duke of Devonshire, was in the main guided by the spirit of the resolutions and findings of the West Africa Commission of 1865, which opposed a forward policy.[99] Thirdly, the Egyptian question was paramount at this time, and all other colonial problems in Africa were but diminutive appendages to it.[100] On the other hand, beneath the caution of the London officials was the conviction that expansion in the future was a possibility. The ever-mounting "imperialist outcry against abandoning to foreign annexation unappropriated territories of colonial and commercial interest" could not be ignored perpetually.[101] Already Lord Kimberley had reacted to it positively, declaring that "we shall get to the Hausa country via Lagos long before the French."[102] The events that unfolded themselves on the Slave Coast after 1885 were instrumental to the realization of this British hope.

The Partition of the Slave Coast after 1885

After the Berlin Conference, the Slave Coast posed the most intricate problem on the west coast of Africa. This five-cornered problem involved the interests of Great Britain, France, Germany, Portugal, and Dahomey. Nowhere else along the Upper Guinea coast were so many powers involved in so short a strip of coastal territory. Though the Portuguese were the first comers to these parts, they had been outdistanced by the French and the Germans in the commercial race there. The uncomfortable nearness of the dynamic British colony of Lagos added another facet to the question. Then there was the added difficulty of the presence in these parts of the two African kingdoms of Dahomey and Porto Novo. France had already acquired Porto Novo as a protectorate. The various European powers involved resolved their claims by diplomatic means, and it was to take a full-scale war to dislodge Dahomey from her portion of the Slave Coast.[103] For purposes of clarity it is better to look at these events country by country than to follow the events in a chronological pattern.

France and Portugal: Conflict and Agreement, 1885–87

After the Berlin Conference, Portugal was the first power to secure new treaty rights on the Slave Coast. Portugal was by no means an intruder in these parts. Indeed, it was Eucaristus de Campos, a Portuguese slave dealer, who founded Porto Novo in 1752 as a new haven for his business. And the Portuguese fort of San Joao Baptista d'Ajuda was a constant reminder of their early relationship with the Slave Coast (until it was abandoned on 31 July 1961).[104] The desire to make their position at Whydah more tenable motivated the Portuguese to initiate talks with King Gléglé's representative, Juliano Felix da Souza, which culminated in the conclusion of a treaty between Portugal and Dahomey on 5 August 1885. This treaty placed the coastline of the kingdom of Dahomey under Portuguese protection. It also gave to Portugal "une foule de concessions au désavantage de Glélé,"[105] especially customs rights over Godomey and Abomey-Calavi. Both Edouard Foà and Robert Cornevin claim that King Gléglé was not well informed by his *chacha* about the forms of the treaty of 5 August 1885. The swift punishment of Juliano Felix da Souza in 1887 by the king vindicates this French claim. But it is interesting to note that this French manner of looking at treaties concluded by rival European powers with African rulers persisted to the end of the partition of west Africa.[106]

Portuguese and French authorities on the Slave Coast clashed when Portugal proceeded to assert her new treaty rights on the Dahomey coast. The hoisting of the Portuguese flag in the environs of Cotonou in September 1885 provoked impassioned protests from Lieutenant Roget, who insisted that the area belonged to France. By 14 September 1885 Roget and his men hoisted the Tricolor in the disputed area.[107] The resolution of this minor local conflict was but the beginning of a long diplomatic tussle. On 21 January 1886, Portugal notified the powers who ratified the General Act of the Berlin Conference of her protectorate on the Dahomey coast, in virtue of the treaty of 5 August 1885. The French Foreign Office raised objections, which were communicated to the Portuguese government by the French ambassador in Lisbon.[108] While diplomats haggled in Lisbon and Paris, there were several parallel developments on the Dahomey coast which affected the trend of events. First of all, the newly appointed commandant of the Portuguese fort, Major Silva da Curado, paid an official visit to Abomey. King Glégé received him cordially but was unyielding over the terms of the doomed treaty of August 1885.[109]

Second, the fort of San Joao Baptista d'Ajuda was always officially classified among the colonial possessions of Portugal.[110] Administratively it was under the jurisdiction of the governor of San Thomé. Following the experience of Major Silva da Curado at Abomey, the governor went to Whydah on the first leg of a proposed official visit to King Glégé to regulate matters arising from the August 1885 treaty. But the Fabian tactics adopted by the chacha Juliano Felix da Souza—probably to cover up his fraud of 1885—kept the governor in Whydah for almost three months without fulfilling his desire to confer with Glélé.[111] The Portuguese did not give up.

Another official Portuguese delegation was dispatched to Dahomey after the governor's report reached Lisbon. They arrived at Abomey in March 1887[112] and found King Glégé as unyielding as ever. These persistent but unsuccessful efforts by Portugal to ascertain her treaty rights from Abomey underlined two facts. First, the treaty of 5 August 1885 was of doubtful value, if not completely null and void. Second, Glélé discovered that his chacha had not only overstepped the bounds of his authority but done so fraudulently. Consequently, Glélé visited on Juliano Felix da Souza that terrible dictatorial wrath which Henri Lefaivre said was not lacking among Dahomey kings.[113]

On the other hand, Portugal found out that her claims to a protectorate over the Dahomey littoral were hollow. It was unprofitable to continue the tedious diplomatic negotiations with France concerning these claims. At the same time Portugal was being harried by Britain in central Africa. Salisbury firmly lectured the Portuguese foreign minister that the British government would not recognize Portuguese sovereignty over territories "not occupied by her in sufficient strength to enable her to maintain order, protect foreigners, and control the natives." [114]

Portugal announced to the powers on 22 December 1887 her renunciation of that protectorate, although she retained her fort at Whydah.[115] The withdrawal of Major da Curado ended the Portuguese threat to French predominance on the Slave Coast.

France and Germany on the Slave Coast, 1885–90

German enterprise on the Slave Coast began in earnest by the middle of the nineteenth century. Before then, German interest in Africa had expressed itself in scientific expeditions and travels. Romance and wanderlust also induced many Germans to journey in several parts of Africa at a time when German publicists and merchants were engaged in forging a "colonial cult." [116] In direct relation to west Africa were the works of Heinrich Barth and Gustaf Mann; the latter's botanical interests led him to the Niger basin to study the flora of the region. Gustav Nachtigal was another important German pioneer in west Africa. German missionaries[117] and traders were the pioneers of German influence on the Slave Coast. The Norddeutsche Missions Gesellschaft, founded in Bremen in 1836, sent four missionaries to the Slave Coast in 1847. These men began work at Christiansborg and Peki, but their premature deaths put an end to the first evangelizing efforts of the Bremen mission on the Gold Coast. They renewed their efforts and in July 1853 sent out a second batch of missionaries, who established themselves at Keta among the Ewe people.[118] By 1860 these missionaries had opened stations at Waya, Anyako, and Wegbe, and their remarkable progress was accompanied by journeys into the hinterland which resulted in the increase of geographical and ethnological knowledge of the area.[119] There were German missionaries on the Gold and Slave Coasts before the arrival of the Ewe Mission from Bremen. R. Cornevin states that Graf von Zinzendorf of Herrenhut had prepared and sent out to Elmina in May 1737 two missionaries—Jacob Protten and Henrick Huckoff.[120] Huckoff died on 15 June 1737, and Protten was unsuccessful in establishing a mission, even though he made two other voyages to the Gold Coast before his death in 1769.[121]

Also, many Germans were in the service of the Basel Mission which began proselytization on the Gold Coast in 1827. Though their initial efforts were undermined and enfeebled by the death of their missionaries, the Basel Mission made persistent efforts which only began to fructify after 1843.[122] The expansion of their field of activity, such as the founding of a new station at Aburi in Akwapim in 1847, resulted in the entry of many Germans into the service of the Basel Mission.

German merchants contributed to the spread of German influence on the Slave Coast. With their British and French competitors they carried on trade along the west coast of Africa and shared in the palm produce of the Bight of Benin.[123] The customs duties levied by the Gold Coast and Lagos administrations forced these traders to seek alternative free ports. The result was the growth of German and French agencies along the Slave Coast at Grand Popo, Agoue, Little Popo (Anecho), Beh Beach (Lome), and Keta.

The rapid growth of German industry added extra impetus to the advance of German maritime commerce. In the Bight of Benin, German trade grew by leaps and bounds. By the 1880s, British and French traders had been overtaken by their German colleagues at Keta, Lome, Grand Popo, and Anecho. That the German firms carried 75% of the palm oil and about 50% of the palm kernels in these ports in 1883 is evidence of their predominance on the western Slave Coast.[124] Baron de Courcel, the sagacious French ambassador to Berlin, was aware of Germany's ever-increasing commercial advance in the Gulf of Guinea. He observed that the German element in the Bight of Benin had reached such proportions "pour que nous devions, desormais, le faire entrer dans nos calculs." He buttressed his views with the statistics of German overseas trade.[125]

Most German expansionists fervently believed that "die Flagge folgt dem Handel." Theo Sommerlad stated that the pioneers of trade should pave the way to colonization for the state.[126] Did not Bismarck ask rhetorically what colonial policy was, adding defiantly that Germany must protect her traders?[127] He went on to protect German traders by acquiring colonies with the unbounded enthusiasm of a novice, in a way that did not escape the comments of his contemporaries.

> Le Prince de Bismarck apporte dans la politique coloniale où il se jette la même énergie d'impulsion, la même hauteur d'aspiration dont il a donné les marques dans sa politique continentale. On ne peut guère douter qu'il ne croie le moment venu de déposséder l'Angleterre de

son hégémonie maritime, comme il a dépossedé, il y a quinze ans, la France de l'hégémonie politique et militaire en Europe.[128]

The German colony of Togo was a result of the above factors.[129] It was founded by the declaration of a protectorate over Bagida, Lome, and the kingdom of Togo on 4 and 5 July 1884. Gustav Nachtigal secured his first treaty of protection from Chief Plakko of Bagida on 5 July 1884, after which followed the ceremony of hoisting the German flag.[130] The next day Henri Randad was nominated provisional consul by Nachtigal, and he held the post till Falkenthal's arrival as Imperial Commissioner of Togo.

After the Berlin Conference, concentrated efforts were made to extend the German protectorate of Togo.[131] Already Captain Herbig had secured a treaty of protection from Chief Mensah of Porto Seguro on 5 September 1884. The French were alarmed by this German move, because they had prior treaty rights at Porto Seguro. Captain Dornian was sent out to assert French rights by the effective occupation of Grand Popo, Petit Popo, and Porto Seguro in April 1885. The German answer was to send Admiral Knorr immediately behind Captain Dornian to safeguard their newly acquired laurels.[132] Back in Paris the new Freycinet Ministry, which came into office after the fall of Jules Ferry, was concerned about this friction with Germany on the Slave Coast. Earlier German efforts to secure a customs agreement with France for this area had petered out because of Ferry's disinclination for such an arrangement. Freycinet and his cabinet were not agreed on a "complete customs union" between their possessions and those of Germany. Other alternative proposals failed.[133] It was in the face of the two-faced problem posed by Portugal and Germany that Freycinet enunciated French policy on the Slave Coast—a policy of consolidation, not expansion.[134] This did not, however, prevent French agents from the conclusion of a treaty of protectorate over Ouatchi on 10 June 1885. Nor did it deter Lieutenant Emmanuel Roget from placing Agoue under French protection on 12 September 1886.[135]

While the French government was seeking a satisfactory diplomatic settlement of the difficulties with Germany on the Slave Coast, Frenchmen who had stakes in the area voiced stiff opposition to German expansion. For instance, in July 1885 the Reverend Menager, a missionary, circulated in France letters by which he intended to activate anti-German pressures on the French government. The Germans, he said, had occupied Gridji and Agbanaken and were so strategically placed that they could cut off French trade at will.[136] Colonel Dorat, who was the French consul at Little Popo and Porto Seguro, complained bitterly about the speed with which the Germans moved into Little Popo.[137] Neither official nor political pressures could shake Freycinet from his conviction that a settlement was imperative. Bismarck was unpredictable. In addition, the memories of Tonkin and the fall of Jules Ferry were so painfully fresh at the Quai D'Orsay that the avoidance of a colonial conflict with Germany was a necessity.

It was clearly realized in Paris that Porto Seguro could not be retained as an enclave in the German protectorate. It had not been possible to obtain Dubreka and a few other comptoirs in Guinea (Rivières du Sud) in exchange for Porto Seguro. Bismarck would not give up his claims to Dubreka. By September 1885 it had become clear to officials in Paris that Porto Seguro was irretrievable. A new basis for a settlement with Germany was found in the persistent demand for German recognition of French rights over Agoue. Baron de Courcel carried the point in Berlin, and the terms for an agreement were drawn up.[138] These terms were studied in Berlin.

A few minor concessions were made by both powers in the course of the exchanges which followed, and the protocol was signed in Berlin on 24 December 1885 by de Courcel and Bismarck.[139] For France, there was no point in hanging on to Anecho and Porto Seguro, the renunciation of which she had endorsed by the signature of the Protocol of December 1885. Accordingly, Colonel Dorat was advised to withdraw from these places. He beat an unwilling retreat, complaining not only of the German acquisitions but also of the manner in which they asserted their rights.[140] In accordance with Article 2 of the Protocol of December 1885, both Germany and France appointed commissioners to delimit the possessions of the two powers on the Slave Coast. For most of 1886 the Imperial Commission, Ernst Falkenthal, and Jean Bayol worked at the partition on the spot of French and German possessions. Their task was completed in the Procèsverbal of 1 February 1887.[141] This agreement fixed the frontier from the coast up to 9° North Latitude. Bayol claimed that by this settlement France obtained freedom of political action in the Ouatchi and Dahomey regions. An island was named after him (Bayol Island), and he proposed to Amédée de la Porte, undersecretary for the colonies, that Falkenthal should be made an officer of the Legion of Honor and Henrich Randad a chevalier of the Legion of Honor.[142]

The settlement of the political problems did not solve the tariff difficulties which bothered French and German traders on the Slave Coast. The Germans had proposed a uniform tariff in March 1886. French traders raised objections against such an economic regime on the grounds that it would do them more harm than good, especially in the liquor trade. Negotiations, however, continued until a satisfactory customs arrangement was arrived at in Berlin on 25 May 1887.[143] This agreement remained in force until it was superseded by another one, concluded in Berlin on 26 December 1889 and put into force on 15 March 1890.[144]

These political and economic arrangements between France and Germany settled the problem of their respective possessions on the Slave Coast. Germany had tried in vain to enlist the support of Portugal in her drive against France. Even by invoking the case of Dahomey, Germany failed to rouse the sympathy of the Portuguese government in her favor and against France.[145] Once the littoral frontiers were settled, both powers began to look toward the interior, the veritable source of commodities for export[146] and the mainstay of the coastal trade.

Britain and Germany: Togo–Gold Coast Boundary, 1885–90

After the events that occurred at Bagida and Lome in July 1884, it became clear that Germany would become Britain's neighbor east of the Gold Coast colony. The eastern limits of the Gold Coast colony were extended in 1879 to Aflao[147] as a preventive measure against the perpetual problem of smuggling, which had a debilitating effect on the revenues of the colony. The success of this measure was, however, partial. By 1884 the Gold Coast administration thought of extending its authority further eastward by acquiring the Beh Beach stretch of coastline, the haven for smugglers whose business was waxing rapidly.[148] Indeed, R. E. Firminger had secured a provisional agreement with the chiefs and headmen of Togo in June 1884, by which they agreed to cede to Britain the Beh seaboard up to Porto Seguro if they failed to get rid of the merchants and traders in this area within a month from 23 June 1884.[149] This was the highest point reached by the Gold Coast administration in the development of the proposal to expand eastward. It had not yet fully dawned on Downing Street that the period of "informal empire" was over and that it no longer had all the time in the world to make up its mind on colonial questions—especially in Africa, where the "game of grab" so passionately deprecated by Lord Salisbury in 1879[150] was now in full play.

The reassertion of the French protectorate over Porto Novo in April 1883 galvanized some London merchants to submit a long memorial to the British government demanding, among other things, the adoption by

Britain of "measures to prevent the further annexation of any of the countries between the Gold Coast possessions and Lagos by any other European Power."[151] But the irresolution of Downing Street continued. A few months later the British government was constrained to absorb the shock of Dr. Gustav Nachtigal's swift annexation of Bagida and Lome to the German empire.[152] Lord Derby pacified Governor W. A. G. Young with the prosaic if not weak-kneed excuse that England had fared very well at the Berlin Conference and would therefore not rock the boat by disputing "the German acquisitions, or criticise further the mode in which they were obtained."[153] Thus the second and final blow was dealt to the British scheme for a colony that would include all the coastline from the Gold Coast to Lagos.[154] British acquiescence in the annexation of Togo by Germany led to some anxiety among the administrative officers of the Gold Coast. Administrative efficiency required a clear definition of the areas of authority of Britain and Germany. Friction was bound to occur in the seaboard between Keta and Bagida as German agents inched their way westward to a portion of the coast that British traders and officials still tended to look at as their exclusive preserve. The Germans, meanwhile, proceeded to aggrandize their tiny coastal enclave by concluding more treaties with native rulers. Between April and June 1885,[155] the two governments exchanged notes "relative to their respective spheres of action in portions of Africa." Continued energetic extension of the German sphere in the interior threatened the flow of the Salaga trade into the Gold Coast and nudged the officials of the Gold Coast to acquire the Akwamu and Krepi regions in reaction to German "annexation of the Agotime, Tavi and Kevi countries which lay behind the Kitta district."[156]

A boundary commission was set up, and its work led to the frontier agreement of 14 July 1886. Dr. Krauel for the German government and C. S. Scott for the British continued work on the boundary question, and their joint recommendation was submitted in September 1887. This recommendation included the proposal for the prolongation of the two-and-a-half mile frontier agreed to in 1886 in such a way that Towe, Kowe, and Agotime would be under German protection and Aquamoo and Creppe (or Peki) would be under British protection. The third paragraph of the joint recommendation envisaged the creation of the "Neutral Zone":[157]

> That a conventional line be drawn on the latitude of the mouth of the River Daka, and that the two Governments shall mutually agree to regard the territories lying to the north of this line, within the limits

marked on the accompanying map, as neutral ground, and to abstain from seeking to acquire within them protectorates or exclusive influence.

By mid-March 1888 both the British and German governments had approved the recommendations, thus giving them the force of an agreement.

In spite of this agreement in principle, the Germans continued their drive toward the hinterland.[158] They began to acquire parts of Krepi and contended that these were not dependent on Krepi. They were operating under the impression that whatever they acquired in the interim would be confirmed as theirs by the boundary commissions to be appointed in the near future. The "disquieting activities" of Germany in the colonial field were not peculiar to west Africa. Sir Valentine Chirol[159] later observed that in British official circles "there was an undercurrent of alarm at the ubiquitous restlessness of German policy." In east Africa[160] Britain faced the restless energies of German agents. Germany was also active in the Far East, (where she had an eye on Kiaochow and Shantung), the Near East, and the Pacific.[161] In the late 1880s Britain's official and public attitude toward German colonial enterprise had not changed much from that of disdain or disapproval of the intrusion of an amateur,[162] though it had become clear in Downing Street that Germany's susceptibilities had to be reckoned with in the imperial arena. Germany, especially under Bismarck, had enormous potential for embarrassing England, and her diplomatic nuisance value had to be contained skillfully.[163]

British agents on the Gold Coast countered the expansion of the Germans by feeble exploration missions to Ho, Adaklu, Kunya, Buem, and the adjacent territories.[164] But the Gold Coast coastline could no longer be extended eastward beyond Aflao, where its slow progress had been halted to Germany. Early in August 1889, France and Britain reached an agreement concerning their respective possessions on the west coast of Africa. This cleared the way for a settlement with Germany by alleviating the burden of the African Department of the Foreign and Colonial Offices. Unfortunately, the tenacity with which Germany held on to her claims over Krepi seemed to preclude a compromise settlement. It was stated in London in December 1889 that "the divergence of the views of the two Governments was as great on the east as on the north, and the Boundary Commission, if it were to meet under present circumstances, would be stopped by this divergence at the very outset of their work."[165] It took six more months of tactful diplomatic activity and a dramatic change in German domestic politics to produce a thaw in the German position. The fall of Bismarck in March 1890 dissolved Lord Salisbury's overcautiousness, and before the negotiations were resumed on 14 May he outlined to Hatzfeldt revised proposals for a general settlement which included the cession of Helgoland to Germany for her "recognition of a British protectorate over Zanzibar."[166] "The tempting bait of Helgoland" was irresistible to the German government, especially to the Emperor.[167] It set in motion forces that disarmed German resistance to British claims in east and west Africa.[168] On 1 July 1890 the Anglo-German agreement respecting Africa and Helgoland was concluded in Berlin.[169] Lord Salisbury expressed his "entire approval of the manner in which Sir Percy Anderson performed the duties intrusted to him in connection with this Agreement and of the tact and ability with which he has carried on the negotiations with the German Foreign Office."[170]

There were those, on both the German and British sides, who criticized the arrangements arrived at after these laborious negotiations. To some Germans, like Carl Peters, they represented a fatal check on Germany's development into a first-rate imperial world power.[171]

The German press reacted with mixed feelings to the agreement.[172] However, it was hoped by a few that Helgoland could play an important part in the growth of German sea power in the North Sea.[173]

In Britain, the Helgoland Agreement, as it came to be known, drew comments in Parliament, from the press, and from the public.[174] To the *Daily Chronicle* it was "the most abject and ignominious surrender of British interests" since the fiasco in virgin America.[175] Sir John Kirk, a veteran of African affairs, hailed the Anglo-German agreement because it gave Witu to Britain and reserved for her "Uganda and a free hand in a good squareblock with an open road to the Nile."[176]

Whether Salisbury and his agents negotiated from strength or from weakness, they did use Helgoland as a sop to Ceberus and thus conditioned Germany for a satisfactory settlement of the nagging colonial questions between Britain and Germany. The treaties of 14 June and 1 July 1890 [177] excluded Germany from the Upper Nile; demarcated British and German spheres of influence in east, west, and southwest Africa; and assured British predominance in Zanzibar.[178]

Back on the Slave Coast, the agents of both Germany and Britain began to explore more carefully those areas which they believed to be under their protection. Several expeditions made their way into the hinterland from the coastal stations in the hope of enhancing the value of their possessions by attracting and even controlling the trade of the interior (see chap. 5 below).

Difficulties between France and Britain on the Slave Coast, 1885–90

The reassertion of the French protectorate over Porto Novo in 1883 lodged the thin edge of a wedge between Lagos and the Gold Coast. Subsequent events showed how vigorously the French drove in this wedge to secure their position on the Slave Coast. Early efforts by British administrators in Lagos to squeeze them out were not successful.[179] Continued attempts to consolidate and extend their position brought the French into constant friction with the British. A way had to be found to eliminate these irritations in the interest of wider political considerations.[180] Progress was slow, and it was not until August 1889 that a general agreement was reached by the two powers.

When, after the Berlin Conference, France embarked on an effective occupation of the Slave Coast, she ran into difficulties not only with Portugal but also with Britain, especially in the reticulation of creeks between Porto Novo and Lagos and over Pokea.[181] The Tickel affair of August 1886 was followed by a clash of British Hausa troops and French *tirailleurs* in the Zunu Creek early in 1887. This clash resulted from renewed efforts by Lagos to shut Porto Novo off from the sea[182] and "to bring the French to their senses."[183]

It was an impossible task to "bring the French to their senses." French colonial enterprise on the west coast of Africa had gathered tremendous momentum, as perceived by the Colonial Office; R. H. Meade had already observed early in 1884 that it appeared "as if the French meant to be more active in the coast than they had been in the past."[184] In Lagos serious concern was felt about French expansion in the Slave Coast. The chances of containing France by diplomacy were very remote, because immediate negotiations were not possible while Britain's official experts on west Africa, especially A. W. L. Hemming, were at the Berlin Conference. After the fall of Ferry, his successor, Freycinet, while trying to find his feet in the quagmire of European politics, advised against further territorial acquisitions on the Slave Coast. A few months later France was thinking of submitting her difficulties with Britain in this area to arbitration.[185] Soon France and Germany reached an agreement on their receptive spheres of influence on the Slave Coast. Lieutenant Roget and, after him, Dr. Pereton seem to have been invigorated by this event, and new pressures were applied on Lagos.[186] The settlement with Germany eliminated all chances of a French withdrawal from the Slave Coast.[187] Pauncefote's tactics of playing for time by postponing further negotiations sine die did not pay off but rather complicated the difficulties that Britain had to face on the Slave Coast and, later, in the hinterland of the Slave Coast. The excuse that official west African experts were away from London was not a plausible one. It may be recalled that several bilateral territorial questions were settled during the Berlin Conference, though outside the conference itself.[188]

By the end of 1885, the course of events on the west coast of Africa and mercantile pressures from Liverpool, Manchester, Lagos, and the Gold Coast[189] induced the British government to divide the administration of the Gold Coast and Lagos. Each colony was erected into an autonomous administrative unit by Queen Victoria's letters patent of 13 January 1886.[190] According to J. P. Schwitzer, by this administrative expedient Britain "tacitly acknowledged her defeat on the Slave Coast by making the Gold Coast and Lagos two entirely separate colonies."[191] This conclusion is not borne out by the evidence about the separation of the Gold Coast and Lagos. First, the clamor for the separation of the administration of the two colonies began as far back as 1883 from various quarters. The main reasons adduced by the memorialists were the decline of commerce, which they blamed on administrative inefficiency; the great distance between Lagos and the Gold Coast, which made it impossible for a single officer to administer both of them efficiently; and the unnecessary expenditure of £8,000 a year for the maintenance of a steamer by which the governor commuted between Lagos and Accra.[192] Second, the London merchants pointed out in paragraph 3 of their memorial that the union of Lagos with the Gold Coast since 1874 had "produced serious inconveniences and had created in the minds of the merchants an earnest desire that the administration of the two colonies should again be separate and distinct."[193] Third, in October 1885 the colonial secretary informed W. B. Griffith of the decision to separate Lagos from the Gold Coast. He stated that the British government had been considering this action for some time and went on:

> Experience also has gone far to show that owing to the nature of the climate, to the difficulties of communication, and to the many important matters requiring his constant presence and attention at Accra, it is not easy for a Governor of united colonies to give to the affairs of Lagos that personal supervision which is necessary and desirable.[194]

The "affairs of Lagos" which needed personal supervision included the tendency of France to expand eastward from Porto Novo. If the British government had "tacitly acknowledged defeat" on the Slave Coast, there would have been no point in strengthening her position in Lagos by restoring a separate administration there "with its own executive and legislature."[195] Finally, the manner in which Britain secured the agreements on the boundaries between Lagos and Porto Novo in 1889 and between Dahomey and the Niger territories in 1898 belies the conclusion that she had conceded defeat in these regions.

Britain's position on the west coast of Africa was further strengthened in 1886 by the establishment of direct cable links between Bonny, Brass, Lagos, Accra, Freetown, and Great Britain by the West African Telegraph Company. A cable station was also installed at Cotonou by 1 November 1886.[196] Rapid communication by telegram was now possible between the Colonial Office and the colonial administrators from their "outposts of progress." Another positive action taken by Britain in 1886 was the granting of a royal charter to the National African Company, which then assumed the name of the Royal Niger Company Chartered and Limited. The founder and mentor of this company was Sir George Taubman Goldie.[197] By July 1886, there were therefore two official agencies to protect British interests in the area: the Royal Niger Company along the Lower and Middle Niger, and the government of Lagos in the littoral of the Gulf of Guinea.

France, on the other hand, was searching for means by which to rectify the mistakes of 1884 whereby Commandant Mattei lost the ground he had gained in the Lower Niger. M. Goldscheider, of the Ministry of the Navy and Colonies, preferred internationalization of the Lower Niger to securing French supremacy on the Upper Niger, but Jules Ferry doubted the wisdom of such a policy.[198] Ferry's successor, Freycinet, and his minister for the navy and colonies, Admiral Galiber, hoped for unhampered access to the Upper Niger through the delta of this river, because the Berlin Act had guaranteed freedom of navigation on the Niger. But, as C. W. Newbury has pointed out, the proclamation of a British protectorate over the seaboard from Lagos to Rio del Rey in June 1885 ruined this French dream.[199]

It was suddenly realized that Britain's preeminence in the Lower Niger was inimical to French interests on that river. Freycinet should not have ratified the General Act of the Berlin Conference until it had been amended to safeguard French interests.[200] To the French foreign minister, the declaration of a French protectorate on the Upper Niger would redress the British announcement of 5 June 1885. Admiral Galiber concurred and suggested details of extent and area.[201] France was already expanding her influence in the Upper Niger, but she had not yet progressed far from the headwaters of the Niger.[202]

It was to General Faidherbe that the French owed the credit for the plan of expansion toward the Niger through Senegambia.[203] In 1884 and 1885 Faidherbe expressed great concern about the Middle Niger in sheer reaction to the British progress in the Lower Niger. He formulated a plan to link the French protectorate of Porto Novo with the Middle Niger at Bussa.[204] Such an extension of French influence would be disadvantageous to British enterprise in the Lower Niger. At the Quai d'Orsay this project met with little or no sympathy, because it was not practical at that time, the power of Dahomey being a reality.[205] Faidherbe's proposals were therefore shelved.

Some other French officials connected with the Slave Coast were fertile with ideas about how to gain control of the Middle Niger. Colonna de Lacca, who combined his post as a business *gérant* with that of a French consular agent, proposed early in 1885 that France should strike northward from Porto Novo through Dahomey and Egbaland to the Niger. These kingdoms were to be conquered and annexed. The result would be the practical hemming in of the National African Company and the colony of Lagos.[206]

In addition, Edouard Viard,[207] after consultations with French missionaries in Porto Novo and Abeokuta, formulated a plan for French expansion into the interior. He stressed the advantages and economy of using the Yorubas against Dahomey[208] to clear the way for a northward expansion of French influence.

An event occurred in November 1887 which was to influence tremendously the development of French influence in the Dahomey area. This was the assumption of office by Victor Ballot[209] as "commandant particular" of France at Porto Novo. Ballot quickly rose from special commanding officer to resident, lieutenant governor, and, in 1894, governor. He guided the formation and the development of the French colony of Dahomey until his retirement in 1899. He had gained considerable administrative experience in Senegal from 1880 to 1887 before his assignment to Porto Novo[210] and had been called "le veritable createur de la colonie du Dahomey." With considerable perception Moloney insisted on the securing of the Lagos hinterland by treaties, in order to "guard against a repetition here of a diversion of trade and influence as we now experience in the Upper Gambia effected by French undermining." Moreover, such a treaty system would erect a formidable bulwark against the undesirable aggression of both the Muhammadans from the north and Dahomey from the west. This plan was approved, with a Foreign Office proviso that the contemplated treaties should neither involve the British government in any additional administrative burden nor violate any legitimate French rights.[211] So, while French experts were pondering how to gain control of the hinterland, British agents were also formulating plans for checkmating their French rivals in the same area.

Both Britain and France recognized the urgency of settling these territorial problems.[212] A shaky truce was declared over the areas in dispute on 2 January 1888, as diplomats made preparations for the delimitation of their spheres of influence in these areas.[213] It was not easy to come to terms about the general bases for negotiations. First, the unstable political situation in France was worsened by the outburst of Boulangism,[214] which almost led to another invasion of France by Germany. Lord Salisbury could not but wish for "another Franco-German war" beneath "the great black cloud" in which he saw "a silver lining" because it would "put a stop to the incessant vexation" caused by France.[215] In May 1887, Lord Lyons, who had "sound judgment, and an almost inhuman impartiality," painfully observed: "I think, in fact, that things look very bad for France both at home and abroad."[216] Two months later Baron Alphonse de Rothschild expressed his fears about the dangers of the European coalition against France. He was anxious to see the outstanding questions producing irritation between Britain and France settled without delay and had told Rouvier that the time had come to translate into action his "anxious desire to establish cordial relations with England."[217] There were several Frenchmen who were in agreement with Lord Lyons's views about the French dilemma.

Second, however, although the French Foreign Office was willing to settle west African questions with Britain, the Colonial Department was not eager to do so. Furthermore, Britain wanted to discuss all outstanding difficulties in west Africa, whereas the French Colonial Department wanted to discuss specific and isolated problems individually. Worse still, the Bureau de l'Afrique resorted to delaying tactics with reference to correspondence concerning these problems.[218]

In the meantime, the modus vivendi of 2 January 1888 had been violated by Edouard Viard, a French explorer whom Sir George Goldie considered "one of the most energetic agents" of French expansion in the Lower Niger.[219] Viard was sent out to investigate the actual and potential commercial situation in the region between Porto Novo and the Middle Niger and was instructed to abstain from "toute ingérence active dans la politique."[220] He flouted ministerial instructions from the start, disembarking at Lagos instead of Cotonou and reaching Porto Novo on 4 March. Ballot prescribed an itinerary for him through north Porto Novo to Oyo, which he did not follow. His actions were predictable,[221] though strangely enough the authorities who sent him out failed to see this. Or they hoped to benefit from his actions if Britain connived at whatever he would do in the area.[222] The newspaper articles on the Viard affair tend to suggest that Viard may have had more than the written instructions we know of, especially those in *Le Matin* and *Le Temps*, some of which were "doubtless inspired by the Colonial Department."[223] Perhaps it was because the French Foreign Office rebuked Jean de la Porte for authorizing Ballot to initiate negotiations for the acquisition of the comptoirs that were to be left by Portugal on the Dahomey coast that the Colonial Department adopted a different attitude toward Viard, whose mission was planned and sanctioned by de la Porte.[224]

When interrogated by Lagos authorities, the chiefs of Abeokuta denied having concluded any treaties with Viard. This was far from the truth, though Moloney was inclined to believe it because he was anxious to secure treaties from Abeokuta and the districts adjacent to it. Abeokuta's recent overtures to the French were prompted by their desire to reestablish their old slave trade connections with Porto Novo and Dahomey.[225]

Because of the storm raised by Britain over Viard's breach of the modus vivendi of 2 January 1888, the French government did not ratify the treaties he collected.[226] The Anglican missionaries in Lagos were incensed by the fact that Edouard Viard received active support from the French Catholic missionaries at Abeokuta. They not only harbored him but also provided him with guides and interpreters and acted as witnesses to the treaty he signed with the Alake of Abeokuta.[227] Therefore, the British missionaries urged the educated Egbas of Lagos to persuade the Alake to conclude a treaty of protection and friendship with Governor Moloney. They also appealed to the Foreign Office for support in their effort to exclude France from the hinterland of Lagos.[228]

Progress toward the conference table continued apace. Ballot and Moloney gave details to Paris and London respectively on the importance of the areas under dispute. Moloney adduced six cogent reasons for striving to include the kingdom of Pokra (Pokea) in the British sphere.[229] These reenforced Hemming's view that England had a "strong and legitimate claim to exercise exclusive influence" in the hinterland of Lagos.[230] According to

Moloney, Addo River was important to Lagos, and the further advantages that would accrue to this colony from the acquisition of Pokra were:

> Extended trade markets of Colony
> Territorial extension in view of increasing population
> Large field of food supplies
> Lever in direction of influencing eventual French withdrawal
> Command of waterway represented by Addo River
> Check of Slave Traffic with Porto Novo.[231]

The efforts of the British government to secure a diplomatic settlement of the territorial questions outstanding between France and Britain in west Africa were unabated by their concern over a possible French invasion of England under the chauvinistic and erratic General Boulanger.[232] Both the Foreign and Colonial Offices wanted a satisfactory and speedy arrangement of the west African disputes. Lord Knutsford, who would have preferred immediate ratification of the commercial treaties concluded by Lagos because of the mounting pressure from merchants and missionaries, instructed Moloney that no action could be taken concerning them until the forthcoming Anglo-French negotiations in Paris had been concluded.[233]

Victor Ballot, on the other hand, exerted himself to persuade the officials in Paris that vital French interests were at stake in Pokra and the Addo River. He argued that these were an integral part of the kingdom of Toffa of Porto Novo. If Britain gained them they would control the Cotonou–Porto Novo waterway. They had already installed themselves at the mouths of the main waterways which link the coasts with the hinterland:

> Ils sont établis à l'embouchure du Volta, de l'Addo, de l'Ogun, de l'Ochoun et du Niger. S'ils parviennent à s'installer à l'entrée de la lagune Kotonou–Porto Novo, ils sont alor maîtres des toutes les voies naturelles ouvertes au commerce de l'intérieur.[234]

Ballot's insistence on the importance of access to the hinterland is noteworthy because the control of the Dahomey-Niger hinterland was to be the keystone of his policy of expansion in the 1890s. There was also considerable pressure on French officials from merchants who had interests on the west African coast. "La grande question est toujours la delimitation des frontiers franco-anglais," reiterated M. Verdier.[235] French missionaries were no less eager to see a resolution of the nagging frontier disputes.[236]

At the Quai d'Orsay, the desire to draw closer to Britain in the face of European unfriendliness toward France disposed the officials to come to an agreement with Britain.[237] Furthermore, the fall of the Flouquet Cabinet in February 1889 furthered the chances of a quick and satisfactory settlement with Britain.[238] To Lord Salisbury the British ambassador in Paris confided:

> I think that the very conciliatory tone of Admiral Barby, the new Minister of Marine and Colonies, coupled with the removal of M. de la Porte, the late obstructive Under-Secretary for the Colonial Department, and the present disposition of the permanent officials of the French F[oreign] O[ffice], which is undoubtedly favourable to an early settlement of disputed questions in a liberal and conciliatory spirit, offer a better opportunity than any we have yet had for a satisfactory negotiation of the Senegal and Gambia question, provided the negotiations opened at once, in a business-like way. . . . But if our object is to settle them as soon as possible, now is the time.[239]

The opportunity offered by this favorable conjunction of circumstances was utilized by both powers. Commissioners were appointed, and Paris was chosen as the seat for the negotiations. The terms of reference for the commissioners were succinct and precise.[240] When the negotiators met, Egerton began by stating the principles which Britain wished to see adopted in west Africa. The French reply was that specific questions, on areas from the Slave Coast to Gambia, should be thrashed out one after the other.[241]

From the start the proceedings of the commission were marked by mutually conciliatory attitudes. The French were "tres coulant," as Nisard had promised earlier.[242] Though the British Colonial Office had expressed its dissatisfaction at the manner in which Lord Salisbury handled west African questions,[243] they were also very accommodating, especially as the responsibility of reaching a settlement rested largely with Hemming.

On the other hand, the French Colonial Department was not quite as conciliatory as Lord Lytton thought it would be with de la Porte out of the way. His successor, Eugene Etienne, was a more ardent imperialist.[244] First, Viard's treaties from Egbaland were forwarded to the Ministry of Foreign Affairs with a long covering letter underscoring French claims and dismissing British claims as invalid.[245] Second, the treaties concluded with Bondoukou in November 1888 were ratified on 4 April 1889. Etienne adjudged that M. de Beckman had lost all "sang-froid" and should be replaced at Porto Novo by M. Tautain, Directeur des Affaires Politiques in Saint Louis.[246] Third, the Bondoukou incident provided another lever with which the Colonial Department tried to upset the smooth progress of the discussions that were then in progress in Paris. Etienne emphasized French treaty rights and demanded compensation from Britain. Spuller, as conciliatory as ever, dismissed these complaints as immaterial.[247]

By a series of reciprocal concessions, the barriers to a settlement were minimized, and the French put together a projet d'entente on which subsequent discussion of all remaining questions of detail would be based.[248] Hemming held on faithfully to Moloney's views about the value of Pokra and the Addo River to Lagos and succeeded in securing these for Britain[249] in the final agreement, which was signed in Paris on 10 August 1889.[250] It was clear in London and in Paris that this agreement was a welcome method of ending the prolonged friction which resulted from the competition for territory on the seaboard of west Africa.[251] But more difficulties were in store. The penetration of the Dahomey-Niger hinterland would be the opening of a veritable Pandora's Box.

The General Act of the Brussels Conference: Mandate for the Occupation of the Hinterland

As the possessions of the European powers on the west African seaboard were being defined, there arose in western Europe a clamor for the suppression of the slave trade and slave raiding in Africa. The *porte-parole* of this movement was Cardinal Lavigérie, who had founded anti-slavery societies for this purpose. He put forward a bold scheme of sending a corps of dedicated volunteers into the African hinterland to combat slave raiders and stop the slave trade.[252] Lavigérie preached an anti-slave trade crusade throughout the capitals of Europe and attracted much sympathy.[253]

What Lavigérie said reminded the powers of their undertaking at Berlin in 1885 to tackle the slave trade question at a subsequent conference. Britain did not wish to lose the initiative in the anti-slavery field to Lavigérie. Salisbury therefore decided to call a conference of all the powers who signed the Berlin Act of 1885. But in order not to attract the suspicion of these powers, especially Portugal and France, it was thought that King Leopold II of Belgium should be asked to invite the powers to Brussels for this conference. The Belgian government accepted the British proposal. Then began a series of diplomatic contacts which finally resulted in the Brussels Conference of 1889–90.[254]

The conference, though summoned for the "purpose of promoting a matter of pure humanity and goodwill, was not entirely devoted to humanitarian questions. Territorial disputes, especially between Britain and Portugal, were a regular feature of the discussions, as is evident from the protocols of the sessions.[255] The deliberations of the conference were skillfully used to further the political, commercial, and fiscal aims of some of its leading participants.

Great concern was expressed for the interior of Africa, which was unanimously regarded as the source of the slave trade. The area involved was that part of Africa between 20° North Latitude and 22° South Latitude, which included practically all the hinterland. To stop the slave trade and slave raiding at its source, it was agreed that this zone had to be controlled, not only by flying columns as envisaged by Lavigérie but by the establishment of European political and commercial authority over the inhabitants of the area.[256] This would keep out the slave raiders or quickly reduce their effectiveness and render less difficult the control of the maritime traffic.[257]

By enjoining the building of railways, the introduction of steamboats, and the setting up of administrative machinery, the General Act of the Brussels Conference implicitly gave the powers the mandate to occupy and govern the interior of Africa in order to suppress the slave trade. The Dahomey-Niger hinterland was included in the specified zone, though at the time in question most slave raids were carried out in eastern and central Africa by Arab traders. The conferences at Berlin and Brussels set the stage and provided the juridical basis for the extension of European influence into the African hinterland from the coastal comptoirs and possessions.

3

The Conquest and Occupation of Dahomey, 1890–1894
The First Dahomey War, 1890

The Kingdom of Dahomey: Foundation and Extent

The foundation of the kingdom of Dahomey probably dates from the seventeenth century, but the establishment of the despotism which was the nucleus of that kingdom occurred in about the sixteenth century.[1] The exact date of the actual foundation of the kingdom is not known, though serious efforts have recently been made to place this event in chronological perspective.[2] M. J. Herskovits pointed out the discord that exists in the chronology of the Abomey dynasty as given by different authors. The work of Edouard Dunglas on this subject appears to be the most reliable to date.[3]

Two legends persist as to the origin of the kingdom of Dahomey. One is based on the etymological and historical explanation of the origin of the name Dahomey;[4] the other on the religious beliefs of the Fon. It will suffice here to recapitulate the central idea of each of these legends, since they have been related in detail by several authors.

The more popular legend attributes the origin of Dahomey to the defeat of Dan at Abomey. The vanquished Dan was not only executed but also cut open ventrally. His intestine was displayed in vengeance. He was subsequently interred at Abomey, whence his inordinate ambition had carried him.[5] Alexander d'Albeca gave a different version of this myth by analyzing the word *Dahomey* etymologically in the Dedji language.[6]

The other legend assigns the foundation of Dahomey to the invincible, demi-god and demi-man Dan, who picked the location of Abomey for religio-political reasons, with the holy city of Cana nearby. By his superhuman attributes Dan assured the invincibility of his dynasty as long as he was worshipped faithfully.[7] This legend appears more credible. It has been pointed out that the name Dahomey (spelled in different forms) appears in atlases[8] published several years before the probable date of the defeat and dissection of Dan (ca. 1610–45), to which the first legend attaches the origin of the name. This raises the question whether the word *Dahomey* was in use before it was ever invented: E. Dunglas recently reinterpreted *Dahomey* to mean "in the House of Dan." [9] This lends great weight to the case for the second legend. Unfortunately, the more sensational legend gained currency because it bore closer affinity to the brutal stereotype of the kingdom of Dahomey created and popularized by the majority of Europeans who wrote about Dahomey from the eighteenth century on. Gross and fantastic exaggerations about Dahomey were not uncommon.[10] To these were added the imaginary embellishments of "voyageurs en chambre," and the result was an image more distorted than ever.[11]

The present République du Dahomey is several times larger in area[12] than the former kingdom of Dahomey. The frontiers of the pre-colonial kingdom were not clearly defined and precise. When asked about the boundaries of their country, Dahomeans usually replied that it was the largest in the world.[13] This imprecision was due to the lack of the knowledge of cartography, which made the delimitation of frontiers in the European style impossible. Theoretically the ancient kingdom of Dahomey was coterminous with the zone over which the authority of the king of Dahomey was unquestioned. Estimates of this territory ranged from 4,000 to 36,000 square miles.[14] In practice, there were customs stations in villages which were considered as frontier outposts. These terminal customs stations on the main arteries of communication and principal caravan routes marked what the court of Abomey considered as points of entry into and exit from the kingdom of Dahomey.[15] The authority of the king of Dahomey extended farther than the points marked by these frontier stations, from which Dahomey intelligence agents watched vigilantly the movements of adjacent tribes such as the Egbas and the Mahis.[16]

It was not until 1888 that a fairly accurate map of Dahomey was produced by Victor Ballot.[17] Even then the exact area of the kingdom remained unknown.[18] In any case, by 1890, when Dahomey came into armed conflict with France, its territories stretched from the Atlantic coast in the south to the country of the Mahi in the north and from Egbaland in the east to Togo (German) in the west. The natural boundaries in the east and the west were the rivers Oueme and Mono, respectively.[19] This whole territory lay in the tropical rain forest belt and was consequently densely wooded. Another important physical feature of this region was the presence of innumerable streams and rivulets as well as the centrally located marshes of Lama.[20]

Development of Diplomatic Relations between Dahomey and France

The French claim that their relations with Dahomey date back to the fourteenth century. But it was not till the second half of the seventeenth century that France obtained her first foothold on the Slave Coast by establishing a fort at Whydah in 1671. However, real diplomatic relations between France and Dahomey were inaugurated on 1 July 1851, when Lieutenant Bouet concluded a treaty with the King of Dahomey confirming French rights to the fort at Whydah and guaranteeing liberty of commerce in all the kingdom of Dahomey to Frenchmen.[21] The French later established themselves at Grand Popo in 1857 and at Porto Novo on 3 February 1863.

Early in Glégé's reign he concluded a treaty with Jean-Baptiste Bonnaud on 19 May 1868, by which he ceded Cotonou to France. Difficulties soon arose which resulted in blockades of the Dahomey coast in October 1867 and again in 1876–87.[22] Glégé was softened if not chastened by these naval exercises, and on 18 April 1878 he concluded a new treaty with (Captain) Paul Serval, by which he confirmed the cession of Cotonou and Porto Novo to France.[23] The renewal of the French protectorate over Porto Novo in 1883 with King Toffa's consent was followed by effective occupation of Porto Novo and then Cotonou, in keeping with the provisions of the General Act of the Berlin Conference.[24] This military assertion of her treaty rights by France led King Glégé to a sudden and unpleasant realization of the full import of the treaties he had signed some years before.[25] He was neither willing to part with any part of his kingdom nor prepared to relinquish his rights to revenue collected in Cotonou. King Glégé enjoyed being a great king. He had inherited the kingdom of Dahomey from his "august father Ghezo, son of Agonglo," at its apogee and would not "abandon its riches to foreigners."[26]

> Ce Glé-Glé a été une manière de Louis XIV nègre, puissant, redouté de ses voisines, entouré, d'une cour nombreuse, très domestiquée, tenant courbes sous sa main de fer les nobles et les vilains, les féticheurs et les guerrièrs. C'est une figure qui n'a pas eu de cadre.[27]

Consequently, Glégé adopted a policy of unilateral disengagement from treaty obligations. First of all, he denounced his treaty with Portugal and punished his agent who was responsible for that treaty (see chap. 2, p. 32 above). His maneuvers succeeded splendidly, and Portugal abandoned her efforts to establish a protectorate over the Dahomey coast in December 1887. Second, Géglé protested to the French resident at Porto Novo in 1887 and bluntly refused to recognize the French military occupation of Cotonou and the protectorate over Porto Novo.[28] In addition he adopted an openly hostile attitude toward King Toffa of Porto Novo, whom he considered the principal architect of the recent developments on the coast.[29]

Unwillingness of Britain and France to Intervene in Dahomey

By the beginning of the nineteenth century, the kings of Dahomey had come under serious criticism in Britain as well as in France, centering around their slave-dealing activities. Moreover, they were seasoned by soul-searing narratives of continual human sacrifices and other forms of savagery. The climax of these unpleasant rites in Dahomey was the annual national festival at Abomey,[30] at which several Europeans had assisted.[31] M. Lartigue, who was an agent of Régis on the Slave Coast, spent some time at Abomey in 1860 and made detailed entries in his diary on the immolation of human beings during the national festival.[32]

Great Britain has always led the anti-slavery movement and always had the initiative in the anti–slave trade campaign.[33] It was principally to put an end to slave-dealing in Lagos that Britain attacked and conquered King Kosoko in 1851.[34] But his collaborator, King Ghezo of Dahomey, was only censured, even though he carried on a much more destructive and ravaging slave-dealing activity than Kosoko and also supplied the Lagos market with slaves.[35] The unwillingness of Britain to intervene militarily in Dahomey continued during the reign of Gléglé. The blockade of Whydah in 1876–79 had limited objectives. Lord Derby reluctantly gave his blessing to Hewett's ultimatum to Gléglé, in order to preserve British prestige on the west coast.[36] Neither Britain nor France wanted to intervene directly in the kingdom of Dahomey at this period.[37] As for England, her expedition against Ashanti in 1874 had driven home the immense difficulties involved in such an exercise —health, sanitation, logistics, and transportation, to mention a few—as well as the cost of such an operation.[38]

When Germany began its acquisition of Togoland, it was thought in the admiralty that Britain should not protest because the "eventual collision with Dahomey would most likely fall to the lot of Germany instead of England." [39] It is clear from this view that British naval officials had not ruled out an ultimate collision with Dahomey. Furthermore, the Foreign Office had considered military intervention in Dahomey but tactfully shied away from it. When Egerton reported that Lieutenant Governor Bayol had confided to him that France would undertake punitive action against Dahomey, the Foreign Office heaved a sigh of relief.[40] As Etienne pointed out, Britain was afraid "de s'immiscer dans les affaires de la cour d'Abomey." [41]

The resident of France at Porto Novo reminded his government in December 1888 that "une expédition au Dahomey serait une gross affaire, mais pas aussi difficile que l'on pourrait le croire." [42] Moreover, early in February 1890, while Jean Bayol was insisting on a war against Dahomey, Captain Leopold Fournier frankly told the Ministère de la Marine that to carry "la guerre sur le territoire Dahomien serait chose grave; . . . il aura pour conséquence de compromettre le pavillon, d'enrayer le commerce, de mettre en peril la vie des résidents européens." The commencement of hostilities against Dahomey at points on the coast would be the prelude to a war more savage than that made by the British against Ashanti, Fournier concluded.[43] The main practical question, then, was who would undertake to bell the cat. As one French observer saw it, the English and Germans wished for only one thing: "c'est qu'une puissance européene, n'importe laquelle, s'empare du Dahomey afin d'être certains qu'ils seront desormais en securité et qu'ils pourront se livrer au négoce ou à leurs autres occupations sans craindre de devinir victimes des Dahoméens pillards." [44]

The International Setting: Britain and Germany Removed from the Dahomey Area by 1889

One of the results of the development of international relations on the Slave Coast from 1884 to 1889 was that the French protectorate of Porto Novo and the kingdom of Dahomey were lumped into the same zone. By the very nature of these two political entities, no symbiosis was possible between them. The interests of France and Dahomey were not only divergent but also mutually exclusive.

The settlement of the frontier between the British colony of Lagos and French Porto Novo on 10 August 1889 covered the area from the coast to 9° North Latitude. To the east of this line, Britain was to have complete freedom of political action; France was to have identical privileges to the west of the frontier line.[45] Thus Britain was, by agreement, excluded from any political action in the kingdom of Dahomey, because it was situated west of the agreed-upon frontier line and did not extend beyond 8° North Latitude. M. Jacques Spuller stressed the fact that the agreement with Britain had clearly defined the area in which France could thenceforth expand freely.[46]

To the west of Dahomey, the Franco-German agreement of 1 February

1887 defined the boundary between Togo and Grand Popo.[47] France had complete freedom of political action to the east of this frontier. This treaty insulated Germany from direct contact with Dahomey and therefore from collision with that state. Furthermore, when Portugal renounced its protectorate on the Dahomey coast in December 1887, a process of elimination, as it were, left France to face the question of Dahomey in her own way and at her own time.[48]

The conclusion of the Anglo-French agreement of 10 August 1889 affected in several ways the course of events on the Slave Coast and its hinterland. First of all, it dampened the vague optimism that prevailed in Lagos and in the Colonial Office in London about the possibility of exchanging the isolated Gambia for Porto Novo and Cotonou.[49] British officials in Lagos considered the increase of revenue that would accrue to the colony from Porto Novo if an exchange of territories were effected. Special emphasis was laid by the Colonial Office on the great difference between "liberty of commerce," which was guaranteed to the nations of both Britain and France, and "free trade." All merchants were subject to the payment of duties.[50] On the French side there was official support for the exchange of the Gambia and Porto Novo. It was forcefully argued that the Gambia was useless to Britain. It was of great interest for France to acquire the Gambia, partly for commercial and fiscal considerations, partly for political reasons, and, above all, for strategic reasons.[51] But the practical, commercial Marseille merchants were opposed to this theoretical, official view.[52]

Second, "any apprehension of the French extending their territory to the back of Lagos and cutting the colony off from the interior" was eliminated by the agreement of 10 August 1889.[53] Consequently, there was no necessity to acquire territory behind Lagos. It was the wish of the British government to maintain friendly relations with the inhabitants of this region and their rulers as well as to "leave them to govern their countries as heretofore themselves." Treaties of commerce and friendship would suffice, Moloney was instructed.[54]

Third, the agreement of August 1889 put an end to the open encouragement which the Lagos administration gave to Dahomey against France at Cotonou,[55] though British traders continued to cooperate with Dahomey.

British merchants, traders, and missionaries were opposed to the Anglo-French agreement of 10 August 1889. They demonstrated their opposition to this agreement by sending a motley deputation to Lord Knutsford,[56] the colonial secretary, to protest against the loss of territories in which British trade and influence had hitherto been predominant. They demanded the revision of the terms of the agreement with respect to the Slave Coast and Sierra Leone. Parties as opposed to each other as Sir George Goldie and the Liverpool Chamber of Commerce joined in common action against what Henry Coke of Liverpool described as "the dread of responsibility owing to the supineness of previous Governments . . ." which favored "the colonizing zeal of the French and the Germans," enabling them to wedge themselves between British possessions.[57] It may be recalled here that the west African section of the Liverpool Chamber of Commerce was organized in 1884 in reaction to the German acquisition of the Cameroons and the apparent loss of trade which it presaged.[58]

However, pressure from commercial and humanitarian quarters did not induce the British government to seek any amendments to the agreement of August 1889. "Imperial interests of a higher order" were evoked by the Intelligence Division of the War Office as causes for which concessions should be made to France. A case in point was the preservation of Sierra Leone harbor, which had been earmarked as a coaling station between Gibraltar and the Cape.[59]

The Foreign Office would neither lose sight of these interests nor ignore Britain's relations with France as a European power because of pressure from parties with vested interests in west Africa. Moreover, as Britain held the key[60] to the rich interior by her control of the major rivers and lagoons, a sense of complacency prevailed in Downing Street. On the other hand, France and her agents had begun assiduously to refashion the lock on the door to the hinterland.[61] Their collision with Dahomey was the most important aspect of this process. For not until the power of Dahomey was destroyed would the road from the coast to the hinterland be open and easily accessible to those Europeans who wished to go yonder. During the struggle with Dahomey, France could count on the neutrality of Britain and even on occasional aid from her.

Remote and Proximate Causes of the First Dahomey War, 1890

The court of Abomey was decidedly against all who in any way aided or abetted the French in their claims over Cotonou. King Toffa of Porto Novo was singled out for all forms of attack by Dahomey, because he was thought to be sympathetic to the gradual dismemberment of the kingdom of Dahomey by France.[62] Gléglé was displeased not only by the pro-French policy of Toffa but also by what he considered rank ingratitude by the king of Porto Novo to the court to which he owed his throne. It was with the aid of Gléglé that Toffa won the fierce struggle for succession to the throne of

Porto Novo by eliminating all his rivals.⁶³ Once solidly in power, however, Toffa manifested remarkable independence and pursued policies that were not to the liking of Dahomey, who expected him to show deference to Abomey. Toffa was by no means a capable and shrewd man. He was given to annoying indiscretions. On several occasions France contemplated his deportation,⁶⁴ but Victor Ballot maintained him at Porto Novo as a figurehead with Bayol's approval.⁶⁵

Both A. L. D'Albeca and Bayol had a low opinion of Toffa and his severe rule. D'Albeca, who knew Toffa very well and had several interviews with him, did not think very much of him. He expressed his assessment of Toffa in a report to Eugene Etienne in November 1889:

> Le roi Toffa n'est ni intelligent ni brave; ce roi indigène est prompt à s'exagérer son importance, quoique ses sujets n'aient pas la reputation d'être des guerriers; son manque de tact, ses notions sommaires de politique lui ont fait commettre des intempérances de langue qui ont poussé le roi Gléglé à énvoyer en Mars 1889 une bande de pillards vers Porto Novo.⁶⁶

By the spring of 1889 Dr. Tautain, who had come from Senegal to replace M. de Beckman in Porto Novo, reported the intensity of the bitterness between Dahomey and Porto Novo. The rivalry between Gléglé and Toffa, he stated, could be seen as "une lutte de race, une haine hereditaire et indestructible." Obviously, he was misled by the rude conflicts between the two kingdoms and the fierce battles of Marel in 1889.⁶⁷ Toffa and Gléglé were not of different races, nor were they traditional enemies. They were both of the same tribe, and their followers, as D'Albeca pointed out, were the same people, spoke the same language, and worshiped the same deities.⁶⁸

Toffa was inextricably caught between France and Dahomey. He could not cope with the vengeance of Dahomey unaided.⁶⁹ The French alliance or protectorate was the only prop on which he could support himself against the military machine of Dahomey.⁷⁰ He did not hesitate to use it to full advantage, just as he had used the might of Dahomey earlier in his reign to entrench himself in power at Porto Novo.

The policy of unilateral renunciation of treaties adopted by Gléglé in the last decade of his reign resulted in strained relations between him and France. Dahomean officials still collected duties at Cotonou. Gléglé had withdrawn the cession of this port to France. He claimed that he had granted the French only the right to trade in Cotonou and emphasized that he would not part with any part of his patrimony, which he considered inalienable by any type of treaty whatever. In the course of 1888, when the Dahomey question became very acute, the hands of the French government were tied by several factors which precluded immediate action by France. First, the modus vivendi of February 1888 prohibited any political action in the hinterland of Lagos and Porto Novo until a permanent settlement could be reached about the delimitation of this area.[71] Jacques Spuller warned Eugene Etienne that any extension of their political action at Porto Novo then would be fraught with dangers and difficulties not only with the indigenous people but also with England.[72] Second, France was then undecided about retaining Porto Novo, which could be exchanged for the Gambia in the ensuing negotiations with England on west African questions,[73] if Britain were willing to go through with such an exchange. Emile Flourens doubted the wisdom of insisting on the acquisition of the Gambia by France. He stressed the changed situation on the west Coast of Africa. The previous negotiation for the exchange of the Gambia with French possessions on the Bight of Benin in 1875 had occurred when France was not installed at Cotonou and when her protectorate over Porto Novo had not been reestablished. Moreover, strong opposition had come from commercial concerns against the abandonment of the French possessions on the Slave Coast.

> En un mot, le commerce de Marseille s'est élévé contre l'abandon des petits établissements au profit des colonies compactes et il a préconisé le système allemand des comptoirs disséminés que le Dr. Nachtigal a été chargé d'appliquer sur le côte occidentale d'Afrique.[74]

Flourens felt that the advantages of such an exchange of territory were more apparent than real and would compromise the future of French expansion in west Africa.[75]

Under the circumstances, therefore, it was imperative to reach a settlement with Britain on west African questions. Relations between Britain and France as major European powers mattered more than that between France and Dahomey. Logically, priority was given to the questions which involved England. The conclusion of an agreement with Britain on 10 August 1889 enabled the French government to turn freely to the Dahomey question. The protectorate of Porto Novo was there to stay. Withdrawal was out of the question. Therefore, a way was to be sought for peaceful coexistence with Dahomey, failing which there would be a war. The French government did not want war with Dahomey. French forces were at this time in action against Sultan Ahmadu of Segu and Samory and Mahmadu Lamine.[76] Moreover, French public opinion had been unfavorable to colonial wars since the fall of Jules Ferry in March 1885 over Tonkin.[77]

Bayol's Mission to Abomey, 1889

To arrive at a negotiated settlement with Dahomey was the aim of the French government. Consequently, a diplomatic mission was dispatched to Abomey soon after the conclusion of the Anglo-French agreement of 10 August 1889. This mission was confined to Jean Bayol, lieutenant governor of the Rivières du Sud, who had represented France along with A. Nisard in the west African negotiations just concluded in Paris. Eugene Etienne, who picked Bayol for this assignment, hoped that he would achieve the same measure of success he had in the Anglo-French talks.[78] Jacques Spuller, in approving the mission to Abomey, paid tribute to Bayol's tact, circumspection, and experience and to his services in the recent negotiations with Britain on west Africa. But the Quai d'Orsay stressed that Bayol should stay within the limits set out in Etienne's instructions. Above all, Bayol should not provoke complications, as Viard had when he undertook political initiative in the course of a purely commercial mission.[79] French agents on the Slave Coast had high hopes about Bayol's mission to Abomey. D'Albeca reported, while the mission was on its way to the capital, that it had produced a great effect by restoring French influence in the area to its former preponderance.[80] He added that "une entente entre la France et le Dahomey, une solution quelconque des questions pendants entre la République et le roi Gléglé feront cesser toute difficulté." [81]

Could Bayol's experience in Fouta Djallon in 1881 stand him in good stead in Abomey in 1889? Was Dahomean diplomacy as supple and accommodating as that of England? Could the pressures which worked when applied to Egerton succeed in negotiations with an absolute monarch[82] who was subject neither to a parliament nor to a bureaucracy? These were the imponderables of the mission. The court at Abomey was used to European visitors, a steady stream of whom had been flowing into the capital since the heyday of the slave trade. Bayol's presence at Abomey would not produce the same type of curious excitement that had attended his visit to the Almany Ibrahim Tory of Fouta Djallon in 1881, when he was sent there to forestall the designs of Britain.[83]

On the French side, an obstacle to a peaceful solution of the Dahomey problem was Jean Bayol himself. A month before he was designated for the political mission to Abomey, he told Egerton that Britain should not give serious consideration to the overtures made by Dahomey for British protection. "In consequence of the horrors and excesses which they had committed lately in the French protectorate of Porto Novo, it would be necessary for the French to take vigorous measures against them and give them a severe lesson," Bayol concluded.[84] With his mind made up in advance about what France should do with Dahomey, Bayol could not be expected to play the role of the angel of peace which Etienne assigned to him early in August 1889.

Jean Bayol was a doctor by education. His love of adventure led him into military service as a naval doctor. He accompanied Gallieni to the Soudan in 1880, and the next year he was sent to Fouta Djallon to secure French interests there. He was made lieutenant governor of Senegal and dependencies in 1882 and later of the Rivières du Sud, and he held this post till 1890. He represented France in the Franco-German partition commission on the Slave Coast in 1886.[85] Bayol had a tendency to be dogmatic. He belonged to the class of colonial administrators who improvised the policy they considered necessary on the spot without waiting to receive instructions from Paris, in the belief that it paid to be audacious and that personal prestige was an asset in dealing with African rulers. He knew from experience that Paris generally accepted faits accomplis as long as the enterprise undertaken was crowned with success.[86]

Bayol's authoritarian traits created utter confusion in the conduct of the French campaign against Dahomey in March 1890, because he could not get along with the naval and military commanders assigned to Porto Novo for the campaign. He was recalled to Paris when it was felt that his continued presence in Porto Novo was a hindrance to the smooth conclusion of peace with Dahomey.[87]

Etienne thought it necessary to acquaint Bayol with the views of the Colonial Department on the questions which he was expected to resolve and "sur le but de la mission importante que vous avez plus particulièrement à remplir." Recent events in Porto Novo indicated a change in the policy of Dahomey toward France. The warm reception which the governor of Lagos accorded to the envoys from Dahomey recently illustrated the aim of Lagos, which was "de tourner au profit de la colonie anglaise le courant commercial dont bénéfice Porto Novo, d'ouvrir aux products du Dahomey une route vers Lagos en évitant les possessions françaises." [88]

The unpredictable attitude of King Toffa in these last incidents seems to have been provoked by persons interested in discrediting France and demonstrating that her establishment in these parts were precarious and insufficient, Etienne observed. He did not possess enough information to enable him to prescribe specific measures for reestablishing French prestige at Porto Novo and to ensure the position of France vis-à-vis Dahomey. Therefore, he could only recommend Bayol "d'étudier avec sang-froid la solution de ces questions et de defendre les interêts de notre pays de la manière que vous paraîtra la plus efficace." [89] Etienne enumerated the problems which needed solution in a descending order of magnitude. Cotonou had pride of place and was to claim Bayol's first attention from a double point of view, both political and fiscal. Second, the governor of Senegal's proposal that Toffa be exiled to Gabon should be studied, and Bayol was to report his findings on this matter by cable. In the third place were other diverse questions, especially Dahomey. For the solution of this third class of problems, Etienne left Bayol "la plus grande initiative, confiant dans [sa] prudence et dans [sa] longue practique des affaires de la Côte d'Afrique." However, he was to act with the greatest circumspection and only after having taken the most meticulous precautions. All prior treaties, both with indigenous rulers and Europeans, were to be scrupulously respected. Edouard Viard would put himself at Bayol's disposal and continue his commercial and political explorations under Bayol's guidance. Any missions to the north of Porto Novo were to stay within the zone considered French and should not intrude into territories tied to Lagos, the Royal Niger Company, or Germany.[90] Bayol was expected to regulate all these questions with the means available in Porto Novo, without the intervention of troops other than those in the area. He was not to make any demands from the Navy but should contact the Colonial Department in case additional organized force was necessary.

By instructing Bayol to defend French interests by any means which appeared to him the most efficacious and by leaving him the greatest initiative, Etienne gave to Bayol what was tantamount to a blank cheque. Moreover, he promised to send Senegalese tirailleurs if these were needed by Bayol. This promise was hedged with the reminder that the French government expected the Dahomey problems to be resolved peacefully. Spuller warned that Bayol should exceed neither the spirit nor the general lines of these instructions.[91] But Bayol was not the modest type; he would not accept failure and would use his initiative to the utmost in order to achieve his aim. This logically led to the first war between France and Dahomey in 1890.

Bayol left Paris for Abomey on 13 August 1889. The king of Dahomey was informed of the proposed visit to Abomey by Bayol. He sent his messengers to Porto Novo to meet Bayol and to conduct him to the capital.[92] Soon after his arrival at Porto Novo, Bayol presided over a meeting called by Toffa on 24 October 1889 of all his notables and others who had run away from Porto Novo because they feared that Dahomey would destroy it. These men were exhorted to return to Porto Novo. Toffa handed out gifts to the more important ones among them to win their confidence. D'Albeca stated that this conference produced a good effect among the people.[93]

By mid-November 1889, Bayol and his entourage left the coast for Abomey. When he arrived at Cana on 20 November he learned that King Glégle had summoned to Abomey all the chiefs of the outlying districts. D'Albeca and Bayol thought that the convocation had been called for the sole purpose of receiving Lieutenant Governor Bayol. Thus D'Albeca jumped to the conclusion that Bayol's mission had produced a "grand effet sur la population du Bénin."[94] But the notables of the kingdom of Dahomey were not convoked to Abomey just to receive Bayol; they were there for the annual festival of their country. Bayol's visit coincided, probably by design, with the celebration of the "coutumes." If Bayol had not wanted to attend these annual festivities, which were known to involve human sacrifices, he could have executed his mission to Abomey without delay after his arrival at Porto Novo. He disembarked at Porto Novo on 1 October but did not arrive at Abomey till 21 November 1889.[95] Furthermore, he had been instructed to give priority to the question of Cotonou, which depended on Dahomey. Therefore, it could be said that Bayol wished to see for himself the annual "bloody" ceremonies of Abomey. He made much of this in his later reports and in his insistence on a punitive expedition against Dahomey.[96]

After a five-day journey, which led him through Abomey-Calavi, Allada, and Cana, Bayol arrived at Abomey on 21 November 1889. He was accorded a grand reception. Eight chiefs accompanied by an escort of soldiers carrying muskets met the mission as it entered Abomey. To Bayol's discomfiture, some of the people assembled to receive him carried the Union Jack! He was later presented to King Glégle, who was described as the greatest king in Africa. His soldiers were invincible. At this the crowd enthusiastically acclaimed the king as the "Lion of Lions." Glégle presented Prince Kondo to Bayol and, with great dignity, mounted his throne again. He had his traditional long pipe in his mouth.[97]

Bayol's pen portrait of Glégle is noteworthy, since it was the last eyewitness description of the king before his death a few weeks after Bayol's arrival at Abomey:

> Sa Majesté Da-Da Gléglé est un homme de haute taille, maigre, à la peau claire. La physionomie est bienveillante, la tête est celle d'un mandingue qui aurait du sang peul. . . . Les extrémités sont assez fines, les oreilles larges, les yeux ont une expréssion indécise. . . . Très fatigué, il a environs 75 ans, il laisse à son fils Kon-Do le soin de régler les affaires intérieures de son royaume, et ne s'occupe que de ses femmes et de ses dévotions pour célébrer la memoire de ses ancêtres, principalement de son père Guezo Apodgi.[98]

The assortment of twenty-three gifts brought from Paris was delivered to Gléglé by Bayol.[99] On 23 November the French envoys were invited to dinner at the Palace of Gime, the residence of Prince Kondo. They were received with "la plus parfaite courtoisie"[100] and were lodged in the former home of M. Sousa, the Chacha of Whydah. It was not until 28 November that Bayol was granted an audience by Prince Kondo. For the first time he expounded the aims of his journey to Abomey, emphasizing the "purely economic aspects of the question" and how it was in the interest of Dahomey to ally itself with France. The French government had pacific intentions toward Gléglé.[101] They were prepared to concede to Dahomey "all customs on imports not in transit to Porto Novo or Lagos." In addition, France would pay 20,000 francs compensation to Dahomey for the occupation of Cotonou.[102] Prince Kondo, in the name of the king, declared that all the previous treaties invoked by France were null and void because they were invented by the French and signed by unauthorized chiefs. He stated that the treaties were the work of M. Germat, a former agent of Mante and Borelli de Régis. "Les Français avaient été autorisés à s'établir comme marchands, jamais à un autre titre," he concluded. This drew tremendous applause from the chiefs present, including the Yevogan of Cotonou, whose post was the main bone of contention.[103]

The suggestion that the question of Cotonou be submitted to arbitration and that Portugal, a nation friendly with Dahomey, be the arbiter was rejected by Prince Kondo.[104] The proposal for the sharing of customs revenue at Cotonou was unfavorable to Dahomey. It meant that approximately 70 percent of the revenue would be in French hands, while Abomey would get a paltry 30 percent. It was estimated that Dahomey officials at Cotonou collected about 40,000 francs annually on liquors alone.[105] Prince Kondo knew what Cotonou meant to the Abomey treasury and was determined not to cede it to France.

It was not possible for Bayol to have a private audience with Gléglé because of the ceremonies going on at Abomey. The French envoys were invited to attend these ceremonies. Furthermore Glégle's ill health was another reason why he did not have any diplomatic talks with the French representatives. Bayol was displeased by the close surveillance to which he and his party were subjected. He wished to complete the ngotiations and return to the coast by mid-December. However, the national festival at Abomey overshadowed all other matters of state at that time of the year. Bayol was frustrated; he consoled himself with the understanding that "tout marche lentement en Afrique." His continued stay at Abomey was of no avail. The rulers of Dahomey would not budge from their uncompromising position on Cotonou. Bayol was made to write the king's views down for the president of France.[106] This was the final act which concluded the unsuccessful negotiations with Dahomey over Cotonou and Porto Novo. The French mission left Abomey on 28 December and returned to Cotonou on 31 December 1889, after a sojourn of thirty-three anxious days at the Dahomey capital.[107]

The failure of Bayol's mission to Abomey doubly embittered him against Dahomey. In his first dispatch after his return to Cotonou he claimed that Prince Kondo had insulted the French republic and that he and his entourage had been virtual prisoners at Abomey, only going out to watch the immolation of victims at the ceremonies.[108] The attacks of malarial fever which Bayol suffered during his stay at Abomey exacerbated his diplomatic difficulties. At one point, according to Bayol, the Dahomey authorities considered holding them as hostages. Moreover, soon after the announcement of the death of Glégle, Bayol warned the Colonial Department in Paris that the heir apparent, Prince Kondo, was hostile toward France.[109] Etienne read this telegram to the Conseil des Ministres on 15 January 1890. In addition, he informed the ministers that Dahomean officials at Cotonou were stirring up difficulties, including the molestation of the tirailleurs stationed there. Immediate action was necessary. The internal disputes at Abomey over succession favored an expedition against the new king, who had begun to mobilize his forces.

The French cabinet was not in favor of an expedition against Dahomey. While informing Bayol of this, Etienne asked him to submit an estimate of the expenses that would be involved, the number and composition of troops that would be needed, the probable duration of the envisaged campaign, and the nature of the resistance and the difficulties that would be met.[110] Bayol was of the opinion that it would take probably one month to defeat and occupy Dahomey. The costs would be met by the ordinary military expenses as well as by the revenue to be collected from customs stations at Cotonou.[111] In these circumstances the intervention of the Chambre des Députés would be avoided. In any case, two companies of tirailleurs from St. Louis were needed to reinforce the troops in Cotonou. With this additional force, Cotonou could be occupied definitively, as could Whydah, Avrekete, Godomey, and Abomey-Calavi. This would be the surest way of protecting European traders.[112] Etienne's immediate reaction was to instruct the governor of Senegal to send two companies of tirailleurs, four cannons, and four mountain guns to Porto Novo to meet Bayol's demand. However, he added that the council of ministers in Paris had not decided whether to embark on an expedition or not.[113] Thus Bayol's hands were strengthened, and he finalized his plans for the occupation of Cotonou, which was executed on 21 February 1890 despite repeated warnings from the Colonial Department that he should only take defensive dispositions.[114] Hostilities had thus been launched between France and Dahomey by the will of Bayol. As has been pointed out, the failure of Bayol's mission to Abomey was the spark that set fire to an already inflammable situation.[115]

Bayol arranged a conference with the Agorigan of Cotonou and his councillors. He made known to them his intention to occupy Cotonou. The Agorigan Houaketome, who was present at the unsuccessful negotiations between Bayol and Prince Kondo (now King Béhanzin) at Abomey, refused to accept Bayol's views. He and his thirty councillors were then arrested and marched off to Porto Novo as prisoners. After this Cotonou was militarily occupied by Commandant Terrillon.[116] Bayol had crossed the Rubicon,[117] as A. L. d'Albeca aptly put it.

The First Dahomey War, February–October 1890: A New King Faces an Old Problem

After the death of Glégié on 29 December 1889, his third and favorite son Kondo, whom he nominated as his successor, took over the reins of power in Dahomey.[118] Glégié had paid special attention to the education of Prince Kondo and had retained the services of the wise Gedegbe, his brother-in-law, as Kondo's teacher.[119] In his later years as king, Glégié groomed Kondo for the kingly office by leaving to him the direction of affairs at Abomey. At the time of his accession to the throne Béhanzin was about forty years of age. "C'est un nègre admirable, bien pris, quoique de taille moyenne, la figure est ouverte, intélligente, le regard franch et droit, il n'a aucun des oripeaux dont on se plait à affubler les rois nègres."[120] His presence was prepossessing, and he was indeed a chip off the old block.[121] The coronation of

Béhanzin produced the first shock of his turbulent reign. After the king-makers had anointed him, they left him alone in the sacred chamber as a part of the ritual. Béhanzin did not fall asleep during this period of isolation, as all previous kings had done. When the king-makers returned to wake him up and complete the coronation ceremony, they saw him wide awake and sitting on his throne. This produced consternation among the king-makers and priests, who took it as an ominous sign of impending danger. When he was presented to his people, he uttered the allegorical statement from which his name Béhanzin was taken.[122] His heraldic emblem was the shark. Would he not be the "Shark of Sharks" (as his father had been the Lion of Lions) and undo all who threatened Dahomey from the sea, especially the French?[123] In any case, a new king had been enthroned to grapple with old problems which were not new to him.[124]

The immediate reaction of Dahomean officials to the imprisonment of their colleagues by Bayol was retaliation. Under the direction of Candido Rodriguez, special secretary to Béhanzin, the Europeans in Whydah were arrested, and those of them who were French were later taken to Abomey as hostages.[125] Bayol's plan for their security when hostilities began did not work. They blamed him for their misfortune.[126] "M. Bayol nous a trompés et nous attendons de lui une réparation avec impatience," declared Consul Bontemps.[127]

On 21 February 1890, when the French military campaign commenced against Dahomey, the total effective force of France in the Porto Novo area comprised 481 men (see table 1), according to Lieutenant Colonel Terrillon, who commanded the troops that conquered and occupied Cotonou "rapidement et brillament."[128]

On the Dahomey side, the exact number of men in arms was not known, though it was estimated that there were about 22,000 regular soldiers, about 1,500 of whom were Amazons. Between 10,000 and 12,000 of them were in Abomey and at the northern and western frontiers of the kingdom; approximately 10,000 of them were stationed at different points in the kingdom itself.[129]

Bayol's estimate of the regular army of Dahomey was exaggerated. The regular army, made up of *soflimatas* and *Amazons* at the time of Béhanzin, consisted of about 12,000 men.[130] But since the principle of "levée en masse" applied to all able-bodied adults in Dahomey, the king was capable of raising several thousand soldiers in times of national emergency.[131]

Bayol's estimate of the population of Dahomey in 1890 was 150,000.[132] This was a fair estimate, because the official figure for 1899 was 181,788.[133]

It is, therefore, highly improbable that about 15 percent of the population of Dahomey in 1890 was in the regular army, as Bayol estimated. Furthermore, if the regular army had as many as 22,000 men, was it not the height of unrealism for Bayol to plan on the conquest and occupation of Dahomey in a matter of one month with fewer than 500 soldiers? [134]

TABLE 1

COMPOSITION OF THE EXPEDITIONARY CORPS ON 21 FEBRUARY 1890

	EFFECTIVES			
	EUROPEANS		AFRICANS	
Names of Officers and Location	Sub. Officers	Soldiers	Sub. Officers	Tirailleurs
COTONOU				
Terrillon, chef de bataillon	...	1	...	...
Collombier, lieutenant	...	1	...	...
Tirailleur Sénégalais				
2nd Company	5	2	4	107
(Lemoine, captain; Huillard, lieutenant)				
4th Company	6	3	4	108
(Pansier, captain; Lagaspie, sous-lieutenant)				
10th Company	1[a]	...	...	24
(Syzmanski, sous-lieutenant)				
Tirailleur Gabonais				
(Oudard, captain; Compérat, lieutenant)	4	...	2	60
28th Batterie	...	5	6	...
26th Batterie	1	6	...	...
PORTO NOVO				
10th Company	3	10	2	116
(Arnoux, captain; Roux, médecin)				
	20	28	18	415

SOURCE: SOM-AN Dahomey V, 2, a, Journal de Marche de la Colonne Expeditionaire, Campagne de 1890, par Lieut. Colonel Terrillon, p. 4.

[a] This figure is missing from the table given in E. Aublet *La Guerre au Dahomey 1888–1893* (Paris, 1894), p. 28.

On the question of the armament of the Dahomean army, Bayol said that most of the soldiers were equipped with long buccaneer guns made in Birmingham, whose range did not exceed one hundred meters. The best weapons of the army were the French carbines of the 1822 model. The Amazons preferred muskets to the long buccaneer guns. They had a good supply of the short blunderbusses sold to the king by the Portuguese, which were "véritable tromblons ou espingoles" of the French infantry a century before. However, some *fusils à répétition* were owned by the Dahomeans. On top of these could be counted a few old cannons of seventeenth century origin, though it is said that the Germans had furnished Béhanzin with a Krupp cannon.[135] That Bayol underestimated the armaments of the army of Dahomey may be shown by official French military reports during the wars and by those of other experts.

> L'armament de l'infantérie était très varié et parcourait toute la série des armes portatives, depuis le fusil à pierre jusqu'aux systèmes les plus récents et les plus perfectionnés: Sniders, Winchester, chassepot, Spencer, Werndl, Peabody, Malinncher, Martini, etc.[136]

Another of Bayol's miscalculations which made him optimistic of an easy victory over Dahomey was that the people of Dahomey would not have the will to resist after a lightning occupation of Cotonou and other points on the littoral. "Les Dahoméens, comme les autres noirs, s'inclinent devant les faits accomplis," he asserted. Furthermore, he felt that the king who was forbidden to see the sea would probably send some chiefs to negotiate with the French, and those chiefs could easily be made to come to terms. Moreover, a rival for the throne of Dahomey would be set up, and efforts to discredit Béhanzin would be intensified. Such a situation would be favorable to the definitive establishment of France at Cotonou and its environs. In conclusion, Bayol remarked that once France was the master of the trading cities on the coast, the territory of Upper Dahomey sooner or later would belong to her, and eventually the then intractable king of Dahomey would seek French protection.[137]

Cotonou was not a natural harbor. A perilous bar separated it from the ocean and made the landing of men and cargo a hazardous affair. In mid-1888 a commission charged to study the feasibility of cutting a canal through the bar reported that it would cost about 300,000 francs. "Il est donc impossible, à notre avis de faire quoiqu'il soit à Kotonou," they concluded.[138] The conclusion of the Anglo-French arrangement of 10 August 1889 led to a renewal of interest in the consolidation of the French position in Porto Novo and Cotonou. A concession was granted to Burdo and Viard for the construction of a wharf at Cotonou early in 1890.[139] The wharf was constructed by Dayde et Pille, and a convention of 7 September 1891 confirmed Viard's concession for fifty years and reserved eighty kilometers of coastline for him.[140]

In addition to the efforts to improve Cotonou for landing purposes,

France sent Captain Albert Septans to Porto Novo in January 1890 to study the question of the defense of French establishments in view of the menacing attitude of Dahomey and a possible French expedition in the area. This did not alleviate the difficulty of complete ignorance of the interior of Dahomey, which was a major handicap for the French during the war against Dahomey.[141]

Two days after the arrest and imprisonment of the officials of Cotonou, the villagers mounted a counterattack against the French soldiers who occupied the city. They failed to regain their village, which was later razed to the ground by the French.[142] French factories were fortified; a telegraph station and a small clinic were established at Cotonou. Reprisals by Dahomey followed swiftly. On 23 February eight French nationals[143] in Whydah were arrested and taken as hostages for the Dahomey officials arrested and detained by Jean Bayol.

The arrest and imprisonment of the eight agents of French commercial and missionary enterprise at Whydah received much publicity in France. The press reports exaggerated allegations of maltreatment of these hostages by Dahomean authorities.[144] This has misled some historians of the events of 1890 in Dahomey into believing that the hostages were ill-treated by zealous subalterns, beaten up, and led in chains to Abomey.[145] According to the account of Consul Bontemps, only Edouard Chaudoin and M. Denlay suffered minor injuries at Whydah. In fact, the hostages were carried in hammocks to Allada and thence to Abomey. They only walked when their carriers had to take some rest. Once in Abomey, they were shown the traditional hospitality which the kings of Dahomey had always shown to all French, and indeed all Europeans, who had visited their capital. "Béhanzin is kind to us and is feeding us well. He has seen to it that we are not molested by his people who are upset by the losses they have suffered in Kotonou," declared the prisoners themselves.[146] The individual recollections and accounts of the victims themselves later on did not bear out the sensational muckraking of the French press.[147]

The next battle after Cotonou was fought on 1 March at Zogbo, to the northwest of Cotonou. The aim of the French officers was to take by surprise a Dahomean contingent reported to be gathering there. But the Dahomean intelligence service, which "joint à une grande perfection de surveillance une perspicacité rare," [148] learned of the French plan in advance. A brief engagement took place between the two sides, with heavier casualties on the French side because they were welcomed by a sustained volley of shots at almost point blank. Low waters on Lake Denham (Nokoué) made a stealthy landing impossible. During the mopping-up operation the French forces discovered a cache of ammunition belonging to Dahomey, which they took back to Cotonou with them. The village of Zogbo was burned by Commandant Terrillon and his troops before they returned to Cotonou.[149]

The first fierce battle of the war was fought on the northern border of Cotonou during the early hours of the morning of 4 March. The Dahomeans, whose tactical specialty was night raids, swooped down on the French posts at about 4 A.M. A French sergeant and his men fled after a brief close combat with the Dahomeans. Those that were overpowered were all killed. However, Captain Oudard and Lieutenant Compeyrat displayed a remarkable presence of mind and did not desert their posts. The Dahomeans feigned retreat and were pursued. But by a surprise maneuver a section of them attacked the rear of the French column and killed Marshal Moreau in the resulting action. Most of the auxiliaries supplied by King Toffa deserted, because they were Dahomean sympathizers at heart. The small resisting company was overwhelmed and massacred. Two hours after dawn the Dahomean soldiers withdrew into the forest.[150] By noon they had regrouped. Their tom-tom of war resounded in the countryside; their war chants reechoed in the outskirts of Porto Novo.[151] Their commandant could be seen on the plain from time to time on his horse. French troops therefore were on the alert for further defensive action when the Dahomeans attacked again. A ferocious pitched battle raged for some hours. A few Amazons participated in this battle: two or three of them were found dead on the field, and one was shot down while she was in the process of beheading a corporal from Gabon who was in the French army. The casualties on the side of the Dahomeans were great because of French fire power, though they fought bravely and desperately against "cette force incomparable des armes perfectionnées entre des mains exercées." [152] The French losses were considerable, too.[153]

The intensity and the savage nature of this first major battle of the war jolted Commandant Terrillon into a sudden realization of the magnitude of the enterprise into which Jean Bayol had led him. It also demonstrated to the Dahomeans the dangers of engaging their adversaries in pitched battles. They fell back on guerrilla warfare, at which they were very efficient and effective. Commandant Terrillon cabled the governor of Senegal for reinforcements and supplies which would bring the forces in Porto Novo to 870 men. The Colonial Department frowned at this figure.[154] Coincidentally, the Quai d'Orsay expressed great concern over the creeping but steady growth of the war in Dahomey, which was being executed before the report of Bayol's pacific mission to Abomey had been received. "Il serait à craindre, en effet, que l'on ne se trouvait ainsi engagé peu à peu dans une expédition ayant Abomey pour but," Spuller warned.[155]

However, the war continued apace. To the disappointment of Bayol, the local population did not rise to join the French against Dahomey, as had been expected. Indeed, some of those recruited by the French deserted to join forces with Dahomey. Furthermore, the French could not count on devoted spies to furnish reliable information on the movements of Dahomean troops.[156] In the meantime, two more French cruisers, *L'Ardent* and the *Kerguelen,* arrived in Cotonou from Senegal and Gabon respectively to augment the French effectives.[157] Efforts were made to bombard Abomey-Calavi and Godome when it was learned that Dahomean troops were concentrated in these towns. The exercise was not very successful.[158] While the storm was gathering for further action on land, Bayol proposed the blockade of the Dahomey coast to prevent the entry of firearms and gunpowder through German and Portuguese firms who were not perturbed by the military action against Dahomey. The jealousy and indiscretion of both French and foreign merchants were more dangerous to the French effort than the army of Dahomey. A blockade of the coast would also force King Béhanzin to swallow his pride and be obliged to negotiate and recognize French treaty rights.[159]

Senator E. Barbey questioned the advisability of a blockade of the Dahomey coast as well as the utility of such an extreme measure: "Il semble donc que le Gouvernement doive murement réfléchir et peser ses decisions avant de recourir à des mesures extraordinaires, d'outre internationals, étant donne que leur utilité n'est rien moins que demonstrée."[160] Meanwhile, a memorandum prepared in the Ministère de la Marine for Barbey concluded that no international complications would be engendered by any French action on the coast between Appa and Bayol Island.[161] It was at this point that the first signs of discord began to appear among the French officials in Porto Novo. Commandant Terrillon was not enthusiastic for a formal blockade of the Dahomey coast. He was of the opinion that a blockade existed in fact since the beginning of the war. A march on Abomey seemed to him a more worthwhile objective than a formal blockade of the coast.[162] The suggestion of an expedition to Abomey drew another warning from the Quai d'Orsay because of the many difficulties which such a measure would create, especially in logistics, tactics, sanitation, provisioning, and communications.[163] Jacques Spuller did not share the views of those merchants and missionaries who stressed how easy it would be to overrun Abomey and loot its riches.[164]

At all events, the blockade of the Dahomey coast was approved by Barbey and Etienne on 3 April 1890, after renewed pressure from Bayol, who was alarmed not only by the sale of arms and ammunition to Dahomey by German merchants but also by the suspect activity of Randad, the German consul at Whydah.[165] Of all the powers, only Portugal raised objections against the French blockade, because it made no reservation for the Portuguese fort at Whydah.[166]

While the diplomatic exchanges were taking place, French and Dahomean troops continued to exchange fire around Porto Novo. On 25 March, an advance party of French troops led by Commandant Terrillon was ambushed by Dahomeans. The French suffered heavy casualties. They fought in retreat under heavy fire by the Dahomeans.[167] Terrillon, determined to redress this defeat of his forces, directed his troops to the left bank of the River Wheme (Oueme), where they were supported by the gunboat *L'Emeraude*. Several villages were bombarded and burned down as the troops marched from Kesounou toward Dangbo. As they entered one of the seemingly deserted villages for a mopping-up operation, Captain Oudard was shot down point blank at the door of a hut he intended to search. Added to this "invisible enemy," as Edouard Foa described it, was the scorching heat of the March sun. Lieutenant Mousset dropped dead from insolation and fatigue soon after Captain Oudard was killed.[168] The French forces retreated to Porto Novo and from there to Cotonou.[169]

By this time the bickering and disaccord among the French military and civilian officials in Porto Novo and Cotonou had led to utter confusion in the execution of the campaign against Dahomey. Bayol, who believed that the main cause of the dissension was difference in rank, was forced to recommend himself for immediate promotion to the rank of third class governor. This would not only raise his prestige before the military and naval authorities but also enable him to deal on equal terms with the Portuguese governor of Sao Tomé on the subject of the fort at Whydah.[170] Leopold Fournier, who was accused of refusing to cooperate with Bayol and Terrillon, was obeying his orders from Paris, which told him to remain *en rade* outside Cotonou and not to land any marines, because "marine ne devoir prendre aucune responsabilité dans evenements du Bènin."[171] Between Bayol and Terrillon the power struggle centered around who would decide the priorities. For instance, whereas Bayol wanted a blockade of the coast, Terrillon wanted to fight the land battles with all the forces at his disposal, with Abomey as his eventual target. Unfortunately for Bayol, the very day he asked for promotion was the day on which his services at Porto Novo were terminated.[172] Five days later, Lieutenant Colonel Terrillon was also recalled, and the Governor of Senegal was instructed to send either Colonel Dodds or Lieutenant Colonel Klipfel to Porto Novo to replace him.[173] Admiral Cavalier de Cuverville was appointed commandant superieur, but Commandant Fournier was charged with the direction of all operations with full military and civil powers until the arrival of Admiral Cuverville.[174] Two facts emerge from this imbroglio:

> Il n'y a pas d'unité de vue.
> Il n'y a pas d'unité d'action.
> C'était l'anarchie pure; il n'en pouvait résulter que
> la confusion, et ça n'a pas manqué.[175]

The unification of both civil and military powers under one commander had a salutary effect on the French war effort. By restoring unity of purpose and action, this measure appreciably augmented the thrust of French forces.

On the other hand, Béhanzin had some dissension in his own camp. Some of his chief advisers favored renewed negotiations with France and an immediate end to the war. Moreover, his fortune-tellers blamed Dahomey's heavy casualties on the king's decision to wage pitched battles by day instead of relying on ambushes and on stealing marches on the enemy by night, on which Dahomey's invincibility depended.[176] The death of the commandant-in-chief of the Amazons aggravated the demoralization of Dahomean troops.[177] Under these circumstances Béhanzin was constrained to apply to Lieutenant Emmanuel Jose dos Santos of the Portuguese fort at Whydah for Portuguese soldiers who would join forces with Dahomey against France.[178] In addition Béhanzin contacted Mantes et Borelli de Régis ainé to mediate between him and the French government. He stressed the uselessness of the war started by Toffa and Bayol, adding that he would agree to a negotiated peace to conserve the integrity of his kingdom. He would release the hostages and come to terms over Cotonou.[179] He even ordered his Yevogans to Whydah and other ports to ensure that French factories were safeguarded against looters and thieves.[180] Above all, Béhanzin was at a loss for the reasons why France was at war with Dahomey, whereas he was only engaged in hostilities against Toffa: "Nous avons toujours été l'ami de la France et jamais nous n'avons rien fait contre cette nation." [181]

Meanwhile, the *Ville-de-Maranhao* docked at Kotonou on 2 April with reinforcements of seventy-five whites and fifty black men from the infantry of the Marine armed with *lebel* rifles.[182] Among them were five officers. This brought the French force to a total of 450 men with twenty officers, six of whom were Africans.[183] This number was appreciably augmented by the auxiliaries whom Commandant Fournier described as "very timid" and who were armed with flint guns.[184]

By the middle of April the Dahomey army was on the warpath again. The head of Toffa of Porto Novo was the objective, according to Toffa's informants.[185] Lieutenant Colonel Terrillon took one-and-a-half companies of tirailleurs and seventy-five disciplinaries to Porto Novo on 16 April, after the resident had informed him of the movement of Dahomean troops. The Dahomeans crossed the River Wheme around Bodji, a few miles northwest of Porto Novo. The French had learned to advance cautiously toward their opponents after their experiences at both Zogbo and Godome. Soon after the French forces assumed battle formation with the timid auxiliaries in the center of the *carré,* the Dahomeans launched a fierce attack against them. Counter-firing by the French with their lethal lebel rifles did not stop the Dahomeans, who surged on steadily, supported by their own artillery. The French retreated "en musique," as Terrillon put it. However, the auxiliaries panicked as the Dahomeans pursued the retreating French forces. It was observed by Terrillon that the Amazons had led the fierce engagement in full force (about 2,000 of them), with Béhanzin in person.[186] The audacity, the maneuvers, the speed of action of the Amazons knew no bounds in the presence of the supreme force of their lives, the king of Dahomey.[187]

This battle of Atchoupa was the last major encounter of the first Dahomey war. The rainy season had begun, making campaigning in tropical Dahomey more perilous than ever. Though the French commandant continued to ask for reinforcements and to entertain thoughts of a march on Abomey,[188] priority was given to strengthening the defences of Porto Novo to enable the French to contain any surprise attack by Dahomey during the rainy season.[189] But only one more noteworthy attempt was made by Dahomey—on the night of 11 May at Cotonou. French troops were alerted in good time by electric danger signals from the *Roland* and the *Naiade,* and they repulsed the invaders.[190] The temporary end to hostilities facilitated negotiations which led to the exchange of hostages early in May,[191] though mutual distrust was by no means abated by this transaction.[192]

French Government's Insistence on Negotiations with Dahomey

Etienne authorized the sending of Senegalese tirailleurs to Porto Novo and Cotonou in January 1890, because Bayol convinced him that with the cooperation of Senegal an expedition in Dahomey would be possible without the intervention of the Chambre des Députés.[193] The Council of Ministers of the second Tirard Cabinet explicitly disapproved of any French intervention in Dahomey which would compel them to go before the Chambre des Députés to ask for credits.[194] Etienne attended cabinet meetings and knew quite well the unfavorable attitude of the French government to "a new Tonkin" in Dahomey, as *L'Intransigeant* put it.[195] The memories of the collapse of the second Ferry Cabinet over Tonkin in March 1885 were fresh in France. The dreaded parliamentary intervention in the Dahomey question came for the first time on 8 March 1890, through an interpellation by François Deloncle on the policy of the French government in Dahomey. How were the Europeans in the menaced area to be protected? Etienne reassured the questioner that appropriate steps had been taken. He underscored Bayol's pacific qualities, presence of mind, and varied experience in African affairs.[196] In the cabinet, Etienne earned the support of Rouvier, the minister of finance, by the affirmation that the costs of the Dahomey expedition would not necessitate any additional expenditure. However, the rapid escalation of the war in Dahomey constrained Rouvier to remind Etienne on 12 March 1890 of this verbal agreement about expenses. He warned that no additional credits would be made available for the Dahomey war unless they were authorized by a vote of Parliament.[197] A few days later the Tirard Cabinet fell, but not because of Dahomey.[198]

This lack of enthusiasm for a war in Dahomey was deepened by the formation of the fourth de Freycinet Cabinet on 17 March 1890.[199] The new minister of foreign affairs, Alexandre Ribot, disapproved of the war in Dahomey and wished to see a quick end to it.[200] Etienne's unique position of exercising ministerial authority without being subject to its concomitant responsibilities was realized by his colleagues. Consequently, the new government transferred the control and direction of the Dahomey affair to M. E. Barbey, the minister for the navy, with the mandate to obtain a negotiated settlement as soon as possible.[201] In his instructions to Leopold Fournier and Admiral Cuverville, Barbey stressed the need to end the affair by a negotiated arrangement.[202] Above all, Barbey confided to his agents on the spot that at the reopening of the Chambre des Députés information would be desired by the members on this subject. He exhorted them to work for a negotiated settlement.[203]

This is the kind of consideration that would not have bothered Etienne as Sous-Secrétaire d'Etat des Colonies, because of the privileged position he occupied in the government.[204] He soon objected against not being consulted about decisions concerning Dahomey and threatened to shift the financial burden of the war from the colonial to the naval budget if the ministry of the navy continued to ignore him. Barbey pacified him by the assurance that nothing was being held back from him but that the very nature of the operations in Dahomey necessitated prompt decisions.[205] The gist of Etienne's argument was that the transfer of the direction and control of the operations in Dahomey to the navy did not remove the area from the territories under the Department of Colonies.

Commandant Fournier had 929 regular soldiers at his disposal when he assumed control of the operations against Dahomey.[206] In addition, there were 290 auxiliaries and gardes civils. These troops were distributed along the seaboard at Cotonou, Porto Novo, Grand Popo, and Agoue, partly to enforce the blockade and partly to protect French establishments from any surprise incursions by the forces of Dahomey[207] (see table 2).

When Fournier reported his initial successes, he was told of the applause this had drawn from the Chambre des Députés but was instructed to "Terminez votre oeuvre par accord même très large. Employez tous moyens, même cadeaux, pour arriver à prompte solution."[208] Four days later, as if to press home the position of the French government, Barbey informed Fournier that the proprietors of Mante and Borelli had proffered the services of M. Siciliano, their former agent in Dahomey, to actuate negotiations between France and King Béhanzin.[209] Siciliano attributed the failure of his efforts in Dahomey to the restrictions imposed upon him by Admiral Cuverville; Cuverville said it was due to Siciliano's lack of influence with King Béhanzin and the absence of any trustworthy confidants in Abomey.[210]

Admiral Cuverville, however, did find another intermediary in Père Dogère, the Catholic missionary who had just been released from captivity in Abomey.[211] Le Père Dogère, of the Société des Missions Africaines de Lyon, left France for west Africa on 8 February 1886 and worked in the Catholic mission at Topo (Whydah) until he went back to France on 10 May 1889. He set out for Whydah again on 23 November 1889 and was there when the war with Dahomey broke out in February 1890. While he was a hostage in Abomey he endeared himself with Béhanzin and wrote

TABLE 2

GARRISONS AT COTONOU, PORTO NOVO, GRAND POPO, ETC., 2 MAY 1890

Porto Novo:	
Infantry	76
Disciplinarians	128
Tirailleurs Sénégalais	329
Artilleurs	28
Total	561
Gardes civil	40
Auxilliares (très peureux), armes fusíl à pierre	250
Total	290
Cotonou:	
Infantry	144
Tirailleurs Sénégalais	37
Artilleurs	17
Marines	83
Total	281
Grand Popo:	
Tirailleurs Sénégalais	14
Tirailleurs Gabonais	57
Total	71
Agoue:	
Tirailleurs Sénégalais	8
Post d'Aguegue:	
Tirailleurs Sénégalais (y compris indisponsibles)	8
Total	16
Grand total	1219

SOURCE: A.C.M., BB4/1989, Fournier to Marine, 2 May 1890; M.A.E., Afrique 126, Fournier to Barbey, 2 May 1890 (tel.).

letters for him to French authorities.[212] "C'est un homme petit, très brun, fortement bronzé, d'un caractère doux en même temps que d'une énergie rare et d'un sang-froid peu commun."[213] He pursued with amazing intrepidity the aims stated by Monsignor de Marion-Bresillac, the founder of the Missions Africaines de Lyon, "travailler à préparer les voies pour pénétrer dans les lieux oú aucun Européen n'a encore pénétré."[214]

Admiral Cuverville believed that the Père Dogère was the only man who could talk to Béhanzin with any chance of success, largely because of his religious habit, which was always respected in Dahomey, and also because he would carry the symbol of the French government. Reverend Dogère was given clear instructions on what to do at Abomey. He was also given a draft treaty on which the negotiations were to be based. He was to find out what had become of the messengers of peace sent to Abomey by Leopold Fournier on 31 May 1890.[215] If Dogère did not return to the coast in a reasonable amount of time, it would be assumed that he had been imprisoned, and a march on Abomey would be the immediate result.[216] Admiral Cuverville was distrustful of the chances of success of peaceful negotiations with Dahomey. Béhanzin was "très actif, astucieux, vindicatif, cruel," and was receiving arms, powder, and mobilizing his forces by levée en masse. He had adopted Fabian tactics to gain time. Colonel Klipfel and Resident Ballot were all agreed on the necessity of an expedition against Abomey without further delay, because the future would render such an expedition more difficult. Victor Ballot, who was in charge of the spy system, counselled a march on Abomey. As Louis Henrique aptly put it, Ballot was "administrator civil par costume, militaire par le tempérament, l'odeur de la poudre est son parfum préféré."[217] The triumvirate of Cuverville, Klipfel, and Ballot proposed to the ministry of the navy that offensive operations against Abomey should commence on 15 September 1890, using the course of the River Wheme. With an effective force of 3,000 men the decisive expedition would not last more than two months, and the considerable results that would be achieved were worth the effort.[218]

In the meantime, serious health problems had beset the French troops. First of all, an outbreak of influenza was brought by the troops from Senegal aboard the *Kerguélen* and spread to the troops aboard the *Sane*.[219] Second, with the rainy season came the general incidence of malarial fever, acute dysentery, gastric biliousness, and vomiting among the troops. Many were incapacitated and put *en dehors de combat* by these attacks.[220]

In addition to these internal health and sanitary problems, Cuverville had to solve the puzzle of transport between Porto Novo and the sea. The numerous accidents that attended the crossing of the bar had caused the loss of several lives and much property. Toward the end of May 1890 the canoe men at Cotonou went on strike. They did not wish to risk their lives any more by crossing the bar in their crude vessels.[221] Wuschlager, an agent of Fabre and Company at Grand Popo, who was a Swiss-German, refused to lend the services of his canoe men for the recovery of goods lost from capsized canoes because he did not want to lose his employees.[222]

The only alternative route was to go through Lagos to Porto Novo. Permission for the use of this route had to be sought from Britain. The governor of Lagos was to be made to understand that France was in Porto

Novo to stay.²²³ The French government should utilize every means at its disposal to publicize its determination to keep its possessions in the Gulf of Bénin.²²⁴

The question of the passage of French gunboats, men, and materials through Lagos was the second international complication which resulted from the war against Dahomey. The first was the blockade of the Dahomey seaboard, proclaimed on 7 April 1890,²²⁵ which provoked protests from the Portuguese because their fort at Whydah was not given special treatment.²²⁶ However, Admiral Cuverville was of the opinion that French passage through Lagos would produce a good effect in Abomey, where it would be reported quickly and fully, because Lagos was "full of Dahomey spies." He wanted to reestablish good relations with Lagos and had sent Captain Fournier to Lagos with this objective in view. Every statement capable of harming public opinion in France and any indiscretion capable of ruining good relations with Lagos while the Dahomey war was still on should be avoided.²²⁷ Waddington contacted Lord Salisbury on behalf of the French government to permit the passage of French gunboats, men, and materials through Lagos. Lord Salisbury granted the request but warned that this was an exceptional case and not a right.²²⁸ Governor Moloney of Lagos was unenthusiastic about allowing the passage of French gunboats through Lagos. When Admiral Cuverville reported this to Paris, renewed efforts were made to get instructions sent to Governor Moloney from London.²²⁹

Another transaction which the French officers had with Lagos in this war period was the delimitation of the Lagos–Porto Novo boundary as provided by the Anglo-French Agreement of 10 August 1889. On the provisional commission France was represented by Lieutenant Tracou, a geodesian, and Britain by Kinstry.²³⁰ The report of the preliminary commission was accepted by the two powers pending minor corrections. Ribot advised the postponement of all delimitation activity till the Dahomey affair was settled, as Admiral Cuverville suggested.²³¹

Père Dogère's Diplomatic Mission to Abomey

Père Dogère obtained permission from his ecclesiastical superiors to go on the diplomatic mission to Abomey for which he had offered his services. The most important asset he possessed for this task was knowledge of the local language, and he was no stranger at Abomey. He was given a hero's welcome, with a hundred cannon shots, ten thousand gun shots, and a parade of chiefs and soldiers.²³² He said mass and reported that there were over eighty communicants.²³³ Béhanzin's reaction was promising. He demanded concessions for Cotonou, but Cuverville rejected these because they showed up France as a defeated party. Béhanzin asked for an annual compensation of £1,500 for Cotonou but added that his officials would administer the city as in the past. He did not want any French garrison at Whydah; he would rather order the Portuguese out, to demonstrate to the French that he did not want foreign military detachments to occupy Whydah.²³⁴ The negotiations continued, and the detente brought about by Dogère's efforts²³⁵ was conducive to optimism. In any case, Cuverville remained unconvinced that success was near. "Jusqu'à présent je ne crois pas à la paix," he confessed.²³⁶ The thaw created by Père Dogère produced the release of thirty-five prisoners held in Abomey, including Bernadin Durand and his colleagues who were sent to Abomey by Captain Fournier.²³⁷ The way was paved for a final settlement before Père Dogère left Abomey. Agreement was reached on the main issues in question; only the details remained to be rounded off. He arrived back in Whydah on 23 August and proceeded to Cotonou to report to Cuverville about his mission.²³⁸ For the successful accomplishment of his difficult task in Abomey, Admiral Cuverville proposed that Dogère be rewarded with the Legion of Honor medal for his "patriotic courage and abnegation." ²³⁹

The envoys of Dahomey came down to Whydah for the final phase of the negotiations for peace. The *Roland* sailed from Cotonou to Whydah for these talks. Admiral Cuverville was converted to optimism by Dogère. He now had great hopes for the success of the negotiations.²⁴⁰ The arrangement for the extradition of criminals between Dahomey and the French possessions was concluded. Cuverville obtained the sanction of Paris to lift the blockade of the Dahomey seaboard at his own discretion. An ultimatum to the Yevogan of Whydah by Cuverville was too late to affect matters one way or the other, since it was issued a day before final agreement was reached ²⁴¹ and the treaty of 30 October 1890 was signed. The conclusion of this treaty marked the end of the first Dahomey war.²⁴²

The treaty of 3 October 1890 provided that King Béhanzin should undertake to respect the French protectorate over the kingdom of Porto Novo and to abstain from all incursions on the territories forming part of this kingdom.²⁴³ Béhanzin recognized French treaty rights over Cotonou, for which France was to pay him an annual compensation of 20,000 francs. There was no provision for the cessation of human sacrifices. In other words, the treaty was not a bill of social and religious reform for Dahomey.²⁴⁴

The Peace Treaty of 3 October 1890

Instead of laying to rest the Dahomey affair, the treaty of 3 October 1890 provoked serious discussions. The result was a widespread agitation against the ratification of this treaty. Moreover, Béhanzin continued to be discredited in a drive to stir up support for a decisive assault against him. The discussion of the Dahomey question in the Chambre des Députés and by the French press elevated it into a public question instead of a departmental one restricted to the governmental bureaus. The development of the Dahomey affair during the interlude of uneasy peace between the conclusion of the treaty of 3 October 1890 and the recommencement of hostilities in May 1892 will now be examined. Why did the French parliament refuse to ratify the treaty with Béhanzin? Why did the missions to Abomey fail to contribute to better relations between France and Dahomey?

The treaty of 3 October 1890 was signed, with the reservation that it had to be ratified by the French government before being regarded as binding on both parties. Admiral Cuverville thought it had set the stage for leading the Dahomeans into civilization. All anterior treaties would be respected by Dahomey. Bayol's proceedings were the cause of the hatred of the French, for he had allowed prisoners of war to be executed in a most barbarous fashion. However, a peace treaty had been concluded,[245] Cuverville jubilantly reported.

When Ribot presented a bill to the Chambre des Députés for the ratification of the treaty with Dahomey, it ran into strong opposition. The Chamber, however, decided to set up a special commission to study the treaty and make recommendations as to whether it should be ratified or rejected.[246] The commission[247] heard the evidence of officials and private individuals who had a knowledge of Dahomey; missionaries, merchants, and ex-soldiers who were well acquainted with Dahomey were heard. The most important submission was made by Cyprien Fabre. At this time Fabre had acquired considerable influence with the French government. He was one of the key figures in the African section of the Conseil Supérieur des Colonies. In addition, he had a respectable following in the commercial circles of Marseille, where he had been unanimously elected president of the chamber of commerce. Cyprien Fabre, moreover, was the proprietor of the most important French trading company on the Dahomey coast.[248] His agent at Whydah was the French consul there as well.

Therefore, Fabre's views on the affairs of Dahomey carried much weight. He submitted to the commission that the treaty of 3 October 1890 was, in his opinion, "mauvais, funeste, pour notre prestige, et compromettant pour nos intérêts." The annual payment of 20,000 francs to Béhanzin was regarded by the Dahomeans as a tribute paid to the king by vanquished France. The increase of prestige which this treaty would confer on Béhanzin was great, and Béhanzin's presence would be inimical for the future of the French colony of Porto Novo. For instance, there was only one German factory on the Dahomey coast before the outbreak of the war in February 1890, but this number had since increased to three. German agents were respected and esteemed, but those of France were not accorded the same treatment. Above all, why should the French parliament ratify a treaty concluded with "un roi nègre"? Was the king of Dahomey free and independent and fit to be treated as a European king? Fabre concluded by suggesting that the treaty in question should not be ratified by the Chambre des Députés and that it would suffice to give official approbation to it.[249] Admiral Cuverville objected to Fabre's views. "Lettre Fabre à Contre-Amiral Valon complétement inexacte," he cabled.[250] This produced little or no effect in Paris, because Fabre's views were corroborated by the reports of Resident Ballot and Ehrmann.[251] Both maintained that the treaty of 3 October 1890 was a result of the intrigues of Père Dogère and Candido Rodriguez with some "autorités véreuses de Whydah." Béhanzin, they claimed, did not know the provisions of the treaty. No one in Porto Novo attached any importance to the treaty in question. Many villages such as Bedji were being deserted by their inhabitants (who were flying away from an imaginary enemy) because they had no faith in the peace treaty with Dahomey. Once in Paris, Victor Ballot stated his views on the treaty to Etienne.[252] Consequently, Père Dogère was dropped from the proposed delegation to Abomey to carry gifts to Béhanzin.[253]

The parliamentary commission on Dahomey was also furnished with the full dossier of the expedition to Dahomey by the Ministère de la Marine, covering the period when this ministry was in charge of executing the affair.[254] There was, therefore, an overwhelming pressure on the commission to reject the ratification of the Dahomey treaty. The colonial administrators in Porto Novo were against the treaty, and they lined up Etienne on their side. He threw his whole weight against the treaty, which was concluded by the Ministère de la Marine without his cooperation. Etienne shared the view expressed by Cyprien Fabre that the treaty with Dahomey would constrict French expansion into the interior of Porto Novo and Dahomey. When he was informed about the reaction of the British press to the Dahomey affair, especially about an article in the *Nineteenth Century,* which said France should be dissuaded from expensive and unprofitable colonial expeditions reminiscent of Tonkin, he said: "Oui, qu'on ait intérêt à décourager toute entreprise qui serait un pas en avant en Afrique."[255]

Admiral Cuverville pressed for the ratification of the treaty because it guaranteed to France all she could get without the use of force. The efforts made by Cyprien Fabre to have the treaty repudiated by the commission were disadvantageous to French commerce, especially to that of Fabre himself. A rejection of the treaty would evoke hostility from Béhanzin and give commercial advantage to the Germans.[256] Cuverville's dilemma was appropriately described by the Paris newspaper *La Lanterne* as follows:

> L'Amiral de Cuverville est, en ce moment, aussi perplexé que le bon Pantagruel, lequel rirait d'un oeil et pleurait de l'autre ne sachant s'il était plus fâché que content ou plus content que fâché. Il voulait faire la guerre et on l'a forcé faire la paix; ceci l'ennuie profondément. Mais cette paix, il a fait par l'intermédiare d'un missionaire, ce qui le réjouit également d'une façon profonde.[257]

The parliamentary commission on Dahomey completed its inquiry and reported its findings and recommendations to the Chambre des Députés on 24 February 1891. They criticized the treaty as intervening between France and ultimate victory over Dahomey. The annual salary of 20,000 francs to the king of Dahomey would be interpreted by the Africans as weakness on the part of France and as a mark of vassalage. This money would enable Béhanzin to procure more guns and ammunition. The treaty did not include any provision for the cessation of human sacrifices and the slave trade in Dahomey. Irrespective of all these criticisms, the commission recommended that the treaty should not be rejected. However, it was not to be ratified by the Chambre des Députés, since this would accord to it an undeserved importance. The government should give it official sanction.[258] That the Chambre des Députés did not ratify the treaty with Dahomey meant the acceptance of the view of the commission that sooner or later France would be "obligés de prendre de nouvelles mesures mieux proportionées à nos intérêts et à la grandeur de la France." Ratification of the treaty by parliament would have bound France in honor to respect it, which would be inimical to the expansion of French possessions into the interior and, by definition, would be opposed to the "interests" of France.

One of the most important results of the work of the commission was that of making the Dahomey affair an open question. Henceforth the

Chambre des Députés was to be aware of what went on in Dahomey. It had to debate the question and, above all, vote money for the pursuance of French policy in that part of west Africa. The Dahomey question had passed from the hands of bureaucrats to those of the parliament, and territorial interests beyond the confines of Dahomey in the vast interior of the Niger basin had been awakened.

4

The Conquest and Occupation of Dahomey, 1890–1894
The Second Dahomey War, 1892–1894

I. Interlude of Uneasy Peace, 1890–92

The period that intervened between the conclusion of the peace treaty of 3 October 1890 and the commencement of the second Dahomey war in June 1892 was one of uneasy peace between France and Dahomey. There was mutual suspicion between them. Both parties continued to prepare for the ultimate collision which would follow a breach of the questionable peace arrangement of 3 October 1890. Béhanzin was in no position then to resume hostilities against the French because of the losses he had suffered in the recent war.[1] The ecstasy of his accession to the throne had quickly been obliterated by the agony of a war with France. Since Dahomey was reputed for her invincibility, he had to do all he could, both spiritually and temporally, to preserve the integrity of his kingdom. Consequently, he ordered raids into the neighboring territories of Abeokuta and Ouatchi for captives who would fulfill the dual purpose of serving as payment for the precision weapons Dahomey was buying in large quantities and as victims for the propitiation of the gods.[2] It appears that he was impelled by an obstinate sense of duty to contain the French in their trading comptoirs on the coast or expel them definitively from the Dahomey seaboard.[3] On the side of France, a move was made to secure definite information about Dahomey with reference to topography and other physical features as well as military strength. Since these were subjects which the local spies had failed to cover reliably, a well-picked group of French officers was sent to Abomey, ostensibly to carry to Béhanzin the presents offered to him by the president of the French republic.[4]

While the fact-finding mission led by Commandant Audeod was carrying out its task, there raged in Paris a debate over what line of action France should take in the Dahomey affair. The conflict was between those who supported an expedition to Abomey in imitation of the British expedition to Kumasi and those who favored a more temporizing policy with the king of Dahomey, with defensive operations on the coast when necessary.⁵ *Le Temps* categorically declared that France should inflict a lesson on Dahomey which would teach her not to question French rights; if France lacked the will to do this, the rights under contest should be renounced.⁶ Finally, though the treaty of 3 October 1890 was ratified by the council of ministers in February 1891,⁷ the payment provided by this treaty was never made to Béhanzin. In other words, the treaty never went into operation. It was a dead letter right from the time it was signed, for neither Béhanzin nor the French government was prepared to abide by it.

Admiral Cuverville's Appeasement Measures

Admiral Cavalier de Cuverville predicted during the negotiations with Dahomey that the probable outcome would be "une paix précaire et une paix armée." ⁸ The measures he recommended after peace was concluded were influenced by these considerations. Six hundred Senegalese tirailleurs were to be stationed at Porto Novo, Cotonou, and Grand Popo "avec les cadres complètes." All European personnel were to be sent back to France or to Senegal, except those who would be placed in charge of the magazine at Porto Novo.⁹

Encouraged by the "great nobility of sentiments" which he had noticed in Béhanzin, Cuverville launched his "peaceful enterprises of appeasement" toward Dahomey.¹⁰ First of all, Victor Ballot was sent to Dekame and the outlying villages of Porto Novo to exhort the villagers to reoccupy their villages; reconstruct their huts and houses, which were razed to the ground in the last war; and settle down to their normal life again. Ballot, who was accompanied by Captain Decoeur, reported that they were received by the Dahomeans with acclamations assuredly more noisy than sincere. His interview with Chief Kedeke of Dekame was pleasant, though Béhanzin had not informed the latter officially of the cessation of hostilities. He reestablished friendship between Kedeke and Toffa.¹¹

Second, it was proposed to send ambassadors of appeasement to Abomey with presents from the president of the French republic to Béhanzin.¹² Victor Ballot was again named by Cuverville to head this delegation to Abomey, but he soon left for France on leave,¹³ and the mission was entrusted to Commandant Audéoud. There was some surprise in the Colonial Department in Paris over the choice of Ballot to lead the proposed mission to Abomey, given Cuverville's scathing criticism of the statics of civil administrators vis-à-vis the court of Abomey.¹⁴ This was a continuation of Etienne's resentment of the direction of the Dahomey affair by the navy.

Cuverville thought that Ballot was "un serviteur d'élite dont le concours dévoué a été precieux à la colonne expéditionnaire du Dahomey" and recommended him for exceptional recompense for his efforts.[15]

The third of the peaceful enterprises proposed by Cuverville was an exploration mission from Grand Popo toward Say on the Niger.[16] This mission was to utilize the Agome River to the west of Dahomey, traverse the Kong region, and proceed to the Niger. Its task would be to explore the region between the Niger and the sea. The appeasement factor in this project was that it would include a Dahomey escort and thus "open a new field of action to Béhanzin other than the Egba." Islam, which was making very serious progress on the right bank of the Niger, was to be opposed among the fetishist populations, who were more responsive to French civilization.[17] This was the grand strategy for diverting the energy of Dahomey into channels which, though equally destructive, would enhance French influence in the Niger hinterland. Unfortunately, this project never got off the ground.

The delegation to Abomey, led by Commandant Audéoud, left Porto Novo on 10 February 1891.[18] The minister for foreign affairs, Ribot, complained to Barbey that his department had not been consulted on the question of sending gifts to Abomey and warned that Commandant Cuverville would be responsible for the initiative he had taken in this respect.[19] But he was reminded that the project had been discussed and endorsed by the French cabinet.[20] The main figures of the mission were Captain Audéoud, Captain Decoeur, Captain Hocquart, Lieutenant Chales, and d'Ambrières, a midshipman. In addition, there were eleven tirailleurs, one corporal, and three representatives of King Toffa, who had his *récade*.[21] When the French officials in Porto Novo informed Béhanzin of their proposal to send a friendly mission to Abomey, he was unenthusiastic about the visit. He did not reply to the French note of 5 December for almost three weeks; on 23 December he wrote, stating that he could not then receive the mission because he would be away from Abomey.[22] Just a year before Jean Bayol had been in Abomey on a friendly mission whose failure sparked off the most terrible war that the Dahomeans had ever known. This could well have generated the lack of interest on the part of Béhanzin in another "friendly mission." But why would he not want to receive the French mission at this particular time of the year? Above all, two important feasts were pending at the time—the anniversary of his father's death on 27 December, and that of his coronation on 1 January. These two feasts would, by custom, involve human sacrifices at which the king would not want

Europeans to be present. The memories of the events of the past year were still raw at Abomey. Moreover, it was reported that Béhanzin was on a recruiting mission in the Mahi country to the north of Dahomey and would not be back in Abomey till the festival date.[23] This accounts for the delay in the departure of the mission for Abomey till February 1891, at which time they were well received and courteously treated.[24]

The declared aims of the mission were twofold, according to Governor Ballay's letter to Béhanzin—to appease Béhanzin and demonstrate to him the friendly intentions of France, and to reconcile him with his relative, King Toffa of Porto Novo. After Audéoud had read the governor's letter to Béhanzin, Béhanzin replied that the mission was sent by Bayol. He was assured that this was not so and that Bayol had been recalled to Paris for his bad services.[25] This reassurance thawed Béhanzin's coldness to the French officers. He told them that Bayol had claimed he was the equal of the king of France when he was at Abomey. After this Béhanzin made an excursus into his unfriendly relations with Toffa, stressing Toffa's ingratitude to Dahomey, to which he owed his throne, and the evils which Toffa had perpetrated against Dahomey. On the question of Cotonou, Béhanzin stated that he could not cede this port because his fetish forbade him to part with any part of his territory. However, he would let things remain as they were with reference to the French military occupation.[26]

A noteworthy event that occurred during the French mission's sojourn at Abomey was the public ceremonial reception accorded to them. On the advice of the chief of Whydah, Kousougan, who was in Abomey with the French delegation, they were made to carry palm branches at their first ceremonial presentation to demonstrate in the traditional manner that peace had been reestablished between France and Dahomey. Captain Audéoud later protested against this incident, which he described as humiliating.[27] The delegation remained at Abomey till 25 March.

Though loads of gifts were delivered to Béhanzin and efforts were made to reconcile him with Toffa, the Audéoud mission had ulterior motives. From reading the reports of the various officers who went on this assignment, one gathers that they had more aims than were stated explicitly. Captain Audéoud's report, which is in three parts, dealt with military and political considerations of Dahomey and offered suggestions about any future campaigns in Dahomey. Lieutenant Chales studied the terrain and the bearing this would have on tactics, logistics, and maneuvering. Captain Decoeur kept the diary of the mission while Captain Hocquart examined the commercial advantages which would accrue to the Porto Novo area with the disappearance of the kingdom of Dahomey.[28] All these studies reveal interesting information on various aspects of Dahomey as they saw them. The fact-finding role of the delegation led by Audéoud was an important one, if not more important than its peacemaking role. It did not reconcile Toffa and Béhanzin, and it did not ease the tension between Dahomey and France.

Béhanzin's Military and Economic Measures Evoke Criticism

One of the most urgent preoccupations of King Béhanzin after the first war with France was the replenishment of his treasury and his armory. The Dahomean army had suffered more serious losses than ever before. Large numbers of their automatic weapons were lost in the battlefields. Immediate rearmament was a prime necessity for reasons of state as well as for the personal prestige of the king himself. The measures which Béhanzin adopted for the achievement of this purpose evoked criticism from France as well as England. The sale of slaves by Dahomey officials to Germans, Portuguese, and Belgians, in addition to the purchase of precision weapons from European merchants, exacerbated relations between France and Dahomey.

The promulgation of new tariffs for Porto Novo, Cotonou, and the French possessions east of Grand Popo in April 1890 [29] was unwelcome news to British officials and traders in Lagos. Soon a demand for uniform tariffs for Lagos and Porto Novo[30] was made, and the French government agreed to this in principle.[31] King Toffa's raids and exaction of customs in the Ajarra Creek districts caused the governor of Lagos to protest to the resident of Porto Novo.[32] It was reported that Toffa's *ilaris* made raids into Badagry and captured and killed several persons.[33] As with Toffa, so with Béhanzin, but on a larger scale: Dahomey raids in Yorbuland were a menace and did much harm to the commercial life of Lagos, it was argued. In the raids which the soldiers of Dahomey made into Abeokuta in June 1890, about 1,200 captives were taken, most of whom were sold as slaves. The discussions of Frederick E. Forbes in 1849 and Thomas Tickel in 1869 with the king of Dahomey about this matter were recalled, and the British government was urged to renew such steps to stop Dahomey from ravaging the hinterland of Lagos.[34] Further pressure was put on the British government to take steps to check Dahomey raids into Yorbuland by British merchants in England.[35] Lord Knutsford asked the Foreign Office to request the French government to control Dahomey, because Dahomey was in the French sphere, according to the agreement of 10 August 1889 between

Britain and France. Lord Salisbury argued strongly against this proposal. Could Britain be asked to control the Mahdists, the tribes of the Congo and the Lake districts, local wars in Ashanti, and so on? Britain's hold on these areas was weaker even than that of France over Dahomey, concluded Lord Salisbury.[36] His views were buttressed by the preliminary investigation of the matter by Egerton in Paris, which showed that "the relations of the French Government with Dahomey were not of a nature which would justify a request of the kind." [37] The French did not claim to exercise any influence over Dahomey, continued Egerton, and both Hanotaux and Haussmann were alarmed by the prospects of free importation of arms into Dahomey through Whydah when the General Act of the Brussels Conference came into operation.[38] Dahomey was a sovereign state and was not party to the Brussels Conference. Therefore, the provisions of the Brussels Act would not be binding on her. Such a situation would defeat the aims of the Brussels Act, since traffic in arms, slaves, and liquor would flourish untrammeled in Dahomey territory, which was included in the zone specified by the Brussels Conference for the prohibition of such traffic.

The Colonial Office approved Denton's proposal to send a strongly worded protest to Béhanzin about the raids of his troops into the hinterland of Lagos, over which Britain had an obligation by the treaty of 1861.[39] As pointed out by Dr. Newbury, European traders of this period were prone to blame any fluctuations in the volume of raw materials coming from the interior on internal wars, although this was not always the case.[40] The protest against Dahomey was motivated by economic considerations, though a few humanitarians and missionaries appended to it the questions of slavery and human sacrifice in Dahomey in order to enlist more support by giving a philanthropic flavor to the case.[41]

French Alarm at Dahomey's Rearmament

In December 1890 Admiral Cuverville was instructed to hand over his powers to Victor Ballot and return to his former post in the Atlantic fleet.[42] The direction of the affairs of Dahomey and Porto Novo was handed back to the Sous-Secrétariat d'Etat des Colonies, to satisfy Eugene Etienne.[43] With Ballot on leave in France, the administration in Porto Novo was in the hands of Resident Ehrmann and Governor Ballay, the latter of whom had been sent there on special mission by Etienne.[44] The first report which Ehrmann made soon after he took office signaled Béhanzin's recruiting mission in the Mahi country.[45] Soon after, Governor Ballay informed Etienne that Béhanzin was being offered a whole range of automatic weapons by

German merchants. It was feared that the king could buy Mauser rifles, which would make his artillery more formidable.[46] These reports did not, however, debar the French government from reaching a decision on 30 April 1891 that an officer should be sent to Whydah to announce the ratification of the treaty with Dahomey. Governor Ballay was instructed to take measures for the payment to the king of the annuity agreed upon in the arrangement of 3 October 1890.[47] But it was in the cumulative effect of these reports that their importance was to be discovered. News of Béhanzin's rearmament continued to trickle into Paris. In May 1891 Ehrmann discovered that the German firm of Volber and Brohm had sold 800 Snider rifles and 15,000 cartridges to the king of Dahomey. In addition, 3,000 rifles and four cannons had been smuggled through Whydah as furniture.[48] This alarmist note was kept up by Resident Ehrmann. The sale of slaves to the Germans for work in the Cameroons and to the Belgians for the Congo formed the theme of one report; another dwelt on the disquieting preparation of canoes by Dahomeans for transporting cannons to attack Grand Popo.[49] This would have been a foolhardy undertaking on the part of the Dahomeans, who were aware of the presence of several French gunboats in the coastal waters.

When the Quai d'Orsay was informed of those reports, Ribot's reaction was to lecture Etienne that it was to the "best interests of France to follow a pacific policy vis-à-vis King Béhanzin."[50] The Colonial Department took the hint and soon informed Ribot that further information from Governor Ballay and Victor Ballot (then in Paris) showed that "the situation was less disquieting than one would be tempted to believe."[51] Ribot criticized the first French war with Dahomey when he came into office and could not be expected to rush precipitately into a new campaign. His caution was the object of criticism by ardent imperialists. He was not too popular in the Chambre des Députés, where his manner was thought too "magistral" and distasteful to the Radicals, led by Georges Clemenceau and Camille Pelletan.[52]

Béhanzin's rearmament program continued apace. Since he did not have enough money to pay for the sophisticated weapons he was acquiring, he raided the adjacent territories for captives, whom he then sold to the Europeans as laborers in their colonies in the Cameroons, the Congo, and the Portuguese islands in the Atlantic. According to Cyprien Fabre, up to five hundred francs were paid for one worker, though the prices varied considerably. Resident Ehrmann observed that Captain de Gravenreuth, who transported over one hundred persons on the *Pollux* to the Cameroons in August 1891, paid 400 francs for each of them. The Belgian ship *Le Souverain* transported about 500 persons from Whydah to the Congo, where Lambote told Fabre's agent that about 4,000 laborers were needed for railway construction.[53] Another shipment of 150 males and about 30 females to the Cameroons took place on 16 September 1891. The French press covered these events. "Ce qui passe actuellement dans cette partie de l'Afrique est une honte. La France doit la faire cesser," admonished Cyprien Fabre.[54] The overwhelming evidence of the recrudescence of the slave trade at Whydah made the French government take steps to end this buying of laborers from Dahomey. The powers concerned were contacted to this effect,[55] and a request was made for the enforcement of the General Act of the Brussels Conference.[56]

The acquisition of precision and automatic weapons by Dahomey was carried on to a much greater extent than was understood by French officials, according to the revelations made when General Dodds seized and examined the records of German firms in Dahomey. After the campaign of 1890, Ernz-Leopold Vitt was the first person to introduce chassepot rifles into Dahomey; he sold 408 of these to Béhanzin early in January 1891. In April he delivered 26,280 cartridges to Dahomey.[57] Trangott-Sollner & Company sold to Béhanzin in April and October 1891 200 Spencer rifles, 40 Snider rifles, 40 chassepots, 12 revolvers, and 32,496 cartridges; in April 1892 they delivered to him 1,150 more cartridges and 200 kilograms of gunpowder. Ernest Barth, a Swiss-born trader at Whydah and associate of Joss of Hamburg, sold to Béhanzin 275 quick-firing rifles and 82,500 cartridges in October 1891; a second sale of 325 quick-firing rifles and 97,500 cartridges was made in April 1892.[58]

Béhanzin's main source of arms supply, however, was the firm of Volber and Brohm, whose representatives at Whydah were Ernest Richter and Peter Buss. They sold arms and ammunition of all sorts to the king of Dahomey, as shown in table 3.

It is clear from these statistics that Dahomey rearmed at a more rapid rate and to a more alarming degree than was known to the French officials. If the facts had been known completely, not even what Lord Lytton described as Ribot's "timidity"[59] could have prevented an immediate preventive war against Dahomey by France. Indeed, the news of the French mission led by Captain Audéoud to Abomey sparked off speculation of another war by France against Dahomey.[60] In any case, the cumulative effect of the reports concerning Béhanzin's rearmament and his desperate efforts to replenish his treasury by the sale of laborers to Europeans was the embitterment of the

TABLE 3

Annex to Volber and Brohm (Richter and Buss)

Dates of Sales	Models and Articles Sold	Quantity	Observation
1891:			
5 February	Peabodys	300	
17 July	Winchesters	60	
18 October	Canons Om 06 Krupp (campagne)	4	
18 October	Canons Om 08 Krupp (campagne)	1	
28 November	Mitrailleuse complète	2	
1892:			
5 March	Winchester	3	
28 February	Winchester	40	
11 April	Winchester	30	
9 August	Mitrailleuse complète	1	
9 August	Petit canon (ballon geschutz)	1	Mark F. Krupp, Essen 1872.
1891:			
February	Cartouches pour Peabody	60,000	
February	Cartouches pour d'exercice	20,000	
July	Cartouches pour Winchester	25,600	
18 October	Obus pour canon de Om 06	300	
18 October	Boites à mitraille de Om 06	100	
18 October	Obus pour canon de Om 06	300	
1892:			
5 March	Cartouches pour Winchester	300	
19 July	Cartouches pour Winchester	200	
28 February	Cartouches pour mitrailleuses	4,024	
9 August	Caisses capsules	6	
9 August	Cartouches pour Winchester	2,000	
9 August	Obus de Om 06	caisse	Le chiffre des caisses
9 August	Boites à mitrailleuses Om 06	caisse	n'est pas indiqué
9 August	Cartouches pour mitrailleuses	caisse	sur le brouillard.

Taken from the books of Volber and Brohm and signed by Richter and Buss.
(Signed) A. d'Albeca
Whydah 5 January 1893.

SOURCE: *Journal Officiel, Etablissements et Protectorats Francais du Golfe de Bénin*, 1 February 1893.

relations between France and Dahomey, thus paving the way to a definitive expedition against Béhanzin.

A final aspect of Béhanzin's economic measures after the 1890 war with France was his agricultural program. The fact that the first war broke out during the planting season meant that normal agricultural production of food crops was interfered with because of the mobilization of persons who in peacetime would have been at work in their farms. Therefore Dahomey's 1890 harvest must have been much below average. Moreover, it must have been an onerous task for the king to provision his forces from February to the end of hostilities in 1890, since previous Dahomean campaigns were not usually of such a long duration, and the troops usually supplied themselves by pillaging the enemy territory. Béhanzin thus gave serious consideration to the question of provisioning his troops in case of another levée en masse. Of course, he had to deal with the temporary shortage of food staples in the immediate post-war period. He could not import foodstuffs from the neighboring territories because of his hostile attitude toward them, whereas the French were able to do so.[61]

He tackled this problem by stepping up work on royal plantations. In order to bring more land into cultivation in the hope of increasing production, more labor was required. This was not to be obtained from Dahomey, since it would mean cutting down total production indirectly. Therefore, a flow of captives from the surrounding territories was the solution. This accounts for the raids that the Dahomeans made into Abeokuta and Ouatchi, though some of the victims of these raids were sold to Europeans for other purposes.[62] Approximately 2,000 captives were taken to work on the royal plantations at Affomayi, Kinkpandu, and Kpokissa, near the fetish river Hlan.[63] It is evident then that Béhanzin had a well-balanced program for the restoration of economic and military normalcy to his kingdom after the nightmare of the new warfare in 1890.

Changed Attitude in France toward War in Dahomey

The first French campaign against Dahomey was organized and unleashed as it were in camera. Only the cabinet and the bureaucrats of the ministries concerned knew what went on before the campaign was made public. In the cabinet there reigned a morbid fear of getting involved in a parliamentary debate of the Dahomey question. Clemenceau, "who, though incapable of forming a government himself was an expert in the art of upsetting Ministers," [64] the Radicals, as well as the Right in French politics were prepared to deal a deadly blow to any republican ministry. Extravagant colonial expeditions offered them a golden opportunity for such a confrontation, as the Tonkin expedition had demonstrated in 1885. However, between 1889 and 1892 rather profound changes had occurred in the internal politics of France; these had tremendous effects on French foreign policy, especially colonial policy.[65]

The fall of General Boulanger, whose "adventurous activity" strengthened the republic, indirectly marked a point of departure in the life of the Third Republic.[66] The growth of republicanism, "in *posse* as well as in *esse*," as Lord Lytton put it, became self-evident. All appreciable possibilities of a monarchical restoration completely disappeared.[67]

Moreover, the intervention of Pope Leo XIII broke the backbone of the Catholic opposition to the Third Republic.[68] One of the most influential of French bishops of the time, the illustrious Cardinal Lavigerie,[69] the Archbishop of Algeria, declared openly for the republican system of government:

> Quand la volonté d'un peuple s'est nettement affirmée, que la forme du gouvernement n'a rien en soide contraire, comme le proclamait dernièrement Léon XIII, aux principes qui seuls peuvent faire vivre les nations chrétiennes et civilisées, lorsqu'il n'y a plus, pour arracher son pays aux abimes qui le menacent, que l'adhésion sans arrière-pensée à la forme du gouvernement, le moment vient de déclarer l'épreuve fait . . . C'est ce que j'enseigne autour de moi, c'est ce que je souhaite de voir imiter en France par tout notre clergé, et en parlant ainsi je suis certain de n'être démenti par aucune voix autorisée.[70]

The definitive establishment of the republic at home was followed by the dispersion of the fear of isolation. A consultative political pact was concluded between France and Russia in August 1890, and two years later the secret military pact which was the binding cement in the Franco-Russian alliance was signed.[71] A third factor which led to the new confidence in France at this time was the downfall of Bismarck. It was this new confidence that ushered in what Jacques Spuller, the veteran politician and former friend of Gambetta, christened "l'ésprit nouveau." [72] With this new spirit the Third Republic entered into its *belle epoque* of conquests in all spheres of endeavor. The adventurous zeal symbolized by the gigantic Eiffel Tower which dominated the exposition of 1889 waxed steadily. France could now undertake to send troops abroad, unlike in the days of Jules Ferry, when such enterprises were unanimously opposed because they spread French forces thinly about and rendered France more vulnerable than ever. The amour propre of the republic had to be defended even in remote parts of the world against the intrigues of Britain and Germany as well as the vanity and arrogance of barbarous despots.[73] The "techniciens de la colonisation" unfolded their well-constructed theories of expansion in their selected areas of operation.[74] For the soldiers "les galons et la gloire" and for the nation "l'amour-propre" became motive forces more than ever. It was in this milieu that the second Dahomey war was shaped.[75]

Why was there a readiness in France to support a decisive campaign against Dahomey in 1892? The answer to this question is to be sought partly in France and partly in the events that occurred in Dahomey itself between 1891 and 1892.

The question of Dahomey occupied the Chambre des Députés on more than twenty occasions from the time it was brought up on 8 March 1890 by François Deloncle to the surrender of Béhanzin on 26 January 1894. After the initial debates over the ratification or nonratification of the peace treaty with Dahomey, the question moved into the more practical and sensitive realms of voting credits for the conduct of the campaign. The first major encounter between the proponents and opponents of an expedition to Dahomey came during the session of 7 April 1892, when Henri Hervieu's interpellation on Dahomey was discussed.[76]

Martineau deplored the precipitate speed at which colonies were being conquered to the neglect of patience and sagacity. Tonkin had hardly been conquered when France had dabbled in Madagascar, where she had not even had reliable treaties. The impression was being given that Africa was inviting France and that the negroes were impatient to receive French authority. "C'est l'age d'or de la politique coloniale," Martineau declared and asked why the chamber was being asked to vote money for yet another expedition. Hervieu suggested an exchange of territory with Germany, Britain, or Portugal and concluded that the alternatives were either a decisive march on Abomey or evacuation of Porto Novo and the Dahomey coast.[77] Emile Jamais, who replaced Etienne as Sous-Secrétaire des Colonies, denied that French policy in Dahomey was an expansionist one. Credits were being demanded for the defense of French interests and to ensure a necessary respect for the flag of France.[78] After ruling out both evacuation and an exchange of territories, Jamais admitted that a march on Abomey had been envisaged but that the problem had been how to inform the chamber about this. He was interrupted:

> François Deloncle: Why talk about it?
> Jules Delahaye: Don't reveal your plans! Béhanzin reads newspapers.
> P. de Cassagnac: Don't give details. A march on Abomey is not outside our reach. We have the forces for it.
> H. Hervieu: March on Abomey or evacuate. There is no other solution.

Jamais was disconcerted. He complained: "If I do not say anything I am reproached for my silence; if I speak I am reproached for saying too much." Deloncle decried military expeditions at the expense of commercial colonization, which animated the colonial group of the chamber, of which he was a key figure. He praised the pacific manner in which Binger acquired vast territories without firing a shot. The credit asked for should be rejected by the chamber because it was for launching a new military expedition.[79] The chamber was reminded by le Provost de Launay that debate on the credits required for the Soudan and Dahomey was "a question in which the honour of France, the blood of our soldiers and the fortune of France were involved. C'est trop!" He also charged that the aim of the colonial policy in west Africa was the junction of Algeria, the Soudan, and the Congo.[80]

Paul Deroulède delivered the sharpest criticism of the policy followed in west Africa. It was Etienne who had replaced the good commercial relations which had existed between France and Dahomey since 1851 with bad military relations.[81] "The greatness of a people is not measured by the extent of their soil space," Deroulède asserted. He emphasized the futility of colonial wars, pointing out that the money spent and men lost in European wars since the Middle Ages could have been used to build a France ten times greater than the empire which Napoleon Bonaparte had wished to create.[82] Alsace-Lorraine, lost for twenty-two years, could not be compensated for by Tonkin or Soudan or Dahomey.

The debate was resumed on 11 April. At the end of it the bill for the occupation of Dahomey was passed by 301 to 177 votes.[83] The Colonial Department obtained the funds it needed for the pursuance of its policy in Dahomey. Shortly afterward the second Dahomey war began.

The discussion of the Dahomey question featured prominently and regularly in the French press from 1890 on.[84] Lord Dufferin reported that it "dominated the Press to the exclusion of other issues" and that there was a general preoccupation in France respecting colonial questions.[85] Of all the newspapers, *Le Siècle* had the best access to official information on colonial questions. It devoted itself "assiduously to colonial affairs and to calling attention to England's plots against French interests."[86] However, *Le Temps* was second to none in the breadth and quality of its coverage of colonial issues, especially the Dahomey affair.[87]

Most of the newspapers and journals cooperated with the ardent imperialists by publicizing their views. Some saw in Dahomey vices to be exterminated;[88] others called for the defense of the French flag, which was being violated by the Dahomeans.[89] The deterioration of the relations between France and Dahomey provided an opportunity for jingoistic calls for French action in Africa, such as the one made by M. G. de Wailly, who had a grand vision of France becoming undisputed master of all west Africa.[90] However, the prospects of the immense wealth of Dahomey and the economic advantages its occupation would bestow on France predominated the case for a march on Abomey. "Commerce, émigration, développement de la vitalité et de la puissance économique d'un 'vieux pays', violà dit-on toujours, la véritable raison d'être des colonies." [91] Commandant Mattei, in a resounding lecture which he delivered in the town hall of Grenoble on 24 March 1890, made a very strong appeal to Frenchmen to embrace the love of colonial expansion, because it was "pour la grandeur et la richesse de la patrie." He pointed out that even in the French army it was being asked why there should be a war against Dahomey. The possession of Dahomey would open to France enormous commercial advantages among other things. Dahomey should be acquired for reasons of trade and for its riches. Add to this the access to the hinterland to the north, which the possession of Dahomey would provide, and Mattei felt that any objections would be answered.[92]

Le Père Chautard underscored the immense vegetable and mineral wealth of Dahomey. The gigantic size of the trees was evidence of the fertility of the soil. He used recent statistics to drive home the economic potential of Dahomey.[93] Nevertheless, the French merchants who had business connections with Dahomey were not all agreed on the glorious and rosy economic picture painted by some of their compatriots. Mantes was cautious and doubted if a prosperous colony could be made out of Dahomey. This opinion was, however, drowned by that expressed by Cyprien Fabre and most of the other merchants that Dahomey was very fertile and had a bright future.[94] M. François lectured the Chambre des Députés on the actual and potential commercial importance of the Dahomey seaboard, while denying any wish to conquer that kingdom. The volume of trade in the Dahomey coast had exceeded 13 million francs, from which France derived more than 400,000 francs annually in customs revenue. This revenue would exceed 1,500,000 francs yearly when the whole coast came under French control and thus assured to French products the vast markets of the hinterland. "Those of us here and outside who love France's Empire in Africa to which M. Etienne imparted form from Algeria to the Congo and the Soudan do not wish to see our soldiers going there to [shoot] but we wish to see our products, our merchandises sold there," he declared.[95] A former missionary in Dahomey, E. Chautard, in a memorandum which he prepared on how to attack Dahomey, pointed out that "immense treasures were accumulated in the palace at Abomey and in the tombs of the Kings of Dahomey at Cana."[96] This was disproved after the capture of Abomey.[97]

To these economic arguments was appended the probable role of Dahomey as the gateway to the rich hinterland of the Niger basin.[98] As *rapporteur* of the Commission du Budget, Chautemps explained to the Chambre des Députés why France should fight for Dahomey and struggle to maintain it:

> Par les immenses territoires dont elle est appelée à etre le débouché naturel, la côte du Dahomey est susceptible d'acquérir une réele importance commerciale. Située à 400 kilometres de Say, elle doit être pour nous la clef de l'Afrique centrale et jouer dans notre politique africaine un rôle autrement prépondérant que le Soudan occidental.[99]

This theme found its way into the newspapers and reviews, where it was expounded with zeal. It was necessary to make this important route accessible without further delay.[100]

Finally, considerations of international competition for colonies entered into the discussion of the Dahomey question as a significant factor. Colonel L. Archinard declared in a lecture to students that to retreat before the blacks would mean giving way to the English and Germans. Père Dogère declared that rich Dahomey, "coveted by the English of Lagos and the Germans of Togo," must be annexed.[101] Thus, during the soul-searching provoked by the Dahomey affair, Frenchmen revealed that economic considerations were foremost in inducing them to acquire Dahomey. Considerations of national prestige and honor carried much weight also. So did the thought of losing ground to Britain, Germany, or even Portugal. During the epoch in question, the French argument that if they evacuated Porto Novo and the Dahomey seaboard, Britain would seize these territories was a valid one. Moreover, if France did not move to reduce the king of Dahomey, she would have had to face the uncomfortable consequences of either a German or British occupation of Dahomey. In order to assure to her coastal comptoirs the undisturbed flow of trade from the hinterland necessary for their viability and development, France undertook the definitive reduction of the kingdom of Dahomey.

Béhanzin's Intransigence

While these fine points of policy were being debated in Paris, events in Dahomey were taking a turn for the worse. Béhanzin's intransigence aggravated matters. His soldiers were on the rampage once again. They attacked villages on the right bank of the Wheme River whose loyalty to Abomey was in doubt. In the meantime armed patrols were on duty all over the kingdom. It was one of these patrols which attacked a French reconnaissance cruise on the *Topaze* as she sailed up the Wheme to Danko, wounding three men and two laptots.[102] Victor Ballot, who was in the reconnaissance party that was attacked, protested to Béhanzin about the conduct of his patrol. Béhanzin did not accept Ballot's protest and pointed out that the statements made by Ballot were wrong. He was displeased by Ballot's effrontery and maintained that he had not raided any French territory. If any African state offended him, he had the right to punish that state, irrespective of Ballot's feelings. If Ballot was not satisfied with this state of affairs, he could do whatever he pleased, including waging another war on Dahomey. At all events, Béhanzin was ready.[103] With this explicit statement by Béhanzin, the already dwindling grounds of compromise shrank to nothing.

This was the culminating point in Béhanzin's intransigence. He had reinstalled at Cotonou the Yevogan Zonohochou in defiance of the treaty of 3 October 1890, and in June 1891 this Yevogan took drastic economic steps against the French factories at Cotonou. He closed the native retail markets opposite these factories and started collecting customs duties for Abomey. There had been Dahomey raids in the valley of the Mono River[104] in territory under French protection, and Blogdomey had been badly ravaged. To these were added the extreme act of attacking a French reconnaissance party on the Wheme River.[105]

The result of the mounting tension was the declaration of war against Dahomey by France early in April 1892. Ballot communicated this decision to Abomey. Béhanzin's reaction was that he was prepared for war if the French so desired. He exhorted the French to remain tranquil at Porto Novo and to concentrate on their commercial activities rather than on his affairs. In this manner, there would be peace between them and Dahomey as heretofore. However, if they wanted a war with him, he was ready. "The first time I did not know how to wage war but now I know," he asserted. His troops, which were more numerous than had been reported to the French, were ready for action. If another war broke out it would be a war of attrition, and he would execute it with all his resources, even if it lasted one hundred years and cost 20,000 men. The amount voted by the French chamber for recommencing the war against Dahomey had been brought to his notice. "Je suis très bien informé," Béhanzin reminded Ballot.[106]

It was in his letters that Béhanzin revealed the application of his cosmology to politics.[107] God, the creator of all things, made both the blacks and the whites and assigned to each their own part of the earth's surface. Harmony was to exist between blacks and whites; none should do evil to the other. Since the whites engaged in commerce, the blacks should have commercial transactions with them on friendly terms. This was as far as their relations should go. This implied that the whites should exercise political authority over those areas of the earth's surface assigned to them by providence, just as the blacks ruled over their own areas. Political interference in the affairs of one another was contrary to natural law. "I am the King of the blacks and the whites do not have to look into my affairs," he declared.[108]

With constancy Béhanzin reiterated that he reserved the right to deal with local African problems as he saw fit. It would be sheer effrontery, even rude intrusion, for the French to concern themselves with his exercise of political authority over Africans. If he extended his authority over French villages in France, then he could understand French protests concerning his actions.[109] Even when Béhanzin was on the verge of defeat in the war with France, he repeated through his messengers, who went to the French camp with a white flag to sue for peace, that the war was a manifestation of divine will. "C'est le bon Dieu qui a voulu la guerre," his representatives told Colonel Lambinet as they outlined to him Béhanzin's peace terms on 29 April 1893.[110] The nature of the Dahomey monarchy, the great influence of priests over the king, and the religio-political functions of Dahomey kings are important factors which influenced Béhanzin's cosmology and his theories of politics.[111]

As for the recent exchange of gunshots on the Wheme, Béhanzin blamed Ballot, whom he had told on several occasions that the river belonged to Dahomey and not to Porto Novo. Any foreigners who intended to travel in Dahomey territory should first of all inform the court of Abomey of their intentions. Since no information had been given to him about a French cruise on the River Wheme, his troops surmised that the gunboat had hostile intentions and consequently attacked it.[112] This expostulation was like crying over spilt milk. On the very day that Béhanzin sent it to Ballot, a presidential decree was signed in Paris appointing Colonel A. Dodds to lead the second campaign against Dahomey.[113] A state of war existed between France and Dahomey once again, after about eighteen months of precarious peace between the two states.

II. The Campaigns of 1892–94

After Emile Jamais had won his battle for credits in the French chamber, he was confronted with the arduous task of how to best apply these funds for the solution of the Dahomey problem. The harmony which now existed between the Colonial Department and the Ministère de la Marine permitted concerted action.[114] As a result, Colonel Alfred-Amédée Dodds, commandant of the fourth regiment of the Infanterie de la Marine, was nominated as commandant supérieur of the French expeditionary force in Dahomey.[115] Colonel Dodds was a mulatto from St. Louis, Senegal. He had been educated in French military colleges and had distinguished himself as a captain at the battle of Bazeilles in 1870 during the Franco-Prussian War. He combined the qualities of leadership, courage, and a rare intelligence with mastery of African affairs.[116] Colonel Dodds carved a niche for himself in the Infanterie de la Marine by his outstanding accomplishments in Senegal and its dependencies. In March 1891 he gained further laurels by his exploits in the Fouta region, which he pacified completely.[117] Etienne suggested in 1890 that either Colonel Dodds or Klipfel should be sent to Porto Novo to replace Terrillon. Colonel Klipfel got the nomination at that time, but Dodds's opportunity came in April 1892. The successful reduction of the king of Dahomey, directed by Dodds and the controversy which centered around him a few years later in Tonkin, made him a very well-known officer of the French army of his time.[118]

The Second Dahomey War Begins

On 28 May 1892 Colonel Dodds landed at Cotonou. The next day Governor Noel Ballay handed over civil powers to him in accordance with ministerial instructions.[119] The difficulties created by Bayol during the campaign of 1890 impressed on the ministry the necessity for a unified command in Dahomey. The French government consulted a committee of experts on west African affairs in mid-April 1892 about future operations in Dahomey and must have received valuable advice from these specialists.[120]

Before the arrival of Colonel Dodds, the movement of the troops of Dahomey had been watched by Governor Ballay with great concern. He was accompanied to Porto Novo by fifty Senegalese tirailleurs. He regretted the absence of a French cruiser at Cotonou, because Béhanzin's troops had been deployed to the north of Porto Novo and the vicinity of Cotonou.[121] In addition, Ballay proposed a blockade of the seaboard to prevent the flow of arms to Béhanzin. To this end the Quai d'Orsay redoubled its efforts to get Britain to instruct her agents in west Africa to enforce the Brussels Act. Hanotaux remarked that Germany had already enforced the Brussels Act and that France had instructed her agents to enforce it as well. Britain was the odd man out. "Mr. Waddington too is in a fuss about this," T. V. Lister said.[122]

Precautionary measures were taken in view of the mobilization by Dahomey. As the fear of surprise attacks by the Dahomeans became greater, French troops were put on the alert night and day. In collaboration with the military officers, Governor Ballay had arms distributed to Europeans and faithful creoles in order that both civil and military elements could be mustered in the event of a surprise attack by Dahomey.[123] It follows that by the time Colonel Dodds arrived at Porto Novo, certain emergency regulations were already in force. At the same time, the inadequacy of French effectives was underscored by the distribution of arms to civilians. With the meager force of 800 soldiers at his command, Dodds could only adopt a defensive posture along the coast while waiting for the rainy season to subside and for reinforcements to arrive.

In order to ascertain where the sympathies of the village heads around Porto Novo lay, Victor Ballot advised Dodds to summon all of them to a conference at Porto Novo, during which the followers of Toffa would renew their pledge to support the French war effort against Dahomey. Prince Sognibo, an anglophile who detested French support for Toffa, did not attend this convocation. The absence of Chief Kekede of Dekame was also significant, because it was believed that friendly relations existed between him and Toffa ever since Ballot's visit to Dekame in November 1890.[124] The lack of local enthusiasm for Toffa demonstrated the hollowness of his "fictitious government," as Captain Charles Jacquot described it.[125] Prince Sognibo and his supporters went over to Abomey, where he became an adviser to Béhanzin.

Cavaignac, the minister for the navy, authorized the formation of a battery of artillery for Dahomey under the command of Captain H. Delestre.[126] On the report of Colonel Dodds, the French government declared a blockade of the Dahomey seaboard on 15 June 1892. Béhanzin retorted by opening hostilities on 26 June, thus forcing Dodds to embark on some offensive action against Dahomean villages on the littoral.[127] Before hostilities began, Dodds and Béhanzin had exchanged hostages who were seized early in June. Two messengers from Whydah were arrested and detained at Porto Novo because they were taken to be Béhanzin's spies. Swift reprisals followed at Whydah, where three French men were seized from the Maison

Fabre et Cie. Fortunately, Captain Vicente de Rosa Rolim of the Portuguese fort at Whydah intervened, and an early exchange of hostages was effected, thus obviating a repetition of the long captivity of hostages that was a feature of the first Dahomey war of 1890.[128]

The minor operations which Dodds sanctioned along the Wheme and Lake Nokoue (Denham) were calculated to prepare the ground for the projected decisive move against Abomey.[129] Thus Dodds kept to his original instructions because he reckoned that they would provide a springboard for further action. He was opposed to the French government's policy of protecting the coastal establishments from Dahomey attacks. After studying the situation, he decided that the only means of inflicting a severe defeat on Béhanzin was by a decisive march on Abomey.[130] This was the only way to break and destroy the power and nuisance value of Béhanzin. After much hesitation the council of ministers approved Dodds's plan of action and gave him a free hand in its execution. Reinforcements were despatched to Porto Novo from Senegal and from Algeria. The *Mytho* and the *Ville de San Nicolas* transported the foot soldiers and the cavalry to Porto Novo, the former vessel bringing along from Toulon half a company of technicians under Commandant Roques.[131]

The zealots of expansionism had won over those who favored with Admiral Cuverville the maintenance of coastal comptoirs. Once the credits were voted by the chamber, the French government went ahead with the expedition to Abomey, which Emile Jamais had denied was the principal aim of his department. Thus was vindicated the contention spearheaded by Paul de Cassagnac, who observed that "d'ailleurs, il y a eu assez de dissimulation dans la politique coloniale. Nous demandons la vérité, la vérité brutale, parce-que c'est la seule qui soit patriotique. Jusqu'à présent, il n'y a eu que des dissimulations et des ménsonges." [132] The "golden age of colonial expansion" had arrived, and protests from the left were impotent against it.

The Expedition to Abomey

The first striking demonstration of military talent by Colonel Dodds was his plan to march toward Abomey, not by the traditional route of Abomey-Calavi-Allada-Agrime-Cana but by the seemingly impenetrable left bank of the River Wheme.[133] The former road was well fortified and defended by Dahomey and would have presented more serious problems to Dodds in logistics and tactics. Since Béhanzin deployed his big guns and most of his forces along the Allada road, this move by Dodds was most disconcerting to him. Furthermore, Commandant Audéoud was sent to operate on the west of Dahomey up the River Mono from Grand Popo in order to distract Béhanzin. The hasty and uncoordinated redeployment of Dahomey forces revealed how distracted the Dahomey command had become. From then on Dodds seized the initiative and continued to dictate the pace of the war till Dahomey was defeated.[134]

The march to Abomey may be divided into two phases for convenience. The first was the advance on the left bank of the River Wheme from Porto Novo to Gbede, where the expeditionary corps crossed the river to the right bank. Colonel Dodds altered his plan for the column to ford the river at Tohoue on 30 September, because of the solid fortifications which Béhanzin's men had amassed at this point, as well as the rise in the water level. As Captain Jacquot observed:

> En effet, on voit difficilement une colonne comprenant près de 3,000 individus avec son artillérie, sa cavalerie et son convoi, traverser une rivière d'un mètre 30 de profondeur environ (au gué) sur plus de 160 mètres de largeur, sous le feu de toute l'armée dahoméenne réunie.[135]

The second phase was that in which the expedition battled its way from the banks of the Wheme to the charred courtyards of the palace at Abomey on 17 November 1892.[136]

Before embarking on the task of marching to Abomey, Colonel Dodds had augmented enormously the meager forces at his disposal when he arrived at Porto Novo. He had 76 officers and 2,088 enlisted men, 930 of which were Africans, mainly Senegalese or Hausa. In addition, there were 2,239 porters, assembled through the efforts of Ballot and Toffa. There were also 132 mules in addition to the cavalry. Beside these land forces, Colonel Dodds had a fleet of five gunboats, four of which were equipped with "canons révolvers à tir rapide." These were under the command of Lieutenant Fésigny of the *Corail*.[137] These gunboats gave vital support to the land forces. They accompanied the column and assured the provisioning of troops, the evacuation of the wounded and the sick, and reserves of ammunition and food. They were therefore a necessary corollary of the land forces.

The first major French incursion into Dahomey territory was the move against Azaouisse, the capital of Dekame, in August. Chief Kekede fled northward rather than surrender to the French and Toffa. He was an old man, as Ballot reported in 1890, and died near Kode from fatigue and exposure.[138] Dekame was reduced, and the forward movement to Dogba began. The infantry was divided into three groups headed by Commandants Riou, Faurax, and Lasserre. All the units except the cavalry were to assemble at Dogba on 14 September.[139] Here a fortified post was erected with the bivouacs on the plateau. Information reached Abomey about the French encampment. Dahomey troops were dispatched to Dogba, where they fought a fierce battle with French forces on 19 September.[140] Colonel Dodds reported that quick-firing rifles were found on Dahomeans who died on the battlefield. The courage of the Dahomeans in battle was amazing. According to one eyewitness, "l'ennemi ripost avec une incroyable énergie, balles et mitraille ne le font pas reculer d'une semelle et nul doute que sans les abatis, il serait venue se jeter sur nos baïonettes."[141] After the battle subsided the French surveyed the field. The wounded were finished off, and about thirty cadavers were burned.[142] What is significant about the battle of Dogba is that the Dahomeans engaged in it without full knowledge of the strength of their enemies. Their intention was to annihilate what was thought to be an advance guard and then continue their march on Porto Novo under the leadership of one of Béhanzin's brothers, Dahomeans captured at Dogba testified.[143] Béhanzin therefore tried to carry out his threat of razing Porto Novo to the ground. But it was a tactical error to have sent his troops down the same route through which the French were advancing northward. If the forces of Dahomey had marched down to Porto Novo via Allada and laid siege on this ill-defended city, they would have put Dodds on the defensive and given a different hue to the conflict.[144]

After the battle of Dogba there was no other major encounter between the warring parties till after the French troops had crossed the Wheme to the right bank. Colonel Dodds changed the plan to cross the river at the Tohoue ford because of the solid fortifications made by the Dahomeans at both Tohoue and Agony. He also changed the date of the passage of the Wheme from 30 September to 2 October. He utilized the opportunity offered by a dense fog to get his men to the right bank from Gbede.[145] The progress of the expedition toward Cana continued cautiously. Engagements were fought at Poguessa, Adegon, Akpa, Koto, and Umbumedi, where the royal plantations were crossed.[146] To the astonishment of the French, they captured four European mercenaries in the Dahomean army: three Germans and one Belgian. They were taken to Colonel Dodds, where they were tried and executed for fighting against the French.[147] This helped to explain the accuracy of the projectiles which the Dahomean artillery fired on the French on the night of 30 September without any fanfare whatever.[148]

The march became more laborious, due to the lack of water and the continual battles with the Dahomeans, prominent among which were those at Koto, Kotopa, and Akpa. In addition, Dodds complained of the paucity of information available to him:

> Le manque complet de renseignements a été la plus grosse difficulté qu'ait recontrée la conduite des operations. Les prisonniers n'ont jamais pu ou voulu parler; les guides qu'on a pu employer ont quitté le Dahomey depuis de longues années et n'ont jamais dépassé Poguessa; en fin, les cartes n'existent pas ou sont fausses, et les renseignements recueillis à Porto Novo sont inexacts ou insuffisants.[149]

To these problems were added the constant desertion of the porters, whose services were of prime importance to the expeditionary corps, and the deterioration of the health of the corps with constant epidemics of dysentery.[150] The attainment of Kotopa was considered by Dodds a major breakthrough in the quest for Abomey, because Kotopa was on the threshold of Cana and Abomey.

> Cana, la ville sainte, n'est plus qu'à quelques kilometres devant nous, à quinze kilometres plus loin s'élève Abomey. Béhanzin veut nous empêcher d'arriver à Cana; notre entrée dans cette ville, notre présence dans le voisinage d'Abomey doivent à jamais compromettre son prestige et anéantir sa puissance.[151]

Béhanzin's Peace Overtures and the Occupation of Abomey, November 1892

The inexorable thrust of the advancing French expeditionary corps, the severe losses suffered by Dahomey in the unequal contest, and the fear of ever being reduced to Toffa's vassal impelled Béhanzin to make overtures of peace to Colonel Dodds. As Dodds correctly pointed out, Béhanzin did not want the invaders to enter Dahomey's holy city of Cana, which they would not only desecrate but destroy in the process of their juggernautic advance to Abomey.

On the morning of 23 October, the first signs of Béhanzin's desire to come to terms with the French were seen. Two Dahomeans with a white flag came to the French camp.[152] They were led to Colonel Dodds, who questioned them on their objectives. They had been sent to announce to the colonel that the king would send him a letter suing for peace. Dodds dismissed them and warned them not to return to the French camp without the king's letter. They returned the next day with Béhanzin's proposals, but Dodds demanded the evacuation of the lines of Koto by the Dahomeans before he could engage in any negotiations with them. On 25 October the reply of Béhanzin was brought to Dodds. The king refused to evacuate Koto and arrogantly added that he still had enough warriors and means to face the French and possibly exterminate them.[153] The first tentatives failed, only to be renewed shortly, as the reality of the situation dawned on Béhanzin.

The expedition pushed on and fought some rude battles with their opponents before they reached Cana. Neither the correspondence from Béhanzin on 27 October, in which he conceded what Dodds demanded and proposed to deal in person with the colonel in the sequestered village of Avlame on the left bank of the Koto, nor the gunfire of his troops could quench Dodd's thirst for Cana. He could not have forgotten that "immense treasures were accumulated in the palace of Abomey and the tombs of the kings of Dahomey at Cana."[154] Captain Audéoud, a recent visitor to Abomey, had no faith in Béhanzin's promises. Colonel Dodds must have shared the views of his officers about the necessity for final victory:

> Il serait pourtant temps d'en finir, l'état de malpropreté dans lequel nous vivons depuis quinze jours, la température accablante qui règne constamment, le manque d'eau persistant, tout cela contribue à affaiblir la santé de nos hommes dont un grand nombre sont atteints de dysenterie ou autres affections intestinales.[155]

The successful entry into Cana on 6 November resounded in Paris, where it was received with "unanimous satisfaction."[156] Consequently Dodds was promoted to the rank of général de brigade on 9 November 1892[157] while he was still at Cana, where Béhanzin renewed his efforts to arrive at a negotiated peace.

Béhanzin's emissaries to the French camp at Cana were led by the Cossugan, his prime minister and chief counselor. They said that the king was prepared to accept French protection. He offered to provision the French expeditionary corps and to conduct them back to the coast through the shorter route through Allada and Whydah. Dodds considered these offers carefully. The way proposed was dangerous because it passed through the marshes of Lama and the hills and forests of Allada. An ambush by the Dahomeans in this region would be very perilous. Dodds's shrewd military sense led him to reject the offer and outline his own terms.

These terms called for Béhanzin to cede all the seaboard and the left bank of the Wheme up to Agony and the Zagnanado district. The abolition of slavery and human sacrifice was to be guaranteed. Dodds further imposed the payment of an indemnity of 15 million francs and the surrender of eight cannons and 2,000 quick-firing rifles. On top of all these, Béhanzin was to deliver three of his notables as hostages to the French and was to permit the expeditionary corps to enter Abomey.[158] Colonel Dodds sent for Ballot for consultations, and he arrived at Cana on 11 November. The terms imposed by Dodds were reported to Béhanzin on 14 November. Dodds gave him twenty-four hours in which to fulfill these terms, failing which the war would be resumed.[159]

It was thought that Béhanzin was reinforcing the fortifications of Abomey and profiting from the truce caused by the negotiations to evacuate the wealth of his treasury and his ammunition. Common sense dictated an immediate march on Abomey before it was rendered impregnable or valueless. Consequently, when Béhanzin sent two cannons, one machine gun, 100 rifles, and 5,000 francs, and two hostages to the French camp on 15 November with promises to pay the remainder, Dodds called off the truce, resumed the march to Abomey, and hostilities were renewed.[160] "La colonne se mettra en marche a 3^h du soir pour aller bivouaquer au palais d'Abomey. On continuera à marcher en carré," he informed his men.[161]

Instead of following the beaten track through Goho, Dodds made a sudden and excellent tactical swerve to go through Djibe and Becon, in order to avoid any fortifications and roadblocks that might have been erected on the former route. From the outskirts of Djibe, the French column observed that Abomey was on fire at 1 P.M. on 16 November.[162] The fire continued through the night. On 17 November the expeditionary corps entered Abomey, whose smoldering ruins dismissed any illusions of loot. Béhanzin, who ordered and supervised the burning of Abomey, fled northward with his supporters and bodyguards.[163] General Dodds proclaimed the victory of the French troops over King Béhanzin and stated that France would thenceforth protect the interests of the people of Dahomey. He promised a new constitution to the country and warned that troublemakers would be "ruthlessly chastised." [164]

General Dodds was convinced that Dahomey would not be truly conquered until Béhanzin was captured. Since this was another formidable task, it was temporarily shelved in order to consolidate the newly won victory. Searches conducted in caches in Abomey yielded large quantities of liquor and munitions, but no treasures. On 25 November about 1,000 laborers were liberated from the royal farms at Affomayi. Goho was chosen and fortified for the four companies left under the charge of Lieutenant Colonel Gregoire before the expeditionary corps was dissolved on 1 December 1892. General Dodds arrived back in Porto Novo on 30 November. Shortly afterward he declared both the fall of Béhanzin and the establishment of a French protectorate over Dahomey.[165]

The occupation of the towns on the seaboard followed. Under Commandant Marquer, Whydah was occupied without incident. Next were Abomey-Calavy, Godome, and Savi.[166] The paramount chiefs of Allada surrendered on 14 December, while Béhanzin was still holding out in the neighborhood of the Mahi country.[167] The blockade of the coast was lifted on 29 December, and Colonel Lambinet was despatched to occupy Allada early in the new year.[168] This made it possible to supply the troops in the Abomey district from Whydah. In addition, a new telegraphic line was established between Whydah and Porto Novo, from where there was already a line up the Wheme to Dogba which served the expeditionary corps. General mopping-up operations were carried out as part of the measures of pacification. Topographical missions were sent out in all directions except the north of Dahomey, where all the Caboceres remained faithful to Béhanzin.[169] While still thinking of the reorganization of Dahomey and the capture of Béhanzin, Général Dodds left for Paris on leave, instructing Colonel Lambinet to resume operations against Béhanzin if pacific methods failed.[170]

Béhanzin Renews Peace Overtures

That the force of his arms had failed to stop the French became evident to Béhanzin by the end of 1892. After his flight from Abomey, he resorted to diplomacy once again for the salvation of his kingdom. When his attempts to reach an agreement with Colonel Lambinet came to nothing, he decided to carry his case to Paris in a last desperate effort to appease France and obtain the restoration of his kingdom to him.

First of all, Béhanzin made advances to Colonel Lambinet toward a reconciliation with France. He complained that Toffa was spreading lies about Dahomey and boasting that he had defeated Dahomey. Toffa should be quieted and reminded that Dahomey could have sacked Porto Novo, had she so desired, before the advent of the French. Even in his apparent humiliation, the fugitive monarch did not shed his rancor for the "despicable Toffa" of Porto Novo. It was on account of Toffa and the Nagos that he had not offered his submission. With the realization that the recent war was ordained by providence and that he had lost, he offered his submission and asked for peace. He would recognize the French protectorate over the littoral, but the plateau of Abomey should be left to him, and all French posts north of the marshes of Lama should be evacuated.[171]

Colonel Lambinet was instructed that it was imperative to negotiate not with messengers nor plenipotentiaries but with Béhanzin himself.[172] But Béhanzin, hidebound by taboos and distrustful of the French, was nowhere to be seen.[173] Convinced of the hopelessness of his position, Béhanzin decided to extend his diplomatic efforts to Paris itself and to enlist international sympathy for his case. Through a manifesto published in the British press, he appealed to the philanthropy and Christian humanity of the great civilized European nations for help against French bullying power. Mighty France was out to exterminate a people "qui ne lui a rien fait et dont le seul crime est d'être ignorant et faible." [174]

Later in the year Béhanzin despatched his envoys to Paris with full powers to reach an agreement with the French government. The delegation was made up of three of his ministers—Princes Chedinga, Ayenkuken, and Tossa. They were accompanied by Béhanzin's press agent Henry Dosso, "a veritable showman" by the name of P. Jackson, editor of the *Lagos Weekly Record*, and a Lagos banker called Neville. On their arrival at Liverpool on 3 November 1893 they gave interviews to the press on the objects of their mission. They did not arrive in Paris till 10 November because Prince Ayenkuken was overcome by the rigors of the climate and was confined in bed for some days in Liverpool.[175]

The envoys said they were empowered by Béhanzin to make a treaty with France on the basis of the convention of Cana of November 1892, which General Dodds accepted but later rejected. Béhanzin would recognize French rights over Porto Novo and Cotonou and would accept a French resident at Abomey and any other cities where it was judged necessary. Human sacrifices would be abolished, and razzias would cease thenceforth. However, Béhanzin would conserve his rights over Whydah and its hinterland between Porto Novo and the Wheme.[176]

The French government refused to deal with these envoys of Béhanzin. Why should they undertake to negotiate with the king's envoy when 7 million francs had been voted in July 1893 for the definitive occupation and administration of Dahomey? [177] Furthermore, General Dodds sailed from Marseille on the *Liban* on 10 August for Cotonou to supervise the annihilation of Béhanzin's power, taking with him 420 officers and men.[178] After one week of frustration in Paris, worsened by the excruciating European winter, the Dahomey mission sent a petition to President Carnot, who refused to receive them at the Elysée. They stated the object of their mission and blamed Toffa for all the misunderstanding between Dahomey and France. "It appears now that the French Government does not wish to receive us and to hear what King Béhanzin has to say. We cannot stand the climate any longer and so we must return to Dahomey."[179] The composition of the Dahomey mission to Paris shows that Béhanzin had the support and advice of some Englishmen who lived in Lagos. The presence of Englishmen in the delegation rendered it more suspect in the eyes of the French, who had been complaining of the anti-French attitudes of Germans and Englishmen on the Guinea coast and who would not want Britain to acquire Dahomey. Furthermore, the delegation to Paris was mistimed and inopportune. Its chances of success were reduced completely, because of its arrival in France after the departure of General Dodds for Porto Novo.[180] Dodds was not only the pacesetter but also the court of appeal for French policy in Dahomey.[181] Above all, the French chamber had decided to fight Dahomey to the finish, and the government could not be expected to rescind the parliamentary decision[182] because of the importunity of unaccredited diplomats from Dahomey. Béhanzin's overtures for peace with France thus petered out woefully.

The Third Campaign, 1893–94: Surrender of Béhanzin, January 1894

The arrival of General Dodds in Porto Novo on 30 August marked a new and final phase in the protracted power-struggle between Dahomey and France. Dodds returned to the west coast, armed with a mandate from France for the "complete disappearance of Béhanzin."[183] As usual he applied himself with tremendous energy and tact to the execution of this mandate till the surrender of the defeated king on 25 January 1894.

With the second Dahomey expedition coming to a successful end, the French chamber was asked to vote more money to defray the expenses incurred in this costly enterprise.[184] As the members of the dissolved expeditionary corps arrived back in France, a plethora of articles, memoirs, and books hit the French public and generated more interest in the Dahomey affair. No wonder then that the first interpellation[185] on Dahomey in 1893 was concerned with government policy and the welfare of the soldiers sent to fight in Dahomey. Montfort was concerned about the violations of the Brussels Act by the sale of arms to Béhanzin and the sanitary condition of the troops in Dahomey in view of the high death rate among them.[186] Le Herissé accused Delcassé of having made himself the executor of the expansion plan outlined by Eugene Etienne before his fall from office. He warned that France had enough of tropical territories and should treat Béhanzin as the English had done in Ethiopia with Theodoros. It was urged by Le Provost de Launay that the nonpolicy of military expeditions was not only disastrous but also a wanton waste of French taxpayers' money. He pointed out that they had been talking about Dahomey in the chamber for one year, and in this period the government had demonstrated that it had no policy but "qu'il se laissait mener au jour le jour, au gré des évenements." Would it not be better to adopt the British method of indirect rule and penetration by missionaries and traders? [187]

Early in April 1893 the French government was again pestered for a definition of its aims in Dahomey in order to avoid a regime of perpetual military expeditions, as in the Soudan.[188] Delcassé responded that he could not give an exact answer until he had consulted General Dodds. However, he had a notion of the type of colony he wanted to establish in Dahomey. It would have a simple administration and would stimulate private initiative so as to attract individual founders of trading comptoirs and agricultural colonies. Delcassé continued frankly:

> Mais je ne fais aucune difficulté de déclarer dès maintenant que la colonie que je rêve, que je voudrais pouvoir installer au Bénin, c'est une colonie où il y aurait le moins de troupes, le moins de fonctionnaires et le plus de cultivateurs et de commerçants possible.
> M. Jaures: C'est le paradis socialiste, cela!
> M. Le Baron Reille: C'est un beau rêve!
> Delcassé: Mais la conquête pour la conquête ne saurait constituer une programme.[189]

Delcassé made the provision that he did not say that the colonial domain of France was forever fixed. "Who could claim to fix the future? Who would try to assign a limit to the force of expansion of the French spirit?" he asked defiantly.[190]

The discussion of the Dahomey affair continued in the French press, especially in *Le Temps, Le Siècle, La Politique Coloniale,* and the *Journal des Débats*. But it came up again in the chamber in July 1893, when an extraordinary credit of 7 million francs was voted for the occupation and administration of Dahomey.[191] On the whole, the majority opinion in France was for a complete victory over Béhanzin. A negotiated settlement would lead to the recuperation of Béhanzin's power, in which could be seen the dangerous germs of future conflicts.[192]

Resumption of Operations for the Capture of Béhanzin

While General Dodds was in France, no serious military incidents or operations occurred. However, there were several minor clashes with pockets of resistant Dahomeans who were still loyal to Béhanzin in the Dekame region.[193] General Dodds had earlier prescribed the maintenance of 3,000 troops in Dahomey until Béhanzin was captured.[194] By utilizing these forces the southern districts of Dahomey were pacified, but the western and northern regions were not yet under French control.

General Dodds planned to secure all these areas before sending his forces to the Agony region. He did not want to risk any outbreaks of violence in the rear of the expeditionary force which would be sent out against Dahomey. The forces were divided into four groups, under Commandants Drude, Boutin, Chmitelin, and de Cauvigny. The fleet was reinforced with the *Mosca,* famous from the Mizon mission of 1890-93, the *Olinda,* and the *Marmet.* After planning the logistics and tactics of the operations, General Dodds left Porto Novo on 13 October to lead the expedition.[195]

All the groups traveled by their assigned routes and met at Zagnanado in order to make a concerted march on Acheribe, where Béhanzin was holding out. When it was learned that Béhanzin might make his way to Lagos, Colonel Dumas was despatched posthaste to seal off the possible escape route. This was a case of the informants distracting the French officers, because Béhanzin was not fleeing to Lagos territory, as subsequent events showed.

The march on Acheribe began on 25 October, and by 3 November a magazine was established at Begohounou and Commandant Chmitelin arrived at Abodugnanli. Then once again the emissaries of Béhanzin appeared at the French camp to negotiate with Dodds.[196] They repeated their offers for peace like a broken record, but General Dodds did not take them seriously and would not order a halt in the operations. How could he engage in peace negotiations with a defeated king whom he had dethroned? Not even the surrender of 476 rifles, four cannons, and two hostages would change the determined mind of the general.[197] On the morning of 9 November thirty-two notables came to Dodds to make their submission, and on this occasion he promised safe conduct to Béhanzin if he surrendered. But the elusive Béhanzin did not believe this promise. By the time Colonel Dumas arrived at Acheribe the next morning, Béhanzin had left for Bedavo with his bodyguard. The pursuit of Béhanzin proved to be a wild goose chase by the French troops. "Il échappe toujours à nos poursuites . . . Béhanzin reste introuvable." [198] Not even the tactical reorganization of the forces by Dodds could end the frustration of an endless hunt for Béhanzin. Rumors continued to circulate about the magical powers and occult strength of the king, who in his flight carried with him his royal amulets and the special amulet of Dahomey, "un bétyle mysterieux d'une éfficacité incalculable." [199] Supernatural powers or not, with the cooperation of the local population, Béhanzin eluded his French chasers like a mirage.

Reorganization of Dahomey by General Dodds

After three months of a fruitless and exhausting search for Béhanzin, General Dodds turned to the positive engagement of the reorganization of Dahomey. In this task he was guided by the views of the French government, those expressed in the chamber on Dahomey, and the contemporary theories on colonial sociology.

Shortly after his successful entry into Abomey, Dodds was instructed by the French government to pursue the clearly defined objective of early installation of indigenous authorities and sending the French troops back to the coast.[200] Dodds reported that the absence of chiefs, most of whom had not surrendered, made it impossible for him to decide whether the kingdom should be dismembered or handed over to one ruler. This question needed careful consideration, he concluded.[201] During the debate on Dahomey in the Chamber, de Launay urged the imitation of the British example of indirect rule. Contemporary theories of colonial sociology based on association[202] rather than assimilation were forcefully expounded, especially by Gustave Le Bon in *Les Lois psychologiques de l'Evolution des peuples* (1891).[203] Earlier Edmond About had pleaded for the making of "these fine Africans" into genuine allies of France. This idea was further developed by A. Burdeau, who postulated that African culture could be transformed by association and education rather than by the imposition of the French way of life by assimilation.[204]

With this background and with most Dahomean chiefs having surrendered, General Dodds proceeded with the territorial and political reorganization of the country.[205] He detached the Mahis, the Dessas, and the Nago of the upper Wheme from Abomey. Above all, he created two independent kingdoms—Allada and Abomey—from the former Dahomey. The future kings of these two kingdoms (or, really, protectorates) would be chosen by the chiefs of each. Their choice was subject to the approbation of the French government.[206]

After the declaration of the new political order, General Dodds ordered the local population to shave their overgrown hair, which had been kept as a sign of mourning for Glégléá. Thus he proved to them that Béhanzin would not return to celebrate the funeral of his father, that his defeat was final.[207] The search for a new king of Abomey began after Dodds had given the blueprint for the political reorganization of Dahomey. Naturally, the chiefs and princes attached more importance to the Abomey kingdom. Therefore, regular meetings of the members of the royal family were held at Abomey, both at the stimulation of General Dodds and spontaneously. Béhanzin was, however, well informed about the trend of events.

In the course of the search for a new king for Abomey, three candidates emerged, all of the royal family of that city. These were Princes Ayidama,[208] Hounhintogban, and Gouchili. At the time Gouchili was in hiding with Béhanzin because he was the Gaou of the Dahomean army and would not forsake his beleaguered brother, the deposed king.[209]

The chiefs would not, however, proceed with such a sacred task as the election of a new king without recourse to the gods. They consulted the oracle, and Hounhintogban and Gouchili were named for the throne. The final choice was, however, made by Béhanzin, who preferred Gouchili as his successor. He sent Gouchili to meet General Dodds and advised him to promise to reveal Béhanzin's hiding place if he was approved as the new king of Abomey.[210] Béhanzin calculated that this quid pro quo would be an irresistible temptation for the general.

The first interview between General Dodds and Prince Gouchili was held in a cordial atmosphere and was marked by warmth and grandeur.[211] The choice of Gouchili was accepted by General Dodds, who proclaimed him king of Abomey on 15 January 1894 in the square of the palace of Simbodji at Abomey.[212] The election and recognition of a king for Allada was completed on 4 February 1894, when Prince Ganhou Hougnon was proclaimed king. He was a representative of the royal family of Ardres and a direct descendant of Meji, the last king of Allada. His chosen name as king was Gi-gla-don-Gbe-nou-maou, a veritable tongue twister.[213]

It is significant to note that Prince Gouchili, who became known as Agoli-Agbo after his coronation, shared Béhanzin's apprehension that Toffa might be offered the throne of Abomey. The allegorical statement he uttered soon after his coronation showed that he was pleased that France did not favor Toffa with such an offer.[214] Therefore Toffa's claim that he defeated Béhanzin was hollow. Satisfied that his inveterate enemy Toffa was never to inherit his throne, deprived of almost all his staunch followers, and tired of continuing the unpleasant life of a hunted fugitive king, Béhanzin decided to give himself up to the French. It is said that he had a farewell dinner with his followers, to whom he delivered a reassuring parting speech on the Adanzun hillock in the vicinity of Abomey.[215] On the morning of 25 January 1894 he surrendered to Dodds. It was arranged at once to deport him to Senegal with his family and to deport his ministers to Gabon.[216] A few days later the treaty which placed Abomey under French protection was solemnly read to a large crowd at the Simbodji palace of Abomey to demonstrate the establishment of a new order.[217] A similar treaty was concluded with Allada on 4 February 1894, sealing the pacification of Dahomey.

King Agoli-Agbo began to lead the life of a monarch in the only way he knew, the grand style of his father, who has been described by P. Mimande as "le roi soleil d'Afrique Noire." But he inherited an almost empty treasury, a ravaged and depopulated kingdom, and all the problems of postwar reconstruction. His request to Porto Novo for tax-farming privileges was refused, and most of the Abomey princes migrated to the richer Allada protectorate.[218] "Very soon it became clear that Agoli-Agbo was unable to find ways of keeping up the appearance of royalty, while dispensing with the authoritarian methods that had held the kingdom together in the past." Slave dealing was forbidden, and the French would not allow the new king to levy taxes.[219] However, his officials collected tolls in the Agony and Sagon districts, because of lack of control by the French in these areas. Agoli-Agbo held on to the Abomey throne precariously till he was deported to the French Congo in February 1900.[220]

Results of the Conquest and Occupation of Dahomey

In the spring of 1894 both General Dodds and Victor Ballot went back to France on leave after the hard campaign.[221] In the interim their positions were filled by Colonel Dumas, one of the key officers of the last campaign. The dearth of civil administrators[222] and the difficulty of controlling the outlying northeastern districts made Colonel Dumas resort to harsh military rule and the severe application of the *indigénat*. Consequently, by the time Victor Ballot returned to Porto Novo in August 1894, several chiefs and elders had been summarily tried and thrown into prison, some for three-year terms.[223]

On the whole, the three expeditions in Dahomey (1890–94) surpassed all the estimates of the experts about the expenses involved, both financial and otherwise. In January 1893, Chautemps, the rapporteur of the budget commission, gave the total expenses on Dahomey as 10,137,000 francs.[224] To the expansionists this was a moderate amount. They were quick to point out that it was not half the 22.5 million francs[225] their English rivals spent on the Ashanti War (1873-74). But the rejoicing was too soon, for the fighting was not yet over. By the time the conquest of Dahomey was achieved in 1894, an additional 11,634,986 francs had been spent, to bring the total military expenditure to almost 22 million francs. The local budget for Dahomey from 1890-93 amounted to 4,084,965 francs, bringing the total recorded expenses to almost 27 million francs.[226] The French taxpayer, then, paid very highly for the acquisition of Dahomey, financially as well as in terms of the hundreds of lives that were lost in the process[227] (see tables 4 and 5).

TABLE 4

CREDITS VOTED FOR THE DAHOMEY WARS, 1890-94

1890 (January)-1893	10,137,000 francs
1893 (28 April and 6 July)	7,900,000 francs
1894	3,734,976 francs
Total	21,771,976 francs

SOURCE: Comptes Définitif des Dépenses: Service Colonial (Ministère de la Marine et des Colonies), appropriate years. These figures correspond with those given in the *Journal Officiel* for the various votes but add the extraordinary votes by decree made subsequent to the parliamentary votes.

TABLE 5

LOCAL WAR BUDGETS OF DAHOMEY, 1890-94

1890	125,864 francs
1891	1,459,965 francs
1892	1,466,436 francs
1893	1,032,700 francs
1894	1,600,000 francs
Total	5,684,965 francs

SOURCE: SOM-AN Dahomey IX, 1, a, b, c, d, e (budgets locaux du Dahomey).

By the conquest of Dahomey, France entrenched herself on the Slave Coast very securely. With such a vast possession behind Porto Novo, there was no more desire to exchange it for the Gambia. This newly gained security affected the territorial negotiations in which Hanotaux and Phipps were engaged on behalf of France and Britain. Having conquered Dahomey, France was unwilling to let its hinterland slip out of her hands.

The disappearance of the strong Fon dynasty of Abomey then opened the road to the Niger hinterland. The curtain was raised, and the energetic act of exploring and acquiring territories in the Niger basin commenced. The "Chad Plan," based on Eugene Etienne's "la perpendiculaire,"[228] acquired new dimensions. Even before the gunsmoke cleared plans were ready to launch expeditions into the Dahomey hinterland through Borgu, Sougou, and Tchantzo to Say on the Niger, in order to shut off the English and the Germans from the rich territory behind the 9° latitude. Binger, whose pacific qualities were greatly admired, was selected to lead the exploration mission,[229] but it was Victor Ballot who, as governor of Dahomey, presided over the destiny of the Dahomey-Niger hinterland till 1898. The conquest of Dahomey, then, ushered in the period of the most intense imperial rivalry among the European powers in the Niger basin, thus vindicating the predictions of D. Kaltbrunner: "Sans être prophète, on peut donc prévoir un conflit, un avenir gros d'orages. En un mot, en Afrique, *ceci mangera cela*."[230]

In addition to the political, the conquest of Dahomey had scientific, military, social, and economic results.[231] It widened the knowledge of geography. Of special importance was the discovery that the Zou was a tributary of the River Wheme. Tropical medicine attracted more attention,[232] and the experiences of the wars enriched military science.[233] On the side of the Africans, it led to closer contact with French culture,[234] economic development, and the chain of political developments, *mutatis mutandis,* which have resulted in the independent republic of Dahomey of today.

In conclusion, the Dahomey wars proved beyond doubt that the kingdom of Dahomey was the strongest state in west Africa in the late nineteenth century. The duration of the wars and the manner in which the battles were fought show how advanced the Dahomean army was in military science. The constitutional structure of Dahomey provided for a strong central administration by the king's court. Free from the handicaps of strong provincial chiefs, such as was the case in Ashanti and Mossi, the Dahomey monarchy developed a formidable military machine armed with Europe's best conventional weapons. The geographical advantage of a long coastline and well-developed ports at Whydah and Cotonou gave Dahomey free access to the sea and, therefore, to European commerce. The Tokolors, the Sofas, and the Ashantis did not have this advantage. The well-established tax system of Dahomey and its natural resources provided a sound economic base which enabled the kings to develop their power and influence.

The king of a well-established kingdom like Dahomey could not have fitted into the French scheme of things, as Toffa did. Béhanzin had clear ideas of his role as a king. These conflicted with the aims of French imperialism; indeed, the two were irreconcilable. What the French offered Béhanzin he already had. His conviction that the establishment of French authority in his dominion was inimical to his existence as king of Dahomey led him to resist France as long as he could and until his defeat. Béhanzin was deported to Martinique through Algeria. He was allowed to take many members of his family with him, including his favorite wives and sons. He died in exile at Blida on 10 December 1906, despite several sustained efforts to secure his repatriation to Dahomey. His remains were returned to Dahomey in April 1928 and reburied at Djime, which was predominantly inhabited by his descendants.

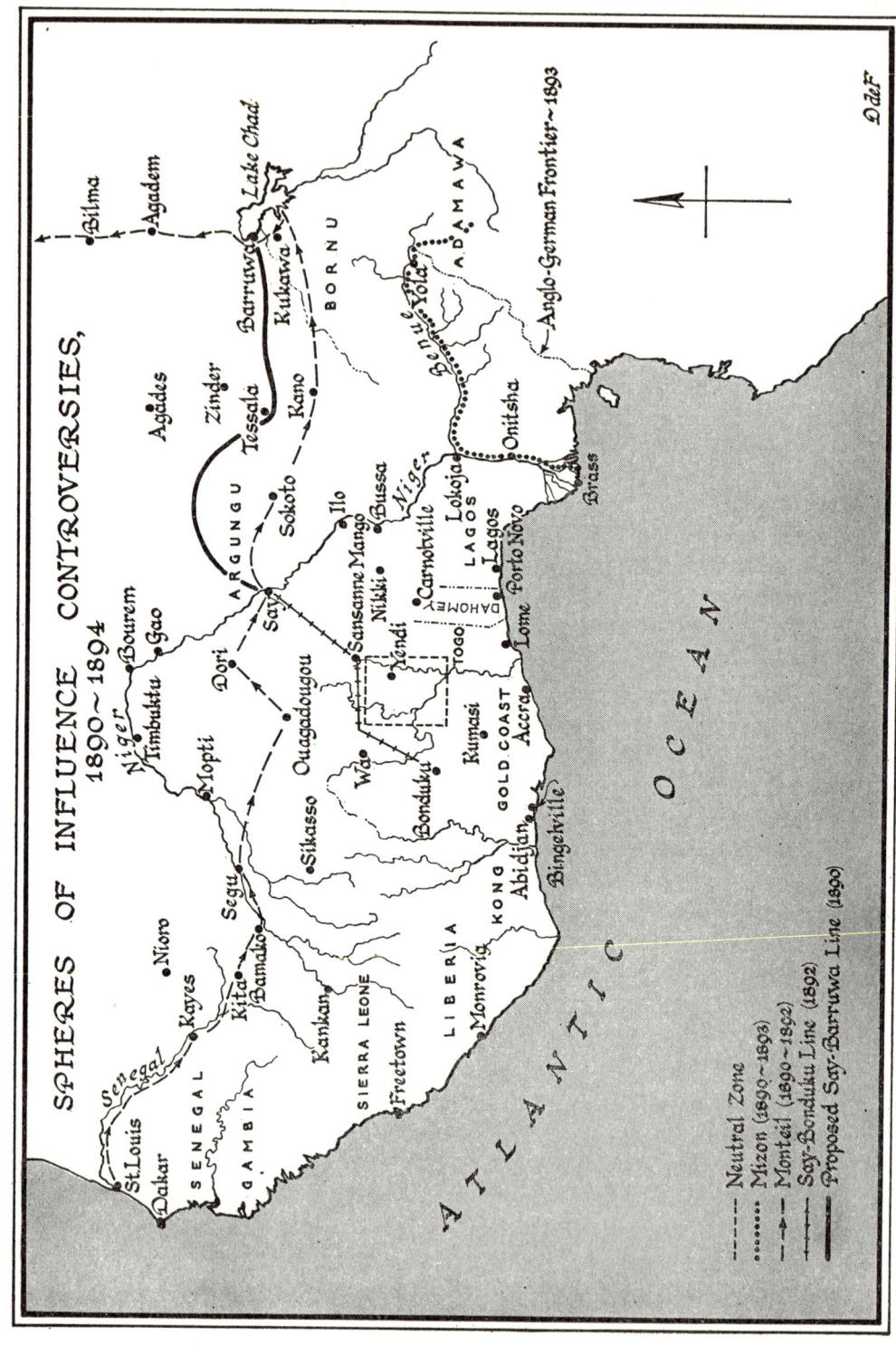

5

European Expeditions into the Hinterland, 1890–1894

The half decade following the signing of the General Act of the Brussels Conference in July 1890 was marked by a series of European exploration missions into the Dahomey-Niger hinterland as well as into central and eastern Africa.[1] In this period the diplomatic tussle which occurred between Britain and Portugal during the Brussels Conference was transposed into practical action in the Zambesi basin.[2] In the vast peneplain of the Niger bend the representatives of Britain, France, and Germany vied for the acquisition of choice and rich territory. Cecil Rhodes had insisted on the acquisition and exploitation by Britain of the tracts of the savage world, whose acquisition and control by other nations would constrict Britain's commerce by hostile tariffs.[3] Fired by identical zeal for the welfare of their fatherland, Frenchmen, Englishmen, and Germans alike tramped and trudged through the tropical forests and savannah of the Niger basin between 1890 and 1895 to extend the influence and commercial interests of their respective countries.[4]

The climax of these expeditions came toward the end of 1894, when various international missions staged a "steeple chase" into Borgu in competition for the acquisition and control of Nikki, its capital. The conquest of Dahomey removed the most serious indigenous obstacle on the road to the Niger hinterland from the Slave Coast. The General Act of the Brussels Conference enjoined the occupation of African territories as a means of eradicating the slave trade and slavery. Since the Anglo-French agreement of 10 August 1889 did not cover the riverine regions of the Middle Niger, these territories were open to competition and became the cockpit of European rivalry after 1890.

Captain L. G. Binger's expedition of 1887–89 opened up areas hitherto unknown. Binger proved that the Kong mountain range, believed to be a barrier to the interior, did not exist as such. Consequently, he demonstrated the possibility of easy access to the Niger bend from the Atlantic coast, as well as of connecting the Guinea coast with the Sudan. The missions of Treich-Laplène reinforced the findings of Binger.[5] Moreover, Dr. Crozat succeeded in visiting Mossi in 1890, adding to the knowledge of the interior of west Africa which was then ever growing.[6] For the Germans, there was the praiseworthy journey of P. von François through Salaga to Mossi, which antedated both those of Binger and Crozat.[7] The empirical data supplied by these explorers enabled the theorists of French expansion in west Africa to formulate new theories and to draw up a grand plan for assuring French domination of the west African hinterland.

Theoretical Bases of French Expeditions

France was second only to Britain as an imperial power. Her politicians and merchants knew from experience the joys and the sorrows of colonization. French intellectuals examined with dedication the question of imperialism and French colonial policy.[8] What Professor A. P. Thornton calls the doctrine of power, profit, and civilization influenced French attitudes to and theories of colonization generally, but in specific cases one of these doctrines usually overshadowed the others. The French experience in Senegal had shown the limitations and possibilities of a tropical colony in west Africa. More colonies were acquired along the coast. The presence of Britain in the area was considered a threat to the French colonies of the littoral. This threat had to be removed, for if Britain gained control of the rich hinterland behind these colonies, their trade would be diverted to British coastal possessions to the detriment of those belonging to France.[9] Therefore, it was imperative to safeguard the hinterland and bring it under French control as quickly as was practicable. Various plans were proposed for this purpose. As Eugene Etienne, the prime mover of French expansion in west Africa, stated, all the representatives of French labor, producers and exporters, had understood that

> la France, qui a marché jadis à la tête des nations colonisatrices, ne pouvait, sous peine de compromettre sans remède sa situation économique, laisser le champ libre aux ambitions coloniales de tous les gouvernements européens, et rester neutre dans ce grand concours des peuples vers de nouveaux débouchés commerciaux et industriels.[10]

In addition to the economic factors enumerated by Etienne, French administrators on the west coast of Africa realized the necessity for prompt action in the spheres still open to political action in the hinterland. Both Colonna de Lecca and A. d'Albeca put forth plans for the penetration of the hinterland at Dahomey.[11] General Faidherbe also formulated a plan for French expansion in the Upper and Middle Niger. Edouard Viard's journey to Abeokuta in 1888 was an application of de Lecca's theory of striking toward the Niger through Egba territory as well as of Faidherbe's contention that the Lower Niger was not a British reserve.[12]

The French ambassador in London, Waddington, had clear ideas about the exploitation of the hinterland of west Africa. After the Anglo-French declaration of 5 August 1890, Waddington unfolded his hinterland plan. What was necessary, he maintained, was to persuade Frenchmen to go out and exploit the new regions, where, up to that time, they had been unenthusiastic about entering. It would be necessary to work for the formation of great colonization companies on the lines of the British Royal Niger Company, the South African Company, and so on. These extensions on the map, he continued, should be made actual markets for French industrial products, to feed French maritime commerce. With considerable realism born out of experience, Waddington concluded: "La simple satisfaction de planter le drapeau français sur les cases d'une centaine de roitelets nègres n'est pas suffisante." [13]

To Etienne's practical mind, it was important to gain full control of the territories in question before embarking on their exploitation. The field was no longer as open and uncompetitive as it was in the 1880s, when Britain's chartered companies were launched into Africa. In 1887, when he first came to the sous-secretariat d'état des colonies, Etienne conceived a dual plan for colonial action.[14] First, it was essential to harness all the forces in France, commercial or otherwise, which would be of service to France in her colonies. Second, these forces were to be unleashed in the colonies of exploitation as well as those of settlement. There was much to be hoped for as far as French colonies were concerned, and Etienne pointed out that the exploitation of those lands "si l'on pouvait grouper les bonnes volontés qui s'ignorent, et réunir en faisceau les forces aujourd'hui disséminées et annihilées par leur propre dispersion."

The French possessions in southeast Asia as well as west Africa were classified by Etienne as colonies of exploitation.[15] These were vast fields of exploitation open to the action of French merchants and industrialists who in time would not fail to discover in these parts considerable and important markets for French products, since there were more than twenty million inhabitants in these colonies. Etienne concluded on an optimistic note:

> Notre prépondérance commerciale ne tardera pas à s'établir dans l'Indo Chine et dans l'Afrique occidentale, si nos commerçants savent montrer

autant d'énergie et de perseverance que nos soldats ont mis de vigueur à leur préparer les voies.[16]

The theory for the occupation of the hinterland of west Africa, especially of the Niger bend and the Lake Chad basin, was crystallized by Etienne and his disciples into what came to be known as the "Chad Plan." Under the energetic and zealous direction of Etienne in the Colonial Department, with the unreserved cooperation of Hanotaux at the Quai d'Orsay,[17] a plan of African colonization emerged. The two features of this plan were the junction of Algeria and Tunisia in north Africa with the Congo and the joining of the west African possessions with those on the banks of Lake Chad. Etienne first enunciated this doctrine of African expansion in the chamber on 10 May 1890, at a very inauspicious moment, as he later pointed out—"à l'occasion de nos misérables difficultés premières avec Béhanzin."[18] His hearers were not only astonished by his visionary *perpendiculaire* but also startled by such a radical proposal as that of making a line drawn from eastern Tunisia through Lake Chad to the Congo the frontier of French West Africa.[19]

The ardor which characterized the colonial activities of Britain, Germany, Italy, and Portugal in 1889 and 1890 was the main factor which led Etienne to state this grand plan so that France would not be outdistanced and driven back by her rivals. The Anglo-German arrangement of 1 July 1890, which was quickly followed by the Franco-British declaration of 5 August 1890, aroused much protest in France and created an atmosphere favorable to Etienne's views. According to Professor H. Brunschwig, the Comité de l'Afrique Française and the "groupe colonial" of the chamber were formed in reaction to the Anglo-French treaty of 5 August 1890.[20] It could, however, be argued that there already existed in the chamber before August 1890 a distinguishable colonial group whose views found expression in *Le Siècle* and who rallied around François Deloncle and Eugene Etienne in debates on colonial affairs. Etienne had been working on the unification of all forces favorable to French colonial expansion since 1887. When he again became Sous-Secrétaire des Colonies in 1889, he resolved to concentrate his energies first on a task which circumstances had made particularly urgent. This was the epoch of great partitions of territories in Africa as well as in Asia and in Oceania, he said, and it was necessary for France to stake her claims. In May 1890, the Conseil Superieur des Colonies was reorganized by Etienne into a more efficient advisory body.[21] The members of the second section (colonies d'Afrique) were men dedicated to French expansion and commercial interests in Africa and constituted, in fact if not in name, a committee for French Africa (see table 6).

Thus, it could be said that what occurred in 1890 was the formalization of a hitherto inchoate group of expansionists and businessmen whose main

TABLE 6

Conseil Supérieur des Colonies: 2e Section Colonies d'Afrique

Names of Members	Remarks
Rouvier	president (2e Section Colonies d'Afrique); former minister of commerce and colonies; Minister of Finances
Admiral Wallon	député for Senegal; Chamber of Commerce of Rouen
François Deloncle	député
Gen. Borgnis-Desbordes	former commandant superior of Upper Senegal
Seignac-Lesseps	former governor of Senegal
Lieut. Colonel Dorat	former resident at Porto Novo
Cyprien Fabre	president, Chamber of Commerce of Marseille; merchant in Dahomey
Theodore Mante	proprietor of Mante Borelli de Régis of Dahomey
Bohn	director of Compagnie Française d'Afrique Occidentale
Verdier	merchant at Grand Bassam and Assinie; ship owner
Medard Beraud	former merchant at Porto Novo and the Congo
Jobet	former trader in Gabon
Buhan	trader in Senegal
Pilastre	delegate of Gabon at the permanent exposition of colonies in Paris
Etienne Trefeu	secretary general of the Société de la Mer Intérieur Africaine
Emile Maurel	merchant (Maison Maurel et Prom of Bordeaux)
Henri Lavertujon	député
Paul Deschanel	député
Thomson	député

Source: SOM-AN C.S.C., Gen. 31, *Organisation et Composition du Conseil Supérieur des Colonies* (Paris, 1890), pp. 20–21; *Almanach National pour 1890: Annuaire Officiel de la République Française* (192e Année) (Paris, 1890), pp. 355–57. Etienne joined this section in 1892 when he fell from office. Hippolyte Percher (Harry Alis) joined this section in 1893.

interests lay in Africa and who had been active in African colonization for a long time. Furthermore, the stated aims of the Comité d'Afrique Française were not new but merely a repetition of Etienne's doctrine of the perpendicular. They were to send diverse missions into the center of Africa. "We are witnessing a unique spectacle in history . . . the actual partition of a scarcely known continent by certain civilized nations of Europe," they declared. They wished to be not idle onlookers but active participants in this unique episode in history. They would give a permanent character to their African action by linking the Congo, the Chad, Sudan-Senegal, and French North Africa for the facilitation of commercial developments in these possessions.[22]

The aims of the Comité were clarified and amplified by its forceful publicist, Hippolyte Percher, whose assumed name was Harry Alis. The execution of the Chad Plan would result in the domination of the central and western Sudan by France. It was hoped to achieve this slowly from the north and more rapidly from the west and south. From the west, Monteil and Menard would advance toward the Chad by separate routes, supported by the columns which were operating in the Upper Niger. From the southwest, Mizon was to use the Benue to reach the Chad basin, while Brazza from the south, as well as Jean Dybowski, would push toward the Upper Ubangi with the Chad as their ultimate destination.[23] Such was the Chad Plan. Before examining how it was unfolded in practice, let us look at the making of the Say-Barruwa Line of 1890, which catalyzed the Chad Plan to produce the scramble for the Niger hinterland in the 1890s.

The Anglo-French Declaration of 5 August 1890

The "absence of mind" theory[24] of Sir John Seeley was illustrated by the action of the Foreign Office in concluding the Helgoland treaty with Germany in July 1890. In negotiating this treaty, Salisbury and his officials lost sight of the Anglo-French arrangement of 10 March 1862 concerning the independence of the sultan of Zanzibar.[25] By assuming protection of Zanzibar and Pemba, Britain committed a diplomatic faux pas by unilaterally breaking the bilateral convention concerning Zanzibar's independence. Britain thus left herself open to justifiable claims for compensation from the French government.

The news of the Anglo-German treaty caused much displeasure in France and provoked discourteous attacks in the chamber, of which Ribot as well as Britain were the victims.[26] Salisbury was blamed for furnishing the occasion for these attacks, because he did not consult France regarding the protectorate he wished to establish in Zanzibar.

The French government was quick in calling Salisbury's attention to the blunder of his administration over Zanzibar. Diplomatic pressures exerted by Waddington on the Foreign Office resulted in an undertaking by Salisbury "to do nothing in Zanzibar without the consent of France." This promise was necessary, said Ribot, because it was a prerequisite for any discussions on the compensations to be accorded to France by Britain.[27] Not even this apologetic gesture by Salisbury could calm the French chamber, who now extended their ill humor to the General Act of the Brussels Conference, contending that the "droit de visite" was among those measures by which Britain wished to whittle down French sovereignty.[28]

The publication of the Anglo-German treaty of 1 July 1890 accentuated anti-British sentiment in the French press. François Deloncle published a sensational tirade against British expansion, underscoring the point that British control of the Chad basin would mean the end of the French proposal for a trans-Sahara railway. *La République Française* declared that no more time should be lost before the acquisition of the hinterland of west Africa from the Niger bend to Lake Chad, which would ensure the desired junction of Algeria, Senegal, and the Niger.[29] There were also press attacks against the French ambassadors in London and in Berlin. They were blamed for not being vigilant and for failing to protect French interests in Africa.[30] Why pay ambassadors who allow us to be cheated by other powers? they asked indignantly. Ribot also came in for strong criticism for the evasive tactics he adopted in the chamber on questions dealing with colonial affairs in which foreign governments were involved.[31]

Behind the scenes, however, Ribot began to demand compensation from Britain because of the Anglo-German treaty. "Britain owes us compensation over Zanzibar either in Madagascar or in Tunisia," he instructed Waddington.[32] The Radicals exploited the Zanzibar affair and raised a public clamor for compensation. Ribot was of the opinion that the anti-government campaign (which was extended to Waddington and Herbette) would not last long if concessions were obtained in Tunisia. In order to be effective, this should be prompt, he stated.[33] Waddington had other ideas about the compensation to be demanded from Britain. Advantages were to be sought in Newfoundland and in Tunisia.[34] But for Ribot, a politician who wished to consolidate his position in the chamber, a compensation in Tunisia was preferable. It would be more effective in dampening the fervor of the radical opposition in the chamber than a compensation over Newfoundland. What France wanted in Tunisia was not considerable and did not conflict with British interests. After all, British trade in Tunisia was about 8 million piasters out of a total Tunisian trade of 52 million piasters. Therefore, Ribot concluded, England should have no difficulty in granting the French request that the treaty of 1875, which had no expiration date but which provided for renewals, should be replaced by a new convention before 31 December 1896.[35]

Salisbury was confronted with the demands of France over Tunisia. He was not disposed to break another treaty in order to satisfy France. "Salisbury's refusal to grant us compensation in Tunisia is deplorable," grumbled Ribot, adding that *Le Temps* had done much harm by the type of publicity it gave the affair.[36] Ribot was consoled by D'Estournelles de Constant, who arrived at the French Embassy in London toward the end of June: "Waddington is best suited to deal with the English. Give him much latitude because he can obtain whatever is obtainable from the English." [37]

Resourceful as ever, Waddington shifted the grounds of compensation to France from Tunisia to Madagascar and the Sudan. On 13 July 1890 he sounded Ribot on the extension of the zone of French influence from the Sudan to Lake Chad. The French foreign minister was responsive to this suggestion but wanted to know the details and still insisted on the urgency of the question of compensations.[38] Waddington presented his proposed compensations to Salisbury. These included the recognition of a French protectorate over Madagascar and the extension of the zone of French influence in the Sudan up to the Niger and to Lake Chad.[39] Tunisia had been dropped from the list. The southern zone of French influence was to be limited by a line from Say on the Niger to Lake Chad's northwestern coast.

Salisbury's ignorance of the region in question led him to consult with the Royal Niger Company authorities. Sir George Goldie observed that a line drawn from Say to Lake Chad would bisect the kingdom of Sokoto, which was presumably under the Niger Company's sphere of influence. Consequently, Goldie proposed a line from Barrum or Gogo, three hundred miles up from Say, to Lake Chad, since such an alternative line would leave all of Sokoto intact under British control.[40] Salisbury believed that "in this matter the interests of Britain are the interests of the Royal Niger Company." [41] Furthermore, Lytton expressed great optimism about the negotiations, despite the unyielding British stand on Tunisia.

> The French will give way about Tunis and content themselves with the concessions made to their wishes about Madagascar and West Africa. Ribot could make a very good show with these results, especially if, in addition to them he practically carries his point about the Egyptian economies.[42]

When Salisbury and Waddington renewed their discussion, the former proposed a Barrum-Chad line instead of one from Say to the Chad. Waddington protested that this would leave France nothing but desert. Eventually, it was agreed to adopt Say as the western departure point for the line to the Chad, provided that the line would be curved northward to leave Sokoto to the Royal Niger Company.[43] However, Salisbury insisted that the territory south of Tunis, which belonged to the Sultan of Turkey, would be excluded from the French sphere.[44] To this the French government raised two objections. It limited the area for eventual French expansion "to the narrow hinterland of Algeria," and by the exclusion of Tunisia it ruled out "des régions au nom desquelles nous avons le droit de traiter," as Ribot asserted.[45] Salisbury sympathized with Ribot's views and was ready to alter the wordings to a certain extent. However, he observed that the French were introducing "a new and startling development of the doctrine of Hinterland," adding that the territory which the French were assuming was not in contact with Tunis at all. "I do not think that the virtue, whatever it is, which converts hinterland into dominion can be allowed to jump over intermediate territory," he continued. He proposed to adopt instead the words "on the south of the Mediterranean possessions of France in Africa," and he pointed out: "I have not noticed the question whether a protectorate can generate Hinterland: but that function would be clearly raised by your language, while it is evaded by mine."[46] It is noteworthy that the question which Salisbury is evading here with satisfaction was to crop up again and again and would be the main bone of contention between Britain and France a few years later, when the Say-Barruwa Line came in for serious criticism by French expansionists.

A few more amendments were made in the draft declaration. For example, Salisbury agreed "to omit all reference to Algeria" in the text, and Waddington perfected the final draft.[47] The operative section of the article on the Say-Barruwa Line was amended by Salisbury himself by the addition of the words "to be determined by the Commission."[48] A boundary commission was to be set up for tracing the line in detail on the spot. The final draft of declaration was officially signed and exchanged on 5 August 1890.[49]

By the first part of this declaration, British authority over Zanzibar and Pemba was recognized by France, and French authority over Madagascar was recognized by Britain. The second part dealt with the recognition of "the sphere of influence of France to the south of her Mediterranean possessions up to a line from Say on the Niger to Barruwa on Lake Chad, drawn in such a manner as to comprise in the sphere of action of the Niger Company all that fairly belongs to the Kingdom of Sokoto, the line to be determined by Commissioners to be appointed." Each power was to appoint two commissioners, who would meet in Paris to settle the details of this line. The commissioners would also be entrusted with the task of determining the respective spheres of influence of the two countries in the region extending to the west and south of the Middle and Upper Niger. Even if these commissioners failed to agree on the details of the line in question, the agreement would remain binding on both powers.[50] One can see in these provisions the creation of the Niger Commission, which only succeeded in delimiting the Niger territories and tracing a Say-Barruwa line[51] acceptable to both powers in June 1898. The use of the loose term *fairly* (*équitablement* in the French version) with reference to the kingdom of Sokoto shows that neither Waddington nor Salisbury wished to use such a strict term as *legally* or *de facto*. The Royal Niger Company would have been hard put to prove the exact extent of the kingdom of Sokoto, since it had not even then entered into solid friendly relations with the sultan of Sokoto.[52]

The French government was pleased with the declaration of 5 August, especially with the speed at which it was concluded. Judging from the press, opinion in France was satisfied about it, "except for the systematic detractors of the Republic and some Radicals like Lockroy and Brisson who would not renounce their opposition."[53] Waddington was sent a laudatory telegram for carrying off almost all his points in the negotiations with Salisbury.[54] Hardly had the French rejoicing begun when it was dampened by Lord Salisbury. In response to accusations by British imperialists that he had signed away too much territory, he declared during his Mansion House speech on 6 August, and later repeated in the House of Lords, that he had only conceded "light land" to the French.[55] Waddington was disconcerted by this statement, which he claimed caused considerable surprise in Paris and had the effect of diminishing very much the good feeling created by the conclusion of the arrangement. He continued: "No doubt the Sahara is not a garden, and contains, as you say, much "light land" but your public comment of the fact was perhaps, you will allow me to say, hardly necessary. You might well have left us to find it out."[56]

Indeed, the French were prepared to find it out. Etienne, who was satisfied with the declaration of 5 August 1890, as he later admitted in the chamber,[57] lost no time in organizing exploration missions to the Niger-Chad region to investigate the Say-Barruwa Line, discover the extent of the kingdom of Sokoto, and lay the foundations of the French empire in these regions.

French Expeditions into the Hinterland

In the wake of the Anglo-French declaration of August 1890 came a series of French exploration missions into the hinterland of the Niger-Chad basin. These were sponsored partly by the French government and partly by private effort. But they were all integral parts of the well-conceived Chad Plan. From the Upper Niger, Lieutenant Monteil was to march through Say to Sokoto and thence to the Chad, from where he would follow the perpendiculaire to Tripoli. Another arm of the western section of the plan was Menard's journey northward from the Ivory Coast toward the Niger bend. This was later expanded by the assignment given to Captain Marchand to link Kenedugu with the Kong region. Of course, the Dahomey affair was still smoldering, and this put in abeyance temporarily the plan to achieve the Niger through northern Dahomey and Borgu. The eastern section of the plan was biforked. Lieutenant Mizon was to travel through the Lower Niger to Adamawa, while Crampel was to travel through the Congo and up the Ubangi River to Lake Chad. A junction of Mizon and Crampel in the Chad basin would cut off both the Royal Niger Company and the Germans of the Cameroons.

It was to Monteil that the task of the reconnaissance of the region traversed by the Say-Barruwa Line was entrusted. With his ability for picking the right man for any given job, Etienne selected this veteran of west African exploration for this difficult assignment.[58] Monteil was instructed to discover the extent and strength of the influence of the Royal Niger Company in the kingdom of Sokoto, to make treaties with indigenous rulers who were not tied to any European power by prior treaties, and to make recommendations on what should be the actual course of the hypothetical Say-Barruwa Line envisaged by the declaration of August 1890. He was to make astronomical observations and study the topography as well as the political structure and commercial potential of the regions he would traverse.[59] In all this he would be supported by the French troops operating in the Sudan campaign.

Monteil left France for St. Louis (Senegal), from where he began his marathon to Lake Chad. He traveled through well-beaten tracks to Segu, where he arrived in October 1890. From there he made his way across the Niger bend region, calling at San, Bobo Diulasso, Lamfiera, Liptako, Wagadugu, Dori, and finally Say, where he concluded a treaty with the local ruler on 24 August 1891. In addition to the treaties he concluded, Monteil took eighty astronomical observations between Segu and Say.[60] His itinerary had taken him, especially between Wagadugu, Dori, and Say, through territory hitherto untraversed by Europeans. He paid tribute to H. Barth, who, despite several errors of detail, deserved homage for "his sincerity and for the exactitude of his work in general." [61]

From Say, Monteil commenced the most important phase of his voyage, which took him through the independent Argungu province into Sokoto. At Sokoto he discovered, to his surprise, that the Royal Niger Company had neither political nor commercial influence, and not even a resident or a treaty. He moved on from Sokoto, after concluding a treaty with the Sultan, through Kaura, Kano, Hadeija, and Borsari to Kukawa on the banks of Lake Chad,[62] where he arrived in the spring of 1892, after about a six-month march from Say. After a brief sojourn at Kukawa, Monteil left Bornu for Tripoli,[63] going through Bilma, Ariguy (Oasis of Kawar), and Murzuk. He returned to France early in 1893.

It was not the hero's welcome and great reception that was accorded to Monteil in Paris, Marseille, Bordeaux, and Lyon, nor the *Grande Medaille d'Or* which the Société de Géographie de Paris awarded him, that made his voyage important.[64] The greatness of his mission lay in his geographical contributions and the recommendations he made to the French government with reference to the Niger bend and the Say-Barruwa Line.[65]

First of all, Monteil gave details of the political organization of the areas in question. In his final report he modified earlier views he had stated from Kano on the relation between Bornu and Sokoto. Bornu was temporally and spiritually independent of the sultan of Sokoto, and the Shehu of Bornu did not recognize the religious title of the Sokoto ruler as "Commander of the Faithful."[66] The Argungu triangle (Djerma, Mauri-Arewa, Argungu) was independent at the time Monteil arrived there in August 1891 but was conquered by the forces of Sokoto in March 1892, thus modifying the political situation of the area. However, France had incontestable rights to claims in both the Argungu triangle and in Bornu.[67]

The aim of the French government in signing the declaration of 1890 with England was not only to partition the French Mediterranean possessions from those of the Royal Niger Company; it was, above all, "de ménager l'accès au Soudan central des products de notre commerce et de notre industrie," argued Monteil. Consequently, a rigid tracing of the Say-Barruwa Line would not correspond to this desideratum.[68] France should not allow herself to be cut off from the major commercial centers of the region between the Niger and the Chad. Most important of these centers was Kano. This commercial metropolis of the Sudan handles an annual volume of trade of approximately 20 to 30 million francs. Products of indigenous industries and imported goods are carried from here to Tripoli, Algeria, Morocco, Arabia, and Turkey. Kukawa is the next center of Sudanese trade, and Katsena is an easy third. "Sokoto is not of great commercial importance," observed Monteil. The importance of Say lay in its location at the crossing point of caravans based in Kano. The acquisition of Say was a necessity for France, because it could be made an entrepot for trade up the Niger to Segu, San, and Djene. Furthermore, Say could be developed into a great market for easy draining of the riches locked up in the forests of Gobir, Maradi, and Zamfara.[69] Above all, it was necessary to carry out immediately the reconnaissance of the Niger from Segu to Say or even Gomba, since no one had explored this section of the Niger since Mungo Park's fateful voyage of 1805.[70]

Finally, Monteil argued forcefully that British influence was absent from the kingdom of Sokoto and that Britain had acted with bad faith in claiming all that fairly belonged to Sokoto. He concluded that his treaty had conferred on France rights which England could not contest since they had no prior treaties with the sultan of Sokoto.[71] France should not lose the trade of the Hausa territories. Just as Commandant Monteil was receiving official instructions about his mission, Lieutenant Mizon left France on 22 September 1890 for another mission, privately sponsored by the Syndicat français de Haut Bénito.[72] Mizon was to travel from the Niger delta up the Benue River to Yola. There was concern in London about the various French expeditions toward the Chad basin. The *Times* alerted the British government and public in December 1890 to what it considered to be an international race toward the Chad for "the most desirable tracts of Africa."[73] This was an opportune remark, because at that time there was a German mission in the region between the Cameroons and the Upper Benue led by Dr. Zintgraff.[74]

François Deloncle, speaking for ardent French imperialists, could not understand why British agents on the Niger should place obstacles in the way of Frenchmen who were going to open up the Niger-Benue basin to civilization.[75] Mizon complained that the Royal Niger Company was deliberately delaying him in order to make it impossible for his boat *Le Réné Caillé* to ascend the Benue during the low water season.[76] This would make impossible the achievement of the ulterior motives of the mission, which, according to the French press, was to join up with the expeditions of Crampel and Monteil and to obstruct German and British expansion in the Chad-Chari basin.[77]

When the Foreign Office learned of these aims of the Mizon expedition, Salisbury wished that Mizon had not been permitted to proceed at all. H. P. Anderson was pleased that the Patani attacked the French expedition, because this "collision with the natives spoilt the game" for Mizon.[78] From then on Mizon was suspect in British eyes. He did get to Yola in August

1891, endeared himself to the Emir, and explored the Adamawa region. He left Yola on 15 December 1891 for the new French post in the Sanagha to the southeast and succeeded in making a treaty with Emir Zubier, but he did not reach Bornu or Lake Chad. Mizon's second mission of 1893 was also full of incidents with the Royal Niger Company, whose agents shared some of Salisbury's views about a French expedition in the Upper Benue.[79] While Etienne praised Mizon for adding to the national patrimony an admirable country, Léon Tharel admonished the French government to make sure that the superb efforts of Commandant Mizon were not lost to the fatherland.[80]

Things did not work out as Mizon would have liked. He had established a bridgehead at Yola for French expansion. But he was not able to link up with Crampel; Crampel and his escort were massacred by followers of Emir Zubier, who was at that time engaged in empire building in central Africa.[81] Above all, Mizon awakened British and German fears of a French occupation of the Benue-Chad region and thus caused them to take steps to exclude France from this area. This resulted in the Anglo-German agreement of November 1893,[82] which was considered by many Frenchmen a new manifestation of the coalition between England and Germany against France.[83]

It appears to have been an error of judgment on the part of the French government to have sent Mizon back to the Adamawa region in August 1892. The complications that arose from his first expedition were not resolved at the time he set out on the second voyage.[84] Mizon reassured Phipps of the pacific and commercial aims of his mission; he had explicit instructions to abide by the provisions of the Brussels Act with reference to the introduction of firearms and munitions of war into Africa.[85]

Once Mizon was actually on his way to central Africa, he revealed that he did have objectives different from those stated in his official instructions. The statements which Mizon made before leaving Bordeaux for Africa "contained views which were considered dangerous for good relations with the Royal Niger Company," as Hanotaux later informed Casimir-Perier.[86] There was something obscure about the Mizon mission, Hanotaux observed, and there appeared to be no complete understanding between Emile Jamais and Commandant Mizon: "L'un disait que ce qu'il souhait dire. Les autre comprenaient ce qu'ils voulaient comprendre." [87]

Soon after Mizon arrived in Adamawa, he proceeded to conclude treaties of protection with the emirs of Mauri (25 August) and Adamawa (22 November). Above all, Mizon telegraphed the sous-sécretaire des colonies and demanded the creation of a French protectorate of central Sudan, made up of the territory covered by his treaties. Without modesty, he proposed that he be named resident of the new protectorate.[88] The Royal Niger Company was alarmed by these proceedings and alerted the British press and government about what Lord Aberdare[89] scornfully described as "Mizon's piracy" in his letter to the *Times*.

In the face of the serious diplomatic difficulties raised by Mizon's presence in the Upper Benue, the French government decided to recall his party,[90] whose intervention in Mauri was outside the terms of reference of his instructions.[91] The French government knew the political difficulties which had arisen from the involvement of French forces in the Sudan in the wars against Ahmadu and Samory. There was the war in Dahomey also. Further involvement in conflict with the British was not adjudged politic. No doubt Mizon was enraged at the unwillingness of the French government to expand in the Upper Benue, and he threatened to reveal the oral instructions which he had received before he set off for central Africa. Casimir Perier was disconcerted by this threat. He asked Ribot for the instructions which were given to Mizon, both verbal and written, because Mizon claimed that he was told he had liberty of action above Ibi. Consequently, he had made treaties with both Adamawa and Mauri and had distributed arms to the followers of Emir Zubier.[92] Ribot doubted whether any verbal instructions to Mizon could have differed in substance from the written instructions, a copy of which he sent to Waddington to reassure the Foreign Office of the purely commercial and pacific aims of the mission.[93]

Mizon's adventures and the international reaction[94] to them demonstrated that the epoch of coastal comptoirs had passed and that the European imperial powers were from then on to concentrate on and scramble over the acquisition of territory in the hinterland—that of the Middle Niger being the most attractive and available.

While Commandant Mizon was probing the political and economic realities of the Upper Benue basin, other French explorers were inching their ways into the territories of the Niger bend, and British and French diplomats were bargaining over the partition of these disputed territories. Ménard was charged with a mission to retrace Binger's route and confirm the treaties concluded by Binger in the interior with the chiefs of Kong, Kjimini, and Anno. Etienne added a note of urgency to this mission, partly because of the Bonduku affair and partly because it was reported to him by the French resident in Grand Bassam that British agents were diverting caravans of the interior from Bonduku to the British possessions in the Gold Coast.[95]

Ménard left Grand Bassam for the hinterland on 22 November 1890.[96] His progress was retarded by constant rains and other troubles. Ménard reinforced the strong belief of the times about the wealth of the hinterland. He painted a more rosy picture about the riches of these areas than Binger had:

> Ces gens-là sont caisses d'or à tout instant on les voit sortir une petite balance qu'ils possèdent tous, et peser de l'or. Le pays est superbe; la végétation y est d'une densité inouïe . . . les arbres ont des proportions gigantesques et tout est d'un vert admirable.[97]

In addition to the tempting natural resources, Ménard reported that the people were warmhearted, judging from the hospitable reception he received and the devotion of his men. Toward the end of December 1890 he still had not arrived in the Bambara country, which was his goal.[98]

British anxiety over the Ménard mission was expressed by Lytton. Her Majesty's government would be prepared to recognize those treaties "subject to future arrangement as to the limit of the territories so recognized," and they earnestly trusted that no stipulations would be confirmed which were "antagonistic to the freedom of British commerce." Since British policy in these west African colonies threw no impediments in the way of French trade, it would be strongly urged that France adopt a system of reciprocity in these areas.[99] As if oblivious of the monopoly exercised by the Royal Niger Company, to which Mizon and Hoenigsberg successfully drew European attention,[100] Lord Lytton warned:

> Monopoly clauses are contrary to the spirit of the various international engagements which have recently been applied to the continent of Africa, and cannot fail, in Western Africa, to impede the settlement of questions between the two countries on the basis of friendly rivalry and of the suppression of mutual jealousies.[101]

Britain wished Captain Ménard to be instructed to refrain from confirming the treaties with Gaman or Bonduku, as relations with these territories were under discussion; in addition, Menard should not make any new treaties in the hinterland of the Gold Coast.[102]

Irrespective of diplomatic pressure from Britain, the French plan "pour ouvrir des routes d'acces vers le haut-pays" of west Africa was pursued relentlessly by Etienne. In 1892 he organized several missions into the Niger bend, led by Binger,[103] Crozat, and Ménard. Unfortunately, Dr. Crozat died before he could reach Mossi, and Captain Ménard was killed at Segala. Binger and his party reached Bonduku on 27 May 1892. From there the mission was subdivided for the return journey to the coast, in order to assure French predominance in a wider territory. Binger and his group returned to Grand Bassam through Djimini and Diamala, where Binger made new treaties while Braulot and the other half of the mission traveled back to the coast through Bona.[104]

During this mission Binger headed the French delegation for the delimitation of the Gold Coast boundary with the Ivory Coast. Captain J. J. Lang was the English delegate. Very little progress was made by the Boundary Commission, because Binger was uncompromising over Nougoua and Bonduku. Captain Lang was dismayed by this attitude, because he had been prepared to meet Binger halfway. "To get as much as possible by means fair or foul is his aim," Lang informed the Colonial Office plaintively.[105] Phipps was displeased by "the very *ex parte* and prejudiced language and attitude" of the British agents on the spot, which rendered his task "a very difficult one." H. P. Anderson disagreed with Phipps's views, and Salisbury delivered one of his rare Olympian judgments in a laconic manner: "I like Captain Lang's tone."[106] This illustrates how Salisbury cherished a tough line but almost always wanted someone else to take the responsibility of stating such disagreeable positions.

Toward the end of 1892, Captain Marchand was authorized to test his hypothesis of linking the Sudan with the Ivory Coast. He started toward the Atlantic coast from Bandama and arrived at Tengrela in February 1892. He had succeeded in linking the Sudan with the coastal possessions of France through the valley of the River Bagoue, an affluent of the Niger.[107]

After the reduction of the power of Béhanzin by French forces, the base of operations shifted from Grand Bassam to Porto Novo, from where the energetic Governor Ballot executed faithfully the blueprint of missions to the hinterland which had been drawn up while the Dahomey war was still raging. Governor Ballot was an archetype of Jules Ferry's idea of what a colonial governor should be,[108] a man of great initiative, courage, and quickness of action.

> Est-ce vous ne savez pas que, dans toutes ces entreprises, les événements, les hommes, l'activité ou l'incapacité des gouverneurs, décident de la fortune ou de la prospérité des entreprises coloniales? . . . Et l'histoire des entreprises coloniales est, plus que toute autre, subordonée à ces caprices des événements, à ces hasards des hommes d'élite ici, des hommes

inférieurs autre part, et à cet esprit, plus ou moins entreprenant, des représentants d'un gouvernement central, qu'il soit parlementaire ou despotique.[109]

Soon after Colonel Dumas handed over administrative powers to Governor Ballot,[110] he concerned himself with the establishment of a base of operations for exploring the territory between northern Dahomey and the Niger. This region was "placed under the direct surveillance of the Governor" by a decree of the French government on June 1894.[111] It formed the third part of the colony of Dahomey and was known as the "territories of political action"; the other two parts were the annexed territories and the protected territories.[112]

Ballot quickly acquired a concession for a new town or post, which he called Carnotville. By an agreement with Chief Chabi of Agbassa, he secured a territory of 400 hectares, two kilometers on each side. Here he planned to install a resident, a Catholic mission, and some European factories.[113] This new post was to be the springboard of the several expeditions which were to be sent into the "territory of political action" extending to Mossi and Gurunsi. Ballot was shrewd to have selected a spot just on the 9° parallel at the limit of the Anglo-French partition between Lagos and Dahomey. Carnotville[114] had definite advantages over Porto Novo and Abomey as a base for launching operations northward into the hinterland. These expeditions had a dual purpose. First of all, they were to exclude the British colony of the Gold Coast from Baoule, Gurunsi, Mossi, Mamprussi, and Dagomba, which were above 9° North Latitude, and at the same time to assure these territories to France by treaties. Second, they were to stop the effort of the Germans in northern Togo and Dahomey, as well as to limit the action of the Royal Niger Company toward Borgu and in this way secure the hinterland of Dahomey up to Say on the Niger.[115] Later these aims were expanded to include the exploration of the Niger from 9° North Latitude up to Timbuktu, the linking of Dahomey with the Ivory Coast through the territory behind Togo and Ashanti, and the junction of Dahomey and the Sudan by acquiring Gurma and Mossi.[116]

Captain Decoeur, who had undertaken a limited mission in Upper Dahomey,[117] was charged with the first expedition into Borgu. Delcassé introduced him to the Comité d'Afrique Française, who financed the expedition.[118] In the company of Captain Baud, Decoeur left Carnotville on 12 October for Nikki, with orders from Governor Ballot to beat the English expedition there under Captain Lugard. In an effort to secure his rear,

Decoeur decided to make a treaty with the king of Gambari, but this ruler was away from Paraku, his capital, on an expedition against Bassila in the west. Decoeur therefore made a detour to Manigri, where he concluded a treaty with its king on 30 October 1894. He then continued on his way to Nikki, where he arrived on 25 November, and the next day he made a treaty with the king of Nikki, the old Siré Toru. Toru denied concluding any treaty with Lugard, who arrived in Nikki before Captain Decoeur.[119]

Governor Ballot was irritated by the retrogression of Decoeur to Manigri, which he rightly feared would give Lugard the advantage of getting into Nikki first. Ballot despatched Administrator Alby posthaste to Nikki, but Alby had no chance of reaching the Bariba capital before either Lugard or Decoeur. In fact, Alby met Decoeur at Perere on his way back to Carnotville, ostensibly to obtain provisions and supplies for his tirailleurs. Alby continued to Nikki and secured a second treaty with the king to supplement Decoeur's.[120]

This was the beginning of a bitter dispute between Governor Ballot and Commandant Decoeur. Decoeur refused to send any reports to Ballot[121]; he preferred to communicate directly with the minister of colonies, because he had been charged with the expedition by the minister. Ballot asked for the recall of Decoeur in December 1894, after the French lost the race to Nikki to Lugard.[122] The brigandage of the troops under Decoeur was deplored by the governor, who felt that the crimes committed by these soldiers would alienate the local population from the French. Furthermore, Ballot remarked that Decoeur might try to exonerate himself of his inaction and lax control of his escort by blaming the administration, as he had the year before with General Dodds.[123] The difficulties between Ballot and Decoeur illustrate the recurrent conflict between the civil administrators of French colonies and the military officers who were in one way or another connected with these colonies.[124] As 1894 drew to a close, Commandant Decoeur and Captain Baud marched off on another exploration journey, Captain Toutée began his voyage across Dahomey to the Niger, and Governor Ballot prepared to ascend to Nikki to verify the situation there for himself. To these we will return later after examining the British reaction to the ever-multiplying expeditions into the hinterland.

British Reaction to the French Expeditions into the Hinterland

Instead of putting an end to territorial competition in west Africa between Britain and France, or even halting it for the time being, the declaration of August 1890 had the opposite effect. The French, dissatisfied with the "light soil" allotted to them, commenced a series of expeditions to discover the extent of what they had acquired and to ascertain the extent of British influence in those territories over which Britain claimed to exercise control through the Royal Niger Company.

Britain's reaction to this French initiative was twofold. An effort was made to solve the difficulties diplomatically. This took the form of the protracted negotiations between Hanotaux and Phipps, who was at the British Embassy in Paris. There was also a practical approach, in the form of counter expeditions under the aegis of the Royal Niger Company or the local administrations of the west African colonies. But the British effort was not as organized or as clearly thought out as was its French counterpart. The rivalries between the Lagos administration and the Royal Niger Company, as well as the lack of contact between these and the Gold Coast administration, militated against their united and effective resistance to the French onslaught on the hinterland.

The Royal Niger Company officials preferred to expand eastward from their Niger territories toward the Nile valley.[125] The company's claims over the kingdom of Sokoto[126] rested on the flimsy evidence of treaties collected in June 1885. The company had no plans for the acquisition of territories, and most of its treaties were not followed up by any form of active influence over the other parties to these treaties. The Royal Niger Constabulary was used solely for "Punitive Expeditions" against local populations whose opposition was considered bad for business. There were fifty-seven such punitive expeditions between 1886 and 1899.[127]

The Lagos administration wished to acquire the whole of Yoruba land after the Anglo-French agreement of 10 August 1889. The Colonial Office consistently refused to accept any new protectorates until pressures from the chambers of commerce in England and from Lagos became irresistible. The difficulty with Ijebu was a case in point. "Great pressure has been brought to bear on this Department by the Chambers of Commerce of Liverpool and Manchester," admitted Lord Knutsford, when he informed the War Office that military action had to be used in Ijebu in order to reopen the closed trade routes to the interior.[128] When Governor Carter of Lagos suggested that Ijebu be placed under British protection after the proposed military action,[129] supporting his views by the rather academic distinction between being willing and anxious to acquire territory and being compelled to acquire territory, he drew criticism from Meade. "This always happens when England wants territory," he observed.[130] Earlier the colonial secretary had raised the delicate question of whether it was just to interfere in the affairs of an independent foreign country simply because that country adopted a tariff system which was disliked. Such a measure, he continued, could be said to be unfriendly but certainly not hostile.[131] The annexation of Ijebu could cause other communities to lose confidence in Britain, since they would start wondering who would be the next victim of British annexation. Even the House of Commons was reassured that England did not plan to annex Ijebu.[132] It appears that Lord Knutsford ignored the fact that the population of Lagos and vicinity was aware of the French war against Dahomey. They could surmise that such an event could happen among them at any time. Thus it is clear that the Lagos administration had no mandate from the Colonial Office to expand into the hinterland; Governor Carter's initiative was alone responsible for the advance to Ibadan in 1893–94.[133]

As for the Royal Niger Company, the first major effort toward the east was the expedition of David McKintosh, one of its agents, to Bornu in 1891. With an escort of three hundred, McKintosh left Ribago, a few miles above Yola, for Kuka. Though the Shehu of Bornu received him, the gifts he brought were rejected. Not even his large escort could soften the Shehu, who refused to sign any type of treaty with McKintosh. Moreover, the expedition was ordered to leave Kuka, where its continued sojourn would make McKintosh a persona non grata.[134] It was reported that the Shehu hoisted the Moslem flag of Turkey during McKintosh's visit to the Bornu capital,[135] probably to demonstrate his independence of Sokoto, which he later confirmed to Monteil. McKintosh's expedition was a disappointment. Salisbury felt that this agent should at least have exacted a promise from the Shehu that he would not enter into alliance with any other European power.[136] The failure was complete when the Shehu received Monteil later in 1892.

Early in 1890 the Royal Niger Company sent Lister to Boussa to make another treaty with the chief.[137] In addition, David Ashford King was sent to Sokoto and Gwandu to conclude treaties. These were the only exertions of a political nature undertaken by the Royal Niger Company till the expedition of William Wallace into Sokoto and Borgu in mid-1894.[138] Wallace made treaties with both Sokoto and Gwandu and then traveled into Gurma and Borgu. He confirmed that these areas were independent of both Sokoto and Gwandu and that not even Ilo had any political ties with Bussa.[139]

These findings by Wallace broke the complacency of the Royal Niger Company about the territories west of the Niger; the conquest of Dahomey heightened the effect. First of all, Goldie wanted to get out of this region the easy way. He proposed that the Foreign Office offer Gurma and Borgu to France in return for French recognition of British rights to the Upper Nile Valley.[140] Second, it was decided to send an expedition westward from the Niger, across Borgu, and into the hinterland of the Gold Coast. For this task Goldie nominated Captain Lugard, whose services he secured mainly because Lugard's efforts to be sent to Uganda again were unsuccessful. Lugard was not enthusiastic about going to the Niger territories at this particular time, as he confided to Sir John Kirk:

> Sir E[dward] Grey says I am not to be sent to Uganda. . . . Regarding my engagement to Sir G[eorge] Goldie I see that one of the points of dispute put forward by France for the settlement is regarding the Hinterland of Dahomey etc. This is the very place I am asked to go to. The F.O. has agreed to discuss all these questions. It therefore appears to me a futile thing for me to start on a filibustering expedition into this territory at the very time when the frontiers are being settled in Europe. I should not be there until about November when in all probability the matter would be settled. Then I should be disowned and discredited, and my work would be useless.[141]

Lugard's sense of the futility of this enterprise would have known no bounds had he known that Sir George Goldie was at that very time urging the Foreign Office to give all of Borgu and Gurma to the French. In any case, he was instructed that "diplomacy and not conquest" was the object of his expedition west of the Niger.[142] Not oblivious of the tragedy of the German Herr Kling or the failures of Wolfe and even Decoeur in this area behind Dahomey, Goldie instructed Lugard to avoid the "exercise of force which could not further the objects of the expedition." Lugard sailed from Liverpool in July for the Niger territories. He arrived at Jebba in September and, after preparations were completed, began his expedition into Borgu through Kishi and Kaiama. From there he went to Nikki, where he arrived on 9 November 1894, beating the French mission under Commandant Decoeur by eight days.[143]

In September 1894, the Lagos press announced the proposed voyage of Captain Bower of the Lagos constabulary into Bariba country. "Only a very small portion of the Bariba country is within the British sphere of influence," declared the *Lagos Echo*. It was hoped that the authorities of Lagos would avoid a collision with their foreign neighbors, namely the

French. The recent unfortunate incident at the frontier of Sierra Leone was recalled as a warning to the officials to be careful in their Bariba venture.[144]

It was the announcement of these two British expeditions into Borgu which sparked off Governor Ballot's reaction. He sent Captain Decoeur to Nikki so that he would arrive there before either Lugard or Captain Bower. In Nikki, Lugard signed a treaty, just as he had done in Kaiama, without bothering to ascertain sufficiently the political status of those who dealt with him. It appears that Lugard was misled by the erroneous statements of Colonel E. Lambinet in 1893 that the Bariba formed an important community at both Porto Novo and Whydah and that they were all Moslems of the Beni-Senusi sect.[145] The consistency with which Lugard blundered in his treaty-making, the keystone of his expedition, raises questions as to the reason for such a slipshod proceeding by a military officer. The argument of Dr. John E. Flint that morals were involved, though well marshalled, is not cogent enough because of Lugard's character.[146] Rather, it seems that the main cause of these shortcomings was Lugard's lack of enthusiasm for the task assigned to him. The despondency arising from his attitude that he was fighting a lost cause may explain why he secured the wrong signatures on the standard treaty forms that were given to him by the Royal Niger Company. Furthermore, he headed back to the Niger by mid-November 1894, contrary to his instructions to go westward to the Gold Coast hinterland.[147]

At the same time that both Lugard and Decoeur were on their way to Nikki, a German expedition led by Dr. Gruner and von Carnap was marching toward the same destination.[148] The Germans were not to be outdone by their French and British rivals.[149] These expeditions produced what M. Vignes has called "an extraordinary carousel of missions" in the Dahomey-Niger hinterland, reminiscent of the *furor consularis* in Samoa described by Robert Louis Stevenson.

The Germans claimed the territory in the hinterland of Dahomey, which they called *Tschantoland*. The existence of this entity was doubted by British officials.[150] However, the German administration in Togo decided to make good its claim. Under the leadership of Gruner, the German expedition left Misahoehe in Togo on 6 November 1894 and wormed its way northward through Bismarckburg to Sansane Mango, where it arrived early in January 1895. Here the expedition was subdivided: the larger section stayed on at Sansane Mango under Gruner to make treaties and consolidate the German position there; the other section, under Lieutenant von Carnap, continued northward to Pama[151] and Gurma, where it ran into Decoeur's expedition, which was operating in this region at that time.[152] Von Carnap went through Matiacuali to Kankantenari, where he had a dispute with Commandant Decoeur, who claimed all of Gurma for France by virtue of his treaty at Fada N'Gurma. Von Carnap advised Decoeur to leave the attribution of territories to the governments of France and Germany. The German expedition continued to Say, from where they descended the Niger to Brass. The journey was full of incidents. They were attacked at Bikini and had to fight their way through. Then there was an outbreak of smallpox among Von Carnap's escort. The section of the German expedition under Gruner marched through Borgu and returned to Misahoehe via Kete-Krachi.[153]

The second but isolated arm of British expeditions into the Niger territories in this period was that sent into Mossi by Governor Branford Griffith of the Gold Coast. The existence of Ashanti as an independent kingdom was a barrier to the expansion of the Gold Coast colony northward into the Niger bend. The creation of the "Neutral Zone" by Britain and Germany was another obstruction to British expansion behind Ashanti, since this zone embraced most of Dagomba and Gonja and a good portion of Brong.[154] Any extension of British influence toward the Niger bend had to be circumvented to avoid these awkward obstacles. Ashanti had survived the defeat of 1873–74 by Sir Garnet Wolseley because the attitude of officials in London was still governed by the report of the parliamentary committee of 1865, which was against further expansion of British territory in west Africa.[155] But as Ashanti was slowly but surely being surrounded by territories linked to Britain, its reduction became a question of time.[156]

The flurry of expansionist activity by the French from the Ivory Coast into the hinterland of the Gold Coast led them into difficulties with the Gold Coast administration, especially over Bonduku, Nugua, and the area around Assinie.[157] As these French pressures mounted in 1891, Governor Brandford Griffith took precautionary measures to save the hinterland of his colony. First, he dispatched George Ekem Ferguson to the Brong region to make treaties with the chiefs of the country. Second, on his own initiative, he proposed to Prempeh I of Ashanti the conclusion of a treaty of protection with the Gold Coast administration acting for Britain.[158]

George E. Ferguson was born in Anomabu. Son of an Englishman and his African wife, he entered the civil service of the Gold Coast after his school days. As a result of the great promise he showed and his outstanding intelligence, he was sent to Britain, where he was trained as a surveyor. He returned to the Gold Coast, where he rendered invaluable service to the administration. His exploration and treaty-making expeditions into the hinterland as far as Mossi made him one of the central figures in the Anglo-French controversy over prior treaty rights in Wagadugu and other towns in the late 1890s.[159] He was killed by Samory's forces on 6 April 1897 at Wa.

Late in 1892 Ferguson was sent on another mission into the Niger bend, Mossi being the destination.[160] In the meantime Ashanti began to cause anxiety both to the administrators and to its neighbors. Consequently, an expedition under Sir Francis Scott was dispatched to Atabubu in September 1893 as a preventive measure against Ashanti raids into the area. In addition to policing the Brong and Nkoranza regions, Scott concluded treaties with the chiefs of these districts.[161] Reverend Fritz Ramseyer of Abetifi, some miles east of Kumasi, reported to Acting Governor Hodgson that it would require little or no effort to reduce Kumasi and annex Ashanti. This report, corroborated by that of Sir Francis Scott, made a great impression on Governor F. M. Hodgson, who was by no means a Little Englander and who was abreast with events in Dahomey, where the French were engaged in the task of conquering Béhanzin. Hodgson therefore pressed the Colonial Office for a forward policy of annexing Ashanti. He found a supporter in J. Bramston of the Colonial Office, who felt that as far as Ashanti was concerned the time had come for "a bold stroke such as tells with savages." [162] But the annexation of Ashanti was shelved for a few more years.[163]

Early in 1894 Hodgson instructed Ferguson to go on another treaty-making expedition into the hinterland, by an eastern route through Salaga, Yendi, Gambaga, Kupela, and Mossi.[164] Ferguson carried out this task with great success. He concluded treaties of commerce and friendship with the chiefs of the countries he traversed. At Wagadugu, Ferguson concluded a treaty with the Mogho Naba, Abu Bukari, on 2 July 1894. Though this treaty was not one extending British protection over Mossi, it did include a clause which provided that the king of Mossi not enter into diplomatic relations with any other European power without first consulting Britain.[165] Ferguson reported to the governor of the Gold Coast his observations of the kingdoms of the hinterland, the commercial activity of the area, and the main commercial centers and important towns.[166]

The controversy created by French expansionists over the treaty-making role of Ferguson was great; it persists even now. Following the tendentious evidence given by the Comité d'Afrique Française, Dr. Elliot P. Skinner stated that Ferguson was at Wagadugu only in December 1894 and that he doubted the validity of the treaty Ferguson concluded there with the Mogho Naba. "One must conclude," added Dr. Skinner, "therefore, that Ferguson, like other European agents of the period, was dishonest." [167]

The evidence available on the Ferguson mission does not give cause to doubt the integrity of the British agent. Ferguson had a long record of voyages into the Gold Coast hinterland.[168] It was Lord Ripon, the colonial secretary, who authorized Ferguson's 1894 expedition into the hinterland to make treaties with Bona, Wa, Lobi, Walembele, and Yariba. Lord Ripon observed:

> It would be much to be regretted if, after the trouble and expense which has been incurred, it should ultimately be found that the object of securing the hinterland of the colony against the encroachments of foreign powers had not been fully attained.[169]

The acting governor of the Gold Coast instructed Ferguson to conclude treaties of friendship and commerce with the native rulers of the hinterland as far inland as Wagadugu, leaving out the Neutral Zone because of its unique position.[170] Ferguson left the coast as soon as preparations were completed for his mission. By early June he arrived at Gambaga, after having dealt with Bona, Wa, and Gambaga. From there he sent the progress report of his mission to the governor, observing that the direct roads to Wagadugu were closed by hostile tribes who robbed caravans. Above all, he expressed his determination to proceed to Wagadugu by an alternative route, which was not free of danger:

> Immediately after despatching this letter, I leave for Mossi. Its importance tempts me to risk the Kupela road. It is the caravan producing country of our hinterland which ought not to be conceded to any foreign power. But not wishing to carry all my eggs in one basket, I enclose herewith duplicates of the treaties made with Bona, Wa, and Gambaga.[171]

Ferguson, then, undertook the laborious voyage to Wagadugu and, according to his orders, concluded a treaty of commerce and friendship with the court of Wagadugu on the printed forms which he brought with him. After this he and his entourage headed southeast into Chakosi and then back into Dagomba, from where he signalled his successful journey to Mossi to Governor Griffith:

I have the honour to report that I arrived at this place Yendi yesterday
... having treated successfully with the authorities of Mossi on 2 July
and with Chakosi on 8 August. . . . I ascertained that previous to my
arrival at Wagadugu three visits had been made by different explorers
at Wagadugu, but that their visits were unattained with political results.[172]

It is clear, then, that Ferguson was in Wagadugu in July 1894. That he concluded a treaty of friendship and commerce was not his fault but that of the Gold Coast administration and the Colonial Office, which instructed him on what to do. At any rate, the British government was not keen on acquiring Mossi. Salisbury advised Phipps early in July 1892 to concede Mossi to France in order to assure British predominance in Borgu and Gurma.[173] While explorers were marching up and down the tropical deciduous forest of the Niger basin, British and French diplomats began negotiations for the delimitation of the spheres of influence of the two powers in the Niger-Chad region.

Anglo-French Niger–Lake Chad Commission, 1892–94

The Anglo-French declaration of 5 August 1890 touched off the controversy which led to the Monteil expedition into the territories between the Niger and Lake Chad. Before Monteil returned, the French Foreign Office initiated negotiations with Britain with a view to delimiting the French and British spheres to the west of the Niger. These negotiations involved mainly an east-to-west frontier between the Niger and western Gold Coast colony and the northward prolongation of the Porto Novo–Lagos boundary above the ninth parallel of latitude.[174] After the return of Commandant Monteil, the negotiations widened to include the discussion and interpretation of the Say-Barruwa Line.

Early in 1891 the French government expressed the wish for the extension of the Lagos–Porto Novo frontier vertically northward to the Niger. But this was not a practical proposition, since the two governments were not yet agreed on the recommendations of the joint boundary commission, which had carried out a geodesic survey of the Lagos–Porto Novo frontier in June 1890. The French government asked for the adjustment of slight discrepancies in the joint report and maps of the boundary commission.[175] By the end of January 1891, Her Majesty's government approved the amendments proposed by France in the recommendations of the boundary commissioners.[176] The urgent question in the area after this was that of the establishment of uniform tariffs between Lagos and Porto Novo, as was provided for by the Anglo-French agreement of August 1889. The Lagos administration pressed the importance of this question and deplored the ever-growing smuggling that went on around Ajara Creek.[177] However, the French Colonial Department was in no hurry to arrange common customs between Lagos and Porto Novo, as Hanotaux remarked to Phipps. Furthermore, there was at this time a general review of French tariffs and commercial agreements by a special commission of the French chamber.[178] When it was threatened that Lagos would establish customs posts on the Ajara, Hanotaux replied that such a measure might shake up the French Colonial Department and quicken a settlement of the common tariff question.[179]

This local tariff problem was soon superseded by the more important general question of the delimitation of the spheres of influence of Britain and France in the territories west of the Niger. Profiting from the lull in the war in Dahomey, Hanotaux proposed the partition of these territories between Britain and France. He wished to avoid a repetition of the type of conflict that had occurred between the two powers in Bonduku and Nougua[180] and in the hinterland of Sierra Leone. There was also the suspicion that the Royal Niger Company might extend its influence farther to the west while France was still engaged in the Dahomey and Sudan campaigns. Since the region in question involved the interests of the Royal Niger Company, Phipps was recalled to London for consultations with Sir George Goldie before he could begin formal talks with Hanotaux. Lord Salisbury was not impressed by the hint that France would be prepared to give all of Borgu to Britain in return for British recognition of French rights over Gurma, which would ultimately mean the extension of French Sudan up to Say. The French would be very tired of west African negotiations after the ordeal of the Dahomey war, he believed.[181] This was not to be so, as was clairvoyantly pointed out by J. W. Lowther: "After they have conquered the King of Dahomey next September will they be very ready to cede the hinterland? They will probably use the old blood and treasure argument."[182]

After the first meeting of the Anglo-French Niger–Lake Chad Commission, Phipps reported the definite proposal of a Say-Bonduku line by Hanotaux, giving to England all the unannexed territory south of this line and to France everything north of it. The proposed line was to run from Say to the northeast corner of the Anglo-German Neutral Zone and from the northwest corner of this zone to Bonduku.[183] After studying the French proposal, the Colonial Office suggested some amendments, which were embodied in Lord

Salisbury's reply to Phipps. The British commissioners should make efforts "to prevent the division of the territory of Gurma which must remain on the English side." Salisbury continued:

> Too much stress should not be laid upon an attempt to limit the French sphere of influence to the eighth parallel of latitude behind Dahomey and Porto Novo, although the Commissioners should be careful that it is clearly secured that the French Government abandon any claim whatever to the hinterland of Dahomey.[184]

This was a case of very poor judgment on the part of Lord Salisbury and the Foreign Office. Was it not presumptuous to expect France to acquiesce in the acquisition of the Dahomey hinterland by Britain after a victorious war against Béhanzin? Perhaps it was the great pressure of domestic politics on Salisbury that forced him into the position of asking the French for what amounted to the impossible.[185]

The amendment to the Say-Bonduku line proposed by England was unacceptable to Hanotaux and more so to the Colonial Department, where plans for an expedition into the hinterland of Dahomey were in the embryonic stage. Not even the offer of the Gambia to France, suggested by A. W. L. Hemming, could produce a shift in the French position, which was to be tremendously strengthened by the exploits of General Dodds in the plains of Abomey. It began to look as if the French expansionists would press their forward policy to the edges of the sphere of the Royal Niger Company.[186]

Though the British amendments killed the Say-Bonduku proposal, negotiations between Phipps and Hanotaux continued on other west African questions, from Sierra Leone to Lake Chad. In January 1893, Phipps suggested to Hanotaux that they should "devote one day to the discussion of the commercial question,[187] since the cause of all friction between the two powers was the policy of commercial restrictions persistently followed by French local agents." To this Hanotaux reacted very favorably, since the main objective was the establishment of the best accord between British and French territories. "I am quite ready to discuss the commercial question with you. I have only one desire, as you know, and it is to arrange all the difficulties and, as you said, to live as good neighbours," replied Hanotaux.[188] However, as the talks progressed, more headway was made with reference to the boundary of the Ivory Coast and the Gold Coast than on the commercial questions. Phipps confided to Hanotaux that the chambers of commerce in England were already criticizing the negotiations and arrangements and that commercial concessions would fortify his position vis-à-vis these chambers of commerce.[189] Those interested in British west African trade, Phipps declared, had strong apprehensions that "every extension of French influence implies corresponding injury to British commercial interests." [190]

After Phipps returned to France from London, where he had found "insuperable difficulties in regard to resigning to France any portion of the Niger bend and the territory therein comprised," [191] the negotiations regarding the Gold Coast–Ivory Coast frontier progressed rapidly, but little or no progress was made with reference to the Niger-Chad question.[192] A totally new element was introduced in the negotiations by the submission of the official report of Commandant Monteil.[193]

The agreement about the Gold Coast–Ivory Coast frontier was signed at Paris on 12 July 1893.[194] This cleared the way for serious work to begin again on the Niger question. Hanotaux proposed to Phipps that the treaties on which both parties based their claims be produced for comparison and discussion. Furthermore, the Say-Barruwa Line was to be reevaluated in the light of the findings made by Monteil.[195] At this juncture, the African question fascinated Hanotaux so much that he contemplated writing a book on Africa's future. In his diary he wrote: "Two beautiful subjects for study when I complete my Richelieu: 'Avenir de politique générale du monde' and 'Ce que sera l'Afrique.' " [196]

For the present the romantic but distant project of forecasting Africa's future was overridden by the immediate and pressing question of the regulation of Anglo-French difficulties in the Niger basin and elsewhere. Hanotaux continued his negotiations with Phipps concerning the hinterland of Dahomey and the Say-Barruwa Line. Early in 1894, Lord Rosebery complained about the "acrimonious attacks of the French press" and demanded that the French government express its disapproval of these attacks and its views on the unilateral repudiation of international obligations by France. He stressed that the Mizon affair, which provided the platform for the press war, was "not a dispute between a French citizen and a British Company. It was a violation of British rights agreed to on 5 August 1890 and reaffirmed by the French Government in August 1892." [197] When no disavowal of the attacks on England was forthcoming, Phipps was instructed to suspend negotiations until the unfortunate incident cleared.[198]

The talks were soon resumed, only to run aground like a floundering ship on the diametrically opposed interpretations of the Say-Barruwa Line by both parties. The French held that this line marked the southern boundary of the Mediterranean possessions of France. It thus excluded the extension of British influence to the north of it, but it did not bar French expansion to the south of it from the Atlantic coast.[199] The brunt of the British case was that France had no right to expand anywhere south of the Say-Barruwa Line and that Mizon's filibustering in the Benue region was a violation of British rights.[200] Phipps drew Hanotaux's attention to the absurdity of the French insistence on the definition of Sokoto before indispensable local information was available.[201] The stalemate over the interpretation of the Say-Barruwa Line led to the suspension of the negotiations. Phipps was instructed to refrain from making overtures for further negotiations.[202] However, Hanotaux continued to seek a satisfactory settlement of all the outstanding problems between France and Britain in Africa, not only in west Africa, as he informed Phipps in April 1894.[203]

Three important events which affected the course of the negotiations when they were resumed in August 1894 occurred in France and in west Africa: the definitive conquest of Dahomey and the exile of Béhanzin by General Dodds and his forces; the establishment of a ministry of colonies in Paris; and the toppling of the cabinet of Casimir Perier in May 1894, which led to Gabriel Hanotaux's appointment as minister for foreign affairs in the Dupuy Cabinet that succeeded Perier's.[204] Moreover, the conclusion of the Anglo-Italian treaty of 5 May, in the wake of which came the Anglo-Congolese treaty of 12 May 1894, affected adversely the attitude of France toward Britain in African colonial matters, since these treaties were considered inimical to French interests in Harrar,[205] Bahr-el-Ghazal, and the Ubangi regions.[206]

In his inaugural speech on 31 May 1894 in the chamber, Charles Dupuy stated that his government favored maintenance of that same continuity of view and of relations (among parties) which, in spite of political rivalry, had permitted France to recover among nations a place worthy of her name and history. In foreign affairs he pledged to watch the interests of France around the world and defend her rights.[207] The new government jumped its first hurdle with perfect poise when Eugene Etienne set this up with a loaded interpellation on French policy in Africa. Hanotaux acquitted himself excellently. At the end of the debate the Dupuy government received a solid and unanimous vote of confidence of 527 votes.[208]

After such a brilliant start, the French government could not but hope for a satisfactory settlement of the outstanding problems with Britain in colonial questions. Moreover, the Liberal government in London was disposed to meet the French government on all these questions "in a most conciliatory spirit." [209] Hanotaux, who had been in charge of the African negotiations as a civil servant, now had to tackle them as a foreign minister.[210] In August he told Lord Dufferin that an endeavor should be made to come to a general understanding on all questions pending between Great Britain and France in east and west Africa. Thus he wished to sandwich the Egyptian question into the talks on west Africa.[211]

Lord Kimberley instructed Lord Dufferin that Britain would be prepared to accommodate French claims elsewhere in Africa "if a satisfactory arrangement is come to upon the question of the British sphere in the Nile watershed." Then, following a memorandum submitted by Sir George Goldie, he expressed a willingness to give most of Borgu to France in return for French recognition of the Say-Barruwa Line and the Anglo-German frontiers east of the Niger, as defined in the arrangements between these two powers concluded in 1886 and 1889 respectively:

> Her Majesty's Government would be prepared to recognize as legitimate the wish of the French Government to reap the advantages of their military operations in Dahomey by obtaining territory in the rear of that kingdom, which would enable them to communicate ... with their sphere in the neighbourhood of the Upper Niger.[212]

Lord Kimberley argued that the hinterland of Dahomey was closed to French expansion into the interior because of England's prior treaty rights in Borgu. However, in the event of French acceptance of the Say-Barruwa Line of 1890 and of Bornu's inclusion in the British sphere, the treaty rights in Borgu would be overlooked in order to make concessions to France to enable her to achieve a junction of her new colony of Dahomey with the Sudan. Two other conditions were laid down in Lord Kimberley's instructions: that the Mizon affair be dropped, and that Hanotaux live up to his promise to Phipps (earlier in the negotiations) about the commercial arrangements involving identic tariffs to be made between British and French possessions in the Sierra Leone and Porto Novo areas.[213]

These proposals were submitted to the Quai d'Orsay, and Phipps, who claimed to "have been given some latitude up to a certain point" and to have been fortified by an interview with Lord Rosebery," [214] went to discuss them with Hanotaux. Very little progress was made in this major conference. Hanotaux stressed the impossibility of French adherence to the proposed Say-Barruwa Line as well as the renunciation of everything from Borgu to

Adamawa.²¹⁵ However, he recognized the conciliatory spirit in which the proposals were made and promised to forward them to the ministry of colonies. Hanotaux told Phipps that he was "more or less a go-between" and that he would have to conciliate the colonial party for any concessions that were made to Britain.²¹⁶

As the negotiations progressed, Hanotaux asked for more important concessions on the right bank of the Niger—that is, in the hinterland of Dahomey. Phipps informed him that Britain was prepared to abandon her treaty rights in Mossi and Borgu if France recognized the Say-Barruwa Line traced according to treaty stipulations. If these proposals were rejected there would be chaos, and France would have to struggle with the Germans, who claimed some territory in the same region of the hinterland. "Isn't it time to terminate this African 'steeple chase'?" asked Phipps.²¹⁷ Delcassé objected to the British interpretation of the Say-Barruwa Line because it amounted to an abandonment of all the results of the explorations of Brazza in the Ubangui basin,²¹⁸ and Britain did not offer adequate compensation in other directions. In the meantime, the French ambassador in London reported that Britain was prepared to guarantee to France the Dahomey hinterland up to Say, thus meeting the French desire for access to the navigable Niger.²¹⁹ The leave of the permanent officials of the Quai d'Orsay, Nisard and Beniot, who were in charge of these affairs, delayed the negotiations.²²⁰ But at the conference of 29 September, Hanotaux was armed with a long note from the colonial ministry, in which Delcassé's views on the various issues were stated. Hanotaux proposed a slight alteration to the map defining the French sphere in the Dahomey-Niger hinterland. He reserved French rights in Adamawa by virtue of Mizon's treaties but remarked that this would be the subject for an entirely separate exchange.²²¹

With most of the difficulties discussed and reduced, Phipps drew up the "project of bases for the settlement of pending African Questions between Great Britain and France." ²²² Further discussions centered on these bases, and common grounds were reached for an agreement.²²³

At this juncture Delcassé, whose ministry had a nonchalant attitude to the negotiations, introduced the difficulty of the passage of the proposed Toutée expedition through the Lower Niger. The Niger Company objected to the navigation of the river by an armed expedition.²²⁴ Hanotaux prevented Toutée from using the Lower Niger, and his instructions were altered so that he began his expedition from Cotonou overland toward the Middle Niger. Delcassé also opposed the proposal for a reciprocal stoppage of expansion missions in the Upper Nile on the grounds that French missions in the Upper Ubangui would get to the Nile before the Colville mission.[225] Then came the fatal blow to the project for an agreement. Governor Ballot telegraphed Delcassé that the delimitation of the Lagos-Dahomey frontier further into the interior could be delayed for many months because it had no immediate utility for France; only the British in Lagos would benefit from an immediate prolongation of the frontier. Delcassé shared Ballot's views on this matter. He communicated his views to Hanotaux and lectured him:

> Il vous appartient, dans ce cas, d'invoquer auprès du Gouvernement anglais des raisons dilatoires, les difficultés d'une organisation administrative toute recent et l'absence d'un personnel spécial par exemple, pour expliquer le retard apporté aux opérations de délimitation.[226]

These developments were ominous for the final draft treaty produced by Hanotaux and Phipps, which was rejected by both governments, each blaming its representatives for undue leniency toward the opponents. Hanotaux later bemoaned the discarding of this treaty so painfully concluded by Phipps and himself. It succeeded, he said, in tying up all the problems between France and Britain in Africa, especially in the Nile valley. It would have saved France the Fashoda fiasco, he later pointed out with hindsight, and was on the whole more advantageous to France than the one that eventually settled these problems.[227] These negotiations failed because France refused to give guarantees to leave the Bahr-el-Ghazal region alone for British enterprise and because the colonial ministry under the influence of Governor Ballot refused to accept an immediate delimitation of the Dahomey-Niger hinterland. Ballot was ready to launch a network of expeditions into this region in order to outdistance the Germans and the British. The ministerial crises in France at this time, coupled with the forward policy of the new ministry of colonies and the colonial group of the chamber, did not favor a negotiated settlement of African problems.[228]

In Britain, though there were those who would have liked "to see a close understanding with France," Lord Rosebery strongly believed that the best course for England was the isolationist one. Both entering the Triple Alliance and concluding a treaty with Italy were not, he stated, "in the range of practical politics for a British Minister at this time. . . . Our only sure policy is to strengthen our fleet and that will be done. . . . Our hands must be free (even in Constantinople): we must co-operate, but not be handcuffed to anyone."[229] Kimberley reinforced the cooperation theme when he asserted that "it would be impolitic for the sake of the acquisition of a strip of land for a road and a telegraph to embroil ourselves with Germany and to encounter all the dangers which would follow from the common action of Germany and France in African questions." [230]

Lord Salisbury foresaw these problems as he was about to leave the Foreign Office after his defeat in the summer of 1892:

> What I am afraid of is a too hurried *rapprochement* with France—involving the abandonment of the Triple Alliance by Italy—a reconstruction of the DreiKaiserbund and Russia on the Bosphorus. . . . I think that the past will be sufficient to warn us against this risk.[231]

The expeditions from 1890 to 1894 awakened the interest of the European imperial powers in the hinterland of the Middle Niger basin. The iron curtain that was the kingdom of Dahomey was lifted with the conquest of Béhanzin, thus opening the way to the Niger bend and adjacent territories. The Hanotaux-Phipps negotiations failed to stem the tide of the aggressive forward policy of France into the heart of Africa and of British intransigence in matters involving the Upper Nile valley. The expedition of Monteil and the international race to Nikki in November 1894 proved the hollow nature of the claims of the Royal Niger Company. The ensuing years became a period of fierce contests between France and Britain in west Africa.

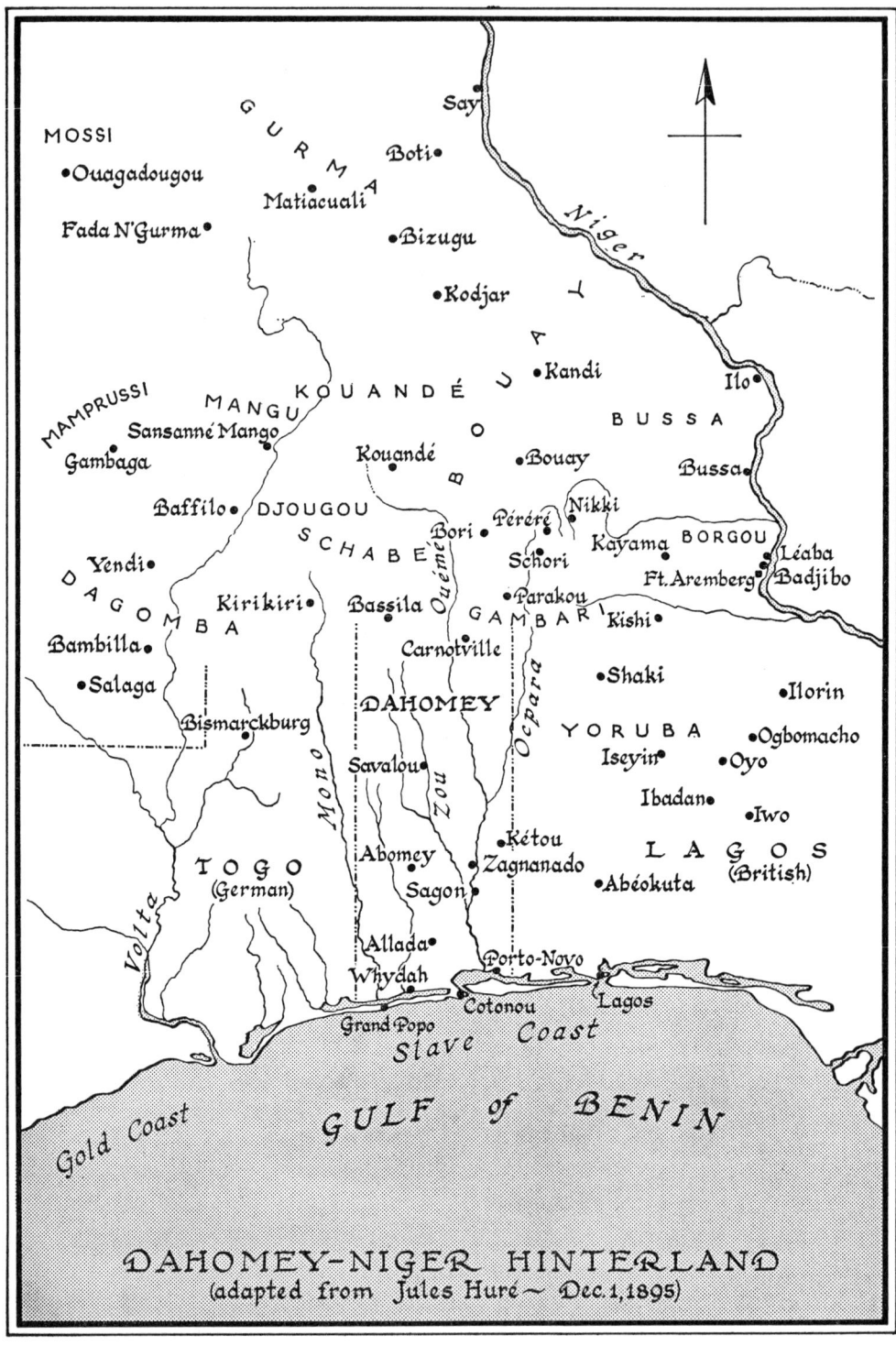

6

The Scramble for and the Occupation of the Hinterland, 1895–1897

> It would be better to let the coming storm blow over before any further delimitation is undertaken.
>
> Dr. Kayser

The German colonial minister cannily forecast accurately the storm of international competition in the Dahomey-Niger hinterland which began to gather early in 1894 and achieved whirlwind intensity by 1897. It was realized that the "recent French success in Dahomey" would necessarily entail an extension of French influence northward.[1] Therefore both Britain and Germany moved to secure the hinterlands of their respective colonies on the Guinea coast against French expansionist activity. The ensuing expeditions, effective occupation, and counter-effective occupation and "dishonorable scramble" for territory in the hinterland was only regulated by a series of diplomatic arrangements in mid-1897 and 1898 between France and Germany, and Britain and France, respectively.

The Changed Situations in West Africa, France, and Britain

During this period, certain political changes occurred in west Africa, France, and Britain, which had far-reaching effects on the undeclared international contest for territory in the Niger bend. The conquest of Dahomey removed the most formidable obstacle in the way of imperial expansion into the interior. The reduction of Prempeh I of Ashanti in 1896[2] meant that the two strong African kingdoms which obstructed easy access to the hinterland from the Atlantic coast were forever removed. Indeed, the gates to the riverine regions of the Middle Niger which remained ajar after the fall of Dahomey were thrown wide open by 1896.[3] The collapse of these two indigenous powers added extra impetus to the scramble by Europeans for territory in the hinterland and was a factor, equally important with European ones, that led to the partition and occupation of this region of west Africa.

In England, the Liberal cabinet of Lord Rosebery, which initiated the British expeditions of 1894, fell from power in the summer of 1895, after a short-lived administration. The third Salisbury administration succeeded it in June 1895, with Joseph Chamberlain as colonial secretary. According to Winston Churchill, Chamberlain, who "grew up in Birmingham in a period when world politics were the well-preserved domain of Whig and Tory aristocracies, and their counterparts in different nations, revealed himself as the first intruder from the new democracy into these select but wide-ranging circles." [4] It has been said that Chamberlain[5] "was the most powerful and the most popular figure in the Salisbury government." Be that as it may, his control and direction of the colonial secretaryship had tremendous effects on British imperialism.

> With Chamberlain's return to the Government there began the full summer of Late Victorian Imperialism which was far more the creation of this erstwhile Radical and Republican, than of the Tories who claimed it as theirs and to whom it has been so readily attributed. It was Chamberlain who planted the Imperialist virus in the Tory body. There may be argument as to whether thanks are due; there can be none as to who deserves them.[6]

Chamberlain watched over those parts of the British empire in Africa with Cerberean vigilance, and no sops from France or Germany could make him budge.[7] Lord Salisbury, who had said earlier in his career that Africa existed for the discomfort of foreign secretaries, learned more about African questions by the time of his third administration[8] than he knew when he made that statement. He commenced his last administration with the blunt realization that international rivalry for territory in Africa and elsewhere was a step toward the strangulation of British commerce by the protectionist policies of France and Germany. He was prepared to do something about this uncomfortable situation, as he declared in Bradford in May 1895:

> If we are to oppose the efforts of all the civilized powers to strangle our commerce by their protective tariffs, it is necessary that we take the measures essential for opening to ourselves new markets among the half-civilized or non-civilized peoples. We need not be dismayed if this effort which is essential for our industries would lead to new responsibilities.[9]

Though Salisbury was not "a man to be guided by others," he comprehended as Chamberlain did that reasons of state and national prosperity made it imperative for his administration to match wits and diplomatic skills with both France and Germany in order to safeguard the far-off markets of Africa.

In the ranks of the permanent civil service officials of both the Foreign Office and the Colonial Office, some noteworthy and rocking changes occurred during this period that could have handicapped the efficiency of the Salisbury administration. First of all, there was the sudden death of Sir Percy Anderson in July 1896. "His power has, both under Lord Rosebery and under the present tenure of Lord Salisbury, been absolute in all matters affecting our African Protectorates," observed Sir John Kirk, who rejoiced at Anderson's passing.[10] Anderson's successor was Sir Clement Hill, who was "equally or more fossil than Anderson and more wedded to the narrowest official views."[11]

Second, the experienced old guard of the Colonial Office gradually but steadily disappeared and was replaced by younger officials whose mettle had not yet been tried.[12] Such a situation gave rise to anxiety among some contemporaries who were closely connected with this office. Kirk observed that

> the Colonial Office, however, at present is in a hopeless state. Hemming went to be Governor of British Guiana from being the head of the West African Department in the Colonial Office. Then Meade retired with 30 years of service, thus breaking the tradition of the office. Next Fairfield died and he was the pay auditor of the C.O. Now Sir John Bramston retires and there are none but junior clerks of no marked or known capacity carrying on. This leaves Chamberlain master but it is a danger for he is cut off from all previous experience and historical knowledge of affairs. He works with mere clerks under him instead of strong men like Herbert, Meade or Fairfield who knew what had been in the past; for Joe with all his smartness is not straight. He is not to be trusted or depended on. He is a match for Rhodes but quite as unscrupulous.[13]

Contrary to the fears expressed by Sir John Kirk, these domestic affairs of the departments concerned did not appreciably hamper their efficiency. Their European counterparts went through more jolting political and administrative changes.[14]

In Paris the ministerial musical chairs which characterized the Third Republic continued its fitful progress. Between January 1895 and 1897 four governments succeeded one another. The Bourgeois Cabinet, which was the most ephemeral of them, lasted for only six months.[15] On the other hand, the Méline Cabinet, formed in April 1896, set a record in longevity for governments of the Third Republic up to that time; it stayed in power till 15 June 1898.[16] In all these cabinets Hanotaux was the minister for foreign affairs, except in the short-lived Radical cabinet of Léon Bourgeois. Therefore, there was a considerable degree of continuity in the work of the Quai d'Orsay, even against the background of ever-changing governments in Paris. It appears, however, that the trend of domestic and foreign affairs was adversely affected by the passage of the Bourgeois Cabinet. Hanotaux complained later of "the embarrassing legacy left for the Méline by the Bourgeois Cabinet which preceded it."[17]

In the young ministry of colonies the contrary was the case. During the first two years of the independent existence of this ministry almost half a dozen ministers presided over it in rather rapid succession.[18] This succession of ministers "like opera scenery" caused some public concern in Paris, because of its neutralizing effect on the new ministry at a time when there were many burning international colonial questions which needed urgent but careful attention. As one publicist put it:

> En outre, par ce temps des graves conflits extérieurs, le ministère des colonies est absorbé par des préoccupations politiques, par des litiges qui se règlent de concert avec le département des Affaires Etrangères. Il défendait son champ, il ne pouvait pas le cultiver.[19]

Another noteworthy development in France at this period was the ascendancy of the colonial group in the Chamber of Deputies and the established popularity of imperial expansion. Hundreds of societies dedicated to the colonial idea were established all over France, just as was the case in Germany.[20] Among these were the Comité d'Etude du Haut-Dahomé, founded in 1895 by Abel Delafosse and Jules Huré, and the Colonization Society of Alsatians and Lorrainians, led by Saudemont.[21] The Comité d'Etude du Haut-Dahomé asked for the "sympathy and encouragement of all those for whom colonial expansion was synonymous with national grandeur and patriotism." They argued that the principle of division of labor applied even in colonial policy. Therefore, they picked one colony—Dahomé, as they preferred to spell it—and wished to do with it what they would wish done to all other French colonies. It was time, they believed, to pass from generalities to specifics.[22] Furthermore, it was necessary to act quickly because of the active competition of their British and German rivals. The efforts of their explorers and diplomats would be futile if they were not followed up and supported by private initiative, and France would once again be outstripped by its rivals.[23]

This private initiative was exemplified by the Alsatian and Lorrainian colonists who selected Dahomey as their field of action. They established their first colony at Lokossa in 1895 and formulated plans for agricultural settlements.[24] Saudemont drew attention to the fact that the life of colons was not comparable to that of troops in campaign and at war. This was done to disabuse those who were hesitant about joining the venture as a result of the hardships they read about in the accounts of the Dahomey war, which were abundant in Paris at this time. Other sites for colonies would be located at Allada, Whydah, and Wesse, he added, boasting that when he returned to Paris by January 1896 he would have his concessions in his pocket and "un plan bien arrêté au sujet de chacune de mes colonies." [25]

In keeping with the Delcassé circular of June 1894,[26] the various chambers of commerce were invited by André Lebon to join the Commerce du Conseil Supérieur des Colonies in 1896. This was a direct method of engaging these chambers of commerce in the colonial enterprise and thereby facilitating the entry of the private sector into colonial exploitation. For the first time, the chambers of commerce from Lille to Marseille and from Bordeaux to Le Havre became involved in the colonial enterprise in an organized manner.[27] In lecture halls, avid expansionists exhorted their audience to give unflinching support to France's colonial enterprise as exploiters—not as conquerors, for the conquests had been accomplished.

> Les idées coloniales ont fait leur chemin. Elles avaient une telle raison d'être qu'en dépit des obstacles qu'elles ont recontrés, elles ont su triompher. Je crois . . . que l'ére des grandes conquêtes est finie . . . la prise glorieuse de Madagascar l'a close. C'est maintenant de la mise en valeur qu'il s'agit.[28]

In the press, the inhabitants of Paris were adjured and admonished to take a leaf from London, Berlin, Hamburg, Amsterdam, and other cities and form effective organs of colonization. France's colonial domain had, since 1870, grown to eight times her continental size and from 5 million to 40 million subjects and protected persons. But the exploitation of this vast patrimony had not kept pace with its growth. Paris, it was urged, should preoccupy itself with this problem of capital importance, because "La colonisation, c'est le *struggle for life;* il y a donc forcément une sélection. Elle se fait d'elle-même. À celui qui a essuyé les platres succède un plus vaillant ou un plus habile qui réussit et grandit." [29] Finally, the change of ambassadors during this period affected in no small way relations between the great European powers. After the departure of Waddington in 1892, the French Embassy in London was not graced with any ambassador capable of exerting considerable influence on the British government until the appointment of Baron Alphonse Chodron de Courcel [30] in December 1894. On the other hand, Lord Dufferin retired as British ambassador to France in October 1896 and was succeeded by Sir Edmund John Monson, who was warmly received in Paris as an Englishman who understood the French.[31] In October 1895 Sir Edward Malet resigned as British ambassador to Berlin after forty years in the public service, the last eleven of which were spent at Berlin.[32] These major diplomatic changes were among the factors which influenced the relations between Britain, France, and Germany in this period. The services of these solid ambassadors were essential in dealing with the west African colonial problems, among others,[33] which were at times accentuated by the actions of zealous proconsuls and explorers on the spot. To these we shall now turn.

French Expeditions and Occupation of the Hinterland, 1895–97

Governor Ballot had suggested the indefinite adjournment of the Anglo-French talks on the northward extension of the Lagos-Dahomey boundary in order to gain time. He wanted to execute the several expeditions which he had planned for the hinterland, and the appointment of a boundary commission in the area would impede his program of expansion to the advantage of Britain and Germany, both of whom, he argued, had plans to cut France off from the navigable Middle Niger. Consequently, the expeditions which he launched in late 1894 were resumed in January 1895 from Carnotville, the base of operations, but this time with a difference in the objectives. These new series of expeditions were not only to collect treaties but to establish posts of occupation as indubitable evidence of French rights over the territories traversed by them. Ballot had boldly inaugurated the "effective occupation" of the hinterland.[34] The trails of French expeditions were marked by military posts of a garrison and a resident and the *Tricolore* fluttering in the African sun.[35] Naturally, Nikki was the starting point of this new policy, because of the controversy over Lugard's treaty there.[36] The tactic of effective occupation was believed by Hanotaux to be a great aid to success in diplomatic negotiations concerning disputed territories;[37] he had long considered answering occupation with occupation. In April 1895 he declared in the French senate that the government had sanctioned effective occupation only to safeguard the rights of the French republic.[38] The Bourgeois Cabinet also continued the tactic of effective occupation, and the ministry of colonies instructed the acting governor of Dahomey in November 1895 "d'établir des postes à Bouay à Kandi, et à Ilo, dans la boucle du Niger, de mannière à occuper effectivement notre ligne d'accès au grand fleuve."[39] France, then, had begun to operate in the west African hinterland on the principle that "effective occupation" was much better than paper claims[40] in establishing title to a territory, especially a contested one. When Britain and Germany reacted to the French maneuver by establishing their own military posts of occupation, the "undignified scramble" for the Dahomey-Niger hinterland began full scale and soon attained a dangerous intensity, and war was only narrowly averted by the settlements of mid-July 1897 and June 1898.

Though Ballot nourished an animosity against Captain Decoeur, the exigencies of the time and situation dictated the continued employment of this officer for further expeditions into the hinterland. By January 1895 the Dahomey-Niger hinterland was swarming with seven French expeditions launched by Ballot.[41]

Commandant Decoeur and Baud were instructed to explore "tout l'arrière-pays jusqu'au Niger" as their mission left Carnotville in December 1894.[42] They marched through Ouari, Ouangara, Birni, and Kouande and arrived at Makka on 31 December 1894, which Decoeur described as a hub of commercial routes. At Birni, Decoeur learned that the German expedition under Kling had left without making any treaties and was in the area. This news was an eye-opener about German objectives in the hinterland.[43] Decoeur therefore decided to subdivide his expedition. This initiative was taken in order to beat the Germans to the Niger and at the same time occupy the Mangu or Chakosi country in advance of the pushy Germans. Baud and Vergoz were to make a rapid march to the Niger with one group while Decoeur and his group headed first for Sansane-Mango and then to the Niger. Baud and his men traveled through Konkobiri, Kodjar, and Kiba and reached the Niger at Bikini, south of Say. From there they marched to Say toward the end of January 1895. On the other hand, Decoeur arrived at Sansane-Mango on 6 January 1895, where he discovered the treaty of friendship and commerce concluded between King Nanbema and G. E. Ferguson of the Gold Coast administration. Despite this, he exacted a treaty of protection from this potentate before he continued his march to Fada N'Gurma. At Pama, he ran into the German expedition under Carnap, who had just concluded a treaty with the chief of Pama in arabic text.[44] When the chief denied he had accepted German protection, Decoeur made a treaty with him on 14 January 1895 by which he placed his territory under French protection. Since Pama was a tributary of Fada N'Gurma, Decoeur headed for the latter city to obtain the ratification of the treaty with Pama and to secure French protection over Gurma.

Gurma (also spelled Gourma) was at this time in a deplorable political ferment. The former authority and great power of the king of Gurma was going downhill rapidly.[45] Chiefs who felt strong enough to do so broke away from the hegemony of Fada N'Gurma. Bilanga was the first to declare itself independent of King Bantchande of Gurma; Tigba and Toucouma followed. In the military effort to regain control over Toucouma, Bantchande's uncle and general was killed. This breakdown of law and order resulted in the occasonal pillaging of villages in Gurma. To these internal problems was added the threat of the troops of Ahmadu of Segu, who was on the run from the French forces in the Sudan. This was a most serious threat, because the Tokolor forces lived off the land by pillage and plunder on their eastward journey to Sokoto.[46]

Under these circumstances, King Bantchande was glad to welcome Decoeur and his military escort. It would be a boon to enlist the aid of the French against both Ahmadu and the recalcitrant local *bato*.[47] Bantchande was, therefore, predisposed to accept French protection, which he formally did by the treaty of 20 January 1895 concluded with Decoeur.[48] This treaty placed all Gurma under French protection. It embodied the central idea of Decoeur's argument against the treaty made by Carnap at Matiacouali and at Kankantchari, where he again met the German expedition. Decoeur protested against the hoisting of the German flag on the top of the chief's house. The two European agents decided to ascertain from the chief whether he recognized the sovereignty of the king of Gurma or whether he was independent. First he agreed that he recognized it, but on further explanation by Carnap's interpreter he expressed reservations, declaring that the king of Fada N'Gurma was supreme in that city but that he himself was sovereign in Kankantchari and that he was "stronger, richer and older."[49] This declaration emasculated Decoeur's contention. Carnap consequently suggested that the affair be decided by their home governments.[50] The French expedition then continued on its way to Say, where it arrived on 1 February 1895, a few days after Baud had concluded a treaty of friendship, commerce, and protection with Sultan Ahmadu of Say.[51] Though Baud arrived at Say only after diverse vicissitudes, he achieved the aim for which the expedition was subdivided at Makka; that is, he ensured French ascendancy at Say. Decoeur had acted as a decoy and had retarded the progress of Carnap's expedition to the Niger by their encounters at Pama and at Kankantchari. Thus Decoeur furthered his own objectives by intersecting the German mission—by design or by accident.[52] After a few days' sojourn at Say, Decoeur sailed down the Niger toward Ilo, while Baud went back to Kodjar to rejoin his group, who were there under Vermeersch. By the time he arrived at Kodjar he discovered, to his chagrin, that his post had been burnt and his men were nowhere to be found. He made a quick decision to rejoin Decoeur on the Niger but only overtook him at Bussa. The aim of the descent of the Niger by Decoeur was to ascertain the extent of the influence of the Royal Niger Company along the river and its right bank. To Decoeur's amazement it was only as far south as Léaba that he saw the first factory of the company under the management of David Ashford King, an African from Sierra Leone. From Léaba, Decoeur returned to Carnotville through Kayama, arriving on 20 March 1895 after about three months of treaty hunting.[53]

The Decoeur mission proved and declared that the authority of the Royal Niger Company was limited to the Lower Niger and could hardly be said to extend to Léaba. Furthermore, it underscored the fact that the territories on the right bank of the Niger were completely independent of both Sokoto and Gwandu and that Nikki and Bussa were separate political entities.

Decoeur and Vergoz headed for the coast, while Baud and Vermeersch were charged with another mission toward Kong to try to join up with the Monteil expedition operating against Samory in the area.[54] They were to cross the north of the Gold Coast and Togo and make treaties with native chiefs in such a manner as to limit the northern expansion of the Gold Coast and Togo. With these clear instructions from Ballot, Baud and Vermeersch set out from Carnotville on 26 March 1895. They passed through Kir-kri and Bafilo and arrived at Sansane-Mango on 12 April. Here Baud made the first payment to King Nanbema of the stipend stipulated in the treaty which this chief had made with Alby on 26 January. This was a very effective measure by the French agents, because it demonstrated that the French "piece of paper" meant something precious—money payments—and that this group of Europeans could be trusted more than the others.[55]

The expedition went on through Gambaga to Walwale, from where they followed Binger's route of 1888 to Wa. At Wa the treaty made by the king with Ferguson was in evidence, but Baud exacted another treaty of protection from this ruler and marched on to Bona, whose king had earlier refused passage to Lieutenant Braulot. Since the right bank of the River Comoe and the Djimini country were under Samory's control, the expedition decided to go down the left bank of the Comoe through Bondoukou to Grand Bassam. They arrived there on 12 June 1895. Though they had linked Dahomey and Ivory Coast, they were unable to create a line of posts through Kong.[56]

Operating simultaneously in the hinterland with the Decoeur-Baud expeditions were those led by Alby, Deville, Mounier, Toutée, and Ballot himself. Mounier was assigned to the Kodokoli region to the northwest of Carnotville; Deville was sent to Bouay on the northeast of Carnotville. By the treaties of 24 February and 9 March 1895, respectively, these areas were placed under French protection.[57] Posts of effective occupation were established at Parakou, Ouari, Bassila, and Schori. Jules Molex was nominated resident of France for Schabe and western Borgou on 17 February.[58] By these measures Governor Ballot intended to secure the rear of the many expeditions operating farther in the interior and prevent their being cut off from the Carnotville base by armed uprising of the unpredictable Bariba.

Alby left Carnotville on 15 January for Mossi. He was instructed to go on to Wagadugu so as to counterbalance the efforts of the British from the Gold Coast. Alby was charged "d'amener le Naba du Mossi à faire alliance" with France. He traveled by way of Ouangara and Kouandé to Sansane-Mango. Here he made a treaty on 28 January with Nanbema, by which all Nanbema's territory was placed under French protection in return for a guaranteed annual salary. Alby's expedition continued northward to Djebiga and thence to Boussourima, on the outskirts of Wagadugu. From this unpretentious village he got into contact with the court of Wagadugu. The Naba refused him entry into the capital, so he returned to Carnotville by way of Pama, Konkobiri, and Kouandé.[59] Alby failed to link Dahomey with Mossi, but his return journey was a desirable complement to the work of Decoeur to the south of Gurma.

Governor Ballot himself contributed equally to the task of assuring French predominance over the Bariba country. After dispatching all the expeditions, he marched off to Nikki and to the Niger with his own escort in order to see things for himself and to ascertain the exact extent of British authority in the coveted hinterland of Dahomey.[60]

> J'ai résolus d'atteindre le Niger par Nikki, en traversant le Bourgou de l'ouest à l'est, afin de m'assurer, par moimême, si, comme l'affirmaient MM Decoeur et Alby, Nikki n'était lié par aucun traité avec l'Angleterre: ce dont je doutais, étant donné que la mission anglais, signalé à Nikki au mois de novembre dernier, ne devait vraisemblablement avoir

d'autre objectif que de placer le Borgou sous le protectorat britannique. Je importait également de savoir si réellement, comme l'affirmait Lord Aberdare, la Royal Niger Company avait des traités avec Boussa et Gomba, et quelle était la valuer de ces conventions, ou bien si ces régions n'étaient pas plus sous le protectorat anglais que le Sokoto, le Gando, l'Adamaoua et le Bornou.[61]

To his great delight Ballot discovered at Nikki that Lugard had made his treaty with the leader of the Moslems and not with the king of Nikki, who alone had the right to execute such a diplomatic instrument. Above all, the Moslem leader in question had no mandate to represent the king. On the contrary, the treaties made by Decoeur and Alby were both signed with the king, Siré Torou, himself; they were therefore reliable guarantees of French rights over Nikki.[62] As a further bulwark of the French claim of Nikki, Ballot secured a declaration from the king to the effect that he was not under British protection and that he accepted French protection. The Moslem leaders who dealt with Lugard were castigated for arrogating to themselves powers that belonged exclusively to the sovereign or his duly appointed representatives.[63]

The next stage of Ballot's journey was to Bussa, where he arrived on 29 January 1895. He recognized that the Royal Niger Company had prior treaty rights in Bussa by the treaties of 10 November 1885 and 20 January 1890, respectively. But, to his dismay, the company exercised no authority over the king of Bussa, who regarded the European "pieces of paper" as mere fantasy and still carried on the extortion of foreigners and the pillaging of Hausa caravans.[64]

Considerations such as these made Ballot underscore the fact that he did not fire a shot on his expedition,

> malgré l'énvie terrible que j'avais de donner une sanglante leçon à ces bandits, et leur faire faire connaissance avec la puissance des nos armes qu'ils semblent ignorer. . . . Je m'étais promis en partant de Porto Novo, d'atteindre le Niger avant le fin de Janvier et sans tirer un coup de fusil. C'est ce que j'ai fait.[65]

It appears that Ballot wanted to ingratiate himself with more members of the colonial group by repeating the pacific nature of his expedition. Had not François Deloncle praised Binger in the chamber not long ago for having accomplished his great mission of 1888–89 without recourse to arms? And had not the French government rewarded him openly with the governorship of the Ivory Coast?[66] Soon after organizing these expeditions, Ballot was promoted to governor second class.[67] Delcassé wired him this good news: "Très satisfait de votre zèle et les mesures prises pour n'être pas dévancé. Viens de signer votre promotion à deuxième classe."

Ballot's dramatic filibustering expedition to Nikki and Bussa had more far-reaching effects in the Anglo-French competition for Borgu than all the other French expeditions to this region. He established beyond doubt that Nikki and Bussa were separate and independent kingdoms in the Bariba or Borgu complex (see chap. 1 on the kingdoms of the hinterland, pp. 7–17). Therefore, a treaty of protection with the king of Bussa could not give any title whatsoever to Nikki, and vice-versa. Ballot thus deflated the claims of the Royal Niger Company over Nikki by virtue of their treaties with Bussa in 1885 and 1890. Second, the company had never had the will or the boldness to make good its title to Bussa by some form of effective control of the king, whose conduct and attitude to foreign traders, in Ballot's opinion, left much to be desired. Consequently, Ballot was convinced that effective occupation ought to constitute the right of sovereignty over any territory. He was further confirmed in this belief after surveying the Oly tributary of the Niger, which drained central Borgu. Third, the realities of the situation led the governor to conclude that France still had the opportunity to expand toward the Niger.

> Tout espoir de conserver notre hinterland n'est donc pas perdu. Il est vrai que l'inaction du Commandant Decoeur a compromis notre situation, mais, j'éstime qu'elle n'est désésperée, si toutfois, l'on veut bien adopter ma manière de voir, qui du reste, est conforme à la vérité: C'est-à-dire, la division du Borgou en trois royaumes indépendants.[68]

Ballot returned to Carnotville through Kayama. He finally got back to Porto Novo on 16 March 1895.[69]

The most controversial of all the expeditions lanuched by Ballot during this period was that of Captain G. Toutée. Right from its inception to the time Toutée was recalled to France, this expedition raised several diplomatic difficulties between Britain and France. It had little of that success which Governor Binger, "un ami pour tous ceux que tente l'Afrique," toasted it over champagne when Toutée stopped over at Grand Bassam on his way to Cotonou.[70] Just as Mizon had harried the Royal Niger Company on the east in 1890–93, so Toutée did on the west in 1895, and some of the problems he raised were not solved until the Anglo-French settlement of 1898.

The Comité d'Afrique Français, which sponsored Toutée's expedition, was chagrined at the refusal of the Royal Niger Company to allow the expedition to go through the Niger delta up the river.[71] Undaunted by this setback, they recast Toutée's instructions, specifying a land journey through Dahomey to 9° North Latitude and then eastward to the Niger, which he was to navigate as far as possible toward Timbuktu.[72] By the time final arrangements were completed in Cotonou concerning logistics and other necessities, Toutée learned that it would be impossible for him to sail up the Wheme to Sagon as planned because of the subsidence of the water level. He traveled by the land route through Abome-Calavi and Allada to Abomey, where he was warmly received by King Agoliagbo, who also gladly provided him with the service of a *récadère* to conduct him and his escort to Zagnanado.[73] In this case the *récade* was "une baguette de 50 centimetres de long avec bec de cane argenté." Toutée remarked: "Ce baton est un symbole représentant le roi lui-même, et sa personne est censée être presenté là où est present son baton. C'est là un usage général dans les pays dahoméens, mahis, ou nagos." [74]

The expedition traveled on from Abomey to Paouignan, where much curiosity and suspicion was raised by its presence. But after Mahmadou, the interpreter, had explained to the people that the column had not come to make war or raid for slaves, the attitude of the local population toward it became sympathetic. The affirmation that the mission would pay for all that it asked for in the way of food and that the leaders of the expedition were "relatives of those who destroyed the kingdom of Dahomey" increased the warmth of the reception accorded to Toutée and his men by the Mahis of Paouignan.[75] The local chief exchanged gifts with Toutée and apologized for his poverty, which was a result of ravages by Dahomey. At Save, Chief Achemu welcomed the expedition with open arms. He expressed his gratitude to the French for having delivered the Mahi from the Dahomean nightmare and asked that the same service be rendered to them with reference to the Bariba, whose terror perpetually hung over the Mahi. He provided carriers for the journey to Tchaourou as well as a *récadère* and gave Toutée precise information on the distance and direction of Tchaki from Tchaourou. Achemu said that the king of Tchaki was his friend. The inquisitive Chief Achemu wanted to know the position of Toffa of Porto Novo under the French, especially whether the new rulers had interfered with Toffa's household. Toutée told him he had seen the seventy-fifth son of Toffa. This reply allayed Achemu's fears about the intolerant nature of European monogamy, because he had many wives.[76]

After having gained the confidence of Chief Achemu, Toutée marched on to Tchaourou, just south of 9° North Latitude, the limit of the Lagos–Porto Novo frontier. He arrived there on 22 January 1895. From Tchaourou Toutée marched directly eastward to Kouboure. It was at this point that the expedition swerved southward to Tchaki, where Toutée made a treaty with the local ruler Chief Ajani and established a post under the charge of Lieutenant de Pas, whom he named French resident of Tchaki.[77]

Toutée met some opposition when he proposed a treaty of protection with the ill and moribund Chief Ajani of Tchaki, both from the chief's head wife and from an ambassador from Oyo who had come to seek the aid of the people of Tchaki for a proposed conflict with the British in Oyo. Kuffo, the delegate from Oyo, remarked that entering into treaty relations with the whites was always the genesis of a multitude of problems. Toutée countered by asserting that relations with Europeans could be on two models, as illustrated by Toffa and Béhanzin. When he asked Bagui, the chief minister of the court of Tchaki, which he preferred, Bagui opted for the Toffa-type relationship.[78] Toutée thus got his way, not only by the many gifts he gave to Chief Ajani but also by coercion and persuasion.

From Tchaki the route of the French expedition curved northward once again through Etchepetei and Bogo, both of which were well below 9° North Latitude, and, like Tchaki, well in the British sphere. The expedition continued due north to Kishi, where Toutée concluded a treaty of protection with Chief Folaouigo, an old man with paralyzed and atrophied legs. No post was created here, but Toutée promised to establish one eventually. Kayama, which was due north of Kishi, was the next large population center where Toutée and his men stopped on their way to the Niger. King Kemura of Kayama did not wish to receive the French expedition. Consequently, Toutée was obliged to spend a night in the village of Banikani on the outskirts of Kayama, while Kemura prepared for the arrival of these intrepid intruders. When Toutée arrived in Kayama the next day he had a rather squalid and prolix conference with King Kemura, whose trumpeters blasted shrill notes to hush their French guest at his first attempt to respond to the king's opening speech. Toutée retaliated. In the end, Kemura agreed to enter into treaty relations with France. He stated that the king of Nikki was his father and that he knew that Sire Torou had accepted "the flag of the whites from Abomey." The treaty was signed with pomp and ceremony.[79]

The French expedition continued on to the Niger; they reached it opposite Badjibo on 13 February 1895.[80] The next day Toutée was visited by Chief Asuma of Badjibo, with whom he entered into friendly relations. Toutée selected a high ground about 500 meters from the Niger for the construction of a post on a rectangular plot 100 meters long and 60 meters wide. He called this post Fort d'Arenberg: "J'ai donné à notre installation ici le nom d'Arenberg me rappelant l'insistance avec laquelle le président du Groupe colonial me demandait d'atteindre le Niger au-dessous de Boussa." [81]

From this post Toutée sailed down the Niger as far south as Jebba, where he said he saw the first agency of the Royal Niger Company, which was under the direction of a certain William from Abeokuta and whose attitude to the French explorers was one of hostility. After this preliminary exercise, Toutée prepared for his important hydrographic mission up the Niger.[82] In the course of this feat, which took him through Bussa, Gwando, Yaouri, Dendi, Gurma, and into the turbulent Touareg country, his party suffered fourteen shipwrecks costing them twelve lives.[83] In the Touareg country he intervened in the civil war against Ahmadu Ali Buri at Kompa. Toutée's armed intervention was beneficial to the relations between France and the inhabitants of this area. Toutée returned to Fort d'Arenberg and sailed down the Niger to the sea at Forcados, from where he returned to Porto Novo via Lagos before he went back to Paris. The storm over the posts he created in what was regarded as British territory led to his recall to France.[84]

Though Hanotaux formally sanctioned the recall of Toutée, he informed the British officials in Paris that France reserved the right to evoke the treaties made by this officer, whose mission was unofficial, in the course of any negotiations involving the respective rights of Britain and France in corps in Paris[86] coupled with indirect pressure through the British press and the House of Commons[87] resulted in the acquiescence of the French government to the withdrawal of the posts created by Toutée at Tchaki and Fort d'Arenberg. Goldie threatened to use force to expel the French from the post on the Niger, because its continued presence there seemed to suggest its permanence.[88] The post at Tchaki was withdrawn on 23 February, because the observations taken by Lieutenant Targe showed that Tchaki was situated at about 8°30′ North Latitude and was therefore in British territory, according to the agreement of August 1889. The ministry of colonies, on

Ballot's advice, agreed with Hanotaux that Tchaki was "incontestably within the British sphere of influence."[89]

The post of Fort d'Arenberg was not so readily evacuated by the French, because Hanotaux wished to retain it for use as a pawn in future negotiations with England for a definitive settlement of the territorial questions concerning the Niger bend. But Chautemps, the colonial minister, argued cogently against the maintenance of Fort d'Arenberg, "établi sur les bords du Niger, en face d'une station anglaise, *et entre deux postes également anglais,* d'après les données fournies par M. le Lieutenant Targe."[90] He underscored the immense difficulties that the provisioning of this post would present in the face of mounting British protest, as well as the diplomatic complications that might arise from its maintenance, asking for Hanotaux's views on the matter. When the Quai d'Orsay continued to prevaricate, Chautemps drafted another letter for Hanotaux on French withdrawal from Fort d'Arenberg, but this letter was never forwarded because the French council of ministers decided to evacuate the post.[91] Instructions were issued to Governor Ballot for the evacuation of Fort d'Arenberg, and the French withdrew in September 1895.[92] The Royal Niger Company pressed home this diplomatic victory by Britain by rechristening the evacuated French post Fort Goldie.[93] But this did not dispel the French desire for a foothold on the navigable Middle Niger.

The German Togo Hinterland Expedition

The French did not have the field to themselves. The German expedition into the hinterland of Togo operated alongside the French missions. Though the German government stated that the expedition under Gruner had no instructions to go to the Niger,[94] the German Colonial Society, which was the main sponsor of the expedition, instructed Gruner to reach the Niger, and the German foreign minister, Kayser, later admitted that Germany wanted access to the Niger through the hinterland of Togo.[95] Even if they were not expressly instructed to make treaties and to go as far as the Niger, Kayser continued, they would do what they could to advance German interests. The German government did not issue express instructions to Karl Peters, Wissman, nor Stetten to make treaties, but these explorers made treaties all the same, and so would Gruner and Carnap.

What was the hinterland of Togo, and what was the German definition of this hinterland? The answer of the German Colonial Department was that "the hinterland of Togo was an elastic and vague term."[96] Marschall even protested that the Royal Niger Company had made treaties in the hinterland of Togo, but he was reassured by Gosselin that the Niger Company made no treaties with the chiefs in the Togo hinterland and that the British government had "consistently shown a desire not to encroach on the Togo hinterland." [97] This lack of precise knowledge of the coveted region was not confined to official circles alone. The *Norddeutsche Allgemeine Zeitung*, in a progress report on the German expedition, declared that Gruner's party spent Christmas at Yendi in the Neutral Zone and planned to take a "northeasterly direction to Sansane-Mango in Borgu." [98] Thus all the territory between the Niger to the east and the Volta to the west lying above 9° North Latitude was loosely called Borgu or included in the German-invented Tschantoland.

In any case, both the German government and the German Colonial Society desired access to the Niger through the north of Togo. The German Foreign Office was prepared to hand the Neutral Zone over to Britain if her wish to extend her possession of Togo to the Niger were granted by England.[99] Kayser said that, from Kaiser William II down to the people, German opinion was aggrieved by the antagonistic attitude of Britain toward Germany's colonial efforts. Despite this, Germany was prepared "to come into conference with maps and rulers and pencils" to settle these matters. Kayser continued:

> But a conference means concessions on both sides; it would not do for England to say that you can't have Samoa for fear of offending New Zealand, nor access to the Niger on account of our Borgu Protectorate. I feel sure it would be in the interest of good relations of both parties were all these causes of misunderstandings and colonial jealousies once for all removed. . . . I can truly say that Germany would be satisfied with a tithe of the concessions which England would have to make before ever she can hope to be on good terms with France in Africa, Asia or elsewhere.[100]

The German expansionists wanted access to the Niger. One of their most militant and vociferous organs, the *Kolnische Zeitung*, accused France of considering Borgu land as "the sole and natural Hinterland of Dahomey," forgetting that it was equally the hinterland of Togo and of Lagos and that it was in the urgent interest of all three colonies to extend themselves to the navigable Niger. After all, Borgu had first been visited by Wolf and Kling, both of whom were Germans. Therefore, Germany could not be excluded from the navigable Niger.[101] A militant forward policy was urged by the

German press. When the German government contradicted Gottlob Adolf Krause's story that the Neutral Zone had been declared a British protectorate by Ferguson, Kayser got himself "into no little hot water" with the colonial enthusiasts.[102] Kayser's attackers included, surprisingly, the *Vossische Zeitung,* an organ which consistently advocated a moderate policy in colonial affairs. It accused Kayser of soft-pedalling and being subservient to English interests in Africa.[103] This accusation was not justified because Kayser and Hatzfeldt had been trying to wrest concessions from England without success. "England grudges us every scrap of territory," complained Kayser. "What we have has been acquired against her will, and she is ever ready to oppose our influence and expansion all the colonial world over."[104]

As these fine points of policy and diplomacy were debated in Berlin, Gruner, Carnap, and Doering were doing the rough work in the Togo hinterland. The expedition began with a bang. The chief fetish priest of Krachi Dente and his assistant were arrested at Nkumi. This priest, Busumfu, and Okra, his assistant, were taken to Krachi and after a summary trial shot by the German authorities on 25 November 1894, ostensibly for plunder and extortion. The local population was said to have been thankful to Gruner for this strong-arm measure.[105] The Germans hoped to show by this execution that they were no less to be reckoned with than the French conquerors of Dahomey or the British who reduced Ashanti. As Governor Griffith of the Gold Coast saw it, the Germans "wanted to invest themselves with a certain amount of prestige upon entering their new station at Krachi,"[106] and there can be little doubt that the execution of the most revered priest of the oracle town of Krachi by the Germans lent them respectability among the local population.

From Kete Krachi the German expedition marched on to Sansane-Mango, where they arrived on 10 January 1895. Gruner and the greater part of the expedition stayed on to conclude treaties with King Nanbema and to secure the rear, while Carnap led the avant-garde of the expedition into Gurma. He made treaties at Pama, Matiacuali, and Kankantenari. The French expedition under Decoeur was in the same area at the same time as Carnap and his men, and naturally a dispute arose over German rights to make treaties in Gurma.[107] Decoeur objected to the hoisting of the German flag at Kankantenari and to the treaty made by Carnap with the chief. He maintained that France had exclusive rights over Gurma because of his prior treaty with the king of Fada N'Gurma. After referring the matter to the chief of Kankantenari, who disclaimed vassalage to Fada N'Gurma, Carnap prevailed on the zealous Decoeur to accept the proposal that the affair be decided by their home governments. After this encounter the two expeditions, rather hostile to each other, parted ways, though both had Say as their destination.[108]

The rear guard of the German expedition under Gruner and Doering marched on from Sansane-Mango[109] to Kankantenari on its way to Say, where it was reunited with Carnap's group.[110] From Say they descended the Niger. Gruner went on to Gwandu, where he concluded a treaty with the Emir. They had to fight off an attack at Bikini, and smallpox broke out among them. Carnap took the sick with him and arrived at Akassa on 5 May 1895; Gruner led the other portion of the expedition through Borgu to Kete Krachi, from where they returned to Misahohe.[111] From now on German expansionists were to claim access to the Niger through the territories traversed by their Togo hinterland expedition.

Britain Tries to Contain French and German Expansionism

All hope of linking the hinterland of Lagos with that of the Gold Coast fizzled out when Lugard retreated from Nikki in the face of Bariba hostility and poisoned arrows.[112] Ferguson, who was engaged in securing the hinterland of the Gold Coast by treaties, returned to the coast in February 1895.[113] Therefore by early 1895 Britain was out of the "race between England, Germany and France which shall reach the coveted land," as Kayser described the competition in October 1894.[114] Although Britain had no expeditions marching up and down the Dahomey-Niger hinterland at this time, her interest in the area was very much alive. She tried to accomplish by shrewd diplomacy what France and Germany were attempting on the spot—to secure as much of this territory as possible for the Gold Coast, Lagos, and the Niger Company.

Unfortunately, rivalry and jealousy between the Royal Niger Company and the Lagos administration[115] hampered concerted action by British agents and left the French unchallenged in their practical efforts to acquire the lion's share of the Niger basin behind Dahomey. Also, both Lagos and the Royal Niger Company had disputes with the administration of the Niger Coast protectorate about the extent of their respective jurisdictions over the Benin-Ondo region and over Ilorin. Early in 1896, Governor Carter envisaged a punitive expedition against Ilorin and its gangs of robbers and bandits. He was of the opinion that Ibadan warriors would gladly participate in such an expedition, which to them would be "a labour of love."[116]

In the Colonial Office it was thought that Lagos would gain access to the Niger by a conquest of Ilorin, and this would be a blow to the monopolistic practices of the Royal Niger Company.[117] But the Niger Company would not brook any intervention by Lagos in the affairs of Ilorin, which it claimed was an integral part of Sokoto-Gwandu.[118] Carter, however, insisted that Ilorin was Yoruba, even though some of its inhabitants were Moslems.[119] Before Carter could act, Goldie quickly moved against Ilorin, pacified it, and also conquered Nupe. Thus instead of cooperating to stem the French onslaught in the Borgu-Gurma region, British agents were intensely divided and absorbed in the partition of spheres between themselves in areas where British predominance was never in question.

Another factor which contributed to the apparent impotence of the Royal Niger Company[120] against French and German expansionism was its preoccupation with the Akassa affair. The raid and sacking of the company's establishments at Akassa by Brassmen, who were exasperated by the Niger Company's monopolistic practices and the unpleasant economic consequences these had on the local population, forced the company to concentrate its constabulary in the Niger delta for preventive and punitive purposes.[121] Thus with the forces of the Niger Company spread out by necessity, with inter-British rivalry between the Niger Company and Lagos, and with the resultant disunity of purpose and lack of cooperation, the guardians of British interests on the spot were militarily weak and unable to check the advance of Germany and France into what had hitherto been regarded as a British sphere of influence by virtue of prior treaties. Consequently, England resorted to diplomacy; she tried to reach an agreement with both Germany and France with reference to their various spheres in the coveted Niger territories. This was a formidable task, because the value of treaties concluded with African chiefs was seriously questioned by Germany as well as by France, who now preferred effective occupation as the criterion for any claim of title to any territory.[122]

> The days of academical African treaties, such as were concluded up to 1890, are past; to have any effect, the Power must have a solid position in the regions in dispute. All appeals to older treaties (affecting territories) with undefined frontiers are of no avail. This is the moment for action.[123]

Earlier Britain had approached Germany for the partition of the Neutral Zone. But the Germans thought the time inopportune, for domestic and external reasons. First of all, Puttkamer of Togo was "shipwrecked and ill" and could not supervise the work of the proposed Anglo-German commission. Another impediment was the rainy season, which would render the work of the commission pernicious. Above all, French success in Dahomey "would necessarily entail an extension of French influence northwards and this was a matter which could not be left out of sight in fixing the limits of the spheres of interest of the three countries in those parts," argued Kayser.[124] When Germany declined to cooperate in the partition of the Neutral Zone, Britain decided to send an officer into this zone to make treaties which would protect Britain's interests "just as Germany's was protected, binding the chiefs not to make treaties with any other Power or to accept the protection of such a Power." [125]

Kimberley decided on this measure because he feared that "Monteil convinced Kayser during his stay in Berlin that British and German interests in those regions [West Africa] are not identical." [126] Kimberley's sharp and perspicacious judgment on this occasion was accurate, for shortly afterward Kayser told Gosselin that France and Germany could cooperate in Africa irrespective of their differences in Europe. With characteristic Prussian realism he remarked: "Who will give us most on the Gold Coast—France or England? This is the question we have to bear in mind." [127] This point of view was again emphasized in what Gosselin described as Kayser's favorite axiom: "There are but three Powers in Africa—England, France and Germany—two of which must inevitably combine against the third." [128] Thinking that he had softened British officials enough by the threat of a hostile Franco-German coalition against Britain in African affairs,[129] Kayser then asked that all the coastline east of the mouth of the Volta be ceded to Germany. If England agreed to this proposal, "Germany would agree to anything England wished with regard to the Neutral Zone and Tschantoland." This would be an effective way of checking French designs on Borgu, continued Kayser, for if matters were allowed to take their course, France would acquire most of Borgu.[130]

Acting on information received from the Gold Coast,[131] the Colonial Office objected to the cession to Germany of the trans-Volta territory, which was an important part of the Gold Coast Colony, "in order to secure the Niger Company in the possession of Borgu, the importance of which to trade there was no means of gauging." The Foreign Office concurred and stressed the fact that "no proposal of the kind would be entertained" by it.[132] To convince Germany that it would make no concessions for what she asked, copies of the British treaties with Bussa were sent to Berlin.[133] These did not impress the German foreign minister, who stressed the question of effective occupation and the position of inland territories with reference to the littoral region already occupied. Marschall added that the readiness with which African chiefs signed treaties with visiting Europeans rendered such treaties questionable.[134] Already the expansionists in Germany were declaring the Niger territories *herrenlos,* adding that the struggle for the conquest of these lands had begun and predicting a repetition of the Cholet-Brazza drama of 1890–91.[135]

As it became clear that England would not cede the seaboard east of the Volta in exchange for Borgu, Germany offered Britain the Neutral Zone in exchange for access through northern Togo to the navigable Niger.[136] At this juncture Goldie's services were enlisted in the negotiations with Germany[137] in the vain hope of an early agreement which would leave France the odd man out, as was the case in 1893, when she was excluded from the Benue basin by the Anglo-German agreement of 15 November. There was no willingness on the part of London to concede to Germany access to the Niger. Instead, a joint commission to the Neutral Zone was proposed to Germany to allay her fears that Ferguson had established British hegemony over the zone.[138] Kimberley communicated to Hatzfeldt a memorandum containing the bases for an agreement on the Togo hinterland, in which the German proposals were not embodied. These British proposals did not, therefore, meet the Germans even halfway, and the Germans commented that they wanted access to the Niger as well as the rich trans-Volta region.[139] The Colonial Office was not pleased with the anti-British proceedings of the Germans in the Togo hinterland[140] and were therefore not as sympathetic to Berlin as was the Foreign Office. Hemming even accused Germany of bad faith in the affair.[141] But the Germans would not give up their demands. They renewed their protests about Ferguson's mission to the Neutral Zone[142] but could not make England budge, and the negotiations were suspended without their achieving their aim.[143]

What emerged from these negotiations was that Germany was not enthusiastic to expand toward the northwest of Togo but rather desired a northeasterly expansion which would link her Togo possessions with the Niger. Therefore, she did not care very much about the Neutral Zone, with its important market town of Salaga, as was demonstrated by the fact that at every step she was prepared to pawn her rights to the zone for what was considered a more profitable acquisition of territory either in the trans-Volta region or toward the Middle Niger.

Negotiations with France

For England, France was a more fastidious neighbor to deal with than Germany, as Kayser rightly pointed out (see p. 185 below). The difficulties between the two powers had grown more complex with time, involving not only the practical question of posts in Borgu or the debate over the principles of the navigation of the Niger[144] but the more alarming differences in the interpretations of the Say-Barruwa Line of 1890. France claimed the right to expand her sphere of influence south of this line, but Britain maintained that France was excluded from all territory south of the line. Then France tried to backtrack from the 1890 agreement. Monteil had told the German Colonial Department in 1894 that Sokoto was "within the sphere of their [France's] further operations."[145] This attitude was clearly against the letter of the Anglo-French agreement of 1890, which left to the Niger Company all that fairly belonged to Sokoto. Furthermore, the proceedings of Toutée and D'Agoult—the commandant of the *Ardent,* which ran aground on the Niger in 1895[146]—demonstrated the determination of the French to acquire part of the navigable Middle Niger and probably part of the Sokoto-Gwandu region. The recall of Toutée[147] and the refloating of the *Ardent* contributed little to Anglo-French understanding in the Niger territories, though these actions paved the way to the abortive negotiations of the spring of 1896.

The questions of the evacuation of the posts established by Toutée and the imperious attitude of the Niger Company toward the grounded *Ardent* and its crew rekindled anti-British outbursts from French expansionists.[148] Britain wished to prevent France from extending her possessions from Dahomey to the Niger, exclaimed *La Politique Coloniale,* but Britain's protests lacked foundation. It concluded reassuringly: "Aussi rien n'empechera l'oeuvre de nos officiers, de nos explorateurs, de subsister avec toutes ses conséquences légitimes, et toutes les rodomontades du *Times,* du Capitaine Lugard et de la Compagnie du Niger ne prevaudront pas contre elle."[149] This newspaper seemed to be speaking for the local administration in Dahomey as well as for the officials of the French government, because the intransigeance they evinced during the negotiations with Britain early in 1896 was mirrored in the views expressed by *La Politique Coloniale.*

Even the effort made by *Le Figaro* to give to its readers the authentic views of Goldie by publishing an interview with him on the Niger question did not allay French fears. It rather aggravated the tension. Etienne's quick response was to berate "perfide Albion" and denounce Goldie's interpretation of the Say-Barruwa Line.[150]

At the official level in Paris, plans were being hatched for the occupation and domination of the Niger bend by France. This was the period of active planning and comparative inactivity on the spot, because the motive force of French penetration of the hinterland, Governor Ballot, was back in France on leave after an action-filled tour of duty in Porto Novo.[151] Any further forward policy had to await his return to Dahomey. In the meantime, he acted in an advisory capacity on matters affecting the Niger territories and the Lagos-Dahomey frontiers.[152] A memorandum was prepared on the hinterland of Dahomey,[153] dealing with the natural divisions of the Niger and the importance of this river on the African continent, the means of penetration into the territories of the Niger bend, the political implications of each of the five means of penetration, and the position of Dahomey vis-à-vis the routes enumerated. This memorandum was the blueprint for French action in the Niger territories and deserves detailed examination.

Five ways of getting to the territories of the Niger bend were enumerated. Two of these were recognized as impracticable, since one, the mouth of the Niger, was in the hands of the Royal Niger Company and the other, the Volta basin, was controlled jointly by Britain and Germany. Only three of the five natural routes to the Niger bend were open to the French: through Senegal, through the "ligne structural" of the Niger basin, and through the Comoe in the Ivory Coast. These three, however, would only lead to the upper section of the territories. Since the middle and eastern sections of the region were desired by France, the plan was stretched to embrace them.[154]

What was the position of Dahomey vis-à-vis the preceding ways of penetration into the territories of the Niger bend? "Dahomey is a narrow corridor and nothing but that. It has the conventional frontiers and does not yield to geographical divisions. It is located between the two natural means of penetration which are in the possession of rival European Powers." This means that in its development it will inevitably face very serious political obstacles. Despite this gloomy prospect, it must develop. "Donc, il ne peut rester comme il est, car il déviendrait une non-valeur et qui est contraire aux principes même d'une politique coloniale." The northward prolongation of Dahomey would lead directly to the Middle Niger at Say, which is at the eastern end of the Niger bend. But this would intersect the most important commercial route of the region which links the Sokoto area with Salaga, the point of convergence of the Volta basin.[155] This would enhance the value of Dahomey, it was believed, because Say was geographically and politically important. Located on the central meridian of the Dahomey corridor, Say could be easily reached without evoking protests from Britain or Germany and could be used as a new base of operations.¹⁵⁶ From Say, the center of the Niger bend would be easily attainable by sailing up the river or by the shortest land route westward to Wagadugu and thence to Segu, which is undisputedly under French control. Wagadugu occupies a central position in the bend and is also the market town for the central trade route of the Voltaic region. Though not yet French, Monteil visited Wagadugu, and Destenave attempted to reach it from the Sudan just as Alby did from Dahomey.

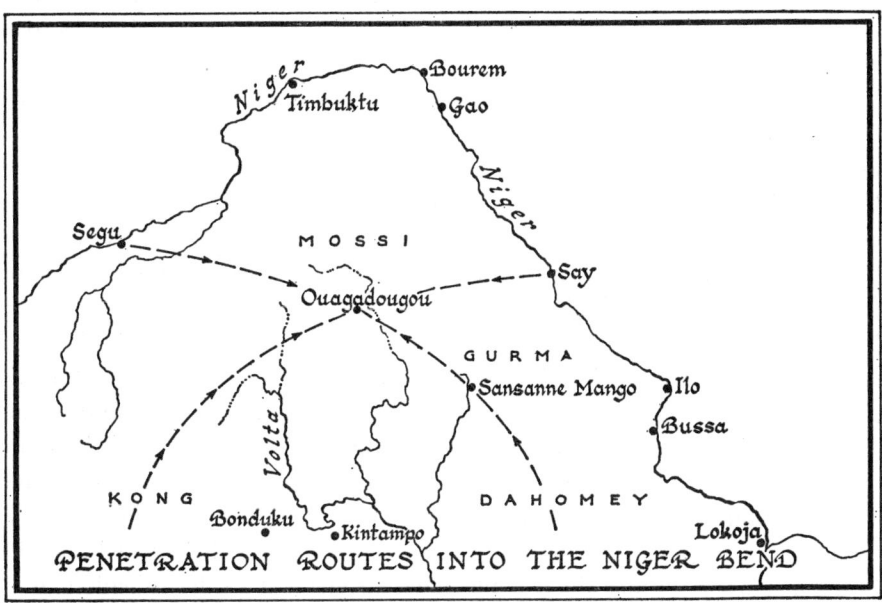

In conclusion, it was stated that France ought to occupy the regions which lead from the coast northward to Wagadugu. In practice this meant the territories extending from Kong to Segu to the west and the territories linking Dahomey to Gurma and Say in the east. Gurma might be contested with Germany, it was felt, but French chances were good there. Samory's presence in the region between Kong and Segu would also raise problems, since it was feared in Paris that Samory was a protégé or ally of Britain.¹⁵⁷ But these would not be insuperable.

In London in this period the Foreign Office took stock of the international situation in the Niger territories.¹⁵⁸ Anderson surveyed the development of the relations between Britain, Germany, and France in the Niger hinterland and underscored the points of difference between Britain and the other two powers. A factor common to both was Britain's determination to exclude them from the navigable Niger. Germany wanted access to a portion of the navigable Niger through a "roomy hinterland." If this were agreed to, argued Anderson, it would have meant "the deposition of Great Britain from her undivided power over the lower river, which was recognized at the Berlin Conference of 1885," and yet it would have been of no immediate benefit to Germany. Though Kimberley's proposal did not grant Germany any portion of the navigable Niger, it was self-denying indeed, because it left the whole Togo-Dahomey hinterland to Germany and France.[159] Both these powers could have been free to adjust, without British interference, their respective claims in this wide-open territory.

With reference to France, Anderson regretted that the Say-Bonduku line offered to Britain by Hanotaux in 1892 was not accepted before it was overtaken by the conquest of Dahomey, which altered French attitudes to the hitherto insignificant and unimportant protectorate of Porto Novo. "The governing idea at Paris has since been, by extending the Dahomey 'Hinterland,' to effect a junction with the regions of the *'boucle'* and to press Britain out of Borgu so as to obtain for France access and control over the Central Niger including the navigable waters below the Boussa Rapids," observed Anderson. This was in keeping with the French dream of a huge African empire from the Mediterranean to Senegal, from the Rivières du Sud to the Upper and Middle Niger, and, if possible, to the Lower Niger and the Gulf of Benin. "In the realization of this idea no fish is too small to be swept into the net; economic value is not gauged."[160] The expansion schemes of the three powers resulted in "the triangular duel" between their expeditions in 1894–95. This triangular duel would have an element of the ridiculous if it did not involve grave international complications, commented Anderson.

Britain learned from these developments that economic value and interests should be the deciding factors for future action in the area, not national prestige and dignity. Western Borgu, which Ballot described as a poor, unhealthy, and unproductive region,[161] should be left to France; so should Gurma, where Britain had no clear title. As a quid pro quo, recognition of the Say-Barruwa Line should be obtained from France, and Britain should keep Bussa and sufficient territory to "leave enough margin on the west of the Niger." The Union Jack should be hoisted at Bussa, with the Niger Company establishing posts on the right bank of the river as far as Bussa Rapids in order to "set effective occupation against non-recognition." In the Gold Coast the status quo should be maintained, and England would have to be prepared to face the consequences in case Germany decided to play the two-to-one game enunciated by Kayser. On no account should the seaboard east of the Volta mouth be ceded to Germany, because of the economic potential of the district around Keta and Denu. However, Wa and Mossi as well as Gurunsi could be left to France. On the other hand, Britain should obtain Dagomba and Gonja.[162]

Compared with the French, the English memorandum was less ambitious and less detailed. Underlying it was that satisfied feeling of the haves,[163] whereas its French counterpart was characterized by the active expansionism and detailed scheming of the have-nots. Britain was given to picking and choosing the choicest territories; France was preoccupied with acquiring as much territory as possible in the hope that the average economic value of all her acquisitions would be worth the effort. It is clear from the French memorandum that economic value was constantly borne in mind in the development of their plans, though Anderson thought this was not the case. It was for their commercial importance that Say, Wagadugu, and a portion of the navigable Niger were high in the French list of priorities concerning expansion in the Niger territories. It was not just for national prestige that France wanted to break the monopoly of the Niger Company on the Lower Niger; the economic potential of all these territories entered into her calculations. Against this background of plans and counterplans, Britain and France resumed negotiations for the regulation of their difficulties in the hinterland of Lagos and Dahomey.

From the records, it is clear that both sides knew exactly what they wanted. The period of "giving away mountains and lakes and rivers" had passed. Soldiers, explorers, and even administrators had increased the knowledge of most of the areas in dispute.[164] This new situation rendered compromise more difficult. A contemporary French observer stated the difficulties succinctly:

> Il ne s'agissait pas de l'embouchure du Niger que personne ne disputait aux Anglais, mais de son hinterland, de celui du Dahomey, des territoires touchant au Tchad et de notre droit, contesté par l'Angleterre, d'avoir un accès sur le Niger inférieur, au-dessous des premières cataractes.[165]

The failure of Britain to reach an agreement with Germany on west African questions in November 1895 [166] forced Britain to step up her efforts to prevent Kayser's two-to-one game from going against her. France could not be allowed to team up with Germany against England. The times were, however, not ripe for such an anti-British combination, because of the intense press war going on between France and Germany over the Togo-Dahomey hinterland. The dispute centered on rival claims to Sansane-Mango and Gurma as a result of Gruner's and Decoeur's expeditions and treaties.[167] Britain had tried in vain in the last few years to wash her hands clean of this area and to leave Germany and France to haggle and adjust their claims as best they could.

England utilized the talks about Siam to pave the way for the renewal of Anglo-French negotiations on those Niger territories which unfortunately were not delimited by the Phipps-Hanotaux effort, which had come to nothing in 1894. In article 5 of the Siam declaration of 15 January 1896, the British and French governments agreed to name commissioners to be charged with the settlement of the territorial questions in the region west of the Lower Niger.[168] However, before this contractual undertaking was agreed to, the ministry of colonies in Paris inquired into the position of France vis-à-vis Britain in the disputed territories. In a long memorandum, Camille Guy[169] surveyed the accomplishments of the various European expeditions into the Niger territories and concluded that France could enter into negotiations about these territories without fear because any arguments hurled against her could be easily refuted. France could win easy access to the Niger, he went on, as well as achieve uninterrupted communication between Dahomey and Ivory Coast.[170]

With the conviction that they would be negotiating from strength, the French government showed an urgent willingness to negotiate. Salisbury restrained them by the plea of Chamberlain's absence from London.[171] In any case, Berthelot asked the ministry of colonies to nominate the official who would represent France at the proposed talks,[172] after Courcel reported that it was desirable to have the work of the commission begun without delay because Sir A. W. L. Hemming, one of the British commissioners, did not have much time before leaving for British Guiana.[173] Commissioners for both powers were accordingly appointed to begin work in Paris.[174]

Salisbury instructed the British representatives to establish a clear interpretation of the Say-Barruwa Line. They were to offer the extension of the Dahomey boundary from the ninth parallel to the Niger at Bikini, failing which they could descend lower to Gomba. This meant that Britain had unilaterally renounced Gurma and western Borgu. Britain's title to Bussa was not to be compromised.[175] On the other hand, the French commissioners were instructed on the grounds for the discussions. These included the regions recently traversed by European expeditions, the interpretation of the Say-Barruwa Line, and the limits of Sokoto. The instructions went farther afield to include questions raised by the Mizon expeditions and the political status of Mauri and Adamawa.[176] What was missing were the concessions, if any, that were to be made to Britain and the type of settlement the French government would accept. Furthermore, the French commissioners did not possess the identical powers of their British counterparts, as Dufferin was quick to point out.[177]

When the commissioners met for the first time on 8 February they were preoccupied with the question of an agenda for their task, in the course of which they agreed to drop the questions of the Mizon affair and the Benue region. The Say-Barruwa Line was given a prominent place. Treaties concluded in the disputed territories were produced, and it was agreed to examine the values of those treaties.[178] In the next session, the treaties presented by the British delegates were discussed, especially those concluded by Ferguson. The French contended that those treaties could not confer political rights since they were "treaties of friendship and commerce." Their value was also doubtful because of the fact that they were concluded by "un homme de couleur." This was the first case, they argued, where a black man made treaties for a European power, and it was doubtful that the natives attached any importance to Ferguson's treaties. These objections were rejected by the British delegates.[179]

It may be noted here that the French always tried to nullify the treaties secured by their rivals on technical grounds, whether they had any basis in international law or not. Already Germany had realized this. In an article in the *Hamburgischer Correspondenz* on the Franco-German dispute over Gurma, it was pointed out that the French were trying to play with the Germans the same game they had played with Britain over Nikki, by alleging that Gruner did not sign his treaty with the real king but with a vassal of the king.[180] The French were guilty of double standards if they accepted the conquest of Dahomey by Dodds, a mulatto, and rejected Ferguson's treaties because he was a colored man.

The fundamental disagreement over the interpretation of the Say-Barruwa agreement of 1890 signed the death warrant of the negotiations. After the first session of the joint commission, Roume's report made Guieysse declare that it was "impossible to accept the British interpretation of the Declaration of 5 August 1890 as the British delegates wanted it to be accepted."[181] On the other hand, Dufferin told Berthelot that the British government would not budge from the interpretation of the line accepted in principle by Hanotaux in 1894.[182] Therefore, on one of the two most important bases of the negotiations, no agreement could be reached because no side was willing to concede anything. The next major question was the definition of the Lagos-Dahomey frontier from the ninth parallel to the Niger. Though peripheral questions such as those of Bona[183] and Kayama were briefly raised, they were not crucial and were primarily used as pawns.

By the end of February Dufferin informed the French government that Colonel Everett would replace Sir A. Hemming, who was to leave for his post in British Guiana.[184] Everett did not possess the rich experience of Hemming in colonial affairs, but this was no handicap to the British delegation because of constant direction from Westminster. On the French side, industrialists and merchants who had interests in west Africa showed great interest in the negotiations. The Société Africaine de France petitioned Berthelot, stating their views on the negotiations but above all asking that explorers who had been in the areas under discussion be attached to the French delegation as technical advisers, in imitation of the example set by England during the Berlin Conference of 1885. The chambers of commerce were not oblivious to their own interests in the area. The ministry of commerce in Paris was petitioned to nominate merchants and industrialists as consultants to the French representatives at the joint commission.[185] These French commercial agencies were not spurred into action by sheer patriotism;[186] that the volume of economic activity in Dahomey had been growing steadily since 1892 was common knowledge to them. A further extension of Dahomey toward the Niger, they reasoned, would lead to a greater growth of French commerce and result in an overall rise in the revenues of Dahomey (see table 7).

Further efforts were made to interpret the Say-Barruwa Line, but without success. Berthelot introduced a new complication to the problem by suggesting that the line be drawn in a meandering manner in order to assure certain areas to France. Salisbury, the only architect of the Say-Barruwa declaration still alive,[187] was rather shocked by the French proposal. He advised Dufferin that the eastern Niger question could be shelved and commented:

> It is a pity that Berthelot's ingenious theory of the coiled boundary should not be preserved for the benefit of future negotiators and students. It is to be noted that Berthelot entirely accepts my contention that all one side of the line is British—all the other side is French; only his notions of a line are eccentric. This is a valuable admission and should not be neglected. . . . The Commissioners should not decide whether

TABLE 7

External Trade of Dahomey, 1892–98

Year	Countries	Imports	Total Imports	Exports	Total Exports
1892	France	1,819,401.21		1,583,173.50	
	Fr. Colonies	18,840.00	6,432,700.97	15,648.80	7,259,910.05
	Foreign	4,595,819.76		5,661,087.75	
	Total	6,432,700.97		7,259,910.05	
1893	France	4,486,946.14		2,353,882.35	
	Colonies	18,203.00	10,456,857.54	....	8,833,460.94
	Foreign	5,951,708.40		6,479,578.59	
	Total	10,456,857.54		8,833,460.94	
1894	France	3,544,473.13		2,725,570.20	
	Colonies	360.00	10,771,789.97	8,245.00	9,973,703.57
	Foreign	7,226,956.84		7,239,888.37	
	Total	10,771,789.97		9,973,703.57	
1895	France	3,407,985.01		3,941,353.78	
	Colonies	....	10,542,220.70	4,997.08	10,521,868.15
	Foreign	7,134,235.69		6,575,517.29	
	Total	10,542,220.70		10,521,868.15	
1896	France	3,716,310.79		3,885,211.40	
	Colonies	....	9,729,249.70	11,119.96	9,224,491.01
	Foreign	6,012,938.01		5,328,159.65	
	Total	9,729,249.70		9,224,491.01	
1897	France	2,938,825.28		1,514,810.95	
	Colonies	....	8,242,957.04	12,874.00	5,778,858.16
	Foreign	5,304,131.76		4,251,173.21	
	Total	8,242,957.04		5,778,858.16	
1898	France	1,953,514.08		2,177,964.00	
	Colonies	1,343,760.36	9,994,567.53	29,569.27	7,538,758.82
	Foreign	6,697,293.09		5,331,243.55	
	Total	9,994,567.53		7,538,758.82	

Source: *Statistiques Coloniales pour l'année 1896: Ministère des Colonies* (Paris, 1899), pp. viii, xii, 575–605 (1892–96). *Journal Officiel du Dahomey*, 15 February 1898 and 15 February 1899, gave the trade figures for 1897 and 1898.

French territory exists on both sides of the line; they are not called upon to decide this point.[188]

The discussion of the treaties which were thought material to the question of the Lagos-Dahomey frontier naturally centered on Borgu. The British delegates claimed that all the places visited by Monteil, Baud, and Decoeur were under the Emir of Gwandu and therefore under British influence.

Consequently, all the French treaties in the hinterland of Dahomey were valueless because they involved areas under Britain by virtue of anterior treaties.[189] This jolted the French government into showing copies of their sixteen treaties with the rulers in the Dahomey-Niger hinterland to the British government. Salisbury did not allay French anxiety by his stern remark to Courcel that these treaties would be submitted to competent authorities in London for scrutiny.[190] Subsequent discussion of the values of both British and French treaties were very involved, technical, and academic, with occasional references to Hausa, Bambara, Mandingo, and other west African languages.[191] The result of this tortuous argument was the decision to discard all treaties. Britain seized the initiative and proposed an extension of the Dahomey frontier to the Niger. Howard told the French delegates that Salisbury had offered them a frontier line commencing at the intersection of the ninth parallel and longitude 1° east of Paris, following this longitude to around Gomba, and crossing the Niger to the Say-Barruwa Line. The French acknowledged Salisbury's conciliatory spirit and agreed to examine the new proposal, adding that they too were animated by the spirit of conciliation.[192]

The British proposal gave to France Gurma, western Borgu, and the Dendi region around Say. These were sizable territories and represented a self-denying concession by Britain at a time when the relentless *koloniale menschen* in Germany were launching a campaign for unity of action between France and Germany "against their common enemy, Britain," because it was in their best interests to do so.[193] That was exactly what Britain did not want to have happen—a hostile coalition of France and Germany against England. But in the eyes of the French the British concessions did not go far enough, because they still excluded France from the navigable Niger.[194] At this juncture the Bourgeois Cabinet was succeeded by the Méline Cabinet, in which Hanotaux, the hard bargainer, was appointed foreign minister.[195] Salisbury would have preferred to deal with Berthelot, despite his warped notions of a line, than with the shrewd Hanotaux, whose anglophobic tendencies were well known.[196]

When the French responded to the generous Salisbury proposals, they asked for more territory. The Dahomey-Lagos frontier, they proposed, should be drawn from the eighth parallel eastward to the Niger, giving them the areas traversed by Toutée and the whole of the western Niger bank from Lokoja upward.[197] This reply bore the imprint of Hanotaux. Salisbury was aroused. He warned sternly that the commissioners had no powers whatever to alter preexisting treaties between France and Britain and that the new

French proposal violated the Anglo-French agreement of 1889 concerning the Lagos–Porto Novo frontier.[198] Even an amended version of the French proposal failed to impress Westminster, because it still gave much of the navigable Niger to France and contravened the Anglo-French agreement of 10 August 1889.[199] The negotiations were terminated without having regulated any of the problems they were constituted to resolve.

The failure of the joint commission to reach an agreement was foreshadowed by the uncompromising attitude adopted by both sides from the beginning of the negotiations. Perhaps most important of all was the fact that Roume, one of the French delegates, had made up his mind long before the discussions began that the whole region in question was a no-man's-land and should belong to the first power to occupy it.

> En résumé la région comprise entre le Niger, au Nord et à l'Est, le 9ᵉ degré de latitude nord, ou tout au plus, le 10ᵉ de latitude nord, (zone neutre de Salaga) au sud, demeure *res nullius* vis-à-vis du droit international de l'Europe, c'est-à-dire, qu'elle doit appartenir au premier occupant.[200]

Therefore, it could not be expected of him to advise or easily accede to the giving away of territories which he, like the German expansionists, considered *herrenlos* and available for effective occupation.

The effort to negotiate an agreement with France was not a complete waste. It checked the formation of a Franco-German bloc against Britain, revealed the determination of France to obtain part of the navigable Niger, and made it clear to Britain that her much-vaunted treaties were not sufficient safeguards for her rights in the Niger territories. She could no longer sit back and enjoy what Salisbury called the "beatitudes of the possidentes"[201] but had to take vigorous action to secure her interests. In addition to demonstrating the rapid growth in the knowledge of the disputed territories, the negotiations also revealed French commercial interest in these areas.[202] Finally, the failure to arrive at a negotiated settlement forced the powers to resort to effective occupation on a massive and unprecedented scale, which plunged them into the crisis of 1897–98.

The Resumption of Effective Occupation and Expeditions

The decree of 16 June 1895 left Dahomey out of the new Government General organized for French west Africa and based at Dakar. This was done to give Ballot enough freedom and initiative for expansion into the hinterland—the area described by him as the region open to political action.²⁰³ During Ballot's leave in France, a new plan for the effective occupation of the hinterland was worked out. Already a hydrographic expedition had been sent to the Niger early in 1896 under the command of Lieutenant Hourst. He was charged to explore and map the Niger from Kuliokoro to the sea. Hourst and his men sailed down the Niger from Timbuktu (Kabara) on 21 January 1896 for Say, where they arrived in the spring.²⁰⁴ They constructed a post on an island in the Niger, where they stayed for about five and a half months, irrespective of the hostility of the sultan of Say, who was a sympathizer of Ahmadu of Segu.²⁰⁵

The French stepped up their measures for the effective occupation of the "boucle du Niger." From the Sudan, it was decided to revive the plan to occupy effectively the central and western territories of the Niger bend—Yatenga, Mossi, Lobi, and Gurunsi—where the French had no treaties as yet but where they feared the English would get in first.²⁰⁶ Captain Destenave was sent to this region in the spring of 1895, but he was refused entrance into Wagadugu by the Naba of Mossi and had to retrace his steps. This time the mission was confided to Lieutenants Voulet and Chanoine with a much larger escort than the unsuccessful Destenave expedition. From Dahomey, Ballot launched with renewed vigor several expeditions into Borgu, Dendi, Mangu, and Gurma. More enthusiastic and zealous than de Trentinian, he charged Baud, Vermeersch, and Bretonnet with the effective occupation of the Dahomey-Niger hinterland, including the disputed capitals such as Nikki, Bussa, and Sansane-Mango. The French had begun to put into operation the official plan for establishing their dominance in the Niger bend (see Map 3 on p. 183 above).

Britain was not idle. Both Everett and Howard proposed that effective occupation was the best way of dealing with the difficulties raised by France.²⁰⁷ These views reinforced those of Chamberlain, who ordered the effective occupation of the Gold Coast hinterland. Since Wagadugu, Bona, Wa, and Lobi were considered important positions, they were to be occupied and garrisoned. The expenses could be borne by the Gold Coast, he affirmed.²⁰⁸ This was in contradistinction to the Niger Company, who were slow in establishing their presence in the vast areas which they claimed as theirs on paper. However, the intransigence of France during the negotiations galvanized the company into action along the Niger in Ilorin and Nupe but not in Sokoto. Not only the Niger Company and the Gold Coast were alerted; Governor Carter of Lagos redoubled his efforts in the Yoruba hinterland of Lagos,[209] and this was continued by Edward Henry McCallum, who succeeded Carter in January 1897 as acting governor.[210]

The powers were, therefore, dangerously poised for a final assault on the Niger territories, which were considered res nullius and which they expected to partition by effective occupation instead of their habitual method of negotiated agreements at peaceful conferences. But they were to revert to the traditional method when effective occupation ran out of hand, as it were, and led them to the dangerous brink of war.

7

The Anglo-French Crisis of 1897–1898

The breakdown of the negotiations between Britain and France in the spring of 1896 ended the moratorium on expeditions into the disputed territories. The French, who had well-worked-out plans for action in these regions, could not but be pleased that British diplomacy did not succeed in destroying their hopes and aspirations in the shell. The junction of the Sudan, the Ivory Coast, and Dahomey was the keystone in the great arch of the envisaged west African empire. Soon after the negotiators disbanded, the French plan was put into action from the book. Britain had realized fully that the resources of the Royal Niger Company, coupled with Goldie's unwillingness to spend much money on effective occupation,[1] were inadequate for containing the French threat. Therefore, steps were taken to strengthen the British presence in the area by the formation of the West African Frontier Force and by bringing in British troops from the West Indies. The tensions that resulted from the presence of British and French forces in the Niger territories, fully armed and in constant friction, forced the two powers to the conference table once again. The differences between them were so great, the stakes so high, and the development so complicated that it took almost nine months of uninterrupted negotiations to reach an agreement acceptable to both sides, signed on 14 June 1898.

Effective Occupation by French Expeditions: The Volta Region

"Avec les Anglais, il faut traiter mais toujours agir, saisir, et nouer promptement. En tout cas, ne jamais perdre le contact."[2] This was the philosophy underlying the actions of Hanotaux, who, as foreign minister, steered the French government through the storm of Franco-British disagreements in west Africa, China, Newfoundland, and Eastern Europe between 1896 and 1898. Indeed, action was the watchword and motto of the French in west Africa in the hectic days of effective occupation. Both Ballot in Dahomey and Trentinian in the Sudan were men who loved action and directed operations with zeal and vigor.

Just as Monteil's expedition and report not only heightened but also solidified French determination to challenge the Say-Barruwa Line, so did Hourst's convince the administration that a thrust toward Say through the center of the Niger bend could no longer be delayed. Hourst's report buttressed Monteil's about the independence of Dendi and Gurma and the existence of Sokoto authority only on the left bank of the Niger.[3] It was therefore decided to attempt the effective occupation of Mossi in the process of the Sudan's steady eastward progress. Destenave had failed because of his ineffective escort, and Mossi was renowned for its invincibility.[4] Lieutenant Voulet, who was charged with the Mossi mission, was provided with an armed escort of about 500 men and sufficient provisions for three months.[5] Destenave reported to Delcassé the stiff opposition he ran into on his way to Wagadugu. It was therefore adjudged that Voulet and Chanoine should have sufficient fire power to overcome any opposition.[6]

Voulet had been in the Destenave mission[7] and had previous knowledge of the terrain to be traversed. He left Bandiagra on 30 July 1896 for Yatenga, Wagadugu, Gourounsi, and Gurma. He was instructed to organize Yatenga and occupy it effectively by creating a residence there. But he was to march rapidly in order to forestall the British at Sati, Kupela, and Wagadugu. Trentinian warned him about the "essentially pacific nature of his role as an agent of penetration." His military escort was like a big stick and should only be used when necessary.

The expedition was received on the outskirts of Yatenga by the fugitive Chief Bagare,[8] a French protégé, whose opponents had expelled him from his capital. With the French, Bagare marched and fought his way back to Ouahigouya, where they arrived on 17 August 1896. The battles at Cun, Salou, Cisse, Youba, and Kambi reduced opposition to Bagare and his French supporters. Rebels were cleared from Ouahigouya, and Voulet had Bagare installed with traditional rituals at the sacred village of Gourcy as the Naba of Yatenga on 24 August. With Yatenga firmly under control, the expedition made its way to Yako, where they were attacked by the troops of the local Naba, just as Destenave was attacked and forced back. But Voulet repelled the attackers at the battle of Samba and continued his march to Wagadugu.[9]

On 1 September a messenger was sent to the court of Wagadugu to announce the imminent arrival of the French.[10] This messenger was not well received at the court and was said to have been maltreated and sent back posthaste to Voulet. Some French alarmists stated that the messenger was whipped for bringing bad news to the Mogho Naba, and Voulet immediately moved in to punish this insult.[11] Others pointed to the flight of the

Mogho Naba at the approach of Voulet as evidence that he flogged the messenger sent to him.¹² This conclusion does not stand up to scrutiny.

First of all, the morbid fear of the Mogho Naba to meet Europeans, based on an oracular prediction, must be taken into account. This was why he refused Destenave entrance to Wagadugu. He told his messenger:

> Si je voyais un blanc j'étais un homme mort. Je sais que les blancs veulent me faire mourir pour prendre mon pays, et d'ailleurs tu prétends qu'ils vont m'aider à organiser mon pays. Mais je trouve mon pays très bien tel qu'il est, je n'ai nul besoin d'eux, j'ai ce qu'il me faut et ce que je veux; j'ai mes marchands, aussi estime-toi heureux que je ne te fasse pas couper la tête. Va t'en donc, et surtout ne reviens plus.¹³

Second, the guide to Voulet's column, Seddo, deserted the French by night and went to the Mogho Naba's palace, where he laid bare the nonpacific tendencies of the French column as well as their military strength. Seddo's information was taken seriously. A cabinet meeting was convoked, at which the alternatives of a capitulation to Voulet or armed resistance were considered. Some ministers thought that presenting the treaty with Britain and the Union Jack should be the course of action. The majority, by deduction, felt that Voulet "would probably humiliate, punish or even kill the Mogho Naba." Consequently, he was advised to flee from his capital, which he did.¹⁴

That the "events leading to the capture of the Mossi capital are not clear," because of a conflict between official sources and the information gathered from the memoirs of witnesses, is not valid.¹⁵ In his official report, Voulet did not mention the whipping of his messenger to the Mogho Naba. Chanoine did not mention it in his private correspondence with his father.¹⁶ Even if the messenger had been received at Wagadugu with royal pomp, that would not have altered the French determination to occupy Mossi effectively before England could do so.¹⁷ Ned Noll, who publicized the whipping of Voulet's messenger, wrote after the publication of the official history of the occupation of the Niger bend. He based his account on this publication, sponsored by Trentinian at a time when the burning of villages and the seemingly perpetual military expeditions of the Sudan were under constant and severe attack in Paris, especially by the Comité pour la Protection et Défense des Indigènes.¹⁸

Voulet marched on Wagadugu on 1 September. Mossi infantry and cavalry attacked the expedition in the vain hope of forcing it to retreat. After about two and a half hours of fierce battle, the Mossi were routed. "It was a thorough stampede; all tried to save themselves and fled in all directions. Some of them in their precipitous flight, even rode past their homes and villages."[19] The power of the quick-firing Lebel rifles of the tirailleurs dissolved the determination and courage of Mossi troops. The French column advanced into Wagadugu and occupied it. The surrounding villages were sacked and burned, but Naba Wobogo and his faithful troops regrouped for a counterattack. The information they received about the smallness of the French force encouraged them. They attacked on 7 September but were repelled. In the pursuit of the hapless Boukari Koutou, Mani and Boussouma were sacked and burned, because their inhabitants sympathized with their fugitive king.[20]

Voulet pursued the fugitive king southward, but without success. The expedition marched on to Sati in Gurunsi, where they concluded a treaty of protection with Chief Hamaria.[21] Voulet then secured a promise from Samory that his forces would not attack Gurunsi, which had come under French protection. Samory's letter was read publicly to reassure Hamaria and his people. After this, Voulet returned to Wagadugu, which he found evacuated at the Naba's orders. He then made a last desperate effort to apprehend Boukari Koutou, who fled to the southwestern region and continually eluded the French column.[22] Here he began gathering troops for another effort to regain his capital. Voulet marched back to Bandiagara through Yatenga in November 1896, fighting incessantly against those African rulers who were opposed to the presence of the French or their protégés in the region. Ostensibly, the object of the return to Bandiagara was to renew supplies and ammunition, but the battles fought to restore Sultan Aguibou's authority in Bandiagara overshadowed everything else. The forcible installation of Bagare at Ouahigouya by the French expedition did not abate the civil war in Yatenga. Voulet had to fight his way back to Wagadugu in December 1896. In the meantime he wrote to Mogho Naba Wobogo, professing his pacific intentions and his desire to enter into treaty relations with him.[23] Who could believe in the pacific intentions of an expedition armed with deadly quick-firing rifles, an expedition which had been burning and sacking villages, fighting battles without provocation, and capturing men, women, children, and livestock at will?[24]

The Mogho Naba fled farther to Koumbi Siguiri, about twenty-five miles to the southeast of Wagadugu, instead of returning to the city. He did not wish to be captured by Voulet in the process of making a treaty with him. No one could predict what the French wanted, and the old oracular statement that the Europeans were a passing phenomenon still had its believers among the Mossi authorities.[25] After the French expedition attacked Wagadugu, Boukari Koutou, who was on the run, is believed to have offered sacrifices to the goddess Tenga, patroness of Mossiland, beseeching her to expel the intruding foreigners and destroy Mazi,[26] who was nominated to succeed him.[27] Coincidentally Mazi died suddenly, probably of poison. This event encouraged the Mossi to go ahead with their plans for a counteroffensive against Voulet, since it appeared to be a quick answer to their prayers to Tenga. But they never succeeded in dislodging the French.

Boukari Koutou's refusal to surrender led to the decision by Voulet to install a successor to the throne with whom he could conclude a treaty of protection which would sanctify the French fait accompli. Mamadou Kouka, a young prince, was nominated and installed by those traditional king-makers of Mossi who had surrendered to the French. It was thought that Mamadou Kouka's youth would make him more amenable to French control than any of his older relatives.[28] Immediately after his installation, he signed a treaty with Voulet placing Mossi under French protection.[29] A fortified post under Captain Scal was established at Wagadugu before Voulet led his expedition into Gurunsi after further clashes with resistant Mossi troops. Mossi resistance petered out when they realized that they were fighting a lost cause.[30] Boukari Koutou, however, continued the fight by diplomacy. He invoked the treaty with Ferguson of 2 July 1894 and sought British intervention to restore him at Wagadugu. He failed in this attempt, just as he had in the use of force.

When Voulet arrived at Koupela in February 1897 he learned of one mission in Gurma and another in southern Mossi. He wrote to both expeditions to remind them that Gurma and Mossi were under French protection. The expedition in Gurma turned out to be a French one from Dahomey; that in southern Mossi was an English expedition under Captain Stewart. Chamberlain urged the forces of the Gold Coast to go on to Wagadugu and establish a post alongside the French post there, when he learned that Voulet had anticipated the British and seized Wagadugu first. Captain Stewart would have done just that, except that the Foreign Office dissuaded Chamberlain.[31]

The two French expeditions met at Tigba on 16 February, proving to the Africans that, though operating from different bases, they were united and had a common aim. For Bantchande of Gurma, Voulet's arrival was a boon. The united French expeditionary force teamed up with his own forces in an attack on Billango on 19 February. They destroyed this village, which was a pocket of resistance to the authority of Bantchande.[32] Voulet went to Tenkodogo (Tengrugu), where he met Captain Stewart. Thinking that the

British expedition was led by Ferguson, Voulet had written Ferguson a menacing letter. He arrived at Tenkodogo in an aggressive mood but was disarmed when he saw Stewart, to whom he apologized.[33] He would have dealt summarily with Ferguson, whose treaty with Wagadugu he had seized.[34] Stewart claimed Tengrugu because he arrived there first and took effective possession of it. Voulet countered that Bussansi was an integral part of Mossi and was under French protection; therefore, Stewart had no rights over Tengrugu. In the end, the two men reached an agreement to refer all these questions to their home governments.[35]

Chanoine went south into Gurunsi and visited Sati and Leo. He made treaties along his route and obtained declarations from village chiefs that they were subject to Gurunsi, especially among the Funssi, Kumpa, and Walembele. He clashed with opposing native forces at Gandiaga, whom he put to flight. They fled to Yarba, where there was a British post.[36] From Leo, Chanoine went to meet the French expedition under Cazemajou at Djebougou, thus ensuring the linkage of operations.

The Voulet-Chanoine success at Wagadugu and in Gurunsi led to the creation of the new administrative unit in February 1897, which was called the Niger-Volta region and placed under Captain Valet.[37] It was the major factor which assured French control of the territories of the Niger bend. The blueprint prepared by the ministry of colonies in 1895 had been faithfully implemented by one of the most ruthless of the French adventurers of the "scramble" period. Voulet was instructed to go back to Wagadugu[38] to consolidate the French position there, while Destenave was sent out to occupy Macina and all the eastern territories to Say. Dori was occupied on 1 May, and Say two weeks later.[39]

A comparison of Mossi resistance to French occupation and that of Dahomey shows that the structural weakness of the Mossi kingdom was a handicap to effective central action. The Nabas of the various provinces of the kingdom enjoyed considerable autonomy of action. Some even challenged the Mogho Naba at will. Yatenga and Lale are examples of this.[40] The absence of a large standing army under central control as in Dahomey meant that the provincial rulers held actual power. They responded favorably to orders from Wagadugu only as long as the mystic which held them to the Mogho Naba lasted. It is true that the Mogho Naba was able to summon thousands of horsemen and foot soldiers overnight to confront Voulet, but the ephemeral nature of the resistance they put up was due partly to the quick surrender of several Nabas and partly to the antiquated weapons with which they were equipped.[41] Jugulating axes and cudgels were no better than fists in battles against sharpshooters armed with automatic repetition rifles—"men who kill from afar," as Gagool put it in *King Solomon's Mines*. Dahomey had a more modernized army, equipped with most of Europe's best weapons. Mossi could not get at these weapons, because it was a landlocked kingdom. The Dahomey economy was much more developed than that of Mossi, so even if they were available the Mogho Naba would not have been able to purchase large quantities of arms.

Expeditions from Dahomey: Baud, Vermeersch, Bretonnet, Ganier, Ricour

Ballot's return to Dahomey in 1896 after his furlough in France marked the beginning of a new phase in the effective occupation of the Niger territories. The preexisting plans were put into operation. Two expeditions were dispatched from Carnotville toward Gurma (and Mossi) and Bussa respectively. When it became evident that the vast territory between these two expeditions could be contested by Britain and Germany, a third unit was sent in to cover this region and link the two previous expeditions. This sudden invasion of the hinterland in all directions excited the inhabitants of these regions, and they took up arms against the foreigners. The result was a quadrilateral conflict in the Niger territories between France, Britain, Germany, and the Africans, which dragged on till June 1898. The partition of the Neutral Zone in 1899 settled all the major contentions in the area.

The assassination of Henri Forget in February 1896 by the son of Chief Sero-Kora Yerima of Yagbasson demonstrated that Borgu was not under French control. The punitive expedition to Yagbasson under Fonssagrives was equally attacked and forced to retreat by the Bariba warriors.[42] Acting Governor Layere was blamed for these unfortunate incidents,[43] which rendered the French claim to Borgu dubious in international circles. Gruner insisted that France had not occupied the hinterland effectively. All they had there, he contended, was a straggling line of isolated posts of a handful of soldiers each. There was no sign of French influence in the whole area, he declared.[44] It was urgent to ensure adequate means of communication between French posts and to occupy the disputed areas so as to convince Britain and Germany that French presence there was real. Bretonnet was assigned to eastern Borgu. He left for the Niger with an armed escort of 100 men and 100 porters. As if to avenge the evacuation of Fort d'Arenberg, he installed himself at Bussa and proceeded to control the right bank of the Niger between Bussa and Ilo as French resident of the Middle Niger.[45]

Chief Kora of Wawa menaced Bussa and the trade routes of the area. Bretonnet took joint action with the king of Bussa against Kora, who fled to Yagbasson, a stronghold of the Bariba.

When Goldie heard of the presence of a European expedition at Bussa, he tried to persuade it to leave on the grounds that Britain had prior treaty rights there. Bretonnet, in typical Mizon fashion, replied defiantly to Goldie's letter. Bussa's relations with the Niger Company were purely commercial, he pointed out, and he was assuming political authority at Bussa.[46] Since Goldie could not dislodge Bretonnet from Bussa by either persuasion or force, he resorted to the Niger Company's old technique of making life difficult for intruders by instigating local opposition by any means.[47] Only several months of diplomatic pressure on France could secure the evacuation of Bussa by French troops.[48]

When Baud left Carnotville in December 1896, he was accompanied by Ballot[49] to Bafilo, where von Seefried had established a German post. Ballot and Seefried held a joint inquiry, during which the local chiefs stated that they made no treaties with Germany. The Germans withdrew. Ballot strengthened the Bafilo post with twenty-five additional soldiers before parting with Baud to confront another German menace at Kirikri, where von Zech had installed a post. Zech contended that Kirikri and Bafilo were dependent on Sokode and could not make treaties on their own. Ballot assembled the chiefs as usual, and they declared they were not vassals of Sokode. The French won again and Zech withdrew from Kirikri.[50]

Baud and Vermeersch continued northward to Fada N'Gurma, creating posts along their route. It is noteworthy that they avoided Sansanne-Mango, where there was a strong German contingent under Thierry. They arrived at Fada N'Gurma on 1 February 1897. Two German soldiers were in the area, sent by Thierry to Chief Adama of Matiacuali. Chief Adama sympathized with Yacom Bato, the ex-king of Gurma, who was opposed to King Bantchande, the French protégé, and his supporters. It was at this juncture that Voulet contacted the Baud-Vermeersch expedition and joined in common military action with them against the opponents of Bantchande at Toucouma and Bilanga, which they occupied on 19 February. After the occupation of Toucouma and Bilanga by the allied forces of Bantchande and France, the troops of the opposition fled, and the power of luckless Yacom Bato was definitively broken. Rather than submit to Bantchande, his rival, he committed suicide by poison.[51]

Chief Adama of Matiacuali still held out against the French. He asked

Thierry for aid against Bantchande and his "protectors."⁵² Before such aid could be sent—if the Germans had enough men and some to spare—Vermeersch marched against Adama, who fled to the German post at Sansanne-Mango. The *Tricolore* was hoisted at Matiacouali, and Vermeersch presided over the election and installation of its new chief. He professed the good intentions of France at the installation ceremony: "We wish that Gourma should be united and peaceful under the legitimate authority of Bantchande; that people should be able to move about in peace from one province of Gourma to another; that Hausa traders should be able to go to and fro without fear of being pillaged; and that Matiacouali recover her former commercial prosperity, the loss of which was due to Adama's pillages."⁵³

The tone of this statement is similar to those made by Ballot, Dodds, Voulet, and other French agents of this period. It has the familiar ring of the humanitarianism and devotion to legitimate commerce of Victorian England. But it was the battles waged by French expeditions that disrupted commerce at this time.⁵⁴

With Vermeersch at Matiacouali, Baud went to Pama to challenge the Germans. He asked the Germans to withdraw from Pama because this was the wish of King Bantchande of Gurma. The Germans did not withdraw, but Baud and Thierry signed an agreement to cease all political action at Pama and Matiacouali pending instructions from their governments on the subject.⁵⁵

The consistent challenge of Germany made the French realize that they had no monopoly of the hinterland. It was felt by the French colonial ministry that the vast territory lying between Fada N'Gurma and the Niger was open to German action. The Germans seemed bent on erecting posts along the routes of Gruner's expedition to the Niger. Efforts had to be made to seal off this territory from the Germans. Lebon reminded Ballot of the danger of the isolation of the two lines of French posts already created by Baud and Bretonnet, respectively. "I leave you to take measures which you deem necessary," he instructed Ballot in January 1897.⁵⁶

What Ballot deemed necessary was the sending of more soldiers into the hinterland to strengthen the already existing posts, establish new posts, subdue resistant districts, and link the points occupied by French troops. Kuandé, whose chief had consistently refused to make treaties with French agents, was to be occupied to forestall the Germans who had an eye on this kingdom.⁵⁷ Ballot, therefore, asked Lebon for an additional company of Senegalese tirailleurs to be employed in this task. He got an affirmative reply:

> Compagnie (de tirailleurs sénégalais) demandée arrivera par *Fraissinet* le 15 Mars. Vous devez l'employer exclusivement à occuper effectivement territoire compris entre Carnotville, Ouagadougou et Ilo et à installer postes dans ce triangle en lui interdisant toute action dans le voisinage, régions occupées par les Allemandes et les Anglais.[58]

The additional detachment from Senegal was placed under the charge of Captain Ferdinand Ganier,[59] sent from Senegal to command this eighth company of Senegalese tirailleurs. The expedition left for the hinterland by sailing up the Wheme to Dogba, from where the overland journey began. Ganier had multiple problems to face. The worst two were the scarcity of foodstuffs along his route and the constant desertion of his porters, made easy by the unmanageable size of the column of 550.[60] The shortage of foodstuffs was due partly to the recent passage through this area of the expeditions under Baud and Bretonnet and partly to the fact that the planting season had begun, ushering in the lean period in west Africa.

Ganier received clear instructions from Ballot before setting out for "the unknown," as Dr. Bartet called it. The primary object of his expedition was to occupy effectively the territory lying between the eastern and western lines of posts already established by Baud and Bretonnet. To this end he was to create a third series of posts from Wangara (Djougou) to Say, through Kuandé, Kodjar, and Botou.

> C'est cette ligne centrale que vous auriez à créer. Elle aura de plus le très grand avantage de vous mettre en rapport avec les deux autres lignes de l'Est et de l'Ouest et d'assurer ainsi plus facilement leurs communications avec le chef lieu. . . . Le premier poste que vous aurez à créer sera Kuandé, le second Konkobiri, le troisième Kodjar. Là devra se borner pour le moment, et à moins d'ordres contraires, la mission que vous aurez à remplir.[61]

Kuandé was earmarked as the first target of the Ganier expedition, because of the uncooperative attitude of its ruler, Woru Wari. He refused to receive Decoeur and Baud in 1895. Subsequent efforts by Alby and Molex to establish relations with him were unsuccessful. Ballot, therefore, judged Kuandé to be a weak spot in the zone France wanted to occupy. Its important geographical position, its commerce, its relations with the Moslems of the Niger, and its large population made the possession of this capital city a desideratum.[62] It was the route center of all roads leading to the east, the west, and the north. Its acquisition would facilitate communication with the French posts in Upper Dahomey, especially above the tenth parallel. Administrator Portes, whom Ballot had recently sent to Kuandé, attributed his failure to the weakness of his forces and above all to the intrigues of the Germans, who were anxious to obtain Kuandé.[63] Ballot declared: "Il est de toute nécessité que nous occupions Kuandé pour ne pas y avoir flotter, avant long-temps, le drapeau allemande. . . . Mon avis est qu'une opération militaire est indispensable et que nous n'obtiendrons rien de roi de Kuandé, tant que nous n'agirons pas vigoureusement contre son pays. En un mot, il faut se hater d'accomplir ce que les Allemands ont l'intention de faire." [64]

Ballot did not rule out the effective occupation of Kuandé by the Germans before the arrival of Ganier at this city. If from Djougou it was ascertained that Kuandé had not been occupied by the Germans, Ganier was to double up and occupy it solidly. He was to employ force only if the king of Kuandé refused him entry to the city, for it would be more advantageous to establish French protection over western Borgu by peaceful methods than by force. If Kuandé was occupied by the Germans[65] before Ganier's arrival, he was instructed to bypass the city and proceed to Lambounti or to Nansougou. In any case, Ballot thought that the king of Kuandé, intimidated by Ganier's armed escort, would not refuse him entry into his capital. At Konkobiri and Kodjar Ganier was to search out the treaties made by Baud in January 1895 with the chiefs of these towns. He was to make copies of these, since the originals had been burned when Baud's baggage caught fire, and renew them in the prescribed manner.

Finally, Ballot underscored the ministerial instructions on the effective occupation of the territory lying in the Carnotville-Wagadugu-Ilo triangle. It was imperative to occupy Kodjar so solidly that the incursions of Ahmadu's troops into the area would be definitively checked. At this time, the fugitive sultan of Segu was installed at Dourga, a few kilometers above Say, with his ally the former Comba of Djabo, Aly Boury N'Diaye. Their soldiers, who were living off the land, ravaged the surrounding villages. Ganier was to contact Destenave, who was operating from Wagadugu, and probably was sent to expel Ahmadu from the right bank of the Niger. He should give Destenave any aid in his power in this arduous task, which he would commence from Dori.[66]

Ganier's progress inland was slow, due to the large size of his escort and the constant desertion of his porters.[67] Ballot rebuked Ganier for his slow progress and accused him of beating his porters and thereby causing their desertion.⁶⁸ Fearing that the Decoeur-Lugard drama at Nikki might be reenacted by the Germans at Kuandé, Ballot urged Ganier to march morning and evening.⁶⁹ Ganier picked up speed after the initial difficulties of logistics, organization, and control of the motley crowd that was his escort. His inexperience⁷⁰ was a factor in his retarded progress, for he was the first to lead a large expedition into the hinterland without having served as a second in some previous expedition.

At Zagnanado, Ganier received valuable information from Villarem, a telegraph official, who had traveled up to Savalu and Badame and back. He was charged with the installation of a telegraph line connecting Porto Novo with Wagadugu, and he had just opened the Zagnanado telegraph station. From Administrator Mounier,⁷¹ Ganier received great help in the way of carriers, whom he constrained the chief of Zagnanado to provide. The expedition marched on to Savalou and then toward Kirikri and Kuandé. To Ballot's surprise Ganier arrived at Kuandé on 30 April. Molex paved the way by reaching an agreement with Woru Wari before Ganier's mission arrived. The expedition was well received, and Woru Wari signed a treaty with Ganier on 30 April 1897, placing his kingdom under French protection.⁷²

With his task cut short at Kuandé, Ganier headed for Konkobiri. In the meantime, he learned of the expulsion of the French officials from the post at Kandi by the king, who acted in concert with the rulers of Bouay and Nikki.⁷³ On the way to Konkobiri, Ganier extended French protection over Guilmoro and Lambounti by treaties with Chiefs Berme Sunon and Zime, respectively. Chief Zime provided guides to lead the expedition to Konkobiri, where King Mandanou Yamfiabou received them warmly. The old king had lost his copy of the treaty he made with Baud in 1895. Ganier renewed a treaty of protection with him, and they exchanged gifts, the French receiving one cattle and ten calabashes of grains.⁷⁴ From Konkobiri, Ganier contacted Baud and was soon joined by Vermeersch. Thus the objective of linking the various arms of French expeditions was achieved in Gurma.⁷⁵

It was at Kodjar that the mission ran into unexpected cold treatment. The new chief, Yankouéré, not only destroyed the treaty which his predecessor had made with Baud in 1895 but also deserted Kodjar with his subjects, saying that he did not wish to meet any white people. When it was discovered that the white men were not in transit but had pitched their tents at Kodjar, Chief Yankouéré returned to his village to face the French.⁷⁶ Intimidated by the large military contingent in his town, he could not but accede to

Ganier's wishes. Accordingly, a post was established at Kodjar with a garrison of seventy-five tirailleurs.[77] This conformed to Ballot's instructions, for Kodjar was of great strategic importance in the Gurma-Niger region. From Kodjar the movements of Ahmadu and his roving troops could be watched, and the Kandi, Matiacouali, and Botou roads could be controlled.

On 25 May 1897 Ganier received additional instructions from Ballot which called for the reestablishment of the post at Kandi at all costs. From Kodjar the expedition marched to Kandi. They met only passive resistance from the chief, who refused to meet them at first but delegated his prime minister to deal with them. Later the chief of Kandi came with an escort of a dozen cavaliers to see the French. The post was reestablished without difficulty. Even Nasara, the prime minister of the chief of Kandi, aided the French in the reconstruction of their post. The rebellious pretender to the Kandi throne also came to terms with the French. The expedition then went back to Kodjar.[78]

It can be seen that the initial success of the Ganier expedition was due mainly to the cooperation of the rudimentary administrative stations which Ballot had established in the hinterland. Through such intermediaries as Administrators Monier, Ravel, Mock, and Molex, the expedition avoided most of the routine difficulties which beset earlier columns. Furthermore, these administrators prepared the local chiefs and kings for the arrival of the French expedition and thus prevented armed conflicts, which would have arisen from panic on both sides.

Germany and Britain did not stand idly by while France beaconed the Niger territories with military posts. Germany was in western Borgu and Gurma simultaneously with France. Zech and Thierry with their aides laid claims on Sansanne-Mango, Pama, and Matiacouali despite French protests. These protests irritated the *koloniale menschen* in Germany and the press. The *Hamburgischer Correspondent* decried the aggressive policy which Ballot had pursued in the hinterland for two years with the backing of the colonial group in the chamber of deputies. From Berlin the *Post* attacked the treaties on which Ballot based his claims to the territories of the hinterland.[79] But the *Deutsche Kolonial Zeitung* urged the government to take vigorous action against the French occupation of Kirikri, Bafilo, and Gurma.[80] Diplomatic pressure on Paris by Germany resulted in Lebon's issuing stern instructions to Ballot against excessive zeal and imprudent language in dealing with the Germans. These could not help but ruin the chances of the success of the proposed negotiations with Germany on the disputed territories and mar the good work which Ballot had done in these areas.[81]

Franco-German Negotiations and the Settlement of 23 July 1897

Prudence and courtesy were not powerful enough shields against the Germans in their drive toward the Niger from Togo. Not even the strong language of the French officials in Dahomey, of which Governor August Kohler of Togo complained, eased the Baud-Thierry conflict at Pama. Gruner was as energetic as Ballot in directing German agents toward the Niger in accordance with the German blueprint for the partition of the Niger hinterland among the three powers involved. Germany would not deny France access to the navigable Niger but would allow her only a small stretch of it. All the right bank of the Niger from just above Bussa to Say was claimed by Germany, including part of the Gwandu emirate, by virtue of Gruner's travels and treaties. The left bank of the Niger was to belong to England,[82] and Germany was to take all of the Neutral Zone.[83] To get to the Niger from Togo, the Germans had to possess Gurma. Consequently, Franco-German clashes were concentrated in Gurma, where France enlisted the support of the paramount ruler, Bantchande, and the Germans entered into relations with local chiefs who were opposed to Bantchande and his French supporters, especially Chief Adama.[84]

In May 1897 serious negotiations opened in Paris between France and Germany for the delimitation of the Togo-Dahomey-Sudan boundaries. According to Hanotaux, these negotiations were furthered by the official visit of Chancellor Hohenlohe to Paris on 27 April 1897.[85] Hanotaux intended to soften Britain by manipulating the German claims in the Niger territories, with the aim of securing definite advantages for France in the end.[86] Germany's desire to expand from Togo to the Niger was unacceptable to France.[87] Against it was pitted France's hinterland theory, which was based on natural dependence and effective occupation of the territories claimed.[88] It was the task of the Franco-German diplomats who met at Paris on 24 May to reconcile the claims of both powers and adjust them in a manner satisfactory to both governments.

An early agreement was not facilitated by the many incidents precipitated by the zeal of the German and French agents in the Niger bend. At first it was in Gurma that the competing officials clashed very often.[89] But soon Gruner began efforts not only to penetrate western Borgu but also to woo Nikki. The favorable response of King Sire Tourou to Germany at the

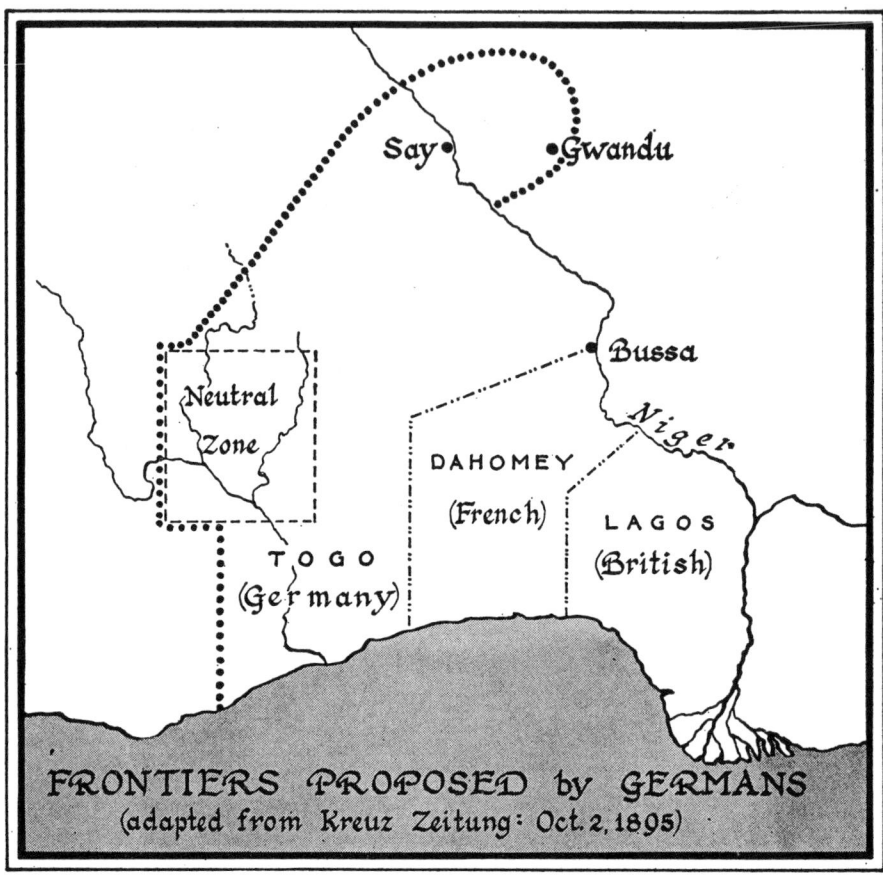

beginning of July 1897 forced Ballot to decide on the effective occupation of Nikki by French forces: "Je suis obligé de faire immédiatement occuper Nikki, autrement les Allemands n'hésiteront pas à le faire et le Borgu tout entier pourrait ainsi nous échapper." [90]

Soon after the opening of the negotiations in Paris, the Germans began to match French effective occupation with their own effective occupation and to give military support to their protégés. The result of this was a sudden burst of German troops in Gurma. They swarmed everywhere, as Captain Ganier reported to Ballot: "Le Gourma se trouve sous le coup d'une véritable invasion allemande. Le Lieutenant Thierry a violé la convention passé avec Baud; il est en marche sur Matiacouali pour rétablir Adama." [91] Lebon instructed Ballot to await the outcome of the negotiations in Paris, which he had no intention to disrupt, especially as Hanotaux was anxious to reach a settlement with Germany because of the diplomatic advantage this would give France in the dispute with England.⁹²

The junction of the various arms of the French expeditions in the Niger territories toward the end of June 1897 at Say and Kodjar had a significant effect on the negotiations with Germany. Destenave and Betbeder marched from Wagadugu to join Ganier at Kodjar, while Bretonnet arrived at Kodjar after a punitive campaign against Kandi.⁹³ French predominance over Gurma was assured by the realization of the objective of the expeditions. Lebon boasted that the Germans gave up their claims to Gurma and that Britain would, in turn, do so.⁹⁴

As a quid pro quo for the loss of Gurma, the whole of Mangu (Chakosi) territory up to 11° North Latitude was granted to Germany. Binger, the ace negotiator for France, struggled to whittle down German claims to the Kodokoli region without much success.⁹⁵ Bafilo and Kirikri, where there were French posts, were awarded to Germany, but Semere and Djougou remained in the French sector. The final agreement was signed on 23 July 1897.⁹⁶ On the whole, it was a great victory for France. All the territory stretching from the 11th parallel to the Niger through Mossi, Gurma, and Dendi was recognized by Germany as belonging to France.⁹⁷ As Germaine Ganier pointed out, Binger, by his diplomatic skill, consolidated for France the area which he was the first to open up in 1887–89.⁹⁸ France now had her hands free to tackle the problems posed by her rivalry with Britain in the Niger territories.

British Reaction to French Expeditions and Effective Occupation

The collapse of the Franco-British talks in May 1896 convinced the British government that France wanted to exclude England from as much of the Niger territories as possible. Chamberlain began immediately to initiate plans to counteract French designs. The military advantage which France had in west Africa was soon neutralized by the formation of the West African Frontier Force, which the British government placed under the command of Lugard. The administrations of Lagos and the Gold Coast were instructed to take active measures to safeguard the hinterlands of their colonies. The Royal Niger Company was pressured into cooperating with other British agencies in resisting French expansionism, and soon after a settlement was reached with France the company's charter was withdrawn. The pressure of these combined Chamberlain measures softened the French government and predisposed it for a negotiated settlement, though both parties not only talked about but also prepared for war.

From the proceedings of the Niger Commission at Paris,[99] it became clear that France was not prepared to recognize Britain's treaty claims in Mossi because Ferguson, who concluded the treaty in question, was a native of west Africa. Chamberlain therefore suggested that an expedition be sent to Wagadugu to get the Mogho Naba of Mossi to confirm Ferguson's treaty. This expedition was to be under a white officer along with Ferguson and other Africans. In addition, Bona Wa, Gambaga, and other neighboring places were to be visited and occupied.[100] When the Foreign Office, in their preoccupation to avoid expenses, suggested that Britain and France take joint action against Samory in the Gold Coast hinterland, Chamberlain demurred and insisted on the unilateral sending of members of the Gold Coast constabulary to Wa and Bona, which were threatened by the sofas under Sarankemory.[101]

The Foreign Office ended its hesitation over the question of an expedition into the hinterland of the Gold Coast when Chamberlain renewed his pressure for the approval of this expedition and communicated to Salisbury a note from the governor of the Gold Coast to the effect that the colony would bear the costs of the expedition.[102] Salisbury concurred. Governor Maxwell was informed that Her Majesty's government had decided to send an expedition to Mossi and adjacent territories "under a white officer." [103] Captain Donald Stewart and Francis B. Henderson were selected by Maxwell to lead the missions into the hinterland. Henderson was charged with the western arm of the expedition to Bona, Wa, Lobi, and Gurunsi; Stewart was in charge of the eastern arm into Mamprussi and Mossi.[104] Both were to proceed to their assigned tasks with 100 men each of the Gold Coast constabulary and 100 rounds of ammunition per man and one maxim gun for each mission. Prudence and courtesy were recommended in any dealings with the French or the Germans as well as with African rulers.[105]

Unfortunately, Chamberlain's plans to secure Mossi for the Gold Coast were robbed of success by the indecision of the Foreign Office and the promptitude of action of the French from the Sudan. Just as Stewart and his men slowly worked their way northward from Kumasi, Voulet occupied Wagadugu and put to flight the Mogho Naba, with whom Britain had a treaty of friendship and commerce.[106] This news produced diverse reactions in London. Chamberlain felt that the British expedition should go on to Wagadugu and install itself beside the French post there.[107] Everett thought that the French planned to use the occupation of Wagadugu as a lever against Britain whenever the sittings of the Niger Commission were resumed. To counteract this, England should delay the reopening of negotiations till the occupation of Bona and Mamprussi (Gambaga) was a fait accompli. The abandonment of Mossi was a trump card in the hands of the British government.[108] But the French expansionists were not moved by British protests over the occupation of Mossi by France. They proposed that France and Germany jointly declare a neutral zone in the Dahomey hinterland, similar to the Anglo-German Neutral Zone in the Salaga region. This, it was argued, would assure the Germans access to the Niger, assure the French the junction of Dahomey and the Sudan, and check the designs of the Royal Niger Company in Borgu and Gurma.[109] The French government did not seize on this idea immediately but continued to seek the resumption of the work of the Niger Commission,[110] though Hanotaux was later to use a Franco-German settlement as a weapon against Britain in the Niger territories.

Stewart's mission met with opposition from the Germans at Gambaga. Lieutenant Massow, who was sent to Gambaga by Gruner to assert Germany's claims, was constrained by Stewart to retrace his steps to Sansanne-Mango. After concluding a treaty with the king of Mamprussi, Stewart proceeded to Tengrugu (Tenkodogo), from where he planned to make a dash for Wagadugu.[111] When Stewart learned of the effective occupation of Mossi by French forces, he decided not to go on to Wagadugu. Instead, he met and conferred with Voulet at Tengrugu. Both decided to leave the delimitation of the French and British spheres to their home governments and to leave Tengrugu unoccupied pending an Anglo-French settlement.[112]

Voulet had come to Tengrugu to deal summarily with Ferguson, who he thought was the leader of the British expedition. Stewart bore witness to French ill will toward Ferguson:

> When Captain Voulet saw the letter in my hands he asked me for a pencil and wrote the following on a piece of paper . . . "It is the first letter, and it is very bad because I believed you were Ferguson. I beg your pardon." I accepted his apology and informed him that Mr. Ferguson was just as fully an accredited officer of the English Government as I was, and that he was entitled to the same courtesies. I then read the letter from which the tone of the P.S. especially the last paragraph, shows how things would have been carried on by the French, if they had found Mr. Ferguson in Tengrugu.[113]

Because of the superiority of the French forces in the Mossi area and of Stewart's caution not to cause unwanted difficulties to the British government, proceeding to Wagadugu was dropped. A deaf ear was given to the persistent plea of Boukari Koutou, the fugitive Magho Naba, for British protection against the French, even though the Colonial Office was convinced that he was entitled to British succor.[114] It is noteworthy that Mogho Naba Wobogo based his demand for British assistance on the treaty he had concluded with Ferguson in July 1894—the very treaty which the French claimed was regarded by Mogho Naba Wobogo as a certificate of hospitality.

The eastern arm of the British expedition under Henderson not only failed in its mission to occupy Wa, Bona, and Gurunsi but also came to grief under the fierce attack of the sofas. Henderson progressed slowly to Dagarti, where he concluded a treaty of protection with King Seidu on 9 January 1897. It was confirmed that the French had no treaty rights in Dagarti, as Baud claimed.[115] At this point the British expedition was flanked on the left by the forces of Samory under his son Sarankemory, and to the northeast the bands of Babatu were only thirty-five miles away.[116] Henderson was worried by the possibility of an attack on the British expedition by either of these two formidable forces. For this reason he requested more soldiers and weapons. The sofas could stop him from reaching Wa, or they could kidnap the chief "to make a treaty impossible" between him and the British.[117] Negotiations with Samory were abortive, and Chamberlain ruled out any joint action with France against this dreaded warrior.[118] In response to Henderson's request for reinforcements, Chamberlain secured the services of six officers from the War Office who were sent to the Gold Coast for service in the hinterland.[119] The sofas struck before any reinforcements could reach Henderson. Sarankemory and his troops were pressing eastward; they were warned by British officials to retreat westward, failing which they should expect vigorous action.[120] The constant British needling, coupled with Henderson's march toward Bona, incited the sofas to swoop down on the British encampment at Dokita. Hard fighting ensued. The military advantage of the sofas constrained the British expedition to retreat toward Wa. The sofas pursued them and turned the retreat into a rout, during which Ferguson was killed. Henderson was taken prisoner and sent to Samory's camp for interrogation.[121] After a short period of captivity, Henderson was released and sent to Maxwell with four delegates from Samory, bringing with him a confidential letter and two large gold ankle rings as presents for the governor.[122] These peace efforts did not succeed; nor did they efface the fact that the sofas checked Henderson's effort to occupy Bona and Lobi.

The French anticipated Stewart at Wagadugu. The sofas decimated Henderson's escort and drove the remainder away from the Bona-Lobi region. This appalling failure obliged Chamberlain to reconsider the "policy of drift, which has already had such disastrous consequences." [123] The British government was to take such dispositions as would effectively counteract French, German, and Sofa aggression in the hinterland.

A West African Force

As Chamberlain saw it, the British government should take those dispositions which would enable her to effectively protect her interests from the aggressive Sofas, the restless French, and the obstinate intrusion of the Germans. Joint action with France against Samory would raise two paramount problems for Britain: it would tie Britain's hands on questions like Mossi and others, and above all, it would "lower British prestige with the natives, who would say Britain was unable, without assistance, to deal with Samory." [124] Therefore, it was time to end the "policy of drift" by adopting "a common definite policy in respect of French and German aggressions . . . applicable to the Gold Coast, Lagos, and the Royal Niger Company's territories." [125]

The Colonial Office was impressed with the gravity of the occupation of Bussa and Mossi by France and the proceedings of the Germans in the Neutral Zone, especially at Yendi.[126] If Germany was "to be prevented from reaping the advantages of the unscrupulous proceedings of German officers," Britain should denounce the Neutral Zone agreements of 1887-88 and authorize the governor of the Gold Coast to occupy Yendi and other places in the Neutral Zone, argued Chamberlain. But Salisbury doubted the legality of such a measure, pointing out that Germany was already in occupation of Yendi and could claim that locality even if the Neutral Zone agreement were denounced unilaterally by Britain.[127] Chamberlain forcefully demolished the objection of the Foreign Office to his bold proposal to snatch the initiative from Germany and to maintain in the Gold Coast hinterland the prestige of "the white man who conquered Ashanti."

French action at Bussa and in Mossi was more irritating to the Colonial Office than that of Germany in the Neutral Zone. Early in May 1897, Salisbury sought Chamberlain's views on a draft letter which was intended for Monson. This letter dealt with the problems of the Niger territories, Britain's objection to French occupation of Mossi, and the resumption of the work of the Niger Commission desired by the French government.[128] Chamberlain suggested that "the proposed despatch should not be sent to Paris," because he hoped shortly to be able to discuss with Salisbury "the whole question of the measures to be taken to stop the advance of the French in the Niger territories as well as in the 'hinterland' of the Gold Coast." Salisbury concurred, and the dispatch was not sent to Monson.[129]

By this time a west African plan had crystallized in Chamberlain's mind. He was convinced that Britain's rights would be flouted continually by European and African powers so long as Britain did not have a formidable military presence in the area. The French believed, Chamberlain observed, that Britain was not in earnest in urging her claims because of the ease with which she had yielded her rights in the past and that Britain would not be willing to incur any expenses to make her claims good by effective occupation. It was imperative to disabuse the minds of the French and to give evidence of British determination "to adopt a different course in the present instance." This evidence could only be "the presence of a force superior to theirs," Chamberlain continued.

> It is possible that on finding themselves confronted by a superior force, and being made aware that we are determined and prepared to substantiate our claims, the French might withdraw from places which we claim under the treaties with native authorities, as the Germans . . . have recently done at Bafilo and Kirikri when confronted by the French themselves.[130]

Elaborating on how to manifest British determination and convince France that the policy of drift was at an end, Chamberlain suggested that Maxwell find out places which Britain "could seize and hold as a material guarantee for dealing with the French seizures of Mossi and Boussa when negotiations are resumed with the French Government." The places to be seized should be above 9° North Latitude and outside the Neutral Zone. For the execution of this policy, a strong force would have to be raised from recruits of the Royal Niger Company and on the spot.

> The question of expense must not be allowed to stand in the way of dealing effectively with the present emergency. It is proposed that the force, although raised in the first instance by the Gold Coast Government, should eventually be employed in occupying the territories claimed as British, not only behind the Gold Coast, but on the Niger, and in that case Lagos and the Niger Coast Protectorate and the Royal

Niger Company would be called upon to contribute towards the cost of what would be in effect a small West African Army.[131]

Here Chamberlain expressed for the first time the idea that later developed into the formation of the West African Frontier Force. Why did Chamberlain stress the recruiting of men for the diminutive west African army he envisaged? Earlier, the War Office had been asked to furnish the Colonial Office with information on British military strength in west Africa as well as Samory's strength in men and arms.[132] The information supplied by the Intelligence Division of the War Office underscored the military weakness of Britain in west Africa. Most of the men under arms in the constabulary of the British colonies and protectorates had no military training whatever and on the whole were ill-equipped. Furthermore, the administrative cleavage and jealousies between the British possessions rendered the mobilization of the available forces difficult, given the enormous distances between these possessions and the difficulties of transportation[133] (see table 8).

Chamberlain, therefore, decided that a west African force under unified command was essential for the execution of British policy in the hinterland. When this scheme was presented to Goldie at an interview in the Colonial Office on 27 May 1897, he refused to discuss "the question of the Niger Company's cooperation with Lagos and the Gold Coast in the defence of their joint interests against French aggression."[134] The Colonial Office, with the approval of Salisbury, increased pressures on Goldie to make him fall in line with the new policy of action in the Niger territories.[135]

Goldie was not impressed by the nonbelligerent attitude of the British government toward the French occupation of Bussa. He insisted that this be treated with the same gravity as a "French occupation of an unoccupied stretch of Australia's coast." But Chamberlain lectured Goldie on the fallacy of the much-vaunted caravan routes of Borgu and repeated Anderson's views on the loss of Borgu, whose economic value was questionable. A settlement with France was to be made "in the wider interests of the Empire." He emphasized that "whatever result might follow from such an invasion of Australia, there can be no question of going to war with France on account of Boussa or Mossi."[136] Goldie did not think that Britain should acquiesce in the loss of places occupied by France and try to secure remaining territories by effective occupation; nor should she sacrifice portions of British claims in the interest of an immediate settlement—if there was continued unwillingness to spend money on extensive effective occupation on the

TABLE 8

Return of Native Troops, Constabulary, and Police on West Coast of Africa, 3 May 1897

Colony or Protectorate	Corps	Hqts. of Corps	Miles from Accra	Offi-cers	Other Ranks	Field Guns	How Armed	Remarks
Gambia	Civil Police	Bathurst	1340	1	83	...	...	No mil. train.
Sierra Leone	Garrison Artillery	Freetown	930	2	100	...	?	natives
	Fortress Engin.	Freetown	930	...	23	...	?	natives
	W. I. Regiment	Freetown	930	22	867	...	LM rifles	
	Frontier Police	Freetown	930	17	487	1 maxim	LM carbine	
Gold Coast	Constabulary	Accra	...	20	1057	16	MH carbine	returns of 31 Dec. 1896
	Volunteers	Accra	...	19	306	...	MH carbine	31 Dec. 1896
Lagos	Constabulary	Lagos	240	10	678	...	Snider rifles	Return 8 Feb. 1893
Gold Coast Protectorate	Constabulary	Old Calabar	250	15	450	6	MH carbines	2 maxims
R.N.C. Territories	Constabulary	Lokoja	500	17	918	28	Snider rifles and a few MH	7 maxims and some odd field guns; Four 2½ pounder Nordenfelt QF guns

Source: CO879/48, War Office to Chamberlain, 8 May 1897.

French pattern. He agreed with Chamberlain's suggestion that England seize some unoccupied places and hold them while waiting for negotiations with France. "British gunboats should be sent to occupy a few points on the Ivory Coast where France has no military posts and which are therefore not effectively occupied according to the novel theory propounded by the French press," declared Goldie.[137] On the home front a west African council should be formed to cover the affairs of the "West African Territories," which would include Lagos, the Niger Coast Protectorate, and the territories of the Royal Niger Company, which for brevity Goldie called Nigeria.[138] The Foreign Office reinforced Chamberlain's pressures on Goldie.[139]

Chamberlain's opposition to Goldie at this time was based not on anticommercial sentiments but on the monopolistic practices of the Niger Company, the international difficulties the company created for the British government, and, above all, Goldie's unwillingness to pay for the effective administration and occupation of all the territories he claimed as British. Chamberlain pointed out the difference between Goldie's understanding of the charter granted to his company and the British government's interpretation of it. Furthermore, the members of Her Majesty's government "do not agree that he is to take all the profits, and that we are to spend hundreds of thousands, or possibly millions, in securing his claims against the French and that he is then to step in and enjoy without cost the security we have secured for him. If this is his view, our best course will be to expropriate him lock, stock, and barrel." [140]

The Foreign Office shared Chamberlain's suspicion of Goldie. Salisbury was displeased with Goldie's refractory and hedgy attitude and, after consulting Chamberlain, directed that discussions with Goldie about the future of the Royal Niger Company would be better dropped.[141] At this juncture Chamberlain was jubilant that his influence was beginning to count in west African affairs.[142] Even Queen Victoria could not but recognize Chamberlain's predominance over the cabinet on these issues. She complained that Chamberlain was very aggressive and would not see the other person's views because of his combative determination.[143] It seems to me, however, that Chamberlain was neither foolhardy nor impervious to reason; he was very determined to terminate the "policy of drift."

The desire to make the British position on the disputed areas of the hinterland clear made Chamberlain appear aggressive.[144] He wished to impress on the French government the degree of displeasure with which Britain viewed the occupation of Bussa and Mossi: "We ought even at the cost of war to keep the hinterland for the Gold Coast, Lagos and the Niger territories. We ought not to allow the Gambia and Sierra Leone business to be repeated." [145] Salisbury was reminded of the French game of making exaggerated claims at the outset with a view to obtaining a larger slice in the end.[146] This was to be prevented. When the French government made repeated overtures for the resumption of the work of the Niger Commission, Chamberlain took a firm line. He set the evacuation of Bussa by France as a prerequisite for the reopening of negotiations.

The French Government should be informed that the Boussa question does not come within the category of questions of doubtful interpretation which might be referred to a Commission, and that Her Majesty's Government must decline to re-enter upon the Niger Commission until this preliminary matter has been settled between the two Governments.[147]

Chamberlain's brinkmanship was therefore born not out of megalomania nor egotism but out of realism.

Meanwhile, Chamberlain pursued the creation of a west African force with vigor. He quickly secured Lugard's consent to command the proposed force in July 1897.[148] The governor of Lagos was instructed to increase the Lagos constabulary to about 2,000 men. For the first time Chamberlain stated that the British government would pay the expenses involved—a deviation from the traditional attitude of the British government since 1865. Mc-Callum was instructed to occupy places above 9° North Latitude in the hinterland of Lagos. All the points in dispute on the west bank of the Niger were detailed to him, and copies of treaties made by the Niger Company were also forwarded to Lagos. Then came the belligerent note in the instructions. Forces from Lagos were to be used to occupy places in Borgu not yet occupied by the French, and several points in the Dahomey hinterland were to be occupied. The number of soldiers at each occupied post should be between 100 and 150, including two European officers and a doctor. In all cases, the force left at each post should be stronger than that in the nearest French installation.[149]

The Foreign Office was formally informed of the proposals for a west African force by mid-August 1897, and the supporting views of the Intelligence Division of the War Office were communicated to Salisbury.[150] It was proposed to organize a west African council in Whitehall, to be made up of Goldie and experts from the Foreign, War, and Colonial Offices. Salisbury, who by this time had developed a strong suspicion of Goldie, objected to his inclusion in the membership of such a council, since he could not be held accountable to the government; he felt that Goldie should only be consulted by the government officials when necessary.[151] Goldie had already succumbed under official and private pressure and thought that the territories of the Royal Niger Company—Nigeria—should be taken away from a private company which was also engaged in trade. He thought this desirable in the interest of empire and added: "The duality of the Niger Company's functions has produced a bitter hostility among a handful of persons in Liverpool, which has had serious international effects."[152] His request that he be given "full prior knowledge" of the future of the Royal Niger Company as a prize for his cooperation with the government[153] was met by the cynical opposition of Salisbury and threats of expropriation by Chamberlain.[154]

With victory over the Niger Company secured, Chamberlain developed with liberty his plan for a west African force. His selection of Lugard turned out to be a wise choice. Lugard was experienced and acceptable to Goldie, but he was disliked by the French, who had not forgotten his anti-French exploits in Uganda against French Catholic missionaries.[155] The news of Lugard's appointment could not but make the French wish for a quick negotiated settlement of the disputes, since it reinforced the earnestness of Chamberlain and fostered his aggressive image. Furthermore, the agreement reached by France and Germany over the Togo-Dahomey frontier increased the desire of Salisbury to resume negotiations with France for reasons of European diplomacy and balance of power.[156] Monson dangled before Salisbury the unfathomable dangers of a hostile combination of the powers of Europe—France, Russia, and Germany—against an isolated Britain. Events in the Far East underscored the possibilities of such a combination, and no amount of territorial acquisition in the Niger territories could offset the consequences of such an isolation of Britain.

Impressed by these arguments, Salisbury informed Chamberlain that Hanotaux's repeated requests for the resumption of negotiations were no longer easy to refuse.[157] To Chamberlain the French initiative was calculated to halt British military preparations, which had disposed the French government more than ever to negotiate. Talks could be resumed, but the military plans would be executed fully, declared Chamberlain.[158] The governors of Lagos and the Gold Coast were instructed to occupy the hinterland of their colonies but not to attack the French.[159] Later Chamberlain secured the passage of a bill to establish a permanent West African Frontier Force by the House of Commons. He presented his case forcefully and won overwhelming support for the bill.[160]

The turning point in British policy in the Niger hinterland was the massacre of the Henderson expedition to Wa and Bona.[161] The tragedy that befell this expedition brought about the sending of two companies of the Second Battalion West Indies Regiment from Sierra Leone to the Gold Coast as well as the dispatch of two gunboats into the area.[162] By mid-May 1897, Chamberlain asked the War Office for more special-service officers to be provided for service in the Gold Coast if necessary.[163] The Foreign

Office counseled prudence and the avoidance of conflict with Samory's forces. But with a large number of British forces in the contested areas and the multiplication of military posts, the number of probable flashpoints of danger increased apace.

The first collision of British and French troops occurred at Asikasso, which was under French possession in late June 1897.[164] This accidental conflict demonstrated how unpredictable the situation in the hinterland had become once France no longer had a monopoly of military expeditions and posts. Soon British troops occupied Bona, Wa, and Lobi, while the French were entrenching their position in Borgu.[165] The occupation of Bonduku by British troops forced Hanotaux to renew requests for negotiations, though he observed that the interests at stake were not worth fighting over.[166] Chamberlain disagreed. The new plans were pursued with vigor. The crisis in the Dahomey-Niger hinterland had assumed alarming proportions by September 1897, and diplomacy was once more resorted to in order to stave off a colonial war which none of the powers wanted but which then appeared imminent.

8

The Work of the Niger Commission, October 1897–June 1898

The desire for the preservation of peace in Europe was one of the major factors which induced Hanotaux to seek a negotiated settlement of all the colonial questions that tended to divide France and England.[1] Though Hanotaux supported the policy of effective occupation pursued by French agents in the Dahomey-Niger hinterland, he never lost any opportunity to ask Britain for the resumption of the work of the Niger Commission, which was broken off in May 1896. Through Baron de Courcel he arranged a personal interview with Salisbury in March 1897, during which the two foreign ministers discussed Franco-British problems and differences. On the Niger question, Salisbury proposed arbitration, to which Hanotaux countered that "it was a difficult principle in policy to refer such matters to arbitration."[2] There was no meeting of minds. Though the meeting produced excellent results on Crete and some other matters, it remained, in Hanotaux's words, "sans influence sur l'issue de la négociation du Niger."[3]

During the six months which elapsed between this conference and the resumption of the work of the Niger Commission, the two governments exchanged several protests over the occupation of points in the disputed areas. These protests were, however, punctuated with pleas by France for the reopening of negotiations. British military measures were put in motion. Chamberlain's chessboard occupation plan had begun to work. French military superiority was at an end in the Niger territories, and Britain could now negotiate from strength. Profiting from the high spirits and good mood created in British official circles by the celebration of Queen Victoria's Jubilee, the French government pressed home their sincerity to negotiate with Britain.[4] Salisbury reacted favorably to the persistent French initiative, and both governments agreed to reconvene the Niger Commission at Paris.[5] The first session of the commission met on 29 October 1897, much later than Hanotaux anticipated, because of Chamberlain's absence from London.[6]

The Niger Commission Resumes Negotiations

There was little doubt about the areas under dispute. What divided the two powers was the manner in which these areas were to be attributed to one or the other power. Three principles were involved in the dispute: the doctrines of hinterland, prior treaties, and effective occupation. Britain wanted the differences to be settled on the basis of either the hinterland doctrine or the treaty doctrine. Salisbury thought that if these two doctrines formed the basis of a settlement, Britain would either get more than all she wanted or secure all the points on which she had set her heart—Bussa, Borgu, etc. "The French, of course, will evade both these doctrines and will try to work by the *occupation doctrine* only," he added.[7] If titles were not good unless supported by occupation, then France's title would only be good to places she actually held for as long as they held them. Any points above the ninth parallel which France did not actually hold would be open to British enterprise. Salisbury continued:

> And as we shall shortly have a much larger force in the region than they have, we can, without any suspicion of collision with them occupy a great many places in the country which they covet most. In a very short time the map will present an appearance of a favourable exception of English and French posts scattered over a vast expanse of desert.

This would displease the French and prove to them that their doctrine of "occupation right is both a logical and a practical failure." They might break the negotiations as a result of this.[8] In any case, Britain placed a high premium on the hinterland of Lagos and would not make any concessions in this area. British aspirations in the hinterland of the Gold Coast would be satisfied by whatever could be obtained there. "But as we shall probably have to give way somewhere," said Salisbury, "we prefer to make our concessions in the still unassigned territory north of the Gold Coast e.g. Wagadugu, etc. and not north of Lagos."

It is true that the French held on tenaciously to the doctrine of effective occupation as the main basis for the regulation of their rivalry with England in the Niger territories.[9] But Hanotaux stated that this principle[10] would be tempered by "a spirit of conciliation" arising out of his keen desire to settle the colonial questions pending between France and England.[11] This spirit of conciliation was reinforced by the belief in official circles in Paris that there would be a danger of a general uprising by Africans if British and French troops clashed in Borgu or in the hinterland of the Gold Coast near Samory's territory.[12]

It could be said, then, that neither Britain nor France issued exact instructions to the negotiators. Both left room for compromise. In the spring of 1898, when it became clear that none of the three major doctrines was acceptable to both as the basis for a settlement, their representatives resorted to compromise and conciliation for the adjustment of the conflicting claims.

There already existed in France an organization formed by "a body of respectable men" whose aim was to promote relations with England and create an entente cordiale between France and Britain. Such a movement also existed in England, under the leadership of Philip Stanhope, M.P. The French Chamber of Commerce in London threw its weight in support of these organizations and made both diplomatic and official contacts for the promotion of a rapprochement between France and Britain.[13] So, beneath the sound and fury of the press and the eager expansionists on both sides, there operated silent but formidable forces for an Anglo-French entente.

The first few sessions of the Niger Commission were taken up by discussions of the validity of the treaties on which territorial claims were based. The controversy centered on Bussa. The French representatives were not prepared to concede the evacuation of Bussa, even in return for Nikki and navigation rights on the Niger. There were no signs that France would budge on those points, which she claimed by the effective occupation doctrine, as discussions of British and French treaty rights proceeded.[14]

Unimpressed by the defensive attitude of the British negotiators, Chamberlain urged that they should seize the initiative. Bussa, which Britain was determined to keep, should be claimed by prior treaty rights and by virtue of the Say-Barruwa Line. Even if the hinterland doctrine were invoked, Bussa would still be British, since it lay directly in the hinterland of Lagos. If the French called off the negotiations because of the tough line England held over Bussa, they would be playing into Britain's hands, since the interim would surely be used for the occupation of more spots in the areas claimed by France. This would result in the entire west African hinterland being checkered with posts bearing the Union Jack and the Tricolor.[15] Convinced by Chamberlain's arguments about Bussa, Salisbury renewed with vigor British protests against French claims based on rudimentary posts of occupation and flag hoisting.[16] The lack of progress in the negotiations led to the recall of Monson to London for consultations, during which he received new briefings from Salisbury. The views were largely Chamberlain's, but Salisbury shared most of them by this time. French insistence on the invalidity of Lugard's treaty at Nikki was based on the fact that the British agent had not treated with the rightful king of Nikki but with an imposter. The British commissioners began to yield to the force of the French case,[17] and Chamberlain was enraged by what appeared to be weakness on the part of the British representatives. Ignoring the fact that the French case was in accordance with the political reality of Nikki, Chamberlain declared that the words of a "military officer of Major Lugard's standing and experience" outweighed all the declarations by blacks collected by the French after Lugard's expedition to Nikki.[18]

The cogency of Chamberlain's arguments convinced Salisbury to instruct Monson to ask the French to name the principle most acceptable to them as a basis for settling their claims—priority of treaties or the hinterland doctrine.[19] British claims, he advised, were to be stated unequivocally. It was thought that by adopting a firm attitude the French would suggest arbitration, in view of the military preparations completed by Britain in west Africa.[20]

It would be erroneous to say that Salisbury was at this juncture acting as a mouthpiece for Chamberlain. The prime minister had his own convictions about the foreign policy aims of the British government, and he stated these on several occasions in 1897.[21] With reference to the scramble for Africa, Salisbury stated the policy of his government at the Lord Mayor's banquet on 9 November 1897:

> Within the last twenty years a vast territory has been cast loose in Africa or has been put up as the object of the desire and acquisition of several enterprising Governments. . . . We desire to be governed by strict principles of right, and by all due and constant regard to the prospects and the interests of the Empire of the Queen. We do not desire any unjust or illegitimate achievements. We do not wish to take territory simply because it may look well to paint it red upon the map. The objects we have in view are strictly business objects. We wish to extend the commerce, the trade, the industry and the civilisation of mankind. We wish to throw open as many markets as possible, to bring as many producers and consumers into contact as possible; to throw open the great natural highways, the great waterways of this

great continent; we wish that trade should pursue its unchecked and unhindered course on the Niger, the Nile and the Zambezi.[22]

Salisbury made this clear statement of purpose shortly after the resumption of the work of the Niger Commission. There can be no doubt that he did not wish to be obstructed in the implementation of this policy. Nor could he be expected to be easily thwarted by the French invocation of the effective occupation doctrine.

The effective occupation of Borgu at this period by British and French troops led to incidents which threatened the progress of the negotiations at Paris. Ballot did not accept the invitation to attend the Jubilee celebrations in Lagos, because he went into Borgu to supervise the progress of the French occupation of Borgu.[23] From reports and observation, Ballot informed Lebon that it was necessary to intervene vigorously in Borgu. Reinforcements were sent to Bretonnet and Ganier. Baud and Vermeersch were to redeploy their forces in Borgu and cooperate with Bretonnet at Bussa and Betbeder at Say.[24] The Franco-German agreement of July 1897 had released troops tied down to French posts at Bafilo, Kirikri, and Kuntum. These troops could now be reassigned into Borgu and elsewhere to strengthen French occupation.[25]

The governor of Lagos reacted to the French presence in the hinterland of Lagos by barring French messengers from routes in the area. As if to impress on Ballot and Bretonnet that Bussa was in the British sphere, letters sent by Bretonnet to the governor were seized and diverted to Lagos.[26] A serious view was taken in London of the presence of French troops in the hinterland of Lagos below the ninth parallel. Monson was instructed to protest against the presence of Lieutenant Brot in this area and even against the occupation of Say by Captain Betbeder.[27] These incidents did not foster the work of the Niger Commission. To prevent their proliferation, Salisbury proposed that identical instructions be issued to the British and French agents in the Niger territories, "in view of the reopening of negotiations."[28] Though French officials blamed London for the slow progress of the talks, Hanotaux asked Lebon to give more freedom of action to the French negotiators.[29] He realized that the unyielding attitude of Binger did not further the negotiations. Courcel was instructed to contact Salisbury and explore why London was taking a tough line.[30] Hanotaux was not surprised when Courcel reported that Salisbury sent him to talk to Chamberlain directly so that he could perceive the nature of the pressures on the Foreign Office. During the interview with Chamberlain at the end of November, Courcel was impressed by the determination of the colonial secretary to take a belligerent course if necessary for the protection of British interests.[31]

Diplomatic pressure from Paris led Salisbury to suggest that France be granted access to the navigable Niger and that a Chinde type concession be made to her around Leaba. This would be a fair exchange for French concessions over the Say-Barruwa Line and elsewhere. Chamberlain opposed these proposals.[32] He felt that no foreign power should be granted any portion of the Lower Niger. France could be allowed freedom of trade on the Niger following a revision of the navigation laws on the river, but access to the Niger should not be a prerequisite for an agreement with France. French invasion of Borgu, as Monson suggested, would be an act of aggression. Such a hostile act would be followed by the withdrawal of the British ambassador at Paris, and vigorous measures would be taken to protect British interests. Monson already reported that the military measures initiated by Chamberlain were producing effects in Paris. Courcel's report of his interview with Chamberlain added to this effect. Continued pressure from the Colonial Office resulted in the dispatch of instructions to Paris on the lines proposed by Chamberlain.[33] The only area in which concessions could be made was Mossi, if the French agreed to the Gold Coast–Ivory Coast boundary which was to run along the River Comoe up to the ninth parallel.[34]

At this point in the diplomatic tussle, Hanotaux wished to introduce into the negotiations the question of the Upper Nile Valley. This would have widened the options and broadened the bases for compromise. The British government refused any discussion on the Sudan. Monson lectured Hanotaux on Grey's speech of 1895, which made it clear that any French advance on the Upper Nile would be "an unfriendly act" and consequently a casus belli.[35] The result was that the French realized that the west African questions were to be resolved in their own context. The Quai d'Orsay and the Foreign Office had to bestir themselves, absorb the public and private pressures exerted on them,[36] and formulate a project on which fruitful discussions could be based.

Controversy over African Treaties

The first three months of the commission were mainly absorbed by the controversy over treaties concluded by French and British agents with African rulers. The validity and the priority of treaties formed the bones of contention. The question of notification as enjoined by the Berlin Act of 1885 was secondary. The French tried to nullify the priority of British treaties by questioning their form, the political status of those who signed them, and even the intentions of the parties to some of these treaties. Consequently, the validity of British treaties in important but disputed places such as Nikki, Mossi, and Bussa was debated or denied by the French.

It is true that treaties are a recognized method of acquiring territory,[37] but the African treaties of this period raise some interesting questions. Could chiefs and kings sign away the sovereignty of their kingdoms and the independence of their people? Did the kings and chiefs own all the land under their rule, and could they sign away the rights of their subjects? There are also the questions of alienable and inalienable rights and of the introduction of written contracts as diplomatic instruments among "states" unused to such instruments.

Land was usually owned by families, who shared it out to their members. Certain plots were owned communally, and it was from such plots that missionaries and other foreign agents received grants of land for their establishments.[38] In most cases it was impossible to define the area covered by the treaties made with European agents, since the chieftaincies or kingdoms in question had no fixed frontiers. For instance, King Bantchande claimed he was supreme ruler over all Gurma when he treated with the French. But his claim was challenged in Pama and Matiacuali, only a few miles away from his seat at Fada N'Gurma.[39] The events in Borgu illustrated the problems of both area and jurisdiction. The Royal Niger Company's treaties with Bussa in 1885 and 1890 were thought to have secured Borgu for Britain. But when it became clear that the ruler of Bussa had no jurisdiction over other parts of Borgu such as Kouande and Nikki, Lugard was dispatched to Nikki in 1894 to conclude a new treaty.[40]

Another difficulty was whether the African rulers understood the ramifications of the treaties to which they appended their marks or seals. Did the interpreters know fully the import of the wordings of the treaties and their legal and political implications? In many cases, the interpreters had only a smattering of the local language and could therefore render a limited service.[41] Even in cases where there was full knowledge of the implications of these treaties, such as the Ferguson treaty at Wagadugu (2 July 1894), the treaties were not taken as seriously as contracts made in the traditional manner—oral and verbal agreements concluded with symbolic acts or solemn oaths. Boukary Koutou sought British aid against Voulet, who drove him out of Wagadugu,[42] and thus destroyed the French claim that he regarded his treaty with Ferguson as a mere certificate of hospitality which was to be shown to any European visitors.[43] The customary contract between Ashanti and Mamprussi on one hand, and Mamprussi and Mossi on the other, may be cited here. These unwritten but solemn contracts were deeply respected. When in 1898 the fugitive Mogho Naba of Wagadugu was offered asylum in Mamprussi, he refused to enter either Gambaga or Nalerigu, the old and the new capitals, respectively. This was because the sovereigns of Mossi and Mamprussi entered into an agreement intended to prevent the conquest of either kingdom by the other. "Each swore a solemn oath, binding on their descendants, that the king of neither country would enter the capital of the other, and the terms of the oath involved a transgressor in certain and violent death." [44] Boukary Koutou settled at Zongoiri, near Gambaga, where he died and was buried in 1904.[45]

Though in some cases the condition of a full understanding of the treaty on both sides was not met,[46] some African rulers entered into treaty relations with Europeans for their own selfish ends. There were times when these treaties were concluded under duress or with the aim of getting rid of the intruding foreigners as quickly as possible. In such cases the treaty was destroyed as soon as the Europeans left; this was what happened in Kodjar.[47] Treaties with Europeans, like umbrellas, could shield the signatories from the attacks of their opponents or rivals. Toffa of Porto Novo and Bantchande of Fada N'Gurma concluded treaties for this purpose.

The attraction of the annual subsidies or salaries usually guaranteed to paramount chiefs in European treaties should not be overlooked. These annual payments, which came easily after a leader appended his mark to a piece of paper, were a boon to personal wealth. They also increased the prestige of the recipient, since they were regarded as payments in recognition of his sovereignty and authority.[48] What is clear, then, is that the debates of the Niger Commission about the validity of those African treaties submitted to it did not include the African rulers' view of the treaties. The declarations produced by the French that Lugard did not treat with the rightful king of Nikki did not affect the fact that the said ruler and his successor were opposed to French presence at Nikki. Only military conquest could secure the French occupation of Nikki.[49]

The Emergence of Draft Conventions

The debate on the validity of British treaties was carried a step further when the French negotiators tendered the expert opinion of Professor Renault.[50] He did not think that the British treaty with Mossi was valid in the light of the Berlin Act of 1885. Above all, the treaty was not binding on any third power which wanted to enter into relations with the ruler of Mossi. It was the onus of the ruler of Mossi to seek British permission to enter into such a relation, not that of the European power, according to the treaty.[51] Though maintaining their stand that French occupation of Mossi was an unfriendly act, the British negotiators could not refute the force of the French argument. They asked London for legal advice with which to counter Professor Renault's opinion.[52]

Meanwhile, the proposals made by Britain in December were accepted by France on the condition that a strip of territory from Nikki to the Niger would be guaranteed to France.[53] France, however, was unprepared to evacuate Bussa. This was in keeping with Courcel's earlier opinion that it was essential for France to obtain an outlet on the navigable Niger below the cataracts of Bussa in order to make the free navigation guaranteed by the Berlin Act a practical reality.[54] The French proposal was rejected by the cabinet on Chamberlain's insistence; the concessions offered to France in Mossi and in Gurunsi were enough. Salisbury suggested a different type of access to the Niger for France.[55] Both Chamberlain and Goldie were opposed to the cession of any territory to France in the Nikki-Niger region. Such a cession, it was argued, would diminish British trade in the area. It would prejudice the territorial integrity of the British possessions and might encourage France to demand similar concessions in other regions of west Africa. The governor of Lagos was instructed to reinforce the forces north of the ninth parallel because of the changed circumstances.[56] Chamberlain did this at the time British negotiators were pleading for a modification of the British position for fear of a conflict with France in west Africa, where France could mobilize Senegalese tirailleurs against Britain.[57]

The discussion of the treaty rights of Britain and France in Gurunsi ended in a stalemate. France claimed Gurunsi by virtue of the treaties of Voulet and Chanoine at Sati and Leo with Hamaria; the British claim was based on the treaties concluded by Henderson with Barbato. The fortunes of civil war in Gurunsi were in Hamaria's favor. The pro-British Barbato was vanquished, and his claims to paramountcy came to nothing.[58] In any case, Britain was prepared to concede Gurunsi and Mossi to France.[59]

On 31 January, Gosselin put the negotiations on a new footing by introducing the question of identic tariffs in both French and British territories.[60] This was a significant step, because identic tariffs were to become an important factor in the final agreement. The French were told that the fear that British commerce would be adversely affected by the expansion of French territories toward the Lower Niger was a paramount factor in the British attitude. French protectionism was disliked, and a determined effort was made to restrict the area in which it operated. The acceptance of the principle of identic tariffs would produce a remarkable thaw in the British position and prove to France that purely territorial considerations were not Britain's concern.

Britain proposed that identic tariffs operate in British and French territories for up to a period of five years. Any differences were to be submitted to arbitration, with the head of customs in Denmark or Belgium called in to adjudicate. The French negotiators expressed willingness to accept the fiscal proposals if France were granted access to the navigable Niger, which they considered a sine qua non in any settlement of the disputes over the Niger territories. France would evacuate Bussa if she were granted access to the Lower Niger; Mossi would also be evacuated. But identic tariffs could not be discussed in detail without German participation, and the Niger Commission was not competent to discuss tariffs.[61] By the beginning of February, then, the major issues before the commission had crystallized into French resistance to identic tariffs and British objections to a band of territory for France on the Lower Niger. Disputes over occupied spots such as Bona, Wa, Lobi, Nikki, and Bussa continued as secondary concerns.[62]

By mid-February, revised instructions were sent to Paris. Britain now had the initiative in the negotiations, and the British press[63] urged the government to be firm in dealing with Hanotaux, who was a tool of the French expansionists. Courcel confirmed that Britain had the initiative. He surmised from his talks with Salisbury that massive reinforcements of troops in west Africa were planned to strengthen the British position. The vague British position at the talks in Paris contrasted greatly with active mobilization of forces in west Africa, the effect of which had become evident in Paris.[64]

The new proposals from London made significant concessions to France. In the Gold Coast hinterland, Britain's claims to Mossi and Gurunsi would be renounced, but Bona, Lobi, Wa, and Mamprussi, and all territory between these and 9° North Latitude would be British. The king of Mossi, Boukary Koutou, was to be reinstated or paid adequate compensation by France. In the hinterland of Lagos, Britain would keep all Bussa and eastern Borgu up to Ilo. Western Borgu, including Nikki and the Dendi region with Say, would be conceded to France. This would have the happy result of linking the French Sudan with Gurma, Liptako, Yagha Torodi, and the kingdom of Nikki. Britain would keep all Sokoto, and France was to recognize the Say-Barruwa Line. On the Niger, Britain would amend the monopolistic regulations of the Royal Niger Company to remove unnecessary restrictions. Above all, Britain would lease land to France on the Niger for commercial purposes only. Such land would be British and under British law and control. For all these concessions, France was to consent to a regime of identic tariffs in the possessions of both powers from the Ivory Coast to the Niger coast protectorate. Finally, France was to withdraw from Bussa, and Britain from Gurunsi.[65]

For the first time, Hanotaux reacted favorably to proposals from London. He appreciated Salisbury's conciliatory attitude and promised to contain the enthusiasm of the colonial group and the intransigence of the protectionists led by Méline.[66] Strong objections were raised about the tariff proposals: the lease should be for ninety-nine years, and freedom of navigation was to be guaranteed on the Niger.[67] Geoffray was instructed to ask Salisbury for a modification of the tariff proposals. He found out that the abolition of differential tariffs was the keystone in the British proposals. Salisbury even suggested that Germany be invited to join the fiscal zone proposed by England. Geoffray suggested to Hanotaux that France draw up a concrete project for agreement without delay, in order to resolve this complicated affair.[68] This did not erode the opposition of the French ministry of colonies to both the tariff and the territorial proposals.[69]

Hanotaux had begun to show signs of suspicion about the policy aims of Britain. The military preparations and measures could not be overlooked,[70] despite diplomatic reports about Salisbury's conciliatory mood. The fiscal proposals would harm French commerce; they might have been thrown in by Britain to precipitate a crisis. France would defend her interests anywhere. If Britain started a conflict or wanted one, France would be ready for it.[71] Hanotaux worked out a war plan. Russia would be asked to tie down British forces in India. British possessions on the Niger could be attacked rapidly through Dahomey. The Turks, who had "an excellent army," would be asked to join France in an assault on Egypt, which they would be eager to regain. Colonial expenses on Tonkin and Annam could be cut to provide funds for a war with Britain in Africa, where her chartered companies were exploiting and molesting the natives—unlike the French, who were raising the natives to their own level.[72]

Why did Hanotaux, who had hitherto asserted that the objects desired in the Niger territories were not worth fighting for, begin to consider the probability of war seriously? He was swayed by the military measures initiated by Britain in the area and the debate in the House of Commons about the creation of a permanent West African Frontier Force,[73] as well as the constant reports from London about the public excitement in Britain concerning questions of the Niger hinterland. According to Courcel:

> L'opinion anglais demeure très excitée par tout ce qui touche à la délimitation des territoires du Niger et aux affaires connexés. . . . Il rest agité passioné, et proie à la conviction presque générale que l'Angleterre a subi, du chel de la France, à la fois un affront à sa dignité et un dommage qui demande réparation. . . . Cette disposition moral tient à un ensemble des causes que j'ai en maintes fois l'occasion de vous exposer dans le détail, et sur lesquelles il me parait superflu de revenir aujourd'hui.[74]

Above all, the news that the British government would take over the territories of the Niger Company and withdraw its charter convinced Hanotaux that Britain meant business.[75] For reasons of state, therefore, it was imperative for him to consider questions of security and advance tentative war plans.[76]

In Britain there was an outbreak of effervescent jingoism over the Niger questions. Courcel was alarmed by the ever-mounting press campaign in Britain against France. He observed that the announcement of the presence of French troops in Argungu (Sokoto) worsened and intensified the attacks in which even serious newspapers like the *Times* and the *Standard* participated.[77] Just as the chauvinistic expansionists across the channel clamored for vigorous action by their government, the jingos in Britain raised battle cries. "What we are now undergoing in China and on the West Coast of Africa we shall undergo everywhere unless and until we fight." This line, taken by the editor of the *South Wales Daily Star*,[78] shows that concern over the disputes with France was not restricted to such metropolitan centers as London, Liverpool, and Glasgow. At the official level, preparedness seems to have been the motto, though Salisbury thought that war was a remote possibility.[79] The mobilization of public opinion and the widespread agitation for war were not neglected by the politicians and diplomats of both countries. It contributed, with other factors, to preparing the ground for a settlement.

Underneath the public furor, French officials studied the British proposals carefully. Their reaction was discussed on 22 February. Bussa was conceded to Britain, but Bona and Lobi were claimed by France. The demand for a tract of territory to connect Dahomey with the Niger was renewed. The fiscal proposals were shelved pending their discussion by the Chamber of

Deputies and consultations with Germany. Binger renewed the French request for an arrangement for the evacuation of invalids through British territory on the model of the Franco-German agreement of 1897. If the proposal by Britain for escort by armed British soldiers were adopted, it would cause constant friction.[80]

When the French position was reviewed at a cabinet meeting in London, the demand for a corridor 100 miles by 30 miles from Dahomey to the Lower Niger was stoutly rejected. The withdrawal of British claims to Mossi was unanimously approved; even Chamberlain conceded this point, in view of the development projects which France had initiated in Mossi.[81] But the French press continued to accuse Chamberlain of bad faith and of the desire to sabotage the efforts of the Niger Commission.[82]

Diplomatic pressure was increased on both sides. Monson told Salisbury that the Méline Cabinet appeared stable enough to last for a long time. There was no need to dillydally, hoping for a change of government in Paris which might bring into office new men more desirous for Anglo-French understanding than Méline and his cabinet.[83] On the French side, Courcel increased his pressure on Hanotaux for a conciliatory attitude instead of stubborn adherence to the effective occupation doctrine. After pointing out that the west African questions were made more difficult by the international situation in Egypt and China, he warned that they could lead to serious conflicts between England and France. Furthermore, the domestic situation in Britain should not be neglected. Though the government had overcome Goldie's obstructionism, there was still the problem of the continued existence of the coalition of Conservatives and Unionists. Salisbury's health was failing. The opportunity offered by his moderating influence should be utilized. If Salisbury left the cabinet, the coalition might come to an end. In such a case power would pass into the hands of the militant imperialists, whose most brilliant leaders were Lord Rosebery and Sir Edward Grey. Such an event would shatter all hopes of a negotiated and peaceful settlement with Britain. Moreover, Queen Victoria was not only advanced in age but also in declining and precarious health. Her moderating influence might be lost at any time. For both domestic and international reasons a quick settlement with Britain would be in the best interests of France.[84]

The first sign of a thaw in the French position was given by Hanotaux on 4 March, during a luncheon in honor of the Prince of Wales at Paris. Hanotaux confided to Gosselin that he had made much progress in assuaging the fears of the protectionist zealots around him. The fiscal proposal of

Britain would be accepted if commensurate territorial concessions were made to France.[85] Hopes of a settlement began to rise. On 15 March Hanotaux presented to Monson the French Projet de la Convention, which, it was hoped, would facilitate the work of the Niger Commission and lead to a quick settlement.[86]

The essence of the French draft convention was that it accepted the principle of equality of treatment of British and French commerce in the possession of both powers. However, it stated that tariffs in British and French territories need not be identical, though freedom of trade was to be guaranteed. This was done in deference to the wishes of the protectionists in the Chamber of Deputies, about seven-eighths of whom represented agricultural constituencies. France would recognize the Say-Barruwa Line if Britain guaranteed her freedom of movement through British territory in Sokoto to the Chad basin, the eastern and northern shores of which France claimed.[87]

The ambiguity of Hanotaux's Chad proposal raised the question of whether France laid claim on all the territory north of Lake Chad up to the Nile valley. The fact that French expeditions were operating in this region at the time accentuated the doubts. But since France had made a significant shift in her opposition to identic tariffs, Monson suggested that a British draft convention be quickly submitted to the Niger Commission. This draft should contain the maximum of British claims.[88]

Courcel met A. J. Balfour at the Foreign Office to discuss the new proposals. Balfour remarked that the ten-year tariff arrangement proposed by Hanotaux was no adequate concession for the loss of Mossi. Though the proposals marked an advance on the French side, they lacked a reciprocity of concessions. As such the British representatives at the Niger Commission had been instructed to reject them.[89] Courcel attributed Balfour's harsh tone to Colonial Office influence. Be that as it may, it had the salutary effect of softening the French government further. Hanotaux now realized that if the negotiations collapsed again, the consequences would be incalculable.

Already the checkerboard policy of counter-effective occupation was proceeding apace in Borgu. The Bariba were up in arms against the French, who believed that British encouragement was not lacking in the widespread uprising against them.[90] The crucial question in Nikki at this time was the succession to the throne following the death of old Sero Torou on 23 December 1897. There were four pretenders. British agents supported Worou Yoro and Sero Kora Yerima; the French favored Ourou Konde and Ali Barca. Ourou Konde was elected amid pomp and pageantry on 25 February

1898. He had been chief of Dounkassa and was earmarked by Ballot as the successor of the grand old Sero Torou.[91] The French protégé was described as "un fantoche sans influence sur la nation Bariba."[92] Such a puppet would fit into the French scheme of things, for at this time it was not in the interests of France to install strong African rulers, since their policies would conflict with those of France at a time when the establishment of French authority was the paramount concern of French agents.[93]

The British, who were not to be outdone, reacted by proclaiming Worou Yoro the king of Nikki and announced that they would march to Nikki to install him. Acting Governor Pascal said that such an act would be humiliating to the French and blamed McCallum of Lagos for the project, which could lead to conflict. Pascal complained that the ministerial instruction which recommended prudence did not envisage developments such as those in Borgu. He advised Ricour to defend himself if British troops attacked his post.[94] Colonel James Willcocks was charged with counter-effective occupation of Borgu. He was to create posts in-between French posts in order to isolate the French posts and render them untenable so as to obtain their evacuation.[95] It was reported that there were approximately 8,000 men in the British forces in west Africa.[96] Paris and Porto Novo reckoned with this force, and its gradual growth affected their attitude to the Niger question.[97]

What French agents in Borgu and the officials in Paris failed to realize was that the opposition to their enterprise was a widespread resistance movement by the Bariba. In eastern and western Borgu, almost every chieftaincy objected to the permanent establishment of French military and administrative authority in its sphere of authority. This resistance led to the widespread battles between the Bariba and the French in the kingdoms of Nikki and Kouande.[98] Even the death in battle at Allio of the popular leader Saka Ycrima did not end the uprising of the Bariba. Rapid communication between the chiefs through messengers on horseback facilitated their simultaneous armed opposition to the French, who were constrained to evacuate their post at Kishi[99] by the intensity of the resistance of the Africans.

At the same time that the Dahomey and Lagos hinterland was being occupied by British and French troops, the Niger Commission grappled with the task of settling the conflicting claims of Britain and France in the area. Monson's advice that a British draft convention be presented to the negotiators was followed. The draft convention produced in London had two prominent features. The first and more important was the proposal for the establishment of identical tariffs in all British and French possessions from the Niger to the Ivory Coast. The second was the repetition of Britain's territorial claims, which refused France any access to the Lower Niger through a corridor of French territory.[100]

Britain restated her claims to Bona and Lobi, irrespective of the French demand for these towns, which were located in auriferous territory. The Dahomey-Lagos frontier was to be prolonged northward to the Niger so as to include eastern Borgu[101] in the British sphere, whereas Nikki and its adjacent districts were to be recognized as French. The frontier line was to hit the Niger in such a manner as to leave within the British sphere Ilo, Gomba, and Bussa and all its environs.

It is of interest to note that France was prepared to give up Nikki in order to obtain some portion of the navigable Niger. Hanotaux communicated to Binger sketch maps showing how France could retain Bussa and a portion of the Lower Niger by offering Nikki to Britain.[102] But the unbending resolution of the British government not to give away any section of the Lower Niger rendered the French plan inoperative.

Britain proposed to revise the regulations on the Niger to ensure freedom of navigation in accordance with the Berlin Act of 1885, but not on the Zambezi pattern. Article 5 of the draft convention proposed that France could lease land on the Niger and at its mouth. No duties whatever would be charged for goods moved from the leased plots to and from French territory. Arms, ammunition, and trade spirits were exemptions. The leased plots of land would remain British territory, and everything on them would be under British jurisdiction. The concessions made to France on the Lower Niger were to be reciprocated on the Upper and Middle Niger.[103]

Overriding and inextricably linked with these territorial proposals was the identic tariff proposal. Nondiscriminatory tariffs were to operate in British and French possessions, excluding Senegal and Gambia. This would throw open to the traders of both nations all the disputed territories and more, since the identic tariff zone was to include all the territory between the Cameroons and Lake Chad and south of the Say-Barruwa Line and the Ivory Coast. British representatives in Paris were instructed to claim all of Mossi, Gurunsi, Mamprussi, Bona, Lobi, and all territory between the ninth parallel and these points if France rejected the fiscal proposals. If Britain claimed Mossi, special treatment was envisaged for the Naba of Wagadugu, since his country would be in the British sphere.[104] In addition to the special treatment of African chiefs, Britain also proposed the subsequent appointment of joint commissions for defining the boundaries agreed to in principle.

The insistence of the British government on the establishment of identic tariffs in each of the French and British territories was mainly due to pressure from British merchants who had commercial interests in west Africa. A repetition of the Sierra Leone type of agreement was undesirable to the merchants as well as to Chamberlain. British chambers of commerce, therefore, sent a strong deputation to Salisbury to express their views on conditions of commerce in west Africa. The deputation emphasized particularly their desire to see the abolition of differential tariffs in French territories and the establishment of a customs union between British and French territories and probably including German possessions. Salisbury received these suggestions favorably.[105] That these proposals were given pride of place in the draft convention sent to Paris shows that both Chamberlain and Salisbury were responsive to the pressures of the chambers of commerce.

Commenting on the effect of the deputation of the chambers of commerce to Salisbury, the French chargé d'affaires in London stated:

> Il est permis d'attacher une certaine importance à cette manifestation qui était annoncée plusieurs jours, et qui se produit avec une entière indépendance, du moins à l'égard de la Compagnie Royale du Niger. ... La réponse de Lord Salisbury parait avoir été très prudente, bien qu'il ait accueilli avec faveur les suggestions des délégués.[106]

Concrete bargaining ensued after the British draft convention was submitted. The proposed Gold Coast–Ivory Coast frontier was acceptable to France if Britain yielded Bona and Lobi. The proposed Lagos-Dahomey boundary was also acceptable to France in principle, but Binger observed that it would involve the withdrawal of French forces from about eight posts. If there were no compensatory British withdrawals, French public opinion would be against the arrangement, since the amour propre of France would be involved.[107] Binger now appeared to be appealing to Chamberlain's doctrine of "territorial concessions for territorial concessions, trade facilities for trade facilities, and nothing for nothing."

The choice before the French was a hard one. If they wanted the vast territories upon which they had set their hearts, they would have to accept the fiscal proposals. If they rejected the identic tariffs, they stood to lose most of the territory they desired or face a breakdown of the negotiations. The latter was now a frightening prospect, given the build-up of British troops in the Niger territories. According to Geoffray, British forces in west Africa "sont actuellement relativement très considerables et dépassent dans des proportions écrasantes le chiffre de nos troupes tel qu'il résulte de l'état que Votre Excellence a bien voulu me communiquer." [108] Furthermore, Courcel, who discussed the proposals with Balfour, warned Hanotaux of the danger of relying on the conciliatory disposition of the Foreign Office, in view of the "special relations" which existed between it and the Colonial Office.[109] This dominance of the Colonial Office in the direction of the negotiations was underscored by Geoffray. He pointed out that the affairs of China and the Spanish-American conflict had diverted public attention from the Niger region. But it appeared that the lull in press attacks would soon be over. This would be pleasing to the Colonial Office, which "affecterait des allures peu conciliantes et qui revendiquerait le droit de suivre les négociations anglo-françaises, en laissant au Foreign Office le simple rôle d'agent de transmission." [110]

The French representatives held out over the fiscal proposals. Courcel discussed the ramifications of these with Gosselin in Paris when he was recalled for consultations. It was pointed out what overwhelming advantages their adoption would give to British commerce, especially British shipping, which carried most French goods and men to west Africa.[111] Toward the end of April, the identic tariff proposal was accepted by France, provided that Mossi would be excluded from the zone in which it would operate. A limit of thirty years was set for the operation of the regime over the selected areas.[112] The reason for the exclusion of Mossi was the French fear that their authority there would be compromised by British economic activity, which could result in the economic integration of Mossi and the Gold Coast. Such a fusion would encourage and facilitate anti-French agitation by the deposed Naba of Wagadugu, who was a refugee in Mamprussi.

Monson signaled that the time was opportune, from the French point of view, for the settlement of difficulties with foreign powers. The Dreyfus affair had shaken up the Méline Cabinet,[113] which was desperate for any accomplishments in foreign affairs which would lend it respectability in the forthcoming parliamentary elections in June. Monson suggested that the French government be met halfway with some concessions, since they had accepted the identic tariff proposal. Under the impulsion of Chamberlain, instructions were sent to Paris restating the British position with no concessions. Salisbury pointed out that French merchants could do business in British possessions as long as they observed the essential principles of "free trade." He argued that identic tariffs in Mossi would benefit both Mossi and the Gold Coast. The French should be told that British public opinion was not easier to placate than its French counterpart in colonial and other matters.[114]

No progress was made when the recent proposals were discussed, even after Gosselin dropped a hint about the future withdrawal of the charter of the Royal Niger Company.[115] Later Lecomte announced the French intention to accept the Mossi demand made by Britain if Britain conceded Bona and Ilo.[116] This was unacceptable to Britain, who also restated their rights over the navigation of the Lower Niger.[117] The major issues of identic tariffs and principal frontier lines had, however, been agreed upon in principle; only the attribution of a few towns held up the final settlement. The two most controversial points were Ilo and Bona. France claimed these two towns for sentimental reasons: Lieutenant Braulot was killed at Bona by Samory's forces on 20 August 1897, and Lieutenant de Bernis was assassinated at Ilo early in February 1898. Therefore, France desired these two spots to honor the valiant officers who died there.[118] Hanotaux appealed to the hinterland theory and to the principle of reciprocal withdrawals to justify his claim to Bona:

> Bona empiète sur l'hinterland de la Cote d'Ivoire et dont l'évacuation par les troupes anglaises pouvait être représenté comme compensant, dans une certain mesure, les abandons considérables que le projet d'arrangement impliquait pour nous sur le Niger comme par notre colonie de la Cote d'Ivoire.[119]

Chamberlain was opposed to the cession of Ilo to France. This would give the French a foothold on the Lower Niger and was consequently inadmissible. It was proposed to compensate France with Simitia in Sierra Leone and some territory in the Sokoto region, but this was not acceptable to France, where the "blood and glory" doctrine made a strong appeal. Salisbury was wary about concessions to France north of Lake Chad because of the policy of excluding France from the Upper Nile Valley.[120] In view of this, Salisbury urged Chamberlain that a quick settlement would be to Britain's interests. "If you wish to come to terms it would be prudent to do so before we take Khartoum. We shall get nothing out of the French Assembly after that event," said Salisbury.[121] After reading the draft of the dispatch intended for Monson, Chamberlain expressed his approval and optimism: "I agree with the suggested amendments. Whatever may be Hanotaux's ideas I think we are equally interested in now getting a quick settlement and I do not want to make difficulties about trifles."[122] When the arch author of British intransigence at the negotiations, who had several times rebuked Gosselin and Everett for their softness, adopted such an attitude, the negotiations could not but be rapidly and successfully concluded.

The domestic situation in France boded ill for the Méline Cabinet. Elections were to take place in the summer of 1898, and there seemed to be writings on the wall indicating the end of Méline's conservative and protectionist ministry. The Dreyfus affair had embarrassed the government. Not even André Lebon's spectacular visit to Senegal [123] could strengthen his political position. He was not reelected at the first ballot in his constituency, and hopes of his winning reelection on the second were as thin as butter on a roadhouse sandwich.[124] Hanotaux himself had been laid down by illness off and on, like Salisbury.[125] There was then, an urgency in the Quai d'Orsay to clinch an agreement with Britain so as to add one more feather to Hanotaux's cap.[126]

On 30 May the French negotiators announced their acceptance of the proposals for the navigation of the Niger. This French gesture was underscored by Hanotaux's resolution not to give up both Ilo and Bona, which had been, as it were, consecrated by "the blood of their soldiers." Soon England conceded Bona but kept Ilo and Simitia.[127] Courcel reported that Chamberlain was the ringleader of the intransigent policy in the cabinet and that other members of the Salisbury ministry who were implacably opposed to concessions rallied around him. It was Chamberlain who dispatched Goldie to Paris to toughen Gosselin and Everett, who he thought were yielding to French pressures easily. Ilo was not to be given up at any cost, despite Monson's telegram to Salisbury that "the fate of negotiations hangs on Ilo."[128]

Finally, Lecomte and Binger informed their British counterparts on 5 June that the French government had accepted the British proposal about Ilo and Bona. The restriction on arms and spirits was dropped by Britain regarding the French leases on the Niger, with the provision that Britain could unilaterally restrict trade in these commodities should the need to do so arise. Likewise, the regulations on the navigation of the Niger could be amended by Britain as she saw fit. France would be notified four months in advance of any such amendments.[129] The troops of both powers were to be withdrawn from the posts ceded, and this reciprocal withdrawal of troops was to be effected within three months of settlement. Instructions were to be issued to colonial governors to see that the evacuation of posts was carried out without incident—especially in Borgu, where British and French posts were juxtaposed and military tempers were high.[130]

The Settlement and Reactions to It

The terms of the settlement were enshrined in the Anglo-French Convention, which was signed at Paris on 14 June 1898.[131] This marked the crowning of the diplomatic labors of about eight months. Gosselin and Everett were praised by Monson for their steadiness and dignity and for the tact with which they dealt with their French colleagues.[132] In Paris, Lebon recommended to Hanotaux that Binger deserved to be made a commander of the Legion of Honor because of his work in the Niger Commission.[133]

In conclusion, it may be pointed out that the most important reason why a settlement was reached was the acceptance by France of the identic tariff proposal made by Britain. Territories which Britain could not acquire directly were placed at her disposal indirectly by the operation of the non-discriminatory tariff policy. France acquired large tracts of barren and thinly-populated country, whereas British acquisitions were fertile and well-populated territories. These arrangements were strongly opposed by many people in France and Britain. As a result of this and the Fashoda affair, the ratification of the convention was postponed till 13 June 1899.

The consideration of the European balance of power as well as of other international issues were also important in deciding the questions in west Africa. The human factors and the domestic affairs in France and Britain helped to bring about a settlement of Anglo-French contentions in west Africa. Of course, the fear of war with Britain, especially after Chamberlain had mobilized the West African Frontier Force under Lugard, was instrumental in disposing the French government to seek a peaceful settlement.

Though a conjunction of all these factors facilitated a settlement of the disputes in west Africa, it cannot be said that the settlement which was reached was mutually satisfactory. In France the fiscal arrangement was attacked viciously by both merchants and politicians. Leading the attack was Etienne, who criticized the niggardly and miserly concessions which Britain condescended to make to France. Though pleased to see the realization of his dream of uniting all French possessions in west Africa by land routes through contiguous territories, Etienne criticized adversely the tariff provisions of the convention. He pleaded with the new Brisson Cabinet[134] to seek an amendment of these provisions before the convention was ratified.[135] Palazot, representative for Dahomey in the Conseil Supérieur des Colonies and in the chamber, also opposed the identic tariff provision of the convention. He contended that it would ruin the business of French merchants in

Dahomey and complained that foreign merchants, especially British, controlled five-sixths of Dahomey's external trade.[136] He objected to the evacuation and abandonment of Bussa and Ilo and expressed bitter dissatisfaction with the Anglo-French Convention. The colonial group in the chamber, supported by their colleagues in the senate, opposed the convention up to the time it was ratified. They even arrogated to themselves the power to establish both political and administrative control over the two leases granted to France by the convention.[137]

This claim by the Comité d'Afrique Française was challenged by a question in the House of Commons, demanding a clarification of the position of the government on the leases before the convention could be ratified. The Foreign Office dismissed the claims as groundless.[138] This did not quiet the press, who quickly pointed out the dangers of the creation by France of a Newfoundland type situation on the Niger.[139] Sir Charles Dilke asked Curzon in the House of Commons to state the territories in which the tariff provisions of article 9 of the convention were applicable.[140] These minor criticisms did not prevent Sir Michael Hicks Beach from declaring that the Niger Convention was "one of the most important diplomatic achievements of the last few years." But Asquith described the foreign policy of the Salisbury government as "characterized by imbecility of purpose and ineptitude of methods." He reproached the government, with reference to west Africa, with "want of consistency and tenacity." These charges were denied by Hicks Beach, who pointed to the Niger Convention as a vindication of the policy of the government.[141] Sir Edward Grey was satisfied with the convention because the most important rights were secured. The convention marked the settlement of a dangerous question in which it was worthwhile to concede something.[142] Alfred Jones, president of the west African section of the Liverpool Chamber of Commerce, criticized the government for not showing enough energy in the Niger affair. Without the agitation launched by Liverpool, he maintained, Britain would have ended up with nothing and would not have acquired the position she now occupied in west Africa.[143]

On the whole, British opinion was favorable to, if not satisfied by, the convention of 14 June 1898. Specific provisions of the convention were criticized, but there was little or no general dissatisfaction with the result of the labors of the Niger Commission. The reverse was the case in France. There, only the officials and politicians involved in the conclusion of the convention expressed some satisfaction with it. Hanotaux saw it as the culmination of the effort to liquidate all colonial disputes with Britain, barring Egypt:

La convention du Niger vient d'être signée et la conclusion de cet arrangement clot la série des difficultés internationales (Siam, Madagascar, Tunis, Chine et Niger) où l'Angleterre pourait chercher à opposer une politique de grief ou de compensations à nos propres revendications dans la question egyptienne. Cette question doit trouver désormais sa solution en elle-même.[144]

He boasted that the convention of 14 June 1898 "consecrated in favour of France the partition of Africa." By it was achieved the junction of Algeria, Tunisia, Senegal, Dahomey, Sudan, Lake Chad, and the Congo with the Bahr-el-Ghazal. This, he contended, made France the most important African power.[145]

The ministry of colonies expressed satisfaction with the convention, in reaction to the shattering attack launched by Palazot and the colonial group of the chamber against it. Binger defended the concessions made to Britain. He pointed out that it was an error to believe that Bussa was important. Furthermore, the economic arrangements would not operate to the disadvantage of French commerce. The differential tariff regime which had hitherto existed in the Ivory Coast "could not be said to be worth much to French commerce and industry in the face of foreign competition in all sorts of manufactured goods. Even the 15% *ad valorem* customs established by the agreement of 10 August 1889 had to be unilaterally lowered to 10% to avoid smuggling and to earn some revenue."[146] It is of interest to note that Delcassé was one of those who criticized Hanotaux's handling of the negotiations of 1898. Speaking to the Académie des Sciences Coloniales in 1931, Hanotaux revealed that Delcassé had rebuked him for failing to obtain all Egypt.[147] This may be due to the fact that Hanotaux left for Delcassé at the Quai d'Orsay the legacy of Fashoda.[148]

The criticisms of the convention of 14 June 1898 were kept alive in France up to the conclusion of the Entente Cordiale between Britain and France in the spring of 1904. In July 1903, while the negotiations for the accord of 1904 were in progress, Etienne visited London. He had an interview with Lansdowne, during which he restated the need for a revision of the Sokoto-Bornu frontier line recognized by the June 1898 convention.[149] The outstanding achievement of the 1898 convention was the settlement in principle of the many nagging colonial questions between Britain and France in the hinterland of west Africa and the transference of political authority in the Dahomey-Niger hinterland from the hands of Africans to those of Europeans. Both powers then began to consolidate their authorities in the areas definitively marked out as theirs. The partition of west Africa was complete, and boundary commissions later delimited the frontiers theoretically recognized on paper. An important step had been taken toward Anglo-French understanding and later collaboration in European power politics.

9

Conclusion

The international competition for the control of the Lower Niger and its basin was initiated by Jules Ferry during the Berlin Conference (1884–85). It dragged on until 1898, when the Anglo-French Convention of 14 June confirmed British predominance on the Lower Niger and marked the ultimate success of Britain's policy of keeping France and Germany out of the navigable Niger and its environs. Chamberlain's intransigence during the final negotiations and his brinkmanship foiled French efforts to secure a portion of the Lower Niger. The triumph of British policy was due more to Chamberlain's realism than to Salisbury's statesmanship.

The General Act of the Berlin Conference and that of the Brussels Conference provided the juridical basis for European expansion into the hinterland as well as for the acquisition of territory on the coast. The Berlin Act had a far-reaching effect on international law affecting colonization. Its articles not only set down the rules of the game but were evoked in almost all disputes which arose from the international rivalry for territories in west Africa. The terms of reference for commissions which were set up to negotiate settlements of territorial questions were drawn up with the provisions of the Berlin Act in mind. The notification of new treaties and territorial acquisitions on the coast or in the hinterland was enjoined by the Berlin Act (articles 34 and 35). Even the hinterland, which was not included in these provisions, came to be treated by the powers in accordance with the Berlin Act.

The coastal region of west Africa was quickly partitioned by the imperial powers after 1885. The hinterland became the only field open for expansion. Merchants and missionaries were keen to see the influence of their home governments extend inland from the coastal colonies and comptoirs. The partition of the hinterland began with the Anglo-French agreement of 10 August 1889 and the Anglo-German Neutral Zone agreement of 1888. By their agreement of August 1889, Britain and France laid the foundation for their future expansion into the hinterland. The frontiers which ran from the coast northward ended at 9° North Latitude, but there was no transverse frontier limiting the extent of the coastal possessions. The ninth parallel was adopted only as a temporary expedient which would be exceeded as European expansionism gathered momentum.

The agents on the spot had much to do with the forward policy which Britain and France adopted in the Niger territories in the 1890s. The competition for territory in the hinterland was primarily a result of the desire to ensure the economic viability of the coastal possessions whose commerce and prosperity depended on the uninterrupted flow of trade. Raw materials were tapped from the hinterland, and manufactured goods were sent from the coast to the African markets in the hinterland. It was necessary to have access to these markets, and gaining exclusive control of them and the populations they served was desirable if not imperative. The exaggerated reports about the economic wealth of the hinterland and the abundance of natural resources, coupled with an unlimited consumer market, were believed by the policy makers and their representatives. Reports by French explorers were read in Westminster, and those of British explorers were avidly studied in Paris. All this was done not only to gain a greater understanding of geography but also to know where the wealth lay and to learn about the most desirable region for expansion.

Britain's claims over Borgu and Gurma can be seen in perspective only in connection with the policy of keeping both France and Germany out of the Lower Niger and its basin. When the Lagos-Dahomey frontier was defined in such a way as to exclude France from the Lower Niger, the rest of Borgu, including Nikki, was conceded to France by Britain. In other words, Borgu was only a shield which Britain used to protect what was considered her vital interests in the Lower Niger. The economic potential of Borgu itself was assessed as poor even by Governor Ballot of Dahomey, who tried energetically to acquire it for France, not for its intrinsic value, but because it would give France access to the waterways of the Lower Niger as well as political control of the territory west of the Niger. If this had been achieved, it would have been easy to divert much of the commerce of the interior from Lagos to Porto Novo. H. P. Anderson had a very poor opinion of the whole Bariba country, based on Ballot's reports as well as those of Lugard and others. This opinion is borne out by the present economic state of all of Borgu, in Dahomey and in Nigeria.

The territories of the Niger bend were coveted for their supposed economic potential. Because of its dense population and the exaggerated reports on its wealth and natural resources, this region was desired as a market and a source of raw materials. Its network of caravan routes and the abundance of large African markets all the way from Wagadugu eastward to Sokoto, Kano, and Kukawa on Lake Chad were given publicity by explorers and merchants.

The auriferous potential of these territories entered into the calculations of the agents of expansionism. Fabulous reports of the abundance of gold in Bonduku, Ashanti, Bona, Lobi, and Mossi were circulated and believed. The exploitation of gold in the Gold Coast and Ashanti at this time lent credibility to these reports, probably on the assumption that the geological formation of these territories was similar if not identical. It is now known that these reports were exaggerated. However, what is important for this study is that such reports were not ignored and that decisions were made on their evidence. The economic value of territories as conceived in those days influenced the struggle for the acquisition of such territories.

When Little Englanders opposed the expenditure of money and men in the acquisition of territory in the Dahomey-Niger hinterland, Chamberlain replied that it was "absurd to measure the possible value of an undeveloped country by its condition." He asserted that the policy of Her Majesty's government was "not the acquisition of new territory, but it is the maintenance of free markets even where that involves the acquisition of new territory and the taking up of a very firm attitude in regard to any attempts which may be made to deprive us of territory which we already possess." Hanotaux also underscored, like Jules Ferry, the cardinal position of economic considerations in French imperial expansion and policy, but he added that "le commerce n'est pas tout; il y a le mouvement de l'âme, et il y a le coeur qui bat."

The Say-Barruwa Line dispute was only an ancillary to the Lower Niger question. It was a prop used by Britain to uphold the policy of keeping France out of the Lower Niger. By forbidding French colonial enterprise in the sultanate of Sokoto and, by implication, in Gwandu and its dependencies, the Anglo-French declaration of 5 August 1890 reinforced the British claim to the exclusive dominance of the Lower Niger. France could only expand from Say upward, which meant exclusion from the navigable Niger between Say and the Atlantic Ocean. This British interpretation of the Say-Barruwa Line was unacceptable to the French because it meant a veritable barrier to French expansion. To be excluded from the richer and more fertile section of the Niger basin and be allotted the "light soil" and desert north of Say and Sokoto was contended by France. Above all, the British interpretation of the Say-Barruwa Line popularized by Goldie meant an obstruction to the Chad plan conceived by Eugene Etienne and patronized by the Comité de l'Afrique Française. France therefore used the Say-Barruwa Line dispute as a crutch to support her atrophied claim to a place on the navigable Niger by challenging the British interpretation of the line. The differing interpretations of the declaration of 5 August 1890 did not cause the difficulties which strained Anglo-French relations in the 1890s. The cause was the energetic insistence of France on reversing the recognition of British authority over the navigation of the Lower Niger as enshrined in the General Act of the Berlin Conference in 1885.

After the conquest of Dahomey in 1894, it was felt in Porto Novo and in Paris that the acquisition of the territory west of the Niger and above 9° North Latitude would place France in a position to challenge the control of the trade and navigation of the Lower Niger by the Royal Niger Company. By acquiring political control of the western Niger territories, it was reasoned, France would ultimately gain equal authority over the Lower Niger with Britain. The expeditions of Toutée and Hourst on the Niger were sent out with this aim in view. Decoeur was dispatched to Nikki to sign a treaty with the Bariba king of this city that would place Borgu under French protection. Lugard got to Nikki first and concluded a treaty there before Decoeur's arrival. Ballot ingeniously discredited Lugard's treaty by proving that he treated with an imposter. Britain did not accept Ballot's view of the Nikki treaties.

The steeplechase to Nikki began a trend which led to serious doubts about the value of treaties as the only title to territories. The scramble for treaties with African rulers by France, Germany, and Britain was soon followed by the "effective occupation" of the territories of the Dahomey-Niger hinterland. French agents on the west coast initiated this system of effective occupation.

The occupation of Bussa by French troops was a last desperate attempt by France to get a foothold on the Lower Niger. Hanotaux, though defending this action publicly against British protests, reproached Lebon privately for conniving at Bretonnet's—or, more properly, Ballot's—neglect of ministerial instructions from Paris, which stipulated that no action be undertaken by French agents of expansion in areas where British rights were established by prior treaties. Through diplomatic pressure, the French post at Bussa was evacuated, and the convention of 14 June 1898 permanently removed the Lower Niger from the orbit of French colonial enterprise.

The Bussa affair is just one of the several cases where the agents of European imperial powers on the spot used their own initiative or neglected official instructions in order to acquire what they considered desirable territories. An ardent expansionist like Governor Ballot of Dahomey represented the extreme type of official who considered himself not only an executive of policies formulated in the metropolitan capital but also an originator of policy and action which he considered to be in the interests of his nation. Dr. Gruner and Governor Gilbert Carter of Lagos could be classified with Ballot in this category. But, then, this independence and initiative of action was among the qualities which Jules Ferry considered indispensable for the success of any proconsul. Such actions as were initiated on the spot in the Dahomey-Niger hinterland—at Tchaki, Pama, Nikki, Sansanne-Mango, and Bussa, for example—had significant effects on the official policies of the metropolitan powers. Men like Lugard, Willcocks, Puttkammer of Togo, and Maxwell possessed initiative and were alive to their responsibilities as agents of expansion, but they did not belong to the same extreme class as Ballot.

All through this study, the contrast between French and British policy in the Dahomey-Niger hinterland has been self-evident. France had a clearly worked out plan of expansion in this part of Africa. It was hoped that the execution of this plan, which was based on solid theoretical bases, would make France the greatest imperial power in Africa. Pierre Lyautey succinctly expressed this French view by his epigram: "Au départ, nos comptoirs. A l'arrivée, un empire."

To achieve this empire, Etienne originated his doctrine of the *perpendiculaire,* which was elaborated into the Chad Plan. The essence of this plan was to unite the Sudan, the Ivory Coast, and Dahomey with the Congo and Algeria by means of an unbroken territory under French possession or protection. Though Etienne intended to carve up the vast tracts of Africa that would thus be acquired into parcels for the exploitation of colonization companies on the British model, he did not fail to reckon with the Zeitgeist, the "throbbing heart" which Hanotaux recognized as seeking expression outside the Fatherland to demonstrate the virility of the Third Republic. National honor was, therefore, an important ingredient in French imperialism generally and in French expansion in the Dahomey-Niger hinterland. The French government always claimed any spot on which any French soldier was killed. The loss of such spots was considered degrading to the amour propre of France. This type of argument was used to persuade Britain to surrender Ilo to France. It was the clamor of the French chamber about the Dahomean insult to French national dignity that sparked off the second Dahomey war against Béhanzin, who was also protesting French encroachment on the integrity of his kingdom.

In contradistinction to the French, Britain began with no designs, theoretical or practical, for the expansion of Lagos and the Gold Coast into the Dahomey-Niger hinterland. The system of "informal empire" was the order of the day until France and Germany began to advance into the interior, when it was realized that Britain would be excluded from the markets of the interior if the hinterland were acquired exclusively by France and Germany. The idea of uniting the Gold Coast and Lagos by acquiring all the territory between them on the littoral was an illusion. Before it was given definitive form, the reestablishment of the French protectorate at Porto Novo in 1883 and the planting of the German flag in Togo in 1884 destroyed its prospects. British activity in the Dahomey-Niger hinterland was a reaction to the stimulus provided by France and Germany. The object was to save the hinterlands of the Gold Coast and Lagos and, above all, to maintain British supremacy on the Lower Niger. There was no theoretical blueprint for British expansion into the Niger territories.

The ever-present instrument of French expansion into the hinterland was the tough infantry of the navy, with its contingents of Senegalese sharpshooters. The use of this force obviated the demand for funds from the French chamber in minor cases. Special funds were only demanded in major cases like the wars in Dahomey and the Sudan. Britain had no standing army for action in the hinterland until she was constrained to create the West African Frontier Force in 1897. The House of Commons was even more unenthusiastic about voting funds for colonial enterprise than the French chamber was all through this period. However, British national honor was also evoked in the disputes over territories in the Niger territories. Commenting on a speech by Salisbury in May 1897, Courcel drew the attention of the French government to the art which Salisbury possessed "to the highest degree of evoking British pride, and the patriotic ambition of his hearers." What Courcel described as Salisbury's "realistic patriotism" was shared by Chamberlain, who never lost an opportunity of comparing British imperial achievements with those of Rome. During the negotiations in Paris and the competitive military action in the Dahomey-Niger hinterland, Chamberlain was irritated by some French demands. He observed: "They would find that courteous diplomacy, and moderate language, and even graceful concessions are not incompatible with a firm maintenance of the honour and the essential interests of the country. And if they were to presume upon this false interpretation of the mind of the Foreign Minister and the mind of the Government, the difficulty of preserving peace would be very much increased." Furthermore, it was national honor which inspired

Chamberlain's call for an Anglo-Saxon alliance between Britain and the United States of America as a shield against any hostile combination of European powers against Britain. Colonial questions, especially in west Africa, east and central Africa, China, and Newfoundland could form the pretext for such an anti-British coalition. Therefore, considerations of the balance of power in Europe affected the handling of colonial disputes at this period.

The influence of local factors on the development of events in the Dahomey-Niger hinterland was considerable. The resistance of some African rulers to European penetration into the interior impeded or slowed down the progress of the imperial forces. In some cases, local resistance forced a change of course on the imperial agents. Resistance by the Bariba against Decoeur's advance compelled him to make a detour. Consequently, Lugard arrived at Nikki before him, even though Ballot made sure that Decoeur had a good head start. The attack of the sofas against Henderson's column in April 1897 stopped the northwesterly advance of British agents and eventually contributed to the loss of Gurunsi by Britain.

Another important local factor that influenced the trend of the partition of the hinterland was the backing of imposters, pretenders whose claim to political authority was shady, and intruders. Britain backed Babato, a freebooter in Gurunsi, against Hamaria, whose authority derived from tradition, though he was not the overlord of all Gurunsi. This initial error by the Gold Coast authorities cost them the acquisition of Gurunsi, where the French backed Hamaria to the hilt. The Nikki affairs illustrate the influence of local factors. First, Lugard concluded his treaty of 1894 with a Moslem imposter. The French proved this error and used it to disallow Britain's claims to Nikki. Second, during the struggle for succession to the throne of Nikki in February 1898, British agents, from a poor knowledge of Bariba ethnology, supported Worou Yoro against Ourou Kondé, whom Ballot had been grooming for the throne for many months. With French support and buttressed by the goodwill of the chiefs of Nikki, Ourou Kondé succeeded Sero Tourou on the Nikki throne. This dealt a second and final blow to British hopes of acquiring Nikki. England settled for Bussa, where she had stronger claims.

French success in Gurma against the Germans was due principally to their support of Bantchande of Fada N'Gurma. German efforts to whittle down the traditional authority of Fada N'Gurma over other districts of Gurma did not succeed as much as they wished, though they profited from the civil war in Gurma by annexing sections of south Gurma. Bantchande provided warriors, guides, and provisions for Franco-Gurmantche campaigns against the chiefs of Pama, Matiacuali, Kodjar, and others. This local support was an essential ingredient in the success of France in Gurma.

What emerges from a study of the local factors is the piecemeal manner in which the kingdoms were conquered and annexed. Rivalries among adjoining territories prevented them from uniting in common action against the invading forces of imperialism. This lack of military alliances on a large scale, defensive or offensive, made concerted action impossible as each entity was quickly reduced and occupied. It was only in Borgu that a widespread resistance movement was encountered. Even then this resistance was not coordinated nor centrally directed. The very chiefs who led the resistance against the establishment of French authority in Borgu were at loggerheads with one another; it was only the advance of the Europeans that forced them to cooperate temporarily. For instance, Toutée reported the cases of the chief of Kouboure, who went to Gobo to discuss the advance of Toutée's mission, and the delegate from Oyo, who came to seek Bariba support in case of military action against Oyo by the forces from Lagos.

The lack of many strong centralized administrations with solid economic bases was a handicap to effective concerted action by African rulers. So was the military organization of these kingdoms. Standing armies were rare, and in most cases the regular army was made up of a small number of men who were poorly trained and ill-equipped. Weapons available to the inhabitants of the hinterland were crude and obsolete. The ease with which Mossi was overrun by French forces under Voulet and Chanoine illustrates the ineffectiveness of muzzle-loaders and flint guns against Lebel rifles and chassepots.

Dahomey proved herself to be the strongest indigenous military power on the west coast of Africa during this period. In the war against France, Dahomeans demonstrated military skills, techniques, and prowess which surprised their adversaries. They were well trained and had access through trade to Europe's latest weapons. King Béhanzin even employed European mercenaries to train his officers and teach them how to operate the munitions of war which he bought from the merchants on the Dahomey coast. The sources of Dahomey's strength were her strong centralized monarchy, her economic prosperity, and her well-organized army of both regulars and reserves. Dahomey was free from the constitutional weakness of Mossi and Ashanti, where strong vassals could question and weaken the power of the monarchy.

The conquest and occupation of the Dahomey-Niger hinterland and the

European rivalry that attended it stimulated the study of traditional African political and social organization, partly for its own sake and partly as an aid to effective administration and control of the annexed territories. The events that occurred in the Dahomey-Niger hinterland between 1885 and 1898 changed the course of African development in this region, probably for the better. But African opposition to European rule, overt and covert, continued for over three generations, until political independence was restored in the 1960s.

Appendix 1

General Act of the Brussels Conference, 2 July 1890

Chapter 1. *Slave Trade Countries. Measures to be Taken in the Places of Origin*

ARTICLE 1

The powers declare that the most effective means for counteracting the Slave Trade in the interior of Africa are the following:

1. Progressive organisation of the administrative, judicial, religious, and military services in the African territories placed under the sovereignty or protectorate of civilized nations.
2. The gradual establishment in the interior by the powers to which the territories are subject of strongly occupied stations, in such a way as to make their protective or repressive action effectively felt in the territories devastated by slave-hunting.
3. The construction of roads, and in particular of railways, connecting the advanced stations with the coast, and permitting of the rivers and streams as are broken by rapids and cataracts, in view of substituting economical and rapid means of transport for the present means of carriage by men.
4. Establishment of steamboats on the inland navigable waters and on the lakes supported by fortified posts established on the banks.
5. Establishment of telegraphic lines, insuring the communication of the posts and stations with the coast and with the administrative centres.
6. Organisation of expeditions and flying columns, to keep up the communication of the stations with each other and with the coast, to support repressive action, and to insure the security of high roads.
7. Restriction of the importation of firearms, at least of modern pattern, and of ammunition throughout the entire extent of the territories infected by the Slave Trade.

Extract from Parliamentary Papers: Africa No. 7 (1890), C. 6048, pp. 20–21.

Appendix 2

Franco-Dahomey Peace Treaty, 3 October 1890

En vue de prévenir les malentendus qui ont amené entre la France et le Dahomey un état d'hostilité préjudiciable aux intérets des deux pays,
  Nous, sous signés:
      Aladaka Dodedji, messager du Roi, assisté de:
      Cussugan, faisant fonction de Yévogan
      Zizidoque, Zounouhoucon, cabécères;
      Ainadou, trésorier de la Gore, designés par
      Sa Majeste le Roi Béhanzin Aidjire,

      et le Capitain de Vaisseau de Montesquiou-Faizansac,
      Commandant le croiseur *le Roland*; le Capitaine
      d'Artillerie Decoeur, designés par le Contre-Amiral
      Cavalier de Cuverville, Commander en Chef des
      forces de terre et de mer, faisant fonction
      de gouverneur de Golfe de Bénin, agissant au
      nom du Gouvernement Français;
  Avons arreté, d'un commun accord, l'arrangement suivant qui laisse intacts tous les traités ou conventions antérieurement conclus entre la France et le Dahomey:

Article Premier: Le Roi de Dahomey s'engage à respecter le protectorat français du royaume de Porto Novo et à s'abstenir de toute incursion sur les territoires faisant partie de ce protectorat. Il reconnait à la France le droit d'occuper indéfiniment Cotonou.

Article Deuxième: La France exercera son action auprès du roi de Porto Novo pour aucune cause légitime de plainte ne soit donnée à l'avenir au roi de Dahomey.

A titre de compensation, pour l'occupation de Cotonou, il sera versé annuellement par la France une somme qui ne pourra en aucun cas dépasser 20,000 francs,
    (or ou argent).
Le blocus sera levé et le present arrangement entrera en viguer à compter du jour de l'échange des signatures. Toutefois cet arrangement ne deviendra définitif

qu' après avoir été soumis à la ratification
du gouvernement français.
Fait à Ouidah, 14 3 Octobre 1890.

    Signé   ALADAKA DODEDJI, CUSSUGAN,
                   ZIZIDOQUE, ZOUNOUHOUCON
                   AINADOU.

    Signé   CANDIDO RODRIGUEZ ALEXANDRE, LES TEMOINS
    Signé   H. DECOEUR
                   Y. DE MONTESQUIOU
    Signé   D'AMBRIERS, DOGÈRE,

                 VU CONTRE-AMIRAL CAVALIER DE CUVERVILLE.

Appendix 3

Delcassé Circular to the Governors of French Colonies, 20 June 1894

CIRCULAIRE
A Monsieurs les Gouverneurs des Colonies

Messieurs,

Les questions coloniales ont pris depuis quelques années, dans les préoccupations de l'opinion publique, une importance et un développement qui imposent au Gouvernement et à l'Administration à tous ses degrés, un redoublement d'effort et de sollicitude.

Grace à l'énergie de nos soldats et de nos explorateurs, grace à l'heureuse ténacité des hommes d'Etat qui ont eu foi dans l'expansion de la France au dehors malgré l'impopularité dont semblaient frappée à une époque encore récente, les entreprises lointaines, notre domains colonial s'est considérablement accru. Le Parlement, le pays ont compris la nécessité des dépenses aussi considérables qui éxigeait l'accomplissement de cette grande oeuvre.

Il resta aujourd'hui à justifier les sacrifices du passé et ceux que reserve l'avenir par els résultats qui seront obtenus. Mettre en valeur les vastes territoires qui nous sont acquis, y créer des exploitations agricoles et par cela même, accroitre leurs relations commerciales avec la France; améliorer ou créer les voies de communication et de pénétration, tel est dans ses grandes lignes, le problème qui s'impose et dont la solution interesse et préoccupe un nombre de jour en jour plus grand d'hommes devoués à la cause coloniale.

Dans cette oeuvre, le role principal appartient à l'initiative privée, a besoin d'être encouragée et soutenue par le Gouvernement et par ses agents.

C'est sur cette question si délicate et si important des relations d'une façon toute particulière votre attention.

On a dit fréquemment que la France n'avait que des colonies de fonctionnaires et de soldats. On s'est plaint et l'on se plaint encore de l'accueil peu encourageant que reçoivent aux colonies ceux de nos concitoyens qui veulent s'y installer des difficultés, des véxations de toute nature qu'ils rencontrent, des entraves qu'apporte au développement des affaires une réglementation routinière et trop fiscale;

SOM-AN Généralité, carton no. 262/1809 (1876–99).

on oppose volontiers à l'attitude de nos fonctionnaires celle des réprésentant des pays étrangers, toujours empressés, dit-on à servir l'intérets de leurs nationaux à faciliter leurs entreprises, à prendre fait et cause pour eux toutes les fois qu'ils ont besoin d'être contenus ou défendus.

Je sais la part d'exagération qu'il y a dans ces récriminations. Je n'ignore pas que le souci de faire respecter la loi et d'assurer au budget les ressources qui lui sont indispensables ne permet pas de donner satisfaction à tous les désidérata du commerce, et de l'industrie:

Mais tout en restant fidèlement attaché à son dévoir professionnel, j'estime que l'Administration peut et doit se considérer comme l'auxiliaire et protectrice désignée des hommes de bonne volonté qui consacrent leur énergie, leurs forces et leurs capitaux à la mise en valeur de notre domaine d'outre-Mer.

L'Administration doit avoir à coeur de les aider, de les renseigner, de leur faciliter leur tache, de briser les entraves que des réglements trop étroits des préjugés la routine ou de fausses considérations fiscales peuvent encore opposer au développement et à la vie meme des entreprises naissantes.

C'est de cet esprit que vous devrez vous inspirer dans les propositions que vous aurez à me soumettre, soit en vue d'amender la réglementation actuellement en vigueur soit dans l'éxamen des demandes et des projets sur lesquels vous serez appelés à formuler un avis.

Je vous prie, d'autre part, de donner aux agents placés sous vos ordres des instructions très précises pour qu'ils se conforment scrupuleusement aux indications qui précèdent.

Vous voudrez bien par un controle incessant, par les enquêtes personnels que vous ferez sur les plaintes dont vous serez saisi, en brisant au besoin par des mésures de rigueur des résistances qui je l'espère, ne se produiront pas, tenir fermenent la main à ce que mes recommandations ne restent dans l'état de lettre morte.

Je vous prie de m'accuser réception de la présente circulaire et de me tenir au courant par des communication fréquentes des mésures que vous croirez utiles de prendre ou de provoquer, pour répondre à ces vues en favorisant le développement économique de la colonie dont le gouvernement vous a été confié.

Recevez Messieurs les assurances de ma considération la plus distinguée.

Le Ministre des Colonies.

(Signed) DELCASSÉ.

Appendix 4

Anglo-Mossi Treaty of 2 July 1894, Concluded by George E. Ferguson

TREATY of FRIENDSHIP and FREEDOM of TRADE made at Wagadugu, this second day of July one thousand eight hundred and ninety-four, between Her Most Gracious Majesty Victoria, Queen of Great Britain and Ireland, Empress of India, &c., &c., &c., Her heirs and successors, by Her Majesty's loyal subject George Ekem Ferguson, an Officer in the Civil Service of the Gold Coast Colony, acting under special instructions received from His Excellency the Officer Administering the Government of the said Colony, also a subject of Her Majesty, and the King, Chiefs, and Principal Headmen of the country of Mossi, on the other part.

Whereas Abu Bukari, King of the country of Mossi and the Chiefs and Principal Headmen of that country, for and on behalf of themselves, their heirs and successors, and people have agreed to enter into a treaty with Her Majesty the Queen of Great Britain and Ireland, Empress of India, &c., &c., &c., Her heirs and successors, by the said George Ekem Ferguson, acting for that purpose for the Officer Administering the Government of the said Colony.

Now, therefore, Abu Bukari King of Mossi, and the Chiefs and Principal men of that country, whose names are herein-after signed to this Treaty, for themselves, their heirs and successors, and the people of Mossi on the one part, and His Excellency the Officer Administering the Government of the said Colony, a subject of, and representing and acting on behalf of, Her Most Gracious Majesty Victoria, Queen of the United Kingdom of Great Britain and Ireland, Empress of India, &c., &c., &c., Her heirs and successors, by George Ekem Ferguson, a subject of Her Majesty (acting for the Officer Administering the Government of the said Colony) on the other part, do hereby enter into this Treaty.

ARTICLE 1

The King of the country of Mossi for himself and his lawful successors, together with the chiefs and principal men of the country of Mossi, whose names are herein-after signed and seals affixed for and on behalf of themselves and their successors and the people of Mossi, hereby declare that they have not entered into any Treaty with any Foreign Power.

ARTICLE 2

There shall be friendship and freedom of trade between the King, Chiefs, Principal Headmen, and people of Mossi and the subjects of Her Most Gracious Majesty the Queen Empress, and it is hereby understood and agreed between the contracting parties to this Treaty that British subjects shall have free access to all parts of Mossi and shall also have the right to build houses and possess property according to the laws of the country of Mossi, and they shall have full liberty to carry on trade or manufacture, and should any difference or dispute arise with regard to any trading transactions or other matters between the subjects of Her Majesty residing or carrying on business at Mossi, and the people of that country the same shall be decided by the proper local authorities according to the Customs and laws existing in that country.

The King, Chiefs, and Principal Headmen of Mossi also hereby declare and engage that they will not extend the rights hereby guaranteed to British subjects to any other persons without first communicating to the Governor of the Gold Coast Colony their intention to grant such rights to persons other than British subjects who may apply to them to be admitted to the same privileges as British subjects.

ARTICLE 3

The King, Chiefs, and Principal Headmen of the country of Mossi, in consideration of their friendly connection with Great Britain and the Gold Coast Colony, by virtue of this Treaty hereby promise to have their principal trade roads kept in order for the advantage of traders passing through, and to the general advantage of the people of the country, that they will encourage trade, and they likewise hereby undertake and bind themselevs not to cede their territory to, nor to accept a protectorate from, or enter into any agreement, arrangement, or Treaty with, any other foreign Power except through and with the consent of the Government of Her Majesty the Queen Empress.

ARTICLE 4

This Treaty shall come into force the date hereof, but power is hereby expressly reserved to Her Majesty the Queen Empress to refuse to approve and ratify the same within eighteen months from the date hereof. In witness whereof the parties to this Treaty have hereunto set their hands and affixed their respective seals.

Done at Wagadugu, in the country of Mossi, this 2nd day of July in the year one thousand eight hundred and ninety-four.

APPENDIX 4

Names of Signatories	Rank	Marks	Seals
Abu Bukari	King of Mossi	X	(L.S.)
Kamsiawnaba	—	X	(L.S.)
Gunnaba	—	X	(L.S.)
Widinaba	—	X	(L.S.)
Laganaba	—	X	(L.S.)
Dapolnaba	—	X	(L.S.)
Wirikumnaba	—	X	(L.S.)
Balamnaba	—	X	(L.S.)
Samannaba	—	X	(L.S.)
Kawmbaunaba	—	X	(L.S.)
Alimami	—	X	(L.S.)
Posiga	—	X	(L.S.)
Panelwelgu	—	X	(L.S.)
Jesubawkasanga	—	X	(L.S.)
Zugawnaba	—	X	(L.S.)
Dannaba	—	X	(L.S.)
Dahanipunaba	—	X	(L.S.)
Lelenaba	—	X	(L.S.)
Wudnorinaba	—	X	(L.S.)
Tansaba	—	X	(L.S.)
Bilbasnaba	—	X	(L.S.)

GEORGE E. FERGUSON, (L.S.)
An Officer in the Civil Service of the Gold Coast Colony for and on behalf of Frederic Mitchell Hodgson, the Officer Administering the Government of the Gold Coast Colony.

MAMA GIMALAH,
Sergeant-Major, Gold Coast Constabulary.

BOSSOMBOY GRUNSHI,
Lance-Corporal, Gold Coast Constabulary.

Signed, sealed, and delivered in our presence, the same having been first read over and interpreted to the King, Chiefs, and people who seemed to understand perfectly the meaning, conditions, and scope of the foregoing Treaty.

Appendix 5

CONVENTION BETWEEN THE UNITED KINGDOM AND FRANCE FOR THE DELIMITATION OF THEIR RESPECTIVE POSSESSIONS TO THE WEST OF THE NIGER, AND OF THEIR RESPECTIVE POSSESSIONS AND SPHERES OF INFLUENCE TO THE EAST OF THAT RIVER

Signed at Paris, June 14, 1898

(Ratifications exchanged at Paris, June 13, 1899)

The Government of Her Majesty the Queen of the United Kingdom of Great Britain and Ireland, Empress of India, and the Government of the French Republic, having agreed, in a spirit of mutual goodwill, to confirm the Protocol with its four Annexes prepared by their respective Delegates for the delimitation of the British Colonies of the Gold Coast, Lagos, and the other British possessions to the west of the Niger, and of the French possessions of the Ivory Coast, Sudan, and Dahomey, as well as for the delimitation of the British and French possessions and the spheres of influence of the two countries to the east of the Niger, the Undersigned, his Excellency the Right Honourable Sir Edmund Monson, Ambassador Extraordinary and Plenipotentiary of Her Majesty the Queen of the United Kingdom of Great Britain and Ireland, Empress of India, accredited to the President of the French Republic; and his Excellency M. Gabriel Hanotaux, Minister for Foreign Affairs of the French Republic; duly authorised to this effect, confirm the Protocol with its Annexes, drawn up at Paris the 14th day of June, 1898, the text of which is as follows:—

PROTOCOL

The Undersigned, Martin Gosselin, Minister Plenipotentiary and Secretary of Her Britannic Majesty's Embassy at Paris; William Everett, a Colonel in Her Britannic Majesty's land forces and an Assistant Adjutant-General in the Intelligence Division of the War Office; René Lecomte, Minister Plenipotentiary, Assistant Sub-Director in the Department of Political Affairs in the Ministry for Foreign Affairs; Louis Gustave Binger, Colonial Governor, unattached, Director of African Affairs at the Ministry of the Colonies; delegated respectively by the Government of Her Britannic Majesty and by the Government of the French Republic in order to draw up, in conformity with the Declarations exchanged at London on the 5th August, 1890, and the 15th January, 1896, a draft of definitive delimitation between the British Colonies of the Gold Coast, Lagos, and the other British possessions to the west of the Niger, and the French possessions of the Ivory Coast, the Sudan, and Dahomey, and between the British and French possessions and the spheres of influence of the two countries to the east of the Niger, have agreed to the following provisions, which they have resolved to submit for the approval of their respective Governments;—

ARTICLE 1

The frontier separating the British Colony of the Gold Coast from the French Colonies of the Ivory Coast and Sudan shall start from the northern terminal point of the frontier laid down in the Anglo-French Agreement of the 12th July, 1893, viz. the intersection of the thalweg of the Black Volta with the 9th degree of north latitude, and shall follow the thalweg of this river northward up to its intersection with the 11th degree of north latitude. From this point it shall follow this parallel of latitude eastward as far as the river shown on Map No. 1, annexed to the present Protocol, as passing immediately to the east of the villages of Zwaga (Soauga) and Zebilla (Sebilla), and it shall then follow the thalweg of the western branch of this river up stream to its intersection with the parallel of latitude passing through the village of Sapeliga. From this point the frontier shall follow the northern limits of the lands belonging to Sapeliga as far as the River Nuhau (Nouhau), and shall then follow the thalweg of this river up or down stream, as the case may be, to a point situated 2 miles (3,219 metres) eastward of the road which leads from Gambaga to Tenkrûgu (Tingourkou), *viâ* Bawku (Baukou). Thence it shall rejoin by a straight line the 11th degree of north latitude at the intersection of this parallel with the road which is shown on Map No. 1 as leading from Sansanné-Mango to Pama, *viâ* Jebigu (Djebiga).

ARTICLE 2

The frontier between the British Colony of Lagos and the French Colony of Dahomey, which was delimited on the ground by the Anglo-French Boundary Commission of 1895, and which is described in the report signed by the Commissioners of the two nations on the 12th October, 1896, shall henceforward be recognized as the frontier separating the British and French possessions from the sea to the 9th degree of north latitude.

From the point of intersection of the River Ocpara with the 9th degree of north latitude, as determined by the said Commissioners, the frontier separating the British and French possessions shall proceed in a northerly direction, and follow a line passing west of the lands belonging to the following places, viz.: Tabira, Okuta (Okouta), Boria, Tere, Gbani, Ashigere (Yassikéra), and Dekala.

From the most westerly point of the lands belonging to Dekala the frontier shall be drawn in a northerly direction so as to coincide as far as possible with the line indicated on Map No. 1 annexed to the present Protocol, and shall strike the right bank of the Niger at a point situated 10 miles (16,093 metres) up-stream from the centre of the town of Gere (Guiris) (the port of Ilo), measured as the crow flies.

ARTICLE 3

From the point specified in Article 2, where the frontier separating the British and French possessions strikes the Niger, viz. a point situated on the right bank of that river, 10 miles (16,093 metres) up-stream from the centre of the town of Gere (Guiris; the port of Ilo), the frontier shall follow a straight line drawn therefrom at right angles to the right bank as far as its intersection with the median line of the river. It shall then follow the median line of the river, up-stream, as far as its intersection with a line drawn perpendicularly to the left bank from the median line of the mouth of the depression or dry water-course, which, on Map No. 2 annexed to the present Protocol, is called the Dallul Mauri, and is shown thereon as being situated at a distance of about 17 miles (27,359 metres), measured as the crow flies, from a point on the left bank opposite the above-mentioned village of Gere (Guiris).

From this point of intersection the frontier shall follow this perpendicular till it meets the left bank of the river.

ARTICLE 4

To the east of the Niger the frontier separating the British and French possessions shall follow the line indicated on Map No. 2, which is annexed to the present Protocol.

Starting from the point on the left bank of the Niger indicated in the previous Article, viz. the median line of the Dallul Mauri, the frontier shall follow this median line until it meets the circumference of a circle drawn from the centre of the town of Sokoto with a radius of 100 miles (160,932 metres). From this point it shall follow the northern arc of this circle as far as its second intersection with the 14th parallel of north latitude. From this second point of intersection it shall follow this parallel eastward for a distance of 70 miles (112,652 metres); then proceed due south until it reaches the parallel of 13°20′ north latitude, then eastward along this parallel for a distance of 250 miles (402,230 metres); then due north until it regains the 14th parallel of north latitude; then eastwards along this parallel as far as its intersection with the meridian passing 35′ east of the centre of the town of Kuka, and thence this meridian southward until its intersection with the southern shore of Lake Chad.

The Government of the French Republic recognises, as falling within the British sphere, the territory to the east of the Niger comprised within the above-mentioned line, the Anglo-German frontier, and the sea.

The Government of Her Britannic Majesty recognises, as falling within the French sphere, the northern, eastern, and southern shores of Lake Chad, which are comprised between the point of intersection of the 14th degree of north latitude, with the western shore of the lake and the point of incidence on the shore of the lake of the frontier determined by the Franco-German Convention of the 15th March, 1894.

ARTICLE 5

The two Governments undertake to appoint within a year as regards the Maps, which are marked 1 and 2 respectively.

The two Governments undertake to appoint within a year as regards the frontiers west of the Niger, and within two years as regards the frontier east of that river, to count in each case from the date of the exchange of ratifications of the Convention which is to be concluded between them for the purpose of confirming the present Protocol, Commissioners who will be charged with delimiting on the spot the lines of demarcation between the British and French possessions, in conformity and in accordance with the spirit of the stipulations of the present Protocol.

With respect to the delimitation of the portion of the Niger in the neighborhood of Ilo and the Dallul Mauri, referred to in Article 3, the Boundary Commissioners shall, in determining on the spot the river frontier, distribute equitably between the two Contracting Powers such islands as may be found to interfere with the delimitation of the river as defined in Article 3.

It is understood between the two Contracting Powers that no subsequent alteration in the position of the median line of the river shall affect the ownership of the islands assigned to each of the two Powers by the *procès-verbal* of the Commissioners, after being duly approved by the two Governments.

ARTICLE 6

The two Contracting Powers engage reciprocally to treat with consideration ("bienveillance") the native Chiefs who, having had treaties with one of them, shall, in virtue of the present Protocol, come under the sovereignty of the other.

ARTICLE 7

Each of the two Contracting Powers undertakes not to exercise any political action in the spheres of the other, as defined by Articles 1, 2, 3, and 4 of the present Protocol.

It is understood by this that each Power will not, in the spheres of the other, make territorial acquisitions, conclude Treaties, accept sovereign rights or Protectorates, nor hinder nor dispute the influence of the other.

ARTICLE 8

Her Britannic Majesty's Government will grant on lease to the Government of the French Republic, for the objects, and on the conditions specified in the form of lease annexed to the present Protocol, two pieces of ground to be selected by the Government of the French Republic in conjunction with Her Britannic

Majesty's Government, one of which will be situated in a suitable spot on the right bank of the Niger between Leaba and the junction of the River Moussa (Mochi) with the former river, and the other on one of the mouths of the Niger. Each of these pieces of land shall have a river frontage not exceeding 400 metres in length, and shall form a block, the area of which shall not be less than 10 nor more than 50 hectares in extent. The exact boundaries of these pieces of land shall be shown on a plan annexed to each of the leases.

The conditions upon which the transit of merchandise shall be carried on on the Niger, its affluents, its branches and outlets, as well as between the piece of ground between Leaba and the junction of the River Moussa (Mochi) mentioned above, and the point upon the French frontier to be specified by the Government of the French Republic, will form the subject of Regulations, the details of which shall be discussed by the two Governments immediately after the signature of the present Protocol.

Her Britannic Majesty's Government undertake to give four months' notice to the French Government of any modification in the Regulations in question, in order to afford to the said French Government the opportunity of laying before the British Government any representations which it may wish to make.

ARTICLE 9

Within the limits defined on Map No. 2, which is annexed to the present Protocol, British subjects and British protected persons and French citizens and French protected persons, as far as regards their persons and goods, and the merchandise, the produce or the manufacture of Great Britain and France, their respective Colonies, possessions, and Protectorates, shall enjoy for thirty years from the date of the exchange of the ratifications of the Convention mentioned in Article 5 the same treatment in all matters of river navigation, of commerce, and of tariff and fiscal treatment and taxes of all kinds.

Subject to this condition, each of the two Contracting Powers shall be free to fix, in its own territory, and as may appear to it most convenient, the tariff and fiscal treatment and taxes of all kinds.

In case neither of the two Contracting Powers shall have notified twelve months before the expiration of the above-mentioned term of thirty years its intention to put an end to the effects of the present Article, it shall remain in force until the expiration of one year from the day on which either of the Contracting Powers shall have denounced it.

In witness whereof, the undersigned Delegates have drawn up and signed the present Protocol.

Done at Paris, in duplicate, the 14th day of June, in the year of our Lord 1898.

(Signed) MARTIN GOSSELIN.
WILLIAM EVERETT.
RENÉ LECOMTE.
G. BINGER.

ANNEXES 1 AND 2

MAPS NOS. 1 AND 2

ANNEX 3

Although the delineation of the lines of demarcation on the two maps annexed to the present Protocol are supposed to be generally accurate, it cannot be considered as an absolutely correct representation of those lines until it has been confirmed by new surveys.

It is therefore agreed that the Commissioners or local Delegates of the two countries, hereafter appointed to delimit the whole or part of the frontiers on the ground, shall be guided by the description of the frontier as set forth in the Protocol.

They shall, at the same time, be permitted to modify the said lines of demarcation for the purpose of delineating them with greater accuracy, and also to rectify the position of the watersheds, roads, or rivers, as well as of towns or villages indicated on the maps above referred to.

Any alterations or corrections proposed by common consent by the said Commissioners or Delegates shall be submitted for the approval of their respective Governments.

(Signed) MARTIN GOSSELIN.
WILLIAM EVERETT.
RENÉ LECOMTE.
G. BINGER.

ANNEX 4

Form of Lease

1. The Government of Her Britannic Majesty grants in lease to the Government of the French Republic the piece of land situated   of the Niger River, having a river frontage   in length, and forming a block of   haectares in extent, the exact boundaries of which are shown on the plan annexed to this lease.

2. The lease shall run for thirty years uninterruptedly, commencing from the   , but in case neither of the two Contracting Powers shall have notified twelve months before the expiration of the above-mentioned term of thirty years its intention to put an end to the present lease, it shall remain in force until the expiration of one year from the day on which either of the Contracting Powers shall have denounced it.

3. The said land shall be subject to the laws for the time being in force in the British Protectorate of the Niger districts.

4. A portion of the land leased, which shall not exceed 10 hectares in extent,

shall be used exclusively for the purposes of the landing, storage, and transhipment of goods, and for such purposes as may be considered subsidiary thereto, and the only permanent residents shall be the persons employed in the charge and for the security of such goods, their families, and servants.

5. The Government of the French Republic binds itself—

(a) To fence in that portion of the said land referred to in Article 4 of this lease (with the exception of the side which faces the River Niger) by a wall, or by a stockade, or by any other sort of continuous fence, which shall not be less in height than 3 metres. There shall be one door only on each of the three sides of the fence.

(b) Not to permit on the said portion of land the receipt or exit of any goods in contravention of the British Customs Regulations. Any act in violation of this stipulation shall be considered as evasion of customs duties, and shall be punished accordingly.

(c) Not to sell nor allow the sale of any goods in retail in the said portion of land. The sale of quantities less in weight or measure than 1,000 kilog., 1,000 litres, or 1,000 metres is held to be sale in retail. It is understood that this stipulation shall not apply to goods in transit.

(d) The Government of the French Republic, or its sublessees or agents, shall have the right to build on the said portion of land, warehouses, houses for offices, and other buildings necessary for the operations of landing, storing, and transshipping goods, and also to construct on that part of the foreshore of the River Niger comprised in the lease, quays, bridges, and docks, and any other works required in connection with the said operations, provided that the designs of all works so to be constructed on the foreshore of the river are furnished to the British authorities for examination, in order to ascertain that these works would not in any way inconvenience the navigation of the river, or be in conflict with the rights of others or with the Customs system.

(e) It is understood that the shipping, landing, and storing of goods on the said portion of land shall be conducted in all respects in accordance with the laws for the time being in force in the British Protectorate of the Niger districts.

6. The Government of the French Republic binds itself to pay annually to Her Majesty's Government, on the 1st January of each year, a rent of 1 fr.

7. The Government of the French Republic shall have the right to sublet the whole or any portion of the land passing under this lease, provided that the sublessees shall not use the land for any other purposes than those stipulated in this lease, and that the said Government shall remain responsible to the Government of Her Britannic Majesty for the observance of the stipulations of this lease.

8. The Government of Her Britannic Majesty binds itself to fulfil towards the lessee all duties incumbent upon it as owner of the said land.

9. At the expiration of the term of thirty years specified in Article 2 of this lease, the French Government, or its sub-lessees, may remain in possession and

in enjoyment for a period of time which, together with the said terms of thirty years, shall not exceed ninety-nine years, of the constructions and installations which shall have been made on the leased land. Nevertheless, the Government of Her Britannic Majesty reserves to itself, on the expiration or determination of the lease, in accordance with the conditions specified in Article 2, the right of purchasing such constructions and installations at a valuation to be determined by experts who will be appointed by the two Governments, on the understanding that notification of their intention be furnished to the French Government ten months, at latest, before the expiration or determination of the lease. In case of disagreement between them, the experts shall choose a referee, whose decision shall be final.

In calculating the value of the above-mentioned constructions and installations, the experts shall be guided by the following considerations:—

(a) In the event of the lease expiring at the end of the first thirty years, the purchase value of the property to be sold shall be the full market value.

(b) In the event of the lease being determined at any time after thirty years, the value of the property to be sold shall be the full market value less a fraction, whose numerator shall be the number of years the lease has run, minus thirty, and whose denominator shall be sixty-nine.

10. The land comprised in the lease shall be measured and marked out without delay.

11. If a difference of opinion should arise between the two Governments as to the interpretation of the lease, or as to any matter arising in connection therewith, it shall be settled by the arbitration of a jurisconsult of third nationality, to be agreed upon by the two Governments.

(Signed) MARTIN GOSSELIN.
WILLIAM EVERETT.
RENÉ LECOMTE.
G. BINGER.

The present Convention shall be ratified, and the ratifications exchanged at Paris within the period of six months, or sooner if possible.

In witness whereof the Undersigned have signed the present Convention and have affixed thereto their seals.

Done in duplicate, at Paris, the 14th June, 1898.

(Signed) EDMUND MONSON.
G. HANOTAUX.

PROTOCOL PROLONGING THE PERIOD FOR THE EXCHANGE OF RATIFICATIONS

Signed at Paris, December 8, 1898

The Undersigned, his Excellency the Right Honourable Sir Edmund Monson, G.C.B., Ambassador Extraordinary and Plenipotentiary of Her Majesty the Queen of the United Kingdom of Great Britain and Ireland, Empress of India, to the President of the French Republic; and his Excellency M. Delcassé, Minister of Foreign Affairs of the French Republic, duly authorised to this effect, have agreed as follows:—

The delay of six months, fixed by the Convention of the 14th June, 1898, for the exchange of the ratifications of the said Convention, is extended by six months and increased to one year.

Done at Paris, in duplicate, this 8th day of December, 1898.

(L.S.) (Signed) EDMUND MONSON.
DELCASSÉ.

DECLARATION

Signed at London, March 21, 1899

(Ratifications exchanged at Paris, June 13, 1899.)

The Undersigned, duly authorised by their Governments have signed the following Declaration:—

The 4th Article of the Convention of the 14th June, 1898, shall be completed by the following provisions, which shall be considered as forming an integral part of it:—

1. Her Britannic Majesty's Government engages not to acquire either territory or political influence to the west of the line of frontier defined in the following paragraph, and the Government of the French Republic engages not to acquire either territory or political influence to the east of the same line.

2. The line of frontier shall start from the point where the boundary between the Congo Free State and French territory meets the water-parting between the watershed of the Nile and that of the Congo and its affluents. It shall follow in principle that water-parting up to its intersection with the 11th parallel of north latitude. From this point it shall be drawn as far as the 15th parallel in such manner as to separate, in principle, the Kingdom of Wadai from what constituted in 1882 the Province of Darfur; but it shall in no case be so drawn as to pass to the west beyond the 21st degree of longitude east of Greenwich (18°40′ east of Paris), or to the east beyond the 23rd degree of longitude east of Greenwich (20°40′ east of Paris).

3. It is understood, in principle, that to the north of the 15th parallel the French zone shall be limited to the north-east and east by a line which shall start from the point of intersection of the Tropic of Cancer with the 16th degree of longitude east of Greenwich (13°40′ east of Paris), shall run thence to the south-east until it meets the 24th degree of longitude east of Greenwich (21°40′ east of Paris), and shall then follow the 24th degree until it meets, to the north of the 15th parallel of latitude, the frontier of Darfur as it shall eventually be fixed.

4. The two Governments engage to appoint Commissioners who shall be

charged to delimit on the spot a frontier-line in accordance with the indications given in paragraph 2 of this Declaration. The result of their work shall be submitted for the approbation of their respective Governments.

It is agreed that the provisions of Article 9 of the Convention of the 14th June, 1898, shall apply equally to the territories situated to the south of the 14°20′ parallel of north latitude, and to the north of the 5th parallel of north latitude, between the 14°20′ meridian of longitude east of Greenwich (12th degree east of Paris) and the course of the Upper Nile.

Done at London, the 21st March, 1899.

(L.S.) (Signed) SALISBURY.
(L.S.) (Signed) PAUL CAMBON.

Abbreviations

A.C.M.	Archives Centrales du Ministère de la Marine, Paris
A.N.	Archives Nationales, Paris
A.N.-A.P.	Archives Nationales–Archives Privées, Paris
A.N.-MI	Archives Nationales–Microfilms, Paris
B.N.	Bibliothèque Nationale, Paris
B.N.-N.A.F.	Bibliothèque Nationale–Nouvelles Acquisitiones Françaises
B.C.E.H.S.	*Bulletin du Comité d'Etudes Historiques et Scientifiques de l'Afrique Occidentale Française*
B.I.F.A.N.	*Bulletin de l'Institut Français d'Afrique Noire*
B.O.	*Bulletin Officiel du Ministère des Colonies* (Paris)
Cab.	Cabinet Papers, Public Record Office, London
C.O.	Colonial Office, London
D.D.F.	*Documents Diplomatiques Françaises*
D.K.Z.	*Deutsche Kolonialzeitung* (Berlin)
E.D.	*Etudes Dahoméennes*
E.H.R.	*English Historical Review*
F.O.	Foreign Office, London
J.A.H.	*Journal of African History*
J.O.	*Journal Officiel* (Paris)
M.A.E.	Ministère des Affaires Etrangères, Paris
M.A.E. C.P.	Ministère des Affaires Etrangères: Correspondances Politique
M.A.E. D.D.	Ministère des Affaires Etrangères: Documents Diplomatiques
M.M.C.	Ministère de la Marine et des Colonies, Paris
P.R.O.	Public Record Office, London
Parl. Papers	Parliamentary Papers, London
R.C.P.P.	*Revue des Colonies et des Pays de Protectorat*
R.D.M.	*Revue des Deux Mondes* (Paris)
R.F.E.C.	*Revue Français de l'Etrangère et des Colonies*

Notes

CHAPTER 1

1. "The Niger," in *Encyclopaedia Britannica* 16 (London, 1957): 437-39; André Lefebre, *De la Création de l'Outillage Public dans l'Afrique Occidentale Française* (Paris, 1904), pp. 222-27.
2. Governor Ballot of Dahomey named this peak in honor of M. Théophile Delcassé, the French minister of the colonies in 1894. See "Map of the Niger Bend," prepared by the service géographique des colonies of the ministère des colonies (Paris, 1897).
3. Emile Auzou, "La Boucle du Niger," in *Revue des Deux Mondes* 147 (1 May 1898): 163-88, 163-166; Urvoy, *Les bassins du Niger: Etudes de géographie physique et de paléogéographie* (Paris, 1942).
4. Henry Hubert, "Afrique Occidentale Française," in *Atlas des Colonies Françaises: Protectorats et Territoires sous Mandat de la France,* ed. G. Grandidier (Paris, 1934), pp. 5, 9-12, 13-15. See B. Hopkins, *Forest and Savanna: An Introduction to Tropical Plant Ecology, with Special Reference to West Africa* (London, 1965).
5. General Toutée, *Dahomé-Niger-Touareg, Récits de Voyage* (Paris, 1917), pp. 150-51; Section d'Outre-Mer des Archives Nationales (hereafter SOM-AN) Soudan II, 1, "Contribution à l'étude de l'Agriculture, de la Zootechnie, de l'Hygiène et de la Pathologie vétérinaire au Soudan Français," par L. O. Petit (1891).
6. Auzou, "La Boucle du Niger," p. 167. See *New Africa* (published by the secretariat of state for cultural affairs and information of the Tunisian government, 1963), p. 78.
7. A. T. Grove, *Africa South of the Sahara* (Oxford, 1967).
8. George P. Murdock, *Africa: Its Peoples and Their Culture History* (New York, 1959), p. 77; André de Beauminy, "Le pays de la boucle du Niger, étude économique," in *Revue Géographique et Commerciale de Bordeaux* 6 (1919): 71-78.
9. See Daryll Forde and P. Kaberry, eds., *West African Kingdoms in the Nineteenth Century* (Oxford, 1967).
10. Colonial Office Confidential Prints, Public Record Office, London, series 879, vol. 50 (hereafter CO879/50, with appropriate series and vol. nos. inserted accordingly), *Account of the Origin and Organisation of the States of the Western Sudan* (translation of treatise by Dr. P. C. Meyer, with maps, 1898).
11. Jacques Lombard, *Structures de type "féodal" en Afrique Noire. Etude des dynamismes internes et des relations sociales chez les Bariba du Dahomey* (Paris, 1965).
12. See G. Parrinder, *The Story of Ketu* (Ibadan, 1956).
13. M. Berge, "Etudes sur le Pays Mahi," in *Bulletin du Comité d'Etudes Historiques et Scientifiques de l'Afrique Occidentale Française* (hereafter B.C.E.H.S.) (1928), pp. 708-55.

14 J. D. Fage, *Reflections on the Early History of the Mossi-Dagomba Group of States,* Historian in Tropical Africa, Special Study No. 5 (London, 1964); R. S. Rattray, "Tribes of the Ashanti Hinterland," in *Journal of the African Society* 30 (1931): 40–57.
15 R. S. Rattray, *The Tribes of the Ashanti Hinterland* (London, 1932), p. 123. See J. H. Greenberg, *Languages of Africa* (Bloomington, 1963).
16 CO879/48, Henderson to Gov. Maxwell, 9 Jan. 1897, 23 Jan. 1897; Gov. Maxwell to Chamberlain, 2 March 1897 (encl. Henderson to Gov. Maxwell, 28 Jan. 1897); Barbato to Henderson, 21 Jan. 1897; H. O. A. McWilliam, "Ferguson, Samori and Barbatu," in *Ghana Teachers' Journal* 27 (July, 1960): 34–43.
17 SOM-AN Afrique III, 26, a, Voulet to Trentinian, 28 Jan. 1897 (copy).
18 Nehemiah Levtzion, "Salaga, a Nineteenth Century Trading Town in Ghana," in *Asian and African Studies: Annual of the Israel Oriental Society* 2 (1966): 207–44.
19 FO64/1357, Malet to Kimberley, 2 Feb. 1895, no. 14, Africa. Malet quoted a notice published in the *Kolonialblatt* about Lieut. Klose's visit to Salaga in October 1894. G. E. Ferguson, "Memorandum on the Brong Tribes" (24 Nov. 1893), in *Accounts and Papers* 57 (1896): C. 7917.
20 CO879/38, Ferguson to Griffith, 19 Nov. 1892 (encl. treaties with Bole, Daboya, Dagomba, and Bimbla).
21 Murdock, *Africa,* p. 80; R. S. Rattray, *Ashanti Hinterland* 1:113.
22 Von Seefried, "Beiträge zur Geschichte des Mangovolkes in Togo," in *Zeitschrift für Ethnologie* (1913), pp. 421–35.
23 *Sansane* means camp or dwelling; thus *Sansane-Mango* means a camp of the Mangos. See Rattray, *Ashanti Hinterland* 1:112–13; R. P. Welsch, "Les Tyokossi du Togo Nord," in *Notes Africaines* 47 (July, 1950): 77–78; R. Cornevin, "Sur le cercle de Dapango (Togo)," in *Le Monde Non-Chrétien,* n.s. 67 (July–Sept. 1963): 182–84.
24 E. P. Skinner, *The Mossi of Upper Volta: The Political Development of a Sudanese People* (Stanford, 1964), p. 138.
25 Ibid., pp. 126–38; SOM-AN Afrique III, 26, "Rapport du Lieutenant Chanoine: Résumé des Renseignements recuillis par le Lieut. Chanoine . . . la Mission au Mossi du 10 Dec. 1896 au 15 Février 1897," 16 Feb. 1897.
26 A. A. Dim Delobson, "Le Morho Naba et sa Cour," in *B.C.E.H.S.,* vol. II, no. 3 (July–Sept. 1928), pp. 386–421.
27 SOM-AN Afrique III, 26, Destenave to Gov. of Sudan, 19 May 1895 (encl. copy of treaty with Yatenga).
28 SOM-AN Afrique III, 26, "Note pour la Iere Direction," by L. Archinard, 24 Oct. 1895. Archinard stated in this note that armed intervention was necessary if France wished to acquire Wagadugu before Britain and Germany. Louis Tauxier, *Le Noir du Yatenga* (Paris, 1917), pp. 109–11.
29 A. A. Dim Delobson, *L'Empire du Mogho Naba* (Paris, 1932), pp. 30–38.
30 M. Delafosse, *Haut-Sénégal-Niger* (Paris, 1912), 1:311–12, 2:149–53.
31 Jules Molex, "Le Gourma," in *Journal Officiel du Dahomey* (1 Aug. 1898), pp. 8–10. Bilanga, Matiacuali, and Pama were in revolt. The other provinces were Fada N'Gurma, Diabo, Yanga, Sobalga, Mali-Konkobiri, Nebba, Bouzougou, and

Botou. See Henri Menjaud, "Documents ethnographiques sur le Gourma" (collected by Administrator Maubert of the *cercle* of Fada N'Gurma and published by H. Menjaud), in *Journal de la Société des Africanistes* 2 (1932): 35–47, facs. 1.

32. W. Buret, "Aperçu politique, agricole et commerciale sur le royaume de Konkobiri," in *Journal Officiel du Dahomey* (15 Aug. 1898). Buret was chief of the French post at Konkobiri, and his report was dated 15 Aug. 1897.

33. Robert Cornevin, *Histoire du Togo* (Paris, 1962), p. 148.

34. Maurice Abadie, *Afrique Centrale: La Colonie du Niger* (Paris, 1927), pp. 114–15; Delafosse, *Haut-Sénégal-Niger* 2:241.

35. Michel Perron, "Le Pays Dendi," in *B.C.E.H.S.* vol. 7, no. 1 (Jan.–March 1924), pp. 51–83. Perron corrected some errors of fact made by both Toutée and Hourst in their accounts of the Dendi; see pp. 67, 69 n. 2.

36. A. Prost, "Notes sur les Songay," in *Bulletin de l'Institut Français d'Afrique Noire* (hereafter *B.I.F.A.N.*) 16 (1954): 167–213. Perron says that the Songhay are the real Dendi.

37. Perron, "Le Pays Dendi," p. 61. See Gouv. Gen. de l'A.O.F., *Monographie de Gaya* (Dakar, 1917), chap. 4.

38. Gouvernement du Dahomey, *Rapport d'ensemble sur la situation générale de la Colonie du Dahomey et Dépendances, 1906* (Porto Novo, 1908).

39. Jacques Lombard, "Un système politique traditionnel de type féodal: les Bariba du Nord-Dahomey," in *B.I.F.A.N.*, vol. 19, Série B (1957), p. 489.

40. Robert Cornevin, *Histoire du Dahomey* (Paris, 1963), p. 183; Ousmany Bouquet, "Notes sur le Borgu: Histoire régionale," in *Bulletin d'Enseignement de l'A.O.F.* (Dakar) 42 (Feb.–March 1919): 65; 45 (Jan. 1921): 32; 47 (April–Sept. 1921): 103.

41. SOM-AN Soudan II, 1, extraits de rapports sur le Borgou, 1895; Rapport Ballot sur la situation politique de la region du Borgou, 17 Feb. 1895; Rapport Deville sur les résultats de sa mission; *Rapport d'ensemble sur la Situation Générale de la Colonie en 1906* (Porto Novo, 1908), pp. 12–13.

42. D. Pierre de Pedrals, *Dans la Brousse Africaine du Dahomey-Borghou* (Cannes, 1946), pp. 96–113. The most recent authoritative work on the Bariba is Lombard's *Structures de type "féodal."*

43. Hubert, "Afrique Occidentale Française," pp. 16–18.

44. Archives Nationales, Microfilms, no. 214 (hereafter A.N. MI 214), Journal du Docteur Alfred Bartet, chap. 9, pp. 68 ff.; Commandant G. J. Toutée, *Du Dahomey au Sahara. La Nature et L'Homme* (Paris, 1899), pp. 164–69.

45. I. Akinjogbin, "Dahomey and Yoruba in the Nineteenth Century," in *Africa in the Nineteenth and Twentieth Centuries,* ed. J. C. Anene and G. N. Brown (Ibadan, 1967), pp. 255-68.

46. Archibald Dalzel, *A History of Dahomey* (London, 1793); J. A. Skertchley, *Dahomey As It Is* (London, 1874); Henri Lefaivre, "Dictateurs Noirs: Les derniers Rois du Dahomey, 1610–1894," in *Revue d'Histoire des Colonies* (1ere trimestre, 1937), pp. 15–76.

47. Paul Mimande, *L'Héritage de Béhanzin* (Paris, 1898), pp. 21–22.

48. A. Le Herissé, *L'Ancien Royaume du Dahomey: Moeurs, Religion Histoire* (Paris, 1911), pp. 82–91; Le Père Chautard, *Le Dahomey* (Lyon, 1890), pp. 7–12; Abbé

Pierre Bouche, *La Côte des Esclaves et le Dahomey* (Paris, 1885), pp. 195–200; W. J. Argyle, *The Fon of Dahomey: A History and Ethnography of the Old Kingdom* (Oxford, 1966), pp. 94–119.
49 Gouvernement du Dahomey, *Rapport d'ensemble de la Colonie du Dahomey en 1899,* pp. 12–13.
50 Murdock, *Africa,* p. 253; Argyle, *The Fon of Dahomey,* pp. 34–54, 55–119.
51 Le Herissé, *L'Ancien Royaume du Dahomey,* p. 83; Montserrat Palau Marti, *Le Roi-Dieu au Bénin, Sud Dahomey, Nigeria Occidentale* (Paris, 1964), pp. 114–41.
52 Le Herissé, p. 91; de Pedrals, *La Brousse Africaine,* p. 103.
53 J. Chanoine, *Documents pour servir à l'histoire de l'Afrique Occidentale Française de 1895 à 1899. Correspondances du Capitaine Chanoine pendant l'expédition du Mossi et du Gourounsi* 13–14 (Paris, 1905); H. Barth, *Travels and Discoveries in North and Central Africa* 3 (London, 1965): 644–49, 202–04 (reprint). Chanoine's report contradicts Barth's view that copper and steel vessels in Mossi were imported from Ashanti.
54 Lt. Col. H. P. Northcott, Report on the Northern Territories of the Gold Coast, in Parliamentary Papers, Intelligence Division, War Office, 14 (London, 1899).
55 G. François, *Notre Colonie du Dahomey* (Paris, 1906), p. 158. The two were Michaut, formerly of the posts and telegraphs of Dahomey, and Drot, an officer of the colonial infantry. L. G. Binger, *Esclavage, Islamisme et Christianisme* (Paris, 1891), pp. 31–32, 70; MacGregor Laird and R. A. K. Oldfield, *Narrative of an Expedition into the Interior of Africa by the River Niger . . . in 1832, 1833 and 1834,* 2 vols. (London, 1837), 2:388.
56 Parl. Papers, Colonial Reports—Annual. No. 377 Northern Nigeria, Report for 1901, C.1388, pp. 60–70, 67.

CHAPTER 2

1 Prof. Dr. Lexis, "Über die Französische Kolonialpolitik," in *Deutsche Kolonialzeitung* (hereafter *D.K.Z.*) (Berlin, 1885), pp. 209–13, 249–56.
2 See correspondence in CO879/21 (9 Aug. 1880–23 July 1884) on Angra Pequena; "Die Angra-Pequena Frage: Deutsches Recht und englische Koloniallust," in *D.K.Z.* (1884), pp. 233–35; S. E. Crowe, *The Berlin West Africa Conference, 1884–1885* (London, 1942), pp. 39–49.
3 E. Banning, "Notes sur ma vie et mes écrits," in *Memoires: Institut Royal Colonial Belge,* ed. by J. Stengers, n.s. 2 (1955): 58–62. In a note to Frère-Oban on 4 December 1882, Banning suggested an international conference to be held at Brussels to discuss African questions by all the interested powers. He suggested a four-point program.
4 Geoffroy de Courcel, *L'Influence de la Conférence de Berlin de 1885 sur le Droit Colonial International* (Paris, 1936), pp. 28–30.
5 Parl. Papers, Africa no. 2 (1884), C.3885, Correspondence Relating to Negotiations between Great Britain and Portugal for the conclusion of the Congo Treaty, 1882–1884; Africa no. 5 (1884), C.4023, Further Papers relating to events connected with the Negotiations with Portugal for a Treaty respecting the Congo River and Adjacent Coast, 1884.

6 E. Banning, *Memoire sur les droits et les prétentions du Portugal à la souveraineté de certains territories de la côte occidentale de l'Afrique* (Paris, 1883).
7 *Allgemeine Zeitung*, 22 April 1883; see article by Gerhard Rohlfs.
8 Deutsches Weissbuch; *Angra Pequena* (11 Dec. 1884); Howard E. Yarnall, *The Great Powers and the Congo Conference in the Years 1884 and 1885* (Gottingen, 1934), pp. 20–25.
9 Ministère des Affaires Etrangères, Correspondance Politique, Allemagne, vol. 59, Bismarck to Courcel, 13 Sept. 1884; Courcel to Ferry, 1 Oct. 1884.
10 M.A.E., Allemagne 59, Ferry to Courcel, 2 Oct. 1884.
11 Parl. Papers, Africa no. 3 (1885), C.4360, Further Correspondence Respecting the West African Conference, p. 3; Africa no. 5, Malet to Granville, 15 Nov. 1884, with enclosure; Africa no. 4 (1885), C.4361, Protocols and General Act of the West African Conference, Protocol 1.
12 FO84/1818, Malet to Granville, 23 Dec. 1884.
13 Toutée, *Dahomé-Niger-Touareg*, p. xiii.
14 Parl. Papers, Africa no. 4 (1885), C.4361, Protocols and General Act of the West African Conference, Protocol 1, p. 12.
15 SOM-AN Afrique VI, 34, c, colonies to M.A.E., 21 Nov. 1883.
16 FO84/1814, Goldie to Anderson, 1 Nov. 1884 (private); *Times* (London), 23 June 1884.
17 *Register of Joint Stock Companies*, 17049:1, "Agreement between the N.A.C. Ltd. and the C.F.A.E.," 31 Oct. 1884. The C.F.A.E. received £60,000 in shares considered fully paid, according to J. E. Flint's "British Policy and Chartered Company Administration in Nigeria, 1879–1900" (Ph.D. diss., Univ. of London, 1959), chap. 2. The published version of this is *Sir George Goldie and the Making of Nigeria* (London, 1960).
18 Edouard Viard, *Au Bas-Niger* (Paris, 1885), p. 43. Of the 63 trading stations in the Lower Niger and Benue by 1883, 31 belonged to French and 32 to British merchants.
19 General Faidherbe, "La Question du Niger," *Revue Scientifique*, no. 3 (17 Jan. 1885), p. 67.
20 FO84/1814, Malet to Granville, 15 Nov. 1884.
21 Yarnall, *Congo Conference*, pp. 43–55; Crowe, *Berlin Conference*, pp. 34–49, 62–71.
22 SOM-AN Afrique VI, 34, c, M.A.E. to colonies, 21 Dec. 1883; "note" (draft), n.d., lists trouble spots in West Africa.
23 SOM-AN Afrique VI, 38, d, Colonies to M.A.E., 30 Dec. 1884.
24 M.A.E., Allemagne 59, Courcel to Ferry, 17 Aug. 1884, minutes by Ferry; Courcel to Ferry, 25 Aug. 1884; *Die Grosse Politik der Europäischen Kabinette*, vol. 3, no. 685, Hatzfeldt to Bismarck, 17 Aug. 1884; no. 687, Hatzfeldt to Bismarck, 25 Aug. 1884; *Documents Diplomatiques Françaises*, 1st series, vol. 5, no. 376, note by Ferry on German proposals.
25 General Duboc, *L'Epopée Coloniale en Afrique Occidentale Française* (Paris, 1938), p. 134; Commandant Antoine Mattei, *Bas-Niger, Bénoue, Dahomey* (Grenoble, 1890), pp. 61–63, 49–63.
26 FO84/1813, memorandum by T. V. L[ister] and by H. P. A[nderson], 14 Oct. 1884.

27 *Die Deutsche Kolonialpolitik* 3 (Leipzig, 1885): 37–38.
28 Parl. Papers, C.4361: Protocols and General Act of the West African Conference, protocol 5, annex no. 17, "Memorandum on the Niger Question," by H. P. Anderson.
29 Ibid., annex no. 15, "Revised Project of the Act of Navigation for the Niger proposed by Great Britain."
30 Yarnall, *Congo Conference*, p. 74; Crowe, *Berlin Conference*, pp. 119–41.
31 SOM-AN Senegal IV, 82, b, governor of Senegal to M.M.C., 24 Sept. 1884; Ferry to Peyron, 20 Dec. 1884; Peyron to Ferry, 24 Dec. 1884. Abdel Kadar stayed in Paris for three weeks. He lived at the Grand Hotel du Louvre, which cost France 2,451 francs (bill, 19 March 1885).
32 FO343/4, Malet Papers, Royal Letter Book and Miscellaneous, Malet to Leopold II, king of the Belgians, 20 Dec. 1884; FO84/1816, Malet to Granville, 5 Dec. 1884.
33 W. H. Dawson, "Imperial Policy in the Old and New World, 1885–1899," in *Cambridge History of British Foreign Policy* 3 (Cambridge, 1923): 209.
34 Public Record Office (London) Cabinet Papers (hereafter P.R.O. Cab.) 37/13, no. 53, Malet to Granville (encl. memorandum by R. H. Meade); FO343/2, Malet Papers, Granville to Malet, 10 Dec. 1884 (private).
35 M.A.E. *Memoires et Documents*, Afrique 109, "Proces-verbaux de la Commission chargée par la Conférence de Berlin de fixer les limites du Bassin commercial du Congo."
36 Parl. Papers, C. 4361, protocol 5, annex, "Report of the Commission charged to examine the projects of Acts of Navigation for the Congo and the Niger," pp. 150–51.
37 Of the 38 articles in the General Act of the Berlin Conference, 27 deal with economic questions concerning the Congo and the Niger. Only 11 articles deal with noneconomic matters. This reinforces the view that the most proximate reason for summoning the conference was economic. Humanitarian considerations were secondary (de Courcel, *La Conférence de Berlin*, p. 125.
38 Maurice Baumont, *L'Essor Industriel et l'Imperialisme Colonial, 1878–1904* (Paris, 1937), p. 97.
39 Ibid., p. 103.
40 See Toutée, *Dahomé-Niger-Touareg*; Lieut. Hourst, *Sur le Niger et au Pays du Touaregs* (Paris, 1897).
41 H. R. Rudin, *Germans in the Cameroons, 1884–1914* (London, 1938), p. 50.
42 M.A.E., Allemagne 62, Courcel to Ferry, 1 Feb. 1885 (encl. *Norddeutsche Allgemeine Zeitung*, 1 Feb. 1885).
43 FO84/1813, Plessen to Granville, 8 Oct. 1884; M.A.E. Allemagne, tome 59, Bismarck to Courcel, 13 Sept. 1884.
44 FO84/1813, memoranda by T. V. Lister, 11 and 14 Oct. 1884.
45 M.A.E., Allemagne 59, Courcel to Ferry, 1 Oct. 1884.
46 De Courcel, *La Conférence de Berlin*, p. 121; Emile Bourgeois et G. Pages, *Les Origines et les Résponsabilités de la Grande Guerre* (Paris, 1921), p. 210.
47 M.A.E., Afrique 108, protocol 7, séance du 7 Jan. 1885.
48 FO343/2, Malet Papers, Granville to Malet, 14 Oct. 1884, 14 Jan. 1885; P.R.O. Cab. 37/13, no. 44, proposed draft of dispatch to Sir E. Malet; no. 51, summary of the results of the west African conference up to 22 Dec. 1884.

49 FO343/2, Malet Papers, Granville to Malet, 23 Dec. 1884 (private); FO343/4, Malet to the Khedive, 19 Jan. 1885 (private).
50 FO84/1820, Granville to Malet, 17 Jan. 1885 (tel.); Malet to Granville, 18 Jan. 1885.
51 FO84/1819, Henry James to Pauncefote, 2 Jan. 1885 (encl. memo by law officers; law officers to F.O., 7 Jan. 1885; "Law Officers' Opinion on Third Basis").
52 FO84/1819, minutes by Lord Chancellor on law officers' report, 3 Jan. 1885; F.O. Confidential Prints No. 4824, memo by E. Herstlet, 24 April 1883.
53 FO84/1819, Pauncefote to Hill, 9 Jan. 1885; FO343/2, Granville to Malet, 14 Jan. 1885 (private).
54 FO84/1819, Granville to Malet, 13 Jan. 1885.
55 Protocols and General Act of the West African Conference, 4361, pp. 201, 214; de Courcel, *La Conférence de Berlin*, p. 83
56 FO84/1819, Granville to Malet, 14 Jan. 1885; Malet to Granville, 15 Jan. 1885 (tel.).
57 M.A.E. *Memoires et Documents*, Afrique 108, protocol 8, annex no. 1, Rapport de la Commission chargée d'éxaminer le Projet de Déclaration rélative aux Occupations nouvelles sur les Côtes d'Afrique (29 Jan. 1885).
58 Mr. J. A. Kasson's proposal on neutrality was ridiculed by Jules Ferry, who remarked that it "se place au contraire à une distance si lointaine et tellement en dehors des réalités qu'en peut la qualifier d'academique" (Ferry to Courcel, 16 Dec. 1884 [private], quoted in de Courcel, pp. 78–79).
59 Ibid., remarks by Busch in the commission.
60 FO84/1819, Granville to Malet, 14 Jan. 1885; Malet to Granville, 15 Jan. 1885; *D.K.Z.* (1885), p. 67.
61 M.A.E. C. P., Allemagne 59, Ferry to Courcel, 16 Jan. 1885 (tel.); M.A.E., Afrique 109, Ferry to Courcel, 16 Jan. 1885.
62 Parl. Papers, 4361, Protocols and General Act of the West African Conference, protocol 8, "Report of the Commission," 29 Jan. 1885.
63 FO84/1819, Malet to Granville, 15 Jan. 1885 (tel.).
64 FO84/1820, Malet to Granville, 16 Jan. 1885 (tel.); FO84/1819, Pauncefote to Hill, 9 Jan. 1885.
65 FO84/1820, Malet to Granville, 29 Jan. 1885, no. 64 Africa; de Courcel, *La Conférence de Berlin*, p. 84.
66 FO84/1820, Malet to Granville, 21 Jan. 1885; 22 Jan. 1885 (tels.). Granville had prescribed this method of approach to Malet. "When new points arise which require reference home, we would be glad to have the opinion of our delegates on the spot" (FO343/2, Malet Papers, Granville to Malet, 23 Nov. 1884 [private]).
67 FO84/1820, Pauncefote to Granville, 23 Jan. 1885; Sir William Horwood, 24 Jan. 1885; Lord Chancellor to Pauncefote, 23 Jan. 1885; Lord Chancellor to Granville, 20 Jan. 1885.
68 Crowe, *Berlin Conference,* p. 189.
69 FO84/1820, Malet to Granville, 24 Jan. 1885 (tel.); Granville to Malet, 26 Jan. 1885 (tel.); Malet to Granville, 31 Jan. 1885 (tel.); *Livres Jaunes: Affaires du Congo et de l'Afrique occidentale, avec Rapport de M. Engelhardt* (Paris, 1885), 26 rapport.
70 P.R.O. Cab. 37/13, no. 53, Malet to Granville (encl. memorandum by R. H.

Meade on his conversation with Bismarck). "I do not find your proposals sufficient," said Bismarck to Meade at the close of a long interview which covered Anglo-German problems in Oceania and in east and west Africa (M.A.E., Allemagne 59, Courcel to Ferry, 23 Nov. 1884).

71 SOM-AN Senegal IV, 82, b, Ferry to Peyron, 20 Dec. 1884; Peyron to Ferry, 24 Dec. 1884.
72 K. Vignes, "Etude sur la rivalité d'influence entre les puissances européenes en Afrique equatoriale et occidentale dépuis l'acte général de Berlin jusqu'au seuil du XXe siècle," in *Revue Française d'Histoire d'Outre-Mer*, vol. 48, no. 1 (1961), p. 33 n. 6.
73 Ibid., p. 35. See also M. Bernheim, *L'Acte général de la Conference africaine de Berlin jugé par la Ligue Internationale de la Paix et de la Liberté* (Bale, 1885); Charles Faure, *La Conference Africaine de Berlin* (Genève, 1885).
74 Baumont, *L'Essor Industriel*, pp. 97–98.
75 For another view see Crowe, *Berlin Conference*, pp. 3–5; and J. D. Hargreaves, *Prelude to the Partition of West Africa* (Edinburgh, 1963), p. 337. Neither Miss Crowe nor Hargreaves, who based his views on Miss Crowe's, read de Courcel's *La Conférence de Berlin*.
76 William L. Langer, *An Encyclopaedia of World History: Ancient, Medieval and Modern*, 3rd ed. rev. (Boston, 1952), p. 841 col. 1.
77 L. Dudley-Stamp, *Africa: A Study in Tropical Development* (New York, 1964), pp. 27–28.
78 J. D. Fage and Derwent Whittlesey, "West Africa," in *Encyclopaedia Britannica* 23 (London, 1957): 522; "Guinea," ibid., 10:971–72.
79 See K. O. Dike, *Trade and Politics in the Niger Delta* (London, 1956); C. Gertzel, "John Holt: An African Trader" (D. Phil. diss., Oxford University, 1962); G. I. Jones, *The Trading States of the Oil Rivers* (London, 1963).
80 de Courcel, *La Conférence de Berlin*, pp. 88, 92, 113–14.
81 E. Hertslet, *Map of Africa by Treaty* 1 (London, 1896): 283–84.
82 German Togo was at this time composed of Lome, Bageida, and their immediate environs (Hertslet 1:320: von Plessen to Granville, 15 Oct. 1884).
83 See A. Akindele and C. Aguessy, *Contribution à l'étude de l'Histoire de l'Ancien Royaume de Porto Novo* (*Memoires de l'I.F.A.N.*), no. 25 (Dakar, 1953), pp. 81–89, on the reign of King Toffa (1874–1908).
84 Hertslet 1:321.
85 The *Yevogan* was the minister in charge of European affairs, called "chief of foreigners and whites" (A. Akindele and C. Aguessy, *Le Dahomey* [Paris, 1955], p. 25).
86 Catherin Coquery, "Le blocus de Whydah (1876–1877) et la rivalité franco-anglaise au Dahomey," in *Cahiers d'Etudes Africaines*, vol. 2 no. 7 (1962), pp. 373–419, 210–14; C. W. Newbury, *The Western Slave Coast and Its Rulers* (Oxford, 1961), pp. 94, 77–95, 97–107, 90–92; M.A.E. M & D, Afrique 76, reports by Serval, 23 and 30 April 1878; note by d'Elteil, 28 April 1879, quoted in Hargreaves: *Prelude*, p. 208. France was to appoint a vice-consul to the Slave Coast and conclude a new treaty with Dahomey so as to gain full control of Cotonou and save it from falling into the hands of Britain. The treaty with Dahomey was signed on 23 April 1878.

87 Cornevin, *Histoire du Dahomey*, pp. 292–93.
88 M.A.E., Afrique 76, d'Elteil to Waddington, 22 Feb. 1879, 1 May 1879; Hargreaves, p. 210.
89 France had decided to hang on to the ancient treaty rights at Porto Novo (23 Feb. 1863) in order to throw them in as a pawn during a general settlement or in the case of an exchange involving the Gambia. Hargreaves, p. 208; M.A.E., Afrique 76; M.A.E. to M.M.C., 16 July 1877; note pour le ministre, 23 July 1877; Newbury, p. 106.
90 FO343/2, Malet Papers, Granville to Malet, 26 Nov. 1884, on the Egyptian question; R. E. Robinson, J. Gallagher, and Alice Denny, *Africa and the Victorians* (London, 1962).
91 M.A.E. Angleterre (C. P. des Consuls), Freetown, 70 di Lacca to M.A.E., 7 April 1883; Newbury, pp. 106–08; Akindele and Aguessy, *L'Ancien Royaume de Porto Novo*, pp. 106–08.
92 M.A.E., Afrique 78, Bories to M.M.C., M.M.C. to M.A.E. (encl. treaty with King Toffa of 25 July 1883), 12 Aug. 1883; Hargreaves, pp. 294–301. The first French protectorate over Porto Novo began with the treaty of 23 Feb. 1863. Ballot to Moloney, 19 Nov. 1887, quoted in Cornevin, *Histoire du Dahomey*, p. 310; J. P. Schwitzer, "British Attitude towards French Colonisation, 1875–1887" (Ph.D. diss., London University, 1954), pp. 295–327.
93 Guilman was succeeded by Germa (Sept. 1883); then came Maignot (March 1884), who was replaced by Colonel L. Dorat in May 1884.
94 Dorat's Report, 26 July 1884, in *Etudes Dahoméennes* 9 (1953): 38–39; Cornevin, *Histoire du Dahomey*, p. 295.
95 A. A. Aderebigbe, "The Expansion of the Lagos Protectorate (1863–1900)" (Ph.D. diss., London Univ., 1959), chaps. 1, 2; Newbury, *Western Slave Coast*, pp. 92–94; Hargreaves, *Prelude*, pp. 211–13.
96 CO147/38, Ussher to Hicks Beach, 7 Oct. 1879, 29 Sept. 1879; Newbury, p. 94.
97 M.A.E., Afrique 77, Bareste to M.A.E., 20 May 1881.
98 R. E. Robinson, "Imperial Problems in British Politics, 1880–1895," *Cambridge History of the British Empire*, vol. 3, *The Empire-Commonwealth, 1870–1919* (Cambridge, 1959), p. 130.
99 Speech by the Duke of Devonshire to colonial premiers in Liverpool on the aims and aspirations of the British Empire League, in *Times* (London), 14 June 1897.
100 See Charles de Freycinet, *La Question d'Egypt* (Paris, 1905), chap. 4.
101 Robinson et al., *Africa and the Victorians*, p. 130.
102 CO87/116, F.O. to C.O., minutes by Kimberley, 4 Aug. 1880, quoted in Hargreaves, *Prelude*, p. 265.
103 Newbury, *Western Slave Coast*, p. 127. See chaps. 3 and 4 below on the Dahomey Wars.
104 A. Akindele and C. Aguessy, *L'Ancien Royaume de Porto Novo*, p. 17; Newbury, pp. 17–20; Hertslet, *Map of Africa*, 1:249.
105 M. d'Autas to F.O., 21 Jan. 1886, quoted in Hertslet 1:253.
106 See E. Foa, *Le Dahomey* (Paris, 1895), pp. 42–44; Cornevin, *Histoire du Dahomey*, pp. 302–03. Similar French charges of bad interpretation of treaty terms and other irregularities will be noted in the cases of G. E. Ferguson (Mossi) and F. D. Lugard (Nikki) in Chapter 5 below.

107 M.A.E., Afrique 82, Roget to M.C.C., 10 and 14 Sept. 1885; M.M.C. to Dorat, Instructions au Lieut. Commandant Disnematin-Dorat.
108 Letters of 16 Feb. 1886 and 23 Feb. 1886, by which France started her prior rights in Whydah, Cotonou, and Porto Novo. See Cornevin, *Histoire du Dahomey*, p. 302; M.A.E., Afrique 82 and 83, for correspondence on Dahomey and Porto Novo.
109 A. L. d'Albeca, *Les Etablissements Français du Golfe du Bénin* (Paris, 1889), p. 25; "Portugal und Dahomé," in *D.K.Z.* (1888), no. 2, p. 13.
110 The Portuguese constitution of 4 April 1838 so classified it. See Hertslet, *Map of Africa* 1:249.
111 For correspondence on King Glégle's relations with Portugal see SOM-AN Afrique IV, 11. This dossier covers the period 1879-88.
112 L. Brunet and L. Giethlen, *Dahomey et Dépendances: Histoire generale, organisation, administration, éthnographie, productions, agriculture, commerce* (Paris, 1900), p. 92.
113 Lefaivre, "Dictateurs Noirs," pp. 15-76.
114 F.O. Handbooks No. 95, pp. 13 ff, Lord Salisbury to Petrie, 2 Aug. 1887; British State Papers, pp. 79, 1063 ff; Sir H. Lauterpacht and R. Y. Jennings, "International Law and Colonial Questions, 1870-1914," *Cambridge History of the British Empire*, 3:679.
115 M.A.E., Afrique 125, notes from Portugal, 22 and 26 Dec. 1887.
116 M. E. Townsend, *The Rise and Fall of Germany's Colonial Empire* (New York, 1930), pp. 34-35.
117 D. Grundemann, "Die Mission in den deutschen Schutzgebieten in West Afrika: Das Togo," in *D.K.Z.* (1888), pp. 227-29. See also C. Mirbt, *Mission und Kolonialpolitik in den deutschen Schutzgebieten* (Tübingen, 1910); A. W. Schreiber, *Bausteine zur Geschichte der Norddeutschen Missions-Gesellschaft* (Bremen, 1911), pp. 90 ff.
118 G. Müller, *Geschichte der Ewe-Mission* (Bremen, 1904), pp. 14 ff.; *Deutsches Kolonial-Lexikon* 2 (Leipzig, 1920): 658.
119 Cornevin, *Histoire du Togo*, p. 128; Müller, pp. 190-92.
120 E. G. Jacob, *Deutsche Kolonialpolitik in Dokumenten* (Leipzig, 1938), p. 16.
121 Cornevin, *Histoire du Togo*, p. 126. Jacob Protten was a mulatto born in Accra. His mother was from the royal family of Anecho (Little Popo), and he visited Popo in September 1737 during his first trip to the west coast.
122 These are not to be confused with the German-speaking Swiss, who formed the majority of the personnel of the Basel mission. See Townsend, *Germany's Colonial Empire*, pp. 43-44; W. E. F. Ward, *A History of Ghana*, 2nd ed. rev. (London, 1958), pp. 204-05; W. W. Claridge, *A History of the Gold Coast*, 2 vols. (London, 1915), 1:424.
123 See Townsend, pp. 44-47, on German traders and German colonies. See also A. Bastian, *Europäische Kolonien in Afrika und Deutschlands Interessen sonst und jetzt* (Berlin, 1884); Prof. Dr. Cheberg, "Über den wirtschaftlichen Wert der Kolonisation für Deutschland," in *Deutsche Kolonialzeitung* (1887), p. 282.
124 Newbury, *Western Slave Coast*, pp. 101-03. Dr. Newbury lists the five leading German firms in these ports. See Jacob, *Deutsche Kolonialpolitik*, p. 68, on Vietor; also Woermann, 2-5.

125 M.A.E. C. P., Allemagne 59, Courcel to Ferry, 10 Oct. 1884 (encl. *Le Commerce de l'Allemagne hors d'Europe*). See *Deutsche Kolonialzeitung* (1886), p. 672, on the Germans in Lagos.
126 Jacob, p. 56. "Das altgermanische Ideal des Individualismus, das einst die Kolonisation des Ostens vollbracht hatte, blieb auch Bismarck's Kolonialideal von Anfang an. Die Pioniere des Handels sollten vorangehen und dem Staate die Kolonialen Wege weisen, ihnen solle er erst folgen mit seinem Schuss" (Theo Sommerlad).
127 *Die Grosse Politik*, 4:64, minutes by Bismarck on Münster to Bismarck, 7 June 1884, quoted in Hargreaves, *Prelude*, p. 320.
128 *Documents Diplomatiques Françaises* (hereafter *D.D.F.*), 1st series 5:551; Courcel to Ferry, 19 Jan. 1885, no. 528.
129 Cornevin, *Histoire du Togo*, pp. 132–34; Newbury, pp. 113–15.
130 Gustav Nachtigal exclaimed: "Vertrag geschlossen, lassen Sie die kaiserliche Flagge an Land bringen." The flag went up and a twenty-one gun salute followed because "Deutschland war auch hier in die Reihe der Kolonialen Mäche eingetreten!" (Jacob, pp. 69–73). This contradicts A. F. Calvert's view that Nachtigal "unostentatiously unfurled the flag of the Fatherland" (A. F. Calvert, *Togoland* [London, 1918], p. 5).
131 Calvert, pp. 3–4.
132 Cornevin, *Histoire du Togo*, p. 135.
133 SOM-AN Afrique IV, 47, Freycinet to Galiber, 4 May 1885; Galiber to Freycinet, 19 June 1885; Legraud to Galiber, 21 July 1885—all quoted in Newbury, *Western Slave Coast*, p. 115.
134 M.A.E., Afrique 81, Freycinet to Galiber, 26 May 1885.
135 Galiber (ministre de la marine et des colonies) sympathized with Lieut. Roget's views and pressed these on Freycinet. M.A.E., Afrique 82, Galiber to Freycinet, 25 Sept. 1885; Hertslet, *Map of Africa* 1:284, no. 250.
136 P. A. de Salinis, *Protectorat Français sur la Côte des Esclaves: La Campaigne du Sane, 1889–1890* (Paris, 1908), p. 540.
137 Cornevin, *Histoire du Dahomey*, p. 305. They quickly erected buildings at Gridji and Little Popo (Anecho).
138 SOM-AN Afrique IV, 47, Freycinet to Galiber, 28 Sept. 1885 (encl. "Projet"). See M.A.E., Allemagne 6, Oaud 61, for correspondence from Courcel. See correspondence on Porto Seguro and the Popos in M.A.E., Afrique 96. These show that the French officials did not care much for Porto Seguro but wished to use it to wrest some concession from Germany.
139 M.A.E., Allemagne 60, reports by Courcel in Oct. and Nov. 1885; M.A.E., Afrique 96, treaty of 24 Dec. 1885. *D.K.Z.*, no. 4 (1886), pp. 102–03, "Vereinbarungen zwischen Deutschland und Frankreich über deren Besitzungen an der Westküste Afrikas und in der Südsee." Hertslet, *Map of Africa* 1:293–96.
140 Cornevin, *Histoire du Dahomey*, p. 305; Newbury, *Western Slave Coast*, p. 115.
141 Hertslet 1:297; M.A.E., Afrique 96, arrangement franco-allemand de 24 Dec. 1885.
142 SOM-AN Afrique IV, 61, Bayol to M.M.C., 1 and 9 Feb. 1887. It was Dr. J. Bayol's habit to recommend all sorts of people for French national honors and for promotion.
143 SOM-AN Afrique IV, 61, a, M.A.E. to Colonies (encl. Herbette to M.A.E., 3 April

1887; "Note sur le régime douanier de la Côte des Esclaves," quoted in Newbury, *Western Slave Coast*, p. 116).

144 Alexander Supan, *Die Territoriale Entwicklung der Europaischen Kalonien* (Gotha, 1906), pp. 273–74.

145 Vignes, "La rivalité d'influence," pp. 43–44; Charles E. Nowell, "Portugal and the Partition of Africa," *Journal of Modern History*, vol. 19, no. 1 (March 1947), p. 1. Nowell gives reasons for Portuguese impotence at this time in European affairs.

146 The Germans had already begun to speculate on the great potential of kola nuts, "diese noch wenig bekannte Frucht, welche für den Welthandel von grosser Bedeutung werden kann" ("Die Kola-Nuss," in *D.K.Z.* [1886], pp. 551–52).

147 Hertslet, *Map of Africa* 1:393–94.

148 CO96/158, Gov. Young to Derby, 30 June 1884. Young buttressed his views by quoting from the report of R. E. Firminger of the district commission at Keta on the growing business of smugglers in Beh Beach and Bagida. G. E. Metcalfe, *Great Britain and Ghana: Documents of Ghana History 1807–1957* (London, 1964), no. 342.

149 The Colonial Office repudiated Firminger's treaty because its terms were "not such as would have been suggested by Her Majesty's Government" (Meade to F.O. 12 Sept. 1884, in C.O. Confidential Print No. 283, p. 136; Metcalfe, no. 347). Firminger's treaty is given in C.O. Confidential Print No. 411, p. 331.

150 FO27/2418, C.O. to F.O., 13 Nov. 1879, minutes by Salisbury, quoted in Schwitzer, "British Attitude," p. 305.

151 Metcalfe, no. 341, p. 414: "Memorial of the Merchants in the City of London, England and Interested in the Trade with the Gold Coast and Lagos" (7 Dec. 1883).

152 CO96/159, Young to Derby, 8 and 9 July 1884; CO96/158, minutes by J. Anderson, 4 Aug. 1884; minutes by Fairfield, 19 Aug. 1884; Young to Derby, 6 Nov. 1884.

153 CO879/22, Derby to Young, 26 Dec. 1884. The type of argument advanced by Governor Young here would later be used by the French against Lugard's treaty at Nikki in Nov. 1894.

154 CO147/36, F.O. to C.O., 16 Oct. 1878, minutes by Hemming, quoted in Schwitzer, p. 306. In 1878 Hemming objected to French intrusion "between the (at present) separate portions of the Gold Coast colony." Even Salisbury considered the Slave Coast part of the Gold Coast. FO27/2414 Lyon to Waddington, 26 Feb. 1879; Lyons to Salisbury, 26 Feb. 1879.

155 Hertslet, *Map of Africa*, 1:394; Paul Steiner, "Land und Leute von Akra," in *Deutsche Kolonialzeitung* (1885), pp. 48–53.

156 Claridge, *Gold Coast*, p. 282. By this time German scholars had begun to analyze their country's colonial experience in Africa. See Herman Soyaux, *Deutsche Arbeit in Afrika: Erfahrungen und Betrachtungen* (Leipzig, 1888); also P.R.O. Cab. 37/14, *German Views on Colonial Matters* (28 Jan. 1885); F.O. Confidential Print No. 5976, *Memorandum on Points of Dispute with Germany in Africa*.

157 The boundary of the Neutral Zone to the north was 10° North Latitude; to the east it was 0°33′ Longitude, and to the west 1°27′ Longitude (Greenwich). The

recommendations were approved by Britain and Germany on 12 and 14 March 1888, respectively.
158 Cf. Dr. Henrici, *Das Deutsche Togogebiet und meine Afrikareise* (Berlin, 1888); C. Benkard, "Reisen in Westafrika," in *D.K.Z.* (1887), p. 250. Dr. Henrici acquired Liati for the Germans in Sept. 1887. See chap. 4 below on expeditions into the hinterland.
159 Sir Valentine Chirol, "The Boer War and the International Situation," *Cambridge History of British Foreign Policy, 1783–1919* 3 (Cambridge, 1923): 270.
160 Otto Arendt, "England and Deutschland in Ostafrika," in *D.K.Z.* (1888), pp. 10–11. See also "Englische Pressestimmen," in ibid., pp. 145–46.
161 "Deutschland in Afrika und in der Südsee," *Die Deutsche Kolonialpolitik*, no. 1; "Deutsche Interessen in der Südsee," ibid, no. 2.
162 M. Adams, "The British Attitude to German Colonisation, 1880–1885," in *Bulletin of the Institute of Historical Research* 15 (1937): 190–93; A. J. P. Taylor, *Germany's First Bid for Colonies* (London, 1938), pp. 32–44.
163 In October 1888 Salisbury had to postpone the preparations for the Brussels Conference to accommodate German activity in Zanzibar (FO541/28, minutes by Salisbury on Vivian to Salisbury, 6 Oct. 1888, Africa no. 52, 26 Oct. 1888). "I think this matter may profitably be suspended while the Anglo-German proposals are pending" (ibid., Africa no. 355). Salisbury to Vivian, 24 Nov. 1888, Africa no. 24. See D. R. Gillard, "Salisbury's African Policy and the Helgoland Offer of 1890," *English Historical Review*, vol. 75 no. 297 (Oct. 1960), pp. 637–38, quoting FO84/1924, Salisbury to Knutsford, 13 July 1888; FO343/3, Malet Papers, Salisbury to Malet, 12 Feb. 1889.
164 G. Trierenberg, *Togo, die Aufrichtung der deutschen Schutzherrschaft und die Erschliessung des Landes* (Berlin, 1914), pp. 2–3.
165 CO879/31, memorandum by A. W. L. Hemming on Krepi, 11 Dec. 1889; C.O. Confidential Print No. 384.
166 Salisbury activated an old plan. See *Parliamentary Debates: House of Commons* 296:1010–18 for proposed cession of Helgoland to Germany and Gorst's observations of 30 March 1885; *Die Grosse Politik*, vol. 8, no. 1676; Gillard, p. 650.
167 The effects of the Helgoland trump on the attitude of Germany to the negotiations were decisive. See *Die Grosse Politik*, vol. 8, nos. 1677–88.
168 Ibid., nos. 1681, 1676 n.; Gillard, p. 653.
169 Parl. Papers, chap. 6046, Africa no. 6 (1890), Correspondence Respecting the Anglo-German Agreement relative to Africa and Helgoland; Africa no. 3, Malet to Salisbury, 1 July 1890 (encl. treaty signed at Berlin on 1 July 1890, art. 4 on west Africa); *D.K.Z.* (1890), no. 16, p. 189, with map; no. 14, p. 171.
170 Parl. Papers, C.6046, Africa no. 6 (1890); no. 2, Salisbury to Malet, 1 July 1890; W. Roger Louis, "Sir Percy Anderson's Grand African Strategy, 1883–1896," in *English Historical Review*, no. 319 (April 1966), pp. 302–03.
171 Carl Peters, *Die Grundung von Deutsch-Ostafrika* (Berlin, 1906), pp. 235–63; Dr. Hubbe-Schleiden, "Deutsche Welthegemonie," in *Deutsche Kolonialzeitung* (1890), p. 182; R. C. Beazley, "Das Deutsche Kolonialreich, Gross Britannien und die Verträge von 1890," in *Die Berliner Monatshefte* (May 1931), pp. 444–59.
172 "Die Denkschrift über die Beweg-gründe zu dem deutscheenglischen Abkommen,"

in *D.K.Z.*, no. 17 (Aug. 1890), pp. 197–99; *Frankfurter Zeitung*, 23 June 1890; *Freisinnige Zeitung*, June and July 1890; L. von Caprivi, *Die Ostafrikanische Frage und der Helgoland-Sansibar Vertrag* (Berlin, 1934).

173 See F. Fabri, *Der Deutsch-Englische Vertrag* (Köln, 1890); Ernst Vohsen, *Zum Deutsch-Englischen Vertrag* (Berlin, 1890); M. von Hagen, *Geschichte und Bedeutung des Helgoland Vertrages* (Berlin, 1916).

174 Parliamentary Debates: House of Commons 347 (24 and 25 July 1890): 743–835; FO84/2083, cutting from *Daily Chronicle* (July 1890), quoted in W. Roger Louis, *Ruanda-Urundi, 1884–1919* (Oxford, 1963), p. 18; *Times* (London), 1 July 1890; *Pall Mall Gazette*, 22 May 1890.

175 Louis, *Ruanda-Urundi*, p. 18.

176 Lugard Papers MSS, British Empire S. 69, Kirk to Lugard, 18 July 1890; **Kirk to Lugard, 15 June 1890**; G. N. Sanderson, "The Anglo-German Agreement of 1890 and the Upper Nile," in *E.H.R.* vol. 78, no. 306 (Jan. 1963).

177 Hertslet, *Map of Africa* 2:642–51.

178 W. O. Henderson, "German East Africa, 1884–1898," in *History of East Africa* ed. V. Harlow, E. M. Chivers, and A. Smith (Oxford, 1965), 2:131; L. W. Hollingsworth, *Zanzibar under the Foreign Office, 1890–1913* (London, 1963), pp. 37–51.

179 Newbury, *Western Slave Coast*, pp. 50–76, 89–95; R. Meade, "Memorandum respecting French Proceedings upon West Coast of Africa," in *C.O. Confidential Print No. 270* (Sept. 1883).

180 Lyons to Granville, 15 and 30 May 1885; Rosebery to Lyons, 3 March 1886; Lyons to Rosebery, 5 March 1886; Lyons to Iddesleigh, 7 Dec. 1886; Lyons to Salisbury, 5 Feb. 1887 and 29 March 1887—all in Lord Newton, *Lord Lyons: A Record of British Diplomacy* (London, n.d.), pp. 507–49.

181 FO403/85, Evans to C.O., 23 Aug. 1886, 1 Sept. 1886.

182 *D.D.F.*, 1st series vol. 5, no. 297, Ferry to Waddington, 7 June 1884.

183 CO147/58 Evans to Holland, 30 March 1887, minutes by Hemming. See Schwitzer, "British Attitude," pp. 295–326, for background material.

184 CO96/162, F.O. to C.O., 24 Jan. 1884, minutes by Meade; *Parliamentary Debates: House of Commons*, 3rd series 279, chap. 1098, statement by Hon. Evelyn Ashley, parliamentary undersecretary to the Colonial Office, 29 May 1883.

185 M.A.E., Angleterre 808, Waddington to Ferry, 11 Jan. 1885; Afrique 81, Freycinet to Galiber, 26 May 1885; Angleterre 812, De Ring to Waddington, 25 Aug. 1885.

186 Both Roget and Pereton had been residents at Porto Novo. Pereton to Gov. of Lagos, 14 March 1887, and F. Evans's reply, in *Etudes Dahoméennes* 9 (1953): 84–85.

187 M.A.E., Angleterre 805, Waddington to Ferry, 10 July 1884; CO96/162, F.O. to C.O., 26 June 1884; C.O. to F.O., 7 July 1884.

188 J. Stengers, *Textes inedits d'Emile Banning, Memoires: Institut Royal Colonial Belge*, n.s. 2 (1955): 43; de Courcel, *La Conference de Berlin*, pp. 113–14; Crowe, *Berlin Conference*.

189 Parl. Papers 56, C.4052; Further Correspondence Regarding the Affairs of the Gold Coast (London, 1884): Manchester Chamber of Commerce to Derby, 4 Dec.

1883, p. 94; London Merchants to Derby, 7 Dec. 1883, p. 95; Rowe to Derby, 19 Feb. 1884 (encl. 1, p. 71, cited in Newbury, *Western Slave Coast*, p. 95). See correspondence in CO96/152 on the problems of merchants in the Gold Coast; also Claridge, *Gold Coast*, 2:302–03.
190 British State Papers 77:991; Metcalfe, *Documents,* no. 350, pp. 420–22.
191 Schwitzer, British Attitude," p. 327.
192 They also asked for the appointment of a resident in Kumasi. Derby dismissed this particular proposal because "strong reasons of policy and prudence" pointed against such an appointment (Claridge 2:302).
193 Parl. Papers, chap. 4052, London merchants to Derby, 7 Dec. 1883, p. 95. They also asked that the British government "adopt measures to prevent the further annexation of any of the countries between the Gold Coast possessions and Lagos by any other European Power." The merging of the administrations of Lagos and the Gold Coast in 1874 was in keeping with the spirit of the report of the Select Committee on Africa (Western) of 1865.
194 CO96/165, F. A. Stanley to Griffith, 14 Oct. 1885; Metcalfe, no. 349, pp. 419–20.
195 CO96/165, Stanley to Griffith, 14 Oct. 1885. J. P. Schwitzer, who observed in her thesis that the Foreign and Colonial Offices were converted to an expansionist mood after 1883, should have seen that the separation of Lagos from the Gold Coast in 1886 followed logically from and was a manifestation of that conversion.
196 Hon. George Peel, "The Nerves of Empire," in *The Empire and the Century*, ed. C. S. Goldman (London, 1905), pp. 265–66; Foa, *Le Dahomey*, p. 49 n.
197 See Flint, *Sir George Goldie*.
198 SOM-AN Afrique IV, 12, b, M.M.C. to M.A.E., 12 Dec. 1884. M. Goldscheider was sous-directeur in the ministère de la marine et des colonies.
199 C. W. Newbury, "The Development of French Policy on the Lower and Upper Niger, 1880–1898," in *Journal of Modern History*, vol. 31, no. 1 (March, 1959), pp. 16–26.
200 SOM-AN Afrique IV, 12, b, note by Goldscheider, 17 July 1885.
201 SOM-AN Afrique IV, 12, b, Galiber to Freycinet, 17 Dec. 1885.
202 See S. Kenya-Forstner, "The French in West Africa: A Study of Military Imperialism" (Ph.D. diss., Cambridge Univ., 1965); General Faidherbe, "L'Avenir du Sahara et du Soudan," in *Revue Maritime et Coloniale* 8 (1863): 221 ff.; H. Dechamps, *Les Méthodes et les Doctrines Coloniales de la France* (Paris, 1953), pp. 113–17.
203 General Faidherbe, *Le Sénégal: La France dans l'Afrique Occidentale* (Paris, 1889).
204 Faidherbe, "La Question du Niger," in *Revue Scientifique*, no. 3 (17 Jan. 1885), pp. 65–68); Faidherbe, "Tombouctou et les grandes voies de communication de l'Afrique," in *Rev. Scientifique* (15 Nov. 1884).
205 M.A.E., Afrique 85, note by Dabey, 24 Jan. 1886; Freycinet to Aube, 10 March 1886.
206 M.A.E., Afrique 81, De Lacca to Faure, 7 Jan. 1885.
207 Edouard R. Viard was connected with Comte de Semelle's C.F.A.E. He went on an exploration mission to Nupe in 1881 and 1882 and was back in the Lagos hinterland in 1888 for treaty-making with the native rulers. See Viard's, *Explora-*

tions Africaines: La France et la Conference de Berlin (Paris, 1885), and his *Au Bas-Niger*.

208 M.A.E., Afrique 85, M.M.C. to M.A.E., 15 Jan. 1886.
209 Ballot was appointed to his new post in September 1887. He arrived at Kotonou on 23 October 1887 and at Porto Novo on 15 November 1887. Papiers Ballot, MI.185 (Archives Nationales, Paris), Ballot to gov. of Senegal, 23 Oct. 1887, 15 Nov. 1887; 29 Nov. 1887.
210 No biography of Victor Ballot exists, except for short sketches by Mlle. G. Ganier, *Papiers d'Afrique: Notes D'Histoire Coloniale*, no. 68 (Dakar, 1963), pp. 3–5. See G. Hanotaux et A. Martineau, *Histoire des Colonies Françaises*, vol. 4, *Afrique Occidentale française* (Paris, 1934), pp. 289–91, 303–09; Duboc, *L'Epopée Coloniale*, pp. 293 ff.; Cornevin, *Histoire du Dahomey*, pp. 309–12; Akindele and Aguessy, *Le Dahomey*, pp. 27–31. The Papiers Ballot do not throw any additional light on the character of Ballot. The documents therein are almost all official in nature and reveal nothing further than what one can glean from the official files and dossiers. He was a man who loved to possess and to exercise authority. Hanotaux and Martineau, p. 290; L. Brunet, "M. Victor Ballot, Gouverneur de Dahomey et Dépendances," in *L'Africaine* (May 1898), pp. 70–74; Louis Henrique, "Victor Ballot," in *Nos Contemporains* 1 (Paris, 1896): 97–101.
211 CO879/26, Moloney to Meade, 15 July 1887; Moloney to Meade, 19 July 1887, no. 139; C.O. to F.O., 27 July 1887; F.O. to C.O., 6 Aug. 1887, no. 163a.
212 Bayol to gov. of Senegal, 21 March 1887, in *Etudes Dahoméennes*, 9:81; Salisbury Papers, A/56, Lyons to Salisbury, 29 March 1887 and 12 July 1887; Egerton to Salisbury, 5 Aug. 1887 and 22 Dec. 1887; Salisbury to Lyons 5 Feb. 1887, 20 July 1887.
213 CO879/28, Anglo-French convention of 2 January, 1888, no. 71 (encl. no. 1). See article 5 (signed by V. Ballot and A. Moloney) in M.A.E., Afrique 125, Flourens to Krantz, 14 Jan. 1888, on the modus vivendi between Porto Novo and Lagos signed according to the instructions received by both representatives from their home governments.
214 On the reaction of Europe to General Boulanger see *Die Grosse Politik* 4, Bismarck to Salisbury, 22 Nov. 1888, and Salisbury's reply, pp. 376–80, 386–88; Bismarck to Hatzfeldt, 11 Jan. 1889, pp. 400–03; Otto Hammann, *Zur Vorgeschichte des Weltkrieges* (Berlin, 1918), pp. 150–59; *Cambridge History of British Foreign Policy*, 3:245–46; A. J. P. Taylor, *The Struggle for Mastery in Europe* (Oxford, 1954), pp. 307–16; Salisbury Papers, A/58. Lytton to Salisbury, 4 April 1889, states causes and results of Boulanger's sudden flight to Brussels, where he later committed suicide. See FO27/3041, Egerton to Salisbury, 1 Oct. 1891, on Boulanger's death.
215 Salisbury Papers, A/56, Salisbury to Lyons, 5 Feb. 1887, 20 July 1887; Newton, *Lord Lyons*, pp. 532–33, 548–49.
216 Newton, pp. 552, 544–545, Lyons to Salisbury, 24 May 1887.
217 Ibid., Lyons to Salisbury, 12 July 1887.
218 Salisbury Papers, A/57, Lytton to Salisbury, 7 and 12 Dec. 1888; SOM-AN Afrique VI, 66, a, Faure to M.A.E., 18 Feb. 1888; M.A.E. to De la Porte, 22 Dec. 1888.

219 CO147/68, Goldie to F.O. (enclosed in F.O. to C.O.), 22 Oct. 1888.
220 *Etudes Dahoméennes,* 9:86–87. Ballot to gov. of Senegal, 25 April 1888, cites ministerial instructions to Viard on 25 January 1888 enclosed in gov. of Senegal to Ballot, 14 Feb. 1888.
221 Viard had gained publicity in 1885 during the discussion of the Niger question. He had also published two works on the Lower Niger in the same year: *Au Bas-Niger* and *Explorations Africaines: La France et la Conférence de Berlin.* He insisted at that time that France had not given up her right to expand in the Lower Niger basin.
222 Salisbury Papers, A/57, Lytton to Salisbury, 26 Dec. 1888; M.A.E., Afrique 125, De la Porte to Flourens, 17 Feb. 1888. De la Porte underlined the unfavorable attitude of the Chambre des Députés to colonial expansion schemes.
223 *Le Matin,* 13 and 14 August 1888, 15 April 1892; *Le Temps,* 15 April 1892; FO84/2208, Dufferin to Salisbury, 19 April 1892, Africa no. 81 (encl. Phipps to Dufferin, 19 April 1892).
224 M.A.E., Afrique 125, gov. of Senegal to M.M.C., 2 Jan. 1888 (conf. tel.); M.M.C. to M.A.E., 11 Jan. 1888, no. 615, minutes ("Mais alors c'est le protectorat du Dahomey. On aurait pu nous consulter avant d'autoriser M. Ballot à engager les negociations"); M.M.C. to gov. of Senegal, 10 Feb. 1888 (tel.); De la Porte to Flourens, 17 Feb. 1888.
225 CO879/28, no. 115 (encl. 10); no. 12 (encl. 4); no. 128; no. 136 (encl. 3); no. 1 (encl. 3). The Viard affair is covered by correspondence contained in these two Colonial Office confidential prints—CO879/28 (355 and 356)—and in SOM-AN Afrique VI, 66, d, M.A.E., Afrique 128.
226 Salisbury Papers, A/57, Lytton to Salisbury, 26 Dec. 1888, no. 87; FO84/2208, Dufferin to Salisbury, 19 April 1892 (encl. Phipps to Dufferin, 19 April 1892). Minutes by C. H. Hill refer to Egerton to Salisbury, 25 July 1888, on the commercial clauses. CO879/28, Egerton to Goblet, 24 Aug. 1888, no. 28 (encl. in F.O. to C.O.).
227 M.A.E., Afrique 128, treaty with Abeokuta, 11 April 1888.
228 CO879/28, no. 1 (encl. 3); Alake Osonekan to Sons & Gentlemen, 16 May 1888; C.O. George to Lagos Egba Committee, 19 May 1888; F.O. to C.O. (encl. C.M.S. to F.O.), 6 Dec. 1888.
229 F.O. Confidential Print No. 5896 (1888), no. 333 (encl. 1, Moloney to Knutsford, 6 Oct. 1888); CO879/28, no. 2 (encl. 1, Alvan Milson's report, 17 May 1888).
230 CO879/28, C.O. to F.O., 3 Oct. 1888; CO147/65, minutes by Hemming, folder no. 19183.
231 F.O. Confidential Print No. 5896, no. 333 (encl. 1, Moloney to Knutsford, 6 Oct. 1888; encl. 3, Milson to Stallard, 4 Oct. 1888).
232 P.R.O. Cab. 37/21, no. 14, French Invasion: alleged inability of British military organisation to protect London (6 June 1888), Salisbury; no. 15, A French Invasion (with map) (8 June 1888), War Office; no. 17, A French Invasion (18 June 1888), Admiralty; no. 18, French Invasion (29 June 1888), Salisbury; Cab. 37/22, no. 32, French Invasion (6 Nov. 1888), Salisbury; no. 35, Colonial Garrisons (7 Nov. 1888), Edward Stanhope; no. 37, A French Invasion (15 Nov. 1888), War Office.
233 CO879/28, Knutsford to Moloney, 24 Sept. 1888; CO147/66, minutes by Knuts-

ford on 22050; CO879/28 Knutsford to Moloney, 18 Oct. 1888; *F.O. Confidential Print No. 5896* (1888), no. 333 (encl. 6, Knutsford to Moloney, 16 Oct. 1888); F.O. 84/1949, Salisbury to Lytton, 31 Jan. 1889, Africa no. 30; Salisbury Papers, A/57, Lytton to Salisbury, 12, 20, and 26 Dec. 1888.

234 M.A.E., Afrique 125, Etienne to Spuller, 9 March 1889, no. 95 (encl. Rapport Ballot [extrait], 24 Jan. 1888); Ballot Papers, AN/MI185, Ballot to gov. of Senegal, 6 Dec. 1887 (encl. "Notice Historique sur Pokea [Pocrah ou Pokrah]").

235 M.A.E., Afrique 125, Verdier to colonies, 24 April 1888; Verdier to Nisard, 28 June 1888 (private); note pour le ministre, 15 Sept. 1888; Fabre to Etienne, 6 July 1889.

236 See Chautard, *Le Dahomey*, pp. 7-12; Abbé Pierre Bouche, *Dahomey* (Paris, 1893); Abel Etienne, *Le Père Dogère, ancien missionaire au Dahomey; récits et souvenirs; conquête du Dahomey* (Toulon, 1909).

237 Lyons to Salisbury, 29 March 1887, quoted in Newton, *Lord Lyons*, pp. 540-41. Lyons concluded that the French were "horribly afraid of being led to join the Italo-Austro-German Alliance" and did not want Britain to "join the others against France and Russia." See A. Leroy-Beaulieu, "Les Rivalités Coloniales, L'Angleterre et la Russie," *Revue des Deux Mondes* (15 Jan. 1886).

238 In the Tirard Cabinet, which took office on 22 February 1889, Jacques Spuller was minister for foreign affairs and Eugene Etienne was the sous-secretaire d'état des colonies. FO84/1950, Lytton to Salisbury, 8 Feb. 1889; Egerton to Salisbury, 8 March 1889.

239 Salisbury Papers, A/58, Lytton to Salisbury, 26 Feb. 1889 (private), 8 March 1889.

240 CO879/29, C.O. to F.O., 22 Feb. 1889; FO84/1950, Lytton to Salisbury, 19 April 1889, Africa no. 48. The British commissioners were A. W. L. Hemming from the Colonial Office and E. H. Egerton from the British Embassy in Paris; the French were Dr. Jean Bayol, lieutenant governor of Senegal, and D'Estournelles from the M.A.E., who was later replaced by A. Nisard of the same ministry.

241 FO84/1950, Lytton to Salisbury, 26 April 1889, Africa no. 53 (encl. Egerton to Lytton, 25 April 1889). Details of the negotiations are contained in correspondence in FO84/1950; CO879/29, nos. 31, 38, 75, 77, 84, 94, 105, 113, 125; SOM-AN Afrique VI, 73, a; and M.A.E., Afrique 128, "Délimitations des possessions anglaises et françaises de l'Afrique Occidentale (1889)."

242 Salisbury Papers, A/57, Lytton to Salisbury, 12 Dec. 1888; A/58, Egerton to Salisbury, 27 June 1889; Lytton to Salisbury, 11 July 1889, 3 Aug. 1889.

243 CO147/73, F.O. to C.O., 16 March 1889, minutes by Meade and Hemming.

244 Louis Henrique, "Eugène Etienne," in *Nos Contemporaines*, 1:25-28; Sylvain Fabre, "Eugène Etienne," in *Bulletin Trimestriel de la Société de Géographie et d'Archeologie d'Oran* 41 (1921): 97-103. See H. Sieberg, *Eugène Etienne und die Franzoesische Kolonialpolitik, 1887-1904* (Berlin, 1970); Roland Villot, *Eugène Etienne* (Oran, 1951).

245 M.A.E., Afrique 125, Etienne to Spuller, 29 March 1889.

246 Ibid., Etienne to Spuller, 5 April 1889. Ballot was in France on leave.

247 Ibid., Etienne to Spuller, 27 June 1889; (Très urgent) note pour le ministre, 28 June 1889. This note was a twenty-page memo. Note complémentaire sur l'affair de Bondoukou, 4 July 1889: "Le Ministre parait d'autant plus autorisé à refuser

248 SOM-AN Afrique 73, a, projet d'entente; M.A.E., Afrique 128, procès-verbaux des séances de la Commission franco-anglais, projet d'entente.
249 Augustus W. L. Hemming was highly commended for the part he played in the satisfactory conclusion of the Anglo-French agreement of 10 August 1889. Later he was knighted by the Queen. CO147/73, minutes by Meade (27/7), and minutes by Lord Knutsford (27/7), folder no. 14250 both praised Hemming's worth.
250 M.A.E., Afrique 128, arrangements franco-anglais du 10 août, 1889; Parl. Papers, Africa no. 3 (1890), 5905, West African Agreement Between Great Britain and France of 10 August 1889, article 4, pp. 3-4.
251 CO879/29, C.O. to F.O., 27 July 1889, no. 124.
252 J. Perraudin, "Le Cardinal Lavigèrie et Leopold II," in *Zaire* 12:171 ff.
253 Except Berlin, where Bismarck was not disposed to receive the cardinal in view of the *Kulturkampf*. (The *Anti-Slavery Reporter*, July-August 1888).
254 FO84/1895, Vivian to Salisbury, 24 Sept. 1888, minutes by Hill; FO541/28, Vivian to Salisbury, 16 Aug. 1888, minutes by Lister and Salisbury; Salisbury to Vivian, 17 Sept. 1888, Africa no. 15; Vivian to Salisbury, 6 Oct. 1888, Africa no. 52. For detailed correspondence on the pre-conference period, see FO541/28 and FO541/37 in particular.
255 Parl. Papers, Africa no. 8A (1890), *Translations of the Protocols and the General Act of the Slave Trade Conference held at Brussels, 1889-1890 with Annexed Declarations.*
256 Ibid., General Act of the Brussels Conference, chap. 1, articles 1-7, see appendix 1.
257 FO84/2103, Kirk to Wylde, 14 May 1890; FO84/2011, Vivian and Kirk to Salisbury, 6 Dec. 1889; FO84/2031, Malet to Salisbury, 13 May 1890. The report of Caprivi's speech in the Reichstag, 12 May 1890, states that "the Bible and the Rifle" must be used in the task of controlling Africa.

CHAPTER 3

1 M. J. Herskovits, *Dahomey: An Ancient West African Kingdom* 1 (New York, 1938): 11-25; Brunet and Giethlen, *Dahomey et Dépendances*, pp. 53-69; Cornevin, *Histoire du Dahomey*, pp. 80-83, 92-100; Dalzel, *Dahomey*, p. 12.
2 Anatole Coissy, "L'Arrivée des Alladahonou à Ouaoue," in *Etudes Dahoméennes*, 13:33-34; E. Dunglass, "Contribution à L'Histoire du Moyen-Dahomey," in *Etudes Dahoméennes* 19 and 20; Coissy, *Tanguieta*, pp. 45-47; R. F. Burton, *A Mission to Glégle, King of Dahomey* (London, 1864), 2:265-302, appendix 4.
3 Herskovits 1:11-13; Le Herissé, *L'Ancien Royaume du Dahomey*, pp. 271-355 (based mainly on oral tradition); Dunglass 19:85-168, 20:3-119; Lefaivre, "Dictateurs Noirs," pp. 15-76.
4 Herskovits 1:15; Capt. Bertin, "Renseignements sur le Royaume de Porto Novo et le Dahomey," in *Rev. Maritime et Coloniale* (1890).
5 Le Herissé, pp. 271-79; Dalzel, *Dahomey*, p. 12. Dahomey = Dan-home = Dan-home = Belly of Dan. Burton 2:242. See also L. K. Waldman, "An unnoticed aspect of Archibald Dalzel's 'The History of Dahomey,'" *Journal of African History* 6 (1965): 185-92.

6 d'Albeca, *Les Etablissements Françaises*, p. 82. Dahomey = Belly of the Serpent = In the Belly of the Serpent. Bouche, *La Côte des Esclaves*, pp. 327–32.
7 de Pedrals, *La Brousee Africaine*, pp. 10–11.
8 Cornevin, *Histoire du Dahomey*, p. 96, citing Mercator's Atlas (1560), Ortelius (1570), Munster and Belleforest (1575), and Leo Africanus's account of his travels in the Sudan in 1507
9 Dunglass, "Moyen-Dahomey," 19:88. Dah-ho-me = In the house of Dan.
10 *Saturday Review*, 4 July 1863, carried an article on the sacrifice of 2,000 human beings on one occasion by the king of Dahomey "in deference to a national prejudice and to keep up the good customs of the country" (quoted in Herskovits, *Dahomey* 1:3).
11 J. de Riols, *La Guerre du Dahomey* (Paris, 1893), p. 13. In recent times a wildly fantastic tale about Dahomey was told by Lobagola (Bata Kindai Angosa ibn) in *Lobagola: An African Savage's own Story* (New York, 1930). Skertchley, *Dahomey As It Is*, pp. 235–38.
12 *West African Directory, 1965–1966* (London, 1965), p. 39. The area of the independent République du Dahomey is 112,000 square kilometers, according to *West Africa Annual*, 1966, ed. L. K. Jakande (Lagos, 1965), p. 38. This is about ten times larger than the area over which the court of Abomey exercised direct authority.
13 "C'est le plus grand pays du monde! Il s'en va tout là-haut . . . tout loin . . . jamais fini" (de Riols, p. 5).
14 Herskovits, *Dahomey* 1:8–10; Burton, *Mission to Glégé* 2:154–55, 230–52; Skertchley, p. 36; John MacLeod, *A Voyage to Africa with some account of the Manners and Customs of the Dahomian People* (London, 1820), pp. 15–16.
15 Le Herissé, *L'Ancien Royaume du Dahomey*, p. 86; Chautard, *Le Dahomey*, p. 7. The frontier guards were called the *onibode* because they collected tolls as well as kept guard. Commandant Grandin, *Le Dahomey* (Paris, 1895), 1:156.
16 Le Herissé, p. 86; John Duncan *Travels in West Africa, 1845–46*, 2 vols. (London, 1847), 2:95–96.
17 Archives Nationales, Papiers Ballot, MI185/1, Cartes nos. 16, 17, 20, 21; see map opposite. M.A.E., Afrique 125, Rapport Ballot, 24 Jan. 1888 (extract).
18 For the expansion of the kingdom of Dahomey, see Cornevin, *Histoire du Dahomey*, pp. 96 ff; J. E. Bouche, "Le Dahomé; son histoire," in *L'Exploration*, no. 70 (Paris, 1876), pp. 581–84; Isaac Akinjobin, *Dahomey And Its Neighbours, 1708–1818* (Cambridge, 1967).
19 Le Herissé, p. 2.
20 P. Bouche, *La Côte des Esclaves*, pp. 201, 318–26; E. Lambinet, *Notice géographique, topographique et statistique sur le Dahomey* (Paris, 1893), pp. 6–16. For the population, revenue, and military organization of Dahomey, see chap. 2 of Lambinet.
21 Documents Parlementaires 1891, Journal Officiel: Chambre des Députés: Annexes aux Procès-Verbaux des Séances, Projets et Propositions des Lois, Exposés des Motifs et Rapports, annexe no. 1235, appendix 2, pp. 613–14. For these treaties see Appendix 2 below.
22 Cathérine Coquery, "Le Blocus de Whydah," pp. 373–419.
23 P. Serval, "Rapport sur une Mission au Dahomey," in *Rev. Maritime et Coloniale*

59 (1878): 186; Documents Parlementaires 1891: Chambre des Députés, annexe no. 1235, p. 614; Archives Centrales de la Marine (hereafter A.C.M.), BB4/1990; Chambre des Députés, no. 1235, rapport par M. de Lanessan; M.A.E., Afrique 125, MMC to M.A.E., 11 Jan. 1888, no. 615. De la Porte stated in this letter that the French fort for garrison was constructed in 1797.

24 Papiers Ballot, MI 185/4; Rapport Bouet, 6 May 1839, p. 38; Alexandre Adande, *Les Recades des Rois du Dahomey* (Dakar, 1962), pp. 24, 26 (song composed by Gléglé in honor of his father Ghezo).

25 Mimande, *L'Héritage de Béhanzin,* pp. 21–22. Gléglé ascended the throne in 1858 and died in Dec. 1889. Brunet and Giethlen, *Dahomey et Dépendances,* pp. 65–69.

26 Feris, "La Cote des Esclaves et les nouvelles possessions françaises," in *Revue Scientifique* (1883), pp. 714–20.

27 See M.A.E., Afrique IV (Dahomey indépendant), dossiers 10 and 11, for treaties and political reports on the independent kingdom of Dahomey up to 1888.

28 SOM-AN Dahomey V, 1, b, Gléglé to president of France, 27 Dec. 1889; Archives Centrales de la Marine, BB4/1990. Chambre des Députés, no. 1235, Rapport par N. de Lanessan citing Gléglé to resident of France at Porto Novo; A.N. Papiers Ballot, MI 185/4, Ballot to gov. of Senegal, 9 Nov. 1887.

29 M.A.E., Afrique 125, Etienne to Spuller, 4 Dec. 1889, no. 366 (encl. Rapport d'Albeca, "Situation politique en Porto Novo," 1 Nov. 1889).

30 Mattei, *Bas-Niger, Bénoue, Dahomey,* pp. 180–81. For a recent analysis of the place of these feasts in the Dahomey state system, see Catherine Coquery-Vidrovitch, "La fête des coutumes au Dahomey: Historique et essai d'interprétation," in *Annales, Economies, Sociétés, Civilisations,* no. 4 (July–August 1964), pp. 696–716; P. Bouche, *La Côte des Esclaves,* pp. 332–36, 341–42.

31 M.A.E., Afrique 126, Haussmann to M.A.E., 3 Jan. 1890 (encl. Bayol to Colonies [tel.], 2 Jan. 1890). Bayol stated that 200 prisoners were sacrificed during his stay at Abomey. SOM-AN Dahomey V, 1, b, Etienne to Spuller, 4 Dec. 1889 (encl. rapport Bayol Mission d'Abomey, 6, Dec. 1889).

32 *Le Figaro,* supplément, 8 March 1890. Extracts from M. Lartigue's diary were published in this issue.

33 FO84/1895, minutes by C. Hill on Vivian to Salisbury, 16 Aug. 1888.

34 Parl. Papers, *Papers relating to the occupation of Lagos; The Colonial Office Lists 1863,* p. 43; *The Colonial Office Lists 1890,* p. 145; R. J. Gavin, "Nigeria and Lord Palmerston," in *Ibadan* (June, 1961).

35 P. Bouche, *La Côte des Esclaves,* pp. 340–42.

36 Hargreaves, *Prelude* 5:201–14; FO84/1464, Admiralty to F.O., 2 May 1876 (encl. Gléglé's reply). The decision of the cabinet on 10 May 1876 is quoted by Hargreaves on p. 203.

37 M.A.E., Afrique 76, Rapport du Contre-Amiral Mottes, 20 April 1879; Coquery, "Le Blocus de Whydah," pp. 418–19.

38 The Ashanti expedition of 1874 cost 22 million francs. See Albert Septans, *Les Expéditions Anglaises en Afrique* (Paris, 1896).

39 P.R.O.30/29/140, Granville Papers, memorandum by Sir F. Richards, 4 Dec. 1884 (encl. in Northbrook to Granville [private], 20 Dec. 1884). Sir F. Richards was an admiralty official.

40 FO84/1951, Egerton to Salisbury, 1 July 1889, Africa no. 90; minutes, 3 July 1889.
41 M.A.E., Afrique 125, Etienne to M.A.E., 5 Aug. 1889 (encl. Etienne to Bayol, 5 Aug. 1889, instructions).
42 M.A.E., Afrique 125, Etienne to Spuller, 31 March 1889 (encl. Beckmann to gov. of Senegal, 18 Dec. 1888, no. 128).
43 Archives Centrales de la Marine, BB4/1989, Fournier to Marine, 8 Feb. 1890.
44 de Riols, *La Guerre du Dahomey*, p. 19. See also M. Hulot, "Rélations de la France avec la Cote des Esclaves," in *Annales de l'Ecole libre des Science Politiques* (Paris, 1894).
45 Parl. Papers, Africa no. 3 (1890), 5905, *West African Agreement Between Great Britain and France of August 10, 1889* (London, 1890), pp. 3–4, art. 4, sec. 4.
46 M.A.E. Documents Diplomatiques, *Delimitation des Possessions Françaises à la Cote Occidentale d'Afrique, 1889–1895*, no. 1, p. 3; Spuller to President of the republic of France, 12 March 1890.
47 SOM-AN Afrique IV, 61, Bayol to Colonies, 1 and 9 Feb. 1887; Hertslet, *Map of Africa* 1:297, no. 79.
48 A.C.M. BB4/1990, memo by E. Peroz, 12 March 1890. Peroz concluded that any French action between Togo and Lagos would not lead to conflict with any European power. See de Riols, p. 19.
49 CO879/29, Memorandum by Hemming on Proposal to cede Gambia to France (Nov. 1888).
50 CO147/81, minutes on 19099; Parl. Papers, Africa no. 3 (1890), C.5905, art. 4, Sec. 5.
51 M.A.E. Waddington Papers, vol. 4, "Notice sur la Gambie," fols. 14 ff.
52 SOM-AN Afrique 66, a, Flourens to Krantz, 13 Jan. 1888.
53 CO879/29, C.O. to F.O., 21 Dec. 1889, no. 161. Edouard Viard's expedition to Abeokuta early in 1888 was resented by Britain because it threatened the hinterland of Lagos.
54 CO879/31, Knutsford to Moloney, 24 Jan. 1890, no. 5 (confidential); CO147/73, minutes by Hemming on 23455.
55 CO879/28, nos. 68, 75; CO879/29, nos. 10, 12.
56 CO879/35, Deputation on West Africa Boundary Questions, 8 Dec. 1891, p. 1, speech by Hon. W. H. Cross. Philanthropic missionaries, ruthless businessmen, and honorable members of both houses of Parliament were included in the list of the supporters of the deputation. Ibid., p. 12, speech by Kimber.
57 Ibid., pp. 3, 13–14, address by Henry Coke, president of the Liverpool Chamber of Commerce, to Lord Knutsford.
58 CO147/65, Moloney to Knutsford, 13 Aug. 1888; W. A. Gibson Martin, *A Century of Liverpool Commerce* (Liverpool, 1950), p. 35. See also Arthur Redford and B. W. Clapp, *Manchester Merchants and Foreign Trade (1850–1939)* 2 (Manchester, 1956): 61–62, 66.
59 CO879/26, memorandum by Brackenbury, deputy quartermaster general, I.D.W.O., 27 June 1887; War Office to C.O., 1 July 1887 (secret) (encl. no. 2).
60 Parl. Papers, Africa 8A (1890), *Protocols and General Act of the Slave Trade Conference held at Brussels 1889–1890 with Annexed Declarations*, p. 34.

61 Mary Kingsley, *West African Studies* (London, 1901), p. 226.
62 M.A.E., Afrique 126, Gléglé to the chiefs of France, 27 Dec. 1889 (encl. Etienne to M.A.E., 6 Feb. 1890, no. 101).
63 Akindele and Aguessy, *L'Ancien Royaume de Porto Novo,* pp. 81–84; G. François, "Le Royaume de Porto Novo," in *Bulletin du Comité de l'Afrique Français* (April 1904).
64 M.A.E., Afrique 126, rapport Bayol, 6 Dec. 1889; FO84/1951, Egerton to Salisbury, 1 July 1889. The governor of Senegal suggested deporting Toffa to Gabon; see Etienne to Bayol, 5 Aug. 1889 (instructions), in M.A.E., Afrique 125.
65 M.A.E., Afrique 126, Etienne to Spuller, 19 March 1890 (encl. rapport, Bayol to Etienne, 10 Jan. 1890). The replacement of Toffa would lead to so many problems that it was decided "à conserver Toffa en pouvoir."
66 M.A.E., Afrique 125, rapport d'Albeca, 1 Nov. 1889 (encl. in Etienne to Spuller, 4 Dec. 1889, no. 366).
67 A.C.M. BB4/1989, Contre-Amiral Brown de Colstoun to Marine, 29 April 1889. In this report it was stated that rebel vassals of Toffa carried out the raid around Porto Novo with the encouragement of Dahomey.
68 Ibid., rapport d'Albeca, 1 Nov. 1889. They were Djedjis or Fon. C. Le Brun-Renaud, *Les Possessions Français de l'Afrique Occidentale* (Paris, 1886), pp. 149–54; Bertin, "Renseignements sur Porto Novo et Dahomey"; d'Albeca, "Les indigènes de l'Afrique occidentale," in *Rev. Scientifique* 2 (1889): 365.
69 A.C.M., BB4/1989, Brown de Colstoun to Marine, 29 April 1889, rapport. "Toffa had neither the men nor the organisation nor the courage to beat back these attacks."
70 Dr. A. Hagen, "La Colonie de Porto Novo et le roi Toffa," *Revue d'Ethnographie* 6 (1887).
71 SOM-AN Afrique VI, 66, d, Spuller to Etienne, 10 April 1889; Flourens to Krantz, 9 March 1888.
72 SOM-AN Afrique VI, 66, d, Spuller to Etienne, 10 April 1889.
73 Papiers Waddington, vol. 4, "Notice sur la Gambie," by Julien de . . . , fols. 14–42. Correspondence relating to the delimitation of the Gambia is contained in SOM-AN Afrique VI, 66, b.
74 SOM-AN Afrique VI, 66, a, Flourens to Krantz, 13 Jan. 1888.
75 Ibid. On the question of the Gambia exchange schemes, see René Catala, "La Question de l'échange de la Gambie britannique contre les comptoirs français du Golfe du Guinée de 1866 à 1876," in *Rev. Hist. des Colonies* 25 (premier semestre 1948): 114–37; Hargreaves, *Prelude,* pp. 174–79; J. M. Gray, *A History of the Gambia* (Cambridge, 1940), pp. 431–43.
76 See SOM-AN Senegal IV, 91, a, b, campagne de 1887–88, rélations avec Lamine, Ahmadu; SOM-AN Sénégal IV, 88, a, b, c, campagne de 1886–87, rélations avec Lamine, Ahmadu, Samory. See S. Kanya Forstner, "The French in West Africa: Military Imperialism" (Ph.D. diss., Cambridge University, 1965); Lieutenant Gatelet, *Histoire de la Conquête du Soudan français 1878–1899* (Paris, 1901), pp. 76–114, 115 ff.; Abdel Kader Mademba, *Au Sénégal et au Soudan Français* (Paris, 1931), pp. 15–26, 27–37, 40–48.
77 F. Goguel, *La Politique des Parties sous la Troisième République* 1 (Paris, 1946):

69–71; Jacques Madaule, *Histoire de France,* vol. 3: *De la IIIe à la Ve République* (Paris, 1966), pp. 43–45, 48; Papiers Hanotaux, vol. 1, Documents personnels et litteraires (1876–1908), "Notes et discours sur Jules Ferry" (22 March 1893).
78 M.A.E., Afrique 125, Etienne to Spuller, 5 August 1889.
79 Ibid., Spuller to Etienne, 12 Aug. 1889 (draft); minutes on Etienne to Spuller, 5 Aug. 1889, approuvé.
80 Ibid., Resident d'Albeca to Etienne, 26 Nov. 1889 (tel. no. 123434 [Copy]).
81 Ibid., rapport d'Albeca, "Situation politique en Porto Novo," 1 Nov. 1889 (encl. in Etienne to Spuller, 4 Dec. 1889, no. 366).
82 See R. E. Dennett, *At the Back of the Blackman's Mind: Notes on the Kingly Office in West Africa* (London, 1906).
83 Jean Bayol, "La France au Fouta Djallon," in *Rev. des Deux Mondes* 54 (15 Dec. 1882): 902–32; Hargreaves, *Prelude,* pp. 268–70.
84 FO84/1951, Egerton to Salisbury, 1 July 1889, Africa no. 90.
85 M.A.E., Afrique 125, Etienne to Bayol, 5 Aug. 1889, instructions, SOM-AN Dossier Administratif: Jean M. Bayol, recommendations.
86 Paul Atger, *La France en Côte d'Ivoire de 1843 à 1893* (Dakar, 1962), pp. 110–17.
87 M.A.E., Afrique 126, Etienne to Bayol, 1 April 1890, no. 353; A.C.M. BB4/1989, Cuverville to Marine, 5 Oct. 1890.
88 M.A.E., Afrique 125, Etienne to Bayol, 5 Aug. 1889, instruction general (encl. in Etienne to Spuller, 5 Aug. 1889 [Très urgent]). The instructions are very detailed and are in a 15-page manuscript. Minutes, approuvé.
89 Ibid.
90 Ibid.
91 Ibid., Spuller to Etienne, 12 Aug. 1889.
92 Ibid., Bayol to Etienne, 16 Nov. 1889 (tel.), no. 119942 (copy).
93 Ibid., rapport Bayol, 4 Nov. 1889; rapport d'Albeca, 1 Nov. 1889 (both encl. in Etienne to Spuller, 4 Dec. 1889, no. 366).
94 Ibid., d'Albeca to Etienne, 26 Nov. 1889 (tel.), no. 123434 (copy).
95 M.A.E., Afrique 126, Bayol to Etienne, 10 Jan. 1890, Rapport Politique (encl. in Etienne to M.A.E., 19 March 1890); Bayol to Etienne, 6 Dec. 1889.
96 Ibid., Etienne to M.A.E., 6 Feb. 1890, no. 101 (encl. Bayol to Etienne, 6 Dec. 1889, "Disposition de la Cour d'Abomey à l'égard de la République Française").
97 Ibid., Bayol to Etienne, 10 Jan. 1890.
98 Ibid., rapport Bayol, 10 Jan. 1890. By March 1888 it was reported by Dahomean envoys to Lagos that Prince Kondo conducted all affairs of state, both internal and external, because of the king's age. F.O. Confidential Prints No. 328, C.O. to F.O., 15 May 1888 (encl. Gov. Moloney to C.O., 29 March 1888).
99 M.A.E., Afrique 126, Haussmann to M.A.E., 3 Jan. 1890 (encl. Bayol to colonies, 2 Jan. 1890 [tel.]).
100 Ibid., Bayol to Etienne, 6 Dec. 1889, rapport.
101 Ibid., Bayol to Etienne, 6 Dec. 1889, rapport.
102 Porto Novo Archives (I.F.A.N.) "Rapport dressé par l'Interprète Xavier Béraud," (12 March 1891), quoted in C. W. Newbury, "A Note on the Abomey Protectorate," in *Africa,* vol. 29, no. 2 (April 1959), p. 148.
103 M.A.E., Afrique 126, Bayol to Colonies, 2 Jan. 1890; Bayol to Etienne, 6 Dec. 1889, rapport.

NOTES TO PAGES 64–67

104 Ibid., Bayol to Etienne, 6 Dec. 1889; Bayol to Etienne, 10 Jan. 1890, "Séjour à Abomey."
105 C. W. Newbury, "The Abomey Protectorate," p. 146; Dunglass, "Moyen-Dahomey," p. 91; d'Albeca, *Les Etablissements Français,* p. 111.
106 M.A.E., Afrique 126, Gléglé to the president of the republic of France, 27 Dec. 1889 (encl. in Etienne to M.A.E., 6 Feb. 1890, no. 101). Bayol; M. Angot, his secretary; and Xavier Béraud, the interpreter signed Gléglé's letter as witnesses.
107 Ibid., Bayol to Colonies, 2 Jan. 1890 (tel.) (encl. in Haussmann to M.A.E., 3 Jan. 1890).
108 Bayol stated that 200 persons were executed at the ceremonies (ibid.).
109 Ibid. "Mort roi Dahomey confirmée Prince héritier Kondo nous hostile." As sous-secrétaire d'état des colonies, Etienne attended meetings of the French cabinet by virtue of the extended powers which his post had acquired under de Freycinet. See François Berge, "Le Sous-Secretariat et les Sous-Secretaires d'Etat aux Colonies: histoire de l'émancipation de l'administration colonial," in *Rev. Fr. d'Hist. d'Outre-Mer,* vol. 47, no. 2 (1960), pp. 303–07.
110 M.A.E., Afrique 126, Etienne to M.A.E., 16 Jan. 1890. The Conseil des Ministres did not want to put such a proposal before the Chambre des Députés. It might lead to the defeat of the government.
111 Duties on spirits passing through Cotonou in 1889 amounted to about 40,000 francs. See Dunglass, "Moyen-Dahomey," p. 91; d'Albeca, *Les Etablissements Français,* p. 111.
112 M.A.E., Afrique 126, Bayol to Colonies (tel.), 19 Jan. 1890, no. 80 (encl. in Etienne to M.A.E., 21 Jan. 1890); Henri Morienval, *La Guerre du Dahomey: Journal de Campagne d'un Sous-Lieutenant d'Infantérie de Marine* (Paris, 1893), p. 74.
113 M.A.E., Afrique 126, Etiene to gov. of Senegal, 20 Jan. 1890 (tel.).
114 Ibid., Bayol to Etienne, 16 Feb. 1890; Etienne to M.A.E., 16 and 18 Feb. 1890; Etienne to Bayol, 19 Feb. 1890; Bayol to Etienne, 22 Feb. 1890.
115 R. Cornevin, "Les divers episodes de la lutte contre le royaume d'Abomey, 1887–1894," in *Rev. Fr. d'Hist. d'Outre-Mer* 47 (2ᵉ trimestre, 1960): 161–212; Cornevin, *Histoire du Dahomey,* p. 321.
116 M.A.E., Afrique 126, Bayol to Etienne, 22 Feb. 1890, no. 218.
117 A. L. d'Albeca, *Les Etablissements Français,* pp. 111–120.
118 "Le Roi du Dahomey," in *L'Intransigeant,* 9 Jan. 1890; SOM-AN Dahomey V, 1, b, Etienne to M.A.E., 3 Jan. 1890 (draft); "Mort de Gléglé: Les Conséquences," in *Rev. Fr. Etr. Col.* vol. 11, no. 86 (15 Jan. 1890), pp. 112–13.
119 This is based on oral evidence given by Gléglé Kakai, whose father Kakai was a nephew of Béhanzin, in July 1961. See Coquery, "Le blocus de Whydah," p. 381.
120 Edouard Chaudoin, "Trois mois de captivité au Dahomey," in *L'Illustration,* no. 2471 (1890), p. 49.
121 Because of his intelligence and his courtesy Gléglé was erroneously said to have been educated at Marseille. King Gezo did send two members of his household to be educated in France, but not the heir apparent Prince Badou, who was later known as Gléglé. See Chautard, *Le Dahomey,* p. 6.
122 Cornevin, "Les divers épisodes," pp. 185–212, "Gbe han zin ai djire."

123 The havoc done by sharks on the Slave Coast was common knowledge. See Hargreaves, *Prelude,* p. 210.
124 *Le Temps,* 3 Feb. 1890.
125 A.C.M., BB4/1990, Bayol to Colonies, 4 March 1890; M.A.E., Afrique 126, Bayol to Etienne, 4 March 1890, no. 273. Rev. Van was released because he was Dutch. Rapport de M. Etienne Bontemps sur les événements du Dahomey, 11 May 1890. Bontemps was French consul at Whydah.
126 M.A.E., Afrique 126, Bayol to Etienne, 7 March 1890 (tel.), no. 299; Bayol to Bontemps, 3 Feb. 1890 (très confidential); Bayol to Bontemps, 14 Feb. 1890; Fabre Maute, and Borelli to Cuverville, 6 Oct. 1890; SOM-AN Dahomey V, 3, a, Cyprien Fabre to Etienne, 29 March 1890; Bontemps to Fabre, 4 April 1890.
127 SOM-AN Dahomey V, 3, a, Bontemps to Fabre, 4 April 1890; French prisoners at Abomey to the president of the republic, 4 April 1890 (copy); rapport sur la captivité des otages au Dahomey du 24 Fevrier au 8 Mai 1890, par E. Bontemps (11 May 1890).
128 A.C.M., BB4/1990, Bayol to Colonies, 22 Feb. 1890.
129 M.A.E., Afrique 126, Bayol to Etienne, 11 Jan. 1890, Enseignements militaires sur le Dahomey. This is a 34-page manuscript giving details of military organization, maneuvers, composition of forces, uniforms and armaments, cavalry, etc. The Amazons were female soldiers who formed the hard core of the army of Dahomey. In Dahomey they were called *Minos* (our mothers). See Leo Woerl, *Dahomey: das Land der schwarzen Amazonen* (Leipzig, 1898); Robert Hartmann, "Uber die Amazonen des Königs von Dahome," in *Verh. Berlin geschichte fur Anthropologie Ethnologie und Vorgeschichte* (1891), 64–71; Chautard, *Le Dahomey,* pp. 10–11.
130 A.C.M., BB4/1989, Cuverville to Marine, 3 July 1890, no. 63. Contre-Amiral Cuverville estimated the regular army of Dahomey to be 12,000 soldiers strong. Burton, *Mission to Glégle* 2:63–85.
131 Grandin, *Le Dahomey* (Paris, 1895), 1:157–63; Victor Nicholas, *L'Expedition du Dahomey* (Paris, 1893), pp. 25–28; Brunet and Giethlen, *Dahomey et Dependances,* pp. 107–111, on the regular and reserve sections of the army of Dahomey.
132 M.A.E., Afrique 126, Bayol to Etienne, 11 March 1890, no. 329 (tel.).
133 Govt. of Dahomey, *Rapport d'Ensemble de la Colonie du Dahomey en 1899* (Porto Novo, 1900), pp. 12–13, population statistics.
134 M.A.E., Afrique 126, Etienne to M.A.E., 21 Jan. 1890 (encl. Bayol to colonies, 19 Jan. 1890 [tel.], no. 80).
135 Ibid., Bayol to Etienne, 11 Jan. 1890, Enseignements militaires sur le Dahomey; Dr. Jean Bayol, "Les forces militaires du Dahomey," in *Rev. Scientifique,* vol. 49, no. 17 (23 April 1892), pp. 520–24. Canons were mainly used for feasts and ceremonies and not as armaments of war. See "Les Intérets Français sur la Cote des Esclaves et au Dahomey," in *La Géographie,* nos. 62 (6 Feb. 1890), 63 (13 Feb. 1890), on the military forces of Dahomey and the future of Dahomey with its natural resources.
136 Brunet and Giethlen, *Dahomey et Dépendances,* p. 111; M.A.E., Afrique 127, Dodds to Marine, 15 Dec. 1892 (copy); SOM-AN Dahomey V, 2, a, Rapport Terrillon: Campagne de 1890.
137 A.C.M., BB4/1990, Bayol to Colonies, 25 Feb. 1890; M.A.E., Afrique 126, Bayol

to Etienne, 11 Jan. 1890. Bayol started the campaign to discredit Béhanzin in France right after the death of Gléglé. "Mort roi Dahomey confirmée. Prince héritier Kondo nous hostile," he cabled Etienne on 2 Jan. 1890.

138 Papiers Ballots, MI185/4, *Rapport sur le crensement du Chenal de la Barre de Kotonou*, par M. Tallenane, chef du service des travaux publics à St. Louis, 21 June 1888, p. 2; "Le Dahomey et son port," in *Europe-France Outre-Mer*, nos. 426–27 (July–Aug. 1965) pp. 9–10.

139 *Revue Française de l'Etranger et des Colonies* (hereafter *R.F.E.C.*), vol. 11, no. 87 (1 Feb. 1890), p. 169.

140 François, *Notre Colonie du Dahomey*, p. 174; Paule Brasseur-Marion, "Cotonou, porte du Dahomey," in *Les Cahiers d'Outre-Mer*, no. 24 (Oct.–Dec. 1953), pp. 364–78. Access to Cotonou and Porto Novo by sea remained difficult, and France had to seek permission from Britain to move men and materials through Lagos during the war with Dahomey.

141 Foa, *Le Dahomey*, pp. 381, 377.

142 Dr. J. Bayol, "L'Attaque de Kotonou," in *Revue Bleue* (1892).

143 Those taken prisoner were Consul Etienne Bontemps, Père Dogère, Edouard Chaudoin, Camille Piétri, Leyraud, Heuze, Denlay, and Thooris. See SOM-AN Dahomey, V, 3, a, C. Thooris to the president of France, 25 March 1890; Mantes and Borelli de Régis to Etienne, 13 March 1890; Etienne to Mantes and Borelli de Régis, 27 March 1890; M.A.E., Afrique 126, Bayol to Etienne, 4 March 1890, no. 273; SOM-AN Dahomey, V, 2, b, Elise Robert to Etienne, 14 March 1890; Elise Robert to the president of France, 20 March 1890; SOM-AN Dahomey, V, 3, c, Madame Leyraud to Etienne, 22 April 1890.

144 *Journal des Débats*, 9 March 1890; *Le Voltaire*, 30 March 1890, no. 4285; *Le Figaro, supplement*, 8 March 1890; Lionel Raidiguet, "La Question du Dahomey," in *R.F.E.C.*, vol. 11 no. 90 (15 March 1890), pp. 355–56. *Le Temps*, 3 Feb. 1890, called for military intervention in Dahomey. In SOM-AN Dahomey V, 3, a, C. Thooris to president of France, 25 March 1890, Thooris complained about the brutal way in which his third son and the other prisoners in Dahomey were treated on the way to Abomey, according to the newspapers. See *Le Lyon Républicain*, 27 Feb., 7, 12, and 31 March, articles on Dahomey by L. Gailliat.

145 Foa, *Le Dahomey*, p. 380; Dunglass, "Moyen-Dahomey," p. 40; Nicholas, *L'Expédition du Dahomey*, pp. 43 ff.; Grandin, *Le Dahomey* 1:262–64; Cornevin, *Histoire du Dahomey*, pp. 326–29.

146 SOM-AN Dahomey V, 3, a, French prisoners at Abomey to the president of France, 4 April 1890 (copy); C. Fabre to Etienne, 23 July 1890 (encl. rapport sur la captivité des otages au Dahomey du 24 Fevrier au 8 Mai 1890, par E. Bontemps, 11 May 1890).

147 Rev. Père Dogère, "Prisonniers au Dahomey," in *Journal des Missions Catholiques*, no. 116 (4 Sept. 1891); Camille Piétri, "93 jours de captivité au Dahomey," in *Journal des Voyages*, no. 699 (30 Nov. 1890); Edouard Chaudoin, "Trois mois de captivité," pp. 49–52.

148 Foa, p. 378.

149 M.A.E., Afrique 126, Bayol to Etienne (colonies), 2 Mar. 1890, no. 258 (tel.). This included several guns and barrels of gunpowder.

150 Ibid., gov. of Senegal to Etienne, 4 March 1890, no. 272 (encl. Terrillon to gov. of

Senegal, 4 March 1890); Bayol to Etienne, 4 March 1890, no. 273. "Dahomey attaque ce matin 5h. avec acharnement inoué, repoussé, est revenu à deux reprises," reported Bayol with surprise; he had thought that the Dahomeans would acquiesce to the armed occupation of Cotonou.
151 On the war and victory songs of Dahomey, see Adande, *Rois du Dahomey,* pp. 24–29. A sample of the battle songs of the Amazons is as follows:

>Nous sommes crées pour défendre
>Le Dahomé, ce pot de miel,
>Objet de convoitise.
>Le pays où fleurit tant de courage
>Peut-il abandonner ses richesses aux étrangères?
>Nous, vivantes, bien fou le peuple
>Oui essayerait de lui imposer sa loi. [Adande, p. 26]

152 Foa, *Le Dahomey,* pp. 383–84.
153 A.C.M., BB4/1989, Fournier to Marine, 5 March 1890; M.A.E., Afrique 126, Terrillon to gov. of Senegal, 4 March 1890 (encl. in gov. of Senegal to Colonies, 4 March 1890, no. 272).
154 M.A.E., Afrique 126, gov. of Senegal to Etienne, 4 March 1890, no. 274 (tel.), minutes: "D'après M. Bayol, M. Fabre, les Missionaires, il suffisait de cent hommes et un corporal pour aller a Ahomey!" Cmdt. Terrillon asked for "section 80 montagne et personnel artillerie pour armer complétement 8 pieces de 4. . . . Envoyés 2 Hotchkiss pour installer sur terrase station télégraphe."
155 SOM-AN Dahomey V, 2, b, Spuller to Etienne, 4 March 1890; M.A.E., Afrique 126, M.A.E. to Etienne, 4 March 1890 (draft), "Affaires du Dahomey."
156 Foa, p. 384; M.A.E., Afrique 126, Bayol to Colonies, 11 March 1890, no. 329.
157 A.C.M., BB4/1988, Marine to Cmdt. de Kerguelen, 6 March 1890 (tel.). The *Sané,* which arrived at Cotonou on 16 February, and the *Emeraude* were there before Terrillon asked for reinforcements. A.C.M., BB4/1989, Fournier to marine, 5 March 1890; BB4/1988, marine to *Sané,* 10 Feb. 1890 (tel.).
158 M.A.E., Afrique 126, Bayol to Colonies, 8 March 1890, no. 306 (tel.).
159 Ibid., Bayol to Colonies, 7 March 1890, nos. 297 (tel.), 299 (tel.); Bayol to Etienne, 11 March 1890, no. 329; Etienne to M.A.E., 10 March 1890 (conf. and urgent); A.C.M., BB4/1990, Bayol to Colonies, 7 March 1890.
160 SOM-AN Dahomey V, 2, b, Barbey to Etienne, 12 March 1890. Senator Barbey was the minister for the navy.
161 A.C.M., BB4/1990, "Note au sujet de la Côte comprise entre les Possessions anglaises de Lagos et allemandes de Togo," par Colonel D. Peroz, 12 March 1890.
162 M.A.E., Afrique 126, Bayol to Etienne, 11 March 1890, no. 329; gov. of Senegal to Colonies, 11 March 1890, no. 330; Bayol to Etienne, 13 March 1890, no. 342; Etienne to M.A.E., 13 March 1890.
163 Ibid., M.A.E. to Etienne, 15 March 1890 (draft); M.A.E. to Colonies, 4 March 1890.
164 SOM-AN Dahomey V, 2, b, "Note: Dahomey," by R. P. E. Chautard; "Dahomey et Porto Novo," by D. Dorat, 12 March 1890; L. Sevin-Desplaces, "Au Dahomey," in *La Géographie,* no. 66 (6 March 1890).

165 A.C.M., BB4/1990, Bayol to Colonies, 13 March 1890, 3 April 1890; SOM-AN Dahomey V, 3, b, Etienne to Barbey, 3 April 1890; M.A.E. to Colonies, 14 and 21 May 1890; *London Gazette,* 11 April 1890; Foreign Office to Waddington, 10 April 1890; *Journal Officiel,* 6 April 1890. The blockade covered the coast between the German possessions of the Popos—6°14′45″ latitude north and 0°10′37″ longitude west of Paris—and the British possessions of Lagos as defined by the Anglo-French agreement of 10 Aug. 1889.
166 A.C.M., BB4/1990, Ribot to Barbey, 14 and 19 April 1890.
167 SOM-AN Dahomey V, 2, a, Journal de Marche, par Terrillon. See E. Aublet, *La Guerre au Dahomey 1888–1893* (Paris, 1894), chap. 2.
168 M.A.E., Afrique 126, Bayol to Etienne, 1 April 1890, no. 445 (tel.).
169 Nicholas, *L'Expédition du Dahomey,* pp. 44–95; Foa, *Le Dahomey,* pp. 385–86; SOM-AN Dahomey, V, 2, a, Journal de Marche, par Terrillon.
170 M.A.E., Afrique 126, Bayol to Colonies, 1 April 1890, no. 445 (tel.). Bayol was fond of recommending people for promotion. He recommended his secretary, M. Angot, for promotion to administrator 4th class in his rapport of 6 Dec. 1889 and Commandant Terrillon for lieutenant colonel in Bayol to Etienne, 23 Feb. 1890, no. 228. "Déjà!" was the answer to this request.
171 A.C.M., BB4/1988, Marine to Commandant *Sané* à Gabon, 10 Feb. 1890 (tel.); Marine to *Sané,* 24 Feb. 1890, 3 March 1890 (tel.).
172 M.A.E., Afrique 126, Colonies to Bayol, 1 April 1890, no. 353.
173 A.C.M., BB4/1990, Etienne to Marine, 27 March 1890. Lieut-Colonel Klipfel was chosen eventually to replace Terrillon.
174 Ibid., BB4/1988, Marine to *Sané,* 5 April 1890; M.A.E., Afrique 126, Etienne to Bayol, 5 April 1890, no. 363 (tel.); Bayol to Etienne, 6 April 1890, no. 464.
175 *Le Petit Journal,* 17 April 1892; Foa, *Le Dahomey,* pp. 379, 387; de Riols, *La Guerre du Dahomey,* pp. 51–58. Foa stated that it was not possible to hold any single person responsible for the conflict between the French officials (p. 379).
176 A.C.M., BB4/1989, Cuverville to Marine, 13 June 1890, quoting Victor Ballot; M.A.E., Afrique 126, Bayol to Colonies, 8 March 1890, no. 306 (tel.).
177 M.A.E., Afrique 126, gov. of Senegal to Etienne, 11 March 1890, no. 330; Bayol to Etienne, 11 March 1890, no. 329.
178 Ibid., Bayol to Colonies, 9 March 1890, no. 315 (tel.). He got a negative reply.
179 SOM-AN Dahomey V, 3, a, Mantes and Borelli to Etienne, 23 April 1890 (encl. Béhanzin to Mantes and Borelli, 2 March 1890).
180 Ibid., Mantes and Borelli to Béhanzin, 23 April 1890 (encl. in Mantes and Borelli to Etienne, 23 April 1890).
181 Ibid., Béhanzin to Ballot, 2 May 1890.
182 The *lebel* was the magazine rifle of the French army (model 1885).
183 Foa, *Le Dahomey,* p. 386.
184 A.C.M., BB4/1989, Fournier to Marine, 2 May 1890. 5,000 bayonet rifles of the old model were requested for these auxiliaries. *Naiade* to Marine, 24 April 1890.
185 Foa, pp. 387–88.
186 A.C.M., BB4/1989, Fournier to Marine, 21 and 22 April 1890; SOM-AN Dahomey V, 2, a, *Journal de Marche,* par Terrillon; M.A.E., Afrique 126, Fournier to Barbey, 21 April 1890 (tel.); Lt. Col. Terrillon, "Le Combat d'Atchoupa, 20 April

1890," in *Journal Officiel* (Etablissements de France au Golfe de Bénin) (1 May 1890), p. 2.
187 Foa, p. 389; Aublet, *La Guerre au Dahomey.*
188 A.C.M., BB4/1989, Terrillon to Fournier, 7 May 1890 (encl. Projet d'Expedition sur Abomey, 6 May 1890); Fournier to Marine, 18 May 1890; M.A.E., Afrique 126, Fournier to Barbey, 22 April 1890; A.C.M., BB4/1988, Marine to *Sané,* 26 April 1890; BB4/1989, Cuverville to Marine, 3 July 1890.
189 Forts were erected around Porto Novo. The most important of these were Fort des Amazones, Fort Oudard, Fort Mousset, and Fort Toffa, all named in commemoration of the outstanding events of the first war. A.C.M., BB4/1989, Cuverville to marine, 3 July 1890, no. 63.
190 Foa, *Le Dahomey,* p. 390.
191 A.C.M., BB4/1989, hostages at Abomey to Bayol, 4 April 1890; Fournier to Marine, 10 May 1890. The canoe which was taking the Dahomean prisoners from the *Kerguelen* capsized at the bar. One person was drowned, not nine as stated in Fournier's telegram; see minutes. M.A.E., Afrique 126, Fournier to Barbey, 28 April 1890; Béhanzin to Ballot, 2 May 1890; Fournier to Barbey, 10 May 1890.
192 A.C.M., BB4/1989, Fournier to Marine, 18 May 1890 (tel.).
193 M.A.E., Afrique 126, Bayol to Etienne, 19 Jan. 1890 (encl. Etienne to Spuller, 21 Jan. 1890).
194 The second Tirard Cabinet was in office from 22 Feb. 1889 to 14 March 1890. See Edouard Bonnefous, *Histoire Politique de la Troisième République* (Paris, 1956), vol. 2; M.A.E., Afrique 126, Etienne to Bayol, 16 Jan. 1890.
195 *L'Intransigeant,* quoted in *Rev. Française de l'Etranger et des Colonies,* vol. 11, no. 95 (1 June 1890), pp. 660–68.
196 *Journal des Débats* (9 March 1890); *Journal Officiel: Chambre des Députés: Débats Parlémentaires* (hereafter *J.O. Chambre Débats*) (9 March 1890).
197 A.C.M., BB4/1990, Rouvier to Etienne, 12 Mar. 1890. After he reorganized the conseil superieur des colonies in May 1890, Etienne made Rouvier the president of the African colonies section (section 2). See SOM-AN Conseil Supérieur des Colonies: Généralités 31, *Organisation et Composition du Conseil Supérieur des Colonies* (Paris, 1890); Rapport au Président de la République, 29 May 1890, par M. Jule Roche; *Almanach National: 1890,* pp. 355–57. Rouvier remained president of the African section of the conseil supérieur des colonies from 1890 to 1898.
198 Andre Daniel, *L'Année Politique 1890* (Paris, 1891).
199 The fourth Freycinet Cabinet was in office from 17 March 1890 to 19 Feb. 1892, the comparatively long term of office due to the *ralliement* in French politics. See Jacques Madaule, *Histoire de France,* vol. 3, *De la IIIe à la Ve République* (Paris, 1966), pp. 57–69; D. W. Brogan, *The Development of Modern France 1870–1939* (London, 1959), pp. 257–67; Alphonse Bertrand, *La Législature 1889–1893* (Paris, 1893).
200 M.A.E. Papiers Ribot, vol. 3, Waddington to Ribot, 22 March 1890 (private); Papiers Waddington, vol. 5, Ribot to Waddington, 8 April 1890: "Il a fallu ensuite d'occuper de l'affaire du Dahomey qui a été mal engagée et que nous avons quelque peine à remettre en bonne voie."
201 Bayol, who was considered a stumbling block to peaceful negotiations with the

king of Dahomey, was recalled to Paris. A.C.M., BB4/1988, Colonies to Bayol, 1 April 1890.
202 A.C.M., BB4/1988, marine to Fournier, 8 April 1890 (draft), 12 and 19 April 1890; Marine to Cuverville, 3 May 1890, Instructions Concernant l'Affaire du Dahomey; Barbey to Ribot, 3 May 1890.
203 A.C.M., BB4/1988, Marine to *Sané,* 2 May 1890; Barbey to Fournier, 11 May 1890.
204 François Berge, "Les Sous-Secrétariat," pp. 305–06.
205 A.C.M., BB4/1990, Etienne to Barbey, 21 Apr. 1890, minutes by Barbey.
206 On Capt. L. Fournier's role in the conquest of Dahomey, see P. A. De Salinis, *Le Protectorat Français sur la Côte des Esclaves: La Campagne du Sané, 1889–1890 d'après des documents inédits* (Paris, 1908).
207 A.C.M., BB4/1989, Fournier to Marine, 2 and 8 May 1890.
208 A.C.M., BB4/1988, Marine to Fournier, 11 May 1890.
209 Ibid., marine to *Sané,* 15 May 1890. Siciliano did go to Dahomey at the expense of Mantes and Borelli, but his efforts bore no fruit.
210 A.C.M., BB4/1990, Siciliano to Marine, 10 Sept. 1890; BB4/1989, Cuverville to marine, 1 Aug. 1890, no. 86; 3 July 1890, no. 63; 13 Sept. 1890, no. 183. It was thought that Mantes and Borelli hoped to gain ascendancy over other French firms in Dahomey by trying to bring about a settlement of the disputed questions. See A.C.M., BB4/1988, Marine to *Sané,* 15 May 1890.
211 See Père Dogère, "Prisonniers au Dahomey"; Paul Lesourd, *L'Oeuvre Civilisatrice et Scientifique des Missionaires Catholiques dans les Colonies Françaises* (Paris, 1931).
212 M.A.E., Afrique 126, Rapport Bontemps, 11 May 1890.
213 de Riols, *La Guerre du Dahomey,* p. 19; Rene F. Guilcher, *La Société des Missions Africaines* (Lyon, 1956), p. 58; Mattei, *Bas-Niger, Bénoue, Dahomey,* p. 167.
214 Grandin, *Le Dahomey* 1:203. See also Abbe E. Describes, *L'Evangile au Dahomey*; A.C.M., BB4/1989, Cuverville to Marine, 3 July 1890, no. 63. Dogère offered to go back to Abomey even at the cost of his life to treat with Béhanzin.
215 A.C.M., BB4/1989, Cuverville to Marine, 1 Aug. 1890 (encl. Rapport: Situation au Dahomey, no. 86); Cuverville to Père Dogère, 11 July 1890, Instructions Confidentielles du Père Dogère, annexe 2, Projet de traité entre la France et le Dahomey. Articles 5 and 7 of this draft treaty specify an end to human sacrifices.
216 A.C.M., BB4/1989, Cuverville to Père Dogère, 11 July 1890.
217 Henrique, *Nos Contemporains* 1:97.
218 A.C.M., BB4/1989, Cuverville to Marine, 3 July 1890, no. 63 (encl. annexe 1, Thème général des opérations contre Abomey, par Cuverville); M.A.E., Afrique 126, Cuverville to Barbey, 27 May 1890.
219 A.C.M., BB4/1989, Fournier to Marine, 8 May 1890.
220 Ibid., Rapport sur l'Etat Sanitaire du Corps Expeditionaire du Bénin pendant le mois de juillet 1890, par Médecin Principal Siciliano, 4 Aug. 1890.
221 Ibid., Fournier to Marine, 10 June 1890.
222 Ibid., Cuverville to Marine, 9 Aug. 1890. Cuverville deplored the fact that French enterprise in the Golfe of Bénin was often represented by foreigners.
223 Ibid., *Sané* to Marine, 28 May 1890; Cuverville to Marine, 13 June 1890; 3 July 1890, no. 63; 7 Aug. 1890.

224 A.C.M., BB4/1989, Cuverville to Marine, 23 May 1890. The Quai d'Orsay was at this time being advised to barter Porto Novo for the Gambia in order to obtain a compact colony of Senegal. M.A.E., Hanotaux Papers, vol. 8, "Note Pour M. Hanotaux: Compte rendu d'une Conversation avec M. le Chatélier sur la pénétration en Afrique," 27 Aug. 1890; M.A.E., Afrique 126, Barbey to Fournier, 10 April 1890 (copy), minutes; Note pour le Ministre par la Direction Politique: Protectorat, 12 April 1890, minutes: "Il n'est pas question du retrait de notre protectorat, mais seulement d'un changement de personne au Porto Novo où le maintain du Roi Toffa pour nous susciter des embarass et des compensation insuffisante."

225 M.A.E., Papiers Waddington, vol. 5, Ribot to Waddington, 8 April 1890; CO879/31, Moloney to Knutsford, 11 April 1890, no. 33 (encl. Fournier to Moloney, 7 April 1890); M.A.E., Afrique 126, Barbey to Fournier, 8 April 1890; A.C.M., BB4/1989, Puttkamer (German Commissioner of Togo) to Fournier, 11 April 1890; SOM-AN Dahomey V, 3, b, Ribot to Colonies, 14 May 1890; Foreign Office to Waddington, 10 April 1890.

226 A.C.M., BB4/1990, Ribot to Marine, 19 April 1890; M.A.E., Afrique 126, note pour le ministre du Portugal à Paris, 23 April 1890.

227 A.C.M., BB4/1989, Cuverville to Marine, 10 and 13 June 1890, 9 Aug. 1890.

228 M.A.E., Afrique 126, Barbey to Fournier, 5 June 1890; Ribot to Colonies, 28 June 1890 (encl. Waddington to Ribot, 4 June 1890); A.C.M., BB4/1988, Marine to Ribot, 4 Aug. 1890.

229 A.C.M., BB4/1989, Cuverville to Marine, 7 and 1 Aug. 1890; BB4/1988, Marine to M.A.E., 25 Aug. 1890, 13 Dec. 1890. The French continued to ask for the passage of their boats through Lagos all through their conflict with Dahomey.

230 CO879/31, Moloney to Knutsford, no. 47 (with enclosures); A.C.M., BB4/1989, Moloney to Fournier, 20 and 31 May 1890; Rapport Tracou, 6 June 1890; A.C.M., BB4/1988, Barbey to Ribot, 17 July 1890.

231 A.C.M., BB4/1990, Ribot to Barbey, 23 Dec. 1890; CO879, Moloney to Knutsford, 31 Dec. 1890, no. 74 (encl. Report on the Kingdom of Pokra, by J. H. Ewart, 1 Nov. 1890).

232 A.C.M., BB4/1990, R. Père Planque (Lyon) to Marine, 1 Oct. 1890. Dogère left for Abomey on 10 Aug. 1890. A.C.M., BB4/1989, Cuverville to marine, 14 Aug. 1890, no. 162.

233 A.C.M., BB4/1989, Cuverville to Barbey, 1 Aug. 1890, "Situation au Dahomey," no. 86.

234 Ibid., Dogère to Cuverville, 9 Aug. 1890 (Abomey); Cuverville to Marine, no. 171.

235 See Père Rene F. Guilcher, *Au Dahomey avec le Père Dogère: L'Activité pacificatrice d'un Missionaire* (Lyon, n.d.); Etienne, *Le Père Dogère,* Dogère, "Prisonniers au Dahomey"; SOM-AN Dahomey V, 4, c, Barbey to Etienne, 13 Aug. 1890.

236 A.C.M., BB4/1989, Cuverville to Barbey, 14 Aug. 1890, no. 62; SOM-AN Dahomey V, 4, 9, Dogère to Cuverville, 15 Aug. 1890.

237 A.C.M., BB4/1989, Cuverville to Marine, 7 Sept. 1890; Journal de M. Bernadin Durand, annexe 3 (encl. in Cuverville to Marine, 5 Sept. 1890, no. 114); SOM-AN Dahomey V, 4, a, Béhanzin to Cuverville, 18 Aug. 1890; Bernadin Durand to Ballot, 15 Aug. 1890, rapport.

238 A.C.M., BB4/1989, *Naiade* to Marine, 25 Aug. 1890, no. 166.

239 Ibid., 30 Aug. 1890, no. 167.
240 Ibid., Cuverville to Marine, 19 Sept. 1890; M.A.E., Afrique 126, Barbey to Ribot, 15 Sept. 1890. Cuverville complained of the hidden opposition of Lagos to the recruitment of African troops by the French.
241 M.A.E., Afrique 126, Cuverville to Yevoghan of Whydah, 2 Oct. 1890.
242 A.C.M., BB4/1989, Cuverville to Marine, 4 Oct. 1890.
243 This was to lead to much misunderstanding in the future, since both parties reached no agreement on the frontiers of Porto Novo.
244 SOM-AN Dahomey V, 4, b, Chambre des Députés, Document Parlementaire No. 1023: Projet de loi portant approbation de l'Arrangement conclu avec le Roi du Dahomey le 3 Octobre 1890, appendix 2.
245 M.A.E., Afrique 126, Cuverville to Barbey, 4 and 5 Oct. 1890.
246 *J.O. Chambre Débats (21 Nov. 1890)*, 22 Nov. 1890, p. 2175.
247 *Journal Officiel*: Chambre des Députés Documents Parlementaires (1890) Annexes aux Proces-Verbaux des Séances, annexe 1023. The commission was composed of Admiral Valon (president), C. Martinon (secretary), François Deloncle, Muller, M. de Lanessan, Henri Hervieu, Felix Faure, Victor Prost, Denizot, and Comte de Kergolay.
248 SOM-AN Conseil Supérieur des Colonies, Gen. 31, Organisation et Composition du Conseil Supérieur des Colonies, par sous-secrétariat d'état des colonies (Paris, 1890), pp. 3–9, 20–21.
249 SOM-AN Dahomey V, 4, b, Vallon to Etienne, 21 Jan. 1891; M.A.E., Afrique 127, Valon to Ribot, 21 Jan. 1891 (encl. Cyprien Fabre to Admiral Valon, 3 Jan. 1891). Fabre's letter is a six-page manuscript. Fabre to Barbey, 3 Jan. 1891 (encl. in Barbey to Ribot, 27 Jan. 1891 [très confidentiel]).
250 A.C.M., BB4/1989, Cuverville to Marine, 12 Feb. 1891 (tel.).
251 Ehrmann took over as acting resident at Porto Novo in December 1890 and held this post during Victor Ballot's leave in France. Ballot left Porto Novo on 9 January 1891 via Lagos on his way back to France.
252 Victor Ballot, "Mission Dahomey et Golfe du Bénin," in *R.F.E.C.* (15 Jan. 1891).
253 M.A.E., Afrique 127, Ehrmann to Ballay, 8 Jan. 1891, "Situation Politique"; Etienne to Ribot, 12 Feb. 1891.
254 A.C.M., BB4/1988, Marine to Admiral Valon, 7 Dec. 1890. The minister kept the originals and sent copies of these to the commission. A.C.M., BB4/1990, Valon to marine, 18 Dec. 1890.
255 SOM-AN Dahomey V, 4, c, Ribot to Etienne, 8 Oct. 1890 (encl. D'Estournelles to Ribot, 3 Oct. 1890); *Nineteenth Century*, Oct. 1890; *The Standard*, 6 Oct. 1890, D'Estournelles to Ribot, 10 Oct. 1890.
256 M.A.E., Afrique 126, Cuverville to Barbey, 11 Oct. 1890; Afrique 127, Cuverville to Barbey, 18 Feb. 1891 (encl. in Barbey to Ribot, 14 March 1891 [personal and confidential]).
257 *La Lanterne*, 7 October 1891; A.C.M., BB4/1989, Cuverville to Marine, 2 Dec. 1891 (encl. Cuverville to editor of *La Lanterne*, 2 Dec. 1891).
258 *Journal Officiel*: Chambre des Députés: Documents Parlementaires (1891) Annexes aux Proces-Verbaux des Séances: Projets et Propositions des Lois, Exposés des Motifs et Rapports, annexe no. 1235 (session ordinaire, séance du 24 Février

1891), Rapport fait au nom de la Commission chargée d'examiner le projet de loi portant approbation de l'arrangement conclu avec le Roi du Dahomey le 3 Octobre 1890, par M. de Lanessan, pp. 608-14. Two members, Henri Hervieu and Victor Prost, voted for the rejection of the treaty (p. 613).

CHAPTER 4

1 CO879/31, F.O. to C.O., 2 July 1891 (encl. Lytton to F.O., 27 June 1891).
2 M.A.E., Afrique 127, Ehrmann to Ballay, 8 Jan. 1891, "Situation Politique"; CO879/31, Denton to Knutsford, 15 March 1891 (encl. inhabitants of Lagos to British govt., Dec. 1890 [received by Denton on 28 Feb. 1891]).
3 SOM-AN Dahomey V, 5, b, Béhanzin to Ballot, 10 April 1892.
4 SOM-AN Dahomey V, 5, a, Ballay to Colonies, 10 Feb. 1891; M.A.E., Afrique 127, Etienne to Ribot, 5 and 12 Feb. 1891.
5 FO84/2208, Dufferin to Salisbury, 20 April 1892, Africa no. 83 (encl. Phipps to Dufferin, 20 April 1892); *Journal des Débats,* 18 April 1892.
6 *Le Temps,* 17 April 1892; *J.O. Chambre Débats,* 8 April 1892, interpellation on Dahomey by H. Hervieu, pp. 491-510.
7 M.A.E., Afrique 127, Etienne to Balley, 5 Feb. 1891; SOM-AN Dahomey V, 4, b, Ribot to Etienne, 18 February 1891; Décret portant Approbation de l'Arrangement conclu entre La France et le Dahomey le 3 Octobre 1890 (Paris, 8 Dec. 1891).
8 M.A.E., Afrique 126, Cuverville to Barbey, 9 Sept. 1890.
9 A.C.M., BB4/1989, Cuverville to Marine, 9 Oct. 1890; BB4/1988, "Note sur les Affaires du Dahomey," 11 Oct. 1890, on effectives.
10 A.C.M., BB4/1989, Cuverville to Marine, 22 Nov. 1890, no. 195, "Situation en Dahomey en Novembre 1890."
11 Archives Nationales, Papiers Ballot, MI 185/4, Rapport Ballot au Amiral Cuverville: Mission dans le Dekame, 12 Nov. 1890; A.C.M., BB4/1989, Cuverville to marine, 22 Nov. 1890, no. 194 (encl. Ballot to Cuverville, 13 Nov. 1890); SOM-AN Dahomey III, 1, c, Ballot, Rapport: Mission dans le Dekame, 12 Nov. 1890.
12 President Sadi Carnot was not aware of this plan. However, the council of ministers approved and endorsed it. M.A.E., Afrique 127, Barbey to Ribot, 16 and 9 Jan. 1890; A.C.M., BB4/1990, Ribot to Barbey, 14 Jan. 1890.
13 SOM-AN Dahomey, V, 5, b, Ehrmann to Gov. Bally, 8 January 1891.
14 M.A.E., Afrique 126, Etienne to Ribot, 18 Dec. 1890, quoting Cuverville to marine, 5 October 1890. Cuverville's criticisms were leveled against Bayol; he rated Ballot very highly.
15 SOM-AN Dossier Administratif: Victor Ballot, Cuverville to colonies, 12 Oct. 1890, recommendations; Cuverville to ministre de la marine, 7 Nov. 1890; Barbey to sous-secrétaire des colonies, 8 Dec. 1890, on Ballot for the Legion d'Honneur.
16 SOM-AN Dahomey III, 2, a, projet de mission à Say par Cuverville, 11 Dec. 1890.
17 Archives Nationales, Papiers Ballot, MI 185/4, Cuverville to Ballot, 11 Dec. 1890; A.C.M., BB4/1989, Cuverville to Cmdt. du Roland, 21 Dec. 1890 (copy).
18 M.A.E., Afrique 127, Etienne to Ribot, 12 Feb. 1891.
19 A.C.M., BB4/1990, Ribot to Barbey, 14 Jan. 1891.
20 A.C.M., BB4/1988, marine to M.A.E., 9 and 16 Jan. 1891. The mission comprised Audeoud, Decoeur, Hocquart, D'Ambrières, and Charles with their guides, porters, and interpreters.

21 A.C.M., BB4/1989, Rapport de M. G. d'Ambrières sur le Voyage de la Mission Française a Abomey, Fevrier–Mars 1891 (29 April 1891); *Journal Officiel* (Rép. Française), March 1891, p. 1017.
22 M.A.E., Afrique 127, Ehrmann to Ballay, 8 Jan. 1891, "Situation Politique."
23 Ibid., Ehrmann to Ballay, 8 Jan. 1891.
24 FO27/3038, Lytton to Salisbury, 2 April 1891; *Journal Officiel,* 2 April 1891.
25 A.C.M., BB4/1989, Rapport de M.G. d'Ambrières, 29 April 1891.
26 SOM-AN Dahomey III, 2, b, rapport, Mission Française à Abomey, par Capt. Hocquart, 2 April 1891; CO879/29, Moloney to Knutsford, 27 June 1889 (encl. Gléglé to the queen of England, 12 May 1889).
27 Audeoud to Gov. Ballay, 3 April 1891, quoted in Cornevin, *Histoire du Dahomey,* p. 335. The carrying of palm leaves into enemy territory did not have identical connotations as the European convention of the white flag.
28 SOM-AN Dahomey III, 2, b, rapports, mission à Abomey, Feb.–March 1891; V, 5, a, b, mission Audéoud.
29 *Journal Officiel,* 2 April 1890.
30 CO879/31, C.O. to F.O., 8 Jan. 1891; F.O. to C.O., 20 Jan. 1891; FO27/3038, Lytton to Salisbury, 24 Jan. 1891.
31 CO879/31, F.O. to C.O., 29 Jan. 1891 (encl. Lytton to Salisbury, 24 Jan. 1891).
32 Ibid., Denton to Knutsford, 2 Feb. 1891 (encl. "Interview with Prince Dosu and Others . . . on board H.M.C.S. "Margaret" off Badagry," 26 Jan. 1891); Denton to Ehrmann, 2 Sept. 1891 (encl. in Denton to Knutsford, 19 Sept. 1891).
33 M.A.E., Afrique 127, Etienne to Ribot, 15 April 1891 (encl. Rapport Gouverneur Ballay, 9 March 1891, on Toffa's harsh rule and razzias in British territory).
34 CO879/31, Denton to Knutsford, 15 March 1891 (encl. inhabitants of Lagos to Lord Knutsford, Dec. 1890). Among those who signed this long petition were Rev. Johnson, John Holt, Witt and Bush, Alf. R. Elliot, G. Wolber, and J. W. Cote.
35 Ibid., Manchester Chamber of Commerce to C.O., 4 June 1891; C.O. to Manchester Chamber of Commerce, 10 June 1891.
36 Ibid., F.O. to C.O., 12 May 1891.
37 Ibid., 2 July 1891 (encl. Lytton to Salisbury, 27 June 1891).
38 FO27/3039, Lytton to Salisbury, 27 June 1891.
39 Lord Salisbury argued that Britain could not shift this obligation to France simply because she could not fulfill it herself. CO879/31, Denton to King Gbéhanzin of Abomey, 9 June 1891; Denton to Lieut. Domville, 10 June 1891.
40 C. W. Newbury, "Victorians, Republicans and the Partition of West Africa," in *Journal of African History,* vol. 3, no. 3 (1962), pp. 493–501.
41 See J. A. Gallagher, "Folwell Buxton and the New African Policy," in *Cambridge Historical Journal* 10 (1950).
42 A.C.M., BB4/1988, Marine to Cuverville, 19 Dec. 1890; Marine to M.A.E., 21 Dec. 1890.
43 M.A.E., Afrique 127, Ribot to Etienne, 10 Jan. 1891.
44 Ibid., Etienne to Ribot, 24 Jan. 1891.
45 Ibid., Ehrmann to Ballay, 8 Jan. 1891.
46 Ibid., Etienne to Ribot, 24 Jan. 1891.
47 Ibid., 30 April 1891 (encl. Etienne to Ballay, 30 April 1891).
48 SOM-AN Dahomey, V, 5, b, Ehrmann to Ballay, 8 May 1891.

49 SOM-AN Dahomey V, 5, b, Ballay to Etienne, 21 Sept. 1891; Ehrmann to Ballay, 8 Nov. 1891; Ballay to Etienne, 28 Dec. 1891 (tel. no. 96).
50 M.A.E., Afrique 127, Ribot to Etienne, 21 November 1891.
51 Ibid., Hausmann to Ribot, 28 Dec. 1891.
52 FO27/3038, Lytton to Salisbury, 22 Jan. 1891; FO27/3039, Lytton to Salisbury, 13 May 1891; Edouard Marbeau, "M. Ribot et l'Afrique," in *R.F.E.C.,* vol. 12, no. 99 (1 Aug. 1890), pp. 129–31.
53 M.A.E., Afrique 127, Etienne to Ribot, 27 Feb. 1892 (with enclosures). Etienne sent Ribot a dossier of information on the question of the recruitment of laborers in Dahomey by European powers. Ballay to Etienne, 19 Jan. 1892, 17 Feb. 1892, 8 Dec. 1891.
54 Ibid., Fabre to Etienne, 26 Jan. 1892; Fabre to Ribot, 9 March 1892; Jamais to Ribot, 26 March 1892 (encl. Béhanzin to Ehrmann, 2 Jan. 1892).
55 Ibid., minutes (n.d.), probably March or April 1892.
56 FO84/2208, Dufferin to Salisbury, 16 April 1892, Africa no. 79.
57 *Journal Officiel*: Etablissements et Protectorats Français du Golfe de Bénin (1 Feb. 1893). Mr. Vitt was expelled by decree on 9 Jan. 1893.
58 This was uncovered by a judicial inquiry ordered by General Dodds. Account Voucher: Béhanzin, Abomey, fol. 66. Barth was deported by decree on 6 Jan. 1893.
59 FO27/3039, Lytton to Salisbury, 13 May 1891.
60 M.A.E., Afrique 127, Etienne to Ribot, 15 April 1891 (encl. Ballay to Etienne, 9 March 1891); *Lagos Weekly Record,* 21 February 1891, "France and Dahomey," extract.
61 The French imported large quantities of food, especially corn, from German Togo during their struggle with Dahomey. See Foreign Office, Miscellaneous Series (1894), no. 346, *Report on the German Colonies in Africa and the South Pacific,* C.7582, p. 7.
62 SOM-AN Dahomey V, 5, b, Ballay to Etienne, 19 Jan. 1892; rapports Ehrmann, 8 Nov. 1891, 8 Dec. 1891, 29 Sept. 1891, 8 Oct. 1891.
63 Edouard Dunglas, "Moyen Dahomey," p. 56; SOM-AN Dahomey V, 2, b, "Les Intérets Français sur la Cote des Esclaves et au Dahomé," in *La Géographie,* 13 Feb. 1890. This article quotes Beraud on the existence of farms worked by slaves.
64 FO27/3038, Lytton to Salisbury, 22 Jan. 1891.
65 Madaule, *Histoire de France* 3:57–69.
66 FO27/3041, Egerton to Salisbury, 1 Oct. 1891.
67 FO27/3038, Lytton to Salisbury, 22 Jan. 1891. See Alexander Sedgwick, *The Ralliement in French Politics,* 1890–1898 (Cambridge, Mass., 1965), for a recent intensive examination of party politics in France in this period.
68 Leo XIII reinforced his advice to the French clergy by his encyclical *Rerum Novarum* (1890) on the state of the working classes and social justice.
69 Lugard Papers, MSS Br. Emp. S69 (Rhodes House), Kirk to Lugard, 19 July 1889. "The Cardinal Lavigerie is a charming man and a man of great wealth and influence," said Sir John Kirk.
70 Toast by Cardinal Lavigerie, 12 Nov. 1890, quoted in Madaule, *Histoire de France* 3:59–60.
71 P.R.O. Cab. 37/30 F.O. "Franco-Russian Relations," 19 Aug. 1891.

72 "C'est l'Ésprit nouveau, c'est l'ésprit qui tend, dans une société aussi profondément troublée que celle-ci, à ramener tous les Français autour des idées de bon sens, de justice et de charité nécessaires à toute société qui veut vivre," according to Jacques Spuller (quoted in Madaule 3:69). See Jacques Chastenet, *Histoire de IIIeme République* (Paris, 1952), vol. 2.

73 See Pierre Renouvin, *Histoire des Rélations Internationales,* vol. 6, *De 1871 à 1914. L'Apogée de l'Europe* (Paris, 1958), pp. 185–203.

74 Ch. A. Julien, *Les Téchniciens de la Colonisation (XIXe–XXe Siècles),* pp. 75–92 (on Faidherbe and west Africa by R. Delavignette).

75 There was opposition to colonial wars, especially by the pacifists. See J. Dumas, *La Colonisation: essai de doctrine pacifiste* (Paris, 1904); P. Louis, *Le Colonialisme* (Paris, 1905); and P. Vigne d'Octon, *La Gloire du Sabre* (Paris, 1900)—all of which are indictments of colonial wars.

76 *J.O. Chambre Débats,* 8 April 1892, pp. 491–512.

77 Ibid., p. 495; Yves de la Brière, "Guerre Coloniale et Theologie catholique," in *Etudes de Sociologie et d'éthnologie juridique,* 5 Sept. 1935.

78 *J.O. Chambre Débats,* 8 April 1892, p. 497.

79 Ibid., p. 500. A very outspoken opposition to colonial wars was Irisson d'Herisson's *La chasse à l'homme, Guerre d'Algerie* (Paris, 1891). This criticism of the conquest of Algeria had a wider implication.

80 *J.O. Chambre Débats,* 8 April 1892, pp. 501–03.

81 Etienne interjected: "Et j'en accept la responsabilité tout entière" (ibid., p. 510).

82 This point was made by Alfred Rambaud in his preface to J. Seeley's *Expansion of England,* according to Deroulede. Ibid., pp. 509–12.

83 A demand for a parliamentary inquiry into the affairs of Sudan and Dahomey was defeated before the voting on the bill. *J.O. Chambre Débats,* 12 April 1891, pp. 540–57, 560–61.

84 Paris newspapers such as *Le Temps, Le Siècle, Le Matin, L'Eclair, Journal des Débats, Journal de Gaulois,* and *La Géographie* and reviews such as *La Nouvelle Revue, Revue Française, Revue Maritime et Coloniale,* etc. competed as it were for pride of place in the coverage of colonial questions. Dahomey and Sudan were the two African questions of any magnitude at this period and as such received much attention.

85 FO27/2208, Dufferin to Salisbury, 20 April 1892, Africa no. 83 (encl. Phipps to Dufferin, 20 April 1892); 21 April 1892, Africa no. 82.

86 FO27/3039, Lytton to Salisbury, 2 Sept. 1891. François Deloncle, who owned *Le Siècle,* had a near relation who was employed in the Colonial Department as one of the chief secretaries; he was P. L. Deloncle.

87 *Le Temps,* 3 Feb. 1890 (special supplement), 22 Jan. 1891, 6 April 1892.

88 G. de Wailly, "Un Regiment Sacré," in *La Nouvelle Revue* 63 (March–April 1890): 390–94.

89 SOM-AN Dahomey V, 2, b, Frank Hardy, "L'Honneur du Drapeau," in *Le Voltaire,* 30 March 1890.

90 G. de Wailly, "L'Afrique Obligatoire," in *La Nouvelle Revue* 75 (1892): 586–92: "C'est par le railway, bien plus surement que par les colonnes expéditionnaires, l'incendie et les balles, que l'Afrique sera conquise et civilisée. . . . C'est une

mission bienfaisante et lucrative, en somme, qui nous appelle au coeur de l'esclavageste Afrique."

91 I. Chessé, "Nos Colonies," in *La Nouvelle Revue* 80 (1893): 614–18. See Pierre Lyautey, *La Battaile Economique* (Paris, 1929).
92 Mattei, *Bas-Niger, Benoué, Dahomey*, pp. 180–86, 187–96.
93 Chautard, *Le Dahomey*, pp. 24–26. He quoted Duncan, J. A. Skertchly, and Burton to support his claims. Trees 150 feet in circumference were common in Dahomey. Skertchly, *Dahomey As It Is*, p. 311; Burton, *Mission to Glégle* 1:125.
94 *Le Temps*, 6 April 1892. Mantes and Fabre also disagreed as to the methods of dealing with Dahomey and the results to be attained.
95 *J.O. Chambre Débats*, 8 April 1892, pp. 499–500.
96 SOM-AN Dahomey V, 2, b, "Note: Dahomey," par E. Chautard (n.d.).
97 A.C.M., BB4/1992, Dodds to marine, 15 Dec. 1892. Dodds reported that guns, canons, mitrailles, Krupp cannons, liquors, etc. were discovered at Abomey, "mais pas d'argent."
98 SOM-AN Dahomey III, 4, 2, Projet de Mission: Hinterland du Bénin, 15 Dec. 1892, Rapport Binger. See *R.F.E.C.* 14 (1 Aug. 1891): 113; 16 (1 Aug. 1892): 97.
99 *J.O. Chambre Débats*, 5 Feb. 1893, p. 403; *Documents Parlementaires: Chambre des Députés* (1893), annex no. 2924, "Exposé des Motifs."
100 Georges Demanche, "Dahomey: route du Niger: situation et population," in *R.F.E.C.*, vol. 18, no. 177 (1 Nov. 1893), pp. 397–406; *Journal des Débats*, 5 Feb. 1893.
101 FO84/2208, Dufferin to Salisbury, 20 April 1892, Africa no. 83; P.R.O. Cab. 37/29, "Development of Trade with the Colonies," by C.O. (Feb. 1891).
102 SOM-AN Dahomey V, 5, b, Ballot to Colonies 28 March 1892.
103 R. Cornevin, "Les divers épisodes de la lutte contre le royaume d'Abomey, 1887–1894" in *Revue Française d'Hist. d'Outre-Mer* 47 (1960): 186–87.
104 M.A.E., Afrique 127, Ballay to Etienne, 19 Jan. 1892; SOM-AN Dahomey V, 5, b, Rapport du M. Cornilleau, vice-résident de France à Grand Popo, 21 Dec. 1891. This dealt with Dahomey raids in the Ouatchi country.
105 The French party was well into Dahomey territory. See E. Foa, "Notice sur le fleuve Wheme, formant la limite entre le royaume de Porto Novo et le Dahomey," in *Comptes Rendus de la Société de Géographie de Paris* (1888), pp. 536–45. They were attacked at Topli. See SOM-AN Dahomey V, 6, b, Rapport de Bataillon Riou sur l'engagement du 27 Mars 1892 à Topli.
106 SOM-AN Dahomey V, 5, b, Béhanzin to Ballot, 10 April 1892.
107 Ibid., V, 4, a, Béhanzin to Cuverville, 18 Aug. 1890; M.A.E., Afrique 127, Jamais to Ribot, 26 March 1892 (encl. Ehrmann to Ballay, 3 Feb. 1892; Béhanzin to resident, 2 Jan. 1892); SOM-AN Dahomey V, 5, b, Béhanzin to Dodds, 10 June 1892.
108 SOM-AN Dahomey V, 6, b, Béhanzin to Ballot, 10 April 1892 (copy).
109 Béhanzin to Ballot, April 1892, cited in Cornevin, "Les divers épisodes," pp. 186–87.
110 E. Dunglas, "Moyen-Dahomey," p. 97.
111 See Marti, *Le Roi-Dieu*, pp. 114–41.
112 SOM-AN Dahomey V, 6, b, Béhanzin to Ballot, 10 April 1892 (copy).

113 Decree of 10 April 1892 signed by President Sadi Carnot. *Journal Officiel*, 11 April 1892; A.C.M., BB4/1992, Dodds to Marine, 29 May 1892, "Ordre Général No. 1."
114 Clashes of personality and opinion between Jules Roche, the new minister of the navy, and Eugene Etienne led to the latter's replacement by Emile Jamais on 8 March 1892. Roche did not want to be a nominal minister, and Etienne exercised wide powers.
115 Col. A. Dodds was born in St. Louis in 1842. M. Silberman, *Souvenirs* (Paris, 1910), p. 45. No biography of General Dodds exists. Contact made with Madame Virginia Derome (née Dodds) in Paris did not yield any private papers of the late general. These were said to have been destroyed during World War II.
116 Brunet and Giethlen, *Dahomey et Dépendances,* pp. 104–05; Cornevin, *Histoire du Dahomey,* pp. 340–41.
117 *Journal Officiel,* 16 March 1891.
118 Morienval, *La Guerre du Dahomey,* pp. 91 ff; *Journal Officiel* (Etablissements et Protectorats de France du Golfe de Bénin), 1 June 1892. M. G. Cavaignac, minister of the navy, proposed Dodds for the post of commandant superior in Dahomey (30 March 1892). This was approved and sanctioned by a presidential decree of 10 April 1892.
119 A.C.M., BB4/1991, Marine to Dodds, instructions au commandant supérieur des établissements de Bénin (draft); *Journal Officiel*: Etablissements et Protectorat Français du Golfe de Bénin, 1 June 1892.
120 FO84/2208, Dufferin to Salisbury, 20 April 1892; *Journal des Débats,* 18 April 1892.
121 *Journal des Débats,* 22 April 1892.
122 FO84/2208, Phipps to Salisbury, 22 April 1892, Africa no. 88, minutes by R.V.L. Earlier Ribot had asked for British enforcement of the Brussels Act. Dufferin to Salisbury, 16 April 1892, Africa no. 79 (encl. Hanotaux to Phipps, 14 April 1892; Dufferin to Salisbury, Africa no. 73.
123 *Le Temps,* 1 May 1892; FO84/2208, Dufferin to Salisbury, 1 May 1892, Africa no 95; 4 May 1892, Africa no. 97.
124 Papiers Ballot, MI 185/4, Rapport: Mission au Dekamé; A.C.M., BB4/1992, Dodds to marine, June 1892.
125 Capt. Jacquot, "Mon Journal de Marche au Dahomey 1892–1893" (unpublished), 31 Aug. 1892. This journal is in my possession, as is the log book kept by Capt. Jacquot during the expedition. I got these through Mlle. Germaine Ganier of Versailles.
126 SOM-AN Dahomey V, 6, c, Cavaignac to rear admiral, 30 May 1892.
127 Foa, *Le Dahomey,* pp. 392–407; SOM-AN Dahomey V, 6, a, Rapport sur les opérations du Corps expéditionnaire du Dahomey en 1892, par A. Dodds.
128 SOM-AN Dahomey V, 5, b, Béhanzin to Dodds, 10 June 1892 (copy); Dodds to Béhanzin, 20 June 1892 (copy).
129 SOM-AN Dahomey V, 6, b, Extract du Journal des Marches et Opérations du Corps expéditionnaire du Bénin du 29 mai au 26 juin 1892, par Commandant Gonard; Journal des Marches et Opérations . . . du 29 juin au 4 aout 1892 inclus, par Gonard.
130 A.C.M., BB4/1992, Dodds to Marine, July 1892.

131 Ibid., Marine to Dodds, July 1892 (draft); Jacquot, "De Geryville à Oran," in "Mon Journal," Twenty-two officers, including Commandant Faurax, and Captains Jacquot, Demartinecourt, and Jouvelet, went with over 150 men to form new units. In addition, there were several officers and men of the cavalry who were included in the reinforcements. These were to join two squadrons of Senegalese *spahis* for active service in Dahomey. A.C.M., BB4/1991, Marine to Cargeurs Reunis, July 1892 (draft); Marine to gov. of Senegal, July 1892 (draft).

132 *J.O. Chambre Débats,* 8 April 1892, p. 496.

133 SOM-AN Dahomey V, 6, a, Rapport sur les opérations du corps expéditionnaire du Dahomey en 1892, par A. Dodds (this is a 77-page manuscript in seven chapters); V, 6, b, Journal des Marches et Opérations du Corps expéditionnaire du Bénin du 29 juin au 4 aout (1892) inclus, par Commandant Gonard.

134 There are several accounts of the Dahomey war, mostly personal memoirs (which are not free from errors) published in French. See Aublet, *La Guerre au Dahomey*; Capt. Fonssagrives, *Au Dahomey: Souvenir des campagnes de 1892–1893* (Paris, 1894); Jules Poirier, *Campagne du Dahomey 1892–1894* (Paris, 1895); Morienval, *La Guerre du Dahomey*; Grandin, *Le Dahomey,* vol. 2.

135 Jacquot, "Mon Journal," 30 Sept. 1892, p. 34.

136 SOM-AN Dahomey V, 6, a, Rapport sur les opérations du corps expéditionnaire du Dahomey en 1892, par A. Dodds.

137 SOM-AN Dahomey V, 6, b, Dossier Fésigny: Rélations des opérations au Dahomey, fuilles numérotés de 1 a 19. The gunboats were *L'Opale, Le Corail, Le Topaze, L'Emeraude,* and the *Ambre. Le Corail* was formerly known as *L'Eclaireur.* There were also 200 canoes for the expedition.

138 Foa, *Le Dahomey,* p. 393. It was supposed that Chief Kékédé was either going to join Béhanzin or fleeing into Lagos territory.

139 The disembarkation of the horses was a cardinal problem.

140 A.C.M., BB4/1992, Dodds to Marine, 19 Sept. 1892 (tel.).

141 Jacquot, "Mon Journal," 19 Sept. 1892, p. 28.

142 Ibid., p. 29. French losses were severe. Commandant Faurax, Lieut. Badaire, and three European soldiers were killed, among others, and 27 were seriously wounded.

143 Jacquot, p. 30.

144 The garrison at Porto Novo comprised "des malingres des différents corps et d'une compagnie haoussas en formation" (ibid.).

145 Notes de Service: 2eme Compagnie, note circulaire, 1 Oct. 1892, par Gonard; note de service, no. 666, 30 Sept. 1892, par Dodds; note de service, 2 Oct. 1892, par Dodds (Gbede rive droite). This Notes de Service, a log book of the expedition, is in my possession.

146 A.C.M., BB4/1992, Ordre General, no. 63, par Dodds, 18 Oct. 1892; SOM-AN Dahomey V, 6, c, Rapport sommaire sur le service de l'Artillerie: Expedition du Dahomey, par Capt. H. Delestre, 4 April 1893.

147 De Riols, *La Guerre du Dahomey,* p. 77, cited in Cornevin, *Histoire du Dahomey.* The three Germans were Schultze, Püch, and Weckel; the Belgian was Anglis.

148 Jacquot, "Mon Journal," p. 34: "Tout-à-coup, jaillit de l'obscurité une vive lueur rouge partie de la rive droite du fleuve, à 1,500 mètres environ du bivouac, puis

une violente détonation se fait entendre en meme temps que le ronflement significatif d'un obus qui passe par-dessus nos têtes et va éclater avec fracas dans le bois voisin; l'artillérie dahoméene nous adresse ainsi une douzaine de projectiles et se tait."

149 A.C.M., BB4/1992, Rapport, par Dodds.
150 Note de service, 27 Oct. 1892, par Dodds; Jacquot, p. 57.
151 Dodds to Marine, 27 Oct. 1892, quoted in Foa, *Le Dahomey,* p. 399.
152 Jacquot, 23 October 1892, p. 56.
153 SOM-AN Dahomey V, 6, a, Rapport, par Dodds; A.C.M., BB4/1992, Dodds to Marine, 23 Oct. 1892 (tel.); Jacquot, 25 Oct. 1892, p. 57.
154 SOM-AN Dahomey V, 2, b, "Note sur le Dahomey," par E. Chautard, former catholic missionary in Dahomey. The major battles fought on the way to Cana were those of Kotopa, Koto, Ouakon, and Diokoue. SOM-AN Dahomey V, 6, c, Rapport: Service de l'Artillérie: Expédition du Dahomey, par Capt. Delestre, 4 April 1893.
155 Jacquot, 25 October 1892.
156 A.C.M., BB4/1992, Dodds to Marine, 6 Nov. 1892 (tel.).
157 A.C.M., BB4/1991, Marine to Dodds, 9 Nov. 1892; *Journal Officiel*: Etablissements et Protectorat Français du Golfe de Bénin, 1 Dec. 1892.
158 These terms were imposed by Dodds and not proffered by Béhanzin, as Cornevin believes (*Histoire du Dahomey,* p. 351). See A.C.M., BB4/1992, Dodds to Marine, 8 Nov. 1892; Dunglas, "Moyen-Dahomey," p. 83; Foa, *Le Dahomey,* p. 400.
159 The terms that needed to be met were the delivery of the arms, payment of half of the indemnity of 15 million francs, and the surrender of three hostages.
160 A.C.M., BB4/1992, Dodds to Marine, 16 Nov. 1892.
161 Notes de service, 15, 16, and 17 Nov. 1892, par Dodds.
162 SOM-AN Dahomey V, 6, a, Rapport sur les opérations du corps expéditionnaire du Dahomey en 1892, par Dodds.
163 Capt. Edouard Martinecourt, "Journal de Marche au Dahomey (1892)" (unpublished). This journal was discovered during my research in Paris. Capt. Martinecourt was an officer in the expeditionary corps. He was in charge of the second group and was in the état-major of the expedition. His journal is now in the possession of Mlle. G. Ganier of Versailles.
164 M.A.E., Afrique 127, Marine to Ribot, 17 Feb. 1893 (encl. proclamation, 18 Nov. 1892); A.C.M., BB4/1992, Dodds to Marine, 18 Nov. 1892, proclamation.
165 A.C.M., BB4/1992, Dodds to Marine, 3 Dec. 1892, déclaration; "Correspondance du Dahomey: Prise d'Abomey et Occupation générale du pays," in *R.F.E.C.,* vol. 17, no. 158, 15 Jan. 1893, pp. 73–77.
166 A.C.M., BB4/1992, Dodds to Marine, 9 Dec. 1892 (tel.).
167 Ibid., Gen. Dodds to Marine, 15 and 16 Dec. 1892.
168 SOM-AN Dahomey V, 6, b, Journal des Marches et Opérations . . . 1er à 31 Dec. 1892, par Gonard. Allada was occupied on 2 January 1893.
169 A.C.M., BB4/1992, Dodds to Marine, 15 Dec. 1892, Rapport Dodds.
170 Ibid., Gen. Dodds to Marine, 8 Feb. 1892, Rapport politique. Lieutenant Colonel Lambinet was the interim head of the French forces in Dahomey while General Dodds was on leave. A.C.M., BB4/1991, Marine to Dodds, 27 Nov. 1892 (tel.).

171 SOM-AN Dahomey V, 8, a, Lambinet to Marine, 29 April 1893. The details of the negotiations are contained in this dossier marked "Négotiations avec Béhanzin."
172 A.C.M., BB4/1991, Marine to Lambinet, May 1893 (draft).
173 Cornevin, *Histoire du Dahomey,* p. 349. The king of Dahomey was forbidden to see the sea. Therefore Béhanzin would not go to Whydah to negotiate in person with French officials. SOM-AN Dahomey V, 8, b, rapport Lambinet.
174 *Bulletin du Comité de l'Afrique Français,* hereafter *B.C.A.F.* (April 1893), p. 6, quoted in Cornevin, *Histoire du Dahomey,* p. 349.
175 Poirier, *Campagne du Dahomey,* pp. 245–49. They stayed at the Northwestern Hotel in Liverpool. M.A.E., Afrique 131, Phipps to Hanotaux, 14 June 1893. Jean Bayol charged that Henry Dosciovo Kagadu was the agent of Governor G. Carter of Lagos at the court of Abomey. See Bayol's article in *Le Temps,* 26 March 1893.
176 *R.F.E.C.,* vol. 18, no. 178 (15 Nov. 1893), pp. 472–74.
177 *J.O. Chambre Débats,* 7 July 1893, p. 2049; 21 July 1893, p. 2228; *Documents Parlementaires: Chambre des Députés 1893,* annexe nos. 2924, 2963, 3009.
178 "Dahomey: Nouvelle Expédition," in *R.F.E.C.,* vol. 18, no. 178 (15 Nov. 1893), p. 472.
179 SOM-AN Dahomey V, 11, b, letter to President Carnot, 17 Nov. 1893; Poirier, *Campagne du Dahomey,* pp. 248–49. Henry Dosso (alias Henry Dosciovo Kagadu) was a Yoruba journalist and had special ties with Béhanzin. See Paul Hazoume, *Le Past du Sang au Dahomey* (Paris, 1937), p. 33.
180 "Rapport Dodds," in *B.C.A.F.* (August 1893), p. 8.
181 *Journal Officiel*: Documents Parlementaires: Chambre 1893, Rapport Chautemps, annexe no. 2553, 28 Jan. 1893; *J.O. Chambre Débats,* 29 March 1893, pp. 1125–28. Theophile Delcassé asserted this view in the Chambre des Députés: "J'affirme enfin que le Gouvernement, qui a donné sa confiance au général Dodds, l'a laisse entièrement libre et maître absolu de son action." Declassé was the sous-secrétaire d'état des colonies at this time (p. 1127).
182 *J.O. Chambre Débats,* 21 July 1893, p. 2228.
183 A.C.M., BB4/1992, Dodds to Marine, 28 Feb. 1893.
184 The sum of 6,236,000 francs asked for was in addition to the 900,000 francs and 3,000,000 francs already voted in April 1892. *J.O.*: Documents Parlementaires: Chambre 1893, "Rapport Chautemps," annexe no. 2552, 28 January 1893.
185 *J.O. Chambre Débats,* 29 March 1893. This was the interpellation by Le Herissé and Montfort on 28 March 1893 (pp. 1125–51).
186 By the end of the campaign in December 1892, 173 Europeans and 32 Africans had died of disease. SOM-AN Dahomey V, 6, a, Rapport Dodds.
187 *J.O. Chambre Débats,* 29 March 1893, pp. 1128–29, 1129–31. The *ordre du jour* was adopted by 312 to 184.
188 De Launay must have been influenced by Capt. E. Peroz's "Le Soudan Français," in *La Nouvelle Revue* 62 (1890): 766–68, and "Le Répeuplement du Soudan Français et l'Esclavage," in *La Nouvelle Revue* 63 (March–April 1890): 380–85. Peroz argued that tropical Sudan was not a colony of settlement and that long years of wars of expansion had destroyed its population.
189 *J.O. Chambre Débats,* 5 April 1893, pp. 407–09.

190 Neither the fall of the Ribot Cabinets (1st and 2nd) nor the movement of the Colonial Department from one ministry to the other affected the Dahomey affair adversely. See André Daniel, *L'Année Politique 1893* (Paris, 1894); I. Chessé, "Pérégrination du Départment des Colonies," in *La Nouvelle Revue* 80 (Jan.-Feb. 1893): 614-18. Chessé was alarmed at the overgrowth of the Colonial Department, with an annual budget of 511,131 francs and 127 civil servants.
191 *J.O. Chambre Débats,* 7, 21, and 12 July 1893.
192 Also, Béhanzin's continuance in office and his possession of the seaboard with his own ports would raise serious problems in the application of the General Act of the Brussels Conference (1890).
193 SOM-AN Dahomey V, 8, b, Rapport Lambinet; V, 8, c, Journal de Marche.
194 A.C.M., BB4/1992, Dodds to Marine, 20 and 28 Feb. 1893; BB4/1991, Marine to Dodds, 19 Feb. 1893; Delcassé to Dodds, 22 Feb. 1893.
195 SOM-AN Dahomey V, 10, a, Rapport Général Dodds: Campagne de 1893-1894. The operations commenced in September, with Comdt. Drude in the Dogba region and Chmitelin in the Abomey district—not on 12 October, as Cornevin points out in *Histoire du Dahomey*.
196 SOM-AN Dahomey V, 10, b, Journal de Marche: Campagne de 1893-1894; V, 11, b, Dodds to marine, 4 Nov. 1893 (copy).
197 Ibid., V, 10, a, Rapport Dodds.
198 Foa, Le Dahomey, p. 406.
199 Cornevin "Les Divers épisodes," p. 196.
200 A.C.M., BB4/1991, Marine to Dodds, 27 Nov. 1892 (tel.); Marine to Ribot, 1 March 1893.
201 A.C.M., BB4/1992, Dodds to Marine, 15 Dec. 1892.
202 See R. F. Betts, *Assimilation and Association in French Colonial Theory, 1890-1914* (New York, 1961).
203 René Maunier, *The Sociology of Colonies: An Introduction to the Study of Race Contact,* trans. E. O. Lorimer, 2 vols. (London, 1949), 1:37-43, 271-340.
204 Edmond About, *Le Dixneuvième Siècle* (Paris, 1890), p. 349; A. Burdeau, *L'Algérie en 1891* (Paris, 1892). See also O. Manoni, *La Psychologie de la Colonisation* (Paris, 1950); Anon., *Le Régime des Protectorats,* 2 vols. (Paris, 1889-99).
205 A.C.M., BB4/1992, Dodds to Marine, 10 Feb. 1894. Dodds opposed direct rule and supported the dismemberment of the old kingdom in order to bring about a quick dislocation of the authority of Abomey.
206 Ibid., 5 Jan. 1894, déclaration; *Journal Officiel*: Etablissements et Protectorat Français du Golfe de Bénin, 1 Feb. 1894, pp. 1-2.
207 SOM-AN Dahomey V, 10, a, Campagne de 1893-1894: Rapport Dodds.
208 The candidature of Prince Ayidama is said to have been supported by Gen. Dodds' interpreter. Cornevin, "Les divers épisodes," p. 200.
209 Paul Hazoume, *Pact du sang,* pp. 36-38.
210 Le Herissé, *l'Ancien Royaume du Dahomey,* p. 351; Adande, *Les Récades des Rois du Dahomey* (Dakar, 1962), p. 9. Béhanzin's surviving brother, Sagbadjou Gléglé, was interviewed by Adande.

211 General Dodds paid tribute to the fighting qualities of Dahomeans, especially their courage, tenacity, and audacity in action. The two leaders had mutual respect for each other. SOM-AN Dahomey V, 6, a, Rapport Dodds (1892).
212 A.C.M., BB4/1992, Dodds to Marine, 15 Jan. 1894; *Journal Officiel*: Etablissements et Protectorat Français du Golfe du Bénin, 1 Feb. 1894, p. 1.
213 Ibid., 15 Feb. 1894, p. 2.
214 "Ago, li agbo! Allada klen afo, ma dja yi o, Frantse, we gni mon [Listen Abomey! The dynasty of Allada stumbled, but thanks to France, it has not fallen]." His name, Agoli Agbo, was coined from the first words of this sentence (Cornevin, "Les divers épisodes," p. 201).
215 Ibid., pp. 201-02.
216 A.C.M., BB4/1992, Dodds to Marine, 26 Jan. 1894; SOM-AN Dahomey V, 11, c, Dodds to Marine, 26 Jan. 1894 (copy); Lieutenant Rittenard, "La capture de Béhanzin," in *Bulletin Militaire d'Information du Dahomey*; G. Riole, "Béhanzin," in *Bulletin du Comité de l'Afrique Français* 2 (1891): 193-96; *Revue du Dahomey et Dépendances*, nos. 8-9 (Aug.–Sept. 1901), "Béhanzin," by J.L.B.
217 This was the treaty of 29 January 1893, which was later given official approbation in Paris. A.C.M., BB4/1991, Marine to Dodds, 19 April 1894.
218 Newbury, "Abomey Protectorate," vol. 29, no. 2 (April 1959), pp. 146-54.
219 A.C.M., BB4/1992, Dodds to Marine, 12 and 15 April 1894.
220 A. L. D'Albeca, a former administrator in Dahomey, opposed the restoration of the Abomey dynasty. See "Le Dahomey en 1894," in *Bulletin de la Société de Géographie de Paris* 16 (1895): 183-210.
221 General Dodds praised Victor Ballot as "an absolutely devoted auxiliary, a sure adviser, and one with an infinitely precious experience" (*J.O. Chambre Débats*, 5 April 1893, p. 409).
222 M.A.E., Afrique 127, Rapport Politique, 8 Feb. 1893, by Dodds. Minutes: "On pourrait trouver des agents dans le personnel des Consulats des Chancelliers."
223 SOM-AN Dahomey V, 8, b, Rapport Dumas; V, 11, d, Rapport Dumas, 21 June 1894; A.C.M., BB4/1992, Dumas to Marine, 21 July 1894.
224 *Journal Officiel*: Documents Parlementaires: Chambre 1893, annexe no. 2553 (28 Jan. 1893), "Rapport fai au nom de la Commission du Budget chargée d'éxaminer le projet de loi portant ouverture au Ministre du Commerce, de l'Industrie et des Colonies, sur l'exercice 1892 de crédits supplémentaires s'élevant à 6,236,000 francs pour frais d'occupation du Dahomey," par M. Chautemps.
225 "Dahomey: Dépenses," in *R.F.E.C.*, Vol. 17, no. 158 (15 Jan. 1893), p. 86; A. Salaignac, "Les Expéditions Anglaises contre les Ashantis," in ibid., vol. 11, no. 93 (1 May 1890), pp. 513-22.
226 These figures are extracted from SOM-AN Dahomey IX, Budget Local et finances, and from Compte Définitif des Dépenses (1890-1894). The credits for 1893 were taken from *Journal Officiel*: Débats (1893).
227 SOM-AN Dahomey V, 10, a, Campagne de 1893-1894: Rapport, by Dodds; Foa, *Le Dahomey*, p. 401. By 1 December 1892, 225 Europeans had died in the campaign and 195 were wounded.
228 Eugene Etienne, *Les Compagnies de Colonisation* (Paris, 1897), pp. 9-10. See *Journal Officiel*: Débats (11 May 1890) on Etienne's speech and the mixed reaction to his *perpendiculaire*: "une perpendiculaire qui tirée de la limite orientale

de la Tunisie et absisée par le lac Tchad jusqu'au Congo, devait constituer la frontière intérieure de l'Afrique occidentale française." See also Jean Dybowski, *La Route du Chad* (Paris, 1893).

229 M.A.E., Afrique 127, Jamais to Ribot, 2 December 1892, minutes by M.A.E.: "Mais cet 'hinterland' est-il suffisamment pacifié à l'heure actuelle pour y risquer un homme ou faire aller la M. Binger?"

230 D. Kaltbrunner, "Les Anglais au Niger," in *R.F.E.C.,* vol. 8, no. 56 (15 Oct. 1888), pp. 462–71, 470.

231 Gaston Chaballier, "La Conquête du Dahomé: ses origines ses résultats," in *Revue des Colonies et des Pays de Protectorat,* no. 6 (Sept. 1895), pp. 511–15; no. 7 (Oct. 1895), pp. 619–22.

232 See Père Joseph Etterle, *Les Maladies de l'Afrique Tropicale* (Brussels, 1892). Note the reports of the doctors in the expedition cited above.

233 Lambinet, *Notice géographique*; extract from the *Rev. Maritime et Coloniale* (Oct. 1893); Nicholas, *L'Expédition du Dahomey.*

234 See Paul Gouzien, *Notice sur le Dahomey,* Office Colonial (Paris, 1899); G. Reste, *Le Dahomey: Réalisations et perspectives d'avenir* (Paris, 1934); H. Adolphe Lara and Ouanilo Béhanzin, *Pour Béhanzin* (Lyon, 1905).

CHAPTER 5

1 Paul Barré, "L'Afrique: les seize traversées," in *La Revue Française,* vol. 11, no. 85 (1 Sept. 1890), pp. 13–14. Barré surveys the history of trans-African exploration from Honorato de Costa (1802–11) to Captain Trivier (1888–89).

2 K.F., "England contra Portugal," in *D.K.Z.* (18 Jan. 1890), pp. 25–26; P.R.O. Cab. 37/26, nos. 19–20, Anglo-Portuguese Colonial differences, by F.O., 19 and 20 March 1890; G. de Wailly "Aux rives du Zambese," in *Nouvelle Revue* 62 (1890): 391–94.

3 Vindex, *Cecil Rhodes* (London, 1900), p. 650. This could apply to west Africa.

4 Compte Rochaid Dahdah, "Commerce Extérieur et Politique Etrangère," in *R.F.E.C.,* vol. 11, no. 90 (15 March 1890), pp. 340–49; "Commerce Extérieur de l'Allemagne et de l'Angleterre," in *R.F.E.C.,* vol. 7, no. 48 (1 May 1888), pp. 582–83. Here it was argued that British trade was holding its own and was not being supplanted by German trade.

5 SOM-AN Afrique II, 3 Missions Binger, 1886–90; Treich-Laplène, 1888–90; L. G. Binger, *Du Niger au Golfe de Guinée par le pays de Kong et le Mossi 1887–1889* (Paris, 1892), 2 vols. G. Valbert "La voyage du Capt. Binger dans la Boucle du Niger" in *Revue des Deux Mondes* (hereafter *R.D.M.*) (1 Feb. 1890), pp. 660–71.

6 Dr. Crozat, "Rapport sur une mission au Mossi, 1890," in *Journal Officiel,* 5 and 9 Oct. 1891, pp. 4820, 4850; G. Valbert, "Deux Missions Françaises dans la Boucle du Niger," in *R.D.M.* (1 Oct. 1891), pp. 684–95.

7 P. von François, "Riese zu Salaga und zu Mossi," in *Mitheilungen von Forschungsriesenden und Gelehrten aus den Deutschen Schutzgebieten* (1888); "Les Allemands dans l'Afrique Occidentale: Exploration de C. von Francois," in *R.F.E.C.,* vol. 9, no. 72 (15 June 1889), pp. 733 ff.

8 P. Leroy-Beaulieu, *De la Colonisation chez les peuples modernes* (Paris, 1874);

C. Pety de Thosée, *Théories de la Colonisation au XIXe siècle et role de l'état dans le développement des colonies* (Bruxelles, 1901–02); A. Murphy, *The Ideology of French Imperialism 1871–1881* (Washington, D.C., 1948); A. P. Thornton, *Doctrines of Imperialism* (New York, 1965); L. Deschamps, *Histoire de la question Coloniale en France* (Paris, 1891).

9 Edouard Marbeau, "Partage Politique de l'Afrique," in *R.F.E.C.*, vol. 8, no. 54 (15 Sept. 1888), pp. 321–29; "Le Commerce français sur la Cote occidentale d'Afrique," in *Rev. Maritime et Coloniale* 78 (1883): 591; M.A.E., Afrique 125, Etienne to Ribot, 3 Oct. 1890 (encl. Rapport Octave Pean, resident *par interim* de la Côte d'Or).

10 Etienne to Muzet, 11 Oct. 1887, in *Bulletin Officiel de l'Administration des Colonies* (1887), pp. 775–78.

11 M.A.E., Afrique 125, Rapport politique, par d'Albeca, 1 Nov. 1889; Afrique 86, Rapport, par Consul de Lecca, 7 Jan. 1885, quoted in C. W. Newbury, "The Development of French Policy on the Lower and Upper Niger 1880–1898," in *Journal of Modern History* (Chicago), vol. 31, no. 1 (March 1959), pp. 16–26.

12 Faidherbe, "La Question du Niger," pp. 65–68; *Le Matin,* 13 June 1885, letter by E. Viard; Roland Malric, "Les Idées de Faidherbe en vue de la découverte des voies d'accès et de pénétration au Soudan," in *Mem. Ecole Nationale de la France d'Outre-Mer* (année scholaire 1936–37).

13 M.A.E., Papiers Ribot, vol. 3, Waddington to Ribot, 11 Aug. 1890; SOM-AN Conseil Supérieur des Colonies, vol. 1, Rapport sur les Compagnies a Charte Anglais, par M. Waddington, ambassadeur de France à Londres, Waddington to Ribot, 1 May 1890.

14 Etienne to Muzet, 22 Sept. 1887, in *Bulletin Officiel de l'Administration des Colonies* (1887), pp. 661–64. Muzet was president of the Delegation Permanente des Chambres Syndicales de France and also of the Paris Chamber of Commerce. Etienne decided to use him to reach the business community of France and to use his services to generate interest in colonization in commercial circles.

15 Ibid. Etienne divided French colonies into three groups: colonies of exploitation (Indo China, Cochin China, Cambodge, Annam, Tonkin, Senegal, and all west African possessions), ancient colonies (West Indies), and colonies of settlement (Tahiti, New Caledonia, Guyane, Algeria).

16 Ibid., pp. 662–63.

17 FO84/2027, Elliot to Salisbury, Africa no. 3, 8 Jan. 1890.

18 Etienne, *Les Compagnies de Colonisation,* p. 9; M.A.E., Afrique 123, Etienne to M.A.E., 18 June 1890.

19 Boissy d'Anglas reacted violently to Etienne's plan. Francis Charmes addressed a remonstrance to Etienne the next day in the *Journal des Débats* (11 May 1890). See also Francis Charmes, *Etudes Historiques et Diplomatiques* (Paris, 1893).

20 H. Brunschwig, "Le Parti Colonial Francais," in *Revue Français d'Histoire d'Outre-Mer,* vol. 46, no. 1 (1959), pp. 49–83.

21 SOM-AN *Conseil Supérieur des Colonies,* Généralité 31, *Organisation et Composition des Conseil Supérieur des Colonies* (Paris, 1890), Rapport du Président de la République, 29 May 1890, par Jules Roche, pp. 3–9. The council was now divided into four specialized sections.

22 *Bulletin du Comité d'Afrique Française,* Jan. 1891. The aims of the committee were defined on 18 Nov. 1890.
23 Harry Alis (Hippolyte Percher), *A La Conquête du Chad* (Paris, 1891); Dybowski, *La Route du Chad.*
24 John A. Seeley, *The Expansion of England* (London, 1883), p. 10.
25 M.A.E., Papiers Waddington, vol. 4, Memoranda et Rapports 1878–92, fol. 158, "Projet de Déclaration à échanger." By the treaty of 10 March 1862, France and Britain jointly guaranteed the independence of Zanzibar.
26 Ibid., vol. 5, Ribot to Waddington, 25 June 1890. "M. Francois Deloncle desires immediately to parade his diplomatic knowledge," Ribot confided to Waddington.
27 M.A.E., Papiers Waddington, vol. 5, Ribot to Waddington, 28 June 1890; C.P. Angleterre 850, Waddington to Ribot, 22 June 1890.
28 Ibid., Ribot to Waddington, 30 June 1891: "Je ne m'attendais pas à cette explosion de mauvaise humeur qui a éclaté à propos de l'acte de Bruxelles et de 'droit de visite.' . . . C'est à l'Angleterre qu'elle avait le parti-pris de faire sentir sa mauvaise humeur."
29 *La République Française,* 10 July 1890; *Le Siècle,* 10 July 1890; M.A.E., Papiers Waddington, vol. 5, Ribot to Waddington, 2 July 1890. Ribot said that a former minister of foreign affairs was among those who inspired the antigovernment press campaign in Paris.
30 Edouard Marbeau, "M. Ribot et l'Afrique," in *R.F.E.C.,* vol. 12, no. 99 (1 Aug. 1890), pp. 130: "MM. Waddington et Herbette était représentés dans les journaux populaires pendus à une potence et un bandeau sur les yeux pendant que l'Allemagne et l'Angleterre dévoraient le gateau africain. . . . A quoi bon payer des ambassadeurs qui nous laissent rouler?"
31 Ibid., pp. 129–31. The press was unaware of the efforts of both the ambassadors and the foreign minister to obtain satisfaction from Britain.
32 M.A.E., Papiers Waddington, vol. 5, Ribot to Waddington, 25 June 1890.
33 Ibid., 2 July 1890.
34 M.A.E., Papiers Ribot, vol. 3, Waddington to Ribot, 1 July 1890.
35 M.A.E., Papiers Waddington, vol. 5, Ribot to Waddington, 2 July 1890. It is important to note that Ribot measured British interests in Tunisia in purely economic terms, i.e., in terms of the volume of British trade there.
36 Ibid., 19 July 1890. The editor of *Le Temps* claimed that he got his news from London. Papiers Ribot, vol. 3, Waddington to Ribot, 9, 11, and 13 July 1890.
37 M.A.E., Papiers Ribot, vol. 3, D'Estournelles to Ribot.
38 Ibid., Waddington to Ribot, 13 July 1890; Ribot to Waddington (confidentiel et particulier, à chiffrer), 20 July 1890.
39 Ibid., Waddington to Ribot, 23 July 1890; Ribot to Waddington, 26 July 1890; Salisbury Papers, A/59, memo by Waddington, July 1890.
40 FO84/2029, F.O. to Lytton, 24 July 1890, Africa no. 5 (tel.); Goldie to Anderson, 25 July 1890.
41 Salisbury Papers, A/59, Salisbury to Egerton, 10 Aug. 1890; Lady G. Cecil, *Life of Robert, Marquis of Salisbury,* 4 vols. (London, 1921–32), 4:320.
42 Salisbury Papers, A/58, Lytton to Salisbury, 24 July 1890.
43 Flint, *Sir George Goldie,* pp. 165–67.

44 M.A.E., Papiers Ribot, vol. 3, Waddington to Ribot, 26 and 31 July 1890; Papiers Waddington, vol. 4, "Memo by Waddington: Bases d'un arrangement intervenu entre le Gouvernement de la République Française et le Gouvernement de S. M. Britannique" 28 July 1890.
45 M.A.E., Papiers Waddington, vol. 4, Ribot to Waddington, 1 Aug. 1890 (personnel et chiffrée): "Il nous est *impossible* d'admettre la dernière rédaction." Ribot warned Waddington not to show this letter to Salisbury.
46 Ibid., vol. 5, Salisbury to Waddington, 2 Aug. 1890.
47 Ibid., 4 Aug. 1890; vol. 4, "Déclaration à échanger," fol. 9; "Notes pour entréntien avec Lord S," "Questions rélatives à l'établissement du protectorat anglais à Zanzibar," W[addington], fols. 172–84. See also FO403/167 for correspondence on these negotiations, especially those between the F.O. and Lytton in 1890.
48 Ibid., vol. 4, fol. 165: "A line so drawn from Say to Barruwa on Lake Chad, as to include in the zone of the Niger Cy. all that fairly belongs to the Kingdom of Sokoto, to be determined by the Commission."
49 M.A.E., Documents Diplomatiques, *Afrique: Arrangements, Actes, et Conventions concernant le Nord, l'Ouest et le centre de d'Afrique, 1881–1898,* no. 25 (Paris, 1898), pp. 211–13; M.A.E., Afrique 129, Declaration Franco-Anglais de 5 aout 1890; Parl. Papers, Africa no. 9 (1890), C. 6130, Declarations exchanged between the Governments of Her Britannic Majesty and the Government of the French Republic with respect to Territories in Africa, Aug. 5, 1890.
50 Parl. Papers, Africa no. 9 (1890), C. 6130, p. 3.
51 The contention of J. E. Flint that "as for Lake Chad, it was an unknown quantity" is not valid. Certainly this was not true of Lake Chad in 1890. In 1823 Walter Oudney, Hugh Clapperton, and Dixon Denham visited it, the first Europeans to do so in the 19th century. They called it Waterloo. In 1850 James Richardson, Heinrich Barth, and Adolf Overweg reached Lake Chad via Tripoli. Overweg was the first European to navigate it in 1851. Then came Edward Vogel (1855) and Gustav Nachtigal (1870). Nachtigal investigated its hydrography in detail. See "Chad" Lake, in *Encyclopaedia Britannica* 5 (London, 1957): 185.
52 Flint, *Sir George Goldie,* pp. 163–67.
53 M.A.E., Papiers Ribot, vol. 3, Waddington to Ribot, 11 Aug. 1890.
54 Ibid., Ribot to Waddington (tel.), quoted in Waddington to Ribot, 11 Aug. 1890.
55 Cecil, *Robert, Marquis of Salisbury* 4:324.
56 Salisbury Papers, A/59, Waddington to Salisbury, 13 Aug. 1890. Waddington's fear of French public opinion was not unfounded. See E. M. Caroll, *French Public Opinion and Foreign Affairs 1870–1914* (New York, 1931); J. E. Howard, *Parliament and Foreign Policy in France . . . during the Third Republic* (London, 1948).
57 SOM-AN Afrique III, 21, a, *Journal Officiel,* 8 June 1894, interpellation of Etienne, Deloncle, and others on the policy of the French government in Africa, p. 931.
58 Lieut. Monteil had rendered distinguished service during his exploration mission in the Upper Senegal in June 1885. See Archives Nationale, Papiers du Colonel Monteil, 66AP/1, Journal d'une Mission topographique dans le Haut-Sénégal,

Feb.–June 1885; 66AP/12, "Quelques lignes sur le caractère de l'homme Monteil," par Madame Monteil.
59 Ibid., 66AP/4, Etienne to Monteil, 15 Sept. 1890, instructions.
60 SOM-AN Afrique VI, 106, a, Monteil to Colonies, 20 Oct. 1890, 15 Jan. 1891, 10 April 1891, "Note du Ct. Monteil sur son voyage jusqu'à Kano" (Kano, Haussa, 6 Jan. 1892); Papiers Monteil, 66AP/2, Journal de Marche de la Mission Monteil au Centre d'Afrique Oct. 1890–24 Sept. 1891. Monteil collected treaties from the rulers of San (14 Jan. 1891), Bobo Dioulasso (20 March 1891), Dafina Lamfiera (3 April 1891), Liptako (23 May 1891), Yagha (16 June 1891), Ouoro Gueladjio (12 Aug. 1891), and Say (24 Aug. 1891). See *Bull. Officiel: Min. des Colonies* 9 (1895): 431 for the ratification of these treaties.
61 SOM-AN Afrique VI, 106, a, Monteil to Colonies, 6 Jan. 1892.
62 Papiers Monteil, 66AP/2, Journal de Marche de la Mission Monteil au Centre d'Afrique 25 Sept. 1891–3 Dec. 1892. The treaty with Sokoto is dated 27 Oct. 1891.
63 Ibid.; see map #2. "Mission Monteil," in *Le Temps,* 24 April 1892; FO84/2208, Phipps to Salisbury, 24 April 1892, Africa no. 91.
64 Papiers Monteil, 66AP/13, press cuttings on Monteil's mission of 1890–92. The Société de Géographie de Lyon established a gold medal award in honor of Monteil. See *Bulletin de la Société de l'Afrique Centrale de Constantine,* May 1893, p. 11.
65 SOM-AN Afrique VI, 106, a, Monteil to Delcassé, 8 April 1893; Delcassé to Develle, 2 May 1893 (draft); M.A.E. to Delcassé, 17 May 1893; Delcassé to M.A.E., 8 June 1893.
66 Ibid., Rapport Monteil sur le trace de la ligne d'influence franco-anglaise en Afrique Centrale: Déclaration du 5 aout 1890, 7 April 1893, p. 4. This is a 24-page manuscript with map. Delcassé felt that Monteil should have a copy of it when he noted: "Le Ct. Monteil qui n'a pas garde copie de ce rapport serait heureux d'en avoir une. Urgent: copie pour Aff. Etr. et pour Ct. Monteil luimeme."
67 Ibid., pp. 5–10; L. Sevin-Desplaces, "La Mission Monteil et la Politique de la France en Afrique du Nord," in *La Nouvelle Revue* 81 (1893): 138–41; Vicomte Eugène-Melchior de Vogué, "L'Exploration du Commandant Monteil," in *R.D.M.* 115 (15 Feb. 1893): 926–41.
68 "Le Lieutenant-Colonel Monteil," in *L'Africaine,* March 1898, pp. 42–46. Monteil's Say-Barruwa exploration made him one of the greatest travelers of the century (p. 45).
69 SOM-AN Afrique VI, 106, a, Rapport Monteil, pp. 11–14.
70 It was to implement this recommendation that both Hourst and Toutée were sent out to the Niger without delay; see above.
71 SOM-AN Afrique VI, 106, a, Rapport Monteil, pp. 15–24. Monteil excused himself for using the German map by Kippert because it had the best scale for the type of work involved in his report. It must have jarred on his patriotic sentiments to use a German map! "L'Expédition du Commandant Monteil," in *L'Afrique Explorée et Civilisée,* vol. 14, no. 1 (Jan. 1893), pp. 22–31.
72 FO84/2028, Lytton to Salisbury, 6 and 12 Nov. 1890. Leon Tharel was chairman of the group that sponsored Mizon's mission, and president of the Société

d'Economie Industrielle of Paris. Louis Mizon, *Explorations en Afrique Centrale 1890–1893* (Paris, 1895).

73 SOM-AN Afrique VI, 82, a, M.A.E. to Colonies (encl. Waddington to M.A.E., 17 Dec. 1890; cutting from the *Times,* 17 Dec. 1890).

74 SOM-AN Afrique IV, 38, a, M.A.E. to Etienne, 24 Jan. 1891 (encl. Herbertte to M.A.E., 6 Jan. 1891); Etienne to M.A.E., 24 Jan. 1891. Etienne suggested that Brazza be informed at once about the German expedition.

75 *Le Siècle,* 7 Nov. 1890; "La Mission Mizon et le Compagnie du Niger," in *R.F.E.C.,* vol. 18, no. 175 (1 Oct. 1893), pp. 321–27.

76 SOM-AN Afrique III, 16, a, Rapport Mizon, 16 July 1892.

77 *Le Siècle,* 14 Nov. 1890, quoting *Tablettes des Deux Charentes; Le Figaro,* 29 Nov. 1890; *Journal des Débats,* 9 April 1891, 27 Dec. 1890. On the details of the Mizon affair see Hanotaux and Martineau, *Histoire des Colonies Françaises* 4:486–92; J. Chauveau, "Mizon à Yola," in *Rev. Hist. Col.,* vol. 41, no. 1 (1954), pp. 227–44; Flint, *Sir George Goldie,* pp. 168–86.

78 FO84/2096, Lytton to Salisbury, 29 Nov. 1890, minutes by Salisbury and Anderson; FO84/2164, Royal Niger Company (hereafter R.N.C.) to F.O., 9 May 1891.

79 See FO403/187 and FO403/200 for correspondence on Mizon; also Louis Mizon, *Une Question Africaine* (Paris, 1895), a 63-page apology.

80 "La Question du Bas-Niger," in *Rev. Colonies et Pays de Protectorat,* no. 6 (Sept. 1895), pp. 490–91; Louis Mizon, "Lettre ouverte à MM. les actionnaires de la Compagnie française de l'Afrique Centrale," in *La Politique Coloniale,* 24 Aug.–3 Sept. 1895; *Le Temps* (supplément special), 10 Aug. 1892, gives Mizon's own account of his first expedition to Yola.

81 Hanotaux and Martineau 4:447–53. Zubier had been a soldier in the Egyptian army. He attracted to himself a formidable force of fanatical followers, who commenced the conquest of the central Sudan by the time Crampel ran foul of them.

82 Louis Mizon, "Résultats scientifiques de ses voyages, 1890–1893," in *Bull. Soc. de Géog. de Paris* 16 (1895): 330–37.

83 "Un nouveau partage politique en Afrique Occidentale: Coalition Anglo-Allemande contre les Français," in *R.F.E.C.,* vol. 18, no. 175 (1 Oct. 1895), pp. 312–17.

84 SOM-AN Afrique VI, 98, c, Ribot to Jamais, 28 July 1892, 18 Aug. 1892 (encl. Waddington to Ribot, 6 Aug. 1892); Waddington to Salisbury, 10 Aug. 1892.

85 Ibid., colonies to Mizon, 2 Aug. 1892.

86 Jean-Paul-Pierre Casimir Périer, député, formed the cabinet which replaced the first Charles Dupuy Cabinet. He was foreign minister as well as president du conseil from 3 Dec. 1893 to 30 May 1894. Casimir Périer died on 11 March 1907.

87 M.A.E., Papiers Ribot, vol. 4, Expansion Coloniale Française, Hanotaux au Conseil, 26 Dec. 1893.

88 SOM-AN Afrique VI, 98, c, Mizon to Colonies, 18 Sept. 1892 (tel.).

89 Lord Aberdare was the chairman of the Royal Niger Company.

90 SOM-AN Afrique III, 16, a, Delcassé to Mizon, 27 June 1893.

91 Ibid., 4 July 1893.

92 M.A.E., Papiers Ribot, vol. 4, Casimir Périer to Ribot, 23 Dec. 1893.

93 Ibid., Ribot to Casimir Périer, 27 Dec. 1893. The correspondence with England on the Mizon mission is contained in SOM-AN Afrique VI, 106, g.
94 A. Channebot, "Le Problem Africain," in *La Nouvelle Revue* 83 (1893): 611–19; D. Kaltbrunner, "Une chemin de fer de Lagos au Niger," in *Bull. de la Société de Géog. Commerciale de Paris* 16 (1894): 114–16. The railway projected by Britain to run from Lagos to the Niger near Bussa and the one in Sierra Leone were seen as a danger, since the trade of the Niger bend would be drained by them for the benefit of the British alone.
95 M.A.E., Afrique 125, Etienne to M.A.E., "Note pour le Ministre des Affaires Etrangères," 19 June 1890. Etienne wrote this memorandum on Bonduku after a meeting of the council of ministers on the same day, at which Bonduku was discussed. Etienne to Ribot, 3 Oct. 1890 (encl. extract from Rapport Pean, resident par interim, Cote d'Or); M.A.E. to Etienne, 25 Oct. 1890 (draft); Lord Lytton to Ribot, 29 Oct. 1890.
96 On the making of the Ivory Coast see F. J. Clozel, "La Cote d'Ivoire: Notice Historique," in *Bull. Soc. de Géog. de Paris* 20 (1899): 249–78; Pierre Lyautey, *L'Empire Colonial Français* (Paris, 1931), pp. 3–34; Atger, *La France en Côte d'Ivoire*, pp. 173–77.
97 M.A.E., Afrique 125, Rapport Ménard, 5 Dec. 1890 (copy).
98 Ibid., 22 Dec. 1890 (copy).
99 Ibid., Lytton to Ribot, 29 Oct. 1890.
100 Antoinne Pillet, "La liberté de navigation du Niger," in *Revue Générale de Droit International Public* (March–April 1896).
101 M.A.E., Afrique 125, Lytton to Ribot, memorandum, 29 Oct. 1890.
102 Ibid., Ribot to Etienne, 6 Dec. 1890 (draft). Etienne's views and observations were sought on the points raised by Lord Lytton.
103 M.A.E., Afrique 127, Projet de mission Binger et Braulot, by Jamais; "Note sur le Bondoukou," 21 March 1891, by L. G. Binger. In this note Binger urged that compensations be made to Britain elsewhere in order to conserve Bondoukou for France. SOM-AN Afrique VI, 97, b, Ribot to Etienne, 22 Dec. 1891 (urgent), instructions from Binger; Ribot to Etienne, 20 Jan. 1892; translation of instructions to Capt. J. J. Lang, Meade to Lang, 11 Dec. 1891.
104 M.A.E., Afrique 127, Jamais to Ribot, 2 Dec. 1892 (encl. Rapport Binger, Dec. 1892).
105 FO84/2208, Capt. Lang to A. Hemming, 2 March 1892 (private).
106 Ibid., Phipps to Anderson, 22 April 1892 (private and confidential), minutes by Anderson and Salisbury; M.A.E., Afrique 130, Rapport Binger: Délimitation franco-anglais dans la Cote d'Or (1892). The conflict between Binger and Lang is dealt with here.
107 Gen. Duboc, *L'Epopée Coloniale,* p. 139; Archives Nationales, 149AP, Papiers Mangin, "Missions Marchand"; *Bull. Soc. d'Afrique Centrale de Constantine* (May 1893), p. 12.
108 Jules Ferry, *Le Gouvernement de l'Algerie* (Paris, 1892), pp. 71–72.
109 *J.O. Chambre Débats,* 27 Nov. 1883. This was contained in a speech by Jules Ferry on 26 Nov. 1884 during which he was attacked by Edward Lockroy and

Andrieux for depending on chance in colonial matters. See Martin Aldao, *Les Idées Coloniales de Jules Ferry* (Paris, 1933), pp. 76–78.

110 SOM-AN Dossier Administratif: Victor Ballot, Ballot to Colonies, 7 Aug. 1894. Victor Ballot was appointed governor of Dahomey by a presidential decree of 22 June 1894 with the title "Governor of Dahomey and Dependencies." Journal Officiel de la Colonie du Dahomey et Dépendances, 1 Aug. 1894. Ballot arrived back in Dahomey on 29 July 1894; he was governor third class.

111 J.O. Dahomey et Dépendances, 1 Aug. 1894 (supplement), pp. 1–2, art. 8.

112 The annexed territories were Grand Popo, Agoue, Whydah, Kotonou, and Abomey-Calavi; the protected territories were Abomey, Allada, Porto Novo, Ouatchi, and Ouéré-Ketu. The northern limit of the protectorates was the Mahi country.

113 SOM-AN Dahomey III, 4, a, Rapport Ballot, 23 Nov. 1894. J.O. Dahomey et Dépendances, 1 Nov. 1894, p. 3. The treaty was signed on 16 Sept. 1894 and was also signed by Chiefs Gobi of Olulungbe and Ywou of Aegou, acting on behalf of the king of Weche.

114 It was named in honor of President Sadi Carnot, who was assassinated in 1894.

115 SOM-AN Dahomey III, 4, a, Projet de Mission concernant l'Hinterland, 15 Dec. 1892.

116 Ibid., Min. of Colonies to Ballot, 17 Dec. 1894 (tel.); Ballot to Colonies, 20 Dec. 1894.

117 SOM-AN Dahomey III, 3, a, Mission Decoeur au Nord Dahomey; III, 4, b, Decoeur to colonies, 1 June 1894. The ministry was surprised by this 4½-page report and the absence of a map of Decoeur's itinerary.

118 SOM-AN Dahomey III, 4, b, colonies to Decoeur, instructions, 24 July 1894; Decoeur to colonies, 17 June 1895. The Comité d'Afrique Française paid 10,000 francs for the expedition.

119 SOM-AN Dahomey III, 4, b, Decoeur to Colonies, 8 Dec. 1894, no. 1; *Ibid*. III, 4, d, Baud to Ollivier, 29 Nov. 1894.

120 SOM-AN Dahomey III, 4, c, Mission Alby, rapport; III, 4, a, Delcassé to M.A.E., 31 Dec. 1894.

121 SOM-AN Dahomey III, 4, b, Decoeur to colonies, 18 Dec. 1894, no. 4; Decoeur to Ballot (tel.): "Je vous ferai remarquer respecteusement que comme Chef de mission je suis sous les ordres du Ministre seul et je telegraphierai au Ministre seul résultat de ma mission" (quoted in Ballot to colonies, 6 April 1895).

122 SOM-AN Dahomey III, 4, a, Ballot to Colonies, 15 Dec. 1894 (tel.).

123 SOM-AN Dahomey III, 4, b, Ballot to Colonies, 11 Jan. 1895; Vermeersch to commandant supérieur, 9 and 12 Dec. 1894; Ballot to Colonies, 6 April 1895, telegrams exchanged with Decoeur. This is an 8-page complaint against Decoeur by Ballot.

124 Toutée, *Dahomé-Niger-Touareg*, p. 24. Capt. Toutée's expedition belongs practically to the 1895 series, though it was planned in mid-September 1894 and he set off from Cotonou on 27 Dec. 1894.

125 FO84/2087, proofs of speech by Lord Aberdare at the annual general meeting of the board of the Royal Niger Company, 29 July 1890.

126 Hertslet, *Map of Africa* 1:122–24, deals with treaties made at Sokoto by Joseph Thomson on 1 June 1885 and at Gwandu on 13 June 1885.
127 *Punitive Expeditions of the Royal Niger Constabulary 1886–1899,* cited in Colonel A. Haywood and F. A. S. Clarke, *The History of the Royal West African Frontier Force* (Aldershot, 1964), p. 28.
128 CO147/84, C.O. to War Office, 23 March 1892, minutes on the draft by Lord Knutsford, no. 5720.
129 Ibid., Carter to Knutsford, 20 June 1892 (confidential).
130 Ibid., minutes by Meade.
131 Ibid., minutes by Lord Knutsford, no. 4863.
132 CO147/85, Knutsford to Carter, 13 May 1892.
133 CO147/91, minutes by Hemming, no. 909. A. W. L. Hemming approved of the informal control of Ibadan by a resident. The same method would have been desirable for Ashanti.
134 FO84/2252, R.N.C. to F.O., 8 June 1891.
135 *The Morning Post,* 9 June 1891.
136 FO84/2174, minutes by Salisbury on *Times* cutting, 14 Sept. 1891, quoted in Flint, "British Policy in Nigeria," p. 306.
137 FO2/167, Treaties between R.N.C. and Native Chiefs, part 1, 1891–98, p. 53. Lister made a treaty at Bussa in Jan. 1890, whereas King made a treaty at Sokoto on 15 April and at Gwandu on 7 April 1890.
138 J. E. Flint points out that H. P. Anderson urged Goldie to expand into Borgu. FO27/3300, Scarborough to F.O., 26 Feb. 1896 (encl. Journal of the Sokoto Expedition, 1894, by Wallace).
139 FO2/167, Treaties between R.N.C. and Native Chiefs, part 1, nos. 137, 139, 26 June 1894, 4 July 1894.
140 FO27/3208, memorandum by Sir George Goldie, 10 July 1894; FO27/3183, Kimberley to Dufferin, 14 Aug. 1894, Africa no. 300.
141 Rhodes' House Library and Archives, Oxford University, Oxford, Lugard Papers, MSS. British Empire S. 69, Lugard to Kirk, 12 June 1894.
142 Goldie to Lugard, 24 July 1894, quoted in M. Perham, *Lugard: The Years of Adventure* (London, 1956), pp. 493, 490–506. See also Flint, *Sir George Goldie,* pp. 223–24; Haywood and Clarke, *Royal West African Frontier Force,* pp. 19–20, 31 n. 1.
143 Lugard made treaties at Kishi (13 Oct. 1894) and Kayama (22 Oct. 1894). See FO2/167, Treaties between R.N.C. and Native Chiefs, nos. 178, 176; Perham, pp. 507–18. Lugard made a treaty at Nikki on 10 Nov. 1894. SOM-AN Dahomey III, 4, a, Delcassé to M.A.E., 19 Dec. 1894, quoting Ballot's telegram.
144 *Lagos Echo,* 22 Sept. 1894; SOM-AN Dahomey III, 4, a, Ballot to colonies, 15 Dec. 1894 (tel.); Delcassé to M.A.E., 27 Dec. 1894 (draft).
145 Lambinet, *Notice Géographique,* p. 20, quoting extract from *Rev. Maritime et Coloniale,* Oct. 1893. Col. Lambinet had been in the Dahomey campaign with Col. Dodds, and his views would have great influence over the military circles of the time.
146 Flint, "British Policy in Nigeria," pp. 463–71; Flint, *Sir George Goldie,* p. 224 n. 1.

147 Perham, *Lugard,* pp. 519–30, 523–30. Lugard's treaty at Nikki was made on 10 Nov. 1894. It was on the standard "Form 12, for Moslems" and was signed by Lafia, a local Moslem who claimed to be a plenipotentiary minister of the king of Nikki.

148 "Explorations Gruner, Lugard et Decoeur, etc. dans la region Borgu-Niger," in *Rev. Française d'Exploration: Gazette de Géographie,* vol. 20, no. 204 (Dec. 1895), pp. 700 ff.

149 A. Weber, "L'Allemagne et l'Imperialisme," in *Rev. Econ. Internationale* (Bruxelles) 1 (1904): 327–66; Dr. Frederic Zahn, "L'Expansion des Allemands à l'Etranger," in ibid. (1906), 1:72–91.

150 M.A.E., Afrique 131, Phipps to Hanotaux, 17 Sept. 1894: "Il est vrai que les Allemands réclament un territoire dérrière le Dahomey auquel ils donnent le nom de 'Tschantoland.' Est-ce qu'il existe vraiment? J'en doute."

151 Pama was shown on German maps (Richard Kiepert's *Deutscher Kolonial Atlas*) as Homma or Fomma.

152 SOM-AN Afrique VI, 133, b, Etude sur les missions Européennes dans la boucle du Niger et sur les négociations relatives au partage, par Camille Guy, chef du service géographique des colonies, pp. 11–13.

153 Full details of the Gruner expedition are given in *D.K.Z.,* June 1895. Von Carnap arrived at Brass on 5 May 1895.

154 Both Salaga and Yendi, the most important commercial centers of this region, were in the Neutral Zone. Kintampo, another important market town, was just outside the southwest corner of the zone. See CO879/31, Gold Coast: Anglo-German Claims: Correspondence 1889–1890, with one map.

155 The Duke of Devonshire deplored the effect of the report of the West African Commission of 1865 on British expansion in west Africa. "For twenty-five years the policy of the Colonial Office in that part of Africa was, in the main, guided by the spirit of those resolutions." "Colonial Premiers at Liverpool: Speech by the Duke of Devonshire," in *Times* (London), 14 June 1897; S. Leighton, "The Colonial Office and the Colonies," in *National Review,* Oct. 1890.

156 On the oscillation of British policy between the annexation of and cooperation with Ashanti in this period, see William Tordoff, *Ashanti Under the Prempehs, 1888–1935* (London, 1965), pp. 31–81.

157 For correspondence on these see CO879/28, Gold Coast: Assinie boundary, Ashanti, Gaman, etc.

158 G. E. Ferguson, *Report on Mission to Atabubu* (London, 1891); CO96/107, C.O. to Griffith, 3 Sept. 1891. The C.O. disapproved of Gov. Griffith's initiative toward Ashanti.

159 Maboth Moseley, "African Surveyor, British Agent," in *West Africa,* 5, 19, and 26 Sept., 17 Oct. 1953; "George Ekem Ferguson of Anomabu," in *Gold Coast Teachers' Journal* 9 (1937): 108–11.

160 Metcalfe, *Documents,* no. 380, Ferguson to Griffith, 19 Nov. 1892; no. 382, C.O. to F.O., 15 Dec. 1892; no. 383, Military Intelligence to C.O., 28 Dec. 1892 (this was the observation of Mil. Int. on Ferguson's report).

161 Parl. Papers, C. 9717, Hodgson (acting governor) to Ripon, 29 Sept. 1893 (with enclosures).

NOTES TO PAGES 147-50

162 CO96/238, Hodgson to Ripon, 13 Nov. 1893 (encl. Ramseyer to acting gov., 31 Oct. 1893), minutes by J. Bramston. Obviously Bramston had the events in Dahomey in mind when he wrote this minute.
163 Accounts and Papers, Parliamentary Papers, C. 7917, Ripon to Hodgson, 30 Jan. 1894; Metcalfe, no. 388.
164 Metcalfe, no. 387, Hodgson to Ferguson, 9 Jan. 1894; CO879/38, Gold Coast: Mission of Mr. Ferguson into the interior. This volume contains the correspondence relative to the expeditions (8 March 1892–26 June 1894).
165 The original copy of the Ferguson treaty at Wagadugu was taken from the Mogho Naba by Capt. Voulet and is in the files of the French Ministry of Foreign Affairs. See M.A.E., Afrique 131, treaty of 2 July 1894 between Ferguson and Abu Bukari and his notables. The large red seal opposite the "X" of the Mogho Naba is a round plastic piece probably from the inside of a bottle cork.
166 CO879/41, Ferguson to Griffith, 18 Aug. 1894. Ferguson made treaties with the chiefs of Sansane Mango, Gambaga, and Wa. These were all treaties of commerce and friendship. Dr. Gruner made treaties of protection with the chief of Sansane Mango after his arrival there on 10 Jan. 1895. McWilliam, "Ferguson, Samori and Babatu," pp. 34–43.
167 Elliot P. Skinner, *The Mossi of Upper Volta: The Political Development of a Sudanese People* (Stanford, 1964), p. 147, citing *Bulletin du Comité de l'Afrique Française* 7 (1897):108–09.
168 He went on a special mission to Krobo and Akwamu (1886); Kwahu and Atabubu (1890); Anglo-German Boundary Commission (1891); and to Bole, Daboya, Dagomba, and Bimbla in 1892. CO879/38, Ferguson to Griffith, 19 Nov. 1892; Memorandum on the Brong Tribes, by G. E. Ferguson, 24 Nov. 1893, in Accounts and Papers, C. 7917 (1896), vol. 58.
169 CO879/38, Ripon to Griffith, 10 March 1893.
170 Ibid., Hodgson to Ferguson, 9 Jan. 1894, instructions.
171 CO879/41, Ferguson to Griffith, 7 June 1894.
172 Ibid., 18 Aug. 1894. The three explorers referred to were Binger, Crozat, and Monteil, who had visited the Mossi capital.
173 FO403/167, Salisbury to Phipps, 6 July 1892.
174 SOM-AN Afrique VI, 115, c, Delcassé to Hanotaux, 24 Sept. 1894. Delcassé suggested that the boundary line should hit the Niger somewhere between Say and Boussa.
175 CO879/31, Lytton to Salisbury (encl. Ribot to Lytton, 24 Dec. 1890). See War Office Intelligence Division to C.O., 17 Jan. 1891, for observations on the report of the Boundary Commission. C.O. to F.O., 22 Jan. 1891.
176 CO879/31, Salisbury to Lytton, 31 Jan. 1891.
177 CO879/33, Denton to Knutsford, 21 July 1891; C.O. to F.O., 8 Sept. 1891; SOM-AN Afrique VI, 97, c, Jamais to Ribot, 16 Dec. 1892; Nisard to Jamais, 22 Dec. 1892; Ribot to Etienne, 25 Feb. 1892; Ribot to Jamais, 10 Dec. 1892.
178 On the voluminous correspondence on this topic see F.O. Confidential Print No. 6185, *Correspondence respecting Commercial Treaties and Tariffs 1889–92*; Lytton to Salisbury, 4 Feb. 1890 (encl. J. A. Growe to Lytton, 3 Feb. 1890); Lytton to Salisbury, 11 and 22 Feb. 1890, 16 June 1890; Lytton to Salisbury, 28 June 1890,

9 Oct. 1890 (encl. Growe to Lytton, 9 Oct. 1890); Memorandum on the French Tariff Bill, 1890, by H. Farnall, 7 Nov. 1890.

179 C.O. Confidential Print No. 409, Egerton to Ribot, 15 Feb. 1890; Egerton to Salisbury, 17 Feb. 1892; Phipps to Salisbury, 22 June 1892; Phipps to Dufferin, 28 May 1892.

180 SOM-AN Afrique VI, 97, b, Ribot to Jamais, 20 April 1892; Dufferin to Ribot, 13 April 1892.

181 Flint, *Sir George Goldie,* pp. 218–20.

182 FO84/2208, Dufferin to Salisbury, 13 May 1892, Afr. no. 108; minutes by Salisbury, H. P. Anderson, and J. W. Lowther, 14 May 1892. J. W. Lowther was the Parliamentary undersecretary for Foreign Affairs.

183 FO403/167, Phipps to Salisbury, 20 June 1892, Africa no. 142. See map 2.

184 CO879/37, Salisbury to Phipps, 6 July 1892; C.O. Confidential Print No. 418, C.O. to F.O., p. 137.

185 At this time Lord Salisbury was preoccupied with the British elections, at which the Conservatives were doing very badly. He sent a note to the diplomatic corps canceling all engagements and saying that he would be away from London. The Gladstonian Liberals had gained 8 seats in Conservative strongholds. "In fact, he knows he will be defeated at the elections," observed Waddington. M.A.E., Papiers Ribot, vol. 3, Waddington to Ribot, 5 July 1892, 25 June 1892.

186 FO84/2210, Phipps to F.O., 23 Oct. 1892; FO84/2211, Phipps to F.O., 30 Nov. 1892.

187 M.A.E., Afrique 131, Phipps to Hanotaux, 23 Jan. 1893 (private).

188 Ibid., Hanotaux to Phipps, 24 Jan. 1893 (private).

189 Ibid., Phipps to Hanotaux, 13 Feb. 1893, 11 April 1893. Phipps pointed out that Lord Rosebery, just as Lord Salisbury, would give Hanotaux's proposals his personal attention.

190 Ibid., 21 May 1893 (private). The French Colonial Department objected to the commercial concessions which Phipps thought should be introduced into the negotiations, claiming that France reserved the right to adopt any fiscal policy she thought desirable. Haussmann to Hanotaux, 3 June 1893 (private).

191 Ibid., Phipps to Hanotaux, 23 April 1893.

192 Ibid., Hanotaux to Phipps, 10 June 1893; Phipps to Hanotaux, 10 June 1893; Dufferin to Develle, 17 June 1893. See FO403/187 for details of the negotiations of the Gold Coast–Ivory Coast frontier.

193 Ibid., Delcassé to Develle, 2 May 1893. Jules-Paul Develle was minister for foreign affairs in the second Ribot Cabinet and the first Charles Dupuy Cabinet from 11 Jan. 1893 to 3 Dec. 1893. He died on 30 October 1919. He was a "deplorable Minister for Foreign Affairs," according to Hanotaux. M.A.E., Papiers Hanotaux, vol. I, Journal d'Hanotaux (June 1887–16 March 1894), 18 Dec. 1893.

194 Parl. Papers, Treaty Series No. 13 (1893), chap. 7108, Arrangement between Great Britain and France fixing the Boundary between the British and French possessions on the Gold Coast (Signed at Paris 12 July 1893); M.A.E., Documents Diplomatique: Afrique: Arrangements, Acts, et Conventions, no. 27, pp. 217–18.

195 FO27/3134, Phipps to Salisbury, 8 Aug. 1893; Phipps to Hill, 25 Aug. 1893.

196 M.A.E., Papiers Hanotaux, vol. 1, Journal d'Hanotaux, 28 March 1893.
197 M.A.E., Afrique 131, Dufferin to Casimir Perier, 4 Jan. 1894. Dufferin added that Lord Rosebery would withhold the publication of a parliamentary paper on the Mizon affair if the French government dissociated itself from the press attacks against England.
198 Ibid., Phipps to Hanotaux, 9 Jan. 1894; note by Hanotaux, 11 Jan. 1894.
199 FO27/3182, Dufferin to Rosebery, 6 March 1894 (encl. Phipps to Dufferin, 3 March 1894).
200 FO403/205, Dufferin to Rosebery, 8 March 1894 (encl. Phipps to Dufferin, 8 March 1894). On the Mizon affair see FO403/200, Niger Territories: Further Correspondence (1894).
201 M.A.E., Afrique 131, Phipps to Hanotaux, 12 March 1894. Phipps was overlooking the fact that the French government was now arguing from the strength of the report of Commandant Monteil.
202 FO27/3182, Kimberley to Phipps, 19 March 1894, Africa no. 93.
203 M.A.E., Afrique 131, Hanotaux to Phipps, 7 April 1894 (draft).
204 Gabriel Hanotaux became the first minister to be selected from outside the Chambre des Députés in the Third Republic. See A. Soulier, *L'Instabilité Ministerielle sous la Troisième République* (Paris, 1939), p. 419; André Daniel, *L'Année Politique 1894* (Paris, 1895), pp. 98–100, 111–12, 158–60; J. Chailley-Bert, "Le Ministère des Colonies," in *R.D.M.* (15 April 1894), pp. 906–24.
205 Documents Diplomatiques Françaises, vol. 11, nos. 112, 116, 174, 181.
206 *Journal Officiel* 8 June 1894 (séance du 7 juin 1894), interpellation by E. Etienne and F. Deloncle and reply by Hanotaux condemning the Anglo-Congolese treaty, pp. 931–40. See also G. Hanotaux, *Le Partage de l'Afrique: Fachoda* (Paris, 1909), pp. 84–85.
207 *J.O. Chambre Débats* (1894) 2:325–36.
208 Ibid., 8 June 1894 (séance du 7 juin 1894), p. 940. For Hanotaux's report of this resounding victory to French ambassadors see D.D.F., vol. 11, no. 134, pp. 205–06. After this Delcassé, minister for the colonies, asked for and obtained 1,800,000 francs for the protection of French interests in Africa by a vote of 438 to 27. *J.O. Chambre Débats*, 10 June 1894, p. 962.
209 FO27/3183, Kimberley to Dufferin, 14 Aug. 1894, Africa no. 300; Robinson et al., *Africa and the Victorians*, p. 392.
210 *Le Nord*, 2 June 1894, "M. Hanotaux, Ministre des Affaires Etrangères."
211 Robinson et al., p. 407.
212 P.R.O. Cab. 37/37, no. 23, Kimberley to Dufferin, 14 Aug. 1894; FO27/3208, memorandum by Sir George Taubman Goldie, 10 July 1894.
213 P.R.O. Cab. 37/37, Kimberley to Dufferin, 14 Aug. 1894. In these negotiations E. C. H. Phipps and Lord Dufferin represented Britain; Hanotaux and Jacques Haussmann represented France.
214 M.A.E., Afrique 131, Phipps to Hanotaux, 29 Aug. 1894.
215 Ibid., Memo Conversation avec M. Phipps, by Hanotaux, 5 Sept. 1894; P.R.O. Cab. 37/37, no. 25; Phipps to Kimberley, 5 Sept. 1894, Africa no. 223. Hanotaux remarked: "Sur tous ces points l'Angleterre nous expose sur *desiderata maxima* et nous les offre comme les concessions."

216 P.R.O. Cab. 37/37, no. 25, Phipps to Kimberley, 5 Sept. 1894; FO27/3187, Phipps to Kimberley, 4 Oct. 1894, Africa no. 260.
217 M.A.E., Afrique 131, note by Hanotaux, 15 Sept. 1894; Phipps to Hanotaux, 17 Sept. 1894. For the first time Phipps introduced the phrase "course au clocher" in these colonial affairs.
218 Ibid., Delcassé to Hanotaux, 18 Sept. 1894; P.R.O. Cab. 37/37, no. 27; Phipps to Kimberley, 22 Sept. 1894, Africa no. 247.
219 SOM-AN Afrique IV, 38, a, Delcassé to Hanotaux, 18 Sept. 1894 (draft); Hanotaux to Delcassé, 23 Aug. 1894; D.D.F., vol. 11, no. 257, D'Estournelle to Hanotaux, p. 386.
220 P.R.O. Cab. 37/37, Phipps to Kimberley, 26 Sept. 1894, Africa no. 250 (printed for the cabinet on 3 October 1894).
221 M.A.E., Afrique 131, memo by Hanotaux, 29 Sept. 1894; Deloncle to Hanotaux, 29 Sept. 1894; SOM-AN Afrique VI, 115, c, note by Deloncle (direction politique et commerciale, ministère des colonies). The minister for the colonies had paid Professor Kanner 200 francs to translate Sir Claude McDonald's report on the Niger Company because this report covered the disputed areas—Sokoto, Bornu, Borgu, Adamawa. Rapport au Ministre, 8 Sept. 1894.
222 M.A.E., Afrique 131, Phipps to Hanotaux, 9 Oct. 1894; note sur le Borgu by M. Deloncle, 5 Oct. 1894; Hanotaux to Phipps, 10 Oct. 1894 (draft).
223 Ibid., Phipps to Hanotaux, 10 Oct. 1894; note by Hanotaux, 21 Oct. 1894; FO403/205, Phipps to Kimberley, 21 Oct. 1894; Dufferin to Kimberley, 1 Nov. 1894.
224 SOM-AN Afrique VI, 115, c, Delcassé to Hanotaux, 15 Nov. 1894; Hanotaux to Delcassé, 13 Dec. 1894 (encl. Dufferin to Hanotaux, 9 Dec. 1894); FO27/3209, R.N.C. to Kimberley, 13 Oct. 1894; FO27/3183, Kimberley to Dufferin, 30 Nov. 1894, Africa no. 414; FO27/3209, R.N.C. to F.O., 24 Nov. 1894.
225 M.A.E., Afrique 131, note by Hanotaux, 21 Oct. 1894. This note formed the basis of a dispatch to the French Embassy in London. Note by Hanotaux, 17 Nov. 1894.
226 M.A.E., Afrique 131, Delcassé to Hanotaux, 12 Dec. 1894 (encl. Ballot to Delcassé, 27 Nov. 1894 [Tel.]). Delcassé convinced the council of ministers about his views on both the Nile Valley and the Dahomey questions.
227 M.A.E., Papiers Hanotaux, vol. 2, Note sur la politique extérieure du Ministère Méline, 1896–98, by Hanotaux (n.d.); Hanotaux, *Fachoda,* pp. 90–91. For an interesting short comparison of Hanotaux and Delcassé see A. J. P. Taylor, "Prelude to Fachoda," in *E.H.R.,* vol. 65, no. 254 (Jan. 1950), pp. 52–80.
228 The Phipps-Hanotaux negotiations succeeded partially, since they led to the agreement on the Sierra Leone–Guinea frontier of 21 January 1895. M.A.E., Doc. Dipl. Afrique: Arrangements, Actes, Conventions, 1881–98, no. 28, pp. 219–21.
229 P.R.O., FO343/3, Malet Papers, Rosebery to Malet, 11 Jan. 1893, 3 Jan. 1894.
230 Ibid., Kimberley to Malet, 19 June 1894. The possibility of cooperating with Germany was considered by Hanotaux over the Niger navigation problem. See SOM-AN Afrique IV, 38, a, "Note de l'ambassadeur d'Allemagne," 16 May 1894; Hanotaux to Delcasse, 23 Aug. 1894; Delcassé to Hanotaux, 18 Sept. 1894 (draft); FO343/3, Rosebery to Malet, 1 Feb. 1893: "The French are putting great pressure all over Europe against British action in Egypt and urging Italy to take action with them at Constantinople. They must indeed be hard pressed."

231 FO343/3, Malet Papers, Salisbury to Malet, 16 Aug. 1892. Salisbury added: "I think there is good hope that the main lines of our policy will not be departed from."

CHAPTER 6

1 CO879/38, Malet to Rosebery, 7 March 1894 (encl. memorandum by Gosselin on conversation with Dr. Kayser, 6 March 1894). The storm did not blow over as quickly as Dr. Kayser had anticipated.
2 CO879/42, Memorandum on Ashanti, by Sir A. W. L. Hemming, Feb. 1895; Haywood and Clarke, *Royal West African Frontier Force*, p. 26.
3 Samory and his forces were still holding out to the west of Ashanti, but they were harried by both French and British expeditions.
4 Winston S. Churchill, *Great Contemporaries* (London, 1959).
5 Robinson et al., *Africa and the Victorians*, pp. 382-83, 405; J. Chamberlain, "The British African Colonies," in *Liberia* (Washington, D.C.), no. 14 (Feb. 1899), pp. 80-82. Chamberlain's knowledge of Africa grew very quickly after he became colonial secretary. See also Achile Viallate, *Joseph Chamberlain* (Paris, 1899).
6 Peter de Mendelssohn, *The Age of Churchill: Heritage and Adventure 1874–1911* (London, 1961), p. 141.
7 See Elizabeth Pakenham, *Jameson's Raid* (London, 1960), pp. 125-36, on Chamberlain.
8 R. C. K. Ensor, *England, 1870–1914* (Oxford, 1936), pp. 224-26. Ensor points out three difficulties inherent in the third Salisbury administration: it was a coalition of Conservatives and Liberal Unionists; Salisbury combined the premiership with the foreign secretaryship; and Chamberlain, who was "the strongest and most popular man" in the administration, was left with the nonprestigious colonial secretaryship, since he was a Liberal Unionist and not a Conservative. However, Chamberlain was allowed "usually the power of a co-Premier and on some rare occasions more." J. L. Garvin, *Life of Joseph Chamberlain* (London, 1934), 3:7.
9 Speech delivered by Lord Salisbury at Bradford on the evening of 23 May 1895, in M.A.E., Correspondance Commerciale: Liverpool (1893–96), vol. 22; Cochelet to Hanotaux, 30 May 1895, no. 65. This extract from the speech is quoted herein. See *Times* (London), 24 May 1895.
10 "Anderson's death has cleared the air not a little and what I say will have more weight. The day of secrecy is going over and there is no one to take his peculiar position, for which we must be thankful. With Anderson much must change and it would have been better had he gone some time ago" Lugard Papers, S70, Kirk to Lugard, 25 June 1896, 23 July 1896, and 9 Aug. 1896.
11 Ibid., Kirk to Lugard, 23 July 1896, 9 Aug. 1896.
12 Sir John Bramston, "The Colonial Office from Within," in *The Empire Review* (April 1901).
13 Lugard Papers, S70, Kirk to Lugard, 6 May 1897.
14 Christian Schefer, *D'un guèrre à l'autre: Essai sur la politique extérieure de la 111ᵉ République* (Paris, 1920).
15 Felix Faure, *Le Ministère Léon Bourgeois* (Paris, 1894), p. 125; *J.O. Chambre Débats*, 24 April 1894. On the weakness of the Radicals in the chamber at this period, see Alphonse Bertrand, *La Chambre de 1893* (Paris, 1893).

16 M.A.E., Papiers Hanotaux, vol. 2, Chronique du Ministère Méline, by Hanotaux (n.d.); Soulier, *Instabilité Ministerielle*. The 3rd Dupuy Cabinet fell on 17 Jan. 1895. It was succeeded by the 3rd Ribot Cabinet, which in turn fell on 28 Oct. 1895. The Radical Cabinet of Léon Bourgeois succeeded it and lasted only till 23 April 1896. Marcellin Berthelot was the foreign minister in this cabinet.

17 M.A.E., Papiers Hanotaux, vol. 2, "Note sur la politique extérieure du Ministère Méline, 1896–1898," by Hanotaux (n.d.).

18 From April 1894 to April 1896 the ministers of colonies were Ernest Boulanger, Théophile Delcassé, Emille Chautemps, Pierre Guieysse, and André Lebon, in that order.

19 Charles Lemire, "Le Role de ville de Paris dans la Colonisation," in *Rev. des Colonies et de Pays de Protectorat* (June–July 1896), pp. 560–66, 561.

20 In Germany the Deutsche Kolonial Geselschaft was the parent society of all the Kolonial-Agitations-Geselschaften, which were spread throughout Germany and had over 19,000 registered members. About 249 branches were affiliated to the Berlin headquarters of the Deutsche Kolonial Geselschaft in 1894. See F.O. Miscellaneous Series (1894), no. 346, *Germany: Report on the German Colonies in Africa and the South Pacific,* [C.7582] Gosselin to Kimberley, 26 Oct. 1894, chap. 7582, sec. 3.

21 G. Saudemont, "Une colonie alsacienne—lorrainne au Dahomey," in *Bull. Soc. de Géog. Commerciale* (Paris) 17 (1895): 1072–73.

22 Jules Huré, "Notre programme," in *Revue des Etudes Dahoméennes,* no. 1 (July 1895), pp. 1–3; Lucien Hubert, "A Nos Lecteurs," in ibid., no. 3 (Sept. 1895), pp. 65–66. The comité rejected the spelling "Dahomey" because it was the English corruption of "Dahomé."

23 Huré, pp. 2–3.

24 M. Sansboeuf, "Au Dahomey," in *Rev. Colonies et Pays Protectorat,* no. 1 (April 1895), pp. 25–27; *Journal Officiel* (Dahomey), 1 June 1898, "Concessions à M. Saudemont."

25 Saudemont, pp. 1072–73. A decree of 19 Oct. 1895 granted Saudemont concessions at Whydah, Allada, and Athieme.

26 SOM-AN Généralité 262/1809, Projet Colonial: Ministère des Colonies: Circulaire aux Gouverneurs des Colonies, by Delcassé, 20 June 1894; see appendix 3. Etienne had sought in 1887 to unite all the chambers of commerce for concerted action in colonial affairs through the Paris Chamber of Commerce. Etienne to Muzet, 11 Oct. 1887, 22 Sept. 1887, in *Bulletin Officiel du Ministère des Colonies* (1887), pp. 661–64, 775–78.

27 SOM-AN Conseil Supérieur des Colonies, Généralité, Min. of Colonies to Chambers of commerce and responses; Le Havre to Colonies, 9 Jan. 1897; Lille to Colonies, 12 Oct. 1896; Lyon to Colonies, 12 Oct. 1896; Rouen to Colonies, 10 Oct. 1896; Marseille to Colonies, 13 Oct. 1896; Bordeaux to Colonies, 12 Oct. 1896; Joannes Convert to Colonies, 13 Oct. 1896 (tel.). Each chamber nominated a representative to the permanent commission of the Conseil Supérieur des Colonies. The permanent commission was instituted by decree on 19 September 1896. See *Journal Officiel,* 20 Sept. 1896, p. 5276.

28 Extract from an address to the monthly meeting of the Société des Etudes

Coloniales et Maritimes of Paris in March 1896 by Prince Henri d'Orleans in *Rev. Colonies et Pays Protectorat* (April 1896), p. 308; M. Blim, "La Conquête de l'Afrique Equatoriale," in ibid. (June–July 1896), pp. 688–99. Blim addressed the Société Française des Ingénieurs Coloniaux in Paris.

29 Lemire, "Le role de Paris," pp. 560–66. A brilliant piece of Darwinism!

30 Hanotaux made this appointment with a view to restoring friendly rapport with Britain. Baron de Courcel (1835–1919) was an experienced and respected man. See Henrique, "Baron Alphonse Chodron de Courcel," in *Nos Contemporains* 2:32–36.

31 Paulin Niboyet, "Sir Edmund John Monson," in *La Revue Diplomatique,* no. 44 (8 Nov. 1896), pp. 1–2; M.A.E. Papiers Hanotaux, vol. 2, "Conversation avec Lord Dufferin," 12 Oct. 1896.

32 FO343/3, Malet to Salisbury, 30 June 1895; Salisbury to Malet, 11 Oct. 1895. Malet was succeeded at Berlin by Sir F. Lascelles.

33 J. McManners, "Imperialism, Diplomacy and War," in *Lectures on European History 1789–1914* (Oxford, 1966), pp. 359–82.

34 SOM-AN Afrique VI, 125, e, Ballot to Colonies, Rapport Politique, 17 Feb. 1895 (affaire du Borgou).

35 M.A.E., Afrique 131, Delcassé to Hanotaux, 27 Dec. 1894; SOM-AN Afrique VI, 125, e, Hanotaux to Delcassé, 18 Jan. 1895.

36 Governor Ballot took away the original Lugard treaty at Nikki of 10 Nov. 1894, concluded on the standard form 12 for Moslems, and sent this to Paris. It is now in the files of the Ministry of Foreign Affairs in M.A.E., Afrique 131.

37 Hanotaux, *Fachoda,* pp. 111–12.

38 D.D.F., vol. 11, no. 163, "Note du Ministre," 20 June 1894, pp. 241–43; *J.O. Sénat Débats* (1895), vol. 1, pp. 469–70; M.A.E., Afrique 131, Confidential Note: Deliberation of the Council of Ministers, by Hanotaux, 17 Nov. 1894.

39 SOM-AN Afrique VI, 124, c, Guieysse to Berthelot, 21 Nov. 1895 (conf.); *Ibid.* VI, 133, b, M.A.E. (Nisard) to Guieysse, 29 Jan. 1896.

40 Frederick L. Schumann, *War and Diplomacy In the French Republic. An Inquiry Into Political Motivation And the Control of Foreign Policy* (New York, 1931), p. 165.

41 These were the missions led by Decoeur, Baud, Toutée, Alby, Mounier, Deville, and Ballot himself.

42 SOM-AN Dahomey III, 4, d, Missions Baud, Baud to Ballot, 25 March 1895, rapport. Lieut. Vergoz replaced Lieut. de Portzamparc as commander of the escort of the Decoeur mission.

43 Commandant Lorho, "Historique de notre expansion dans l'Hinterland dahoméen," in *Revue des Troupes Coloniales,* vol. 3, no. 16 (Oct. 1903), pp. 480–508.

44 Von Carnap-Quernheimb, "Bericht uber den Marsch von Sansane-Mangu nach Pama und Gurma," in *D.K.Z.* (22 June 1895): 195–97.

45 Molex, "Le Gourma," pp. 8–10. Jules Molex was the resident of France at Fada N'Gurma, from where he wrote this report in June 1898.

46 Delafosse, *Haut-Sénégal-Niger* 2:149–53.

47 *Bato* was the title of the ruler of one of the main chiefdoms of Gurma. Each was elected by the notables of his villages, and his election was validated by the king of Gurma.

48 SOM-AN Dahomey III, 4, a, "Notes sur les traités passés les puissances européennes dans les pays de la boucle du Niger," by E. Roume (directeur des affaires politiques et commerciales, min. des colonies), 17 May 1895.
49 Duboc, *L'Epopée Coloniale,* p. 297.
50 Von Carnap-Quernheimb, "Bericht uber den Marsch" (22 June 1895), pp. 195–97; (29 June 1895), pp. 202–04.
51 SOM-AN Dahomey III, 4, d, Baud to Ballot, 25 March 1895. The treaty was signed on 30 Jan. 1895. See *Bull. Off. (Min. of Colonies)* 9 (1895): 766.
52 A. Terrier, "Mission Baud-Vermeersch," in *B.C.A.F.* (1898), p. 127.
53 SOM-AN Dahomey IV,3 (Hint. Dah.), Rapport Baud, 25 March 1895. See L. Vermeersch, *Historique de la Mission Baud-Vermeersch: Le Dahomey, 1894–1895* (Paris, 1897); SOM-AN Traités, 12.
54 Papiers Monteil, 66AP/6, Journaux des Marches de la Colonne de Kong, 1894–95; 66AP/9 and 66AP/10, Opérations contre Samory; Rapports, cartes, bulletins des opérations, 1894–95; P. L. Monteil, *La Colonne de Kong* (Paris, 1902).
55 SOM-AN Dahomey III, 4, d, Rapport Baud, 21 June 1895.
56 Ibid.; Vermeersch, *La Mission Baud-Vermeersch.*
57 SOM-AN Dahomey III, 4, b, Ballot to Colonies, 25 March 1895; SOM-AN Soudan II, 1, Rapport Deville sur les résultats de sa mission (1895); *Bull. Off. (Min. des Colonies)* 9 (1895): 766.
58 *Journal Officiel de Dahomey,* vol. 6, no. 7 (1 April 1895), pp. 1–2; A. Deville, "Le royaume de Bouay" in *B.C.A.F.* (1895), pp. 258–60.
59 SOM-AN Dahomey III, 4, c, Rapport Alby; III, 4, a, "Itinéraires suivis par les missions envoyées dans l'Hinterland du Dahomey et traités passés par elles d'après les cablogrammes et les rapports adressés au Department, by Ballot; Note pour le Ministre, 27 May 1895.
60 Dahomey III, 4, a, Ballot to Colonies, 17 Feb. 1895. Governor Ballot's expedition was made up of 25 Senegalese tirailleurs, 50 civil guards, and 200 porters. Ballot was proud that he did not fire a single shot on his expedition. He boasted that he did not want to imitate Captain Lugard, the "hero" of the Uganda massacres of women, children, and all.
61 Ibid.
62 Ibid., 5 Feb. 1895 (tel.); Colonies to M.A.E., 1 April 1895 (draft); FO27/3252, Dufferin to Salisbury, 19 July 1895. Africa no. 202 (encl. declaration obtained by Ballot at Nikki).
63 SOM-AN Dahomey III, 4, a, Ballot to colonies, 21 Jan. 1895; colonies to M.A.E. 23 April 1895 (draft); III, 4, b, Ballot to colonies, 25 March 1895; treaty with King Siri Tourou of Nikki, 20 Jan. 1895; declaration of King Siri Tourou, 21 Jan. 1895.
64 Germaine Ganier, "Les rivalités franco-anglaise et franco-allemande de 1894–1898. Dernière phase de la course au Niger: La Mission Ganier dans le Haut-Dahomey, 1897–1898," in *Revue Fr. d'Hist. d'Outre Mer,* vol. 49, no. 2 (1962), pp. 181–261.
65 SOM-AN Dahomey III, 4, a. Ballot to Colonies, 17 Feb. 1895.
66 *La France en Côte d'Ivoire,* pp. 122 ff, André Clérici, ed., *Histoire de la Cote d'Ivoire* (Abidjan, 1962), pp. 76–79.
67 *Journal Officiel de Dahomey,* vol. 6, no. 6 (15 March 1895), p. 1; SOM-AN Dossier Administratif: Victor Ballot, Delcassé to Ballot, 25 Jan. 1895.

68 SOM-AN Dahomey III, 4, a, Ballot to Colonies, 17 Feb. 1895. Convinced that the Schabe were not part of Borgu and that Bouay was an independent kingdom, Ballot sent A. Deville to make treaties of protection with their rulers. He dispatched Mounier, who was the chief escort of his mission, to the Kodokoli region to collect treaties of protection and to establish posts of occupation.
69 *Journal Officiel de Dahomey,* vol. 6, no. 7 (1 April 1895), p. 1.
70 Toutée, *Dahomé-Niger-Touareg,* p. 18.
71 Goldie claimed that the "freedom of navigation" of the Niger excluded armed parties and that as such Toutée's expedition did not qualify to use the Lower Niger. FO27/3209, R.N.C. to Kimberley, 13 Oct. 1894; FO27/3183, Kimberley to Dufferin, 30 Nov. 1894, Africa no. 414; SOM-AN Afrique VI, 115, c, Hanotaux to Delcassé, 13 Dec. 1894; Delcassé to Hanotaux, 15 Nov. 1894 (draft); VI, 124, c, Delcassé to Hanotaux, 16 Jan. 1895 (draft).
72 Toutée, *Dahomé-Niger-Touareg,* pp. 23–30; Toutée to Colonies, 15 Jan. 1895, quoted in *Dahomé-Niger-Touareg,* p. 81.
73 Ibid., pp. 68–71. The *récadère* was an official representative of the king, who carried the royal baton as an identity card for introducing himself and others to local rulers. The *récade* performed the function of a modern passport.
74 Ibid., p. 69. See Adande, *Les récades des rois du Dahomey.*
75 Toutée, *Dahomé-Niger-Touareg,* pp. 87–89. Toutée explained to the chief, through Abdul his interpreter, what the exile of Béhanzin meant, since the Mahi had no idea of what the island of Martinique was like. He had never seen the sea (p. 90).
76 Ibid., pp. 98–99, 103–04, 102. Capt. Toutée, "Par le Dahomey et le Niger Moyen au Sahara Francais," in *Bull. de la Soc. Géog. Commerciale (Paris)* 18 (1896): 11–20. This was the published version of a lecture delivered by Toutée to the Société de Géographie Commerciale de Paris on 27 Dec. 1895.
77 Toutée, *Dahomé-Niger-Touareg,* pp. 150, 153, 164–68.
78 Ibid., pp. 147–49. "Celle de Toffa, car nous savons que vous l'avez défendu et qu'il est heureux," replied Bagui. SOM-AN Dahomey III, 4, e, Toutée to Colonies, 9 March 1895 (tel.) "Tchaki est une agglomération considerable agricole et industrielle en case de rétrocession," declared Toutée in this telegram. Toutée left a resident at Tchaki with a view to influencing the choice of a pro-French successor to Chief Ajani whose death was then imminent.
79 Ibid., *Dahomé-Niger-Touareg,* pp. 183–84, 193, 197–98, 202–03.
80 SOM-AN Soudan III, 2, b, Toutée to Colonies, 15 Feb. 1895. In recognition of his important mission to the Niger in 1894–95, Georges-Joseph Toutée was promoted to the grade of officer by a decree of 11 July 1896.
81 Ibid., 11 March 1895; Toutée, *Dahomé-Niger-Touareg,* p. 234.
82 SOM-AN Dahomey III, 4, e, Toutée to Colonies, 11 March 1895.
83 These details were given by Toutée in a lecture to the Old Boys of the Ecole Coloniale de Paris at the Mairie de Saint-Suplice in Paris. See *Rev. des Colonies et de Pays Protectorat* (1896), pp. 504–06.
84 SOM-AN Afrique VI, 124, c, Hanotaux to Chautemps, 11 May 1895 (encl. Howard to Hanotaux, 9 May 1895); FO27/3257, memorandum by C. H. Hill, "On the Position of the Niger Company," 6 May 1895; FO27/3234, Howard to Kimberley, 8 May 1895, Africa no. 13.

85 SOM-AN Afrique VI, 124, c, Hanotaux to Chautemps, 11 May 1895.
86 FO27/3234, Howard to Kimberley, 8 May 1895; FO27/3229, Kimberley to Dufferin, 24 May 1895, Africa no. 164.
87 J. W. Lowther asked Sir Edward Grey, assistant undersecretary for foreign affairs, about the Toutée mission on 10 May. Again on 15 May, Grey was again asked about the same misson. See *Hansard H. C. Debates* (1895); *The Standard,* 10 and 15 May 1895; "France and England on the Niger," in *The Times* (London), 11 May 1895; *The Daily News,* 10 May 1895.
88 FO27/3257, R.N.C. to F.O., 16 and 21 May 1895; FO27/3258, R.N.C. to F.O., 22 Aug. 1895.
89 SOM-AN Afrique VI, 124, c, Hanotaux to Chautemps, 18 May 1895; Chautemps to Hanotaux, 22 May 1895 (draft); Hanotaux to Chautemps, 7 June 1895.
90 SOM-AN Afrique VI, 124, c, Colonies to M.A.E., 22 May 1895.
91 Ibid., Chautemps to Hanotaux, June 1895 (draft and fair copy), minutes by Chautemps. "Cette lettre n'a pas été envoyée par suite d'un accord intervenu au Conseil des Ministres et qui la rendent inutile." M.A.E. C. P., Angleterre 904, "Note pour l'ambassadeur d'Angleterre," 18 May 1895.
92 SOM-AN Afrique VI, 124, c, Hanotaux to Chautemps, 27 June 1895; Chautemps to Hanotaux, 8 Aug. 1895; Hanotaux to Chautemps, 9 Sept. 1895 (encl. Howard to Hanotaux, 31 Aug. 1895); FO27/3232, Dufferin to Salisbury, 10 Sept. 1895, Africa no. 244 (encl. Hanotaux to Howard, 9 Sept. 1895).
93 FO83/1387, R.N.C. to F.O., 23 Dec. 1895.
94 FO64/1334, Malet to Kimberley, 5 Oct. 1894, Africa no. 110 (conf.) (encl. "Memorandum on a Conversation with Dr. Kayser on the German Expedition into the Togo Hinterland," by Gosselin, 4 Oct. 1894).
95 Ibid., 2 Dec. 1894 (encl. "Memo on a Conversation with Dr. Kayser," by Gosselin, 1 Dec. 1894).
96 Ibid., Gosselin to Kimberley, 17 Nov. 1894, Africa no. 139.
97 Ibid., Gosselin to Marschall, 17 Nov. 1894.
98 *Norddeutsche Allgemeine Zeitung,* 15 Feb. 1895 (encl. in FO64/1357, Malet to Kimberley, 16 Feb. 1895).
99 FO64/1334, Malet to Kimberley, 2 Dec. 1894 (encl. "Memo on a Conversation with Dr. Kayser," by Gosselin, 1 Dec. 1894).
100 Ibid. Dr. Kayser realized the magnitude of the differences between France and Britain and was accurate in assessing the costly nature of a settlement between the two powers. As it turned out, Germany and France reached an agreement in the Dahomey-Niger hinterland before Britain and France did so, and an entente between them had to wait until 1904.
101 FO64/1334, Gosselin to Kimberley, 29 Oct. 1894, Africa no. 129 (encl. "The French and English in Borguland and the German Togo Expedition," in *Kolnische Zeitung.*
102 *Reichsanzeiger,* 7 Nov. 1894; FO64/1334, Gosselin to Kimberley, 7 Nov. 1894, Africa no. 133 (encl. *Kreuz Zeitung,* 6 Nov. 1894, in which Krause's letters were also published).
103 FO64/1334, Gosselin to Kimberley, 10 Nov. 1894, Africa no. 136.

104 Ibid., Malet to Kimberley, 2 Dec. 1894, Africa no. 150 (encl. "Memo on a Conversation with Dr. Kayser," by Gosselin, 1 Dec. 1894).
105 FO64/1357, Malet to Kimberley, 1 Feb. 1895, Africa no. 13; Gosselin to Marschall, 15 March 1895.
106 CO879/41, Griffith to Ripon, 22 Jan. 1895 (encl. Ferguson to governor, 15 Dec. 1894); F.O. to C.O., 7 March 1895 (encl. Kimberley to Malet, 6 March 1895, Africa no. 43), Griffith to Ripon, 24 Jan. 1895 (encl. Ferguson to governor, 23 Dec. 1894).
107 Von Carnap-Quernheimb, "Bericht uber den Marsch" (22 June 1895), pp. 195–97; FO64/1357, Malet to Kimberley, 27 April 1895, Africa no. 54.
108 *Kolnische Zeitung*, 20 Feb. 1895; FO64/1357, Malet to Kimberley, 21 Feb. 1895, Africa no. 24; Dr. Gruner, "Die franzosischen Anspruche auf das Hinterland von Togo," in *Deutsche Kolonialzeitung*, 30 Nov. 1895, pp. 377–78.
109 Dr. von Doering, "Von Mangu nach Kankantschari, 9 Jan.–5 Feb. 1895," in *D.K.Z.*, 6 July 1895, pp. 210–12; *Kolnische Zeitung*, 20 Feb. 1895.
110 FO64/1357, Gosselin to Kimberley, 25 March 1895, Africa no. 38 (encl. *Norddeutsche Allgemeine Zeitung*, 23 March 1895; *D.K.Z.*, 23 March, 1895.
111 Dr. Gruner, "Die Deutsche Togo Expedition," in *Verhandhlingen der Gesellschaft fur Erdkunde* (1895), pp. 76, 698; Von Carnap-Quernheimb, "Bericht uber den Marsch" (29 June 1895), pp. 202–04 (a map of the routes taken is on p. 203).
112 Perham, *Lugard*, pp. 519–30.
113 CO879/41, C.O. to F.O., 16 Feb. 1895; Kimberley to Hatzfeldt, 5 April, 1895 (encl. "Memorandum on the Missions of Ferguson in the Gold Coast Hinterland in 1892, 1893, and 1894," 5 April 1895).
114 FO64/1334, Malet to Kimberley, 5 Oct. 1894 (encl. "Memo by Gosselin on a Conversation with Dr. Kayser," 4 Oct. 1894).
115 Aderibigbe, "Expansion of the Lagos Protectorate," pp. 308–18.
116 CO147-104, Carter to Chamberlain, 11 Jan. 1896, 6 April 1896.
117 Ibid., 6 Feb. 1896; minutes by J. B[ramston], 26 March 1896; 5 April 1896 (tel.); minutes by H. J. Read, 6 April 1896.
118 CO147/109, F.O. to C.O., 18 April 1896 (encl. R.N.C. to F.O., 17 April 1896); F.O. to C.O., 15 Aug. 1896 (encl. R.N.C. to F.O., 2 June 1896).
119 CO147/109, "Memorandum on Ilorin," by H. J. Read, correction by Carter on Minute Paper No. 9801, 19 May 1896.
120 Anene and Brown, *Africa in the Nineteenth and Twentieth Centuries*, p. 126.
121 FO403/217, Sir John Kirk's Report: The Royal Niger Company and the Chiefs of Brass: Investigation into the trouble between, and plans for the future (1895).
122 FO64/1334, Gosselin to Kimberley, 1 Nov. 1894, Africa no. 130 (encl. Marschall to Gosselin, 29 Oct. 1894).
123 *Kreuz Zeitung*, 1 Nov. 1894 (encl. in FO64/1334, Gosselin to Kimberley, 1 Nov. 1894, Africa no. 130. The *Kreuz Zeitung* said that neither British nor French claims to Borgu should be recognized, and it referred to an article in *Kolnische Zeitung*, 29 Oct. 1894.
124 FO64/1333, Malet to Rosebery, 7 March 1894 (encl. "Memorandum on a con-

versation with Dr. Kayser," by Gosselin, 6 March 1894); Marschall to Malet, 8 March 1894 (encl. in Malet to F.O., 9 March 1894).

125 FO64/1341, Kimberley to Hatzfeldt, 3 May 1894; Hatzfeldt to Kimberley, 17 May 1894.
126 FO27/3182, Kimberley to Phipps, 19 March 1894, Africa no. 93.
127 FO64/1333, Gosselin to Kimberley, 4 May 1894.
128 CO879/41, F.O. to C.O., 3 Sept. 1894 (encl. Gosselin to Kimberley, 30 Aug. 1894).
129 FO343/3, Malet Papers, Kimberley to Malet, 19 June 1894 (private).
130 CO879/41, Gosselin to Kimberley, 30 Aug. 1894. See the article in *Kreuz Zeitung,* 27 Aug. 1894, on French intentions in the hinterland of Dahomey.
131 CO879/41, Ferguson to governor, 18 Aug. 1894 (encl. in Griffith to Ripon, 28 Aug. 1894).
132 CO879/41, C.O. to F.O., 11 Sept. 1894; F.O. to C.O., 15 Sept. 1894.
133 FO64/1326, Kimberley to Malet, 16 Oct. 1894, Africa no. 165.
134 FO64/1334, Gosselin to Kimberley, 1 Nov. 1894, Africa no. 130 (encl. Marschall to Gosselin, 29 Oct. 1894).
135 *Kreuz Zeitung,* 6 Oct. 1894, "Des Hinterland von Togo" (encl. in FO64/1334, Gosselin to Kimberley, 9 Oct. 1894).
136 CO879/41, Malet to Kimberley, 2 Dec. 1894, Africa no. 150 (encl. memo by Gosselin, 1 Dec. 1894).
137 FO64/1372, Goldie to F.O., 11 Jan. 1895 (encl. Vohsen to Goldie, 9 Jan. 1895).
138 It was with great reluctance that Lord Ripon agreed to this proposal. See CO879/41, F.O. to C.O., 11 Feb. 1895; C.O. to F.O., 16 Feb. 1895; F.O. to C.O., 1 March 1895; C.O. to F.O., 9 March 1895; C.O. to Maxwell, 15 March 1895 (tel.).
139 FO64/1367, Kimberley to Hatzfeldt, 16 March 1895 (encl. Hatzfeldt to Kimberley, memorandum, 28 March 1895).
140 CO879/41, Griffith to Ripon, 6 April 1895 (encl. Ferguson to governor, 22 Feb. 1895).
141 Ibid., C.O. to F.O., 10 May 1895 (encl. "Memo by Hemming on German Treaties in the Hinterland," 4 May 1895); C.O. to F.O., 23 May 1895.
142 FO64/1367, Kimberley to Hatzfeldt, 5 April 1895 (encl. memo on Ferguson's missions in the hinterland in 1892, 1893, and 1894, 5 April 1895); Hatzfeldt to Kimberley, 20 May 1895; Kimberley to Hatzfeldt, 1 June 1895. The German expedition had reached the Niger, and even Gruner had made treaties with the Emir of Gwandu.
143 FO64/1367, Kimberley to Hatzfeldt, 14 June 1895; FO64/1358, Gosselin to Kimberley, 19 June 1895, Africa no. 74 (encl. "From the Togo Hinterland," in *Kolonialblatt,* 15 June 1895); FO64/1359, Gosselin to Salisbury, 26 Oct. 1895, Africa no. 136; FO83/1368, "Memorandum on the Negotiations of November, 1895," by H. P. Anderson, 28 Nov. 1895.
144 A. Duchene, "Le droit de la navigation dans le Niger," in *Revue générale de Droit International Public* (Paris, 1895); SOM-AN Afrique VI, 124, c, "Régime legal de Navigation du Bas Niger, 1895," by Toutée, 4 Nov. 1895.
145 FO27/3182, Kimberley to Phipps, 19 March 1894, Africa no. 93.

146 SOM-AN Afrique VI, 124, c, "Note rélative à la lettre adressée le 16 Juillet 1895 au Ministre des Affaires Etrangères à propos de *l'Ardent* par l'Ambassadeur d'Angleterre," 24 Oct. 1895; Colonies to M.A.E., 10 Dec. 1895 (draft); "Situation de l'Ardent dans le Niger" (draft), n.d.
147 Ibid., Chautemps to Hanotaux, 8 Aug. 1895; Hanotaux to Chautemps, 9 Sept. 1895 (encl. Howard to Hanotaux, 31 Aug. 1895).
148 Ferdinand de Béhagle, "Le Noupé et les prétentions de la Compagnie Royale du Niger," in *Revue de Géographie* (May 1895).
149 Africanus, "La France et l'Angleterre sur le Niger: Réponse au *Times*," in *La Politique Coloniale*, 14 May 1895; *The Times* (London), 11 May 1895.
150 *La Politique Coloniale,* 20 Aug. 1895, quoted in Flint, *Sir George Goldie.*
151 SOM-AN Dossier Administratif: Victor Ballot, Ballot to colonies, 23 July 1895 (tel.), no. 55, minutes by Chautemps "Faites le nécéssaire, pressé."
152 SOM-AN Afrique VI, 124, a, Guieysse to Berthelot, 20 Nov. 1895 (draft), no. 216.
153 SOM-AN Afrique IV, 38, a, "Sur l'Hinterland du Dahomey." (no date, this six-page manuscript has no date but was probably prepared late in 1895).
154 Ibid., "Sur l'Hinterland du Dahomey: Moyens de pénétration dans la boucle du Niger."
155 Levtzion, "Salaga," pp. 207–44.
156 SOM-AN Afrique IV, 38, a, "Description géographique de l'Hinterland du Dahomey," by Camille Guy, n.d. This memorandum was illustrated with a sketch map of the hinterland between the Niger and the Bismarcksburg-Carnotville line.
157 Ibid., "Sur l'Hinterland du Dahomey: Etat de la Question," minutes, "Allégation un peu téméraire?"
158 F.O. Confidential Print No. 6659, Memorandum on the International Situation East and West of the Niger, by H. P. Anderson, 31 Aug. 1895 (21 pages).
159 Ibid., pp. 2–7.
160 Ibid., pp. 7–14.
161 Ibid., p. 17. Ballot observed that Borgu was "au nombre des contrées les moins favorisées par la nature et les plus déshonorées par l'homme. Il est difficile d'imaginer un pays plus triste, plus malsain, avec des habitants plus inhospitables et plus ivrognes, plus rapaces et plus voleurs. . . . La misère est-elle extrême. Le pays, peu fertile, ne produit que juste ce qu'il faut pour nourrir ses habitants." Nonetheless, France wanted Borgu, for though it was apparently not favored by nature, its inhabitants were potential consumers of French products. It would also bring Dahomey nearer to navigable Niger.
162 F.O. Conf. Print No. 6659, Memorandum on the International Situation East and West of the Niger, pp. 17–21. Anderson was of the opinion that the situation regarding Germany was a difficult one, noting that Hohenlohe, who succeeded Caprivi, had been an active expansionist.
163 Salisbury Papers, A/119, Salisbury to Dufferin, 26 July 1895 (private).
164 Cf. M. Sabatier, *Touat, Sahara et Soudan* (Paris, 1891); Monteil, *De St. Louis à Tripoli par lac Tchad* (Paris, 1896); C. H. Robinson, *Hausaland or Fifteen Hundred Miles through the Central Soudan* (London, 1896); Toutée, *Dahomé-Niger-Touareg*; Lugard, "An Expedition to Borgu," in *The Geographical Journal* (Sept.

1895), pp. 211–18. The reports of Ballot, Deville, Wallace, and others contributed to the knowledge of the area.
165 Dr. G. Renouard, *L'Ouest Africain et les Missions Catholiques: Congo et Oubanghi* (Paris, n.d.), p. 39.
166 FO83/1368, "Memorandum on the Negotiations of November 1895," by H. P. Anderson, 28 Nov. 1895.
167 FO403/216, Dufferin to Salisbury, 7 Dec. 1895 (encl. "L'Allemagne et la France au Togo," in *La Politique Coloniale,* 5 Dec. 1895); "La France et L'Allemagne au Nord du Dahomey: Réponse au Dr. Gruner, Chef de la Mission allemande au Togo," in *La Politique Coloniale,* 7 Dec. 1895; Dufferin to Salisbury, 25 Oct. 1895 (encl. "Du Dahomey au Niger," in *La Politique Coloniale Illustrée,* Oct. 1895).
168 M.A.E., Doc. Dipl., Afrique 197, *Arrangements, Actes, et Conventions concernant le nord, l'ouest et le centre de l'Afrique, 1881–1898,* no. 30, p. 231.
169 Camille Guy was head of the geographical service of the ministry of colonies. He worked with almost all the explorers and soldiers on their return from the Niger territories and prepared maps of the regions traversed by these explorers. He was therefore abreast with the developments in these areas.
170 SOM-AN Afrique VI, 133, b, "Etude sur les missions Européennes dans la boucle du Niger et sur les négociations rélatives au partage," by Camille Guy, chef du service géographique, ministère des colonies. In this 16-page manuscript, Guy condemned Toutée for establishing a post at Tchaki and making treaties at Kishi and Tchaki. See note by Duchene.
171 Chamberlain had begun to make his weight felt in these international negotiations. See FO64/1372, C.O. to F.O., 20 Jan. 1896; CO879/43, C.O. to F.O., 20 Dec. 1895.
172 SOM-AN Afrique VI, 133, b, Berthelot to Guieysse, 30 Jan. 1896.
173 M.A.E., C. P., Angleterre 911, Courcel to Berthelot, 20 Jan. 1896. Sir A. Hemming was made governor of British Guiana from his post in the Colonial Office. He worked in the Colonial Office from 1869 to 1896.
174 The other British commissioner was H. Howard of the Paris embassy. The French commissioners were Roume, director of political and commercial affairs, ministry of colonies, and Larrouy, minister plenipotentiary and undersecretary for protectorates, ministry of foreign affairs. SOM-AN Afrique VI, 133, b, Guieysse to Berthelot, 1 Feb. 1896; Berthelot to Guieysse, 4 Feb. 1896.
175 FO27/3273, Salisbury to Dufferin, 7 Feb. 1896; FO403/233, Salisbury to Dufferin, 31 Jan. 1896.
176 SOM-AN Afrique VI, 133, b, Guieysse to Berthelot, 7 Feb. 1896 (draft).
177 Ibid., Berthelot to Guieysse, 19 Feb. 1896 (urgent).
178 SOM-AN Afrique VI, 134, b, Négociations franco-anglais: Séance du 8 Feb. 1896; FO27/3274, Dufferin to Salisbury, 8 Feb. 1896, Africa no. 21 (encl. Howard to Dufferin, 8 Feb. 1896). See François Berge: "Le Ministère Léon Bourgeois et la politique étrangère de Marcellin Berthelot au Quai d'Orsay, 2 Nov. 1895–29 Mars, 1896," in *Rev. d'Histoire Diplomatique* (1957), pp. 93–125.
179 SOM-AN Afrique VI, 134, b, Séance du 22 Feb. 1896; FO403/233, Dufferin to Salisbury, 22 Feb. 1896 (encl. Howard to Dufferin, 22 Feb. 1896); FO27/3274,

Dufferin to Salisbury, 15 Feb. 1896 (encl. Hemming and Howard to Dufferin, 15 Feb. 1896).
180 SOM-AN Afrique VI, 133, b, Cor to Berthelot, 8 Feb. 1896.
181 Ibid., Guieysse to Berthelot, 20 Feb. 1896 (urgent), "Note rélative à la Séance du 26 février 1896." This deals with the technical examination of treaties.
182 SOM-AN Afrique VI, 134, b, "Note du Ministre," 22 Feb. 1896. In this interview Dufferin referred Berthelot to Hanotaux to Phipps, 10 Oct. 1894; Séance du 24 Feb. 1896; Salisbury Papers, A/114, Dufferin to Salisbury, 28 Feb. 1896; F.O. Conf. Print. No. 6631, *Negotiations with France respecting Africa (1894)*, tabular summary, p. 5.
183 SOM-AN Afrique VI, 133, b, "Note pour M. Roume," by Camille Guy, 21 and 24 Feb. 1895.
184 Ibid., Nisard to Guieysse, 4 March 1896 (encl. Dufferin to Berthelot, 29 Feb. 1896). Col. Everett was from the Intelligence Division of the War Office.
185 Ibid., G. Lesner, president, Société Africaine de France, to Berthelot, 13 Feb. 1896; min. of commerce to Berthelot, 11 March 1896 (encl. chamber of commerce of Le Havre to min. of commerce, 3 March 1896); Berthelot to Guieysse, 18 March 1896. The chambers of commerce of Marseille and Dunkirk petitioned Berthelot.
186 See Georges Borelli, *Réssources économiques et avenir commerciale du Dahomey* (Paris, 1900), pp. 360–62, for trade figures. Borelli was a member of the chamber of commerce and the geographical society of Marseille. He had important business establishments in Dahomey in Mante and Borelli Ltd.
187 Waddington, who was coauthor of the Say-Barruwa declaration of 1890, died in 1893. It should be remembered that both Salisbury and Waddington prepared this declaration—much of it drafted on scraps of paper—in a very short time and without any public discussion of its implications.
188 Salisbury Papers, A/119, Salisbury to Dufferin, 3 March 1896 (private).
189 SOM-AN Afrique VI, 134, b, "Note rélative à la Séance du 26 Feb. 1896"; VI, 133, c, Decrais to colonies, 10 April 1896 (encl. "Memorandum on the Political Situation in the Borgu country," 27 March 1896).
190 M.A.E. C. P., Angleterre 913, Courcel to Berthelot, 11 March 1896 (encl. Salisbury to Courcel, 9 March 1896); SOM-AN Afrique VI, 133, b, Nisard to Guieysse, 28 March 1896.
191 FO403/235, Niger Negotiations at Paris: Correspondence, part 1 (1896), Dufferin to Salisbury, 21 March 1896, Africa no. 53 (encl. Howard and Everett to Dufferin, 21 March 1896); memorandum by British commissioners on Borgu, 27 March 1896; SOM-AN Afrique VI, 133, b, "Réponse aux Memoranda presenté par les Commissaires Anglais pour la délimitation des territoires du Niger sur la Situation Politique du Borgu," by M. Lerrouy, 20 April 1896.
192 SOM-AN Afrique VI, 134, b, "Séance du 27 Avril 1896."
193 SOM-AN Afrique VI, 133, b, Cor to Berthelot, 23 April 1896 (encl. *Hamburgischer Correspondent,* with an article on the Franco-British negotiations); Hanotaux to Lebon, 30 April 1896.
194 FO27/3275, Dufferin to Salisbury, 30 April 1896 (encl. Howard and Everett to Dufferin, 28 April 1896).

195 Andre Lebon was made minister for colonies, and Binger soon became head of the Africa department of the ministry of colonies.
196 M.A.E. C. P., Angleterre 915, Courcel to Hanotaux, 7 May 1896.
197 FO403/235, Dufferin to Salisbury, 8 May 1896 (encl. Howard and Everett to Dufferin, 8 May 1896).
198 FO27/3273, Salisbury to Dufferin, 12 May 1896, Africa no. 139.
199 FO27/3275, Dufferin to Salisbury, 23 May 1896, Africa no. 88 (encl. Howard and Everett to Dufferin, 23 May 1896).
200 SOM-AN Dahomey III, 4, a, "Note sur les traités passés entre les Puissances européennes dans les pays de la boucle du Niger," by E. Roume (directeur des affaires politiques et commerciales), 17 May 1895.
201 Salisbury Papers, A/119, Salisbury to Dufferin, 26 July 1895 (private).
202 SOM-AN Afrique VI, 133, b, "Délimitation des sphères d'influence française et anglaise du Soudan Central: Nécéssité de l'attribution à la France de la ville de Kouka au point de vue économique," by George Roland, ingénieur en chef des mines, 18 April 1896; George Roland to Lebon, 7 May 1896.
203 L. Faulong, *Les Rapports Financiers de la Métropole et de l'Afrique Occidentale Francaise dépuis 1825 à nos jours* (Paris, 1910), p. 68. Dahomey entered the government general by the decree of 17 Oct. 1899, after the settlement of the hinterland question by the Franco-British agreement of 14 June 1898. *Bull. Officiel Min. des Colonies* 9 (1895): 531. The governor of Dahomey was only required to send in duplicate to the governor general of A.O.F. all his military and political reports. See "Rapport au Président de la République Française suivi d'un décret instituant un gouvernement général de l'Afrique Occidentale francaise," by E. Chautemps.
204 CO879/45, acting governor of Lagos to Chamberlain, 30 Oct. 1896; "Mission Hourst," in *Rev. Colonies et Pays des Protectorat* (April 1896), p. 403.
205 "Mission hydrographique du Niger: Lettres du M. Hourst," in *Bull. Soc. Géog. Commerciale de Paris* 18 (1896): 134, 300, 480, 927–28, 931, 947. Among Hourst's instruments was a phonograph for recording the music and chants of the local population. See Duboc, *L'Epopée Coloniale*, pp. 157–59; CO879/48, F.O. to C.O., 13 Jan. 1897 (encl. Monson to Salisbury, 26 Dec. 1896, Africa no. 234).
206 Minister of colonies to Grodet, 16 Feb. 1895, quoted in Duboc, pp. 151–52. Colonel de Trentinian succeeded Gov. Grodet in the Sudan, where the latter was adjudged to be too pacific and inert.
207 FO27/3276, Howard to Salisbury, 5 Aug. 1896, Africa no. 147; CO879/45, C.O. to F.O., 13 July 1896 (encl. memorandum by Everett).
208 FO27/3301, F.O. to C.O., 18 Aug. 1896; C.O. to F.O., 14 Sept. 1896, 27 Nov. 1896.
209 Auzou, "La Boucle du Niger," p. 185.
210 Aderibigbe, "Expansion of the Lagos Protectorate," pp. 316 ff.; *Colonial Office List 1898*, p. 441.

CHAPTER 7

1 J. L. Garvin, *Life of Chamberlain* 3:209–10.
2 Hanotaux, *Fachoda*, p. 70.
3 SOM-AN Soudan III, 26, a, Mission Hourst: Rapport.

4 Skinner, *Mossi of Upper Volta*, p. 138.
5 See Voulet, *Mission au Mossi et au Gourounsi* (Paris, 1898). Lieut. Chanoine was the chief of the escort. The other three Europeans were Sergeants Loury and Jarriel and Dr. Henric. There were 203 tirailleurs, 50 spahis, and 250 porters.
6 SOM-AN Sénégal I, 96, bis., Note au President de la République, November 1895.
7 Captain Destenave was the resident of Bandiagara. SOM-AN Afrique III, 26, note, 24 Oct. 1895.
8 Naba Bagare (Bakare) was installed by Destenave, who profited from the civil war in Yatenga in 1895 and occupied this western province of Mossi. But rival princes for the office of Naba of Yatenga forced Bagare to flee after the French left. See Tauxier, *Le Noir du Yatenga*, pp. 109–10.
9 SOM-AN Afrique III, 26, a, Rapport Voulet (1897).
10 Chanoine, *Documents*, annexe 5, "La Mission de MM. les Lieutenants Voulet et Chanoine," in *L'Africaine* (Nov. 1897), pp. 15–16.
11 Ned Noll, "Le Mossi: La Mission du Lt. Voulet," in *La Tour du Monde* 33 (14 Aug. 1897): 257.
12 Skinner, *Mossi of Upper Volta*, pp. 149–53.
13 SOM-AN Afrique III, 26, note, 24 Oct. 1895.
14 Dim Delobson, *Mogho Naba*, p. 38. Dim Delobson was a local chief of Mossi extraction and a Roman Catholic. Voulet's proceedings in Yatenga and Yako were known at Wagadugu.
15 Skinner, p. 149. Dr. Skinner's work is the most recent authoritative study of the Mossi people from a social anthropological point of view, but it contains errors of historical facts because of his over-reliance on the propaganda publications of the Comité d'Afrique Française and the writings of expansionists who sought to justify the ruthless actions of their soldiers.
16 J. Chanoine to General Chanoine, 21 Feb. 1897, in Chanoine *Documents*, p. 15.
17 SOM-AN Sénégal I, 96, bis., "Note au Président de la République," Nov. 1895.
18 Capt. Morisson, *Histoire Militaire et Historique: Résumé de la Pénétration dans la Boucle du Niger* (Notice Générale sur le Soudan publiée par ordre du Colonel de Trentinian, Lieut. Governeur Partie 2ᵉ, Mai 1897). See *La Politique Coloniale*, 10 Nov. 1896; FO27/3276, Gosselin to Salisbury, 13 Nov. 1896, Africa no. 196.
19 Dim Delobson, *Mogho Naba*, p. 39 ff., quoted in Skinner. *Mossi of Upper Volta*, p. 150.
20 Both Voulet and Chanoine attested to the unflinching devotion of the Mossi to their Mogho Naba and rulers. Chanoine, *Documents*, p. xii.
21 SOM-AN Afrique III, 26, a, Rapport Voulet. The treaty with Hamaria was signed on 19 September 1896.
22 Voulet, *Mission au Mossi et au Gourounsi*; *La Politique Coloniale*, 7 Nov. 1896. The British Embassy in Paris reported Voulet's success at Wagadugu. FO403/234, Gosselin to Salisbury, 13 Nov. 1896, Africa no. 96.
23 Chanoine, *Documents*, p. xx.
24 CO879/45, Stewart to governor (encl. in Maxwell to Chamberlain). 19 Nov. 1896.
25 "Le blancs ne font que passer et ne s'établiront jamais au Mossi" was the belief. Chanoine, annexe, p. x; Crozat, "Une Mission au Mossi," pp. 4820–50. Crozat

reported that Mogho Naba Wobogo trusted to charms and consulted diviners (pp. 4835–36).

26 Mazi was a brother of Boukari Koutou and the eldest of the other princes. Chanoine, p. xii.

27 Lieut. Chanoine to General Chanoine, 21 Feb. 1897, in Chanoine, p. 17; Lucien Marc, *Le Pays Mossi* (Paris, 1909), p. 156; Skinner, *Mossi of Upper Volta*, pp. 133–34.

28 Mamadou Kouka assumed the name of Mogho Naba Sighiri at his investiture. SOM-AN Afrique III, 26, a, Rapport Voulet.

29 Captain Lambert, "Le Pays Mossi," in *Bull. Soc. Géog. de l'A.O.F.* (June 1908), p. 73. Mamadou Kouka was installed on 27 January 1897.

30 Archives of the Gouvernement Général de l'A.O.F. (Dakar), Doc. 15G, 190, May 1897, quoted in Skinner, *Mossi of Upper Volta*, p. 216 n. 46. See Morisson, *La Pénétration dans la Boucle du Niger*.

31 FO27/3301, C.O. to F.O., 27 Nov. 1896; F.O. to C.O., 30 Nov. 1896.

32 Général Bénoit, *Histoire militaire de l'Afrique Occidentale Française* (Paris, 1937); Pierre Deloncle, *L'Afrique Occidentale Française: Decouverte, Pacification, mise en valeur* (Paris, 1934), pp. 202–06.

33 CO879/45, F.O. to C.O., 23 Nov. 1896 (with encl.); CO879/48, Stewart to governor, 18 Dec. 1896.

34 SOM-AN Afrique VI, 149, a, Ferguson's treaties and Voulet's letters.

35 CO879/45, F.O. to C.O., 23 Nov. 1896 (encl. memo by Everett); SOM-AN Afrique III, 26, a, Rapport Voulet, no. 10 (Feb. 1897); agreement with Stewart, 9 Feb. 1897.

36 Chanoine, *Documents*, pp. 108–14. A map of the itinerary is appended to this volume.

37 Morisson, *Le Pénétration dans la Boucle du Niger*.

38 See M. Piguet, *La Mission Voulet au Mossi et au Gourounsi* (Paris, 1898).

39 SOM-AN Soudan III, 3, Mission Destenave (1897), Rapport Destenave.

40 Chanoine, *Documents*, pp. xiv–xv: "Le Mossi se divise en principautés dont les six principales sont: Ouagadougou, Boussoumo, Yatenga, Rissima, Yako, et Lale. Les Nabas reconnaissent tous l'autorité du Naba de Ouagadougou, mais ne lui paient de redevance que quand bon leur semble, lui font la guerre parfois." See Skinner, *Mossi of Upper Volta*, p. 110.

41 George Cheron, *L'Exploration et la Conquête du Mossi* (sample manuscript) in SOM-AN, Bibliothèque, R429d; R. Pageard, "Refléxions sur l'histoire du Mossi," in *L'Homme*, no. 1 (Jan.–Feb. 1962), pp. 111–15.

42 "La Mission Fonssagrives et l'affaire Yagbasson," in *Rev. Col. et Pays Protectorat*, no. 7 (July 1896), pp. 783–86; SOM-AN Dahomey IV, 3 (Hint. Dah.), Lebon to Hanotaux, 27 Nov. 1896 (draft).

43 A.N. MI 214, Journal Bartet, p. 66.

44 Hans Gruner, "Die Franzosischen Auspruche aus das Hinterland von Togo," *D.K.Z.*, no. 48 (30 Nov. 1895), pp. 377–78.

45 "Mission Bretonnet," in *B.C.A.F.*, March 1898, p. 91. H. E. Bretonnet (1864–99) was a lieutenant in the colonial detachment from 1892. He was chief of the escort of the Mizon expedition of 1892–93. He headed an expedition in the Ivory Coast hinterland in 1895 to Diamala and Djimini and the French expedition to

the Niger, Dec. 1896 to January 1898. He was in the Chari expedition, October 1898 to July 1899. He died in battle at Togbao near Lake Chad.

46 Flint, *Sir George Goldie,* pp. 225–57, quoting FO27/3368, Goldie to officer commanding the European expedition, reported at Boussa, 17 Feb. 1897; Bretonnet to Goldie, 23 Feb. 1897 (encl. Goldie to F.O., 8 April 1897).

47 G. Ganier, "La Mission Ganier dans le Haut Dahomey, 1897–1898," in *Revue Fr. d'Histoire d'Outre-Mer,* vol. 49, no. 2 (1962), p. 201.

48 FO27/3408, Salisbury to Monson, 27 Jan. 1898; FO27/3410, Monson to Salisbury, 14 Jan. 1898, Africa no. 19; 1 Feb. 1898; SOM-AN Afrique VI, 149, c, colonies to M.A.E., 12 Feb. 1898; Monson to Hanotaux, 29 Jan. 1898, minutes by Binger.

49 Baud's escort was under the charge of Veermersch. There were 30 Senegalese tirailleurs, 50 men from the Dahomey civil guards, and 100 porters.

50 Von Zech, "Vermischte Notizen uber Togo und das Togo Hinterland," in *Mittheilungen aus den deutschen Schutzgebieten* (1898), p. 89. See also *Deutsche Kolonialblatt* 7 (1896) on his expedition from Krachi to Salaga.

51 SOM-AN Dahomey IV, 3 (Hint. Dah.), Baud to Ballot, 17 Feb. 1897, 23 March 1897.

52 Ibid., 17 Feb. 1897.

53 "Mission Baud-Vermeersch," in *B.C.A.F.,* April 1898, pp. 127–30.

54 The disruption of trade as a result of the expeditions of 1897–98 is reflected in the trade figures for exports for these years. Exports of Dahomey dropped from 9,224,491 francs for 1896 to a paltry 5,778,858 francs for 1897 and 7,538,758 francs in 1898. See table 7, p. 189 above.

55 "Mission Baud-Vermeersch," p. 130.

56 SOM-AN Dahomey IV, 3 (Hint. Dah.), Lebon to Ballot, 22 Jan. 1897 (encl. note by Binger). The triangle formed by Carnotville, Wagadugu, and Ilo was to be effectively occupied, said Lebon.

57 A.N., MI 214, Journal Bartet, pp. 18–23. Dr. Alfred Bartet was the medical officer attached to the Ganier expedition. His diary was discovered during my research in 1965 by the aid of Mlle. Germaine Ganier. Dr. Bartet was then 96 and lived in Rheims. He died in 1968. His carefully kept diary is a valuable source of information on the occupation of Borgu, Gurma, and the situation of these kingdoms during the period.

58 Ibid., p. 19. The *Thibet* brought the tirailleurs from Senegal instead of the *Fraissinet* mentioned in Lebon's letter to Ballot.

59 Captain Ferdinand Ganier (1848–1900) fought in 1870–71 as a sublieutenant in the army of the Loire. He chose French citizenship after the annexation of the Vosges by the Germans. He quickly rose to lieutenant and then captain in the infantry of the navy. He served in New Caledonia and was posted to Senegal in November 1896. He led the Dahomey hinterland expedition of 1897–98, was recalled to Senegal in 1899, and died on 2 August 1900 of yellow fever in St. Louis. See Ganier, *Papiers d'Afrique,* p. 28.

60 A.N., MI 214, Journal Bartet, pp. 13–15. The empty villages were due to the effort by young men to avoid being drafted as porters and to the fact that many people were out in the farm lands preparing their fields for the planting season.

61 Ibid., p. 19. Dr. Bartet copied Ballot's instructions to Ganier verbatum "to fill the afternoon of forced rest" at Zagnanado on April 4, 1897.

62 Papiers Ganier, carton 1, Ballot to Ganier, 22 March 1897, "Objets de la Mission:

Instructions Politiques," pp. 18–23. This 20-page manuscript contains the original instructions to Ganier. The private papers of F. Ganier are in the possession of Mlle. G. Ganier at Versailles.

63 A.N., MI 214, Journal Bartet, p. 20, quoting Portes to Ballot, 7 March 1897
64 Ibid., "Instructions politiques," p. 21. Ganier's seconds were Sublieutenants L. P. Drot and P. E. Aymes.
65 SOM-AN Dahomey IV, 3, Ballot to Lebon, 21 Feb. 1897; Lebon to Ballot, 30 Jan. 1897.
66 A.N., MI 214, Journal Bartet, pp. 21–23; SOM-AN Dahomey IV, 3, Lebon to governor general of A.O.F., 28 Jan. 1897. In this letter Lebon stressed the necessity for cooperation with Dahomey and Sudan for the success of French policy.
67 SOM-AN Dahomey IV, 3, Ballot to Lebon, 23 March 1897. Ganier had 500 porters, 6 of whom were charged with loads of gifts for native chiefs.
68 A.N., MI 214, Journal Bartet, pp. 25–27, 36. About 150 porters escaped by the time Ganier got to Zagnanado. One carrier was shot dead as he tried to escape. "A sordid example, but a necessary lesson," observed Dr. Bartet.
69 SOM-AN Dahomey IV, 3, Ballot to Lebon, 23 April 1897. Lebon was told that at Ganier's rate of progress he would not get to Kuandé till 10 May 1897. A.N., MI 214, "Journal Bartet," Ballot to Ganier, quoted on p. 17.
70 A.N., MI 214, Journal Bartet, p. 23.
71 Ibid., pp. 16–17. Mournier was Ballot's brother-in-law.
72 Papiers Ganier, carton 1, "Journal de marche du Capitaine Ganier, 1 March 1897 à 12 Jan. 1898"; SOM-AN Dahomey IV, 3, Rapport Ganier, Journal de marche, March 1897–Jan. 1898.
73 Papiers Ganier, carton 2, Molex to Ballot, 1 May 1897 (copy). The documents in carton 2 were copied from Porto Novo Archives.
74 Ibid., Ganier to Ballot, 11 May 1897.
75 Ibid., 12 May 1897.
76 Dr. A. L. Bartet, "Colonne expéditionnaire dans le Haut-Dahomey, 1897–1898," in *Archives de médecine navale* (July, Aug., and Sept. 1898), quoted in Ganier, "La Mission Ganier," p. 217. Mlle. Ganier did not know that Dr. Bartet was still alive when she wrote her article. G. Ganier to B. Obichere, 4 Jan. 1965.
77 Papiers Ganier, carton 2, Ganier to Ballot, 19 May 1897 (copy).
78 Ibid., Molex to Ballot, 30 May 1897; Molex to Ballot, 3 June 1897; SOM-AN Dahomey IV, 3 (Hint. Dah.), "Journal de Marche du Capt. Ganier, Mars 1897–Janvier 1898."
79 SOM-AN Afrique VI, 142, a, Lebon to Hanotaux, 4 May 1897. The French consul in Hamburg sent the extracts from the *Hamburgischer Correspondent* to Hanotaux on 25 March 1897. *Die Post*, 19 March 1897.
80 "Die Abgrenzung in Hinterland der Togokolonie," in *D.K.Z.,* no. 20 (15 May 1897), p. 193.
81 SOM-AN Dahomey IV, 3 (Hint. Dah.), Lebon to Ballot, 20 May 1897; Lebon to Hanotaux, 22 March 1897; Hanotaux to Lebon, 13 March 1897, minutes by Binger: "Le cabinet a câblé hier au Dahomey."
82 SOM-AN Afrique VI, 127, a, extract of the German plan published with a map in *Kreutz-Zeitung,* 2 Oct. 1895; "Die Eingabe uber das Hinterland von Togo," in *D.K.Z.,* no. 16 (17 April 1897), pp. 152–54 (with map).

83 See F.O. Confidential Print No. 7229, *Correspondence relative to Anglo-German Boundaries on the Gold Coast, 1896–97.*
84 "Die Abgrenzung in Hinterland der Togokolonie," p. 193. Gruner's treaty with Turuturiba Adama was evoked in this article. "Uber Gurma," in *D.K.Z.*, no. 14 (3 April 1897), p. 135; "Koloniale Grenzfragen," in *D.K.Z.*, no. 10 (6 March 1897), p. 92.
85 M.A.E., Papiers Hanotaux, vol. 2, "Note sur la politique extérieure du Ministère Méline, 1896–1898," by Hanotaux, p. 15. The Togo question was discussed by Hanotaux and Hohenlohe in "Chronologie du Ministère Méline."
86 SOM-AN Afrique IV, 38, b, Hanotaux to Lebon, 3 June 1896, 11 Dec. 1896.
87 SOM-AN Afrique VI, 144, a, Lebon to Hanotaux, 26 Jan. 1897; SOM-AN Dahomey I, 17, colonies to Ballot (draft), 26 March 1897.
88 "La Mission allemande dans le Boucle du Niger," in *B.C.A.F.*, Nov. 1895; *La Politique Coloniale,* Oct. 1895.
89 "Vom Bogen des Niger und dem Tschadsee," in *D.K.Z.*, no. 12 (20 March 1897), p. 114; "Vom Bogen des Niger," in *D.K.Z.*, no. 15 (10 April 1897), p. 144; SOM-AN Dahomey IV, 3 (Hint. Dah.), Ballot to Lebon, 23 June 1897 (encl. Ganier to Ballot, 7 June 1897).
90 SOM-AN Dahomey IV, Ballot to Lebon, 11 July 1897, quoted in Ganier, "La Mission Ganier," p. 233.
91 SOM-AN Dahomey IV, Ganier to Ballot, 7 June 1897 (encl. in Ballot to Lebon, 23 June 1897).
92 M.A.E., Correspondence Politique, Grande Bretagne n.s.8 (1897–98), Hanotaux to Courcel, 4 July 1897 (tel.).
93 SOM-AN Dahomey IV, Ballot to Lebon, 29 June 1897; Bretonet to Ballot, 28 June 1897; Papiers Ganier, carton 2, Molex to Ballot, 17 July 1897.
94 SOM-AN Afrique VI, 142, a, Monson to Hanotaux, 12 May 1897 (encl. extract from *Le Temps*); Lebon to Hanotaux, 17 June 1897.
95 "Zur Frage des Togo-Hinterlandes," in *D.K.Z.*, no. 21 (22 May 1897), p. 205; "Die Togokonferenz," in *D.K.Z.*, no. 22 (29 May 1897), p. 213. See *B.C.A.F.*, May 1897. The German negotiators were Dr. Zimmermann, Messrs. Muller, Kohler, and Vohsen, and Professor Dankelmann. See *Der Reichsanzeiger* (Berlin) Oct. 19, 1897.
96 M.A.E., Doc. Dipl. *Convention relative à la délimitation des possessions francaises du Dahomey et du Soudan et des possessions allemandes du Togo* (Paris, 1897); *Beilage zur D.K.Z.*, no. 22 (May 1897), pp. 95–96 (with map). "Das deutschfranzosische Abkomen uber die Abgrenzung von Togo," in *D.K.Z.* no. 44 (30 Oct. 1897) pp. 445–46.
97 There was adverse criticism of the convention in Germany. See "Die Togokonferenz," in *D.K.Z.*, no. 30 (24 July 1897), p. 295; "Die Togo Vertrag," *D.K.Z.*, no. 32 (7 Aug. 1897), p. 315.
98 Ganier, "La Mission Ganier," p. 232.
99 FO403/235, F.O. to C.O., 30 May 1896 (encl. "Reports of British Representatives on the Niger Commission").
100 CO879/45, C.O. to F.O., 13 July 1896; F.O. to C.O., 30 July 1896 (encl. "Memorandum on the proposed Mission in the Hinterland of the Gold Coast," by Col. W. Everett, 23 July 1896).

101 CO879/45, C.O. to F.O., 7 Aug. 1896; F.O. to C.O., 18 Aug. 1896 (encl. "Memorandum on proposed Missions to Wagadugu, Bona, Wa," by Henry Howard, 5 Aug. 1896).
102 CO879/45, C.O. to F.O., 14 Sept. 1896 (encl. minutes by Gov. Maxwell, 5 Sept. 1896); FO27/3301, C.O. to F.O., 26 Sept. 1896; F.O. to C.O., 1 Oct. 1896.
103 CO879/45, C.O. to Maxwell, 3 Oct. 1896.
104 Ibid., Maxwell to Chamberlain, 2 Nov. 1896, 10 Dec. 1896 (tel.).
105 Ibid., 19 Nov. 1896 (encl. instructions to Capt. Stewart, resident of Kumasi [Secret], and to F. B. Henderson, traveling commissioner, 18 Nov. 1896).
106 CO879/45, F.O. to C.O., 10 Nov. 1896 (encl. Gosselin to Salisbury, 7 Nov. 1896); FO27/3276, Gosselin to Salisbury, 13 Nov. 1896, Africa no. 196 (encl. *Politique Coloniale,* 7 Nov. 1896).
107 FO27/3301, C.O. to F.O., 27 Nov. 1896; F.O. to C.O., 30 Nov. 1896. Chamberlain contended that the French occupation of Mossi was "an unfriendly act."
108 CO879/45, F.O. to C.O., 23 Nov. 1896 (encl. "Memorandum on the Reported Occupation of Mossi by Lieut. Voulet," by William Everett, 19 Nov. 1896); Chamberlain to Maxwell, 1 Dec. 1896 (tel.).
109 FO403/234, F.O. to C.O., 2 Dec. 1896 (encl. "Les Allemandes et la Compagnie du Niger," in *Journal des Débats,* 26 Nov. 1896).
110 CO879/45, F.O. to C.O., 29 Dec. 1896 (encl. Monson to Salisbury, 26 Dec. 1896, Africa no. 14 [Tel.]); FO27/3226, Monson to Salisbury, 27 Dec. 1896, Africa no. 236.
111 CO879/48, Maxwell to Chamberlain, 23 Feb. 1897 (tel.); Maxwell to Chamberlain, 29 Jan. 1897 (encl. Stewart to governor, 16 Dec. 1896; Henderson to governor, 1 and 2 Jan. 1897); Hodgson to Stewart, 5 Jan. 1897; Maxwell to Chamberlain, 26 Feb. 1897 (conf.).
112 CO879/48, Maxwell to Chamberlain, 5 Feb. 1897 (encl. Stewart to governor, 29 Dec. 1896 [Gambaga]); C.O. to F.O., 22 March 1897 (encl. Maxwell to Chamberlain, 18 March 1897 [tel.]); Maxwell to Chamberlain, 30 March 1897 (tel.).
113 CO879/48, Maxwell to Chamberlain, 31 March 1897 (encl. Stewart to governor, 18 Feb. 1897); Voulet to Monsieur, 6 Feb. 1897, 30 Jan. 1897. In the postscript Voulet stressed that a filibustering adventurer was outside the laws and protection of a civilized power. "Entente Provisoire conclué dans un but de Conciliation entre les Représentants de la France et de l'Angleterre à (Tengrugu) Tenkodogo," 9 Fevrier 1897.
114 CO879/48, Stewart to governor, 1 and 3 Feb. 1897; C.O. to F.O., 27 April 1897; Stewart to governor, 29 Dec. 1896 (private); C.O. to F.O., 6 and 30 April 1897.
115 CO879/48, Henderson to governor, 9 Jan. 1897 (encl. treaty with Wa [Dagarti]).
116 Ibid., Maxwell to Chamberlain, 2 March 1897 (encl. Henderson to governor, 28 Jan. 1897); Barbatu to Henderson (received 21 Jan. 1897).
117 Ibid., Henderson to governor, 9 and 10 Jan. 1897 (private).
118 CO879/45, C.O. to F.O., 16 Dec. 1896; F.O. to C.O., 24 Dec. 1896; CO879/48, Maxwell to Chamberlain, 6 March 1897; F.O. to C.O., 29 March 1897 (encl. Salisbury to Monson, 25 March 1897); Chamberlain to Maxwell, 4 June 1897 (confidential).
119 CO879/48, Chamberlain to War Office, 29 Jan. 1897; War Office to C.O., 23 Feb. 1897, 3 March 1897; Maxwell to Chamberlain, 8 April 1897 (encl. "Instruc-

tions for the Guidance of Officers employed in the Gold Coast Hinterland, 1897," 7 April 1897).
120 Ibid., Maxwell to Chamberlain, 6 March 1897.
121 Ibid., 26 April 1897 (tel.), 1 May 1897; Chamberlain to F.O., 27 April 1897; C.O. to War Office, 27 April 1897; C.O. to Admiralty, 27 April 1897. Chamberlain enclosed a copy of Maxwell's telegram in each of these letters. Maxwell to Chamberlain, 7 May 1897 (encl. Leland to governor, 15 April 1897); Stewart to Maxwell, 26 April 1897.
122 CO879/48, Maxwell to Chamberlain, 3 June 1897 (encl. Henderson to Maxwell, 17 May 1897).
123 Ibid., Chamberlain to Goldie, 1 July 1897.
124 CO879/48, Chamberlain to Maxwell, 4 June 1897 (confidential).
125 Ibid., Chamberlain to Goldie, 1 July 1897.
126 FO64/1421, Salisbury to Lascelles, 17 Feb. 1897, Africa no. 20; FO64/1409, Gough to Salisbury, 8 April 1897, Africa no. 41.
127 CO879/48, C.O. to F.O., 13 May 1897; F.O. to C.O., 19 May 1897; C.O. to F.O., 17 June 1897.
128 FO403/248, F.O. to C.O., 7 May 1897 (encl. draft letter to Monson).
129 CO879/48, C.O. to F.O., 19 May 1897; F.O. to C.O., 26 May 1897.
130 CO879/48, Chamberlain to Maxwell, 4 June 1897 (confidential).
131 Ibid.
132 Ibid., C.O. to War Office, 30 April 1897.
133 Ibid., War Office to C.O., 8 May 1897 (encl. "Memorandum on the Estimated Military Strength and Resources of Samory, Chief of the Sofas," by Major Northcott, Intelligence Division of the War Office, 3 May 1897).
134 CO879/48, Goldie to Chamberlain, 28 May 1897; C.O. to F.O., 26 June 1896; F.O. to C.O., 30 June 1897.
135 Ibid., Chamberlain to Goldie, 1 July 1897.
136 CO879/48, Chamberlain to Goldie, 1 July 1897. This view arose from Chamberlain's conviction that France would withdraw when confronted by a force superior to hers. This conviction was shaken by the tenacity of the French, and by autumn of 1897 Chamberlain's views had changed on the possibility of war with France in west Africa. See Chamberlain to Selborne, 29 Sept. 1897, quoted in Garvin, *Life of Chamberlain* 3:211.
137 CO879/48, Chamberlain to Goldie, 1 July 1897; Goldie to C.O., 19 July 1897; CO96/308, Goldie to C.O., 19 July 1897.
138 CO879/48, Goldie to C.O., 21 July 1897. This is the first time the name Nigeria was used in official correspondence.
139 FO83/1530, C.O. to F.O., 16 July 1897; FO27/3370, F.O. to R.N.C., 23 July 1897; R.N.C. to F.O., 27 July 1897.
140 Chamberlain to Selborne, 19 Sept. 1897, quoted in Garvin 3:209–210.
141 FO83/1533, "Memorandum on Meeting with Goldie," 7 Sept. 1897; Hill to Goldie, 10 Sept. 1897; Goldie to F.O., 14 Sept. 1897; Chamberlain to F.O., 22 Sept. 1897; R.N.C. to F.O., 24 Sept. 1897, minutes by T. H. S[anderson] and Salisbury. On Goldie and the British government at this period, see Flint, *Sir Georgie Goldie,* pp. 264–312.
142 Chamberlain Papers, J.C. 11/6, Chamberlain to Selborne, 12 Sept. 1897 (secret).

143 George Earl Buckle, *The Letters of Queen Victoria,* 3rd series, 1886–1901 (London, 1930–32), 3:209–12.
144 Maurice Crouzet, "Joseph Chamberlain," in *Les Politiques d'expansion imperialiste* (Paris, 1949), ed. Pierre Renouvin, pp. 179–81.
145 Chamberlain Papers, J.C. 11/6, Chamberlain to Selborne, 29 Sept. 1897, quoted in Garvin, *Life of Chamberlain* 3:211.
146 Chamberlain Papers, J.C. 11/6, Chamberlain to Salisbury, 6 June 1897.
147 CO879/48, Gosselin to Salisbury, 1 July 1897, Africa no. 200; C.O. to F.O., 14 July 1897. Chamberlain was incensed by the fact that dispatches from Paris showed that Hanotaux regarded the question of Bussa as one to be settled by the Niger Commission. Monson to Hanotaux, 1 July 1897 (encl. in Monson to Salisbury, 1 July 1897, Africa no. 201).
148 Perham, *Lugard,* p. 637. Lugard's appointment as commandant was gazetted on 26 Aug. 1897. See Haywood and Clark, *Royal West African Frontier Force,* pp. 31–32.
149 CO147/115, Chamberlain to McCallum, 23 July 1897.
150 CO879/48, C.O. to F.O., 14 Aug. 1897; C.O. to F.O., 25 Aug. 1897 (encl. Intelligence Division of the War Office to C.O., 17 Aug. 1897).
151 CO147/124, F.O. to C.O., 19 Aug. 1897; FO83/1538, Goldie to Sanderson, 30 Nov. 1897, minutes by Salisbury.
152 CO879/48, Goldie to C.O., 21 July 1897.
153 FO83/1533, Hill to Goldie, 10 Sept. 1897; Goldie to F.O., 14 Sept. 1897.
154 Ibid., F.O. to Goldie, 23 Sept. 1897 (draft by Salisbury); Chamberlain to Selborne, 19 Sept. 1897, quoted in Garvin, *Life of Chamberlain* 3:209–10.
155 SOM-AN Afrique VI, 149, c, Pontarice to minister of war, 10 May 1898. Chamberlain's statement to the Royal Colonial Institute that "the doors of the Temple of Janus are never closed in the wide dominions of the Queen" did not allay French fears. M.A.E. C.P., n.s.29, Empire Britannique: Dossier Général, 1897–1901; Geoffrey to Hanotaux, 1 April 1897 (encl. *The Times* [London], 1 April 1897); SOM-AN Afrique VI, 142, a, Lebon to Hanotaux, 11 Sept. 1897.
156 CO875/48, F.O. to C.O., 12 July 1897 (encl. Monson to Salisbury, 10 July 1897 [tel.]), Africa no. 4; FO27/3339, Monson to Salisbury, 5 and 17 Sept. 1897; FO27/3343, Monson to Salisbury, 16 Sept. 1897.
157 FO27/3372, F.O. to C.O., 21 Sept. 1897.
158 CO147/124, C.O. to F.O., 17 Sept. 1897; FO27/3372, C.O. to F.O., 27 Sept. 1897.
159 FO27/3372, C.O. to F.O., 30 Sept. 1897 (encl. instructions to the governors of Lagos and the Gold Coast).
160 House of Commons Debate, 24 Feb. 1898, *Hansard,* 4th series, vol. 53, cols. 1617–28; Garvin, *Life of Chamberlain* 3:215; A. F. Madden, "Changing Attitudes," in *Camb. Hist. of The Brit. Empire* 3:389. See CO879/51, West African Frontier Force: Papers (23 July 1897–24 March 1898).
161 "Les Anglais dans l'arrière pays de la Cote d'Or," in *Journal des Débats,* 5 May 1897.
162 CO879/48, Maxwell to Chamberlain, 26 April 1897; C.O. to Admiralty, 27 April 1897; C.O. to War Office, 27 April 1897; C.O. to F.O., 27 April 1897; War Office to C.O., 29 April 1897; Admiralty to C.O., 29 April 1897; McCallum to Chamber-

lain, 28 April 1897; "Les Anglais dans l'Ouest Africain," in *Le Temps,* 4 Oct. 1897. The *Heron* and the *Jackdaw.*

163 Ibid., C.O. to War Office, 19 May 1897; Maxwell to Chamberlain, 14 May 1897, 17 May 1897 (tel.); F.O. to C.O., 28 May 1897.

164 Ibid., Maxwell to Chamberlain, 26 June 1897 (tel.); SOM-AN Afrique VI, 142, a, Nissard to Lebon, 6 July 1897 (encl. Gosselin to Hanotaux, 30 June 1897).

165 SOM-AN Afrique VI, 142, a, Hanotaux to Lebon, 8 July 1897 (encl. Courcel to Hanotaux, 24 June 1897; Salisbury to Courcel, June 1897 [Copy]); CO879/48, McCallum to C.O., 31 May 1897.

166 FO27/3339, Monson to Salisbury, 5 Sept. 1897.

CHAPTER 8

1 M.A.E., Papiers Hanotaux, vol. 2, "Notes sur la politique étrangère de la France," Draft by Hanotaux, Sept. 1896. In this note Hanotaux gave top priority to the maintenance of the general peace in the foreign policy aims of France. Chamberlain would seek an Anglo-German alliance in the spring of 1898. J. A. S. Grenville, *Lord Salisbury and Foreign Policy: The Close of the Nineteenth Century* (London, 1964), pp. 110–12, 123.

2 M.A.E., Papiers Hanotaux, vol. 2, "Compte rendu Entrevue avec Lord Salisbury," 27 March 1897. The interview took place on 26 March at the French Foreign Office and the British Embassy. Hanotaux's notes are the only extant full account of the interview. The Salisbury Papers contain none. See A. L. Kennedy, *Salisbury, 1830–1903: Portrait of a Statesman* (London, 1953), pp. 280–82.

3 M.A.E., Papiers Hanotaux, vol. 2, "Note sur la politique extérieure du Ministère Méline, 1896–1898," by Hanotaux, p. 15; SOM-AN Afrique VI, 142, a, Hanotaux to Lebon, 30 March 1897 (confidential); Lebon to Hanotaux, 15 April 1897; Hanotaux to Lebon, 3 May 1897.

4 SOM-AN Afrique VI, 142, a, Monson to Méline, 19 Aug. 1897; Méline to Monson, 26 Aug. 1897.

5 Ibid., Hanotaux to Lebon, 20 Sept. 1897; Lebon to Hanotaux, 22 Sept. 1897, 6 Oct. 1897; Salisbury Papers, A/119, Salisbury to Monson, 19 Oct. 1897; M.A.E. C.P., n.s.29 (Grande Bretagne), Geoffrey to Hanotaux, 12 Oct. 1897.

6 M.A.E. C.P., n.s.29 (Grande Bretagne), Geoffrey to Hanotaux, 12 Oct. 1897; SOM-AN Afrique VI, 142, b, "Protocols des Séances de la Commission du Niger: Reprise des conferences en 1897," 1ere Séance, 29 Oct. 1897.

7 Salisbury Papers, A/119, Salisbury to Monson, 19 Oct. 1897.

8 Ibid. Salisbury added that he did not think war would result from this policy.

9 The British representatives at the resumed Niger Commission were Martin Gosselin of the Paris Embassy and Col. William Everett of the Intelligence Division, War Office. The French were represented by G. Binger, head of the Africa department of the Ministry of Colonies, René Lecomte, and Capt. Toutée.

10 SOM-AN Afrique VI, 142, a, Hanotaux to Lebon, 15 Oct. 1897. See K. Vignes "Etude sur les relations diplomatiques Franco-Britanniques qui conduisirent à la Convention du 14 Juin 1898," in *Revue Fr. d'Histoire d'Outre-Mer,* vol. 52, nos. 188–89 (1965), pp. 352–403.

11 M.A.E. C.P., n.s.11 (Grande Bretagne: Relations avec la France, 1897–98), Hano-

taux to Courcel, 4 July 1897 (tel.); SOM-AN Afrique VI, 142, a, Hanotaux to Lebon, 3 Oct. 1897; Lebon to Hanotaux, 6 Oct. 1897.

12 SOM-AN Afrique VI, 142, a, Lebon to Hanotaux, 6 Oct. 1897 (urgent and conf.), minutes by G. Binger (n.d.).

13 M.A.E. C.P., n.s.11 (Grande Bretagne), French Chamber of Commerce of London to Hanotaux, 22 April 1897; Hanotaux to Courcel, 27 April 1897 (draft); Geoffrey to Hanotaux, 21 May 1897. The leader of the Entente Association in Paris was de Lanessan; the London group was led by Leon Clerc.

14 FO403/251, Negotiations at Paris: Further Correspondence, part 2, Oct. 1897–June 1898, Gosselin to Salisbury, 30 Oct. 1897, 5 Nov. 1897 (with enclosures); FO27/3343, Gosselin to Salisbury, 29 Oct. 1897, Africa no. 27 (tel.); 10 Oct. 1897.

15 CO879/50, C.O. to F.O., 10 Nov. 1897; F.O. to C.O., 11 Nov. 1897; C.O. to F.O., 12 Nov. 1897; Memorandum on the Boundary Questions in the Bend of the Niger, by Col. W. Everett, 30 Oct. 1897.

16 FO27/3336, Salisbury to Gosselin, 11 Nov. 1897, Africa no. 351; Chamberlain Papers, J.C. 11/6, Chamberlain to Selborne, 12 Sept. 1897; J.C. 5/7, Salisbury to Chamberlain, 17 Sept. 1897.

17 FO27/3340, Monson to Salisbury, 14 Nov. 1897, Africa no. 368.

18 FO83/537, memorandum by Chamberlain, 16 Nov. 1897; CO879/50, Memorandum on Claims of Great Britain and France in the Territories adjacent to the Gold Coast, by Antrobus, 3 Nov. 1897; CO879/50, C.O. to F.O., 22 Nov. 1897.

19 FO27/3336, Salisbury to Monson, 23 Nov. 1897, Africa no. 367; 26 Nov. 1897.

20 FO403/251, Monson to Salisbury, 24 Nov. 1897, Africa no. 37. See Margery Perham and Mary Bull, *The Diaries of Lord Lugard* (London, 1963), pp. 326–34 (1st diary, July 1894–April 1895; 2nd diary, Oct. 1897–June 1898).

21 M.A.E. C.P., n.s.8 (Grand Bretagne), Courcel to Hanotaux, 7 May 1897, no. 228; Salisbury's speech to the Primrose League in the Albert Hall; n.s.11 (Grande Bretagne), Courcel to Hanotaux, 17 Nov. 1897, no. 492; Salisbury's speech on the policy of the Unionists, delivered at the Albert Hall.

22 M.A.E. C.P., n.s.8 (Grande Bretagne), Geoffrey to Hanotaux, 10 Nov. 1897, no. 485 (encl. *The Standard,* 10 Nov. 1897 [Extract]).

23 CO879/48, McCallum to Chamberlain, 31 May 1897 (encl. Ballot to McCallum, 25 May 1897); 5 May 1897 (encl. *Journal Officiel du Dahomey,* 15 April 1897).

24 SOM-AN Dahomey IV, 3 (Hint. Dah.), Ballot to Lebon, 2 Aug. 1897; Rapport Politique, by Ballot, 22 Aug. 1897; Lebon to Ballot, 26 Aug. 1897.

25 Ibid., Ballot to Lebon, 18 and 22 Sept. 1897; Papiers Ganier, carton 2, Ganier to governor, 8 Sept. 1897; Vermeersch to Ganier, 20 Sept. 1897. Kouande and Wassa in western Borgu were trouble spots at this time.

26 FO27/3372, C.O. to F.O., 15 Oct. 1897 (encl. McCallum to Chamberlain, 13 Oct. 1897); Ballot Papers, MI 185/4, Ballot to McCallum, 20, 28, and 30 Oct. 1897, 5 Nov. 1897; CO879/50, C.O. to F.O., 11 Nov. 1897 (encl. letters seized from French messengers); SOM-AN Afrique VI, 142, a, Lebon to Hanotaux, 16 Nov. 1897.

27 SOM-AN Afrique VI, 142, a, Monson to Hanotaux, 28 Sept. 1897; Hanotaux to Lebon, 28 Sept. 1897 (très urgent); Lebon to Hanotaux, 29 Sept. 1897.

28 SOM-AN Afrique IV, 38, b, Monson to Hanotaux, 28 Nov. 1897 (encl. in Hanotaux to Lebon, 2 Dec. 1897); Lebon to Hanotaux, 14 Oct. 1897, no. 519 (confidential); VI, 149, c, Hanotaux to Lebon, 25 Jan. 1898.
29 SOM-AN Afrique VI, 142, a, Binger to Hanotaux, 5 Nov. 1987; Hanotaux to Lebon, 27 Oct. 1897.
30 SOM-AN Afrique IV, 38, b, Lebon to Hanotaux, 27 Oct. 1897; M.A.E. to Lebon, 20 Oct. 1897 (encl. Geoffrey to Hanotaux, 9 Oct. 1897 [Copy]).
31 SOM-AN Afrique VI, 142, a, Courcel to Hanotaux, 2 Dec. 1897 (copy); M.A.E. C. P., Angleterre 920, Geoffrey to Hanotaux, 26 Nov. 1896.
32 FO83/1538, memorandum by Salisbury, 30 Nov. 1897; memorandum by Chamberlain, 1 Dec. 1897. A Chinde-type concession meant the application to the Niger of the navigation regulations for the Zambezi which Britain imposed on Portugal to protect the interest of Nyasaland and the British South Africa Company.
33 CO879/50, C.O. to F.O., 27 Dec. 1897 (encl. memorandum, 25 Dec. 1897); C.O. to F.O., 29 Dec. 1897; FO27/3374, C.O. to F.O., 29 Dec. 1897.
34 FO27/3336, Salisbury to Monson, 30 Dec. 1897, Africa no. 438.
35 M.A.E., Doc. Dipl. *Affaires du Haut-Nil et du Bahr-El-Ghazal, Fachoda, 1897–1898* (Paris, 1898), pp. 1–3; Monson to Hanotaux, 10 Dec. 1897; Hanotaux to Monson, 24 Dec. 1897. At this time Marchand was on his way to Fachoda. Hanotaux provided 25,000 francs for Marchand's mission from the *fonds speciaux* of the Ministère des Affaires Etrangères. See Hanotaux Papers, vol. 11, "Fonds Secrets, 1898."
36 On the "polemic battle" between the British and French press which seemed to hinder an amicable settlement, see Monson to Salisbury, 6 March 1898 in G. P. Gooch and H. Temperley, eds., *British Documents on the Origins of the War, 1898–1914*, 11 vols. (London, 1926–30), vol. 1, no. 173, pp. 146–47. Many documents pertinent to these negotiations are printed in Gooch and Temperley.
37 M. F. Lindley, *The Acquisition and Government of Backward Territory in International Law* (London, 1926), pp. 188–206. See Eugène Ortolan, *Des Moyens d'acquérir le Domaine International* (Paris, 1851).
38 Recent studies of customary land laws in the territories under investigation include N. A. Ollennu, *Principles of Customary Land Law in Ghana: Law in Africa No. 2* (London, 1962); M. O. Onwuamaegbu, *Law of Landlord and Tenant in Nigeria: Law in Africa No. 12* (London, 1966); L. T. Chubb, *Ibo Land Tenure* (London, 1961). See also T. O. Elias, *Nigeria Land Law and Custom* (London, 1954).
39 SOM-AN Dahomey IV, 3, Ballot to Lebon, 23 June 1897 (encl. Ganier to Ballot, 7 June 1897); Ballot to Lebon, 21 July 1897; Ganier to Ballot, 8 Aug. 1897.
40 F. D. Lugard, *Dual Mandate in Tropical Africa* (Edinburgh, 1922), pp. 9–29, 32–42.
41 Lindley, *Backward Territory*, pp. 182–88, 172–74.
42 CO879/48, Stewart to Gov. Maxwell, 1 and 3 Feb. 1897.
43 Duboc, *L'Epopee Coloniale*, pp. 162–63.
44 Northcott, *Northern Territories of the Gold Coast*, pp. 14–15. Boukary Koutou did not refuse to enter Gambaga "because of the tradition that if he ever saw the

Gambaga ruler, both of them would die," as Dr. E. P. Skinner stated. Northcott, who had personal contact with Boukary Koutou, presents more reliable evidence. See Skinner, *Mossi of Upper Volta*, p. 152.

45 Colonial Reports, Northern Territories of the Gold Coast, 1905; Dim Delobson, *Mogho Naba*, p. 45.
46 Lindley, *Backward Territory*, pp. 172–74.
47 Ganier Papers, carton 2, Ganier to Ballot, 19 May 1897.
48 Lugard, *Dual Mandate*, pp. 14–15. The case of Béhanzin of Dahomey and the treaty of 3 Oct. 1890 with France illustrates this point.
49 Lindley, chap. 19, pp. 137–59, on effective occupation. See Gaston Jèze, *Etude théorique et practique sur l'Occupation comme mode d'acquérir les Territories en Droit International* (Paris, 1896).
50 Professor Renault was professor of international law at the Sorbonne and legal adviser to the Quai d'Orsay.
51 FO27/3410, Proceedings of the Niger Commission, 7 Jan. 1898.
52 Ibid., Monson to Salisbury, 11 Jan. 1898, Africa no. 159.
53 FO403/251, Monson to Salisbury, 14 Jan. 1898.
54 D.D.F., 1st series, vol. 13, no. 46, p. 46, Courcel to Hanotaux, 17 Dec. 1896.
55 FO27/3410, Monson to Salisbury, 11 Jan. 1898, Africa no. 159, minutes by Salisbury.
56 CO537/14, memorandum by Chamberlain, 25 Jan. 1898; C.O. to F.O., 28 Jan. 1898; FO27/3410, Monson to Salisbury, 20 Jan. 1898, Africa no. 31 (encl. memorandum by Gosselin and Everett).
57 FO27/3410, Gosselin and Everett to Salisbury, 28 Jan. 1898.
58 McWilliam, "Ferguson, Samori and Barbatu," pp. 34–43; FO27/3410, Gosselin to Salisbury, 20 Jan. 1898.
59 SOM-AN Afrique VI, 149, a, Compte rendu: 14e Séance, by Binger.
60 FO403/251, Monson to Salisbury, 1 Feb. 1898, with enclosures.
61 FO403/251, Monson to Salisbury, 1 Feb. 1898, Africa no. 39; Gooch and Temperley, *Documents*, vol. 1, no. 164, p. 139, Monson to Salisbury, 31 Jan. 1898.
62 FO27/3410, Monson to Salisbury, 5 Feb. 1898, with enclosures.
63 *The Times* (London), 5 Feb. 1898; *Manchester Guardian*, 5 Feb. 1898. There is a volume of extracts from British newspapers on the Niger crisis of 1897–98 in Rhodes House Library donated by Matthew Nathan, former governor of the Gold Coast.
64 *D.D.F.*, 1st series, vol. 14, no. 32, p. 55, Courcel to Hanotaux, 28 Jan. 1898; no. 35, pp. 62–63, Hanotaux to Courcel, 1 Feb. 1898; FO403/251, Monson to Salisbury, 2 Feb. 1898.
65 FO27/3408, Salisbury to Monson, Africa no. 87, 15 Feb. 1898; Gooch and Temperley, *Documents*, vol. 1, no. 65, p. 140; Rouire, "La France et l'Angleterre dans la Vallée du Niger," in *R.D.M.* (15 Oct. 1898), pp. 864–97.
66 H. du Basty, "M. Méline," in *Rev. d'Hist. Contemporaine* (1888), pp. 84–87.
67 FO27/3411, Monson to Salisbury, 22 Feb. 1898; 25 Feb. 1898, Africa no. 93.
68 *D.D.F.*, 1st series, vol. 14, no. 61, pp. 108–09, Geoffray to Hanotaux, 22 Feb. 1898; FO403/251, Monson to Salisbury, 19 Feb. 1898, Africa no. 26.

69 SOM-AN Afrique IV, 38, c, Hanotaux to Lebon, 23 Feb. 1898 (encl. Monson to Hanotaux, 21 Feb. 1898); Binger to Hanotaux, 17 Feb. 1898 (with encl.).
70 Ibid., Courcel to Hanotaux, 2 and 10 Feb. 1898.
71 *D.D.F.,* 1st series, vol. 14, no. 35, p. 63, Hanotaux to Courcel, 1 Feb. 1898; no. 45, p. 79, Hanotaux to Lebon, 8 Feb. 1898.
72 M.A.E., Papiers Hanotaux, vol. 2, "Note sur l'Angleterre et les colonies Françaises" (1898), by Hanotaux.
73 See CO875/51, West African Frontier Force: Papers, 23 July 1897–24 March 1898.
74 M.A.E. C.P., n.s. 11 (Grand Bretagne), Courcel to Hanotaux, 12 March 1898 (encl. "Note pour l'Ambassadeur," by du Pontarice; Henry Norman, "An Inquiry into French Opinion: West Africa," in *The Daily Chronicle,* 12 March 1898. Norman concluded that the French did not want war. Mercadier to Courcel, 12 March 1898. Mercadier was regarded generally as "un informateur sur et habile," according to Courcel.
75 F.O. Conf. Print No. 6857, Memorandum on Effects of Withdrawing rights from the Royal Niger Company (1898); *The Times,* 25 May 1897 (encl. in Afrique IV, 38, b, Hanotaux to Lebon, 3 June 1897 (très confidential); Geoffray to Hanotaux, 25 May 1897; "La France et l'Angleterre au Niger," in *La Dépêche Coloniale,* 11 Oct. 1897, quoting the *Morning Post.*
76 SOM-AN Afrique IV, 38, c, Hanotaux to Lebon, 16 Feb. 1898, no. 437 (confidential); Hanotaux to Lebon, 1 March 1898, no. 527 (encl. Courcel to Hanotaux, 22 Feb. 1898).
77 M.A.E. C.P., n.s. 8 (Grande Bretagne), Courcel to Hanotaux, 22 Feb. 1898; SOM-AN Afrique IV, 38, c, Hanotaux to Lebon, 18 March 1898, no. 769 (encl. extracts from the *Daily Chronicle,* 14 March 1898, 9 Feb. 1898); "England and France" in *Freeman's Journal* (Dublin), 7 March 1898; Hanotaux to Lebon, 1 March 1898, no. 526.
78 "China and West Africa" (editorial), *South Wales Daily Star,* 30 March 1898.
79 See F.O. Conf. Print No. 7915, Correspondence re Colonial Defence 1896–1901.
80 FO27/3411, Monson to Salisbury, 24 Feb. 1898, Africa no. 32, with enclosures.
81 FO27/3411, Foreign Office memorandum, 25 Feb. 1898.
82 FO27/3412, Monson to Salisbury, 3 March 1898, Africa no. 97 (encl. *Le Temps,* 3 March 1898); SOM-AN Afrique IV, 38, c, Hanotaux to Lebon, 18 Feb. 1898, no. 433 (Conf.) (encl. Courcel to Hanotaux, 30 Jan. 1898).
83 FO27/3411, Monson to Salisbury, 2 Feb. 1898; Andre Lebon, "La Boucle du Niger 1896–1898," in *R.D.M.* (15 Sept. 1900), pp. 356–83.
84 *D.D.F.,* 1st series, vol. 14, no. 80, p. 133, Courcel to Hanotaux, 12 March 1898. Courcel's appraisal of the chances of the Liberals was perhaps overly optimistic.
85 FO27/3412, Monson to Salisbury, 6 March 1898, with enclosures. Count Munster, the German ambassador in Paris, also dropped a hint about Hanotaux's efforts to meet the British halfway.
86 FO27/3412, Monson to Salisbury, 16 March 1898, Africa no. 174, with enclosures; FO27/3434, C.O. to F.O., 17 March 1898.
87 FO403/251, Monson to Salisbury, 16 March 1898 (encl. Projet-Convention).
88 FO27/3412, Monson to Salisbury, 16 March 1898.

89 *D.D.F.*, 1st series, vol. 14, no. 98, p. 161, Courcel to Hanotaux, 22 March 1898; FO27/3408, Salisbury to Monson, 22 March 1898; SOM-AN Afrique IV, 57, c, Hanotaux to Lebon, 26 April 1898; Gooch and Temperley, *Documents,* vol. 1, no. 175, pp. 148–49, Balfour to Monson, 28 March 1898.

90 SOM-AN Dahomey IV (Hint. Dah.), Pascal to Lebon, 6 and 9 Jan. 1898; Lebon to Hanotaux, 8 Jan. 1898; Lebon to Pascal, 13 Feb. 1898; Pascal to Lebon, 2 March 1898; Perham, *Lugard,* pp. 683–91.

91 SOM-AN Dahomey IV, Pascal to Lebon, 22 March 1898; "Rapport politique," by Commandant Supérieur Ricour, 13 Feb. 1898.

92 SOM-AN Afrique IV, 38, c, Hanotaux to Lebon, 18 March 1898 (encl. Geoffray to Hanotaux, 14 March 1898); *Daily Chronicle,* 14 March 1898.

93 See P. Vuillot, "La France et l'Angleterre sur le Niger," in *Questions Diplomatiques et Coloniales* (1 April 1898), pp. 404–30; F. A. Edwards, "The French on the Niger," in *Fortnightly Review* (April 1898), pp. 576–91; SOM-AN Afrique VI, 149, c, Monson to Hanotaux, 10 Jan. 1898.

94 SOM-AN Dahomey IV, Pascal to Lebon, 22 March 1898 (tel.); SOM-AN Afrique VI, 149, c, Lebon to Hanotaux, 22 March 1898 (confidential).

95 Haywood and Clarke, *Royal West African Frontier Force,* pp. 29–31; Perham, *Lugard,* pp. 683–91.

96 SOM-AN Afrique IV, 38, c, Geoffray to Hanotaux, 14 March 1898 (copy).

97 SOM-AN Dahomey IV, Pascal to Lebon, 9 May 1898.

98 On the Bariba political system, see J. Lombard, "La vie politique dans une ancienne société de type féodal les Bariba du Dahomey," in *Cahiers d'Etudes Africaines,* no. 3 (Oct. 1960); J. Lombard, "Un System politique traditionnel de type féodal: les Bariba du Nord-Dahomey," in *B.I.F.A.N.* 19 série B (1957).

99 SOM-AN Afrique VI, 149, c, Binger to M.A.E., 7 June 1898 (drafted in May); Hanotaux to Lebon, 27 May 1898.

100 FO27/3416, "Proceedings of the Niger Commission," 4 April 1898 (encl. British Draft Convention).

101 The towns of Okuta, Bere, Ashigere (Yashikera), and Bete were to be in the British sphere.

102 M.A.E., Papiers Hanotaux, vol. 9, d'Agoult to Hanotaux, 12 Feb. 1896; "Note relative à l'internationalism des eaux du Niger et à leur extraterritorialité," by Comte d'Agoult, député du Sénégal, 12 Feb. 1896; SOM-AN Afrique VI, 133, b, sketches by Binger on the attribution of Bussa and Nikki. The sketches are identical with those in Hanotaux Papers, vol. 9.

103 SOM-AN Afrique VI, 149, c, Protocols des Séances de la Commission du Niger: Séance du 4 Avril 1898.

104 FO27/3416, British Draft Convention, 4 April 1898. See Auzou, "La Boucle du Niger," pp. 163–88.

105 *The Daily Telegraph,* 24 Feb. 1898.

106 SOM-AN Afrique VI, 149, c, Geoffray to Hanotaux, 24 Feb. 1898 (copy); Hanotaux to Lebon, 23 March 1898.

107 FO403/251, report of the proceedings of the Niger Commission, 21 April 1898; FO27/3416, Monson to Salisbury, 26 April 1898, with enclosures; SOM-AN Afrique VI, 149, c, colonies to M.A.E., 9 April 1898 (draft).

108 SOM-AN Afrique VI, 149, c, Geoffray to Hanotaux, 30 April 1898; Pontarice to M.A.E., 30 April 1898; Binger to M.A.E., 10 and 11 May 1898 (draft); IV, 38, c, Binger to Hanotaux, 5 May 1898 (draft).
109 *D.D.F.,* 1st series, vol. 14, no. 119, Courcel to Hanotaux, 2 April 1898; SOM-AN Afrique VI, 149, c, Geoffray to Hanotaux, 29 April 1898 (encl. extract from *The Standard,* 29 April 1898, on House of Commons debate of 28 April 1898), dealing with Sir Charles Dilke's question to Chamberlain.
110 SOM-AN Afrique VI, 149, c, Geoffray to Hanotaux, 30 April 1898 (copy); Geoffray to Hanotaux, 5 May 1898 (copy), on Chamberlain's speech on Mossi in the House of Commons; *Le Matin,* 15 April 1898, attack on Chamberlain.
111 The Elder Dempster Lines were mentioned specially. SOM-AN Afrique VI, 149, b, séance du 21 Avril 1898; FO27/3412, Gosselin to Salisbury, 22 April 1898.
112 FO27/3413, Monson to Salisbury, 29 April 1898, Africa no. 154. See John Westlake, "England and France in West Africa," in *Contemporary Review,* April 1898, pp. 582–92.
113 FO27/3413, Monson to Salisbury, 1 May 1898.
114 FO27/3409, Salisbury to Monson, 6 May 1898.
115 FO27/3413, Monson to Salisbury, 13 May 1898 (encl. "Memorandum on a Conversation with René Lecomte," by Gosselin, 13 May 1898).
116 FO403/251, Monson to Salisbury, 16 May 1898.
117 FO27/3409, Salisbury to Monson, 18 May 1898; FO27/3440, C.O. to F.O., 26 May 1898 (encl. memorandum by Chamberlain, 26 May 1898); SOM-AN Afrique VI, 149, c, Geoffray to Hanotaux, 7 May 1898 (copy). Hanotaux based his claim to Ilo on the assassination of de Bérnis there. See Lorho, "Expansion dans l'Hinterland dahoméen," pp. 704–05.
118 *Le Figaro,* 23 May 1898.
119 *D.D.F.,* 1st series, vol. 14, no. 207, p. 315, Hanotaux to Courcel, 1 June 1898; SOM-AN Afrique VI, 149, c, Geoffray to Hanotaux, 23 May 1898 (copy), quoting *Daily Chronicle* and *Daily Mail,* 22 May 1898; Hanotaux to Lebon, 27 May 1898.
120 FO27/3409, Salisbury to Monson, 20 May 1898; FO27/3440, C.O. to F.O., 4 June 1898.
121 Garvin, *Life of Chamberlain* 3:220. The Anglo-French crisis over the Nile came as a result not of British occupation of Khartoum but of Marchand's occupation of Fashoda. See Heinz Kossatz, *Untersuchungen uber den Französisch-Englischen Weltgegensatz im Fachodajahr* (Breslau, 1934), pp. 23 ff.
122 FO27/3409, Chamberlain to Hopwood, 20 May 1898, minutes by Chamberlain.
123 Eugene Lagrillière-Beauclerc, *Missions au Sénégal et au Soudan: Voyage de M. André Lebon, Ministre des Colonies, Octobre-Novembre 1897. Rapport* (Ministère des Colonies) (Paris, 1897).
124 Lebon had 10,752 votes against Maussabre's 10,487. *Journal Officiel du Dahomey* (15 May 1898), p. 4.
125 FO27/3413, Monson to Salisbury, 23 May 1898; M.A.E. (Grande Bretagne), n.s.8, Geoffray to Hanotaux, 30 April 1898, no. 244.
126 M.A.E., Papiers Hanotaux, vol. 2, "Note sur la politique extérieure du Ministère Méline, 1896–1898," by Hanotaux, p. 17. "M. Hanotaux avait agrandi la France!" declared Méline one day in the Chamber of Deputies.

127 *D.D.F.*, 1st series, vol. 14, no. 207, p. 315, Hanotaux to Courcel, 1 June 1898; FO27/3409, Salisbury to Monson, 29 May 1898, Africa no. 268; FO27/3413, Monson to Salisbury, 3 and 5 June 1898; Hanotaux to Monson, 9 June 1898 (copy).

128 *D.D.F.*, 1st series, vol. 14, no. 211, p. 321; Gooch and Temperley, *Documents,* vol. 1, no. 180, p. 155; Chamberlain to Salisbury, 2 June 1898, quoted in Garvin, *Life of Chamberlain* 3:219-20.

129 FO27/3413, Monson to Salisbury, 5 June 1898, Africa no. 197; Gooch and Temperley, vol. 1, p. 156.

130 FO27/3414, Monson to Salisbury, 12 and 16 June 1896; SOM-AN Afrique VI, 149, c, Hanotaux to Lebon, 11 June 1898; *D.D.F.*, vol. 14, no. 225, pp. 333-34; Hanotaux to Courcel, 15 June 1898.

131 M.A.E., Doc. Dipl. (Livre Jaune), *Convention entre la France et la Grande-Bretagne fixant la délimitation des possessions françaises de la Côte d'Ivoire, du Soudan, et du Dahomey, des colonies Britanniques de la Côte d'Or et du Lagos et des autres possessions britanniques à l'Ouest du Niger, ainsi que des possessions françaises et britanniques et des sphères d'influence des deux pays à l'est du Niger, signée à Prais le 14 Juin 1898* (Paris, 1898); Herstlet, *Map of Africa* 2:785-96. See p. 263 above.

132 FO27/3414, Monson to Salisbury, 15 June 1898, Africa no. 212. Gosselin was later knighted.

133 M.A.E., Papiers Hanotaux, vol. 11 (Fonds Secrets 1898), Lebon to Hanotaux, 14 June 1898.

134 The second Brisson Cabinet succeeded the Méline Cabinet and was in power from June to October 1898. It was succeeded by the 4th Dupuy Cabinet in November 1898.

135 E. Etienne, *L'Oeuvre Coloniale, algerienne et politique de Eugène Etienne,* Coll. and ed. Dépeche Coloniale (Paris, 1907), 1:312-13, 324. FO27/3414, Monson to Salisbury, 18 July 1898, Africa no. 250.

136 SOM-AN Afrique VI, 149, c, E. Palazot to min. of colonies, 13 July 1898; FO27/3414, Monson to Salisbury, 18 July 1898, Africa no. 248.

137 *B.C.A.F.*, July 1898. See Alphonse Bertrand, *Le Sénat 1897* (Paris, 1898); *Quinzaine Coloniale,* 25 March 1898. The groupe colonial in the senate included R. Waddington, de Freycinet, Constans, Ernest Boulanger, Peytral, Tirman, and Reynal.

138 FO27/3766, memorandum on the French leases, 19 July 1898.

139 *Daily Graphic,* 18 July 1898; *St. James' Gazette,* 18 July 1898.

140 SOM-AN Afrique VI, 149, c, Nisard to Trouillot, 30 June 1898 (encl. Geoffray to Delcassé, 25 June 1898); *The Times* (London), 25 June 1898.

141 Speech of Sir Michael Hicks Beach at the lord mayor's banquet. *The Times* (London), 23 June 1898; M.A.E. C.P. (Grande Bretagne), n.s.8, Geoffray to Delcassé, 24 June 1898, no. 344.

142 M.A.E. C.P. (Grande Bretagne), n.s.8, Geoffray to Delcassé, 8 July 1898; *The Standard,* 8 July 1898.

143 M.A.E. C.P. (Grande Bretagne), n.s.8, Rocher to Declassé, 24 June 1898. Rocher

was French consul at Liverpool. See Diplomaticus, "Where Lord Salisbury has failed," in *Fortnightly Review* 69 (1898):518.
144 M.A.E., Papiers Hanotaux, vol. 11 (Fonds Secrets 1898), Hanotaux to French ambassador in Egypt, 21 June 1898 (draft), affaires du Niger, May–June 1898.
145 Hanotaux asserted that Jules Ferry gave France her empire in Indochina and Hanotaux gave France "le plus bel empire que la France pouvait ambitionner en Afrique." M.A.E., Papiers Hanotaux, vol. 2, "Note sur la politique extérieure du Ministère Méline, 1896–1898," by Hanotaux (n.d.), pp. 16–17.
146 Ibid., "Note: Renseignements demandes par le Ministre," by Binger, 21 June 1898; SOM-AN Afrique VI, 149, c, Trouillot to Delcassé, 16 Aug. 1898 (confidential) (draft); Nisard to Trouillot, 22 July 1898, with enclosure.
147 C. Vergniol, "Fachoda, II," *La Revue de France* (July–Aug. 1936), pp. 639–42.
148 On Fashoda, see the newly opened private papers of Delcassé. M.A.E., Papiers Delcassé, vols. 3 (Paul Cambon) and 4 (Baron de Courcel).
149 FO27/3767, Lansdowne to Monson, 2 July 1903, Africa no. 325.

Selected Bibliography

PRIMARY SOURCES

I. Manuscript Sources: Official Correspondence

A. *British*

Foreign Office Correspondence, Public Record Office, London
  Foreign Office Papers, series 84, Great Britain, 1883–92 (FO84/. . .).
  Foreign Office Papers, series 83, Great Britain, 1893–98 (FO83/. . .).
    Africa, Drafts and Various Dispatches; Diplomatic and Domestic; Lyons; Lytton; Dufferin; Gosselin; Egerton; Monson; Howard; Everett; Waddington; D'Estournel; Geoffray; Courcel.
  Foreign Office Papers, series 2 (FO2/. . .).
    Slave Trade, Africa, Treaties
  Foreign Office Papers, series 64, Germany, 1884–98
    Africa Drafts and Dispatches; Africa (Various) Diplomatic Dispatches, Diplomatic Drafts; Correspondence with Malet, Gosselin, Gough, Lascelles, Hatzfeldt, Jenisch, Hohenlohe, Caprivi.
  Foreign Office Papers, series 94 (treaties)
    Volume 785 (FO94/785), Anglo-French convention of 14 June 1898, with additional declaration of 21 March 1899, ratified in Paris on 6 June 1899.
  Foreign Office Confidential Prints, series 403 (FO403/. . .).
  Selected volumes, 1884–98.
  Parliamentary Papers (1884–98), selected volumes.
  Cabinet Papers, Public Record Office (P.R.O. Cab. 37/. . .).
  (Photographic copies of Cabinet Papers)
    For the purposes of this book the most valuable collection of Foreign Office correspondence has been series 27 (France). I have attempted to use these systematically in the effort to determine the process of the formulation of British and French policies toward the Dahomey-Niger hinterland and the relation between this part of west Africa and the overall African policies of the two powers concerned.
    Series 84 and 83 were also very valuable for this study. Correspondence in these series not only clarified several points in the diplomatic dispatches but also revealed the influence of domestic British politics on the formulation of British policy concerning the Niger territories. Correspondence in series 64 (Germany) were necessary adjuncts to the foregoing and

showed how considerations of Germany and European alliances affected British and French action in the Niger territories.

Colonial Office Correspondence, Public Record Office, London

Colonial Office Papers, series 147, Lagos, 1885–98 (CO147/. . .).

Dispatches; Miscellaneous; Minutes; Drafts; Reports. Colonial Office Colonial Office Papers, series 96, Gold Coast, Selected Volumes, 1885–98 (CO96/. . .).

Colonial Office Papers, series 445, Africa (west), West African Frontier Force, 1898–1900.

Colonial Office Papers, series 537, Africa (west), supplementary correspondence, 1897–1899.

Colonial Office Confidential Prints, series 879, African (west) (CO879/. . .).

These were formerly classified under series 806 but were reclassified in 1965 as series 879.

Selected volumes, 1884–98.

In addition to the documents contained in Colonial Office Correspondence, series 96 (Gold Coast) and 147 (Lagos), extensive use has been made, in this study, of Colonial Office Confidential Prints dealing specially with territorial questions in the Niger basin and with territorial disputes with France and Germany in the hinterlands of the Gold Coast (Ghana) and Lagos.

B. *French*

Ministère des Affaires Etrangères: Archives Diplomatiques, Quai D'Orsay, Paris

Memoires et Documents, Fonds Divers, Série Afrique

AFRIQUE, vols. 78–85, Etablissements françaises du Golfe de Guinée, 1883–87.
    Afrique 125, 188–90.

    Afrique 126, 1890, Evénements du Dahomey.
    Afrique 127, 1891–94, Affaires du Dahomey.

AFRIQUE, vols. 86, 128–31, Possessions anglaises de la Cote Occidentale, 1883–94; Délimitations des possessions anglaises et françaises de l'Afrique Occidentale, 1889.

AFRIQUE, vols. 95–06, 134, Possessions allemandes de la Côte Occidentale de l'Afrique, 1884–95.

AFRIQUE, vols. 108–09, Conférence de Berlin 1884–85.
    Afrique 108, Protocoles et documents annexés.
    Afrique 109, Correspondances et documents divers; Procès-verbaux de la commission chargée par la Conférence de Berlin de fixer les limites du Bassin commercial (conventional) du Congo, Nov. 1884.

AFRIQUE, vols. 114–19, Conférence Anti-Esclavagiste de Bruxelles, Novembre

1889–Décembre 1891; Correspondances et documents divers, 1889–91; Projets de protocoles; notes et documents divers; Tarifs douaniers au Congo; Conférence de Bruxelles, Protocoles imprimés.

Ministère des Affaires Etrangères: Correspondance Politique

ANGLETERRE: vols. 807–90, 1884–90 (Waddington).

    vols. 891–99, Jan.–Dec. 1894 (Decrais, D'Estournelles de Constant, Baron de Courcel).

    vols. 900–10, Jan.–Dec. 1895 (Courcel and Geoffray).

    vols. 911–21, Jan.–Dec. 1896 (Courcel, Geoffray, Saint-Genys, De la Chausée).

ALLEMAGNE: vols. 59–62, 1884–85 (Courcel, Bismarck, Ferry).

Ministère des Affaires Etrangères: Correspondance Politique et Commerciale, Nouvelle Série, 1897–1914

GRANDE BRETAGNE

    n.s.1, Politique Interièure: Dossier général, 1897–1902 (1 vol.).

    n.s.8, Politique Etrangère: Dossier général, 1897–98 (1 vol.).

    n.s.11, Politique Etrangère: Relations avec la France, 1897–98 (1 vol.).

    n.s.25, Politique Etrangère: Relations avec l'Allemagne, 1897–1907 (1 vol.).

    n.s.29, Empire Britannique: Dossier général, 1897–1901 (1 vol.).

    n.s.39, Affaires commerciales: Relations et Conventions avec la France, 1897–1908 (vol.).

ALLEMAGNE

    n.s.60, Relations avec l'Angleterre, 1897–1914 (1 vol.).

    n.s.63, Questions Coloniales, 1897–1903 (1 vol.).

Ministère des Affaires Etrangères: Correspondance Consulaire et Commerciale, 1793–1901

LIVERPOOL: vols. 21–23, Jan. 1886–Dec. 1901.

MANCHESTER: vols. 4–7, July 1884–June 1899.

LONDON: vols. 85–101, Jan. 1884–August 1898.

Ministère des Affaires Etrangères: Documents Diplomatiques: Livres Jaunes

No. 157, Affaires du Congo, 1884–87 (Paris, 1890).

No. 160, Conférence internationale de Bruxelles, 18 Nov. 1889–2 Juillet 1890, Protocoles et acte finale (Paris, 1891).

No. 161, Conférence internationale et Commission de Bruxelles, Nov. 1889–Febrier 1891, Correspondance diplomatique (Paris, 1891).

No. 179, Délimitation des possessions françaises de la Côte Occidentale de l'Afrique, 889–95.

No. 192, Convention relative à la délimitation des possessions françaises du Dahomey et du Soudan et des possessions allemandes du Togo (Paris, 1897).

No. 196, Convention entre la France et la Grande-Bretagne fixant le délimitation des possessions françaises de la Côte d'Ivoire, du Soudan, et du Dahomey, des colonies Britanniques de la Côte d'Or et du Lagos et des autres possessions françaises et britanniques et des sphères d'influence des deux pays à l'est du Niger (signée à Paris, 1898).

No. 197, Afrique—arrangements, actes, et conventions concernant le nord, l'ouest et le centre de l'Afrique, 1881–98 (Paris, 1898).

No. 202, Affaires du Haut-Nil et du Bahr-El-Ghazal, Fachoda 1897–98 (Paris, 1898).

No. 205, Déclaration additionelle du 21 Mars 1899, à la Convention Franco-anglaise du 14 Juin, 1898 (Paris, 1899).

No. 206, Correspondance et documents relatifs à la Convention Franco-anglaise du 14 Juin 1898, 1890–1898 (Paris, 1899).

No. 216, Affaires de Siam, 1893–1902 (Paris, 1902).

Section d'Outre-Mer des Archives Nationales, Rue Oudinot, Paris (formerly Archives du Ministère de la France d'Outre-Mer).

AFRIQUE VI: AFFAIRES DIPLOMATIQUES

43 and 44, Conférence de Berlin, 1884–85.

80 and 81, Conférence de Bruxelles, 1889–90.

66 and 73, Angleterre, 1888–89.

97 and 98, Angleterre, 192.

106, Angleterre, 1893.

114 and 115, Angleterre, 1894.

124, c, Affaires du Niger, 895, Mission Toutée; etc.

125, e, Missions Decoeur, Alby, et Monteil; Affaire du Borgu.

133, b, c, Affaires du Niger, Borgu (1896).

134, b, Negociations franco-anglaises (1896).

142, a, Délimitation au Niger, correspondance, incidents, etc. (1897).

b, Délimitation au Niger (1897), protocoles, commission, etc.

149, a, Commission de Délimitation dans la région du Niger, protocole.

b, Convention du 14 Juin, 1898.

c, Délimitation au Niger, correspondance (1898).

150, c, Rapports entre le Dahomey et le Lagos.

d, Tariffs douaniers dans l'Afrique Occidentale et au Congo.

4, Mission Marchand.

DAHOMEY III, Explorations and Missions (1889–1900) Dossiers 1–9. Decoeur, Baud, Vermeersch, Toutée, Alby. Projets des missions.

DAHOMEY IV, Hinterland du Dahomey, expéditions.

DAHOMEY V, Dossiers 1–12, Expéditions militaires (1889–95); Campagne de 1890; Campagne de 1892; Rapport Dodds; Négociations avec Béhanzin; Campagne de 1893–94; Journal de Marche; Correspondance diverse.

DAHOMEY IX, Carton 2710, Dossier 3 (finances, 1893–1900).
SOUDAN III Missions: Toutée.
AFRIQUE IV Dossiers 9, 10, 11, Dahomey Independant, (1845–88).
AFRIQUE III Dossiers 19, 21, 26, Missions Monteil, Voulet, Chanoine; Correspondance diverse.
CONSEIL SUPERIEUR DES COLONIES, GENERALITES, Dossiers I bis, 3 and 31.
DOSSIER ADMINISTRATIVE, Victor Ballot, Gouverneur du Dahomey.

Archives Centrales du Ministère de la Marine, Paris. Inventaire BB⁴, Campagnes E.M.G.

BB4/1988
BB4/1989, Dossiers de la Première Expédition du Dahomey, 1890–1891.
BB4/1990
BB4/1991, Dossiers de la 2ᵉ Expédition du Dahomey, 1892–1894.
BB4/1992
BB4/2022, Expéditions Coloniales diverses, 1885–1900; Affaire de Kotonou, Telegrammes, 1890.

These were invaluable for the study of the wars against Dahomey. These documents have hitherto not been used in the study of the conquest of Dahomey. It was only through the use of them that the discovery of the dispute between the Colonial Department and the Ministry of the Navy over the conduct of the Dahomey war was made.

It is difficult to gain access to the Archives Centrales de la Marine since it is a departmental and military rather than a public archive.

II. MANUSCRIPT SOURCES: PRIVATE PAPERS
  A. *British*
   1. The Papers of Robert Arthur Talbot Gascoyne Cecil, Third Marquis of Salisbury (Christ Church, Oxford).
      The volumes which were most useful for this were those containing Salisbury's private correspondence with the officials of the British embassy in Paris, especially vols. 56–60 (1886–92) and 114–19 (1895–1900).
   2. The Papers of Joseph Chamberlain (Birmingham University Library, Birmingham).
      Only the correspondence with Selborne and Salisbury yielded some additional information for this study to the official correspondence available at the Public Record Office.
   3. The Papers of Sir Edward Malet (Public Record Office, London, FO343/1–13). The volumes used for this study were:
      FO343/2, 1884.
      FO343/3, 1889–95.
      FO343/4, Royal Letter Book and Miscellaneous, 1 Nov. 1884–29 June 1889.

B. *French*
1. Papiers Hanotaux (Archives Diplomatiques, Ministère des Affaires Etrangères, Quai d'Orsay, Paris).
   Vols. 1–3, Notes et souvenirs personnels de G. Hanotaux.
   Vols. 4–12, Mémoires et Documents rassamblés par G. Hanotaux.
   Vol. 13, Correspondances addressés à G. Hanotaux.
   These papers were opened last year and were used extensively in this study. Only vol. 3 was not found useful.
2. PAPIERS DELCASSÉ (Archives Diplomatiques, M.A.E., Paris).
   These were recently opened after they were classified and bound. They were donated by Madame Nogués (née Suzanne Delcassé), who still keeps the Vatican Dossier and the letters of Nisard, ambassador to the Vatican, 1898–1904. These papers were not found useful for this study because they do not include any documents dealing with the period when Delcassé was minister for the colonies or undersecretary of state for the colonies. They are, however, invaluable for the study of the Fashoda affair and the making of the Entente Cordiale of 1904, especially vols. 3 and 4 (Paul Cambon and Baron de Courcel). They contain no letters by Delcassé himself.
3. Papiers Waddington (William Henry) (Archives Diplomatiques, M.A.E., Quai d'Orsay, Paris).
   Vols. 1–5 bis. These were invaluable, especially for the examination of the making of the Say-Barruwa Line of 1890. Most of the original documents in the declaration of 5 August 1890 are to be found in vols. 4 and 5 bis. Volume 3 deals with Egypt (1878–88).
4. Papiers Ribot (Archives Diplomatiques, M.A.E., Quai d'Orsay, Paris) (1890–93).
   Vols. 1–4. Only vols. 3 (Rapports Franco-Anglais, 1890–93), and 4 (Expansion Coloniale Française, 1890–93) provided valuable evidence for this thesis.
5. Papiers Ganier (These are in the possession of Mlle. Germaine Ganier, Avenue de Paris, Versailles).
   Carton 1 (1885–98); carton 2 (1897–1899) is mostly copied from Porto Novo Archives by Mlle. Ganier.
   The Papiers Ganier were important for the study of the expeditions for the effective occupation of Borgu and Gurma in 1897–98.
6. Papiers Ballot (Victor) (Archives Nationales, Rue Francs-Bourgeois, Paris 3).
   These are microfilmed in four reels (MI 185).
7. Journal du Dr. Alfred Bartet (Archives Nationales, Paris).
   Donated by Mlle. Ganier and microfilmed (MI 214). This recently discovered diary gives detailed information on the country and people of

the Dahomey hinterland. It was kept by Dr. Bartet during the Ganier expedition of 1897–98.
8. Papiers du Colonial Monteil (1885–1940) (Archives Nationales, Paris). Donated by Madame Monteil (66 AP), vols. 1–18. Volumes 2, 3, and 4 deal with the Monteil expedition of 1890–92 from St. Louis to Lake Chad and Tripoli.
9. Papiers Etienne (Eugène) (Bibliothèque Nationale, Rue Richelieu, Paris), N.A.F. 24.327.
These were not found useful for this study.
10. Manuscript Section (Bibliotheque Nationale, Paris).
There are additional manuscript collections and private papers in the Bibliothèque Nationale for Hanotaux, Delcassé, Méline, Felix Faure, André Lebon, Ribot, and Berthelot. All these are classified under N.A.F. (Nouvelles Acquisitions Françaises). Most of these manuscripts, however, deal mainly with domestic politics and affairs and did not yield any evidence for this study.
11. "Journal de Marche au Dahomey, 1892–1893," by Capt. Charles Jacquot (1858–1935).
This diary is in my possession. It was valuable for following the progress of the Second Dahomey War.
12. "Notes de Service" of the Dahomey Expedition, 1892, by Capt. Demartinecourt.
This is in my possession.
13. "Journal de Marche au Dahomey, 1892–1894," by Capt. Demartinecourt, Adjutant-Major, 2ᵉ Compagnie du Bataillon Etranger et Commissaire Rapporteur.
This diary is in the possession of Mlle. G. Ganier, Versailles.

III. PRINTED COLLECTIONS OF OFFICIAL CORRESPONDENCE
1. *Documents Diplomatiques Françaises*, Ministère des Affaires Etrangères, Paris (Paris, 1914, 1929–65).
2. Gooch, G. P., and Temperley, H., eds. *British Documents on the Origins of the War, 1898–1914*. 11 vols. London, 1926–30.
3. Lepsius, Johannes, Mendelssohn Bartholdy, Albrecht, and Thimone Frederich, eds. *Die Grosse Politik der Europaischen Kabinette, 1871–1914*. Berlin, 1922–27.
4. Metcalfe, G. E., ed. *Great Britain and Ghana: Documents of Ghana History, 1807–1957*. London, 1964.

SECONDARY SOURCES

Adams, M. "The British Attitude to German Colonisation, 1880–1885." *Bulletin of the War, 1898–1914*. 11 vols. London, 1926–30.
Adande, Alexandre. *Les Récades des Rois du Dahomey*. Dakar, 1962.

Aderebigbe, A. A. B. "Expansion of the Lagos Protectorate, 1863–1900." Ph.D. dissertation, London University, 1959.

Akindele, A., and Aguessy, C. *Contribution à l'Etude de l'histoire de l'Ancien Royaume de Porto Novo.* Dakar, 1953.

———. *Le Dahomey.* Paris, 1955.

Akinjobin, Isaac. *Dahomey and Its Neighbours, 1708–1818.* Cambridge, 1967.

Albecca, A. L. d'. *Les Establissements Français du Golfe de Bénin.* Paris, 1889.

Aldao, Martin. *Les Idées Coloniales de Jules Ferry.* Paris, 1933.

Alis, Harry. *À la Conquête du Tchad.* Paris, 1891.

———. *La Mission Monteil.* Paris, 1894.

Anene, J. C., and Brown, G. N., eds. *Africa in the Nineteenth and Twentieth Century: A Handbook for Teachers and Students.* Ibadan, 1967.

Angoulvant, Gabriel. *La Pacification de la Côte d'Ivoire, 1908–1915: Methodes et Resultâts.* Preface du Général Gallieni. Paris, 1916.

Arendt, Otto. "England und Deutschland in Ostafrika." *Deutsche Kolonialzeitung* (1888).

Arnold, Rosemary. "A Port of Trade: Whydah on the Guinea Coast." In *Trade and Market in the Early Empires,* edited by K. Polanyi, C. W. Arensbert, and H. W. Pearson. Chicago, 1957.

Atger, Paul. *La France en Côte d'Ivoire de 1843 à 1893.* Dakar, 1962.

Aublet, E. *La Guerre au Dahomey 1888–1893.* Paris, 1894.

Aubreville, A. "Les forêts du Dahomey et du Togo." *Bulletin du Comité d'Etudes Historiques et Scientifiques de l'Afrique Occidentale Française* 6–7 (December 1937).

Auzou, Emile. "La Boucle du Niger." *Revue des Deux Mondes* (1 May 1898).

Ballot, Victor. *Le Chemin de fer du Dahomey.* Paris, 1900.

Banning, E. *Le Partage de l'Afrique.* Brussels, 1888.

———. *Mémoire sur les droits et les prétentions du Portugal à la souveraineté de certains territoires de la côte occidentale de l'Afrique.* Paris, 1883.

———. "Textes Inedits: Notes sur ma vie et mes écrits." *Mémoires: Institut Royal Colonial Belge,* n.s.2 (1955), edited by J. Stengers.

Bastian, A. *Europaische Kolonien in Afrika und Deutschlands Interessen sonst und jetzt.* Berlin, 1884.

Basty, H. du. "M. Meline." *Revue d'Histoire Contemporaine* (1888).

Baumont, Maurice. *L'Essor Industriel et L'Imperialisme Colonial, 1878–1904.* Peuples et Civilisation: Historie Générale, vol. 18, under the direction of Louis Halphen and Philippe Sagnac. Paris, 1937.

Bayol, Jean. "La France au Fouta Djallon." *Revue des Deux Mondes* 54 (15 Dec. 1882).

———. "L'attaque de Kotonou." *Revue Bleue* (1892).

Beazley, R. C. "Das deutsche Kolonialreich, Gross-Britannien und der Vertrag von 1890." *Die Berliner Monatshefte* (May 1930).

Behagle, Ferdinand de. "Le Noupe et les prétentions de la Compagnie Royale de Niger." *Revue de Géographie* (May 1895).

Benkerd, C. "Reisen in Westafrika." *Deutsche Kolonialzeitung* (1887).

Benoit, Général. *Histoire militaire de l'Afrique Occidentale Française.* Paris, 1931.

Berge, Francois. "Le Sous-Secrétariat et les Sous-Secrétaires d'Etat aux Colonies: Histoire de l'imancipation de l'administration colonial." *Revue Française d'Histoire d'Outre-Mer* 47 (1960).

Bernheim, M. *L'Acte général de la Conférence africaine de Berlin jugé par la Ligue Internationale de la Paix et de la Liberté.* Berne, 1885.

Bertha, Jacques. "Notes concernant les rois de Nikki." *Notes Africaines* (July 1947).

———. "Races et langues du bas Dahomey et du bas Togo." *Grands Lacs* (Numero Special, July 1946).

Bertin, Capt. "Renseignements sur le Royaume de Porto Novo et le Dahomey" in *Revue Maritime et Coloniale* (1890).

Burton, R. F. *A Mission to Gléglé, King of Dahomey.* Vol. 2. London, 1864.

Bertrand, Alphonse. *Le Sénat de 1897.* Paris 1898.

Bettencourt Vasconcellos Corte Real do Cauto, Vital de. *Descripcao historica, topographica e ethnographica do dictricto de S. Joao Baptista d'Ajuda e do reino de Dahomena Costa da Mina.* Lisbon, 1869.

Betts, R. F. *Assimilation and Association in French Colonial Theory, 1890–1914.* New York, 1961.

Beurdeley. *La Justice Indigène en Afrique Occidentale Française.* Paris 1916.

"Bibliographie du Dahomey." *Journal de la Société des Africanistes* 6 (fasc. 2). Paris, 1936.

Binger, L. G. *Du Niger au Golfe de Guinée par le pays de Kong et le Mossi, 1887–1889.* Paris, 1892.

———. *Esclavage, Islamisme et Christianisme.* Paris, 1891.

Blondel, F. *Bibliographie géologique et minière de la France d'Outre-Mer.* 2 vols. Paris, 1940–41.

Borelli, Georges. *Resources économiques et avenir commerciale du Dahomey.* Paris, 1900.

Bouche, Abbé Pièrre. *Sept ans en Afrique Occidentale: La Côte des Esclaves et le Dahomey.* Paris, 1885.

Bouche, J. E. "Le Dahomey: son histoire." *L'Explorateur* (1896).

———. "Les établissements de la Côte des Esclaves et les visées de l'Angleterre." *Revue de France* 52 (1876).

Bourgeois, E., and Pages, G. *Les Origines et les Résponsabilites de la Grand Guerre.* Paris, 1921.

Bridgman, J., and Clarke, David E. *German Africa: A Selected Annotated Bibliography.* Stanford, Calif., 1965.

Brogan, D. W. *The Development of Modern France, 1870–1939.* London, 1959.

Brunet, L., and Giethlen, Louis. *Dahomey et Dépendances: Histoire générale, organisation, administration, ethnographie, productions, agriculture, commerce.* Paris, 1900.

———. "M. Victor Ballot, Gouverneur du Dahomey et Dépendances." *L'Africaine* (May 1898).

Brunschwig, H. "Le Parti Colonial Française." *Revere Française d'Histoire d'Outre-Mer,* vol. 46, no. 1 (1959).

Buxton, T. Folwell. *The Remedy.* London, 1840.

———. *The Slave Trade and Its Remedy.* London, 1840.

Calvert, A. F. *Togoland.* London, 1918.

Cardinall, A. W. *A Bibliography of the Gold Coast.* Accra, 1931.

Carnap-Quernheimb, von. "Bericht über den Marsch von Sansane-Mangu nach Pama und Gurma." *Deutsch Kolonialzeitung* (22 June 1895).

Caprivi, L. von. *Die Ostafrikanische Frage und der Helgoland-Sansibar Vertrag.* Berlin, 1934.

Chamberlain, Joseph. "The British African Colonies." *Liberia,* no. 14 (Washington D.C., Feb. 1899).

Chanoine, J. *Documents pour servir à l'Histoire de l'Afrique Occidentale Française de 1895 à 1899. Correspondence du Capt. Chanoine pendant l'expédition du Mossi et du Gourounsi.* Paris, 1905.

Charmes, Francis. *Etudes Historiques et Diplomatiques.* Paris, 1893.

Chaudoin, Edouard. "Trois mois de captivité au Dahomey." *L'Illustration,* no. 2471 (1890).

Chautard, Le Rev. Pierre, *Le Dahomey.* Lyon, 1890.

Cheberg, Prof. Dr. "Über den wirtschaftlichen Wert der Kolonisation für Deutschland." *Deutsche Kolonialzeitung* (1887).

Cherneau, M. "Carte du Dahomey." *Mouvement Géographique,* vol. 11, no. 11 (1892).

Cheron, George. "L'Exploration et la Conquête du Mossi" (sample manuscript). In SOM-AN, Bibliotheque, R429d.

Chirol, Sir Valentine. "The Boer War and the International Situation." In *Cambridge History of British Foreign Policy, 1783–1919* 3. Cambridge, 1923.

Chubb, L. T. *Ibo Land Tenure.* London, 1961.

Churchill, Winston S. *Great Contemporaries.* London, 1959.

Claridge, W. W. *A History of the Gold Coast.* 2 vols. London, 1915; 2nd ed. 1964.

Clérici, André. *Histoire de la Côte d'Ivoire.* Abidjan, 1962.

Coissy, Anatole. "L'Arrivée des Alladahonou à Ouacoue." *Etudes Dahoméenes* 13.

Cook, A. N. *British Enterprise in Nigeria.* Philadelphia, 1943.

Coquery, Catherine. "Le Blocus de Whyday (1876–1877) et la rivalité franco-anglaise au Dahomey." *Cahiers d'études africaines,* vol. 2, no. 7 (1962).

Coquery-Vidrovitch, Catherine. "La fête des coutumes au Dahomey: Historique et essai d'interprétation." *Annales, Economies, Sociétés, Civilisations,* no. 4 (July–August 1964).

Cornevin, R. *Histoire du Dahomey.* Paris, 1962.

———. *Histoire du Togo.* Paris, 1962.

———. "Les divers episodes de la lutte contre le royaume d'Abomey, 1887–1894." *Revue Française d'Histoire d'Outre-Mer* 47 (2e trimestre 1960).

Cortez da Silva Curado, A. D. *Dahome.* Collacao d'uma serie de artigos publicados no Commerio de Portugal. Lisbon, 1887.

Couchard, A. *Au Moyen-Dahomey. Notes sur le cercle de Save, suivies d'essais sur la population Nagot-Schabe* (Paris, 1911).

———. "Au Moyen-Dahomey." In *La Géographie* 25. Bourdeaux, 1911.

Courdioux. *Notes sur la Côte des Esclaves.* Paris, 1875.

Courtet. "Aperçu historique de la colonisation au Dahomey." *Bulletin de la Société Naturelle d'Acclimatation de France* 12 (1905).

Crose, R. Louis. "Le chemin de fer du Dahomey." *Nouvelle Revue,* no. 1 (1905).

Crouzet, Maurice. "Joseph Chamberlain." In *Les Politiques d'expansion impérialiste,* edited by Pierre Renouvin. Paris, 1949.

Crowe, S. E. *The Berlin West African Conference, 1884–1885.* London, 1942.

Crozat, Dr. "Rapport sur une Mission au Mossi, 1890." *Journal Officiel* (5 Oct., 9 Oct. 1891).

Courcel, Geoffroy de. *L'Influence de la Conférence de Berlin de 1885 sur le Droit Colonial International.* Paris, 1936.

D'Horel, P. *Afrique Occidentale: Senegal, Guinée, Côte d'Ivoire, Dahomey, Congo.* Paris, 1905.

Dahdah, Comte Rochaird. "Commerce Extérieur et Politique Etrangère." *Revue Français de l'Etranger et des Colonies,* vol. 11, no. 90 (15 March 1890).

"Dahomey et Dépendance: Importations et exportations pendant l'année 1896." *Revue Coloniale* (1897).

"Dahomey: Mouvement Commercial." *Bulletin du Comité de l'Afrique Français* (hereafter *B.C.A.F.*) (1895).

Dalzel, A. *Dahomey.* London, 1723.

Daniel, Jean. *Le Palmier à Huile en Dahomey.* Paris, 1902.

Dawson, W. H. "Imperial Policy in the Old and the New World 1885–1899." In *Cambridge History of British Foreign Policy* 3. Cambridge, 1923.

Dechamps, H. *Les Méthodes et les Doctrines Coloniales de la France.* Paris, 1953.

Delavaud, Louis. "Carte du Dahomey par M. d'Albeca." *Revue de Géographie* 5 (1892).

———. *La Politique Coloniale de l'Allemagne.* Paris, 1887.

Deloncle, Pierre. *L'Afrique Occidentale Française: Découverte, Pacification, mise en valeur.* Paris, 1934.

Demanche, George. "Dahomey, route du Niger: situation et population." *Revue Française de l'Etranger et des Colonies,* vol. 18, no. 177 (1 Nov. 1893).

Demaret, Emile. *Organisation Coloniale et Fédération: Une Fédération de la France en de ses Colonies.* Paris, 1899. Preface by Eugene Etienne.

Dennett, R. E. *At the Back of the Blackman's Mind: Notes on the Kingly Office in West Africa.* London, 1906.

Deschamps, L. *Histoire de la Question Coloniale en France.* Paris, 1891.

Describes, Abbé. *L'Evangile au Dahomey—Missions de Lyon.* Lyon, n.d.

Deutsches Kolonial-Lexikon. 3 vols. Leipzig, 1920.

"Die Denkschrift über die Beweggründe zu dem Duetsche-Englischen Abkommen." *Deutsche Kolonialzeitung,* no. 17 (August 1890).

"Deutsche Interessen in der Sudsee," In *Die Deutsche Kolonialpolitik.* No. 1. Leipzig, 1885.

"Deutschland in Afrika und in der Sudsee." In *Die Deutsche Kolonialpolitik.* No. 2. Leipzig, 1885.

Die Lage in Afrika: Unmittelbar vor und nach dem Deutsche-Englischen Vertrag vom politischen Standpunkt aus betrachtet. Dresden and Leipzig, 1890.

Dike, K. O. *Trade and Politics in the Niger Delta, 1830–1885.* London, 1956.

Dim Delobson. A. A. *L'Empire du Mogho Naba.* Paris, 1932.

Diplomaticus. "Where Lord Salisbury has failed." *Fortnightly Review* 69 (1898).

Dodds, Général A. *Rapport.* Paris, 1894.

Doot. "Notes sur le Haut-Dahomey." *La Géographie* (1904).

Dubarry, Armando. *Voyage au Dahomey.* Paris, n.d.

Duboc, Général. *L'Epopée Coloniale en Afrique Occidentale.* Paris, 1938.

Duchene, A. "Le droit de la Navigation dans le Niger." *Rev. Générale de Droit International Public* Paris, 1895.

Dudley-Stamp, L. *Africa: A Study in Tropical Development.* 2nd ed. New York, 1964.

Dunglas, E. "Contribution à l'Histoire du Moyen-Dahomey." *Etudes Dahoméennes* 19 and 20.

Dybowsky, Jean. *La Route du Chad.* Paris, 1893.

Elias, T. O. *Nigerian Land Law and Custom.* London, 1954.

"Englische Pressestimmen." *Deutsche Kolonialzeitung* (1883).

Ensor, R. C. K. *England, 1870–1914.* Oxford, 1936.

Etienne, Abel. *Le Père Dogère ancien Missionaire au Dahomey. Récite et Souvénirs: Conquête du Dahomey.* Toulon, 1909.

Etienne, Eugene. *Les Compagnies de Colonisation.* Paris, 1897.

———. *L'oeuvre Coloniale, algérienne et politique de Eugène Etienne.* Collected and edited by *Dépêche Coloniale.* Paris, 1907.

Fabri, F. *Der deutsch-englische vertrage.* Koln, 1890.

Fage, J. D., and Whittlesey, Derwent. "West Africa." In *Encyclopaedia Britannica* 23. London, 1957.

Faidherbe, Général. "La Question du Niger." *Revue Scientifique,* no. 3 (17 January 1885).

———. "L'avenir du Sahara et du Soudan." *Revue Maritime et Coloniale* 8 (1863).

———. *Le Sénégal: La France dans l'Afrique Occidentale.* Paris, 1889.

———. "Tombouctou et les grandes voies de communication de l'Afrique." *Revue Scientifique* (15 November 1884).

Faulong, L. *Les Rapports Financiers de la Métropole et de l'Afrique Occidentale Française depuis 1825 à nos jours.* Paris, 1919.

Faure, Charles. *La Conférence Africaine de Berlin.* Genève, 1885.

Favitski de Probobysz, Comte de. *Répetoire bibliographique de la littérature militaire et coloniale française depuis cent années.* Paris and Liege, 1935.

Feris. "La Côte des Esclaves et les nouvelles possessions françaises." *Revue Scientifique* (1883).

Ferry, Jules. *Le Gouvernement de l'Algérie.* Paris, 1892.

Fieldhouse, D. D. *The Colonial Empires, a comparative survey from the 18th century.* London, 1966.

Flint, John Edgar. *Sir George Goldie and the Making of Nigeria.* London, 1960. This is the published and condensed version of "British Policy and Chartered Company at Administration in Nigeria, 1879–1900." Ph.D. dissertation, London University, 1959.

Foa, E. *Le Dahomey.* Paris, 1895.

Fonsagrives. *Notice sur le Dahomey.* Paris, 1900.

"Français, anglais et allemands dans l'arrière-pays du Dahomey." *B.C.A.F.* (1895).

François, G. *Notre Colonie du Dahomey.* Paris, 1905.

François, Georges. "La Mise en Valeur du Dahomey." *B.C.A.F.,* no. 11 (1905).

Francolini, B. "Die Europaer in Afrika." *Junges Europa* (1942).

Freycinet, Charles de. *La Question d'Egypte.* Paris, 1905.

Gaffarel, Paul. *Notre Expansion Coloniale en Afrique de 1870 à nos jours.* Paris, 1918.

Gaillard, R. "Etude sur les lacustres du Bas-Dahomey." *L'Anthropologie* 18 (1907).

Ganier, G. "Les Rivalités franco-anglaise et franco-allemande de 1894 à 1898; Dernière phase de la course au Niger: La Mission Ganier dans le Haut-Dahomey, 1897–1898." In *Revue Français d'Histoire d'Outre-Mer,* vol. 49, no. 2 (1962).

———. *Papiers d'Afrique.* Dakar, 1963.

Garvin, J. L. *Life of Joseph Chamberlain* 3. London, 1934.

Gaston, Joseph. "Monographie de la ville de Bondoukou." *B.C.A.F.* (Dec. 1915).

Gatelet, Lieutenant. *Histoire de la Conquête du Soudan français 1878–1899.* Paris, 1901.

Gavin, R. J. "Nigeria and Lord Palmerston." *Ibadan* (June 1961).

Gibson, Martin W. A. *A Century of Liverpool Commerce*. Liverpool, 1950.

Gillard, D. R. "Salisbury's Helgoland Offer: The Case against the Witu Thesis." *English Historical Review,* vol. 80, no. 316 (1965).

———. "Salisbury's African Policy and the Helgoland Offer of 1890," *English Historical Review,* vol. 75, no. 297 (October 1960).

Goguel, F. *La Politique des Parties dans la Troisième République* 1. Paris, 1946.

Goldie, Sir George. "Britain's Priority on the Niger." *National Review* (April 1898).

Gooch, G. P., and Temperley, H., eds. *British Documents on the Origins of the War, 1898–1914*. 11 vols. London, 1926–30.

Gouzien, Paul. *Notice sur le Dahomey*. Office Colonial. Paris, 1899.

Grandin, Commandant L. *A l'Assaut du pays des Noirs: Le Dahomey*. 2 vols. Paris, 1895.

Grenville, J. A. S. *Lord Salisbury and Foreign Policy: The Close of the Nineteenth Century*. London, 1964.

Grundemann, D. "Die Mission in den deutschen Schutzgebieten in Westafrika: Das Togo." *Deutsche Kolonialzeitung* (1888).

Guilcher, René F. *Au Dahomey avec le Père Dogére: L'Activité Pacificatrice d'un Missionaire*. Lyon, n.d.

Guinand. "Notes sur les Populations du Dahomey." *B.C.A.F.,* no. 1 (1904).

Hagen, A. "La Colonie de Porto Novo et le roi Toffa." *Revue d'Ethnographie* 6 (1887).

Hagen, M. von. *Geschichte und Bedeutung des Helgoland Vertrages*. Berlin, 1916.

Hanotaux, G., and Martineau, A. *Histoire des Colonies Françaises*. Vol. 4, *L'Afrique Occidentale Française*. Paris, 1934.

Hanotaux, G. *Le Partage de l'Afrique: Fachoda*. Paris, 1909.

Hargreaves, J. D. *Prelude to the Partition of West Africa*. London, 1963.

Hartmann, Robert. "Über die Amazonen des Königs von Dahomey." *Verh. Berlin, Geschichte für Anthropologie Ethnologie und Vorgeschichte* (1891).

Haywood, A., and Clarke, F. A. S. *The History of the Royal West African Frontier Force*. Aldershot, 1964.

Hazoume, Paul. *Doguicimi*. Paris, 1938.

———. *Le Pact du Sang au Dahomey*. Paris, 1937.

Heggoy, A. A. "The Colonial Policies of Gabriel Hanotaux in Africa 1894–1898." Ph.D. dissertation, 1963. University microfilms, Ann Arbor, Michigan.

Henderson, W. O. "German East Africa, 1884–1898." In *History of East Africa* 2, edited by V. Harlow, E. M. Chivers, and A. Smith. Oxford, 1965.

Henrici, Dr. *Das Deutsche Togogebiet und meine Afrikareise*. Berlin, 1888.

Henrique, Louis. *Nos Contemporains: Galérie, Coloniale et Diplomatique*. 2 vols. Paris, 1896.

Henry, Yves. "Le Coton en Dahomey." *Bulletin de la Société de Géographie,* nos. 5, 11, 12 *Commerciale de Bordeaux* (1904).

Herissé, A. le. *L'Ancien Royaume du Dahomey.* Paris, 1911.
Herskovits, M. J. *Dahomey: An Ancient West African Kingdom.* 2 vols. New York, 1938.
Hertslet, E. *Map of Africa by Treaty.* 3 vols. London, 1896.
Heutsch, H. *Deux années au Dahomey, 1903–1905.* Nancy, 1916.
Histoire de Louis Anniaba; Roi d'Essenie en Afrique, sur la Côte de Guinée. Amsterdam, 1740.
Hollingsworth, L. W. *Zanzibar under the Foreign Office, 1890–1913.* London, 1963.
Hubert, H. "Distribution des mouches tse-tse au Dahomey." *La Géographie* (1907).
———. "Esquisse préliminaire de la Géologie du Dahomey." *Comptes Rendus de l'Académie des Sciences* (Paris) 145 (1907).
———. "La Barre au Dahomey." *Annales de Géographie* (Paris) no. 92 (1908).
———. "La Carte géologique du Dahomey." *La Géographie.* (1908).
———. *Mission Scientifique au Dahomey.* Paris, 1906.
Hube-Schleiden, Dr. "Deutsche Welthegemonie." *Deutsche Kolonialzeitung* (1890).
Hulot, M. "Rélations de la France avec la Côte des Esclaves." In *Annales de l'Ecole libre des Science Politiques.* Paris, 1894.
Huré, Jules. *L'Expansion Française au Dahome: Voie nouvelle de pénétration dans le Soudan Central et la Boucle du Niger. Chemin de fer de l'Ouemé à Kouande.* Paris, 1896.
Jacob, E. G. *Deutsche Kolonialpolitik in Dokumenten.* Leipzig, 1938.
Jakande, L. K. *West Africa Annual 1966.* Lagos, 1965.
Jeze, Gaston. *Etude théoretique et practique sur l'Occupation comme mode d'acquérir les Territoires en Droit International.* Paris, 1896.
Jolly, Jean. *Dictionnaire des Parlementaries Française: Notices biographiques sur les Ministres, Députés.* 3 vols. Paris, 1963–64.
Joucla, E. *Bibliographie de l'Afrique Occidentale Française.* Société d'Editions géographiques, maritimes et coloniales. Paris, 1937.
Kaltbruner, D. "Les Anglais au Niger." *Revue Français de l'Etranger et des Colonies,* vol. 8, no. 56 (15 Oct. 1888).
Kanya-Forstner, S. "The Conquest of the Western Sudan: A Study in French Military Imperialism." Ph.D. dissertation, Cambridge University, 1966.
Kingsley, Mary. *West African Studies.* London, 1901.
Koloniales Schrifttum in Deutschland (Kolonialpolitischen Amtes). Berlin, 1941.
Kossatz, Heinz, *Untersuchungen uber den Französisch-Englishen weltgegensatz im Fachodajahr.* Breslau, 1934.
"La France dans l'Afrique Occidentale: Lettre du Taout 1863." *Annales de Géographie* (1891).

"La France et l'Angleterre au Niger." *B.C.A.F.* (1896).
"La France et l'Angleterre sur le Niger, la Benoue et le Haut-Dahomey." *B.C.A.F.* (1895).
Laffite, R. *Le Pays des Negres et la Côte des Esclaves.* Tours, 1885.
Lagrillière-Beauclerc, Eugene. *Missions au Sénégal et au Soudan: Voyage de M. André Lebon, Ministre des Colonies, Octobre–Novembre 1897: Rapport.* Paris, 1897.
Laird, MacGregor, and Oldfield, R. A. K. *Narrative of an Expedition into the Interior of Africa by the River Niger, 1832, 1833, and 1834.* 2 vols. London, 1837.
Lambinet, E. *Notice géographique, topographique et statistique sur Dahomey.* Paris, 1893–94.
Langer, William L. *An Encyclopaedia of World History: Ancient, and Modern.* 3rd rev. ed. Boston, 1952.
———. *The Diplomacy of Imperialism.* 2nd ed. New York, 1960.
Lara, H. Adolphe, and Béhanzin, Ouanilo. *Pour Béhanzin.* Lyon, 1905.
"Le Commerce du Dahomey en 1895." *Revue Coloniale* (1896) and *Annales de Géographie* (1896).
"Le Dahomey." *Comptes Rendus des Séances de la Société de Géographie de Paris,* no. 9 (1890). "Le Dahomey" in *Mouvement Géographique,* vol. 4, no. 17 (1892).
Le Garrères, R. "Dahomey: Cercle du Borgu. Le Secteur de Parakou." *Revue Coloniale,* n.s. 8.
LeFaivre, Henri. "Dictateurs Noirs: Les derniers Rois du Dahomey, 1610–1894." *Revue d'Histoire des Colonies,* no. 1 (1937).
Lemire, Charles. "Le Rôle de Ville de Paris dans la Colonisation." *Revue des Colonies et de Pays de Protectorat* (June–July 1896).
Lemoine, Fredéric. *Le Dahomey.* Melum, 1911.
Lenfant, E. *Le Niger, voie ouverte à notre commerce africain.* Paris, 1902.
Leroy-Beaulie, P. *De la Colonisation chez les peuples modernes.* Paris, 1874.
Lesourd, Paul. *L'Oeuvre Civilisatrice et Scientifique des Missionaires Catholiques dans les Colonies Françaises.* Paris, 1931.
Levtzion, Nehemiah. "Salaga, A Nineteenth Century Trading Town in Ghana." *Asian and African Studies: Annal of the Israel Oriental Society* 2 (1966).
Lewin, Evans. *Subject Catalogue of the Library of the Royal Empire Society: The British Empire Generally, and Africa* 6. London, 1930.
Lexis. "Über die Französische Kolonialpolitik." *Deutsche Kolonialzeitung* (1885).
Lindley, M. F. *The Acquisition and Government of Backward Territory in International Law.* London, 1926.
Lobagola (Bata Kindai Amogozaibn). *An African Savage's Own History.* New York, 1930.
Lombard, Jacques. "Aperçu sur la technologie et l'artisanat Bariba." *Etudes Dahoméenes* 18.

———. *Structures de type "féodal" en Afrique Noire. Etude des dynamismes internes des relations sociales chez le Bariba du Dahomey*. Paris, 1965.

Lorho, Capt. "Historique de notre expansion dans l'Hinterland dahoméen," *Revue des Troupes Colonials,* vol. 3, no. 17 (Nov. 1903).

Louis, W. Roger. "Anderson's Grand Strategy." *English Historical Review* (April 1966).

———. *Ruanda-Urundi, 1884–1919*. Oxford, 1963.

Lugard, F. D. *Dual Mandate in Tropical Africa*. Edinburgh, 1922.

Lyautey, Pierre. *L'Empire Colonial Français*. Paris, 1931.

Madaule, Jacques. *Historie de France*. vol. 3, *De la IIIe a la Ve République*. Paris, 1966.

Madden, A. F. "Changing Attitudes and Widening Responsibilities, 1895–1914." In *The Cambridge History of the British Empire*. vol. 3, *The Empire-Commonwealth, 1870–1919*. Cambridge, 1963.

Mademba, Abdel Kader. *Au Sénégal et au Soudan Français*. Paris, 1931.

Madrolle, Claudius, *En Guinée* (Paris 1895).

Marbeau, Edouard, "M. Ribot et l'Afrique" in *Revue Française de l'Etranger et des Colonies,* Vol. XII, No. 99 (1 Aug. 1890).

Marc, Lucien, *Le Pays Mossi* (Paris 1909).

Marti, Monserrat Palan, *Le Roi-Dieu au Benin, Sud Togo, Dahomey, Nigeria Occidentale* (Paris 1964).

Martineau, Alfred; Roussier; and Tramond. *Bibliographie d'histoire coloniale, 1900–1930*. Société de l'Histoire des Colonies Françaises. Paris, 1932.

Mattei, Antoine, Commandant. *Bas-Niger, Bénoue, Dahomey*. Grenoble, 1890.

McManners, J. *Lectures on European History, 1789–1914*. Oxford, 1966.

McWilliam, H. O. A. "Ferguson, Samon and Barbatu." *Ghana Teachers Journal,* no. 27 (July 1960).

Mendelssohn, Peter de. *The Age of Churchill: Heritage and Adventure, 1874–1911*. London, 1961.

Merlo, Christian. "Synthèse de l'activité fetichiste aux Bas-Togo et Dahomey." in *Bulletin d'Institut Français de l'Afrique Noire,* vol. 12, no. 4 (Oct. 1950).

Messimy, A. *Notre oeuvre coloniale*. Paris, 1918.

Metcalfe, G. E. *Great Britain and Ghana: Documents of Ghana History, 1807–1957*. London, 1964.

Mimande, Paul. *L'Héritage de Béhanzin*. Paris, 1898.

Ministère de la Guerre, Section Historique. *Bibliographie militaire*. 4 vols. Paris, 1930–35.

Ministère des Colonies. *Cinq Cent Livres sur la Communauté Française: Bibliographie Succincte*. Paris, 1945.

Mirbt, C. *Mission und Kolonialpolitik in den deutschen Schutzgebieten*. Tubingen, 1910.

Mizon, Louis. *Explorations en Afrique Centrale, 1890–1893*. Paris, 1895.

———. *Une Question Africaine.* Paris, 1895.
Molex, J. "Le Gourma." *Journal Officiel du Dahomey et Dépendances* (1 Aug. 1898).
Mondjannagni, Alfred. "Quelques aspect historiques, économiques et politiques de la frontière Dahomey-Nigeria." *Etudes Dahoméennes,* n.s. no. 1 (1963–64).
Monnier, Marcel. "De la Côte D'Ivoire au Soudan meridional: Mission Binger." *Compte Rendu de la Société de Géographie* (Paris) (1892).
———. *Mission Binger: France Noire, Côte d'Ivoire et Soudan.* Paris, 1894.
Monteil, L. *De St. Louis à Tripoli par le Lac Tchad.* Paris, 1896.
Monteil, Lieut.-Col. P. L. *Une Page d'Histoire Militaire Coloniale: La Colonne de Kong.* Paris n.d.
Morienval, Henri. *La Guerre du Dahomey: Journal de Campagne d'un Sous-Lieutenant d'Infantérie de Marine.* Paris, 1893.
Morin, Lieut. E. *Conférence sur le Dahomey.* Paris, 1890.
Morrison, Capt. *Histoire Militaire et Historique: Résumé de la Pénétration dans la Boude du Niger* (Notice Générale sur le Soudan, publiée par ordre du Colonel de Trentinian, Lieutenant-Gouverneur, partie 2e, May 1897).
Moulignié. *La Conquête de Dahomey.* Paris, 1893.
Murphy, A. *The Ideology of French Imperialism, 1871–1881.* Washington, D.C., 1948.
Ned, Noll. "Le Mossi: La Mission du Lt. Voulet." *La Tour du Monde* 33 (14 Aug. 1897).
Newbury, C. W. "A Note on the Abomey Protectorate." *Africa,* vol. 29 no. 2 (April 1959).
———. "The Development of French Policy on the Lower and Upper Niger, 1880–1898." *Journal of Modern History,* vol. 31, no. 1 (March 1959).
———. *The Western Slave Coast and Its Rulers.* Oxford, 1961.
Niboyet, Paulin. "Sir Edmund John Monson." *La Revue Diplomatique,* no. 44 (8 Nov. 1896).
Nicholas, Victor. *L'Expedition du Dahomey en 1890 avec un aperçu géographique et historique.* 2nd ed. Paris, 1893.
Noir, Louis. *Au Dahomey: Une Amazon de Behanzin.* Paris, 1892.
———. *Les Amazons au Sahara.* Paris, 1899.
———. *Prisonnières au Dahomey: La Venus de Whydah.* Paris, 1892.
Northcott, H. P. *Report on the Northern Territories of the Gold Coast* (1899).
Nowell, Charles E. "Portugal and the Partition of Africa." *Journal of Modern History,* vol. 19, no. 1 (March 1947).
Ollenu, N. A. *Principles of Customary land law in Ghana: Law in Africa, No. 2.* London, 1966.
Onwuamaegbu, M. O. *Law of Landlord and Tenant in Nigeria: Law in Africa, No. 12.* London, 1966.
Ortolan, Eugene. *Des Moyens d'acquérir le Domaine International.* Paris, 1851.

Ortroy, F. van. *Conventions Internationales definissant les limites actuelles des possessions, protectorats et spheres d'influence en Afrique (d'après les textes authentiques)*. Bruxelles, 1899.

Pageard, R. "Reflexions sur l'histoire du Mossi." *L'Homme*, no. 1. (Jan.–Feb. 1962).

Pasquier, Georges. "L'Organisation des Troupes indigènes en Afrique Occidentale Française." Doctorat d'Etat Droit, Paris, 1912.

Pasquier, Roger. "Chronique de l'Histoire Coloniale: l'Afrique Noire d'expression française." *Revue Française d'Histoire d'Outre-Mer*, vol. 48, nos. 3, 4 (1961), pp. 438–57.

———. "Chronique d'Histoire d'Outre-Mer: L'Afrique Noire d'expression française." *Revue Française d'Histoire d'Outre-Mer*, vol. 1, no. 1 (1963), pp. 74–129.

Pawlowski, A. "Bibliographie raisonnée des ouvrages concernant le Dahomey." *Revue Maritime et Coloniale* (May–June 1895).

Pedrals, D. Pierre de. *Dans la Brousse Africaine: Au Dahomey-Borghou*. Cannes, 1946.

Peel, Hon. George. "The Nerves of Empire." In *The Empire and the Century*, edited by C. S. Goldman. London, 1905.

Perham, M., and Bull, M. *The Diaries of Lord Lugard*. London, 1963.

Perham, M. *Lugard: the Years of Adventure, 1858–1898*. London, 1956.

Peters, Carl. *Die Gründung von Deutsch-Ostafrika*. Berlin, 1906.

———. *Willenswelt und Weltwille: Studien und Ideen zu einer Weltanschauung*. Leipzig, 1883.

Pillet, Antoine. "La Liberté de Navigation du Niger." *Revue Générale de Droit International Public* (March–April 1896).

Piquet, M. *La Mission Voulet au Mossi et au Gourounsi*. Paris, 1898.

Poirier, Jules. *Campagne du Dahomey, 1892–1894*. Paris, 1895.

Polanyi, Karl, and Rotstein, Abraham. *Dahomey and the Slave Trade: An Analysis of an Archaic Economy*. Seattle, 1966.

Prudencio, Eustache. *Les Rois d'Abomey 1625–1898*. Dakar, n.d.

Quellien, Alain. "La Politqiue Musulmane dans l'Afrique Occidentale Francaise." Dectorat d'Etat Droit, Paris, 1910.

Quenum, Maximilien. *Au Pays des Fons: Us et Coutumes du Dahomey*. 2nd ed. Paris, 1938.

Redford, Arthur, and Clapp, B. W. *Manchester Merchants and Foreign Trade, 1850–1939* 2 Manchester, 1956.

Reichenbach, J. "Etude sur le Royaume d'Assinie." *Bulletin de la Société de Géographie de Paris* 11 (1891).

Renouard, G. *L'Ouest Africain et les Missions Catholiques: Congo et Oubanghi*. Paris, n.d.

Renouvin, Pierre. *Histoire des Relations Internationales*. Vol. 6, *Le XIXe Siecle: De 1871 à 1914: L'apogée de l'Europe*. Paris, 1958.

République du Dahomey, Service d'Information. *Connaissez-vous le Dahomey?* (Paris 1962).

———. *Enquête démographique 1961. Données de base sur la situation démographique qu Dahomey en 1961.* Paris, 1962.

———. *Le Dahomey: Naissance d'une Nation.* Paris, 1963.

Reste, G. *Le Dahomey: Réalisations et perspectives d'avenir.* Paris, 1934.

Reste, J. F. *Le Dahomey Réalisations et Perspectives d'avenir.* Paris, 1934.

Riols, J. de. *La Guerre du Dahomey.* Paris, 1893.

Robinson, C. H. *Hausaland or Fifteen Hundred Miles through the Central Sudan.* London, 1896.

Robinson, R. E., and Gallagher, J. A., with Denney, Alice. *Africa and the Victorians.* London, 1961.

Robinson, R. E. "Imperial Problems in British Politics, 1880–1885." In *Cambridge History of the British Empire.* Vol. 3, *The Empire-Commonwealth, 1870–1919.* Cambridge, 1959.

Rouard de Card, E. *Les Traités de délimitation concernant l'Afrique Française.* Paris, 1910.

———. *Les Traités de protectorat conclus par la France en Afrique de 1870 à 1895.* Paris, 1897.

Rouire. "La France et l'Angleterre dans la Vallée du Niger." *Revue des Deux Mondes* (15 Oct. 1898).

Rudin, H. R. *Germans in the Cameroons, 1884–1914.* London, 1938.

Sabatier, M. *Touat, Sahara et Soudan.* Paris, 1891.

Salinis, P. A. de. *Protectorat Français sur la Côte des Esclaves: La Campaigne du Sane, 1889–1890.* Paris, 1908.

Sanderson, G. N. "The German Agreement of 1890 and the Upper Nile." *English Historical Review,* vol. 78, no. 306 (Jan. 1963).

Saudemont, A. *Exposé de la Colonisation au Dahomey.* Paris, 1896.

Saudemont, G. "Une Colonie alsacienne-lorrainne au Dahomey." *Bulletin de Société de Géographie Commerciale* (Paris) 17 (1895).

Schreiber, A. W. *Bausteine zur Geschichte der Norddeutschen Missions-Gesellschaft.* Bremen, 1911.

Schwitzer, J. P. "The British Attitude to French Colonisation, 1875–1887." Ph.D. dissertation, London University, 1954.

Seeley, John. *The Expansion of England.* London, 1883.

Sell, M. *Das Deutsche-Englische Abkommen von 1890.* Berlin, 1926.

Septans, Albert. *Les Expéditions Anglaises en Afrique.* Paris, 1896.

Serval, P. "Rapport sur une mission au Dahomey." *Revue Maritime et Coloniale* 59 (1878).

Sieberg, H. *Eugène Etienne uad die Franzoesische Kolonialpolitik, 1887–1904.* Berlin, 1970.

Skertchley, J. A. *Dahomey As It Is.* London, 1874.

Skinner, E. P. *The Mossi of Upper Volta*. Stanford, 1964.
Smigielski, Basile. "Histoire Médicale de la Campagne du Dahomey en 1892." Doctorat d'Etat-Médécine, Paris, 1896–97.
Sonolet, L. *L'Afrique Occidentale Française*. Paris, 1918.
Soulier, A. *L'Instabilité Ministérielle sous la Troisième République*. Paris, 1939.
Soyaux, Herman. *Deutsche Arbeit in Afrika Erfahrungen und Betrachtungen*. Leipzig, 1888.
Sprigade, Paul. "Die französiche kolonie Dahomey." *Mitt. Deutsch Schutzgebiete* 2 (1918).
Steiner, Paul. "Land und Leute von Akra." *Deutsche Kolonialzeitung* (1885).
Stengel, Karl von. *Deutsche Kolonialzeitung*, no. 17 (Aug. 1890).
Tauxier, Louis. *Le Noir du Soudan*. Paris, 1912.
———. *Le Noir du Yatenga*. Paris, 1917.
Taylor, A. J. P. *Germany's First Bid for Colonies*. London, 1938.
Ternaux-Compa, S. H. *Bibliotheque asiatique et africaine ou cataloque des ouvrages relatifs à l'Asie et l'Afrique, qui ont Paru depuis la decouverte de l'imprimérie jusqu en 1700*. Paris, 1841.
Terrier, A., and Mourey, C. *L'Expansion Française et la Formation Territoriale: L'Oeuvre de la Troisième République en Afrique Occidentale*. Paris, 1910.
Thornton, A. P. *Doctrines of Imperialism*. New York, 1965.
Thosee, C. Pety de. *Théories de la Colonisation au XIXe Siecle et Rôle de l'Etat dans le développement des Colonies*. Bruxelles, 1901–02.
Toutée, Capt. G. J. *Dahome-Niger-Touareg*. Paris, 1895.
———. *Du Dahomey au Sahara: La Nature et l'Homme*. Paris, 1899.
Townsend, M. E. *The Rise and Fall of Germany's Colonial Empire*. New York, 1930.
Trautman, René. *La Littérature populaire à la Côte des Esclaves Contes, Proverbs, devinettes*. Paris, 1927.
Trierenberg, G. *Togo die Aufrichtung der deutschen Schutzherrschaft und die Erscheliessung des Landes*. Berlin, 1914.
Urvoy, Y. *Les bassins du Niger: Etudes de géographie physique et de paléogéographie*. Paris, 1942.
Verger, Pierre. "Painted Palaces of Dahomey: An Illustrated Commentary." *Geographical Magazine* (March 1942).
Vergne de Tressan, Lieut. *La Pénétration Française en Afrique*. Paris, 1906.
Vergniol, C. "Fachoda, II." *La Revue de France* (July–August 1936).
Vermeersch, L. *Historique de la Mission Baud-Vermeersch: Le Dahomey 1894–1895*. Paris, 1897.
Viallate, Archile. *Joseph Chamberlain*. Paris, 1899.
Viard, Edouard. *Au Bas-Niger*. Paris, 1885.
———. *Explorations Africaines: La France et la Conférence de Berlin*. Paris, 1885.

Vignes, K. "Etude sur la rivalité d'influence entre les puissances européenes en Afrique equatorial et occidentale depuis l'acte générale de Berlin jusqu'au seuil du XXe siècle." *Revue Française d'Histoire d'Outre-Mer*, vol. 48, no. 1 (1961).

Vindex. *Cecil Rhodes, His Political Life and Speeches, 1881–1900*. London, 1900.

Violle, Raoul. "Rapport de route et de mission dans le Haut-Dahomey." *Annales d'Hygiène et de Médécine Coloniales*. No. 2. Paris, 1905.

Vohsen, Ernst. *Zum Deutsch-Englishen Vertrag*. Berlin, 1890.

Voulet. *Mission au Mossi et au Gourounsi*. Paris, 1898.

Wailly, G. de. "Un Regiment Sacré." *Nouvelle Revue* 63 (March–April 1890).

Waldman, L. K. "An unnoticed aspect of Archibald Dalzel's 'The History of Dahomey.'" *Journal of African History* (1965).

Ward, W. E. F. *A History of Ghana*. 2nd rev. ed. London, 1958.

Waterlot. "Les Bas-Réliefs des Bâtiments Royaux d'Abomey." *Travaux et Memoires de l'Institut d'Ethnologie*. Paris, 1926.

Weber, A. "L'Allemagne et l'Impérialisme." *Rev. Econ. Internationale* (Bruxelles) 1 (1904).

West African Directory, 1965–66. London, 1965.

Williams, Joseph S. *Africa's God: Dahomey*. Vol. 1, no. 2. Anthropological Series, Boston College Graduate School. Boston, 1936.

Winks, Robin W., ed. *The Historiography of the British Empire-Commonwealth: Trends, Interpretations and Resources*. Durham, N.C., 1966.

Woerl, Leo. *Dahomey: Das Land der Schwarzen Amazonen*. Leipzig, 1898.

Wright, Harrison M. "British West Africa." In *The Historiography of the British Empire-Commonwealth: Trends, Interpretations and Resources*, edited by Robin W. Winks. Durham, N.C., 1966.

Yarnall, Howard E. *The Great Powers and the Congo Conference in the Years 1884 and 1885*. Gottingen, 1934.

Zahn, Dr. Frederic. "L'Expansion des Allemandes à l'Etranger." *Rev. Econ. Internationale* 1 (1906).

Zech, von. *Deutsche Kolonialblatt* 8 (1896).

———. "Vermischte Notizen über Togo und das Togo Hinterland." *Mitteilungen aus den deutschen Schutzgebieten* (1898).

Index

Abdel Kader, 21
Abeokuta, 86, 95; Dahomean raids in, 90; and Viard's expedition, 46, 48, 125
Aberdare, Lord, 137
Abetifi, 147
Ablada, 63
Abodugnanli, 115
Abomey, 16, 32, 57, 112; Audéoud's mission to, 86–90, 93; Bayol's mission to, 60–66, 88; Dogère's mission to, 79–81; expedition to, debated, 97–99; in First Dahomey War, 70, 72–73, 77, 79; French protectorate, 118; history, legendary, 51; human sacrifice at festival, 54, 63, 65, 88–89; in interval between wars, 86–89; kingdom, 116–17; Toutée in, 171; treasures, false reports of, 100, 109, 110; Whydah hostages in, 70, 77, 81
—in Second Dahomey War: burned, 110; expedition to, 105–08, 110; occupation of, 110–11
Abomey-Calavi, 31, 63, 66, 72, 111, 171
About, Edmond, 116
Abu Bukari, 147, 260
Aburi, 34
Achemu, Chief, 171–72
Acheribe, 115
Acts of Navigation, Berlin Conference, 22
Adaklu, 39
Adama, chief of Matiacouali, 201–02, 207
Adamawa, 23, 133, 136, 137, 155, 187
Addo River, 47, 49
Adegon, 107
Affomayi, 111
Aflao, 37, 39
Agbanaken, 35
Agoli-Agbo, king of Abomey (Prince Gouchili), 117–18, 171
Agome River, 88
Agony, 107, 110, 115
Agotime, 38
Agoue, 34–36, 77
Aguibou, sultan of Bandiagara, 197
Ahinson, 15

Ahmadu, sultan of Segu, 3, 11, 13, 60, 137, 166, 173, 192, 204, 206
Ajani, chief of Tchaki, 172
Ajara (Ajarra) Creek, 90, 150
Akassa, 177, 178
Akpa, 107, 108
Akwamu (Aquamoo), 38
Akwapim, 34
Alby, administrator in Dahomey, 141, 167–69, 183, 203
Algeria, 131, 134; in Chad Plan, 126, 129, 249; forces from, in Second Dahomey War, 105
Ali Barca, 234
Alis, Harry (Hippolyte Percher), 128
Allada, 105, 107, 109, 111, 163; French protectorate, 118; kingdom, 116, 117
Allio, 235
Alsace-Lorraine, colonists in Dahomey from, 163
Aly Boury N'Diaye, 204
Amazons, 67, 75
Ambrières, d' (midshipman), 88
Anderson, H. P., 135, 139, 183–85, 215, 246
Anderson, Sir Percy, 40, 161
Anecho (Petit Popo), 34–36
Anglo-Congolese Treaty of 12 May 1894, 153
Anglo-French Agreement of 10 August 1889, 39, 55, 123, 150, 190, 245
Anglo-French Convention of 14 June 1898, 241–45; text, 263–72
Anglo-French Declaration of 5 August 1890, 125, 126, 128–32, 134, 141–42, 149, 181, 247, 248
Anglo-German Agreement of November 1893, 136, 180
Anglo-German Agreements of 1890, 40, 126, 128
Anglo-Italian Treaty of 5 May 1894, 153
Anglo-Portuguese Treaty of 1884, 18–19
Angra Pequena affair, 18–19
Annam, 231
Anno, 137

Anyako, 33
Appa, 72
Arabia, 134
Archinard, Colonel Louis, 100
Ardent (gunboat), 72, 181
Argungu, 134, 232
Ariguy, 134
Ashanti, 140, 146, 147, 228, 247, 252; people, 120
Ashanti War, 54, 119
Asia, southeast, French possessions in, 125–26
Asikasso, 220
Asquith, Herbert Henry, 242
Assinie, 146
Asuma, chief of Badjibo, 173
Atabubu, 147
Atakora range, 7
Atchoupa, 75
Audéoud, Commandant H. M.: mission to Abomey, 86–90, 93; in Second Dahomey War, 105–06, 109
Avrekete, 66
Ayenkuken, Prince, 112
Ayidama, Prince, 117
Azaouisse, 106

Babato (Babatu, Barbato), Chief, 10, 213, 229, 251
Badagry, 90
Badame, 205
Badjibo, 173
Bafilo, 167, 201, 206, 209, 225
Bagare, Chief (Naba), 11, 195, 197
Bagida, 35, 38
Bagoue River, 139
Bagui (person), 172
Bahr-el-Ghazal, 153, 156
Balfour, A. J., 234, 238
Ballay, Noel, 89, 91, 92, 103, 104
Ballot, Victor, 5, 44–47, 52, 58, 118, 120, 174, 182, 184, 194, 235, 246, 248, 249, 251; Béhanzin's correspondence with, 101–02; in Borgu, 225; and Decoeur, hostility between, 141, 165; expedition (personal) to Nikki and Bussa, 168–70; expeditions to Dahomey-Niger hinterland promoted, 139–41, 145, 164, 165, 167, 191–92; in First Dahomey War, 79; in French-British negotiations, 156; in interval between wars, 87–89, 91, 92, 101; and military occupation of Niger territories, 200–08; in Second Dahomey War, 104, 106, 110; treaty in First Dahomey War, 83
Bandama, 139
Bandiagara, 11, 195, 197
Banikani, 172
Banning, Emile, 18, 26
Bantchande, king of Gurma, 12, 13, 166, 198, 201, 202, 207, 227, 228, 251–52
Baoule, 140
Barbato. *See* Babato
Barbey, E., 72, 73, 76–77, 88
Bareste, French consul, 29, 30
Bariba, country, 144–45, 170, 246
—people, 9, 13–14, 16, 168, 171, 200, 201, 234, 251, 252; Moslems in Nikki, 145, 169; resistance movement, 235
Barrum, 130
Bartet, Alfred, 203
Barth, Ernest, 93
Barth, Heinrich, 33, 133
Basch, 25
Basel Mission, 34
Bassila, 141, 168
Baud, Captain, 189, 192, 204, 207, 212; first expedition, 140, 141; second expedition, 165–68; Vermeersch and, in military occupation, 201–03, 205, 225
Baumont, Maurice, 26
Bayol, Jean, 36, 54–55, 89, 103; character and career of, 61; in First Dahomey War, 67–74, 76, 82; mission to Abomey, 60–66, 88
Bayol Island, 36, 72
Beckman, M. de, 48–49, 58
Becon, 110
Bedji, 83
Begohounou, 115
Béhanzin, king of Dahomey, 16, 121, 139, 147, 153, 157, 172, 249, 252; agricultural program, 94–95; armaments and military forces, 90–94; Ballot's correspondence with, 101–02; coronation of, 66–67; Dogère's mission to, 78–79, 81; French mission received, 88–89; in interval between wars, 86–95, 100–02; name, origin of, 67; political ideas, cosmology in, 102; as Prince Kondo, 63–66; successor chosen, 117; Toffa and, 89, 111, 117
—in First Dahomey War, 69, 70, 72, 74, 75, 77; treaty problems, 81–84, 87
—in Second Dahomey War, 101, 103–16; Abomey burned, 110; peace overtures, 108–

13, 115; pursuit of, 115–16; surrender of, 118
Beh (Bey) Beach, 34, 37
Belgium: in Berlin Conference, 21; in Congo question, 18
Benin, Bight of, 28, 34, 59
Benin-Ondo region, 177
Beniot, 155
Benito, 28
Benue River, 128, 135–37, 187
Berlin Conference (1884–85), 2, 4, 19–28, 42; Acts of Navigation, 22; General Act, 26–28, 32, 43, 53, 236, 245, 248
Berme Sunon, chief of Guilmoro, 205
Bernis, Lieutenant de, 239
Berthelot, Pierre Eugène, 186–88, 190
Betbeder, Captain, 209, 225
Biaba Lompo, king of Gurma, 13
Biafra, Bight of, 28
Bikini, 146, 165, 177, 186
Bilanga (Billango), 166, 198, 201
Bilma, 134
Binger, Louis Gustave, 98, 167, 169–70; expeditions, 120, 123, 138–39; in Niger Commission negotiations, 225, 236, 237, 240, 241, 243
Birni, 165
Bismarck, Count von, 34, 36, 39, 96; and Berlin Conference, 19, 21, 23, 25–26; resignation of, 40
Bismarckburg, 145
Blogdomey, 101
Bobo Diulasso, 133
Bodji, 75
Bogo, 172
Bona (Bouna), 5, 148, 167, 188, 192, 210–12, 219, 220, 247; in Niger Commission negotiations, 230, 232, 236, 237, 239, 240
Bonduku (Bondoukou), 48–49, 137–39, 146, 150, 168, 220, 247; Say-Bonduku Line, 150–51, 184
Bonnaud, Jean-Baptiste, 53
Bontemps, consul at Whydah, 67, 70
Borgu, 5, 8, 120, 123, 149, 168, 215, 220; expeditions to, 133, 140, 143, 144, 146, 192; French and British rights to, 144, 149, 150, 154, 155, 170, 181, 184, 186, 190, 200, 230, 234–36, 246; French and British troops in, 218, 225, 240; German claims in, 175, 179, 206; resistance movement in, 252; territory and group, 9, 13–14, 170; treaties, validity of, 227
Bornu, 134, 143, 154, 226, 243
Bornu, Shehu of, 143
Borsari, 134
Botou, 203
Bouay, 13, 168
Bouet, Lieutenant, 53
Boukari Koutou, king of Mossi, 197, 198, 212, 227–28, 230
Boulanger, General Georges, 47, 95–96
Boulangism, 45
Bourgeois, Léon, 161–62, 190
Boussa. See Bussa
Boussouma, 197
Boussourima, 168
Boutin, Commandant, 115
Bower, Captain, 144
Bramston, Sir John, 147, 161
Brass (place), 146
Brassmen, 178
Braulot, Lieutenant, 139, 167, 239
Brazza, Pierre Savorgnan de, 128, 155
Bremen Mission, 33
Bretonnet, Captain H. E., 192, 200–03, 209, 225, 248
Brisson, Eugène Henri, 132, 241
Britain: African possessions, 18, 28; in Berlin Conference, 19–27; and Brussels Conference General Act, 104; colonial policy, lack of, 250; in Dahomey, 44–45, 54–57; Dahomey-Niger territory claimed by, 3–4, 45–49, 123; and Dahomey peace delegation to France, 113; Niger–Lake Chad Commission, Anglo-French, 149–57; political changes, 159–61; slave trade opposed, 54
—France and: crisis of 1897–98, 194, 209–20; in Dahomey-Niger hinterland, 124, 125, 129, 136, 140–57, 159, 177–79, 181–93; Entente Cordiale, 5–6, 223, 243; Niger Commission negotiations, 221–44; Slave Coast partition, 29–31, 41–49, 55–57
—Germany and: in Borgu, 175; crisis of 1897, 213; negotiations, 178–80; Togo—Gold Coast boundary, 37–41
Brong, 146, 147
Brot, Lieutenant, 225
Brunschwig, H., 126
Brussels Conference (1889–90), 3, 49–50; General Act, 50, 91, 93, 104, 123, 129, 245; article 1, text, 255

Buem, 39
Burdeau, A., 116
Burdo, 69
Buri, Ahmadu Ali, 173
Busch, 25
Buss, Peter, 93
Bussa (Boussa), 5, 8, 44, 143, 167, 173, 179, 192, 200, 249; Ballot's expedition to, 169–70; Bretonnet in, 200–01; British oppose French occupation of, 213–15, 217–18, 225, 229–32, 236; British rights in, 184, 186; French evacuation of, 248; kingdom, 9, 13, 170; Niger Commission negotiations on, 223, 242, 243, 251; treaties, validity of, 227
Bussansi, 199
Busumfu, priest of Dente at Kete-Krachi, 176
Busumo, 11

Cameroons, German, 27, 28, 57, 133; slaves in, 92–93
Campos, Eucaristus de, 31
Cana, 63, 108–10
Carnap, Lieutenant von, 145–46, 165–66, 174, 176–77
Carnot, Sadi, 112–13
Carnotville, 7, 140, 164, 165, 167, 168, 200, 201, 204
Carter, Governor Gilbert, 142, 143, 177, 178, 192–93, 249
Casimir-Périer, Jean Paul Pierre, 136, 137, 153
Cassagnac, Paul de, 97, 105
Cauvigny, Commandant de, 115
Caviagnac, G., 104
Cazemajou, Captain G. M., 199
C.F.A.E. (Compagnie Française de l'Afrique Equatoriale), 20, 21
Chabi, Chief, 140
Chacha, 31, 32, 64
Chad Plan, 120, 126, 128, 129, 132, 247–49. *See also* Lake Chad
Chakosi, 165, 209; kingdom, 9–11; people, 10
Chamberlain, Joseph, 5, 186, 192, 198, 247, 250–51; as colonial secretary, importance of, 160–61; in French-British crisis of 1897–98, 209–10, 212–20; and Niger Commission, 221, 223–26, 229, 233, 237–40, 245; and West African Frontier Force, 214–19, 241
Chanoine, Lieutenant J., 192, 229, 252; in Voulet's expedition to Mossi, 195, 196, 199

Chasles, Lieutenant, 88, 89
Chaudoin, Edouard, 70
Chautard, Père E., 99–100
Chautemps, Emile, 100, 118, 174
Chedinga, Prince, 112
Chirol, Sir Valentine, 39
Chmitelin, Commandant, 115
Christiansborg, 33
Churchill, Winston, 160
Cisse, 195
Clemenceau, Georges, 92, 95
Coke, Henry, 57
Colonization Society of Alsatians and Lorrainians, 162, 163
Comité d'Afrique Française, 126, 127, 140, 147, 171, 242, 248
Comité d'Etude du Haut Dahomé, 162
Comité pour la Protection et Défense des Indigènes, 196
Comoe River, 167–68, 182, 226
Compeyrat, Lieutenant, 71
Congo, 126, 128, 133, 249
Congo, Belgian, 93
Congo question, 18–19, 22
Congress of Vienna (1814–15), 19–21
Constant, d'Estournelles de, 130
Corail (gunboat), 106
Cornevin, Robert, 1, 31, 33
Cossugan, 109
Cotonou (Kotonou), 15, 29, 56, 57, 87, 89, 112, 120, 155, 171; Bayol's negotiations on, 62, 64–66; Béhanzin's actions in, 101; cable station, 43; in First Dahomey War, 66, 67, 69–70, 73–75, 77, 81; Portuguese and French dispute for, 32; in Second Dahomey War, 103; tariffs, 90; treaty ceding to France, 53, 54, 58–59; wharf, construction of, 69
Courcel, Alphonse Chodron, Baron de, 19, 21, 24, 26, 34, 36, 164, 186, 190, 250; in Niger Commission negotiations, 221; 225–26, 229, 230, 232–34, 238, 240
Crampel, Paul, 133, 135, 136
Crozat, Dr., 123–24, 138–39
Cun, 195
Curzon, Lord, 242
Cuverville, Admiral Cavalier de, 105; and Dogère's mission, 78, 79, 81; in First Dahomey War, 74, 76, 79, 80; in interval between wars, 87, 88, 91; and treaty after First Dahomey War, 82–84

INDEX 389

Dagari, 10
Dagarti, 212
Dagomba, 9, 10, 140, 146, 185
D'Agoult, Comte, 181
Dahomey, 3, 7–9, 14–16, 36, 37, 44, 123, 133, 137, 140, 147, 153, 154, 157, 159, 231; Bayol's mission to Abomey, 60–66, 88; Béhanzin's military and economic programs, 90–94; British and French conflicts of interest, 44–45, 54–57; colonial development, French plans, 162–63; colonists from Alsace and Lorraine, 163; corridor to Niger proposed, 232, 233; economic conditions between wars, 90–91; external trade, 189, 242; French peace treaty (1890), text, 256–57; French protectorate established, 111; French reasons for conquest, 97–100; French relations with, 53–54, 82–103; kingdom, 9, 14–16, 31, 51–52; -Lagos frontier, 182, 185, 186, 188–91, 235–37, 246; Lagos raided from, 90–91; military strength, 252; name, meaning of, 51–52; Niger bend routes affecting, 182–83; origin, legends of, 51–52; physical geography and resources, 7, 8; political group, 9; population, 67–68; Portuguese treaty and rights, 31–33, 53–54; reorganized by Dodds, 116–18; republic, modern, 52; slave trade, 54, 90–93, 95; Sudan and Ivory Coast linked with, 139, 140, 154, 194, 249; Togo-Sudan boundaries, 207–09, 219. *See also* Dahomey War, First; Dahomey War, Second
Dahomey-Niger hinterland: area included in, 1, 7; climate and vegetation, 8–9; European expeditions (1890–94), 123–57; French expeditions, 124–28, 132–41, 164–74, 191–93, 248; French military occupation, 164–65, 173–74, 191–207; German claims, 4, 123, 145, 159, 183–85, 202, 250; German expeditions, 145–46, 165–67, 174–77; maps, 122 158, 208; mineral resources, 8, 247; partition of, summarized, 245–53; peoples, 9–14; physical features, 7–8; political situation, 9–17; and Second Dahomey War, 119–21. *See also* Britain: in Dahomey, Dahomey-Niger territory claimed by, and Dahomey peace delegation to France; Germany: in Dahomean situation, Dahomey-Niger hinterland
Dahomey War, First, 66–85; armed forces and armaments in, 67–69, 78; blockade of coast, 72–73, 80; causes of, 57–60, 65–66; Dogère's mission to Abomey, 78–81; health problems, 79; negotiations on, 76–80; plans for, 65–66; transportation problems, 79–80; treaty, 81–85, 87
Dahomey War, Second, 103–21, 249; Abomey expedition, 105–08; Abomey occupied, 109–11; armed forces and armaments in, 106; Béhanzin's peace overtures, 108–13, 115; Béhanzin's surrender, 118; expenses of, 118–19; French attitude toward, 97–100, 113–14, 116; French declaration of, 98, 101, 102; results, 118–20; treaties, 118
Daily Chronicle (London), 40
Dakar, 191
D'Albeca, Alexander L., 51, 58; and Bayol's mission to Abomey, 60, 63, 66; and expeditions to hinterland, 124
Dan (legendary character), 51
Dangbo, 73
Danoe, 185
Decoeur, Captain H. A., 87–89, 168, 169, 186, 189, 203, 205, 251; Ballot's hostility to, 141, 165; Carnap meets, 165–67, 176–77; expedition to Nikki, 140–41, 144–46, 248; second expedition, 165–68
Dekame, 87, 106, 115
Delafosse, Abel, 162
Delahaye, Jules, 97
Delcassé, Théophile, 113, 114, 140, 163, 170, 195; Anglo-French negotiations criticized by, 243; Circular to the Governors of French Colonies (20 June 1894), text, 258–59; and Niger–Lake Chad Commission, 155–56
Delestre, Captain H., 104
Deloncle, François, 76, 97, 98, 126, 129, 135, 169
Dendi, 13, 173, 190, 192, 195, 209, 230; people, 13
Denlay, M., 70
Denton, Captain G. C., acting governor of Lagos, 91
Derby, Earl of, 38, 54
Deroulède, Paul, 98
Dessa people, 116
Destenave, Captain, 11, 183, 192, 195, 196, 199, 204, 209
Deutsche Kolonial Zeitung, 206
Deville, A., 168
Devonshire, Duke of, 30

Diamala, 139
Dilke, Sir Charles, 242
Djebiga, 168
Djebougou, 199
Djene, 135
Djerma, 134; people, 13
Djibe, 110
Djimini, 139, 167
Djougou. *See* Wangara
Dodds, Colonel (General) Alfred-Amédée, 74, 93, 141, 151, 153, 187, 202; Abomey expedition, 105–08, 110–11; Béhanzin offers peace terms to, 108–10; Béhanzin surrenders to, 118; character and career of, 103; Dahomey reorganized by, 116–18; promoted to general, 109; in Second Dahomey War, 102–18
Doering, 176, 177
Dogba, 106–07, 111, 203
Dogère, Père Alexandre, 77–78, 83, 100; mission to Abomey, 78–81
Dokita, 212
Dopkwe, Dopkwegan, 15
Dorat, Colonel L., 29–30, 35–36
Dori, 133, 199, 204
Dornian, Captain, 35
Dosso, Henry, 112
Dourga, 204
Dreyfus affair, 238, 240
Drude, Commandant, 115
Dubreka (Rivières du Sud), 28, 36
Dufferin, Lord, 98, 154, 164, 187, 188
Dumas, Colonel, 115, 118, 140
Dunglas, Edouard, 51, 52
Dupuy, Charles, 153
Durand, Bernardin, 81
Dybowski, Jean, 128

Egbaland, 48, 52
Egba people, 52
Egerton, Edwin H., 48, 54, 60, 61, 91
Egypt, 29, 30, 231
Ehrmann, French resident at Porto Novo, 83, 91, 92
Elmina, 33
Elteil, Antin d', 29
Emeraude (gunboat), 73
England. *See* Britain
Etchepetei, 172
Ethiopia, 114
Etienne, Eugene, 48–49, 55, 58, 59, 98, 99, 103, 113, 120, 153, 181, 243, 247, 249; Anglo-French Convention criticized, 241–42; and Bayol's mission to Abomey, 60–62, 65, 66; and expeditions in hinterland, 124–26, 132, 133, 136–38; in First Dahomey War, 73, 76, 77; in interval between wars, 87, 91; treaty in First Dahomey War, 83–84
Everett, Colonel William, 188, 192, 210, 240, 241
Ewe people, 33

Fabre, Cyprien, 82–84, 92, 93, 99
Fabre et Cie., Maison, 104–05
Fada N'Gurma, 8, 12, 146, 165, 166, 176, 201, 227, 251
Faidherbe, General Louis Léon Cesar, 20, 44, 124, 125
Falkenthal, Ernst, 35, 36
Fashoda, 156, 241, 243
Faurax, Commandant, 107
Ferguson, George Ekem, 10, 165, 167, 176, 177, 180, 198; death of, 212; expeditions and treaties, 146–49, 210–12, 227–28; prejudice against, 187, 199, 210, 211; Mossi treaty (Wagadugu, 2 July 1894), text, 260–62
Ferry, Jules, 35, 36, 41, 43, 60, 76, 96, 139, 245, 247, 249; in Berlin Conference, 2, 19–21, 23, 24, 26
Fésigny, Lieutenant, 106
Figaro, Le (periodical), 181
Firminger, R. E., 37
Flint, J. E., 145
Flourens, Emile, 59
Foa, Edouard, 31, 73
Folaouigo, Chief, 172
Fongha, 13
Fon people, 9, 15–16, 51, 120
Fonssagrives, Captain, 200
Forbes, Frederick E., 90
Forcados, 173
Forget, Henri, 200
Fort d'Arenberg, 173, 174, 200
Fort Goldie, 174
Fournier, Leopold, 55; in First Dahomey War, 73–77, 80
Fouta Djallon, 7, 60, 61
France: African possessions, 18, 28; armed forces in Africa, 250; in Berlin Conference, 19–22, 26; colonial policy, 96–100, 124–28,

INDEX 391

162–64, 249–50; colonization plans, 162–63; Comité d'Afrique Française, 126, 127, 140, 147, 171, 242, 248; Conseil Supérieur des Colonies, 126–27, 163; Dahomey peace treaty (1890), text, 256–57; German war with, threatened, 45; Niger–Lake Chad Commission, Anglo-French, 149–57; politics of Third Republic, 95–96, 161–64; Portugal and, in Slave Coast partition, 31–33; Russian alliance with, 96. *See also* Britain, France and; Dahomey; Dahomey War, First; Dahomey War, Second
—Dahomey-Niger hinterland: claims, 3–5, 44–49, 123; expeditions, 124–28, 132–41, 164–74, 191–93, 248; military occupation, 164–65, 173–74, 191–207
—Germany and: in Dahomey-Niger hinterland, 186, 187, 251; negotiations and settlement of 23 July 1897, 207–09, 225; Slave Coast partition, 33–37
François, G., 99
François, P. von, 124
Freycinet, Charles de, 35, 36, 41, 43, 76
Funssi people, 199

Gabon, 62
Gaiser, G. L., 28
Galiber, Admiral C. E., 43, 44
Gallieni, General Joseph Simon, 61
Gaman, 138
Gambaga, 147, 148, 167, 210, 211, 228
Gambari, 141
Gambia, 27, 56, 59, 119, 151
Gandiaga, 199
Ganhou Hougnon, Prince (Gi-gla-don-Gbe-nou-maou), king of Allada, 117
Ganier, Captain Ferdinand, 203–06, 208–09, 225
Ganier, Germaine, 209
Gaya, 13
Gbe, 15
Gbede, 106, 107
Gedegbe, 66
General Act of Berlin Conference (1884–85), 26–28, 32, 43, 53, 236, 245, 248
General Act of Brussels Conference (1889–90), 50, 91, 93, 123, 129, 245; article 1, text, 255
Geoffray, chargé d'affaire, French Embassy, London, 231, 237–38
German Colonial Society, 174, 175

Germany: African possessions, 18, 28; armaments bought from, 92–94; in Berlin Conference, 19, 21–25; and Brussels Conference General Act, 104; colonial enterprise, 39; in Dahomean situation, 54–56; French military occupation and German posts, 201, 202, 204–06; French opposition to colonial expansion, 136, 140; French war with, threatened, 45; Helgoland ceded to, 40, 128; merchants in Africa, 34–35, 83; missionaries in Africa, 33–34; Niger, claims on, 207–09; Togo expedition, 174–77; Togo protectorate, 28, 35, 38, 54. *See also* Britain, Germany and; France, Germany and
—Dahomey-Niger hinterland: claims in, 4, 123, 145, 159, 183–85, 202, 250; expeditions in, 145–46, 165–67, 174–77
Germat, 64
Ghezo (Gezo), king of Dahomey, 15, 53, 54
Gi-gla-don-Gbe-nou-maou (Prince Ganhou Hougnon), king of Allada, 117
Gladstone, William Ewart, 25
Gléglé, king of Dahomey, 15, 31, 32, 117; and Bayol's mission to Abomey, 63–64; death of, 65, 66; descriptions of, 53, 64; French relations with, 53–54, 58–59; son trained as his successor, 66; Toffa and, 54, 57–58
Glover, Governor John H., 29, 30
Gobir, 135
Godome, 31, 66, 72, 74, 111
Gogo, 130
Goho, 111
Gold, 8, 247
Gold Coast, 4, 5, 8, 27, 142, 144, 145, 167, 184, 192, 209, 213, 222, 238, 247, 250; British exploration of, 39; British military forces in, 210, 219–20; expeditions from, 146–49; French efforts in, 140, 146; German missionaries in, 33–34; German trade with, 34; –Ivory Coast boundary, 139, 151, 152, 226, 237; Lagos and, French and British dispute, 41–43; –Togo boundary, British and German negotiations, 37–41
Goldie, Sir George, 20, 43, 45, 57, 178, 194, 229, 233, 240; Chamberlain's opposition to, 215–19; and Fort d'Arenberg, 173, 174; and French expedition to Bussa, 201; French interview with, 181; in negotiations with France, 143–44, 150, 154; in negotiations with Germany, 180; Say-Barruwa Line

proposed, 130, 247; and West African Frontier Force, 215–19
Goldscheider, 43
Gomba, 135, 186, 190, 236
Gonja, 146, 185
Gosselin, Martin, 175, 179, 229, 233, 238–41
Gouchili, Prince (Agoli-Agbo), 117–18
Gourcy, 195
Gourma. *See* Gurma
Gourounsi. *See* Gurunsi
Grand Bassam, 27, 137, 139, 168
Grand Popo, 34, 35, 53, 56, 77, 88, 92, 106
Granville, Lord, 23, 24, 27
Gravenreuth, Captain de, 92–93
Great Britain. *See* Britain
Gregoire, Lieutenant Colonel, 111
Grey, Sir Edward, 144, 226, 233, 242
Gridji, 35
Griffith, W. Branford, governor of the Gold Coast, 42, 147, 148, 176
Gruner, Hans, 186, 187, 200, 202, 207, 211, 249; expedition, 145–46, 174–77
Guieysse, Pierre, 187
Guilmin, 29
Guilmoro, 205
Guinea, Spanish, 27, 28
Guinea Coast, Upper, 27
Gurma (Gourma), 2, 5, 173, 183, 184, 192, 195, 198, 200, 205; French and British claims in, 140, 144–46, 149–51, 186, 190, 246; French and German claims in, 186, 206, 207, 209, 251; French protectorate established, 166; French success in, 251–52; German expedition to, 176; kingdom, 9, 10, 12–13; physical geography, 7, 8; trade routes, 12–13; Voulet's expedition to, 195
Gurmantche people, 9
Gurunsi (Gourounsi), 5, 9, 10, 140, 185, 192, 210, 212; British and French rights in, 229–31, 236; British errors in, 251; people, 9; Voulet in, 195, 197–99
Guy, Camille, 186
Gwandu, 143, 173, 177, 207, 247
Gwandu, Emir of, 189

Hadeija, 134
Hamaria, Chief, 10, 197, 229, 251
Hamburgische Correspondenz, 187, 206
Hanotaux, Gabriel, 4, 5, 91, 104, 119, 126, 162, 184, 186, 187, 190, 247, 249; in British and French negotiations (1897–98), 194, 211, 219, 220; and Dahomey-Niger hinterland expeditions, 136, 142, 164–65; in German and French negotiations (1897), 207–09; and military occupation of hinterland, 164–65, 173–74, 248; in Niger Commission, 221, 222, 225, 226, 230–34, 236, 238–43; in Niger–Lake Chad Commission, 150–57
Harcourt, Sir William, 25
Harrar, 153
Hatzfeldt, Count von, 40, 176, 180
Haussa territories, 135
Haussmann, Jacques, 91
Hazoumé, Paul, 15
Helgoland, 40, 128
Hemming, Sir A. W. L., 25, 41, 46, 48, 49, 151, 161, 180, 186, 187
Henderson, Francis B., 210–12, 219, 229, 251
Henrique, Louis, 79
Herbette, 129
Herbig, Captain, 35
Herskovits, M. J., 51
Hertslet, Sir E., 24
Hervieu, Henri, 97
Hewett, Edward Hyde, consul, 30, 54
Hicks Beach, Sir Michael, 242
Hill, Sir Clement, 161
Ho, 39
Hocquart, Captain, 88, 89
Hodgson, F. M., 147
Hoenigsberg, 138
Hohenlohe, Prince von, Chancellor, 207
Hombor mountains, 7
Houaketome, 66
Hounhintogban, Prince, 117
Hourst, Lieutenant E. A. L., 13, 22, 192, 195, 248
Howard, Henry, 190, 192
Huckuff, Hendrick, 33
Human sacrifice: abolition of, proposed, 110, 112; at Abomey festival, 54, 63, 65, 88–89
Huré, Jules, 162

Ibadan, 177
Ibrahim Tory, 60
Ijebu, 142–43
Ilaris, warriors of Porto Novo, 90
Ilo, 5, 167, 200, 204; kingdom, 9, 13; in Niger Commission negotiations, 230, 236, 239, 240, 242, 249
Ilorin, 177–78, 192

INDEX

Indigénat, 118
Institut de Droit International, 18, 21
Islam. *See* Moslems
Ivory Coast, 133, 146, 168; –Gold Coast boundary, 139, 151, 152, 226, 237; Sudan and Dahomey linked with, 139, 140, 194, 249; tariff, 243

Jackson, P., 112
Jacquot, Captain Charles, 104, 106
Jamais, Emile, 97–98, 103, 105, 136
Jebba, 173
Jones, Alfred, 242
Journal des Débats, 114

Kaiama (Kayama), 144, 145, 167, 170, 172, 188
Kaltbrunner, D., 120
Kambi, 195
Kandi, 206, 209
Kankantchari (Kankantenari), 146, 166, 167, 176, 177
Kano, 13, 134, 247
Kasson, John A., 24
Katsena, 134
Kaura, 134
Kayser, Dr. Paul, German Foreign Office, 159, 174–77, 179, 181, 185
Kekede (Kedeke), chief of Dekame, 87, 104
Kemura, king of Kayama, 172–73
Kenedugu, 133
Kerguelen (ship), 72, 79
Kesounou, 73
Keta, 33, 34, 38
Keta-Krachi, 146, 176, 177
Ketenu, 29, 30
Ketu kingdom, 9
Kevi, 38
Kiaochow, 39
Kiba, 165
Kilinga, 10
Kimberley, Lord, 30–31, 154, 156–57, 179, 180, 184
King, David Ashford, 143, 167
Kings, African, treaties made by, 227–28
Kinstry, 80
Kipirsi heights, 7
Kirikri (Kir-kri), 167, 201, 205, 206, 209, 225
Kirk, Sir John, 40, 144, 161
Kishi, 144, 172, 235
Kjimini, 137
Kling, Captain, 144, 165, 175

Klipfel, Lieutenant Colonel, 74, 79, 103
Knutsford, Lord, 47, 56, 90, 142, 143
Kodjar, 165, 167, 203–06, 209, 228, 252
Kodokoli region, 168, 209
Kohler, August, 207
Kölnische Zeitung, 175
Kondo, Prince: Bayol's negotiations with, 63–66. *See also* Béhanzin
Kong region, 133, 137, 168, 183
Konkobiri, 165, 168, 204, 205
Kora, chief of Wawa, 201
Koransa, 147
Kosoko, king of Lagos, 54
Koto, 107–09
Kotonou. *See* Cotonou
Kotopa, 108
Kouande (Kuandé), 165, 168, 202–05, 227; Bariba resistance movement, 235; kingdom, 9, 13
Koubouré, 172, 252
Koumbi Siguiri, 197
Kousougan, chief of Whydah, 89
Kowe, 38
Krachi, 176
Krauel, Dr., 38
Krause, Gottlob Adolf, 176
Krepi (Creppe), 38, 39
Kuandé. *See* Kouande
Kuffo, 172
Kuka, 143
Kukawa, 134, 247
Kuliokoro, 192
Kumasi, 86, 210
Kumpa people, 199
Kuntum, 225
Kunya, 39
Kupela (Koupela), 147, 195, 198

Lacca, Bonaventura Colonna de, 29, 44, 124, 125
Lagos, 4, 27, 31, 61, 209, 222, 250; armed forces in, 218, 229; Dahomean raids in, 90–91; Dahomey frontier, 182, 185, 186, 188–91, 235–37, 246; and exploration of hinterland, 142–45; in First Dahomey War, transport problems, 79–80; French difficulty with Britain over, 41–43, 56, 225, 230; Gold Coast separated from, 42; intervention in Porto Novo, 29; Porto Novo boundary, 55, 80, 149, 191; Royal Niger Company and, 177–78; slave trade in, 54; tariff, 90, 150

Lagos Echo, 144
Lake Chad, 126, 129–32; Chad Plan, 120, 126, 128, 129, 132, 247–49; explorations near, 132–35; French claim territory near, 234. *See also* Niger–Lake Chad Commission
Lake Nokoue (Denham), 105
Lale, 199
Lama Marsh, 7, 52, 109
Lambermont, Baron Charles Auguste (1819–1905), 26
Lambinet, Colonel E., 102, 111, 112, 145
Lambounti, 204, 205
Lamfiera, 133
Lang, Captain J. J., 139
Lansdowne, Lord, 243
Lanterne, La (periodical), 84
Lartigue, Lieutenant, 54
Lasserre, Commandant, 107
Launay, Le Provost de, 98, 114, 116
Lavigérie, Charles, Cardinal, 49, 96
Layere, 200
Léaba, 167, 226
Lebon, André, 163, 202–03, 207–09, 225, 240, 241, 248
LeBon, Gustave, 116
Lecomte, René, 239, 240
Lefaivre, Henri, 32
Le Herissé, A., 113–14
Leo (place), 199, 229
Leo XIII, Pope, 96
Leopold II, king of the Belgians, 49
Liban (ship), 112
Liberia, 28, 29
L'Intransigeant (periodical), 76
Liptako, 133
Lister, T. V., 104, 143
Liverpool Chamber of Commerce, 57, 142
Lobi, 5, 148, 192, 210, 213, 220, 247; in Niger Commission negotiations, 230, 232, 236, 237
Lockroy, Edward, 132
Lokoja, 190
Lokossa, 163
Lombard, Jacques, 14
Lome, 34, 35, 38
Lorho, Commandant, 1
Lowther, J. W., 150
Lugard, Captain Frederick D., 5, 16, 164, 177, 205, 224, 227, 228, 246, 249, 251; expedition to Nikki, 5, 140–41, 144–45, 169, 248, 251; West African Frontier Force commanded by, 209, 218, 219, 241
Lyautey, Pierre, 249
Lyons, Lord, 45
Lytton, Lord, 48, 93, 96, 130, 138

McCallum, Edward Henry, 193, 235
Macina, 199
MacKintosh, David, 143
Madagascar, 97, 129–31
Mahi: highlands, 7; people, 9, 14, 52, 116, 171; territory, 9, 111
Mahin Beach enclave, 28
Mahmadu, 171
Mahmadu Lamine, 60
Makka, 165
Malet, Sir Edward, 164; in Berlin Conference, 19–21, 23-25, 27
Mamadou Kouka, prince of Wagadugu, 198
Mamprussi, 5, 8, 16, 140, 210, 211, 230, 236; agreement with Mossi, 228; political group, 9–13
Manchester Chamber of Commerce, 142
Mandanou Yamfiabou, King of Konkobiri, 205
Mango people, 11
Mango Ture, 11
Mangu (Mangou), 165, 192, 209
Mani, 197
Manigri, 141
Mann, Gustav, 33
Mantes, Theodore, 99
Mantes et Borelli de Régis ainé, 74, 77
Maradi, 135
Marchand, Captain J. P., 133, 139
Marel, 58
Marion-Bresillac, Monsignor de, 78
Marmet (ship), 115
Marquer, Commandant, 111
Marschall, 174, 180
Martineau, député, 97
Massow, Lieutenant Valentin von, 211
Matiacouali, 8, 146, 166, 176, 202, 206, 227, 252
Matin, Le (newspaper), 46
Mattei, Commandant Antoine, 20, 43, 99
Mauri, 136, 137, 187
Mauri-Arewa, 134
Maxwell, Governor William, 210, 212, 214, 249
Mazi, 198

INDEX

Meade, R. H., 25, 41, 142, 161
Méline, Félix Jules, 162, 190, 231, 233, 238, 240
Menager, Reverend, 35
Ménard, 128, 133, 137–39
Mensah, chief of Porto Seguro, 35
Mimande, Paul, 118
Misahoehe, 145, 146, 177
Missionaries: German, 33–34, 135; in Lagos, 46
Mizon, Lieutenant Louis A. A., 26, 170, 187; expedition, 128, 133, 135–38; treaties, 136–37, 152–55
Mock, 206
Mogho Naba of Wagadugu (Wobogo), 11, 147–48, 195–97, 199, 200, 210, 212, 228, 238
Molex, Jules, 12, 168, 203, 205, 206
Moloney, Governor Alfred, of Lagos, 30, 44, 46–47, 49, 56, 80
Mono River, 52, 101, 106
Monson, Sir Edmund John, 164, 213, 214, 219, 224–26, 233–35, 238–41
Monteil, Lieutenant P. L., 143, 149, 152, 157, 167, 179, 181, 183, 189, 194–95; expedition, 128, 133–35
Montfort, 113
Moreau, Marshall, 71
Morgho Naba. *See* Mogho Naba of Wagadugu
Morocco, 134
Mosca (ship), 115
Moslems, 203; Bariba, in Nikki, 145, 169; Dendi, 13, 14; French opposition to, 88
Mossi, 2, 5, 16, 124, 140, 155, 185, 192, 200, 209, 247, 252; Alby's expedition to, 168; British expeditions to, 146–49, 210–12; British oppose French claims in, 213–15, 217; British treaties, validity of, 228–29; Ferguson's treaty (Wagadugu, 2 July 1894), text, 260–62; French occupation of, 11–12; kingdom, 9–12; and Mamprussi agreement, 228; in Niger Commission negotiations, 226, 229, 230, 233, 234, 236, 238, 239; people, 9, 16, 20; physical geography and resources, 7, 8; trade routes, 16; Voulet's expedition to, 195–99, 252
Mounier, 168, 205, 206
Mount Delcassé, 7
Mousset, Lieutenant, 73
Moynier, G., 18

Murzuk, 134
Mytho (ship), 105

Nachtigal, Gustav, 33, 35, 38, 59
Nago people, 116
Naiade (ship), 75
Nalierigu, 228
Nanbema (Nambema), King, 10, 11, 165, 167, 168, 176
Nansougou, 204
Naouri peak, 7
Nasara, 206
National African Company, 20, 43, 44
Neutral Zone, 146, 211, 213, 245; British and German partition discussed, 178–80; partition of 1899, 200
Neville, Lagos banker, 112
Newbury, C. W., 43, 91
Newfoundland, 129
Niger: area of, 7; Berlin Conference, discussion of, 2, 19–23; British dominance of, 4; British policy on, 2, 19–21; French expeditions to, 133, 135, 140, 155, 165, 167, 192; French negotiations on, 4–5, 43–44, 185; German and French negotiations on, 207–09; navigation rights, 2, 5, 21–22, 181, 184, 236, 239, 240; Niger Commission, discussions of, 226, 230, 231, 236, 239, 240; Toutée's expedition to, 170–74, 248. *See also* Dahomey-Niger hinterland
Niger, Lower, 133, 236, 239, 245–48; British control of, 20–23, 250; French claims in, 43
Niger, Middle, 23, 200
Niger, Upper, French occupation of, 18, 26, 43–44
Niger bend, 182–83, 192; economic potential of, 246–47; French control of, 199
Niger Commission, 5, 210, 211, 213, 217; work of (1897–98), 221–44
Niger Delta, British protectorate, 27, 28
Nigeria, 217, 218
Niger–Lake Chad Commission, Anglo-French, 149–57
Niger-Volta region, 199
Nikki, 5, 123, 157, 167, 187, 192, 227, 228, 230, 246, 249, 251; Ballot's expedition to, 168–70; Bariba resistance movement, 235; British errors in, 251; Decoeur's expedition to, 140–41, 144–46; French occupation of, 164, 207–08; king, choice of, 234–35, 251; kingdom, 9, 13, 170; Lugard's expedition

to, 5, 140–41, 144–45, 169, 248, 251; Niger Commission negotiations on, 223, 224, 230, 236
Nile, Upper, 4, 40, 144, 155–57, 226
Nineteenth Century (periodical), 83–84
Nisard, A., 48, 60, 155
Nkumi, 176
Noll, Ned, 196
Norddeutsche Allgemeine Zeitung, 175
Norddeutsche Missions Gesellschaft, 33
Nugua (Nougoua), 139, 146, 150
Nupe, 192; people, 14

Oil Rivers, 21, 28
Okra, priest of Dente at Kete-Krachi, 176
Olinda (ship), 115
Oly River, 170
Ouahigouya, 195, 197
Oua-Lembele people, 199
Ouangara. *See* Wangara
Ouari, 165, 168
Ouatchi, 35, 36, 86, 95
Oudard, Captain, 71, 73
Oueme River. *See* Wheme River
Ourou Konde, 234–35, 251
Oyo, 172, 252

Palazot, E., 241, 243
Pama, 145, 165–68, 176, 202, 206, 207, 227, 249, 252
Pandjari basin, 7–8
Paouignan, 171
Paraku, 141, 168
Park, Mungo, 135
Pas, Lieutenant de, 172
Pascal, acting governor, 235
Patani people, 135
Pauncefote, Sir Julian, 23–25, 42
Peki, 33, 38
Pelletan, Camille, 92
Pemba, 128, 131
Percher, Hippolyte (Harry Alis), 128
Perere, 141
Pereton, Dr., 41
Périer. *See* Casimer-Périer
Perron, Michel, 13
Peters, Carl, 40, 174
Petit Popo (Anecho), 34–36
Phipps, E. C. H., 4, 119, 136, 139, 149, 186; and Niger–Lake Chad Commission, 150–57
Plakko, chief of Bagida, 35

Poguessa, 107
Pokra (Pokea), 41, 46–47, 49
Politique Coloniale, La (periodical), 114, 181
Pollux (ship), 92
Popo. *See* Grand Popo; Petit Popo
Porte, Amédée de la, 36
Porte, Jean de la, 46, 48
Portes, 204
Porto Novo, 46, 47, 59, 61, 65, 83, 112, 139, 145, 170, 173, 184, 246; in First Dahomey War, 66, 67, 70, 71, 73, 75, 77, 79–81; founding of, 31; French protectorate, 28–31, 37, 41, 44, 53–55, 81, 250; Gambia possibly exchanged for, 56, 59, 119; in interval between wars, 87, 91, 97; –Lagos boundary, 55, 80, 149, 191; in Second Dahomey War, 104, 106, 107; tariffs, 90, 150, 154; telegraph line to Wagadugu, 205; transportation problems, 79–80
Porto Seguro, 35, 36
Portugal: African possessions, 18, 123; in Berlin Conference, 22; Dahomey, treaty and rights in, 31–33, 53–54, 56; in First Dahomey War, 73, 74, 80; France and, in Slave Coast partition, 31–33; Germany wants help from, 37
Post (Berlin), 206
Prempeh I, king of Ashanti, 146, 159
Protten, Jacob, 33–34
Puttkamer, Jesco von, governor of Togo, 1889–95, 179, 249

Quittah, 185

Ramseyer, Reverend Fritz A., 147
Randad, Henri, 35, 36, 73
Ravel, 206
Renault, Professor, 228–29
René Caillé (boat), 135
République Francaise, La (periodical), 129
Rhodes, Cecil, 123
Ribago, 143
Ribot, Alexandre, 76, 80, 82, 88, 92, 93, 137; and Anglo-French Declaration of 5 August 1890, 128–31
Richter, Ernst, 93
Ricour, Commandant, 235
Rio de Oro, 27, 28
Riou, Commandant, 107
Ripon, Lord, 148
Rissama, 11
Rivières du Sud (Dubreka), 28, 36

Rodriguez, Candido, 67, 83
Roget, Lieutenant Emmanuel, 32, 35, 41
Roland (ship), 75, 81
Roques, Commandant, 105
Rosa Rolim, Vicente de, 105
Rosebery, Lord, 152, 154, 156, 159–60, 233
Rothschild, Alphonse, Baron de, 45
Roume, Etienne, 187, 191
Rouvier, Pierre Maurice, 45, 76
Rowe, S., 30
Royal Niger Company, 4, 43, 125, 145, 150, 151, 157, 182, 192, 194, 211, 248; and Anglo-French Declaration of 5 August 1890, 130–32, 181; authority of, on Niger, 167, 184, 185; charter withdrawn, 209, 232, 239; and French expansion, 177–79; and French explorations, 133–37, 140, 142, 143, 155, 169–73; and French occupation of Bussa, 201; Niger Commission negotiations on, 231; and Togoland, 174–75; and West African Frontier Force, 214–19
Royal Niger Constabulary, 142
Russia, 231; French alliance with, 96

Sagon, 171
St. Louis, Senegal, 133
Salaga, 10, 147, 180, 182
Salisbury, Lord, 33, 37, 250; and Anglo-French Declaration of 5 August 1890, 128–32; on Anglo-German Agreement of 1 July 1890, 40; in British relations with France, 45, 48, 49, 80, 91, crisis of 1897–98, 210, 212–15, 217–19; and Dahomey-Niger hinterland expeditions, 135, 136, 139, 143, 149; and Niger Commission, 221–26, 229–33, 237–40, 245; and Niger–Lake Chad Commission, 150–51, 157; as prime minister, third administration, 160–61; in Say-Barruwa Line interpretations, 186, 188–91
Salou, 195
Samba, 195
Samory, Touré, 3, 60, 137, 147, 167, 183, 197, 210, 212, 213, 215, 220, 239
San, 133, 135
Sanagha, 136
Sané (ship), 79
San Joao Baptista d'Ajuda (fort), 31, 32
Sansanne-Mango, 8, 10, 11, 145, 165, 167, 168, 176, 177, 186, 192, 201, 202, 206, 211, 249

Santos, Emmanuel Jose dos, 74
Sarankemory, 210, 212
Sari, 195
Sati, 197, 199, 229
Saudemont, G., 162, 163
Savalu, 205
Savi (Save), 15, 111, 171
Say, 8, 88, 120, 130–31, 140, 146, 165, 166, 185, 203, 225, 230; French expeditions to, 133–35, 192, 199, 209; German expedition to, 177; Niger bend routes from, 182–83
Say-Barruwa Line, 4, 5, 128, 131–34, 149, 152–55; interpretation of, 181, 184, 186–90, 247–48; in Niger Commission negotiations, 223, 226, 230, 234
Say-Bonduku Line, 150–51, 184
Scal, Captain, 198
Schabe, 9, 168
Schori, 168
Schwitzer, J. P., 42
Scott, C. S., 38
Scott, Sir Francis, 147
Seddo, 196
Seefried, von, 201
Seeley, Sir John, 128
Segala, 139
Segu, 133, 135, 183
Seidu, king of Dagarti, 212
Selborne, Lord, 24, 25
Semere, 209
Senegal, 124, 129, 182, 240
—forces from: in First Dahomey War, 66, 71, 76, 87; in French occupation army, 203, 250; in Second Dahomey War, 105
Senegambia, 18, 44
Septans, Captain Albert, 70
Sero Kora Yerima, Chief, 200, 234
Sero Tourou. *See* Siré Tourou
Serval, Paul, 29, 53
Shantung, 39
Siam Declaration of 15 January 1896, 186
Siciliano, 77
Siècle, Le (periodical), 98, 114, 126
Sierra Leone, 27, 57, 145, 150, 154, 219, 239; –Liberia frontier, 28, 29
Silva da Curado, Major, 32, 33
Simitia, 239, 240
Siré Tourou (Sero Tourou), king of Nikki, 5, 141, 169, 172–73, 207–08, 234, 251
Skinner, Elliot, P., 1, 147–48
Slave Coast, 14, 27–31; British plans for

annexation of, 29–31; France and Britain, difficulties of, 29–31, 41–49, 55–57; France and Germany, claims of, 33–37; France and Portugal, claims of, 31–33
Slavery, abolition proposed, 110
Slave trade, 15; British efforts against, 54; Brussels Conference on, 3, 49–50, 123; in Dahomey, 54, 90–93, 95; forbidden, 118; Lavigérie's crusade against, 49
So, 15
Société Africaine de France, 188
Sofa people (Sofas), 120, 212–13, 251
Sognibo, Prince, 104
Sokoto, 13, 153, 186, 195, 201, 230, 232, 234, 239, 247; in Anglo-French Declaration of 5 August 1890, 130–32, 181; Bornu frontier, 243; British expansion in, 142, 143; French explorations in, 133–35
Sommerlad, Theo, 34
Songhay people, 13
Sougou, 120
Soui Marsh, 7
South African Company, 125
South Wales Daily Star, 232
Souverain (ship), 93
Souza, Juliano Felix da, 31, 32, 64
Spain, Rio de Oro protectorate, 27, 28
Spanish Guinea, 27, 28
Spuller, Jacques, 49, 55, 59, 60, 62, 72, 96
Standard (London), 232
Stanhope, Philip, 223
Stetten, Rittmeister von, 174
Stewart, Captain Donald, 198–99, 210–13
Sudan, 137, 192, 195, 196, 210, 226, 230; in Chad Plan, 128, 130, 249; Ivory Coast and Dahomey linked with, 139, 140, 154, 194, 249; Togo–Dahomey boundaries, 207–09
Sunon Sero, 13
Syndicat Français du Haut Bénito, 135

Targe, Lieutenant, 173, 174
Tariffs, 5, 150, 154; in Dahomey, 90; German, on Slave Coast, 36–37; Lagos and Porto Novo, 90, 150, 154; Niger Commission discussions of, 229–31, 234, 236–39, 241, 243
Tautain, Dr., 49, 58
Tavi, 38
Tchaki, 171–74, 249
Tchantzo, 120
Tchaouru, 171, 172

Telegraph communications, 43, 111, 205
Tem, 10
Temps, Le, 46, 87, 98, 114, 130
Tengrela, 139
Tenkodogo (Tengrugu), 198–99, 211
Terrillon, Commandant, 66, 103; in First Dahomey War, 71–75
Tharel, Léon, 136
Theodore, king of Abyssinia, 114
Theodoros, emperor of Ethiopia, 114
Thierry, Captain, 201, 202, 206, 207
Thornton, A. P., 124
Tickel, Thomas, 41, 90
Tienga people, 13
Tigba, 166, 198
Timbuktu, 7, 26, 140, 171, 192
Timbuktu, Djerma of, 21
Times (London), 135, 137, 232
Tirailleurs, senegalese, 103, 105, 106
Tirard, Pierre Emmanuel, 76
Toffa, king of Porto Novo, 29, 30, 47, 53, 54, 57–58, 113, 121, 172, 228; and Bayol's mission, 61–63; Béhanzin's relations with, 89, 111, 117; family of, 171–72; in First Dahomey War, 71, 74, 75; Gléglé opposes, 54, 57–58; in interval between wars, 87, 88, 90; in Second Dahomey War, 104, 106, 111
Togo, 4, 52, 140, 145, 167, 180; Dahomey hinterland, 184, 186; Dahomey–Sudan boundaries, 207–09, 219; German expedition in, 174–77; German move toward Niger from, 207–09; German protectorate, 28, 35, 38, 54, 250; –Gold Coast boundary, British and German negotiations on, 37–41; –Grand Popo boundary, 56
Tohoue, 106, 107
Tokolors, 11, 120, 166
Tonkin, 36, 60, 76, 95, 97, 103, 231
Topaze (gunboat), 101, 102
Tossa, Prince, 112
Touaregs, 173
Toucouma, 166, 201
Toutée, Captain Georges-Joseph, 8, 13, 22, 141, 155, 168, 181, 190, 252; expedition to Niger, 170–74, 248
Towe, 38
Tracou, Lieutenant, 80
Trade routes: in Gurma, 12–13; in Mossi, 16
Trangott-Sollner & Company, 93
Treaties, validity of, 226–28
Treaty of Frankfurt (1871), 21

Treich-Laplène, 123
Trentinian, Colonel L. E., 192, 194–96
Tripoli, 133, 134
Tsafa, Chief, 10
Tschantoland, 145, 175
Tunisia, 126, 129–31
Turkey, 231
Twiss, Sir Travers, 18, 25

Ubangi region, 153, 155
Ubangi River, 128, 133, 156
Uganda, 40
Umbumedi, 107
United States: in Berlin Conference, 21, 24; Chamberlain proposes alliance of, with Britain, 251
Ussher, Governor H. T., 29, 30

Valet, Captain, 199
Verdier, A., 47
Vergoz, 165, 167
Vermeersch, Captain L., 167, 192, 201–02, 205, 225
Viard, Edouard, 20, 44, 48, 60, 62, 69; expedition, 45–46, 125
Victoria, Queen, 217, 233
Vignes, Kenneth, 1, 145
Villarem (telegrapher), 205
Ville de Maranhao (ship), 75
Ville de San Nicolas (ship), 105
Vitt, Ernz-Leopold, 93
Voltaic peoples, 9, 10
Volta River, 7, 179–80, 182
Vossische Zeitung, 176
Voulet, Lieutenant P. G. L., 192, 201, 202, 227, 229; expedition to Mossi, 195–99, 210, 252; prejudiced against Ferguson, 211

Wa, 147, 148, 167, 185, 192, 210, 212, 219, 220, 230
Waddington, William Henry, 80, 104, 125, 137, 164; and Anglo-French Declaration of 5 August 1890, 128–32
Wagadugu, 5, 11–12, 133, 168, 185, 192, 204, 236, 247; Ferguson's missions to, 147–49, 210–11, 227–28; Ferguson's treaty (2 July 1894), text, 260–62; Niger bend routes from, 183; telegraph line to Porto Novo, 205; treaties, validity of, 227–28; Voulet in, 195–99, 210
Wagadugu, Mogho Naba of (Wobogo), 11, 147–48, 195–97, 199, 200, 210, 212, 228, 238
Wailly, G. de, 99
Walembele, 148
Wallace, William, 143
Walwale, 167
Wangara (Ouangara, Djougou), 16, 165, 168, 203, 209
Waya, 33
Wegbe, 33
Wesse, 163
West Africa: native troops and police in, 216 (table); partition of, after Berlin Conference, 3–4, 26–28, 245–46; partition of, after Convention of 1898, 243–44
West Africa Commission of 1865, 30
West African Frontier Force, 5, 194, 209, 214–20, 231, 241, 250
West African Telegraph Company, 43
Wheme (Oueme) River, 52, 73, 75, 79, 116, 120, 171, 203; in Second Dahomey War, 105–07, 110; *Topaze* attacked, 101, 102
Whydah, 15, 28, 66, 112, 120, 145, 163; in Béhanzin's preparations for war, 92, 93; British blockade of, 54; in First Dahomey War, 67, 70, 73, 74, 77, 80, 81; French rights in, 53; Portuguese possession of, 31–33; in Second Dahomey War, 104–05, 109, 111; slave trade in, 93
Willcocks, Colonel James, 235, 249
Wissman, von, 174
Witu, 40
Wobogo. *See* Wagadugu, Mogho Naba of
Wolber and Brohm, 92, 93
Wolf, Dr. Ludwig, 144, 175
Wolseley, Sir Garnet, 146
Worou Yoro, 234, 235, 251
Woru Wari, chief, of Kouande, 1883–97, 203, 205
Wuschlager, 79

Yacom-Bato, king of Gurma, 12, 13, 201
Yagbasson, 200, 201
Yako, 195
Yankouéré, chief of Kodjar, 205–06
Yaouri, 173
Yarba, 199
Yariba, 148
Yatenga, 11–12, 192, 199; Voulet in, 195, 197
Yendi, 10, 147, 213

Yerima, Saka, 235
Yerima, Sero-Kora, Chief, 200, 234
Yevogan, 28, 29, 64, 74, 280
Yola, 135–36
Yoruba, 90, 192–93; people, 9, 44
Yorubaland, 142
Youba, 195
Young, W. A. G., 38

Zagnanado, 110, 115, 171, 205
Zambesi, 21, 22, 123
Zamfara, 135
Zangoiri, 228
Zanzibar, 40, 128–29, 131
Zech, Julius von, governor of Togo, 1904–10, 201, 206
Zime, chief of Lambounti, 205
Zintgraff, Dr., 135
Zinzendorf, Graf von, 33
Zogbo, 70–71, 75
Zonohochou, 101
Zou River, 120
Zubier, Emir, 136
Zunu Creek, 41